Paratexts are those liminal devices and conventions, both within and outside the book, that form part of the complex mediation between book, author, publisher, and reader: titles, forewords, epigraphs, and publishers' jacket copy are part of a book's private and public history. In *Paratexts*, an English translation of *Seuils*, Gérard Genette shows how the special pragmatic status of paratextual declarations requires a carefully calibrated analysis of their illocutionary force. With clarity, precision, and an extraordinary range of reference, *Paratexts* constitutes an encyclopedic survey of the customs and institutions of the Republic of Letters as they are revealed in the borderlands of the text. Genette presents a global view of these liminal mediations and the logic of their relation to the reading public by studying each element as a literary function. Richard Macksey's foreword describes how the poetics of paratexts interacts with more general questions of literature as a cultural institution, and situates Genette's work in contemporary literary theory.

Literature, Culture, Theory 20

Paratexts: thresholds of interpretation

Literature, Culture, Theory 20

❖❖

General editors

RICHARD MACKSEY, *The Johns Hopkins University*

and MICHAEL SPRINKER, *State University of New York at Stony Brook*

The Cambridge *Literature, Culture, Theory* Series is dedicated to theoretical studies in the human sciences that have literature and culture as their object of enquiry. Acknowledging the contemporary expansion of cultural studies and the redefinitions of literature that this has entailed, the series includes not only original works of literary theory but also monographs and essay collections on topics and seminal figures from the long history of theoretical speculation on the arts and human communication generally. The concept of theory embraced in the series is broad, including not only the classical disciplines of poetics and rhetoric, but also those of aesthetics, linguistics, psychoanalysis, semiotics, and other cognate sciences that have inflected the systematic study of literature during the past half century.

Selected series titles

The subject of modernity
ANTHONY J. CASCARDI

Critical conditions: postmodernity and the question of foundations
HORACE L. FAIRLAMB

Introduction to literary hermeneutics
PETER SZONDI
(translated from the German by Martha Woodmansee)

Anti-mimesis from Plato to Hitchcock
TOM COHEN

Mikhail Bakhtin: between phenomenology and Marxism
MICHAEL F. BERNARD-DONALS

Poetry, space, landscape: toward a new theory
CHRIS FITTER

The object of literature
PIERRE MACHEREY
(translated from the French by David Macey)

Rhetoric, sophistry, pragmatism
edited by STEVEN MAILLOUX

Derrida and autobiography
ROBERT SMITH

Novels behind glass: commodity culture and Victorian narrative
ANDREW H. MILLER

Kenneth Burke: rhetoric, subjectivity, postmodernism
ROBERT WESS

Rhetoric and culture in Lacan
GILBERT D. CHAITIN

Gérard Genette
Paratexts
Thresholds of interpretation

❖❖❖

Translated by
JANE E. LEWIN
Foreword by
RICHARD MACKSEY

CAMBRIDGE
UNIVERSITY PRESS

Published by the Press Syndicate of the University of Cambridge
The Pitt Building, Trumpington Street, Cambridge CB2 1RP
40 West 20th Street, New York, NY 10011–4211, USA
10 Stamford Road, Oakleigh, Melbourne 3166, Australia

Originally published in French as *Seuils*
by Éditions du Seuil 1987
and © Éditions du Seuil
First published in English by Cambridge University Press 1997 as
Paratexts: Thresholds of Interpretation
English translation © Cambridge University Press 1997

A catalogue record for this book is available from the British Library

Library of Congress cataloguing-in-publication data applied for

ISBN 0 521 41350 8 hardback
ISBN 0 521 42406 2 paperback

Transferred to digital printing 2001

Contents

Contents

Contents

Contents

❖❖❖

Foreword

❖❖

RICHARD MACKSEY

Pausing on the threshold

Read, read, read, read, my unlearned reader! read, – or by the knowledge of the great saint *Paraleipomenon* – I tell you before-hand, you had better throw down the book at once; for without *much reading*, by which your reverence knows, I mean *much knowledge*, you will no more be able to penetrate the moral of the next marbled page (motley emblem of my work!) than the world with all its sagacity has been able to unravel the many opinions, transactions and truths which still lie mystically hid under the dark veil of the black one.   Sterne, *Tristram Shandy*, III, 36

Laurence Sterne, that pioneer anatomist of the physical body of the book, is offering advice to one of the much put-upon fictive readers of his antic text. What follows is indeed a literal "marbled page," which by the convention of eighteenth-century binders marks the outermost limits of the text and by the nature of its production is both unique and stylized. Sterne had already presented his reader with his celebrated "black page" marking the innermost and overdetermined limits of the text itself.[1] The marbled page is part of the frame containing both the text itself and all the liminal devices – titles, signs of authorship, dedications, epigraphs, prefaces, notes, intertitles, epilogues, and the like – that mediate the relations between text and reader. As the Russian formalist critic Viktor Shklovsky[2] long ago pointed out, *Tristram Shandy* "lays bare" the constructional principles of the

---

[1] Some of Sterne's commentators claim that "the veil of the black one" refers to Satan. It seems more reasonable, however, to assume the reference is to the "black page" (I, 12). Significantly, the black page, overdetermined to the point of illegibility, is a memorial to Sterne's alter ego, Yorick.

[2] "Sterna – Stilistichesky Kommentary" was originally published in Petrograd in 1921 as a monograph; it was reprinted slightly revised in Shklovsky's brilliant collection, *O teorii prozy* (Moscow, 1929; 2nd edition). For an English version, see *Theory of Prose*, translated by Benjamin Sher (Elmwood Park, IL, 1990).

novel as genre by a series of devices (*priemy*) that fundamentally disturb the narrative conventions of the book. In the case of the liminal devices or "paratextual" elements, this means the radical dislocation of readerly expectations: dedications and prefaces are scattered within the text (and on one occasion a dedication is put up for sale); notes, glosses, intercalations, and misplaced chapter headings interrupt the conventional diegetic progress of the narrative. The signs of authorship are repeatedly undone: the author (whose name does not appear on the title page of the original edition), the narrator, and the dramatized reader change places; the author's sermon (intercalated in II, 17) is judged a plagiarism and reattributed to Yorick, a character within the novel, and a name which will eventually become the author's pseudonym when his own sermons are collected. What Sterne as theorist in jester's motley invites, with all these dislocations, is a serious reflection on the poetics of the novel. And an important part of this reflection is the function of the elements that surround and contextualize the text. As the present epigraph suggests, this interrogation of the frontiers between the text and its public demands a dedicated reader, in the senses both of one widely read and of one alert to every artful disruption, intrusion, and lacuna (under the patronage of "St. Paraleipomenon").

Gérard Genette, the most intrepid and persistent explorer in our time of the relations between criticism and poetics, is the legitimate inheritor of Sterne's pioneer enterprise. He shares with Sterne a broad erudition and a sharp eye for the anatomy of discursive practices and narrative strategies. The mordant wit with which he seasons his textual scholasticism is also Shandean in its flavor. Although Genette has long been an authoritative figure in narratological circles, the full compass of his work is probably less well known to the anglophone audience than that of any other major French critic of his generation. Until recently, only a small fraction of his *œuvre* has been available in English translation. This relative neglect is not so much a function of any inherent difficulty in his method or style. (Derrida, Barthes, and, *a fortiori*, Blanchot and Lacan present much greater challenges to the translator.) It is not even a matter of the company he has kept, since he has been a key figure among the critics associated with two of the most influential Parisian journals of our era, *Tel quel* and *Poétique*. It remains rather a matter of the vagaries of

publishing activity and perhaps Genette's stubborn refusal to be
easily categorized: he has at various times been called many
names – structuralist (both "high" and "low"), narratologist,
historian of discursivity, rhetorician, semiotician of style, postmodern poetician, mimologist, transtextualist;[3] but throughout
his career certain preoccupations and a characteristic rigor have
marked all his publications. Thanks in large part to the efforts of
Jane E. Lewin, the admirable translator of the present book, six
volumes of his work have already appeared in English, but most
have been relatively short works. Happily this situation is at last
about to be remedied. In addition to *Seuils* (*Paratexts*), a translation of one other large volume has just appeared (*Mimologiques*)
and another is about to be published (*Palimpsestes*), which will
allow his English readers a much more comprehensive survey of
Genette's achievement.[4]

His first book, *Figures [I]*, a series of critical essays on subjects
ranging from baroque literature to Proust, Valéry, Borges, and
Robbe-Grillet, was received in 1966 with considerable critical
acclaim. It opened a number of his abiding concerns: the relation
of classical rhetoric to contemporary discursive practice, the
reciprocations between criticism and poetics, the nature of *littér-
arité*, the unceasing play between the specific text and the larger
literary figuration of which it is a continuous part. His second
collection of essays, *Figures II*, appeared three years later and
extended his presiding concerns with narrative theory and the
poetics of language. In 1972 *Figures III* collected important essays
on "Critique et poétique," "Poétique et histoire," "La Rhétorique
restreinte," and "Métonymie chez Proust," but the largest part of
the book was devoted to an extended narratologic discussion of
the syntax of narrative, with Proust as the exemplary text. His
systematic analyses of the order, duration, frequency, mood, and
voice of narrative structure have become canonical among students of fiction. At the level of applied criticism, *pari passu*, the

[3] "Narratology" is a term first coined in 1969 by Genette's colleague and
collaborator Tzvetan Todorov. "Mimologist" refers to Genette's "voyage to
Cratylusland" in *Mimologiques* and "transtextualist" to his detailed analyses of
textual transcendence in his trilogy *Introduction à l'architexte*, *Palimpsestes*, and
Seuils (the French title of the present work).
[4] The University of Nebraska Press published a translation of *Mimologiques*
[*Mimologics*] by Thaïs E. Morgan in 1995 and has announced a forthcoming
translation of *Palimpsestes* by Channa Newman.

subtle readings of the case texts, which are at once illustrative of narrative functions and uniquely Proustian in their transgressions, constitute a major contribution to Proust studies. (Jane Lewin translated this section of the book as *Narrative Discourse: An Essay in Method* in 1980.) More than a decade later, in *Nouveau discours du récit* (1983), which he modestly styled "a sort of postscript," Genette returned to his classic formulation of the fundamental elements of narrative, tightening his definitions, refining the systematic presentation with renewed attention to the connections among the choices of *mood* ("point of view"), *voice* ("person"), and narrative *level* ("embedding"). And throughout, the author replies directly and amusingly to his critics. (Lewin translated this text under the English title of *Narrative Discourse Revisited* in 1988.)

Turning in 1976 to an issue in the poetics of language that had engaged Peirce, Benveniste, Gardiner, Jakobson, and Lévi-Strauss among many others before him, Genette produced an immense study of "cratylism," of authors since Plato who have questioned the arbitrary nature of the linguistic sign.[5] With great wit and erudition *Mimologiques* traces the metamorphoses of the debate from its first engagement by Cratylus, Hermogenes, and Socrates through its restaging in the exchanges between Leibniz and Locke in the seventeenth century and the rise of comparative philology in the nineteenth century, to its survival in contemporary linguistic theory. Attending to the cultural as well as epistemological implications of resurgent "Cratylan" arguments, Genette discusses theories of language origins, hieroglyphs, onomatopoetics, mimographisms, mimophonies, and other representational schemes.[6] Along the way Mallarmé, Valéry, Claudel, Proust, Ponge, and their peers are invited to join the debate.

With a small volume in 1979, *Introduction à l'architexte* (also translated by Lewin), Genette opened a new phase in his mapping of a general poetics. The topology he is exploring here includes the various borderlands between the text and the

[5] For additional perspectives on the long debate opened by Plato's *Cratylus*, see: Josef Derbolav, *Platons Sprachphilosophie im Kratylos und in den Späteren Schriften* (Darmstadt, 1972), Bernard E. Rollin, *Nature and Conventional Meaning* (The Hague, 1976), and, most recently, Joseph F. Graham's provocative study, *Onomatopoetics: Theory of Language and Literature* (Cambridge, 1992).

[6] Thus his incisive treatment of Ernest Renan's fierce Eurocentrism and *géomimologie* anticipates by several years Edward Said's discussion in *Orientalism*.

Republic of Letters, the "outside" to which it relates. He states the project modestly enough in the imaginary interview that concludes the book: "[F]or *the moment* the text interests me (only) in its *textual transcendence* – namely, everything that brings it into relation (manifest or hidden) with other texts. I call that *transtextuality* ...""[7] This general project will extend his "moment" for almost a decade and include two large succeeding volumes, of which the present book forms the tentative conclusion. The particular form of transcendence that he considers in the *Architexte* is the traditional domain of generic criticism, which Genette extends to include modes of enunciation and types of discourse. He defines the relationship more generally as one "of inclusion that links each text to the various types of discourse it belongs to. Here we have the genres, with their determinations that we've already glimpsed: thematic, modal, formal, and other" (82). He thus joins the enterprise initiated by Aristotle in the *Poetics*, a systematic text that Genette seeks to disentangle from a long tradition of wrong-headed readings.[8]

Genette's transtextual project continued with the publication of *Palimpsestes* in 1982, where he considers what he calls "literature in the second degree." Here, in the early pages, he redefines and extends his system of transtextualities into a five-part schema (elaborated on below). He then proceeds to consider specifically the relations that he styles "hypertextual." As his governing image of the palimpsest suggests, these are new texts "written over" older ones, inviting a kind of double reading. The most obvious modern example is Joyce's *Ulysses* ("hypertext") superimposed on Homer's *Odyssey* ("hypotext"), but the relationship covers all forms of imitation, adaptation, parody, and pastiche.[9] Its incidence can be studied from the most localized cases of stylistic and thematic mirroring to designs on the grandest scale like Joyce's novel or Mann's Biblical tetralogy or *Doktor Faustus* (which Mann insisted on calling "parodies"). Borges too is a rich

---

[7] *The Architext: An Introduction*, translated by Jane E. Lewin (Berkeley and Los Angeles, 1992), 81.

[8] One of Genette's significant contributions to contemporary poetics is his rescue of Aristotle from what he sees as a tradition of romantic misreading.

[9] Of course the hypertextual relationship of *Ullysses* to Homer's epic is less than obvious without the novelist's chapter titles, which Joyce suppressed in the published version of the book. Genette works out the complex network of correspondences between the eighteen chapters of the novel and Homer's original narrative in a detailed diagram; see *Palimpsestes* (Paris, 1982), 356.

mine of hypertextual games, often intradiegetically: thus before turning to Cervantes, his indefatigable Pierre Menard had undertaken "a transposition of the *Cimitière marin* into alexandrines." Although some earlier theorists extend the term "intertextuality" to include filiations and reinventions such as these, Genette restricts the older term to the much narrower sense of citational and related uses.

Before considering the present volume, which completes the "transtextual trilogy," to bring Genette's publishing itinerary up to date, we should note two more recent books: *Fiction et diction* (1991, translated by Catherine Porter in 1993) and *L'Œuvre de l'art* (1994). The first of these is a series of four essays, that returns to some of his earliest concerns about "literariness," what it is that makes a text an aesthetic object. But like the volumes of the trilogy it also investigates the unstable frontiers between realms, between the literary and the nonliterary but also between the two modes of "fiction" (which depends for its force on the imaginary nature of what it describes) and "diction" (whose efficacy depends on its formal characteristics). He extends these border distinctions in discussions of how speech acts relate to fictional statements and of the differences between fictional narratives and those based on fact (autobiography, history). The collection concludes with a semiotic definition of style.

And finally, in *L'Œuvre de l'art* Genette announces an ambitious new project that will take him from the domain of poetics to that of general aesthetics, addressing at a higher level of abstraction the status and functions of art. In his title he plays on the double sense of "the work of art" (*l'œuvre d'art*) and "the *work* of that art-work." Once again, however, he is concerned with mapping "regimes" or zones of governance, the primary distinction being between those of "immanence" (the type of object of which the work consists) and of "transcendence" (the various ways in which a work exceeds or "overflows" this immanence). Following Nelson Goodman, he further distinguishes kinds of immanence between the "autographic" and the "allographic."[10] His provisional definition of the work itself is

[10] See Nelson Goodman, *Languages of Art* (Indianapolis, 1968), 112–22. Genette adopts Goodman's distinction between the status of those art works where the authenticity of the immanent object is crucial (e.g., painting or sculpture) and those where it is not (e.g., a literary text or a musical composition). The former

rigorously intentional: "a work of art is an intentional aesthetic object, or, which amounts to the same thing: a work of art is an artifact (or human product) [enlisted] to an aesthetic function."[11] He underscores the viewer's or reader's share in this intentional process: one never sees the same painting twice; one never reads the same book twice. "The work is never reducible to its immanent object, because its being is inseparable from its action."[12]

Paratexts (whose French title, *Seuils*, surely contains a sly wink at his long-time publisher, Editions du Seuil) is (as the French title also tells us) about "thresholds," the literary and printerly conventions that mediate between the world of publishing and the world of the text. In a brief introduction to a special issue of *Poétique* devoted to essays on the paratext by members of a seminar at the Ecole des Hautes Etudes, Genette speaks of their topic as "this fringe at the unsettled limits that enclose with a pragmatic halo the literary work."[13] And writing of this undecidable space, which is neither quite container nor contained, he adds: "Now the paratext is neither on the interior nor on the exterior: it is both; it is on the threshold; and it is on this very site that we must study it, because essentially, perhaps, *its being depends upon its site.*" As a key work in Genette's career, *Paratexts* is itself a resolutely liminal book: it completes (for the time being at least) his transtextual poetics, but in its complex mediations between author, publisher, and audience it broaches issues related to the adjacent realms of fiction and fact that are discussed in the much briefer *Fiction et diction* that follows it. In a self-contained work, *Paratexts* also presents some of the characteristic virtues of Genette's criticism early and late. These virtues include clarity of exposition, systematic precision, a vast range of literary example – all products of an agile and original theoretical mind. As a major player in contemporary poetics and narrative theory, Genette is able to situate even his most detailed analyses within

are styled "autographic," the latter "allographic." Note that Genette here departs from his earlier use of "allography" in the first chapter of *Paratexts* (see footnote 8 and the translator's comment).

[11] *L'Œuvre de l'art* (Paris, 1994), 10. Translation mine. This book is the first volume of an announced pair.

[12] From the author's *prière d'insérer* for *L'Œuvre de l'art*.

[13] "Paratextes," *Poétique* 69 (Paris, 1987), my translation. Genette has been for many years *Directeur d'études* in the history and theory of literary forms at the Ecole des Hautes Etudes en Sciences Sociales.

the framework of larger critical issues. To his perseverance in systematic development must be added that Shandean humor noted earlier, which explodes jokes amid the soberest topics, a rare quality in the higher reaches of contemporary poetics.

At this point, since the terminology is precise but occasionally at variance with the usages of other critics, the reader of *Paratexts* may find it useful to see the work situated within Genette's general poetics of transtextuality, alluded to above. Writing in *Palimpsestes* he observes that the following five-element schema is arranged in ascending order of "abstraction, implicitation, and globality."[14]

1. *Intertextuality:* A textual transcendence that Genette defines in what he admits is "an undoubtedly restrictive manner":[15] "a relation of co-presence between two or more texts, that is to say, eidetically and most often, by the literal presence of one text within another" (8). Quotation, the explicit summoning up of a text that is both presented and distanced by quotation marks, is the most obvious example of this type of function, which may also include plagiarism and allusion of various kinds. Since Genette feels this form of transtextuality has been vigorously studied in recent years, he sees no need for another book on the subject.

2. *Paratextuality:* The subject of the present book, comprising those liminal devices and conventions, both within the book (*peritext*) and outside it (*epitext*), that mediate the book to the reader: titles and subtitles, pseudonyms, forewords, dedications, epigraphs, prefaces, intertitles, notes, epilogues, and afterwords – all those framing elements that so engaged Sterne; but also the elements in the public and private history of the book, its "epitext," that are analyzed in the latter part of this volume: "public epitexts" (from the author or publisher) as well as "private epitexts" (authorial correspondence, oral confidences, diaries, and pre-texts).

---

14 *Palimpsestes*, 8–12. The translations from this passage in the schema are mine. (This five-element system is a refinement on the presentation in the *Architexte*, where Genette had made do with four levels of transtextuality.)

15 Very generally he associates his "classic" notion of intertextuality with that of Julia Kristeva in *Sèméiôtikè* (Paris, 1969) rather than with the much broader sense of the term enlisted by Michael Riffaterre in *La Production du texte* (Paris, 1979; English translation, New York, 1983) and elsewhere. For a historical account of the practice of citation, see Antoine Compagnon, *La Seconde Main* (Paris, 1979).

3. *Metatextuality:* The transtextual relationship that links a commentary to "the text it comments upon (without necessarily
citing it)." In the *Architexte* Genette remarks, "All literary
critics, for centuries, have been producing metatext without
knowing it" (82). Since a systematic discussion of metatextuality would require a comprehensive survey of all
literary criticism (whether explicit or implicit), the author
feels such a task must be deferred to the indefinite future.
4. *Hypertextuality:* The "literature in the second degree" discussed above: the superimposition of a later text on an earlier
one that includes all forms of imitation, pastiche, and parody
as well as less obvious superimpositions.[16] This relationship
is the terrain of *Palimpsestes.*
5. *Architextuality [or architexture]:* The most abstract and implicit
of the transcendent categories, the relationship of inclusion
linking each text to the various kinds of discourse of which it
is a representative. (Conventionally, the paratextual elements
– title or preface – can be enlisted to define an architext.)
These generic and modal relationships are surveyed in *Introduction à l'architexte.*[17]

Much as Genette delights in the systematic deployment of
categories, functions, and domains, he is even more fascinated by
the fringes and borderlands between regimes that these explora-
tions open up. *Paratexts* is especially rich in these regions of
ambiguity. Thus the terrain of the paratext poses intriguing
problems for any speech-act analysis, situated as it is between the
first-order illocutionary domain of the public world and that of
the second-order speech-acts of fiction. As Genette suggests in his
Introduction, the special pragmatic status of paratextual declarations requires a carefully calibrated analysis of their illocutionary
force. While he charts a topology that abounds in precisions (and
neologisms), repeatedly drawing distinctions reminiscent of High

[16] For a recent account of parody and pastiche that is both analytic and historical,
see Margaret A. Rose, *Parody: Ancient, Modern, and Postmodern* (Cambridge,
1993).
[17] At the beginning of *Palimpsestes*, Genette notes that Louis Marin had already
used the term *architexte* in "Pour une théorie du texte parabolique," an essay in
Claude Chabrol and Louis Marin, *Le Récit évangélique* (Paris, 1974), 167f.
Genette remarks, however, that this usage for an originary text can be easily
assimilated to his own term *hypotexte*, adding with mock impatience: "It's
about time that some Commissioner of the Republic of Letters impose on us a
coherent terminology" (7).

Structuralism (e.g., *spatial*: peritext/epitext; *temporal*: original/
later/delayed; *enunciatory*: authorial/allographic/actorial),
Genette is never satisfied with purely taxonomic mappings. Each
element is studied as a literary *function*. He is thus equally
concerned with the anatomy and physiology of the devices.
Similarly, he is constantly alert to ways in which these paratextual devices can be both conventional in their form and highly
original in their deployment.

From authorial "pre-texts" to public and private "epitexts,"
Genette is lucidly systematic in his development and often
brilliantly apt in his illustrations. These literary examples range
over nearly three millennia from Homer and Virgil to Nabokov,
Pynchon, Perec, and (inevitably) Proust. The references are also
strenuously "comparative," drawing from a wide range of national literatures and conventional practices. (He points out, for
instance, that one of the most familiar forms of public epitext, the
"interview," arrived only very late in France, 1884, and was
based on an American model. Similarly, he is able to distinguish
the francophone *prière d'insérer*, often implicitly or explicitly the
voice of the author, from the anglophone *blurb* or jacket copy,
which issues from the publisher.) In its scope and exactitude
Paratexts constitutes an encyclopedic survey of the customs and
institutions of the Republic of Letters as they are revealed in the
borderlands of the text, a neglected region that the book maps
with exceptional rigor. Other scholars have studied the literary
use of individual paratextual elements, but Genette seems to be
the first to present a global view of liminal mediations and the
logic of their relation to the reading public.

Any book of this magnitude inevitably casts the shadow of
what it does not propose to do. Genette is explicit about this. In
his epilogue he mentions three aspects of paratextuality that he
has omitted: *translation*, particularly when the author is colla-
boratively engaged in the process; the issuing of the text *in
serialized form*; and the inclusion of *illustrations*, especially those
supplied by the author. But there are other aspects of scholarship
that are deliberately refused. Although the literary examples
cover the canon of Western literature, the study is resolutely
synchronic, "un essai de tableau général," and does not claim to
be a *history* of paratextuality. Save for his local and often brilliant
accounts of specific paratextual devices, Genette is not concerned

with the evolution of forms but with their functions, defined with as much precision as possible. His meticulous anatomies and taxonomic distinctions trace an exhaustive list of logical relationships and modal inflections: of "text" to "book" and of the book to the audience; of the status of the writer; and of enunciative temporalities – the "anterior" and degrees of the "ulterior" and "posterior," the "anthumous" and the "posthumous," etc. Thus the discussion of prefaces (*pace* Sterne) generates a nine-element grid for situating the writer according to "rôle" and "régime" (see the chart in Chapter 8 under "Senders"). These precisions could have proven exhausting as well as exhaustive (an ambition the author explicitly denies) were it not for Genette's humor and richness of illustration. As in the case of Sterne, this humor and richness are pervasive, a signature of his style (nicely captured here by his translator): the sentences are *alive*, not wooden or routine or mechanical. The author's personal tone informs even what would normally be the dullest material or the most academic demonstrations.

In addition to studying these mediating devices, *Paratexts* also resumes, in isolated passages, questions of the hypertext and readership that had been approached from another angle in *Palimpsestes*. This could be seen as an invitation to the reader to push beyond the poetics of liminal structures toward a consideration of the way these discursive functions interact with the more general question of literature as a cultural institution. While such an exploration would extend into another kind of pragmatic borderland, this may be a direction – already implicit in his work – that Genette will explore in subsequent books. The author's reticence before the "institutional question" may reflect a more general contemporary reluctance about addressing the social consequences of theory.

Pausing on the threshold of *Paratexts*, we return finally to Sterne's liminal invitation to his reader at the marbled page, poised on the cusp of the synecdochic relationship between the text and its container. The invitation (and challenge) is to *read*, with vigilance as well as knowledge, and, as Sterne also reminds us, to become through this reading a collaborator in the on-going literary construction. And by recognizing the complex conventions of "the book" we are thus invited to understand how we unwittingly are manipulated by its paratextual elements. Genette too challenges us to *read through* the conventions of the paratext to the discursive life of the book, which in turn enables the reading with renewed vigor of other books.[18]

[18] Speaking of the dynamic role of his "transtextualities," Genette asserted the constructive power of critical reading as long ago as an interview that appeared in the *Magazine Littéraire* (192, February 1983): "So far critics have only interpreted literature; it is now a question of transforming it" (41).

Books by Gérard Genette

Figures. Paris: Editions du Seuil, 1966.
>   [*Figures of Literary Discourse,* eleven essays selected from this
>   and the next two volumes, translated by Alan Sheridan:
>   New York: Columbia University Press, 1982]

Figures II. Paris: Editions du Seuil, 1969.

Figures III. Paris: Editions du Seuil, 1972.
>   [*Narrative Discourse: An Essay in Method,* a substantial portion
>   of this volume ("Discours du récit"), translated by Jane E.
>   Lewin: Ithaca: Cornell University Press, 1980]

Mimologiques: Voyage en Cratyle. Paris: Editions du Seuil, 1976.
>   [*Mimologics,* translated by Thaïs E. Morgan: Lincoln: University
>   of Nebraska Press, 1995]

Introduction à l'architexte. Paris: Editions du Seuil, 1979.
>   [*The Architext: An Introduction,* translated by Jane E. Lewin:
>   Berkeley and Los Angeles: University of California Press,
>   1992]

Palimpsestes: La littérature au second degré. Paris: Editions du Seuil,
1982.
>   [An English translation by Channa Newman is forthcoming
>   from the University of Nebraska Press]

Nouveau discours du récit. Paris: Editions du Seuil, 1983.
>   [*Narrative Discourse Revisited,* translated by Jane E. Lewin:
>   Ithaca: Cornell University Press, 1988]

Seuils. Paris: Editions du Seuil, 1987.
>   [*Paratexts,* translated by Jane E. Lewin: Cambridge University
>   Press, 1997]

Fiction et diction. Paris: Editions du Seuil, 1991.
>   [*Fiction and Diction,* translated by Catherine Porter: Ithaca:
>   Cornell University Press, 1993]

L'Œuvre de l'art: Immanence et transcendance. Paris: Editions du
Seuil, 1994.

Genette has edited a number of collaborative volumes, notably the following titles:

[with R. Barthes and T. Todorov], *Recherches de Proust*. Paris: Editions du Seuil, 1980.

[with R. Debray-Genette and Todorov], *Travail de Flaubert*. Paris: Editions du Seuil, 1983.

[with P. Bénichou and Todorov], *Pensée de Rousseau*. Paris: Editions du Seuil, 1984.

[with Todorov], *Théorie des genres*. Paris: Editions du Seuil, 1986.

Esthétique et poétique. Paris: Editions du Seuil, 1992.

Genette has also published a valuable edition of Dumarsais's *Les Tropes* (1730) with commentary by P. Fontanier from the Paris edition of 1818 (Geneva: Slatkine, 1984).

Translator's note

Throughout this text, the word *classical* refers to the French seventeenth century, except where the context makes clear that some other country or period is meant.

All bracketed material in both the text and the footnotes is the translator's, except bracketed comments within quotations: those are the author's.

Every title mentioned is identified by author the first time it appears in a chapter, except titles of works in the following two categories: (1) works originally written in English and (2) non-English works that are considered classics (for example, the *Iliad*, the *Decameron*, *Madame Bovary*, *War and Peace*, *The Trial*).

Although the author often illustrates his points with references to French literature, readers who are not familiar with the works or authors he invokes will have no trouble grasping his points – most of the time. Thus, annotations of material that in itself may be unfamiliar are generally not necessary. Only when the author's point would be unclear without an explanation have I supplied one.

Some sources of quotations from works originally published in English or from published English translations of works originally written in a language other than English are given in the notes; all others are listed following page 410. Unattributed translations of quotations originally written in French are mine. Unless otherwise stated, the place of publication of French works is Paris.

Possessive adjectives and personal pronouns that refer to authors in general, or to publishers, editors, readers, and critics in general, are in the masculine.

For the English translation, the author added a number of explanatory passages.

1

Introduction

A literary work consists, entirely or essentially, of a text, defined (very minimally) as a more or less long sequence of verbal statements that are more or less endowed with significance. But this text is rarely presented in an unadorned state, unreinforced and unaccompanied by a certain number of verbal or other productions, such as an author's name, a title, a preface, illustrations. And although we do not always know whether these productions are to be regarded as belonging to the text, in any case they surround it and extend it, precisely in order to *present* it, in the usual sense of this verb but also in the strongest sense: to *make present*, to ensure the text's presence in the world, its "reception" and consumption in the form (nowadays, at least) of a book. These accompanying productions, which vary in extent and appearance, constitute what I have called elsewhere the work's *paratext*,[1] in keeping with the sometimes ambiguous meaning of this prefix in French[2] (I mentioned adjectives like "parafiscal" [a "taxe parafiscale" is a special levy] or "paramilitary"). For us, accordingly, the paratext is what enables a text to become a book and to be offered as such to its readers and, more generally, to the public. More than a boundary or a sealed border,

---

1 *Palimpsestes* (Seuil, 1981), 9.
2 And undoubtedly in some other languages, if this remark by J. Hillis Miller, which applies to English, is to be believed: " 'Para' is a double antithetical prefix signifying at once proximity and distance, similarity and difference, interiority and exteriority, ... something simultaneously this side of a boundary line, threshold, or margin, and also beyond it, equivalent in status and also secondary or subsidiary, submissive, as of guest to host, slave to master. A thing in 'para,' moreover, is not only simultaneously on both sides of the boundary line between inside and out. It is also the boundary itself, the screen which is a permeable membrane connecting inside and outside. It confuses them with one another, allowing the outside in, making the inside out, dividing them and joining them" ("The Critic as Host," in *Deconstruction and Criticism*, ed. Harold Bloom et al. [New York: Seabury Press, 1979], 219). This is a rather nice description of the activity of the paratext.

1

1 Introduction

the paratext is, rather, a *threshold*,[3] or – a word Borges used apropos of a preface – a "vestibule" that offers the world at large the possibility of either stepping inside or turning back. It is an "undefined zone"[4] between the inside and the outside, a zone without any hard and fast boundary on either the inward side (turned toward the text) or the outward side (turned toward the world's discourse about the text), an edge, or, as Philippe Lejeune put it, "a fringe of the printed text which in reality controls one's whole reading of the text."[5] Indeed, this fringe, always the conveyor of a commentary that is authorial or more or less legitimated by the author, constitutes a zone between text and off-text, a zone not only of transition but also of *transaction*: a privileged place of a pragmatics and a strategy, of an influence on the public, an influence that – whether well or poorly understood and achieved – is at the service of a better reception for the text and a more pertinent reading of it (more pertinent, of course, in the eyes of the author and his allies). To say that we will speak again of this influence is an understatement: all the rest of this book is about nothing else except its means, methods, and effects. To indicate what is at stake, we can ask one simple question as an example: limited to the text alone and without a guiding set of directions, how would we read Joyce's *Ulysses* if it were not entitled *Ulysses*?

The paratext, then, is empirically made up of a heterogeneous group of practices and discourses of all kinds and dating from all periods which I federate under the term "paratext" in the name of a common interest, or a convergence of effects, that seems to me more important than their diversity of aspect. The table of contents of this book undoubtedly makes it unnecessary for me to list these practices and discourses here, except that one or two

---

3   [The French title of this book is *Seuils*, which means "thresholds."]

4   This image seems inevitable for anyone who deals with the paratext: "an undefined zone ... where two sets of codes are blended: the social code as it pertains to advertising, and the codes producing or regulating the text" (C. Duchet, "Pour une socio-critique, ou Variations sur un incipit," *Littérature* 1 [February 1971], 6); "an intermediary zone between the off-text and the text" (A. Compagnon, *La Seconde Main* [Seuil, 1979], 328).

5   Philippe Lejeune, *Le Pacte autobiographique* (Seuil, 1975), 45. What follows this phrase indicates clearly that the author was partly aiming at what I am calling paratext: "... name of author, title, subtitle, name of series, name of publisher, even the ambiguous game of prefaces."

2

terms are provisionally obscure, and these I will soon define. As far as possible, my approach follows the order in which one usually meets the messages this study explores: the external presentation of a book – name of author, title, and the rest – just as it is offered to a docile reader, which certainly does not mean every reader. In this respect, my saving everything I call "epitext" for the end is no doubt especially arbitrary because many future readers become acquainted with a book thanks to, for example, an interview with the author (if not a magazine review or a recommendation by word of mouth, neither of which, according to our conventions, generally belongs to the paratext, which is characterized by an authorial intention and assumption of responsibility); but the advantages of putting the epitext at the end will, I hope, turn out to be greater than the drawbacks. In addition, this overall arrangement is not so strict as to be especially coercive, and those who ordinarily read books by beginning at the end or in the middle will be able to apply the same method, if it is one, to this book, too.

Furthermore, the paratextual messages inventoried here (in a preliminary, condensed, and doubtless incomplete way) do not constitute a uniformly unvarying and systematic presence around a text: some books lack a preface, some authors resist being interviewed, and in some periods it was not obligatory to record an author's name or even a work's title. The ways and means of the paratext change continually, depending on period, culture, genre, author, work, and edition, with varying degrees of pressure, sometimes widely varying: it is an acknowledged fact that our "media" age has seen the proliferation of a type of discourse around texts that was unknown in the classical world and *a fortiori* in antiquity and the Middle Ages, when texts often circulated in an almost raw condition, in the form of manuscripts devoid of any formula of presentation. I say an *almost* raw condition because the sole fact of transcription – but equally, of oral transmission – brings to the ideality of the text some degree of materialization, graphic or phonic, which, as we will see, may induce paratextual effects. In this sense, one may doubtless assert that a text[6] without a paratext does not exist and never has existed. Paradoxically, paratexts without texts do exist, if only by

---

[6] I now say *texts* and not only *works* in the "noble" sense of that word (literary or artistic productions, in contrast to nonliterary ones), as the need for a paratext

accident: there are certainly works – lost or aborted – about which we know nothing except their titles. (Some examples: numerous post-Homeric epics or classical Greek tragedies, or *La Morsure de l'épaule* [published in English as *The Shoulder Bite*], which Chrétien de Troyes takes credit for at the beginning of *Cligès*, or *La Bataille des Thermopyles*, which was one of Flaubert's abandoned projects and which we know nothing else about except that the word *cnémide* [greave] was not to have appeared in it.) These titles, standing alone, certainly provide food for thought, by which I mean they provide a little more than many a work that is everywhere available and can be read from start to finish. Finally, just as the presence of paratextual elements is not uniformly obligatory, so, too, the public and the reader are not unvaryingly and uniformly obligated: no one is required to read a preface (even if such freedom is not always opportune for the author), and as we will see, many notes are addressed only to *certain* readers.

The approach we will take in studying each of these elements, or rather each of these types of elements, is to consider a certain number of features that, in concert, allow us to define the status of a paratextual message, whatever it may be. These features basically describe a paratextual message's spatial, temporal, substantial, pragmatic, and functional characteristics. More concretely: defining a paratextual element consists of determining its location (the question *where?*); the date of its appearance and, if need be, its disappearance (*when?*); its mode of existence, verbal or other (*how?*); the characteristics of its situation of communication – its sender and addressee (*from whom? to whom?*); and the functions that its message aims to fulfill (*to do what?*). This questionnaire is a little simplistic, but because it almost entirely defines the method employed in the rest of this book, no doubt a few words of justification are in order at the outset.

A paratextual element, at least if it consists of a message that has taken on material form, necessarily has a *location* that can be situated in relation to the location of the text itself: around the text and either within the same volume or at a more respectful (or more prudent) distance. Within the same volume are such

is thrust on every kind of book, with or without aesthetic ambition, even if this study is limited to the paratext of literary works.

elements as the title or the preface and sometimes elements
inserted into the interstices of the text, such as chapter titles or
certain notes. I will give the name *peritext* to this first spatial
category[7] – certainly the more typical one, and the focus of
Chapters 2–12. The distanced elements are all those messages
that, at least originally, are located outside the book, generally
with the help of the media (interviews, conversations) or under
cover of private communications (letters, diaries, and others).
This second category is what, for lack of a better word, I call
epitext; it will be dealt with in Chapters 13 and 14. As must
henceforth go without saying, peritext and epitext completely
and entirely share the spatial field of the paratext. In other words,
for those who are keen on formulae, *paratext = peritext + epitext*.[8]

The *temporal* situation of the paratext, too, can be defined in
relation to that of the text. If we adopt as our point of reference
the date of the text's appearance – that is, the date of its first, or
original,[9] edition – then certain paratextual elements are of prior
(public) production: for example, prospectuses, announcements
of forthcoming publications, or elements that are connected to
prepublication in a newspaper or magazine and will sometimes
disappear with publication in book form, like the famous
Homeric chapter-titles of *Ulysses*, whose official existence proved
to be (if I may put it this way) entirely prenatal. These are
therefore *prior* paratexts. Other paratextual elements – the most
common ones – appear at the same time as the text: this is the
original paratext. An example is the preface to Balzac's *Peau de
chagrin*, a preface produced in 1831 along with the novel it
introduces. Finally, other paratextual elements appear later than
the text, perhaps thanks to a second edition (example: the preface
to Zola's *Thérèse Raquin* – four months later) or to a more remote

[7] The notion of "peritext" overlaps with that of "périgraphie," proposed by
A. Compagnon, *La Seconde Main*, 328–56.
[8] Even so, I must add that the peritext of scholarly editions (generally posthumous) sometimes contains elements that do not belong to the paratext in the
sense in which I define it. Examples of such elements would be extracts from
allographic reviews (see the Pléiade edition of Sartre, the Flammarion edition
of Michelet, and so forth). [The word "allography" in its various forms refers
to a text (preface, review, etc.) that one person writes for another person's
work.]
[9] Here I will disregard the sometimes pronounced technical (bibliographic and
bibliophilic) differences among *first trade edition, original [limited] edition, editio
princeps*, and so on, to summarily call the earliest one *original*.

new edition (example: the preface to Chateaubriand's *Essai sur les révolutions* – twenty-nine years later). For reasons of function that I will elaborate on below, here we have grounds for differentiating between the merely *later* paratext (the Zola case just mentioned) and the *delayed* paratext (the Chateaubriand case). To designate elements that appear after the author's death, I – like everyone else – will use the term *posthumous;* to designate elements produced during the author's lifetime, I will adopt the neologism proposed by my good master Alphonse Allais: *anthumous* paratext.[10] But this last antithesis is applicable not solely to delayed elements; for a paratext can be at one and the same time original and posthumous, if it accompanies a text that is itself posthumous – as do the title and the (fallacious) genre indication of *La Vie de Henry Brulard, écrite par lui-même. Roman imité du Vicaire de Wakefield* [*The Life of Henry Brulard, written by himself. A novel in imitation of "The Vicar of Wakefield"*].

If, then, a paratextual element may appear at any time, it may also disappear, definitively or not, by authorial decision or outside intervention or by virtue of the eroding effect of time. Many titles of the classical period have thus been shortened by posterity, even on the title pages of the most reliable modern editions; and all of Balzac's original prefaces were deliberately deleted in 1842 at the time his works were regrouped to form the whole known as *La Comédie humaine*. Such deletions, which are very common, determine the life span of paratextual elements. Some life spans are very short; to my knowledge, the record is held by the preface to *La Peau de chagrin* (one month). But I said above, "may disappear *definitively or not*": an element that is deleted – for example, when a new edition comes out – can always reemerge upon publication of a still newer edition. Certain notes in Rousseau's *Nouvelle Héloïse*, absent from the second edition, lost no time returning, and the prefaces Balzac "deleted" in 1842 are present today in all reliable editions. The duration of the paratext is often intermittent, therefore, and this

[10] [Allais (1854-1905) was a humorist who wrote light verse, tales, and sketches.] *Anthumous* is the term Allais used to designate those of his works that had appeared in a collection during his lifetime. We should also remember that *posthumus*, "after burial," is a very old (and wonderful) false etymology: *postumus* is merely the superlative of *posterus* ["following" (compar. *posterior*: "following after"; superl.: "hindmost, last")].

intermittence, which I will speak of again, is very closely linked to the basically functional nature of the paratext.

The question of a paratextual element's *substantial* status will be settled, or eluded, here – as it often is in practice – by the fact that almost all the paratexts I consider will themselves be of a *textual*, or at least verbal, kind: titles, prefaces, interviews, all of them utterances that, varying greatly in scope, nonetheless share the linguistic status of the text. Most often, then, the paratext is itself a text: if it is still not *the* text, it is already *some* text. But we must at least bear in mind the paratextual value that may be vested in other types of manifestation: these may be iconic (illustrations), material (for example, everything that originates in the sometimes very significant typographical choices that go into the making of a book), or purely factual. By *factual* I mean the paratext that consists not of an explicit message (verbal or other) but of a fact whose existence alone, if known to the public, provides some commentary on the text and influences how the text is received. Two examples are the age or sex of the author. (How many works, from Rimbaud's to Sollers's, have owed part of their fame or success to the glamor of youth? And do we ever read "a novel by a woman" exactly as we read "a novel" plain and simple, that is, a novel by a man?) Another example is the date of the work: "True admiration," said Renan, "is historical"; in any case, it is indisputable that historical awareness of the period in which a work was written is rarely immaterial to one's reading of that work.

I have just tossed together the most unsubtle and patently obvious characteristics of the factual paratext, but there are many others, some more trivial and others more basic. Examples of the more trivial are membership in an academy (or other exalted body) or receipt of a literary prize. Examples of the more basic (and these we will meet again) are the implicit contexts that surround a work and, to a greater or lesser degree, clarify or modify its significance. These implicit contexts may be authorial (the context formed around, for example, *Père Goriot* by the whole of *La Comédie humaine*), generic (the context formed around the same work [*Père Goriot*] and the same whole [*La Comédie humaine*] by the existence of the genre known as "the novel"), historical (the context formed, for the same example, by the period known as "the nineteenth century"), and so forth. I will not undertake here to specify the nature or gauge the weight of these facts of contextual affiliation, but we must at least remember that, in principle, every context serves as a paratext.

The existence of these facts of contextual affiliation, like the existence of every kind of factual paratext, may or may not be brought to the public's attention by a mention that, itself, belongs to the textual paratext: a genre indication, the mention on a band[11] of a prize, the mention in a "please-insert"[12] of an author's age, the indirect disclosure of an author's sex by way of his or her name, and so forth. But the existence of these facts does not always need to be mentioned to be a matter of "common knowledge." For example, most readers of *A la recherche du Temps perdu* are aware of the two biographical facts of Proust's part-Jewish ancestry and his homosexuality. Knowledge of those two facts inevitably serves as a paratext to the pages of Proust's work that deal with those two subjects. I am not saying that people must know those facts; I am saying only that people who do know them read Proust's work differently from people who do not and that anyone who denies the difference is pulling our leg. The same is true, of course, for the facts of context: reading Zola's *Assommoir* as a self-contained work is very different from reading it as an episode of *Les Rougon-Macquart*.

The *pragmatic* status of a paratextual element is defined by the characteristics of its situation of communication: the nature of the sender and addressee, the sender's degree of authority and responsibility, the illocutionary force of the sender's message, and undoubtedly some other characteristics I have overlooked.

The sender of a paratextual message (like the sender of all other messages) is not necessarily its *de facto* producer, whose identity is not very important to us: suppose, for example, that the foreword of *La Comédie humaine*, signed Balzac, had in fact been written by one of Balzac's friends. The sender is defined by a putative attribution and an acceptance of responsibility. Most

---

[11] [The band is a strip of brightly colored paper – about 2-1/2 inches from top to bottom – that encircles a book or journal across its lower third. Some bands are unbroken and prevent the casual reader from flipping through the book or journal; others have a front and back flap that fold over the front and back covers of the book or journal. Printed on the band may be various kinds of publisher's information, as discussed in Chapter 2, "The Publisher's Peritext."]

[12] [The "please-insert" (*le prière d'insérer*) is what nowadays is called jacket copy. It is the subject of Chapter 5.]

often the sender is the author (*authorial* paratext), but the sender may equally well be the publisher: unless a please-insert is signed by the author, it customarily belongs to the *publisher's* paratext. The author and the publisher are (legally and in other ways) the two people responsible for the text and the paratext, but they may delegate a portion of their responsibility to a third party. A preface written by this third party and accepted by the author, such as Anatole France's preface to Proust's *Les Plaisirs et les jours*, still belongs (it seems to me), by the mere fact of this acceptance, to the paratext – which this time is an *allographic* paratext. There are also situations in which responsibility for the paratext is, in a way, shared: one example is an interview with the author in which someone else poses the questions and generally "collects" the author's remarks and reports them, faithfully or not.

The addressee may be roughly defined as "the public," but this is much too loose a definition, for the public of a book extends potentially to all of humankind. Thus some qualifications are called for. Certain paratextual elements are actually addressed to (which does not mean they reach) the public in general – that is, every Tom, Dick, and Harry. This is the case (I will come back to it) of the title or of an interview. Other paratextual elements are addressed (with the same reservation) more specifically or more restrictively only to readers of the text. This is typically the case of the preface. Still others, such as the early forms of the please-insert, are addressed exclusively to critics; and others, to booksellers. All of that (whether peritext or epitext) constitutes what I call the *public* paratext. Finally, other paratextual elements are addressed, orally or in writing, to ordinary individuals, who may or may not be well known and are not supposed to go around talking about them: this is the *private* paratext. Its most private part consists of messages the author addresses to himself, in his diary or elsewhere: this is the *intimate* paratext, so designated by the mere fact of its being addressed to oneself, regardless of its content.

By definition, something is not a paratext unless the author or one of his associates accepts responsibility for it, although the degree of responsibility may vary. From the language of politics I will borrow a standard distinction, one easier to use than to define: the distinction between the official and the unofficial (or semiofficial).[13] The *official* is any paratextual message openly accepted by the author or publisher or both – a message for which the author or publisher cannot evade responsibility. "Official," then, applies to everything that, originating with the author or publisher, appears in the anthumous peritext – for example, the title or the original preface, or even the comments signed by the author in a work for which he is fully responsible (for example, Tournier's *Vent Paraclet* [a book of essays about Tournier's own novels]). The *unofficial* (or *semiofficial*) is most of the authorial epitext: interviews, conversations, and confidences, responsibility for which the author can always more or less disclaim with denials of the type "That's not exactly what I said" or "Those were off-the-cuff remarks" or "That wasn't intended for publication" or indeed even with a "solemn declaration" like Robbe-Grillet's at the Cerisy colloquium. There he refused outright to grant any "importance" to "[my] journal articles haphazardly collected in a volume under the name of Essays" and, "all the more," to "the oral remarks I may make here, even if I agree to their later publication" – a declaration amounting, I imagine, to a new version of the paradox of the Cretan.[14] Also and perhaps especially unofficial is what the author permits or asks a third party (an allographic preface-writer or an "authorized" commentator) to say: see the part played by a Larbaud or a Stuart Gilbert in the diffusion of the Homeric keys to *Ulysses*, a diffusion Joyce organized but did not publicly take responsibility for. Naturally there are many intermediary or undecidable situations in what is really only a difference of degree, but these shadings offer the author an undeniable advantage: it is sometimes in one's interest to have certain things "known" without having (supposedly) said them oneself.

A final pragmatic characteristic of the paratext is what – making free with a term used by philosophers of language – I call the *illocutionary force* of its message. Here again we are dealing with a gradation of states. A paratextual element can commu-

---

[13] [The French words are *officiel* and *officieux*. *Officieux* means indistinguishably "unofficial" and "semiofficial" and will be rendered "unofficial" except in contexts in which only "semiofficial" makes sense.]

[14] *Colloque Robbe-Grillet* (1975) (Paris: 10/18, 1976), 1:316. [The Centre Culturel International of Cerisy-la-Salle was the site of a colloquium on "Robbe-Grillet: Analyse, théorie." The paradox: A man from Crete says, "All Cretans are liars." If the statement is true, he must be lying . . .]

nicate a piece of sheer *information* – the name of the author, for example, or the date of publication. It can make known an *intention*, or an *interpretation* by the author and/or the publisher: this is the chief function of most prefaces, and also of the genre indications on some covers or title pages (*a novel* does not signify "This book is a novel," a defining assertion that hardly lies within anyone's power, but rather "Please look on this book as a novel"). It can convey a genuine *decision*: "Stendhal" and *"Le Rouge et le noir"* do not mean "My name is Stendhal" (which is false in the eyes of the registry office) and "This book is named *Le Rouge et le noir*" (which makes no sense), but "I choose the pseudonym Stendhal" and "I, the author, decide to give this book the title *Le Rouge et le noir*." Or it can involve a *commitment*: some genre indications (autobiography, history, memoir) have, as we know, a more binding contractual force ("I commit myself to telling the truth") than do others (novel, essay);[15] and a simple notice like "First Volume" or "Volume One" has the weight of a promise – or, as Northrop Frye says, of a threat. Or a paratextual element can give a word of advice or, indeed, even issue a *command*: "This book," says Hugo in the preface to *Les Contemplations*, "must be read the way one would read the book of a dead man"; "It must all," writes Barthes at the head of *Roland Barthes par Roland Barthes*, "be considered as if spoken by a character in a novel"; and some permissions ("You may read this book in one-or-another sequence," "You may skip this or that") indicate just as clearly, although discreetly, the peremptory potential of the paratext. Some paratextual elements entail even the power logicians call *performative* – that is, the ability to perform what they describe ("I open the meeting"): this is the case with dedications and inscriptions. To dedicate or inscribe a book to So-and-So is obviously nothing more than to have printed or to write on one of its pages a phrase of the type "To So-and-So" – an extreme

---

[15] [The words "contract" and "contractual" as used in this book are based on Philippe Lejeune's studies of autobiography. Lejeune makes the point that "autobiography is a *contractual* genre," and he speaks of "the implicit or explicit contract proposed by the *author* to the *reader*, the contract that determines how the text is read" ("The Autobiographical Contract," in *French Literary Theory Today: A Reader*, ed. Tzvetan Todorov, trans. R. Carter [Cambridge University Press, 1982], 219). In *Palimpsestes* Genette points out that "the term [contract] is obviously highly optimistic as to the role of the reader, who has signed nothing and who can take this contract or leave it. But it is true that the genre or other indications *commit* the author" (9).]

case of paratextual efficiency, for saying it is doing it. But there is already much of that in affixing a title or selecting a pseudonym, acts that mimic any creative power.

These comments on illocutionary force, then, have brought us imperceptibly to the main point, which is the *functional* aspect of the paratext. It is the main point because, clearly and except for isolated exceptions (which we will meet here and there), the paratext in all its forms is a discourse that is fundamentally heteronomous, auxiliary, and dedicated to the service of something other than itself that constitutes its raison d'être. This something is the text. Whatever aesthetic or ideological investment the author makes in a paratextual element (a "lovely title" or a preface-manifesto), whatever coquettishness or paradoxical reversal he puts into it, the paratextual element is always subordinate to "its" text, and this functionality determines the essence of its appeal and its existence.

But in contrast to the characteristics of place, time, substance, or pragmatic regime, the functions of the paratext cannot be described theoretically and, as it were, *a priori* in terms of status. The spatial, temporal, substantial, and pragmatic situation of a paratextual element is determined by a more or less free choice from among possible alternatives supplied by a general and uniform grid; and from these possible alternatives, only one term – to the exclusion of the others – can be adopted. A preface, for example, is necessarily (by definition) peritextual; it is original, later, *or* delayed; authorial *or* allographic; and so forth. This series of options and necessities strictly defines a status and therefore a type. Functional choices, however, are not of this alternative, exclusive, either-or kind. A title, a dedication or inscription, a preface, an interview can have several purposes at once, selected – without exclusion of all the others – from the (more or less open) repertory appropriate to each type of element (the title has its own functions, the dedication of the work its own, the preface takes care of other or sometimes the same functions), without prejudice to the subcategories specific to each paratextual element (a thematic title like *War and Peace* does not describe its text in exactly the same way a formal title like *Epistles* or *Sonnets* does; the stakes for an inscription of a copy are not those for a dedication of a work; a delayed preface does not have the same purpose as an original preface, nor an allographic preface the same purpose as an authorial preface; and so forth). The functions of the paratext therefore constitute a highly empirical and highly diversified object that must be brought into focus inductively, genre by genre and often species by species. The only significant regularities one can introduce into this apparent contingency are to establish these relations of subordination between function and status and thus pinpoint various sorts of *functional types* and, as well, reduce the diversity of practices and messages to some fundamental and highly recurrent themes, for experience shows that the discourse we are dealing with here is more "constrained" than many others and is one in which authors innovate less often than they imagine.

As for the converging (or diverging) effects that result from the composition around a text of the whole of its paratext – and Lejeune has shown, apropos of autobiography, how delicately complex these effects may be – they can depend only on an individual, work-by-work analysis (and synthesis), at whose threshold a generic study like this inevitably leaves off. To provide a very elementary illustration (elementary because the structure in question is limited to two terms): a full title (or titular whole) like *Henri Matisse, Roman* [Aragon's *Henri Matisse, A Novel*] obviously contains a discordance between the title in the strict sense (*Henri Matisse*) and the genre indication (*Roman*) – a discordance that the reader is invited to resolve if he can (or at least to integrate into an oxymoronic figure of the type "to lie true" [*mentir vrai*]) and to which perhaps only the text will give him the key, which by definition is individual even if the formula seems likely to attract a following[16] or, indeed, to become stereotyped into a genre.

One last point, which I hope is unnecessary: we are dealing here with a synchronic and not a diachronic study – an attempt at a general picture, not a history of the paratext. This remark is prompted not by any disdain whatever for the historical dimension but, once again, by the belief that it is appropriate to define objects before one studies their evolution. Indeed, basically this work consists of dissolving the empirical objects inherited from

---

[16] Philippe Roger, *Roland Barthes, Roman* (Grasset, 1986).

tradition (for example, "the preface"), on the one hand analyzing them into more narrowly defined objects (the original authorial preface, the delayed preface, the allographic preface, and so forth) and on the other hand integrating them into broader wholes (the peritext, the paratext in general). Thus this work consists of bringing into focus categories that, until now, have been disregarded or misperceived. The articulation of these categories describes the paratextual field, and their establishment is a precondition for any attempt to provide historical perspective. Diachronic considerations will not, however, be omitted: this study, after all, bears on the most socialized side of the practice of literature (the way its relations with the public are organized), and at times it will inevitably seem something like an essay on the customs and institutions of the Republic of Letters. But diachronic considerations will not be set forth *a priori* as uniformly crucial, for each element of the paratext has its own history. Some of these elements are as old as literature; others came into being – or acquired their official status, after centuries of "secret life" that constitute their prehistory – with the invention of the book; others, with the birth of journalism and the modern media. Others disappeared in the meantime; and quite often some replace others so as to perform, for better or worse, an analogous role. Finally, some seem to have undergone, and to be undergoing still, a more rapid or more significant evolution than others (but stability is as much a historical fact as change is). For example, the title has its fashions – very obvious ones – which inevitably "date" any individual title the minute it is uttered; the authorial preface, in contrast, has changed hardly at all – except in its material presentation – since Thucydides. The general history of the paratext, punctuated by the stages of a technological evolution that supplies it with means and opportunities, would no doubt be the history of those ceaseless phenomena of sliding, substitution, compensation, and innovation which ensure, with the passing centuries, the continuation and to some extent the development of the paratext's efficacy. To undertake to write that general history, one would have to have available a broader and more comprehensive investigation than this one, which does not go beyond the bounds of Western culture or even often enough beyond French literature. Clearly, then, what follows is only a wholly inceptive exploration, at the very provisional service of what – thanks to others – will perhaps come after. But enough of the excuses and precautions, the unavoidable themes or clichés, of every preface: no more dawdling on the threshold of the threshold.[17]

[17] As one might suspect, this study owes much to suggestions from the various audiences who participated in its development. To everyone, my deep gratitude and my performative thanks.

2

The publisher's peritext

I give the name *publisher's peritext* to the whole zone of the peritext that is the direct and principal (but not exclusive) responsibility of the publisher (or perhaps, to be more abstract but also more exact, of the *publishing house*) – that is, the zone that exists merely by the fact that a book is published and possibly republished and offered to the public in one or several more or less varied presentations. The word *zone* indicates that the characteristic feature of this aspect of the paratext is basically spatial and material. We are dealing here with the outermost peritext (the cover, the title page, and their appendages) and with the book's material construction (selection of format, of paper, of typeface, and so forth), which is executed by the typesetter and printer but decided on by the publisher, possibly in consultation with the author. All these technical givens themselves come under the discipline called *bibliology*, on which I have no wish to encroach; here my concern with them extends only to their appearance and effect, that is, only to their strictly paratextual value. Besides, this paratext's dependence on the publisher basically assigns it to a relatively recent historical period, whose terminus *a quo* coincides with the beginnings of printing, or the period historians ordinarily call modern and contemporary. This is not to say that the (much longer) pre-Gutenberg period, with its handwritten copies that were really even then a form of publication, knew nothing of our peritextual elements; and below we will have reason to ask how antiquity and the Middle Ages handled such elements as the title or the name of the author, whose chief location today is the publisher's peritext. But what the pre-Gutenberg period did not know anything of – precisely because of the handwritten (and oral) circulation of its texts – is the publisher's implementation of this

16

peritext, which is essentially typographical and bibliographical in nature.[1]

Formats

The most all-embracing aspect of the production of a book – and thus of the materialization of a text for public use – is doubtless the choice of *format*. Over time, the meaning of this word has changed once or twice. Originally it designates two things: one is the manner in which a sheet of paper is or is not folded to end up as the "leaves" of a book (or, in common parlance, as the book's *pages*, one recto-verso leaf naturally making two pages, even if one of the two remains blank);[2] the other is the size of the original sheet itself, conventionally designated by a type of watermark (*shell, Jésus, bunch of grapes*, and so forth).[3] The manner of folding thus did not by itself indicate the flat dimensions of a book; but it quickly became a shorthand way of estimating them: a folio volume (folded once, hence two leaves, or four pages per sheet) or a quarto volume (folded twice, hence four leaves, or eight pages per sheet) was a large book; an octavo (eight leaves [*8vo*]) was a medium book; and a duodecimo (*12mo*), a sextodecimo (*16mo*), or an octodecimo (*18mo*), a small book. In the classical period, "large formats" (quarto) were reserved for serious works (that is, works that were religious or philosophical rather than literary) or for prestige editions that enshrined a literary work. Montesquieu's *Lettres persanes*, for example, appears in two octavo volumes, but his *Esprit des lois* in two quarto volumes; the

---

[1] Among the many works that deal with the history and prehistory of the book, I refer readers particularly to Lucien Febvre and Henri-Jean Martin, *L'Apparition du livre* (Albin Michel, 1958) [tr. *The Coming of the Book: The Impact of Printing 1450–1800*, trans. David Gerard (London: NLB, 1976)]; A. Labarre, *Histoire du livre* (PUF, 1970); and H.-J. Martin and R. Chartier, *Histoire de l'édition française* (Promodis, 1983–87).

[2] The practice of folding and assembling sheets and binding the resulting unit with either a flexible or a stiff material actually predates the use of paper: it goes back to the third and fourth centuries, when the *codex* of parchment replaced the *volumen* of papyrus; but the techniques of producing paper helped to standardize – and therefore codify – the practice.

[3] [In *Lost Illusions*, Balzac mentions *Coquille* (Shell), *Jésus*, and *Raisin* (Grapes) as "names given to the different sizes of paper ... [and drawn] from the watermark stamped in the middle of the sheet" (Penguin, p. 108). The "Jésus" watermark was the monogram "I. J. S."]

Lettres persanes is not awarded the honor of a quarto until the big collected edition of the *Œuvres* of Montesquieu in three volumes (1758). Rousseau's *Nouvelle Héloïse* and *Emile* come out in 12mo; the big edition of the "complete" works of 1765 appears in six quarto volumes. Bernardin de Saint-Pierre's *Paul et Virginie* likewise goes into quarto for the "recherché" and illustrated edition of 1806.[4] This way of assigning a work to a size is certainly not applied universally (the first edition of the *Fables* of La Fontaine, in 1668, is quarto), but it definitely predominates.

At the beginning of the nineteenth century, when large volumes had become rarer, the dividing line between serious and nonserious shifted: 8vo was used for serious literature, and 12mo and smaller were used for the cheap editions reserved for popular literature. We know that Stendhal spoke contemptuously of the "small 12mo novels for chambermaids."[5] But even then, serious works that also proved commercially successful could be put out in a new edition in "small format" for a more casual and more ambulatory reading. The first separate edition of *Paul et Virginie* (1789)[6] was 18mo, "for the benefit," said the author, "of women who want my works to fit into their pockets"; the same explanation accompanied the fourth edition of Chateaubriand's *Génie du christianisme* – "one of those books," says the foreword, "that people like to read while in the country and enjoy taking along when they go for a walk."

The foregoing examples no doubt suffice to indicate the paratextual value conveyed by these distinctions of format, distinctions that already had the same weight and ambiguity as our contrast between "trade edition" and "pocket edition" – with the pocket format capable of connoting equally well a work's "popular" nature or its admission into the pantheon of classics.

Aside from the contrast between trade and pocket edition, to which I will return, the modern, purely quantitative meaning of

---

4 The other great deluxe edition of this text with the enviable fate was, from Curmer in 1838, a "large 8vo" in a printing of thirty thousand copies; it was hailed as "the most beautiful book of the century."

5 "Printed by M. Pigoreau, ... where the hero is always perfect and ravishingly beautiful, very well built and with big, protuberant eyes," and "read much more in the provinces than the 8vo novel printed by Levavasseur or Gosselin, whose author is trying to achieve literary excellence" (letter to Salvagnoli about *Le Rouge et le noir*, itself 8vo from Levavasseur).

6 [When first published, *Paul et Virginie* was volume 4 of Bernardin de Saint-Pierre's *Etudes de la nature* (1787).]

the word "format" is certainly less freighted with paratextual value. The dimensions of our trade editions have become standardized or stereotyped at about the average formats of the nineteenth century, with variances, depending on publisher or series, that no longer have much relevance in themselves, except that during the past two or three decades publishers have gotten into the habit of using a relatively large format (about 6-1/2 x 9-1/2 inches) for supposed best-sellers, those famed "beach books" that (as has been said over and over again) have to be large enough for the cover in the store window to seem like a poster, and heavy enough for the book itself to prevent a beach towel from being gone with the wind. That practice could be considered a notable reversal of the classical contrast, though a limited one, as it is seasonal and is contradicted at least by the persistence, or resurgence, of prestigious large formats like the 7-1/2 x 9-1/2 that Gallimard reserves for graphically ambitious books such as Aragon's *Fou d'Elsa* or for certain very spatialized texts by Butor, such as *Mobile, Description de San Marco, 6,810,000 litres d'eau par seconde, Boomerang,*[7] and so on.

The latest accepted meaning of the word *format* is obviously no longer connected either with the manner of folding (the generalized use of trimming has almost entirely erased our awareness of this feature) or, despite appearances, with the notion of size: the latest accepted meaning of "format" is the one that has become attached to the undoubtedly transitory expression *format de poche* [pocket size]. The contrast between "trade edition" and "pocket edition" is, as we know, based on technical and commercial features, the most important of which is certainly not size (ability to fit into a pocket), even if for some years size did constitute an undeniable selling point.[8] The contrast between trade and pocket,

---

7 [In *Mobile*, for example, the white spaces on the page – their relations to the printed words – play a major role in the effect created and in the expression of theme.] *Boomerang* pushes the exploitation of graphic resources so far as to use three colors of ink: black, blue, and red. This procedure is no doubt costly, but it is potentially so very effective that one is astonished to see it used so rarely outside of textbooks.

8 Those years were by no means softbound series' earliest years: the designation "pocket" was not used either in the nineteenth century by Tauchnitz or in the twentieth by Albatross (1932), Penguin (1935), or Pelican (1937); its first appearance was not until 1938 with the American Pocket Book and its symbol, Gertrude the Kangaroo. And Pocket was only one softbound series among several (Seal, then Avon, Dell, Bantam, Signet, and so forth), not all of which singled out size for attention. The nearly-twenty-year quasi monopoly of the

as a matter of fact, has much more to do with the old distinction
between books bound in a stiff material and books bound in a
flexible material – which has been perpetuated in English-
speaking countries in the distinction between hardcover and
paperback – and with the very long history of popular series,
which goes back at least to the small Elzevier 12mo of the
seventeenth century; then, via the 12mo or 32mo of the Bibliothèque bleue troyenne, to the eighteenth century; and then, via
the railway series, to the nineteenth. This is obviously not the
place to repeat a tale that has already been told more than once,[9]
the tale of the history and prehistory of the "pocket-size" book,
nor is it the place to reexamine the controversy that greeted the
emergence of this phenomenon, at least among the French
intelligentsia.[10] This controversy, just like the ones that accompanied the birth first of writing and then of printing, was located on
a terrain that was typically axiological, not to say ideological: it
all came down to knowing, or rather saying, whether the "culture
de poche" (in Hubert Damisch's phrase) was a good or a bad
thing. Such value judgments obviously lie outside our present
subject matter: good or bad, source of cultural wealth or cultural
poverty, the "culture de poche" is today a universal fact; and – all
evaluation aside – Damisch's phrase has proven to be wholly
accurate, for the "pocket edition" (that is, simply the republication at a low price of old or recent works that have first undergone the commercial test of the trade edition) has indeed become
an instrument of "culture," an instrument, in other words, for
constituting and, naturally, disseminating a relatively permanent
collection of works *ipso facto* sanctioned as "classics." A glance
over the history of publishing shows, moreover, that from the
very beginning this was indeed the intention of forerunners like
Tauchnitz (early nineteenth century: Greek and Latin classics) or,
a century later, the founders of Albatross (1932; first title: Joyce,

French *Livre de poche* [Pocket book] (1953) is what made the reference to format
a fixture in the French language.

9 See in particular Hans Schmoller, "The Paperback Revolution," in *Essays in the
History of Publishing*, ed. Asa Briggs (London: Longman, 1974), 283–318;
Y. Johannot, *Quand le livre devient poche* (PUG, 1978); Piet Schreuders, *Paper-
backs, U.S.A.: A Graphic History, 1939–1959*, trans. Josh Pachter (San Diego: Blue
Dolphin, 1981); G. de Sairigné, *L'Aventure du livre de poche* (H.C., 1983); and the
dossier published by *Le Monde* on March 23, 1984.

10 See H. Damisch, "La Culture de poche," in *Mercure de France* (November 1964),
and the ensuing discussion in *Les Temps modernes* (April and May 1965).

Dubliners): to republish ancient or modern classics at low prices
for use by a basically "university" public – that is, undergradu-
ates. This was still, before World War II, the intention of Penguin
and Pelican. The strictly "popular" orientation, introduced in
about 1938 in the United States and facilitated by the war, was
unquestionably secondary; and the present competition among
the serious and indeed scholarly "pockets" (in France: Folio
classique, Points, GF, among others) – everything that German
publishing professionals call "books à la Suhrkamp"[11] – is little
more than a return to the pocket book's roots, a return inspired
by the obvious (current) profitability of the university market.
The very pronounced development of the critical and documentary apparatus, moreover, parallels the development manifested
in semicritical trade series (such as the Classiques Garnier) or in
relatively sumptuous series (such as the Pléiade) – one encountered as well in the publishing of art books or record jackets:
erudition at the service of culture, or one could say, more
caustically, erudition as a sign of culture – and culture as a sign of
what?

Today, therefore, "pocket size" is basically no longer a format
but a vast set or nebula of series – for "pocket" still means
"series" – from the most popular to the most "distinguished,"
indeed, the most pretentious; and the series emblem, much more
than size, conveys two basic meanings. One is purely economic:
the assurance (variable, and sometimes illusory) of a better price.
The other is indeed "cultural" and, to speak of what interests us,
paratextual: the assurance of a selection based on *revivals*, that is,
reissues. Occasionally someone speculates about the possibility of
reversing the flow – publishing works first in pocket size, then
producing in more expensive editions those titles that have
triumphantly passed the first test – but this seems contrary to all
the technical, media, and commercial givens, even if in particular
situations certain books have taken this paradoxical journey and
even if certain pocket series welcome, as experiments, some
previously unpublished works that are thus immediately can-
onized. For undoubtedly the pocket edition will long be synonymous with canonization. On that account alone, pocket format is

[11] [Suhrkamp is a German publisher of intellectual books packaged for a
relatively wide readership – something of a German equivalent to Gallimard.]

a formidable (although ambiguous – indeed, because ambiguous) paratextual message.

Series

That brief detour across the immense continent of the pocket edition has thus taken us, paradoxically, from the old notion of format to the more modern notion of series, which undoubtedly is itself only a more intense and sometimes more spectacular specification of the notion of publisher's emblem. The recent development of the use of series, whose history and geography I will not attempt to trace here, certainly responds to the need felt by big-name publishers to demonstrate and control the diversification of their activities. Nowadays that need is so powerful that the lack of series (books published not as part of any series) is experienced by the public, and articulated by the media, as a sort of implicit or *a contrario* series: for example, people speak of Gallimard's "white series" – an almost legitimate misuse of the term – to designate anything in that publisher's output that does not bear a specific emblem.[12] We know the symbolic power of this degree zero, whose unofficial name produces a highly effective ambiguity, "white" doing the work of a sign in the absence of a signifier.

The series emblem, even in this mute form, therefore amplifies the publisher's emblem, immediately indicating to the potential reader the type of work, if not the genre, he is dealing with: French or a foreign literature, avant-garde or tradition, fiction or essay, history or philosophy, and so forth. We know that for a long time, the catalogues of pocket series have included genre specifications symbolized by the choice of color (as early as the Albatrosses, then the Penguins of the 1930s: orange = fiction, grey = politics, red = theatre, purple = essays, yellow = miscellaneous), by the choice of geometric form (Penguin after World War II: square = fiction, circle = poetry, triangle = mystery, diamond = miscellaneous; Idées-Gallimard: open book = literature, hourglass = philosophy, crystal = science, trio of cells = human sciences – a whole study, and an entertaining one at that, could be done of those broad symbolizations), or, in Points, by what is

---

[12] [The French word for "white" is *blanc*, which also means "blank."]

done with any given term, in color, on a fixed list. With these sometimes very emphatic forays into the area of generic or intellectual choices, the paratext that most typically derives from and depends on primarily the publisher obviously encroaches on the prerogatives of an author, who thought himself an essayist but ends up a sociologist, linguist, or literary theorist. Publishing (and therefore society) is sometimes structured like a language, the language of the Conseil supérieur des universités or of the Comité national de la recherche scientifique; it is, in other words, structured by subject (and for some very straightforward reasons). To be admitted into the pocket-book club, the main thing is not always to be a certain size but rather to fit a certain "profile," and to face up to it.

The cover and its appendages

Except in technical bibliographies and, naturally, in the 10/18 series, which has made its measurements into an emblem, the folding and dimensions of a book are generally not stated, and the reader must make them out for himself. To pass from size to emblem, therefore, is to pass from a feature that is all-embracing and implicit to a feature that is localized and explicit. The place for the emblem is the publisher's peritext: the cover, the title page, and their appendages, which present to the public at large and then to the reader many other items of information, some of which are authorial and some of which are the publisher's responsibility. In the rest of this chapter I will draw up a rough and probably incomplete inventory of these items of information; in the next few chapters, I will return to the most important ones.

The printed cover – a cover made of paper or board – is a fairly recent phenomenon and seems to date from the early nineteenth century. In the classical period, books appeared inside a leather binding that was mute except for a short version of the title and sometimes, on the spine, the author's name. Said to be one of the first examples of a printed cover is that of Voltaire's *Œuvres complètes*, put out by Baudoin in 1825. At that time the title page was the main site of the publisher's paratext, but once the possibilities of the cover were discovered, they seem to have been exploited very rapidly. So here is a basic list (unless I have omitted something) of what may appear, in no special order, on a cover, with all periods and all genres mixed together – and presented with the understanding that all these possibilities have never been exploited at one and the same time and that nowadays the only items virtually (if not legally) obligatory are the name of the author, the title of the work, and the emblem of the publisher.[13]

Cover 1 (front cover):

- Name or pseudonym of the author(s)
- Title(s) of the author(s) [e.g., professor of ..., member of ..., etc.]
- Title(s) of the work
- Genre indication
- Name of the translator(s), of the preface-writer(s), of the person(s) responsible for establishing the text and preparing the critical apparatus
- Dedication
- Epigraph
- Likeness of the author or, for some biographical or critical studies, of whoever is the subject of the study
- Facsimile of the author's signature
- Specific illustration
- Name and/or colophon of the series
- Name of the person(s) responsible for this series
- In the case of a reprint, mention of the original series
- Name or trade name and/or initials and/or colophon of the publisher (or, in the case of a co-publication, of both publishers)
- Address of the publisher
- Number of printings, or "editions," or "thousands"
- Date
- Price

Usually these localized verbal, numerical, or iconographic items of information are supplemented by more comprehensive ones pertaining to the style or design of the cover, characteristic of the publisher, the series, or a group of series. Simply the color of the paper chosen for the cover can strongly indicate a type of book. At the beginning of the twentieth century, yellow covers were synonymous with licentious French books: "I remember,"

---

[13] See P. Jaffray, "Fiez-vous aux apparences ou Les politiques de couverture des éditeurs," *Livres-Hebdo* (March 31, 1981).

writes Butor, "the scandalized tone of a clergyman, in a British railway car, who thundered at a friend of mine: 'Madame, don't you know that God sees you reading that yellow book!' That accursed and indecent signification is certainly the reason Aubrey Beardsley named his quarterly *The Yellow Book*."[14] More subtly and specifically, not too long ago the cover of the French translation of Thomas Mann's *Doctor Faustus* (*Docteur Faustus*, Albin Michel, 1962) showed a sheet of paper very faintly imprinted with a musical score.

Covers 2 and 3, the inside front and back covers, are generally mute, but this rule admits of exceptions: magazines often put publisher's information there, and that is where the volumes in the small-sized series Microcosme du Seuil always include an illustration that can – or rather *cannot not* – serve as a paratext. In the volume *Roland Barthes par Roland Barthes*, two handwritten instructions were placed there, the first of which I mentioned in the previous chapter: a real (albeit fictional) genre contract.

Cover 4, the back cover, is another strategically important spot, which may contain at least the following:

• Reminder, for the benefit of those with deep amnesia, of the name of the author and the title of the work
• Biographical and/or bibliographical notice
• Please-insert [see Chapter 5]
• Press quotations or other laudatory comments about earlier works by the same author or, indeed, about this work itself, if it is a new edition or if the publisher has been able to obtain such comments before publication (this latter practice is what the British and Americans customarily refer to by the evocative term *blurb* or, more literally, *promotional statement*, an equivalent of the French *bla-bla* or *baratin* [patter]; sometimes these even appear on cover 1)
• Mention of other works published by the same house
• Genre indication, like those I evoked apropos of pocket-book series
• Series statement of principles, or intent
• Date of printing
• Number of reprintings
• Mention of the cover's printer

[14] M. Butor, *Les Mots dans la peinture* (Skira, 1969), 143.

- Mention of the designer of the cover art
- Identification of the cover illustration
- Price
- ISBN (International Standard Book Number); the ISBN system was created in 1975; the first numeral indicates the language of publication, the second the publisher, the third the book's own number within this publisher's output, and the fourth – I am told – is an electronic control key
- Magnetic bar code, in the process of being generalized for obvious practical reasons; this is undoubtedly the only piece of information the reader can do absolutely nothing with, but I imagine that bibliophiles will end up investing a portion of their neurosis in it
- "Paid" advertisement – that is, paid to the publisher by a manufacturer outside of publishing (for I doubt that a publisher will ever accept an ad from a competitor); it is up to the reader to establish an ad's relation to the theme of the book; an example: an ad for American cigarettes on Dashiell Hammett's *Sang maudit* [*The Dain Curse*] (Carré noir, 1982).

I've surely forgotten some of the items that may go on cover 4, but it is necessary to say that sometimes, *a contrario*, cover 4 is almost mute, as occasionally with Gallimard, Mercure, and Minuit, especially for poetry series: this reserve is obviously an external sign of nobility.

The *spine*, a narrow site but one with obvious strategic importance, generally bears the name of the author, the colophon of the publisher, and the title of the work. And here a technical quarrel rages between those who favor horizontal printing and those who favor vertical, and, among the latter, between those who favor an ascending vertical (most French publishers) and those who favor a descending vertical (a few French and most foreign publishers, who argue that this arrangement is compatible with the position of a book lying flat on its back, allowing both its front cover and its spine to be read); there are, in addition, a few cases of coexistence between horizontal and vertical. John Barth claims to have had, while writing *The Sot-Weed Factor*, two equally important aims: the first was to construct a plot even more complicated than the plot of *Tom Jones* (mission accomplished); the second was to write a book long enough, and therefore thick enough, so that its title could be printed in a single horizontal line on the spine. I don't know if the original edition fulfilled his wish, but the paperback editions scoff at it. In any case, one need not write a long text, one need only choose a short title. The ideal would undoubtedly be to make the one proportional to the other and, at any rate, to prohibit titles that are longer than their texts.

Finally, the cover can include folds, or flaps, atrophied vestiges of an earlier tuck-taking,[15] which nowadays can accommodate some of the items I have already listed (or reminders of them), particularly the please-insert, the statement of principles of the series, and the list of works by the author or in the same series. Here again, a mute fold, like every wasteful act, is a sign of distinction.

But as a matter of fact the cover is not always – and in the current state of development of the publisher's presentation, is less and less often – the first manifestation of the book offered to the reader's perception, for more and more publishers are clothing the cover itself wholly or partially with a new paratextual support: the *dust jacket* (or *wrapper*) or the *band* [see Chapter 1, note 11], generally one *or* the other. The material feature that these two elements have in common, which allows us to look on both of them as appendages of the cover, is their detachable character, as if they were constitutively ephemeral, almost inviting the reader to get rid of them after they have fulfilled their function as poster and possibly as protection. Originally the band was even fastened together[16] – perhaps to keep people from thumbing through the book in the bookstore (a purpose served nowadays by some transparent and generally mute wrappings) – which made its conservation even more problematic, after the book was slid out or the band broken apart. Some functional features are plainly connected to this physical feature: most likely the paratextual messages that appear on the jacket and band are

---

[15] [These are the flaps (re)folded in from the front and back covers to give an effect very like a dust jacket, but these flaps are integral with the cover binding.]

[16] The technical term is "bande de lancement" [launching band] or "bande de nouveauté" [new-publication band]. The term clearly indicates the provisional nature of the object, which is not meant to accompany the book beyond its early editions and whose typical message – today outmoded, doubtless for obvious reasons – used to be: "Just Published."

also meant to be transitory, to be forgotten after making their impression.

The most obvious function of the jacket is to attract attention, using means even more dramatic than those a cover can or should be permitted: a garish illustration, a reminder of a film or television adaptation, or simply a graphic presentation more flattering or more personalized than the cover standards of a series allow. The jacket of Sollers's *Paradis*, in 1980, offers an excellent example: it contained no illustration, but the title and especially the name of the author were ostentatiously displayed in large letters on a red background. The jacket likewise included, on a line by itself (I will return to this), the genre indication *roman* [a novel].

Of course, the jacket may also not appear until later, with a new edition or a new printing or simply when it seems warranted by some event, such as (and this is the preeminent example) the arrival of a film adaptation; and even for an edition in the process of being distributed, a jacket can be a convenient way of acquiring a new image.

The back of the jacket, its spine, and one and/or the other of its flaps can, if necessary, augment one or another element of the cover paratext. I will not begin to list the thousand and one variations of this game except to point to the rare case of certain Classiques Garnier jackets, on the insides of which were printed selections from the catalogue, and to the case of the Pléiade jackets, nowadays open along the spine to reveal, like some decolletage, the skin of the book itself.

The band – to spin out these metaphors of clothing – is a sort of mini jacket that covers only the lower third of the book, and its means of expression are, in general, purely verbal – but the custom of placing an illustration or a likeness of the author on the band seems to be gaining ground. The band may repeat in larger letters the name of the author; it may display the name of a literary prize the work has already won;[17] or it may carry a phrase, either authorial (see Noel Burch, *Praxis du cinéma*:

---

[17] Or of an honorable mention: after *Les Jeunes Filles en fleurs* was awarded the Goncourt, in 1919, that work's unsuccessful rival, *Les Croix de bois* by Roland Dorgelès, was adorned, in turn, with a band that bore in large letters "Prix Goncourt" and, in very small letters, "Quatre voix sur dix" ["Four votes out of ten"].

"Contre toute théorie" ["Against all theory"]) or allographic (Denis Hollier, *Politique de la prose*: "L'empire des signes, c'est la prose" ["The empire of signs is prose"] – Sartre). In all these cases, especially the last two, the paratextual function is obvious: it is the function served by the epigraph, which we will meet again in its canonical place, but here an epigraph both fleeting and more monumental. Hard to say whether it thereby gains more than it loses, or the reverse. A book of Queneau's, I can't remember which one, bore this dialogue on its band: "*Staline*: Qui aurait intérêt à ce que l'eau ne s'appelât plus l'eau? *Queneau*: Moi." ["*Stalin*: To whose advantage would it be if water were no longer called water? *Queneau*: Mine."] Nor can I remember which book of Jean-Claude Hémery's bore on its band this pre-1968 slogan: "A poêle Descartes!" ["Descartes to the stake!"]. For other recent examples see Jan Baetens's article "Bande à part?"[18] which rightly (particularly in connection with certain initiatives by Jean Ricardou) speaks of a "textualization" of the band: an authorial takeover of one of the publisher's elements, imbuing that element with the spirit of the text. For Ricardou's *La Prise de Constantinople*, for example, the title's transformation on the back cover into *La Prose de Constantinople* [*The Storming of Constantinople* / *The Prose of Constantinople*] was mirrored by a transformation of the slogan on the band from (recto) "La machine à détraquer le temps" into (verso) "Le temps a détraqué la machine" ["The machine for turning time upside down" / "Time has turned the machine upside down"]. Or, for Ricardou's *Lieux-dits, Petit guide d'un voyage dans le livre*, this ambiguous invitation, entirely adapted to the text: "Devenez un voyageur à la page" [*Localities: A short guide to a journey within the book* / "Become a traveler on the page / in the know"]. Since that time Ricardou's publisher, Seuil, has more or less abandoned the expensive practice of using bands, so in 1982 Ricardou printed on the cover of *Théâtre des métamorphoses*, in trompe l'oeil, this false band: "Une nouvelle education textuelle" ["A new textual education"]. Perhaps that is the solution of the future – I don't mean the slogan, but the technical procedure, altogether parallel to the conversion undergone by the please-insert, which not long ago consisted of an expensively inserted sheet but which now appears on cover 4.

---

[18] Jan Baetens, "Bande à part?" *Conséquences* 1 (Autumn 1983).

Let's not take leave of the detachable elements without saying a word about certain expressive or historiated slipcases, preferably for bound books whose covers can't really take any lettering. That support, too, could well be textualized someday. On the other hand, a practice that is on the way out – undoubtedly for economic reasons – is the use of the attached *ribbon*, or *bookmark*, which could also include information, valuable or not, specific or not.

A very special case – and an especially important one, given the role this series has played in French culture in the second half of the twentieth century – is that of the jackets of the Pléiade series,[19] which have other characteristics besides being (recently) slit at the spine. Because these books have mute bindings, their jackets obviously play the role of cover, generally (the standards have varied for a half-century) bearing not only the name of the author and a titular apparatus (to which I will return) but also the name of the person responsible for establishing and annotating the text, and a likeness of the author. And because the multi-volume editions, such as those for Balzac's *Comédie humaine*, Zola's *Rougon-Macquart*, or Proust's *Recherche*, obviously require several likenesses, collecting and arranging these pictures must occasionally pose some problems for those in charge. For example, five pictures of Zola and twelve of Balzac had to be found, and an arrangement had to be decided on – an arrangement that cannot fail to generate inferences (intended or not) about meaning. Because *La Comédie humaine* is a whole whose arrangement is not chronological but thematic, perhaps the arrangement of Balzac's pictures was left to chance; and Zola's pictures do not seem to have been chosen to correspond to the temporal progression of the volumes. In the case of the *Recherche*, however, the choice and arrangement of pictures give the impression that the 1954 editors[20] selected for the first volume a picture of Proust as a young man; for the second, a worldly Proust, flower in his buttonhole; and for the third, an aging Proust,

[19] [The Pléiade series (published by Gallimard) is comparable to the Library of America in textual authority and quality of paper and binding. There are, however, two main differences between these series: the Pléiade volumes are smaller, and whereas the Library of America publishes works by American authors exclusively, the Pléiade publishes both French and non-French classics.]

[20] [The 1954 edition of the *Recherche* was the first to be based on Proust manuscripts that had not been available until the early 1950s.]

devoted to his art; and the connotations are obvious, albeit invalidated by the actual dates of these pictures, which are 1891, 1895, and 1896, respectively; that is, all three date from well before the *Recherche* was planned and thus have no link to the chronology of its writing. For the reader, who certainly pays less attention to the dates given on the flaps than to the look of the pictures themselves, a significant connection is irresistibly established not so much with the chronology of the book's composition as with the internal chronology of the narrative – that is, the age of the hero. For the reader, therefore, these three pictures evoke at the same time the aging of Proust and the aging of the narrator-hero, thus inevitably drawing the *Recherche* toward the status of autobiography. Actually, I by no means wish to claim that such an interpretation is wholly illegitimate (I will come back to this) but simply that it is generated, or reinforced, surreptitiously by a paratextual arrangement that in theory is wholly innocent and secondary. I do not know what choice will be made with regard to photographs for future editions. And with the cover illustrations chosen for the volumes in the GF set, which is apparently committed to Bonnard as the Folio set was to Van Dongen,[21] there will no doubt be other kinds of evocation, apposite or not. In any case, we may well miss – if they are not revived – the subtle montages that, thanks to Pierre Faucheux, adorned the covers of the Livre de poche set: montages of yellowed photographs, manuscripts "en paperoles," and hints of the Gallimard white cover. But in the meantime, with a boost from the justified popularity of genetic criticism, the "manuscript page" has become a cover stereotype. There is no escaping it.

Paradoxically, the effect of this whole group of peripheral elements has been to push the cover strictly speaking (?) back toward the inside of the book and to make it into a second (or rather, a first) title page. In the early days of the printed book, the title page was the preeminent place of the publisher's paratext. The printed cover came along to repeat the title page, or relieve it

---

[21] [The covers of the volumes in the GF and Folio sets of the *Recherche* are reproductions of paintings. In the next sentence of the text: "paperoles" were the sometimes very long pieces of paper that Proust attached to the galleys of the *Recherche* as he endlessly reworked and extended his text, to the despair of his typesetters and publisher; and Gallimard was the initial publisher of all volumes of the *Recherche* except the very first *Swann* (published by Grasset in 1913).]

of some of its functions. Today the jacket, the band, and the slipcase, if any, are doing the same thing for the cover; and this is the sign of an expansion – some will say an inflation – of at least the opportunities (that is, of the possible supports) for a paratext. One could imagine other stages in this evolution, involving the packaging: protective boxes, covers for the boxes, and so forth, not to mention the deployment of ingenuity invested in the promotional material intended solely for bookstores and ultimately for their clientele: posters, blow-ups of covers, and other gimmicks. But at that point we leave the peritext behind.

The title page and its appendages

After the cover and its various appendages, the publisher's paratext next zeroes in most obviously on the very first and very last pages, which are generally unnumbered. I will inventory them in the order that is most common today, at least in French publishing, for the site of most of these items of information is pretty much a matter of whim.

In principle, pages 1 and 2, called the *flyleaf*, remain "blank" – or more exactly, unprinted. Page 3 is reserved for the "half title": this page bears only the title, possibly shortened. I do not know the reason for this redundant custom, but the minimal naming makes the half-title page the optimal site for the inscription, which we will meet again on its own account. Pages 4 and 6 may be used for various items of information from the publisher, such as the title of the series, the mention of deluxe editions (and, in the copies of these editions, the identification number), the frontispiece, the list of works by the same author (which we will also meet again), the list of works published in the same series, some legal information (copyright, which gives the official date of first publication; ISBN; reminder of the law concerning reproductions, whose dissuasive power has stood the test of time; for translations, mention of the original title and copyright; in the United States, Library of Congress Cataloging-in-Publication data; and so forth), and sometimes – too rarely – an identification of the typeface used. Yes, too rarely, for this identification seems to me entirely necessary. The reader has the right and sometimes even the *duty* (I will return to this) to know the typeface used for the book he holds in his hands, and he cannot be expected to be able to recognize it by himself. Page 5 is the *title page*, which – after the colophon of medieval manuscripts and the early incuna-bula – is the ancestor of the whole modern publisher's peritext. It generally includes, besides the actual title and its appendages, the name of the author and the name and address of the publisher. It may include many other things, particularly the genre indication, the epigraph, and the dedication – or, at least in the classical period, the mention of the dedication (along with the name and titles of the dedicatee), giving notice of the actual dedication to follow, that is, the dedicatory epistle, which generally begins on the next right-hand page.[22] But above all, as we will see below, the classical title – generally more expanded than ours – often constituted a veritable description of the book, a summary of its action, a definition of its subject, a list of its appendixes, and so forth. The classical title could also contain its own illustration, or at least its own ornamentation, a sort of more or less monumental portico entrance called a frontispiece. Later, when the title page got rid of this decoration, the frontispiece took refuge on the left-hand page facing the title page, before disappearing almost completely in modern times.[23]

The final pages, too, may include some of the information just mentioned, except, no doubt, for the legally required data. Only the final pages include the printer's colophon – the printer's mark indicating that his work has been completed: the name of the printer, the date of completion, the serial number, and perhaps the date of the book's *dépôt légal*.[24]

Typesetting, printings

But those localized peritextual elements do not exhaust the repertory of the publisher's paratext borne by the book. We have

---

[22] The right-hand, or *recto*, page is the side that generally has the advantage, perceptually speaking, at least in our system of writing. The left-hand page is called *verso*. [In French the right-hand and left-hand pages are also referred to, respectively, as "la belle page" and "la fausse page."]

[23] We should remember that, under the *ancien régime*, the pages immediately after the title (or sometimes the very last pages) were in principle reserved for publication of the *privilège* [license to print] by which the king granted the author and his bookseller exclusive right to sell the work. Certain modern critical editions reproduce this document's text, which is never devoid of historical interest.

[24] [Legally required deposit in the Bibliothèque Nationale.]

still to consider two features that constitute the basis of the book's material realization: the typesetting and the choice of paper. The typesetting – the choice of typeface and its arrangement on the page – is obviously the act that shapes a text into a book. This is not the place to discuss the history or aesthetics of the art of typography; I will simply note that typographical choices may provide indirect commentary on the texts they affect. No reader can be completely indifferent to a poem's arrangement on the page – to the fact, for example, that it is presented in isolation on the otherwise blank page, surrounded by what Eluard called its "marges de silence," or that it must share the blank page with one or two other poems or, indeed, with notes at the bottom of the page. Nor can a reader be indifferent to the fact that, in general, notes are arranged at the bottom of the page, in the margin, at the end of the chapter, or at the end of the volume; or indifferent to the presence or absence of running heads and to their connection with the text below them; and so on. Likewise, no reader should be indifferent to the appropriateness of particular typographical choices, even if modern publishing tends to neutralize these choices by a perhaps irreversible tendency toward standardization. When one reads a Montaigne or a Balzac, for example, it is certainly a pity to be deprived of the very distinctive look of a classical or romantic written form, and here one understands the requirements of bibliophiles keen on original editions or, more modestly, facsimiles. These considerations may seem trivial or marginal, but there are cases in which the graphic realization is inseparable from the literary intention: it is hard to imagine certain texts by Mallarmé, Apollinaire, or Butor deprived of this dimension, and one can only regret the abandonment – apparently accepted by Thackeray himself in 1858 – of the Queen-Anne-style characters in which the original (1852) edition of *Henry Esmond* had been typeset. Those characters gave the book its "bewigged and tapestried" look and contributed greatly to its effect as pastiche. It must at least be admitted that two versions of that book exist: one in which the imitative intention is extended to the typographical (and orthographical) paratext, the other in which the imitative intention is limited to theme and style. This very division becomes paratextual.

Much less significant, no doubt, is the role played by the

different choices of paper that constitute the deluxe printings of an edition;[25] some people reserve the term *original edition* for these printings. The difference among copies depending on whether they are printed on vellum, on Japan paper, or on ordinary paper is obviously less relevant to the text than a difference in typesetting, no doubt because, if the typesetting is only a materialization of the text, the paper is only an underpinning for that materialization, even further removed from the constitutive ideality of the work. Here, therefore, the real differences are only aesthetic (attractiveness of the paper, quality of the impression), economic (the market value of a copy), and possibly material (greater or lesser longevity). But these real differences also – and perhaps especially – serve as the grounds for a fundamental symbolic difference, one that results from the fact that these deluxe printings are by nature "limited." For bibliophiles, this limitedness somewhat counterbalances the ideal and thus potentially limitless nature of literary works that deprives them of almost all the value of ownership. This limitedness – in other words, this scarcity (emphasized, moreover, by the allocation of a number) – is what makes each copy of a deluxe printing absolutely unique, if only in this one slight detail. Each copy may in fact be unique in two or three other ways, but these no longer pertain exactly to the publishing of the copies: a personal binding, a handwritten inscription, an inscribed or illustrated bookplate, handwritten notes in the margin. The publisher itself, however, may contribute to such exercises in value-increasing singularization. The most arresting example – but perhaps not the only one of its kind – is that of those fifty folio copies of Proust's *Jeunes Filles en fleurs* printed in 1920 (after the book received the Goncourt prize), each of which included some pages

---

[25] Nothing is more confusing than the use of the word "edition": it may extend to all copies put out by the same publisher ("the Michel Lévy edition of *Madame Bovary*"), even if the text was modified several times during a reprinting, or it may be limited to each block of a thousand or five hundred copies of a single printing (a limitation sometimes favored by publishers for promotional reasons). Technically, the only accurate terms are *typesetting* and *printing*, or *impression*. From the same typesetting, one can get an indefinite (unless the machinery wears out) number of printings and therefore of sets of copies that are, in theory, identical. But each printing may be the occasion for minor corrections, and the classical period did not refrain from making corrections even in the course of one printing, a practice that introduced textual differences into copies from a single set. See R. Laufer, *Introduction à la textologie* (Larousse, 1972).

of the genuine manuscript, which in this way was exhaustively distributed (apparently without the author's having been consulted) among these particular copies, not all of which have yet been recovered: an odd blend of publishing and the trade in autographs.

In the case of deluxe printings, the irony is that, for obvious technical reasons, notice of these printings ("proof of printing") is printed in *all* copies, including the ordinary ones that are not in any way affected by it. But it does not follow that readers of these ordinary copies have no interest in the notice, for to them it is a piece of bibliographical information like any other, and perhaps the occasion for regret – and the thought of their regret can only increase the pleasure of the privileged few. For it is not enough to be happy; one must also be envied.

3

The name of the author

❖❖❖

Place

Nowadays it seems both necessary and "natural" to record the name – authentic or fictive – of the author in the peritext, but this has not always been so, if we judge by the common use of anonymity in the classical period. That common classical practice (which I shall say more about below) shows that the invention of the printed book did not impose this particular paratextual element (the name of the author) as quickly and firmly as it imposed certain others. Recording the author's name was even less necessary and natural in the era of ancient and medieval manuscripts, a period lasting for centuries, when there was, so to speak, no place available to put such information as the name of the author and the title of the work, except for a reference incorporated, or rather buried, in the opening (*incipit*) or closing (*explicit*) sentences of the text. It is in this form of an incorporated reference (which we will meet again in connection with titles and prefaces) that we have the names of, for example, Hesiod (*Theogony* line 22), Herodotus (first word of the *Histories*), Thucydides (same location), Plautus (prologue of *Pseudolus*), Virgil (closing lines of the *Georgics*), the romance-writer Chariton of Aphrodisias (at the head of *Chaereas and Callirhoe*), Chrétien de Troyes (at the head of *Perceval*) and Geoffroy de Lagny (Chrétien's successor for *Lancelot*), Guillaume de Lorris and Jean de Meung (whose names are recorded at the juncture of their respective works, at line 4059 of *Roman de la rose*), "Jean Froissart, treasurer and canon of Chimay," and of course Dante (canto 30, line 55, of *Purgatory*). I don't count the mysterious Turold of *Roland*, whose role in that work (author, narrator, copyist?) is not defined. And quite obviously I omit dozens of others, but it is nonetheless the case that the number of authors' names recorded

37

3 The name of the author

in the text is much smaller than the number of authors' names –
beginning with Homer's – that have been passed on to us only by
tradition or legend and have caught up with the posthumous
paratext only after very long delays.[1]

The paratextual site of the author's name, or of what serves as
such, is today both very erratic and very circumscribed. Erratic:
along with the title, the name of the author is strewn throughout
the epitext, in advertisements, prospectuses, catalogues, articles,
interviews, conversations, news items, or gossip. Circumscribed:
the canonical and official site of the author's name is in practice
limited to the title page and the cover (cover 1, with possible
reminders on the spine and cover 4). Other than that, the author's
name appears nowhere else in the peritext – which means, in
short, that signing a work is not, like signing a letter or a contract,
the usual thing to do, even if an author sometimes feels the need
to indicate where or when the work was written (and some
authors, such as Cendrars, insist on providing such indications).
But this negative standard admits of exceptions. Péguy's *Jeanne
d'Arc*, for example, which has no author's name on its cover, has
two on its title page (Marcel and Pierre Baudouin – the first of
which can be considered a sort of dedication to a friend who has
died) and then only one, as signature, on its last page (Pierre
Baudouin, which is then, strictly speaking, the pseudonym of the
author, itself a form of tribute).[2] In a more playful vein, Queneau
signed his poem "Vieillir" in *L'Instant fatal* with these two closing
lines: "Qu-e-n-e-a / U-r-a-i grec-mond."[3] And we know how
Ponge ended *Le Pré* with his name printed beneath the line
drawn under the last verse, an affectation that has since been
imitated in various ways.

But recording the name on the title page and recording it on
the cover fulfill two different functions. On the title page the
name is printed modestly and, so to speak, legally, and generally
less conspicuously than the title. On the cover the name may be

[1] See Ernst Robert Curtius, "Mention of the Author's Name in Medieval
Literature," Excursus XVII of *European Literature and the Latin Middle Ages*,
trans. Willard R. Trask (New York: Pantheon Books, 1953; reprint, New York:
Harper Torchbook, 1963).

[2] [Marcel Baudouin, Péguy's closest friend, died before *Jeanne d'Arc* was
finished; Péguy took the pseudonym "Pierre Baudouin" for his early works.]

[3] [These two lines in effect spell the name (last name first) "Raymond Queneau":
in French, the name of the letter "i" is pronounced "ee" and the name of the
letter "y" is pronounced "ee-grec."]

38

printed in varying sizes, depending on the author's reputation; and when the requirements of a series prevent such variations in size, a dust jacket provides a clear field, or a band allows the name to be repeated in more insistent letters, sometimes minus a first name, to make the author appear more famous. The principle governing this variation is apparently simple: the better known the author, the more space his name takes up. But this proposition requires at least two modifications. First, the author may be famous for extraliterary reasons, before he has published anything whatsoever. Second, magical thinking (act as if it were so, and you'll make it happen) occasionally leads the publisher to engage in promotional practices that somewhat anticipate glory by mimicking its effects.

Onymity

Theoretically, in modern practice there is no mystery about when the name appears: it appears with the first edition, and with all subsequent editions, if there are any. Thus, except when the initial attribution is wrong and is later corrected (for example, in the case of apocrypha), the original recording of the name is definitive. Actually, however, the norm of recording a name at the time of the original edition is by no means universally adhered to: the author's name may appear after a delay or, indeed, may never appear, and these variations obviously derive from the diversity of ways in which authors choose to designate themselves.

The name of the author can in fact appear in three main conditions, not to mention some mixed or intermediate states. Either the author "signs" (despite the above-mentioned reservation, I will use this word to make a long story short) with his legal name: we can plausibly surmise (I am not aware of any statistics on this matter) that this is most commonly the case; or he signs with a false name, borrowed or invented: this is *pseudonymity*; or he does not sign at all, and this is *anonymity*. For referring to the first situation, it is fairly tempting to follow the model of the other two and coin the term *onymity*. As always, the most ordinary state is the one that, from habit, has never received a name, and the need to give it one responds to the describer's wish to rescue it from this deceptive ordinariness. After all, to sign a work with one's real name is a choice like any other, and nothing authorizes us to regard this choice as insignificant.

Onymity is sometimes motivated by something stronger or less neutral than, say, the absence of a desire to give oneself a pseudonym, as is evident (in the case alluded to above) when someone who is already famous produces a book that will perhaps be successful precisely because of his previously established fame. The name then is no longer a straightforward statement of identity ("The author's name is So-and-So"); it is, instead, the way to put an identity, or rather a "personality," as the media call it, at the service of the book: "This book is the work of the illustrious So-and-So." Or at least the illustrious So-and-So claims to be the author of this book, even if some insiders know he didn't exactly write it himself and perhaps hasn't read the whole book, either. My reason for evoking here the practice of using a ghostwriter is to remind readers that paratextual indications are matters of legal responsibility rather than of factual authorship: under the rules of onymity, the name of the author is the name of whoever is putatively responsible for the work, whatever his real role in producing it; and a possible "inspection to verify" does not fall within the jurisdiction of a paratextologist.

The indirect effects of onymity are not entirely limited to cases of previous fame. The name of a wholly unknown person may indicate, beyond the logicians' purely "strict designation," various other features of the author's identity: often the author's sex (which may have crucial thematic relevance), and sometimes the author's nationality or social class (the nobiliary particle, if I may say so, still makes an impression) or kinship with some better-known person. In addition, in our society the surname of a woman is not exactly a simple matter: a married woman *must* choose among her father's name, her husband's name, or some combination of the two; the first two choices – but not the third – are, in principle, opaque to the reader, who will therefore not be able to infer marital status from them; and many careers of women of letters are punctuated with these onymous variations that reveal marital, existential, or ideological variations (here, I offer no example). I'm certainly forgetting other equally relevant cases, but the ones I've mentioned are no doubt enough to confirm that "keeping one's name" is not always an innocent gesture.

The author's name fulfills a contractual function whose importance varies greatly depending on genre: slight or nonexistent in
fiction, it is much greater in all kinds of referential writing, where
the credibility of the testimony, or of its transmission, rests
largely on the identity of the witness or the person reporting it.
Thus we see very few pseudonyms or anonyms among authors
of historical or documentary works, and this is all the more true
when the witness himself plays a part in his narrative.

The maximal degree of this involvement is obviously autobiography. Here I can do no better than refer to Philippe
Lejeune's works, which show the decisive role that the name of
the author, in a relation of identity with the name of the hero,
plays in constituting the "autobiographical contract," its several
variations, and its possible fringes.[4] In terms of what interests us
here, I have only one word to add: the name of the author is not a
given that is external to and coexistent with this contract. Rather,
the name of the author is indeed a constituent element of the
contract and has an effect that blends with the effects of other
elements, such as the presence or absence of a genre indication
or – as Lejeune himself specifies[5] – one or another statement in
the please-insert or in any other part of the paratext. The genre
contract is constituted, more or less consistently, by the whole of
the paratext and, more broadly, by the relation between text and
paratext; and the author's name obviously is part of it all,
"included within the bar separating text and off-text."[6] For us
this bar has become a zone (the paratext) broad enough to
contain a number of items of information that may contradict
each other and that, above all, may vary over the course of a
work's history. For example, in some disguised autobiographies
the author gives his hero a name different from his own (like the
Pierre Nozière of Anatole France, or the Claudine of Colette), an
act that denies these works the status of autobiography strictly
speaking; but a broader or more delayed paratext draws them
into that field in one way or another. As an element of the genre
contract, the author's name is caught up in a complex whole
whose boundaries are hard to trace and whose constituent parts

[4] [See Chapter 1, note 15.]
[5] See the first two chapters of *Moi aussi* (Seuil, 1986).
[6] Lejeune, *Le Pacte autobiographique* (Seuil, 1975), 37.

41

are equally hard to inventory. The contract is what it all adds up to – which is almost always provisional.

Anonymity

Although anonymity is degree zero, it, too, includes gradations. There are false anonymities, or cryptic onymities, like that of Rojas's *Celestina*, where the author's name appeared in an acrostic in an introductory poem. There are *de facto* anonymities, which derive not from any decision but rather from an absence of information, an absence permitted and perpetuated by custom: such is the case for many medieval texts, particularly the *chansons de geste* (it was not customary for anyone to claim responsibility for them, and no latter-day investigation has been able to solve the mystery of their authorship), and also for *Lazarillo*. Throughout the classical period there were anonymities of convenience, characteristically used by persons of high estate who would doubtless have thought it demeaning to sign so unaristocratic a work as a book in prose. Examples are Mme de La Fayette (at the head of *La Princesse de Clèves*, a note from the publisher to the reader indicates fairly ironically that "the author has not felt able to declare his identity; he was afraid that his name might diminish the success of his book") or La Rochefoucauld (whose name, or rather initials, did not appear, unless I am mistaken, until 1777). But more generally during the classical period, putting the author's name on a book other than drama or heroic poetry was not really customary, and many authors – aristocrats or commoners – did not feel obligated to announce their authorship or would have even considered such an announcement immodest or inopportune. See Boileau, who signed "sieur D***" ["Mr. D ..."] until the "favorite" edition of 1701, with its "sieur Boileau-Despréaux"; or La Bruyère, who did not sign his *Caractères* until the sixth edition of 1691, and even then did so only indirectly, by mentioning in the chapter "De quelques usages" his ancestor Geoffrey de La Bruyère; and then, in the 1694 edition, by attaching to the text the speech he gave on being inducted into the French Academy.

Other noteworthy anonymities in the eighteenth century include Montesquieu's *Lettres persanes* (in the introduction, the author justifies his use of anonymity in these terms: "I know a woman who walks quite gracefully, but she limps as soon as anyone looks at her") and *Esprit des lois*; Marivaux's *Effets surprenants de la sympathie* and *Voiture embourbée*; Prévost's *Mémoires d'un homme de qualité*; in England, *Robinson Crusoe* and *Moll Flanders*, *Pamela*, *Tristram Shandy*, and *Sense and Sensibility* (*Pride and Prejudice*, published two years later, has instead of the author's name the phrase "By the author of *Sense and Sensibility*"). Exceptions to this practice are [Lesage's] *Gil Blas, Tom Jones*, and the novels Marivaux wrote after his career as a dramatist: *Télémaque travesti*,[7] *Pharsamon, Marianne*, and *Le Paysan parvenu*. This type of anonymity generally had nothing to do with a fiercely protected incognito: quite often the public knew the identity of the author by word of mouth and was not in the least surprised to find no mention of the name on the title page.[8] Other anonymities were somewhat better kept, at least as official fictions, either because they constituted a precautionary measure in the face of persecution by state or church (see Voltaire, Diderot, and others) or because they satisfied a doggedly held whim on the part of the author.

The most striking example of an author with this last motivation is certainly Walter Scott. Known and respected as a man of law and as a poet, he refused to sign his first novel, *Waverley*, and then signed most of the subsequent ones with the phrase (apparently in imitation of Jane Austen, but destined here for more glory – and for new imitations) "By the author of *Waverley*." It seems that in the interim the reason for the anonymity had changed; and Scott, great literary strategist that he was, had discovered that his incognito, by arousing curiosity, was contributing to the success of his books. In the incognito, he would say after the fact, he also found deeper satisfaction, thinking himself (like some Italian actor) a better writer when disguised (this justification is not too far removed from the one Montesquieu gave for the *Lettres persanes*) and believing that a true novelistic vocation is inseparable from a certain proclivity for suddenly disappearing, that is, in short, for clandestineness. Besides, from

[7] Marivaux's authorship of this work is nevertheless disavowed in a notice by the publisher in the fourth part of *Marianne*.

[8] Here I omit an intermediary situation we will encounter below: works bearing the name or initials of the author, who claims in a preface to be only the "editor" of the text (see Rousseau's *Nouvelle Héloïse* or Laclos's *Liaisons dangereuses*).

1816 on he adds to this (almost) uncomplicated anonymity a fairly complex game of pseudonyms, fictitious authors, and imaginary preface-writers, of which I will have occasion to speak again. In the interim, also, that same incognito had been penetrated in various ways: certain critics had established meaningful connections between the *Waverley Novels* and the poetic works of Walter Scott, and at least since 1818 Defauconpret's French translations of the novels had been appearing under the name of "Sir Walter Scott." But the game continued, and not until 1827, in the preface to the *Chronicles of the Canongate*, does Scott officially acknowledge his work, recounting – with a goodly number of picturesque and dramatic details – how, on February 23 of that same year, he had been induced to unmask himself at a gathering of Scottish writers. The definitive edition of his novelistic works appears "under his name" starting in 1829.[9]

Like all badges of discretion or modesty, this one can just as easily be charged to coquetry. Balzac will do so, deciding in 1829 to sign *Le Dernier Chouan* and obviously taking aim at Walter Scott and Scott's imitators (including Balzac himself, no doubt, for the works of his youth): "[The author] has reflected that, today, perhaps signing a book evinces modesty, at a time when so many people are flaunting their anonymity." The best part of that is that Balzac had first thought of attributing this novel to an imagined author, "Victor Morillon," whom he credited, in a pseudo-allographic foreword that we will meet again, with the modesty that lies in signing one's own work.

In actual fact, the common use of anonymity, whether or not an expression of pride, did not die out in the nineteenth century as quickly as one might think. As evidence (limiting ourselves only to France), these several works stand out: *Méditations poétiques* (1820), *Han d'Islande* (1823), *Bug-Jargal* ("By the author of *Han d'Islande*," 1826), *Armance* (1827), *Le Dernier Jour d'un con-*

---

9   The formula, used in the general preface, is this: "The Author, under whose name they are for the first time collected." As I haven't been able to see for myself a copy of this edition (Cadell, 1829–33, known as "Magnum Opus"), and catalogues and bibliographies being what they are, I would not vouch for the official presence of Walter Scott's name on the title page; and on the strength of a later reprinting (Cadell, 1842–47), I would believe, rather, the reverse. But the advertisement and preface, which are very autobiographical, leave no doubt about the identity of the author, who dates them from his very well known residence of Abbotsford. A signature, then, that is still indirect but completely transparent.

damné (1829), and *Notre-Dame de Paris* (1831).[10] In all these cases the author's name comes along very quickly, with the second or third edition, so that anonymity then seems a sort of affectation of mystery reserved for the original edition. In England, and quite obviously as an effect of the eighteenth-century-style pastiche, *Henry Esmond* still, in 1852, observes this purely conventional ritual.

The formula "By the author of ..." became relatively common after Austen and Scott. We have just seen it with Hugo, and Stendhal uses it at least four times: for the original edition of *L'Amour* ("By the author of *L'Histoire de la peinture en Italie* and of *Les Vies de Haydn* ..."), the original editions of *Les Mémoires d'un touriste* and *La Chartreuse* ("By the author of *Rouge et noir* [*sic*]"), and the original edition of *L'Abbesse de Castro* ("By the author of *Rouge et noir, La Chartreuse de Parme,* ..."). Closer to our own time, we are familiar with "By the author of *Amitiés amoureuses.*"[11] That phrase in itself constitutes a highly devious form of the statement of identity: it is a statement of identity precisely between two anonymities, explicitly putting at the service of a new book the success of a previous one and, above all, managing to constitute an authorial entity without having recourse to any name, authentic or fictive.[12] Philippe Lejeune says somewhere that someone doesn't become an author until his second publication, when his name can appear at the head not only of his book but also of a list of works "By the same author." This witticism is perhaps unfair to authors of only a single work, such as Montaigne, but there is some truth in it, and in this respect the Austen-Scott formula has the merit of being paradoxically economical.

These "modern" anonymities (that is, for the most part, classical in type) are obviously not all meant to last, and in fact they have not been preserved. For each of them, then, we have (at the cost of some digging in the library, for even critical editions are not

[10] [*Méditations poétiques* is by Lamartine, *Armance* is by Stendhal, and the other four are by Hugo.]

[11] [An author later revealed to be Mme Lecomte du Nouy.]

[12] I would not say as much for the use, on the original edition of Gide's *Caves du Vatican* (1914), of the formula "By the author of *Paludes*," for *Paludes* was not anonymous.

always very loquacious on this point, which they no doubt judge to be trivial) what can be called an official date of attribution – which we should not be too quick to call an admission of authorship, for these delayed onymities are sometimes posthumous. For Walter Scott, 1827 is indeed a date of admission (somewhat forced upon him), but La Rochefoucauld's name, as I have said, does not appear in the official peritext of the *Maximes* until long after his death. In these cases, then, it is better to say that posterity effects an attribution without worrying much about the wishes of the deceased author. When one thinks of the care scholars take to "establish" a text that conforms to the last anthumous revisions, such forceful paratextual takeovers make one wonder. But we will come across many others, some of which are no doubt more serious.

Given the existence of these posthumous attributions, let us keep in mind at least the thought that the sender of the author's name is not necessarily always the author himself; and as we will see, one of the normal functions of the preface is to give the author the opportunity to officially claim (or deny) authorship of his text. But the name on the title page and cover? I fully realize that, anthumously, the name should not be there except with the author's consent, but does it necessarily follow that he is (legally) the one who puts it there? Clearly such is not necessarily always the case, and this is one of the features that distinguish the act of putting a name on a cover or title page from the act of signing the text. It would be more correct, it seems to me, to say that with respect to the cover and title page, it is the publisher who *presents* the author, somewhat as certain film producers present both the film and its director. If the author is the guarantor of the text (*auctor*), this guarantor himself has a guarantor – the publisher – who "introduces" him and names him.

Pseudonymity

The use of a fictive name, or pseudonym, has long fascinated amateurs and inconvenienced professionals – here I mean bibliographers in particular – and the inconvenience and fascination are by no means mutually exclusive, but rather the opposite. Hence a certain proliferation of commentaries, not all of which concern us, fortunately. It is doubtless appropriate for us to begin by placing pseudonymity within the larger set of practices that consist of putting at the head of a book a name that is not the legal name of its author (this larger set is what classical bibliographers called quite simply "pseudonym").

The first of these practices, which we have just encountered, consists of the complete omission of the name; this is obviously anonymity (example: *Lazarillo*). The second consists of the real author's fallacious attribution of the text to a known author: this is *apocrypha* (example: *La Chasse spirituelle*, attributed in 1949 to Rimbaud by Nicolas Bataille and Mme Akakia-Viala). The third, a variant of the second, is that of *apocrypha with permission*, which, for a real author who does not want to be identified, consists of finding another author who is willing to sign in his place; this variant is fairly rare, but Chapelain is said to have occasionally lent his name in this way to none other than Richelieu, and we will see below that Balzac undoubtedly used such loaner names for one or another of his prefaces. The fourth practice is the reverse of the second: someone fallaciously attributes to himself, and thus "signs" with his own name, another person's work. This is *plagiarism*, and we know that a good, or bad, part of Stendhal's early work owes its existence to plagiarism (true, he didn't sign these items with his name, or even with his future illustrious pseudonym). The fifth practice is both a variant of the fourth and the reverse of the third: that of *plagiarism with permission* (from the plagiarized author, of course, and upon remuneration), which we have already met under the term *ghostwriting*. To give only an old example: it is well known that Alexandre Dumas *père* often received help from (among others) a professional writer named Auguste Maquet. This, then, is the penholder, the reverse of the loaner name. The sixth practice is another variant of the second: the real author attributes a work to an author who, this time, is imaginary but provided with some attributes. This practice is known as *imagining the author*, and a very generic illustration of it is the dramatic work that Mérimée attributed to a certain "Clara Gazul"; but the practice entails countless subtle gradations, which we will meet in connection with prefaces. The seventh practice could be described as a variant of the sixth: a real author attributes a work to an imaginary author but does not produce any information about the latter except the name – he does not, in other words, supply the whole paratextual apparatus that ordinarily serves to substantiate (seriously or not) the existence of the imagined author.[13] Although there are intermediary or undecidable states between the sixth practice and the seventh, it is doubtless wise to cut all theoretical connections between them and describe the latter simply as the fact, for the real author, of "signing" his work with a name that is not – or not exactly or not entirely – his legal name. This is obviously what we generally think of as pseudonymity, and it is the subject of most of the rest of this chapter.

Classical and modern bibliographers who have taken an interest in this practice have sought above all to discover what Adrien Baillet, the first of them, called the "motives" and "manners" of adopting a pseudonym, and they have also sought to establish a jurisprudence of pseudonymity, whose essential point is to determine an author's (or any other user's) right of ownership (and, if necessary, of transmission) to his pseudonym.[14] Theoretically, nothing in all of this concerns us, because the pseudonym of a writer, as it generally appears in the paratext, is not accompanied by any mention of that kind of thing and because the reader receives the pseudonym – still theoretically – as the author's name, without being able either to evaluate or to question its authenticity.

What concerns us about the pseudonym as a paratextual element is – independently, if possible, of all consideration of motive or manner – the *effect* produced on the reader, or more generally on the public, by the presence of a pseudonym. But here we must distinguish between the effect of *a given pseudonym*, an effect that may very well coincide with the reader's total ignorance of the fact of the pseudonym, and the *pseudonym-effect*, which, in contrast, depends on the reader's having information about the fact. Let me explain. The names "Tristan Klingsor" or "Saint-John Perse" may, in a reader's mind, induce one or another effect of glamor, archaism, Wagnerianism, exoticism, or

---

13 See Jean-Benoît Puech, "L'Auteur supposé. Essai de typologie des écrivains imaginaires en littérature," thesis (Ecole des Hautes Etudes en Sciences Sociales, Paris, 1982). Valéry Larbaud insisted several times on the difference between a pseudonym and an imagined author. For example: "Don't forget," he wrote to a translator, "to say clearly that Barnabooth is not a pseudonym but the hero of a novel, the way Clara Gazul is not a pseudonym of Mérimée or, better yet, the way Gil Blas is not a pseudonym of Lesage."

14 On this research tradition, see M. Laugaa, *La Pensée du pseudonyme* (PUF, 1986).

what have you, which will influence the way he reads the work of Léon Leclerc or Alexis Léger,[15] even if he is wholly unaware of the conditions ("motives," "manners") of the choice of pseudonym and, even more, if he takes the pseudonym for the author's real name. After all, connotations equally strong, although different, could certainly adhere to a wholly authentic name such as Alphonse de Lamartine, Ezra Pound, or Federico García Lorca. The effect of a pseudonym is not in itself different from the effect of any other name, except that in a given situation the name may have been chosen with an eye to the particular effect; and incidentally, it is very curious that the bibliographers who have wondered so much about motives (modesty, cautiousness, oedipal dislike for one's patronymic or not, concern to avoid homonymy, and so forth) and about manners (taking the name of a place, lifting a name from the book itself, changing a first name, turning a first name into a last name, doing without a first name, using abbreviations, elongations, anagrams ...) have paid so little attention to the mixture of motive and manner that adds up to the calculation of an effect.

As for the pseudonym-effect, it assumes that the fact of the pseudonym is known to the reader: this is the effect produced by the very fact that one day Mr. Alexis Léger decided to use a pseudonym, any pseudonym. The pseudonym-effect necessarily blends with the effect of *this* pseudonym, either to reinforce it ("The choice of this name is in itself a work of art") or possibly to weaken it ("Ah, it's not his real name? Then that makes it too easy ..."); or else to end up being weakened itself ("If, with a name like Crayencour, I had to choose a pseudonym, I certainly wouldn't have chosen the anagram Yourcenar") – or, indeed, disputed ("*Alexis Léger* was better than that ridiculous *Saint-John Perse*"). As Starobinski rightly says: "When a man conceals or disguises himself with a pseudonym, we feel defied. This man refuses to give himself to us. And in return we want to *know* ..."[16] Even then, this qualification has to be added: *if at least we*

---

[15] And/or reciprocally: "*Saint-Léger Léger: Eloges* [author: Saint-Léger Léger; title: Eloges] is constructed with the same consonants and gives the cover of the book its euphonious unity. And here is *Saint-John Perse: Anabase*, which also gives a nice unit of sound evoking an image of Asia" (A. Thibaudet, *Honneur à S.-J. P.* [Gallimard, 1965], 412). See J.-P. Richard, "Petite remontée dans un nom-titre," *Microlectures* (Seuil, 1979).

[16] J. Starobinski, "Stendhal pseudonyme," *L'Œil vivant* (Gallimard, 1961).

already know we are dealing with a pseudonym (and this is perhaps the main point).

Thus from the moment the truth of the patronymic is disclosed by a more remote paratext, by a piece of biographical information, or more generally by fame, the reader's reverie about the pseudonym ceases to be a straightforward speculation based more or less on what the name itself suggests (either the speculation the author expected when offering the reader something more felicitous than his legal patronymic, or some other one). I am certainly not claiming that every reader of Voltaire, Nerval, or Marguerite Duras knows the legal names concealed beneath those pseudonyms, or knows even that they are pseudonyms. I think merely that disclosure of the patronymic is part of the biographical renown that lies on the horizon, near or distant, of literary renown (that of the works themselves). I mean: biographical renown eventually catches up with literary renown or surrounds it like a halo. Consequently no pseudonymous writer can dream of glory without foreseeing this disclosure (which does not much concern us here), but reciprocally, no reader who is more or less interested in the pseudonymous author can avoid being exposed to that particular bit of information. Once the reader has the information, the pseudonym is included in his image, or idea, of that particular author, so that inevitably (although in varying degrees from reader to reader) he considers pseudonym and patronymic together, or in alternation; and thereby, no less inevitably, he distinguishes within his image or idea the figure of the author from the figure of the private man (or of the author in a different public role: Alexis Léger the diplomat). This is the point at which a more or less unrestricted (because more or less well informed) inquiry into the "motives" and "manners" of the choice of pseudonym takes over: So-and-So took his mother's name, So-and-So changed his first name, So-and-So patched together an anagram, someone else – a woman – took a man's name,[17] and so forth. I will spare my own reader a hopelessly empirical taxonomy and list of examples that clutter

---

[17] Besides, it is curious how these masculine pseudonyms, once known to be such, become transparent, with no effect of transsexuation: for me, at least, *George Sand* and *George Eliot* are women's names just as surely as are *Louise Labé* and *Virginia Woolf*. The femaleness of the person designated completely blots out the "maleness" of the designating word.

up all the gossip sheets. The important thing, it seems to me, is to be aware that single pseudonymity (Molière, Stendhal, Lautréamont) always tends more or less to split into a sort of dionymity – Molière/Poquelin, Stendhal/Beyle, Lautréamont/Ducasse – and that this dionymity resulting from the coexistence of the patronymic and a pseudonym is in itself only a special case of polyonymity (that is, of the use, by one writer, of several pen names). For the underlying idea is that the multiple pseudonym is to some small degree, as the case of Stendhal plainly illustrates, the true nature of the single pseudonym and the state it naturally inclines toward.

Here if we wished to classify, we would undoubtedly have to show – in a double-entry table that, for once, I will refrain from presenting – the intersection of at least two simple categories. An author can "sign" some of his works with his legal name (Jacques Laurent) and can sign others with a pseudonym (Cecil Saint-Laurent). Such an opposition is, of course, open to an unsophisticated interpretation: the works signed with the patronymic are allegedly more "owned up to," more "acknowledged," because in them the author is allegedly more himself, for reasons of personal preference or literary dignity. This is doubtless the case for Laurent, but one should not put too much faith in this criterion, for an author may also, for social reasons, acknowledge serious and professional works and use a pseudonym to conceal the novelistic or poetic works he personally "cares" about much more, according to the principle of the "violin d'Ingres."[18] Examples? Let us venture, to his credit, the novels of Edgar Sanday, pseudonym of Edgar Faure.[19] Polyonymity may also actually be polypseudonymity, which is when an author signs exclusively with various pseudonyms. Apart from the complication of the short-lived presence of a loaner name, this is the case of Romain Gary / Emile Ajar. In this case and others, one of the pseudonyms may appear more "pseudo" than the other and lead people to believe in the authenticity of the latter. But it is now becoming known that "Gary" was not more authentic than

---

[18] [The painter Ingres took great pride in his violin playing. Thus, the principle of the "violin d'Ingres" is that someone who is a professional in one area cares deeply about his performance in another area lying far outside his specialty.]

[19] [Edgar Faure, a French political leader for many decades, served as prime minister twice in the 1950s.]

"Ajar" and perhaps one or two others, for the pseudonym habit is very much like the drug habit, quickly leading to increased use, abuse, even overdose.

Moreover, the author's various signatures may be simultaneous (more exactly, alternating), such as those I have just evoked, or successive, such as those used by, for example, Rabelais and Balzac. Rabelais signed *Pantagruel* and *Gargantua* "Me Alcofribas, abstracteur de quintessence" and then took on the *Tiers*, then the *Quart livre* as "François Rabelais, docteur en médecine"; Balzac, in his youth and in a sequence I have forgotten, signed his works "Lord R'Hoone," "Horace de Saint-Aubin," or "Vieillerglé" before adopting in 1830 an "Honoré de Balzac" that was itself somewhat pseudo, for the registry office that he would one day compete with[20] knew him only by the more plebeian name of Honoré Balzac. For even in simple pseudonymity there are degrees, because there are degrees in the distortion of a patronymic, but I have no intention of incorporating that given.[21] Henry Beyle was, successively, "Louis-Alexandre-César Bombet" for the *Lettres sur Haydn* and then, for *L'Histoire de la peinture*, "M. B. A. A." (M. Beyle, ancien auditeur [Monsieur Beyle, former Commissioner]),[22] and finally (I greatly simplify), starting with *Rome, Naples et Florence en 1817*, "M. de Stendhal, officier de cavalerie," later just "Stendhal." That adds up to only three and one-half pseudonyms (not counting an anonymous work such as *Armance*), which is ultimately not very many for someone obsessed with the private, indeed the intimate, nickname.[23]

I don't know whether some Guinness book has registered the world record for pseudonyms, mixing indiscriminately all periods and all categories. Kierkegaard is alleged to have used a good many, and we know of at least the three "ghosted" works by Pessoa; but here we verge on the practice of imagining the author, for in Kierkegaard's case and, even more so, in Pessoa's,

---

[20] [In *La Comédie humaine*, Balzac created more than two thousand characters.]

[21] One of the most economical of such distortions is undoubtedly the Frenchification of Mondriaan into Mondrian. But a pseudonym, too, may be distorted or shortened: an edition of Voltaire's *Lettres philosophiques* appeared in 1734 under this name, whose transparency is two degrees removed: "By M. de V...."

[22] But one hundred copies had this fuller mention: "By M. Beyle, ex-auditeur au Conseil d'Etat."

[23] See Starobinski, "Stendhal pseudonyme."

each of these hypostases is endowed with a fictive identity by paratextual means (prefaces, biographical notices, and so forth) and even, or especially, by textual means (thematic and stylistic autonomy). For us, let the symbolic recordholder be, a little arbitrarily, Renaud Camus, who seems to have invested a considerable amount of his creativity in a truly stunning polyonymic game, one in which I know for sure I will get lost – but I suppose that is its function. By way of illustration, here is what I think I know at the moment: 1975, Renaud Camus, *Passage*, with a character named Denis Duparc; 1976, Denis Duparc, *Echange*; 1978, Renaud Camus and Tony Duparc, *Travers*, which announces the forthcoming appearance of a work by Jean-Renaud Camus and Denis Duvert named *Travers 2*;[24] J. R. G. Camus and Antoine du Parc, *Travers 3*; J. R. G. Du Parc and Denise Camus, *Travers Coda et Index*; the appendix to that last work: Denis du Parc, *Lecture* (or *Comment m'ont écrit certains de mes livres* [*Reading, or How Certain of My Books Wrote Me*]). In the meantime and since, there have been various other texts signed merely Camus (Renaud), in which a list of works by the same author – a list without that actual heading – modifies my list above in various ways. I am intentionally unaware, of course, whether "Renaud Camus" is a pseudonym. But we should remember that an author who has become famous under his patronymic may, under exceptional circumstances and at least in England, legally change his name. On August 30, 1927, Mr. Thomas Edward Lawrence was granted the right to call himself thenceforth Mr. Thomas Edward Shaw. From that day on, did "T. E. Lawrence" become, retroactively, a pseudonym?

Before leaving pseudonymity, I had planned to mention also that, among the arts, the use of pseudonymity is limited basically to two domains: literature and, far behind, the theatre (names of actors), a realm that today encompasses the broader field of show business. Done. I had also planned to be surprised at that limitation and to seek the reasons for the privileging of literature and the theatre: why have so few musicians, painters, or architects used pseudonyms? But at this point, the surprise would be much too factitious: use of a pseudonym unites a taste for masks

---

[24] In fact published under the title *Eté* (POL Hachette, 1982). The whole group is to constitute the "trilogy in four books and seven volumes" of the *Eglogues*.

and mirrors, for indirect exhibitionism, and for controlled histrio-
nics with delight in invention, in borrowing, in verbal transformation, in onomastic fetishism. Clearly, using a pseudonym is
already a poetic activity, and the pseudonym is already somewhat like a work. If you can change your name, you can write.

A possible appendage to the author's name is the mention of his
"titles" [honors, etc.]. Down through the centuries, these have
included all kinds of nobiliary ranks and all kinds of functions
and distinctions, honorific or real. I will not rehash all of that, but
we have already seen Beyle plead his ex-function as commissioner on the Council of State. English neoclassical authors
readily styled themselves, for lack of anything better, "Esquire";
Rousseau styled himself "Citoyen de Genève" (not for lack of
anything better, and only at the head of whichever of his works
were likely to do credit to this title); and Paul-Louis Courier,
reediting and revising the translation of Longus by "Monsieur
Jacques Amyot, during his lifetime bishop of Auxerre and master
chaplain of the court of the kings of France," gives himself the
title "Winegrower, member of the Legion of Honor, formerly a
mounted gunner." The titles that French authors still use are, it
seems to me, of two kinds: one indicates membership in an
academy (the French Academy, the Institute of France, the
Goncourt Academy) and the other a university rank or function
(*agrégation, doctorat,* professor at a university or at the Collège de
France). None of that is very sexy, but if we were to go digging in
remote regions, we would surely find more picturesque formulae.
  Certain formulae, as we know, are obligatory. Others – sometimes the same ones – are good for business. As for the rest,
applying dime-store psychology, we can be fascinated by their
wholly indistinguishable blend of childish vanity and deep
humility. My excellent sire liked to call himself a "user of gas."
But after all, at the turn of the century that must've been a sign
that one was well off and distinguished; it must've been a
privilege and, indeed, a mark of favor. He also styled himself, in
a phrase whose humor I long found unfathomable, *recipient of the
Cross of War, for military reasons.* Here I will end this domestic
digression.

4

❖❖

Titles

❖❖

Definitions

To a greater extent than perhaps any other paratextual element, the title raises problems of definition and requires careful analysis: the titular apparatus as we have known it since the Renaissance (I will discuss its prehistory below) is very often not so much precisely an element as a rather complex whole – and the complexity is not exactly due to length. Some very long titles of the classical period, such as the original title of *Robinson Crusoe* (which we will meet again), were relatively simple in status. A much shorter whole, such as *Zadig ou La destinée, Histoire orientale* [Voltaire's *Zadig or Destiny, An Oriental Tale*], forms a more complex statement, as we will see.

One of the founders of modern titology,[1] Leo H. Hoek, writes very correctly that the title as we understand it today is actually (and this is true at least of ancient and classical titles) an artificial

---

[1] It was, I think, Claude Duchet who gave the name *titology* [French "titrologie," after "titre," the word for *title*] to this little discipline, which to date is the most active of all the disciplines – if any – concerned with studying the paratext. Here is a selective and incomplete bibliography of titology: M. Hélin, "Les Livres et leurs titres," *Marche romane* (September–December 1956); Theodor Adorno, "Titles" (1962), in *Notes to Literature*, vol. 2, trans. Shierry Weber Nicholsen (New York: Columbia University Press, 1992); Charles Moncelet, *Essai sur le titre* (BOF, 1972); Leo H. Hoek, "Pour une sémiotique du titre," working paper, Urbino (February 1973); C. Grivel, *Production de l'intérêt romanesque* (Mouton, 1973), 166–81; C. Duchet, "La Fille abandonnée et la bête humaine, Eléments de titrologie romanesque," *Littérature* 12 (December 1973); J. Molino, "Sur les titres de Jean Bruce," *Langages* 35 (1974); Harry Levin, "The Title as a Literary Genre," *Modern Language Review* 72 (1977): xxiii–xxxvi; E. A. Levenston, "The Significance of the Title in Lyric Poetry," *Hebrew University Studies in Literature* (spring 1978); H. Mitterand, "Les Titres des romans de Guy des Cars," in *Sociocritique*, ed. C. Duchet (Nathan, 1979); Leo H. Hoek, *La Marque du titre* (Mouton, 1981); John Barth, "The Title of This Book" and "The Subtitle of This Book," in *The Friday Book: Essays and Other Nonfiction* (New York: G. P. Putnam's Sons, 1984); C. Kantorowicz, "Eloquence des titres," Ph.D. diss. (New York University, 1986).

object, an artifact of reception or of commentary, that readers, the public, critics, booksellers, bibliographers, ... and titologists (which all of us are, at least sometimes) have arbitrarily separated out from the graphic and possibly iconographic mass of a "title page" or a cover. This mass includes, or may include, many appended bits of information that the author, the publisher, and their public did not use to distinguish as clearly as we do now. After much of that was set aside – the names of the author, the dedicatee, and the publisher; the address of the publisher; the date of printing; and other introductory information – it gradually became customary to retain a more limited whole as the title. But to get at its constituent elements, we still need to analyze it. The terms of the analysis have given rise to a debate between Leo Hoek and Claude Duchet, which I now loosely summarize.

Let's take the title, given above, of what today we call *Zadig*.[2] Hoek (1973) proposed (using other examples) to consider the first part, up to my comma (that is, *Zadig ou La destinée*), as the "title," and the rest (*Histoire orientale*) as the "subtitle." Rightly finding this analysis too cursory, Duchet proposed distinguishing three elements: the "title," *Zadig*; the "second title" (marked here by the conjunction *ou*, and elsewhere by a comma, an indentation, or any other typographical device), *ou La destinée*; and the "subtitle" (generally introduced by a term indicating the work's genre), here, of course, *Histoire orientale*. Hoek (1981), taking this suggestion into account but not especially charmed by the somewhat clumsy term "second title" (borrowed from early-nineteenth-century terminology), made a counterproposal: "title" (*Zadig*), "secondary title" (*ou La destinée*), "subtitle" (*Histoire orientale*).

Anxious to put my mark, too, on the brief history of titology, I will suggest that the terminological distinction between "secondary title" and "subtitle" is a little too slight to gain a foothold; and because, as Duchet clearly saw, the principal feature of his "subtitle" is its more or less explicit inclusion of a genre indication, the simplest and most expressive thing to do might be to call the third element exactly by that feature, thereby freeing up "subtitle" to revert to what is already its commonest meaning. Hence these three terms: "title" (*Zadig*), "subtitle" (*ou La destinée*), and "genre indication" (*Histoire orientale*). What we have here is

---

[2] The original title in 1747 was actually *Memmon, Histoire orientale*; the present title appeared in 1748.

the most complete form of a virtual system; in our present culture, only the first element is obligatory. Today we more commonly encounter defective forms of the system, for example, title + subtitle (*Madame Bovary, Mœurs de province*) or title + genre indication (*La Nausée, Roman* [Sartre's *Nausea, A Novel*]), not counting really simple titles, that is, those reduced to the single element "title," without subtitle or genre indication, such as *Les Mots* [Sartre's *The Words*], or deviant arrangements like this obviously parodic one: Viktor Shklovsky's *Zoo or Letters Not about Love: The Third Heloise*.

Defective or not, titles do not always separate out their elements in so formal a way. The third element, especially, is frequently incorporated into the second (*L'Education sentimental, Histoire d'un jeune homme* [Flaubert's *Sentimental Education: The Story of a Young Man*]) or into the first (*Le Roman de la rose; Life of Johnson; Essai sur les mœurs* [Voltaire]; and so forth), or it may even wholly constitute the first, as with *Satires, Elegies, Writings,* and so on. When these genre indications are incorporated and more or less deviant or original in wording (*Chronique du XIXe siècle* [*Chronicle of the 19th Century*], the subtitle of *Le Rouge et le noir;*[3] *Méditations poétiques* [Lamartine]; *Divagations* [Mallarmé]), they may generate a good deal of uncertainty or controversy: in *Ariel ou La vie de Shelley* [Maurois's *Ariel or The Life of Shelley,* published in English as *Ariel: A Shelley Romance*], is or isn't "La vie" a disguised genre indication, another way to say *biography*? Is the *Mœurs de province* of *Bovary* a straightforward subtitle, or is it a sort of variation on the (Balzacian) genre formula *Etude de mœurs* [*Study of Manners*]? Depending on the response, this element will be classified under either "subtitle" or "genre indication." But (despite appearances) my concern is not to classify but to identify the constituent elements, whose functions in the constituted wholes may be infinitely varied or shaded. We will not pursue them that far.

As a matter of fact, in relation to the elements that I will henceforth call title and subtitle, the genre indication is somewhat

[3] This was the subtitle at least on the general title page. But at the head of book 1, a repeat of the title is accompanied by a new subtitle, *Chronique de 1830*, all the more inexplicable in that it shamelessly contradicts the fiction of the foreword, according to which the novel was written in 1827. Apparently no comment from the specialists.

incongruous, for the first two are defined formally and the third functionally. So despite the various disadvantages of doing so, I have decided to save my discussion of the genre indication for a study of its own, which appears at the end of this chapter. For now, let us simply remember that the genre indication can serve as a relatively autonomous paratextual element (like the mention "a novel" on our contemporary covers), or it can take over – to a greater or lesser degree – the title or subtitle. I am also reserving for later in the chapter – for my study of the title's functions – a consideration of simple titles with the value of a genre indication, titles of the type *Satires* or *Meditations*.

Let us also note, apropos of the structure of the title thus reduced (title + subtitle), that the two elements may be more or less tightly integrated. I imagine my readers have already noticed that *Ariel ou La vie de Shelley* is a more closely linked double title than *Madame Bovary, Mœurs de province*, undoubtedly at least because, whatever graphic arrangements the author and publisher adopt, the "*ou*" does more to bind than to sunder. The same observation applies to *Pierre or The Ambiguities*, *Anicet ou Le panorama* [Aragon], *Blanche ou L'oubli* [Aragon], and some others. Moreover, *Anicet* has this distinctive feature: Aragon specified that the genre indication "Roman" ["A Novel"] be incorporated into the title (despite the original comma). This seemingly quite disjunct title, *Anicet / ou Le panorama, / Roman*, must, by authorial decision, function as a whole: *Anicet-ou-Le-panorama,-Roman*. The same recommendation, I would imagine, for *Henri Matisse, Roman* [Aragon].

One especially paradoxical case is that of *Le Soulier de satin* [*The Satin Slipper*, a play by Claudel], which includes a subtitle, but only as spoken (in the prologue) by the Announcer, who is supposed to mention it at each performance. Contrary to normal theatrical practice, the (complete) title exists, if I may say so, only orally. But this orality is immediately belied or subverted by the typically graphic layout of it in the printed text of the prologue: LE SOULIER DE SATIN / OU / LE PIRE N'EST PAS TOUJOURS SUR / ACTION ESPAGNOLE EN QUATRE JOURNEES [THE SATIN SLIPPER / OR / THE WORST IS NOT ALWAYS SURE / A SPANISH ACTION IN FOUR DAYS] – a layout the Announcer is undoubtedly instructed to reconstitute with gestures, pantomime, or various vocal modulations.

Definitions

In the contemporary period, the subtleties of titular presentation have multiplied, and I will not pursue them through all their vagaries. Some of these presentations, in any case, must surely be the despair of bibliographers, who find the fanciful graphics of these presentations impossible to transcribe faithfully. See the titular presentations of Maurice Roche, each of which resorts to so distinctive a kind of lettering that all I can do here is evoke them by description: *Circus* in "illuminated" characters, *Codex* in a sort of capital Roman script with the letter *x* lengthened into a Greek χ; and so forth. I would have as much or more trouble reproducing an oral mention, even if it goes unnoticed (one finesses the graphic detail), but conversely Doubrovsky's title *Fils*, a snap to copy out, cannot be pronounced accurately because, in saying it, one inevitably disambiguitizes it.[4] Here one copes by means of buccal contortions. I also see that, in the case of titles whose elements are originally arranged one above the other, too often even in writing the original layout is violated (sometimes by the publisher first of all, on the half-title page – make no mistake about that). Examples of such titles are

Sade	*Ouï*	*Donnant*	*Le Soupçon*
Fourier	*dire*	*donnant*	*le désert*
Loyola	[Deguy],	[Deguy],	[Jabès],
[Barthes],			

and others. Less difficult to respect is the written form of LETTERS, by John Barth: for pressing reasons, he requires seven capitals.

Simple or complex, the titular apparatuses I have evoked so far bear on single works, or works presented as single, such as a novel (*Madame Bovary*) or a collection (*Satires*), and this is obviously the most common situation because most collections (of poems, novellas, or essays) present themselves as undivided wholes. But matters can get complicated when the book itself professes to be a factitious and purely material grouping of works that were previously published one at a time and whose specificity must not be eliminated or even diminished by their presence in a collection. Complications can also arise when,

---

[4] [The French word *fils* means both "son" (singular or plural) and "threads" (plural) – but when the meaning is "son(s)," the "l" is not pronounced, and when the meaning is "threads," the "s" is not pronounced.]

conversely, a work originally published separately in book form is presented as part of a larger whole.

I said *can* get complicated. Complications are not inevitable, and many a collection of more or less complete *Poetic Works* is presented under this straightforward title or something equivalent; likewise, for example, *The First Forty-Nine Stories* of Hemingway brings together three previous collections (*In Our Time, Men Without Women, Winner Take Nothing*) without indicating that fact anywhere except in the table of contents. But the author of a new collection may also be anxious to mention in the title the individual constituent works. In that case we see the appearance of a two-level titular apparatus, one level constituted by the title of the whole (for example, *Les Lois de l'hospitalité* [Klossowski], or *Volume One* [Ponge], or *Poems* [Bonnefoy]) and the other by the list of titles gathered together (*La Révocation de l'édit de Nantes, Roberte ce soir, Le Souffleur* [Klossowski]; *Douze Petits Ecrits, Le Parti pris des choses, Proèmes,* ... [Ponge]; *Du mouvement et de l'immobilité de Douve, Hier régnant désert,* ... [Bonnefoy]).

An author can even refuse to federate under a common title works whose autonomy he wishes to maintain; in such a case the method is, instead, confederal, a method dear (for example) to Michaux (*Plume, précédé de Lointain intérieur* [... *preceded by* ...]) or to Char (*Le Marteau sans maître, suivi de Moulin premier* [... *followed by* ...]); but without fail this approach makes the first title seem the main one – which may not be what the author desired. All of which goes to show that it is not so easy for several works to cohabit inside one book without confusion.

I do not know whether the term *overarching title* is commonly used for a general title assigned after the event, such as *Volume One,* but it seems to me that we would do better to save that term for the reverse situation: for whole works consisting of several volumes, each of which has its own title. We find this situation especially with novelistic sets, exemplified by Zola's *Rougon-Macquart,* Proust's *Recherche,* Romains's *Hommes de bonne volonté,* and so forth. Balzac's *Comédie humaine,* which was assembled after its constituent works were published and has a looser unity than the other sets, is again a separate case. In reality, each of the novels or novellas of this whole-to-come appeared separately, in serial and/or book form, and this mode of presentation was maintained to the end, concurrently with the publication of more or less partial groupings: *Scènes de la vie privée* (1830), *Romans et contes philosophiques* (1831), *Etudes de mœurs au XIXe siècle* (1835) (already subdivided into *Scènes de la vie privée, de la vie de province, de la vie parisienne*), *Etudes philosophiques* (1835), and finally *La Comédie humaine* (1842), in which these divisions, as well as some others, reappear in a structure of several levels: thus *La Cousine Bette* is the first episode in *Les Parents pauvres*, which belongs to *Scènes de la vie parisienne*, which belongs to *Etudes de mœurs*, which ultimately belongs to *La Comédie humaine*. Obviously this structure appears only in the collected editions of *La Comédie humaine*; the innumerable separate editions often do not even mention the existence of such a whole. Moreover, other groupings of Balzac's works are possible, even if clearly unfaithful to the author's intentions: for example, a grouping by chronological order of publication or by chronological order of the action, not to mention the facsimile republication of the copy of the Furne 1842 edition in which Balzac wrote his corrections.[5] The possibility of all these variations derives from the fact that the sequence of *La Comédie humaine*, although quite loosely thematic (see the author's own hesitations), is in any case not chronological.

The whole of Zola's *Rougon-Macquart* clearly has a stronger, or more obvious, unity, one the author basically had in mind from the beginning. Thus the first volume of the set, *La Fortune des Rougon*, bore on its title page and cover the overarching title *Les Rougon-Macquart*, as did each volume published during Zola's lifetime. Actually, the situation was even more complex, for here the overarching title itself has a subtitle (sub-overarching title): *Histoire naturelle et sociale d'une famille sous le Second Empire*. I suspect that the very numerous and sometimes very inexpensive posthumous editions of such a popular work have not always scrupulously respected this arrangement, one the author definitely wanted. To spare ourselves an exhausting retrospective investigation, I offer a very sketchy picture of how the matter now stands in France: the overarching title appears neither on the Livre de poche set nor on the GF set nor (for obvious reasons) on the lone *Germinal* put out by Garnier. The only present series that

---

[5] See the *Œuvres de Balzac* provided by R. Chollet (Rencontres, 1958–62); *L'Œuvre de Balzac publiée dans un ordre nouveau*, by A. Béguin and J. A. Ducourneau (Formes et Reflets, 1950–53); and the *Œuvres complètes illustrées*, by J. A. Ducourneau (Bibliophiles de l'originale, 1965–76).

show it are Folio and, of course, Pléiade – and the latter, to tell the truth, is meticulous in the opposite direction, putting on its dust jackets only the overarching title with its subtitle, and listing the novels grouped in each volume only on the jacket flap and title page.

Diegetic integration is stronger still in the *Recherche* because there the succession of "parts" is governed by the single chronological thread of the life of the narrator-hero, and we know that Proust originally hoped to publish this work in a single thick volume, entitled either *A la recherche du Temps perdu* or *Les Intermittences du coeur* [*Irregularities of the Heart*]. Quickly resigned to an unavoidable division, in October 1912 he suggested to Fasquelle a work entitled *Les Intermittences du coeur* and divided into two volumes: *Le Temps perdu* and *Le Temps retrouvé*.[6] At first the Grasset edition was supposed to hold to that bipartite division, but then, as the announcement of 1913 attests, it adopted the tripartite division *Du côté de chez Swann*, *Le Côté de Guermantes* (note the change in the article, a change we know Proust insisted on), *Le Temps retrouvé*. Ideally these volumes would have been printed without paragraph indentations, even for the dialogue: "That makes the talk enter more into the continuity of the text."[7] According to André Maurois, it was Louis de Robert who persuaded Proust to accept some indentations, in the more traditional presentation put out by Grasset and then by Gallimard. Proust obviously agreed to these divisions into volumes and indented units as concessions to custom and to publishing requirements, as these two confidences to René Blum attest: "As a concession to habit, I'm giving different titles to the two volumes. ... However, maybe I'll put a general title at the top of the cover the way Anatole France, for example, did for *Histoire contemporaine*"; and "I pretend that [the first volume] is a small whole all by itself, like *L'Orme du mail* in *Histoire contemporaine* or *Les Déracinés* in *Le Roman de l'énergie nationale*."[8] In this way – reluctantly – Proust little by little, or inch by inch, gave up the initial unitary structure in favor of a binary division, then a

---

[6]   *Correspondance*, ed. Philip Kolb (Plon), 11:257. The initial capital of "Temps" is constant in Proust's writings. I am not sure that this wish has always been fully respected.

[7]   Letter to Louis de Robert, June 1913, ibid., 12:212.

[8]   February 20, 1913, ibid., 79; and early November 1913, ibid., 295. [*Le Roman de l'énergie nationale* is by Barrès.]

ternary division that, in 1918 and still under the pressure of circumstances, became a division into five "volumes" (*Swann, Jeunes Filles, Guermantes, Sodome, Temps retrouvé*) and finally into seven volumes, with *Sodome et Gomorrhe III* subdivided into *La Prisonnière* and *La Fugitive*.

The publisher's rendition of this structure, then, starting with the Grasset *Swann* of 1913, was an overarching title, *A la recherche du Temps perdu,*[9] positioned above the volume title, *Du côté de chez Swann*, an arrangement that obviously highlighted the partial title to the detriment of the general title. Gallimard kept that arrangement for the set of fourteen, then fifteen volumes constituting the current edition in the Collection Blanche, but greatly increased the type size of the general title, thus favoring the latter. In 1954, the Pléiade presentation gave an even greater advantage to the general title; and for some years now – in keeping with the new norms of the series – the section titles (as for the *Rougon-Macquart*) have totally forsaken the front of the jacket and the spine and are relegated to the back of the jacket. This paratextual evolution obviously, even if fortuitously, conformed to Proust's original intentions but perhaps not to his final intentions, which I will have occasion to speak of in another chapter. In any case, the fact remains that since 1913 two or three generations of readers will have had different perceptions of Proust's work and accordingly will doubtless have read it differently, depending on whether they were receiving it as a set of autonomous works or as a unitary whole, with a single title, in three volumes. Pocket editions, since the 1960s, have unavoidably brought about a return to the division into sections, mitigated by a presentation that is more compact than the one in the Collection Blanche (eight volumes rather than fifteen) but aggravated by covers that give less and less prominence to the general title. In Livre de poche, the general title appears in very small letters *under* the section title, and in Folio the general title is relegated to the back cover. The culmination of this evolution is reached by the new GF edition, even though its general editor is an eminent Proustologist: on the covers of the volumes that have appeared thus far (*La Prisonnière, La Fugitive*, and *Le Temps retrouvé*), the only reference to the whole is buried in the text of the please-insert. In all these

---

[9] Set entirely in capital letters, which evaded the question of what to choose for the first letter of *Temps*.

cases, of course, the title page makes up for things in a location that, from the bibliographical point of view, remains the most official and perhaps the only reliable one, but for the "general" reader, such compensation is a little late and no doubt too inconspicuous. I do not know what the various editions to come hold in store for us, but in one sense the diversity – indeed, the incoherence – that lies ahead will at least have the fortunate effect of liberating this text from a presentation that is today a little too canonical, and thus from a paratext that, given its monopoly, is a little too imperious.

Place

For centuries the title, like the name of the author, had no site reserved for it, except sometimes, in the case of the *volumina* of antiquity, a sort of label (*titulus*) more or less firmly affixed to the knob (*umbilicus*) of the roll. Unless the opening or closing lines of the text itself mentioned the title, thus making it inseparable from the future life of the work (as we have seen in connection with the name of the author), the title was more a question of oral transmission, of knowledge by hearsay, or of scholarly competence. The invention of the *codex* did not really improve the title's material situation: the text began on the first page (or its second side, after a mute first side), in the same conditions as in antiquity. The first printed books, which were designed to look just like the manuscripts they were reproducing, did not yet include what we call a title page. The reader had to search for the title at the end of the volume, in the colophon, along with the name of the printer and the date of printing; the colophon is therefore in many respects the ancestor or embryo of our publisher's peritext. The title page did not appear until the years 1475–80, and for a long time – until the invention of the printed cover – the title page remained the only location of a title often loaded down, as we have seen, with various items of information that for us are appendages. With the invention of the printed cover, that page was then called simply *title*, and not from metonymy: rather, bit by bit our ideal notion of the title had worked its way free of the initial textual and later paratextual jumble in which it had been buried without a really specific status, as when Herodotus started his work with "What Herodotus the Halicarnassian has learnt by inquiry is here set forth" or Robert de Clari started his work with "Here begins [the literal translation of the Latin *incipit*] the history of those who conquered Constantinople."

In our present scheme of things, the title has four almost obligatory and fairly redundant locations: the front cover, the spine, the title page, and the half-title page (which, as a rule, has nothing on it but the title, possibly in shortened form).[10] But often one still finds the title repeated on the back cover and/or as the running head, that is, along the tops of all the pages, a position it may share with the chapter titles, the practice in that case being to use the top of the left-hand page for the title of the work. When the cover is concealed by a dust jacket, the title of the work is inevitably, again, repeated – or, to put it differently – advertised there. I know of no equivalent in (modern) literature of a terminal title, like those of Debussy's *Préludes*, which, I may add, are in effect titles of the parts, with the general title clearly appearing at the head of the score. The most ingenious exploitation of this multiplicity of locations is the one (cited in Chapter 2) that Ricardou thought up for *La Prise de Constantinople*, the title of which changes in form and meaning when repeated on the back cover, which is presented as a second front cover: *La Prose de Constantinople*. This is perhaps the only such exploitation, a fact perhaps showing that avant-garde writers have not really invested in this type of resource, or rather that the requirements set by technical and commercial standards, which are very rigid in this area, have deterred them from doing so.

Books bound in leather (or Leatherette) often omit the name of the title from the front cover but for obvious reasons keep it on the spine, which is the only surface visible in a library and often in a bookstore and which, today, could therefore be the second obligatory location, after the title page. Obligatory and not in the least insignificant, for the spine's narrowness often requires a telltale abbreviation (some early bindings include juicy ones – a result of the classical period's casualness in this regard) or a sometimes difficult choice (one I have already mentioned) between a horizontal and a vertical printing.

---

[10] But Gallimard's Le Chemin series includes no half title, and this exception is undoubtedly not unique.

Time

The time of the title's appearance raises no problem, in theory: the title appears upon publication of the original (or the pre-original, if any) edition. But there are some subtle variations, or twists.

Let us not completely discount (because information about it often ends up incorporated in the paratext of scholarly editions) the genetic prehistory, or prenatal life, of the title – that is, the author's hesitations about his choice, hesitations that may last for quite a long time and may entail quite a lot of thought. Baudelaire's *Fleurs du mal* was first entitled *Les Lesbiennes* or *Les Limbes*; Stendhal's *Lucien Leuwen* (unfinished, to be sure, and with a posthumously chosen title) was at various times going to be called *L'Orange de Malte*, *Le Télégraphe*, *L'Amarante et le noir*, *Les Bois de Prémol*, *Le Chasseur vert*, *Le Rouge et le blanc*; and in the pre-text (or pre-paratext) of Zola's *Bête humaine*, Claude Duchet has counted no fewer than 133 proposed titles. That is undoubtedly a record of sorts, but Zola's lists are not at all immaterial to the reader and are even less so to the critic, for they stress various thematic aspects unavoidably sacrificed by the definitive title, and this pre-paratext is a wholly legitimate part of the posthumous paratext.[11] No Proustian who is the least bit knowledgeable is unaware today that the *Recherche* was almost entitled *Les Intermittences du coeur* or *Les Colombes poignardées* [*The Stabbed Doves*] (!); that is important to our reading, like knowing that Giono's *Un roi sans divertissement* was first called *Charge d'âme*. These are two examples from among thousands, even if some of those pre-titles were, for their authors, perhaps no more than working titles – provisional, and manipulated as such, as *The Trial* and *The Castle* were (according to Brod) and as *Work in Progress* must have been before becoming *Finnegans Wake*. Even or especially when provisional, a formula is never completely

---

[11] H. Mitterand, in the Pléiade edition of Zola's novels, specifies that the list for *La Bête humaine* is the most copious one. He also cites fifty-four pre-titles for *L'Œuvre*, and C. Becker counts twenty-three for *Germinal* (Garnier, p. lv). The title *L'Argent*, in contrast, emerged right at the start. As for *Le Ventre de Paris* [*The Belly of Paris*], at first the work was to be entitled *Le Ventre*, which, Zola said, "I found much broader and more forceful. I yielded to my publisher's wish" (letter to J. Van Santen Kolff, July 9, 1890).

unimportant, except when the author resorts to a plain serial number.

We also know that some authors, inclined to pseudonyms in everything, give their works – even after publication – kinds of nicknames for intimate or private use: Stendhal, for example, preferred to designate the *Rouge* by the name of its hero, *Julien*, and to designate *Les Vies de Haydn* by the name of its pseudonymous author, *Bombet*. And I am not talking about mere abbreviations, or rather I am: Chateaubriand's first work is officially entitled *Essai historique, politique et moral sur les révolutions anciennes et modernes considérées dans leurs rapports avec la Révolution française* [*Historical, Political, and Moral Essay on Ancient and Modern Revolutions Considered in Their Relations with the French Revolution*]. We have reduced that title to the form *Essai sur les révolutions*, but the author himself always shortened it to *Essai historique*. That difference is not minuscule.

The reverse case – a title hit upon all of a sudden, and sometimes well before the subject of the book – is by no means uncommon, and still less is it unimportant, because then the preexisting title has every probability of functioning like some opening words (see Aragon, or the famous "first line" whispered to Valéry by the gods),[12] that is, like an instigator: once the title is there, the only thing left to produce is a text that justifies it ... or doesn't. "If I write the story before finding the title, the story generally aborts," claims Giono apropos of *Deux Cavaliers de l'orage*. "A title is needed because the title is the sort of banner one makes one's way toward; the goal one must achieve is to explain the title."[13]

But an author's hesitations about the title, when these exist, may persist after the manuscript is submitted and, indeed, after the work is first published. At that point the author is no longer alone (assuming he has been up until then): he has to deal with

[12] [In *Je n'ai jamais appris à écrire ou Les incipit* (Skira, 1969), Aragon mentioned the inspirational power, for him, of the first sentence. Valéry, in "Au sujet d'*Adonis*," in *Variété* (*Œuvres*, Pléiade 1:482), wrote, "The gods, graciously, give us a first verse *for nothing*; but it is our task to fashion the second, which must harmonize with the first and not be too unworthy of its supernatural brother" [tr. *Variety*, trans. Malcolm Cowley (NY: Harcourt, Brace, 1927), 71].]
[13] See R. Ricatte, "Les Deux Cavaliers de l'orage," *Travaux de linguistique et de littérature* 7, no. 2 (1969): 223. We know that this is not true for all of Giono's works, but the fact remains that one may draw inspiration from a title and then, after the text thus inspired is finished, prefer another title for it.

4 *Titles*

his publisher, the public, and sometimes the law. Everyone now knows that, without Gallimard, Sartre's *Nausée* would have been entitled *Melancholia* and that Proust had to give up *La Fugitive*, a title Tagore had already used, in favor (provisionally) of *Albertine disparue*.[14] Balzac's *Cousin Pons* had first been advertised to readers of the *Constitutionnel* under the title *Les Deux Musiciens* (below, I will discuss the reasons for this change). Numerous substitutions of this type, proposed or imposed by publishers, will never be known, but sometimes the author complains officially in a preface or unofficially in an interview, confidence, or personal note, and these semi-repudiations, too, belong to the paratext. A marginal note in *Armance* indicates that the title Stendhal wanted (after dropping *Olivier*, which at that time "exposed" the subject) was *Armance, Anecdote du XIXe siècle*. The note goes on to say that "the second title [that is, the present complete title, *Armance ou Quelques scènes d'un salon de Paris en 1827*] was thought up by the bookseller; without bombast, without charlatanism, nothing sells, said [this bookseller] Mr. Canel." What would he say today? But the author may just as easily be stubborn about a title and then regret it later. This is apparently the case with Flaubert, who, having "irrevocably" forced *L'Education sentimentale* on Michel Lévy ("It is *the only* title that conveys the idea of the book"), issues a retraction in his dedication to Henry Meilhac: "The title really should have been *Les Fruits secs*." We also know that in 1920 Proust was perfectly ready to complain about his title and wished he had kept the alleged initial title, *Le Temps perdu*.[15]

Above I said that hesitations about the title may persist after the work is first published, but what I meant was first published during the author's lifetime and with his consent. Thus *Albert Savarus*, which was serialized under this title in 1842 and was immediately reprinted under the same title in the first

---

[14] Provisionally because the Pléiade edition, since 1954, has restored *La Fugitive*; the pocket editions, however, have kept *Albertine disparue*, and J. Milly, for GF, gives *La Fugitive*, followed in parentheses by *Albertine disparue*. So we are apparently heading toward a situation of synonymy of the same type as *Spleen de Paris / Petits Poèmes en prose* [two titles given to a posthumous collection of poems by Baudelaire].
[15] Flaubert, *Lettres inédites à Michel Lévy* (Calmann-Lévy, 1965), 154; Proust to Jacques Rivière, July 26 or 27, 1920.

volume of *La Comédie humaine* (which constituted its original edition), resurfaced in 1843, in a collection of works by various authors, under the new title *Rosalie*. In the same collection, *La Muse du département* reappeared under the new title *Dinah*. To my knowledge, specialists propose no explanation for these changes in title, which are accompanied by no significant modifications of the text. The same cannot be said of the change from *Le Dernier Chouan ou La Bretagne en 1800* (1829) to *Les Chouans ou La Bretagne en 1799* (1834): the latter presents what is actually a new text (but as we know, the earlier text was initially going to be entitled *Le Gars*). The most economical approach is certainly the one taken by Senancour, who in 1804 published a work called *Oberman*, then in 1833 a revised version under the new title *Obermann*. Unfortunately he did not continue along that route for the third edition, more extensively revised, of 1840, which does not have a third *n*. But because the reworkings of 1833 were minor, Senancour's (too few) fans have a very easy way of distinguishing the two main versions of this text, at least in writing: on the telephone, a little emphasis would be needed.

A final mode of official transformation may emerge as a reaction to a successful adaptation made under a new title – a title it is thought advantageous for the book to appropriate. For example, Simenon's novel *L'Horloger d'Everton* [*The Clockmaker of Everton*] (1954) was reissued in 1974 with a cover bearing an illustration based, of course, on the Bertrand Tavernier movie and with this strange title: George Simenon / *L'Horloger de Saint-Paul* / d'après le roman [adapted from the novel] / *L'Horloger d'Everton*. The title page gives only the original title, which undoubtedly shows that only the outside is new. Another example: Pierre Bost's novel *Monsieur Ladmiral va bientôt mourir* [*Mr. Ladmiral Is Going to Die Soon*], published in 1945, became in 1984 a movie (also by Tavernier) entitled *Un Dimanche à la campagne* [*Sunday in the Country*]. In the meantime, Pierre Bost had died. The publisher rushed to put out a new edition, whose title – on the cover and title page – remained *Monsieur Ladmiral* (etc.) but whose dust jacket, illustrated by the advertising poster for the movie, had as an overarching title, in much thicker letters, *Un Dimanche à la campagne*. Such tactics are economical and equivocal, but they may turn out to be only transitional steps

4 Titles

toward a definitive change in title: all that would be needed, no doubt, would be for the new title, timidly advanced in this way, to have lasting popularity.[16]

For the main agent of titular drift is probably neither the author nor even the publisher but in fact the public, and more precisely the posthumous public, still and very properly called posterity. Its labor – or rather, in this case, its laziness – generally tends toward a reduction – actually, an erosion – of the title.

The simplest form of this reduction is possibly omission of the subtitle. Omission is, moreover, selective and has a variable impact: the educated public still knows *Candide ou L'optimisme,* *Emile ou De l'éducation,* and perhaps *Les Caractères ou Les mœurs de ce siècle*[17] (for [Rousseau's] *Julie,* very exceptionally, posterity has promoted the original subtitle to title: *La Nouvelle Héloïse*);[18] but can anyone now, without hesitating, give the subtitle (already cited) of *Le Rouge et le noir* or of *L'Education sentimentale* (also already cited), not to mention the subtitle of [Balzac's] *Eugénie Grandet* (only its serial version carried *Histoire de province*) or of *Père Goriot* (the original subtitle of 1835, *L'histoire parisienne,* disappeared at the time of the first regrouping)? Publishers sometimes unfortunately help this omission along, for in many modern editions, even scholarly ones, subtitles disappear from covers and, indeed, from title pages. An example: the subtitle of *Bovary,* which was nevertheless present in all the editions Flaubert revised and is obviously of thematic importance, did not

16 Furthermore, we should remember the very common habit of modifying the title for the translation of a work. We could use a whole study of this practice, which is not without paratextual effects. Lacking such a study, I offer this example, chosen by the luck of the stepladder: the English translations of [Malraux's] *La Condition humaine* and *L'Espoir* are, respectively, *Man's Fate* and *Man's Hope,* translations that suggest a tolerably apocryphal symmetry between the two works – but I do not know whether the author was consulted on this point.
17 [*Emile* is by Rousseau, *Les Caractères* by La Bruyère.] As a matter of fact, in the seventeenth and eighteenth centuries it was always *Les Caractères de Théophraste traduits du grec avec les caractères ou les mœurs de ce siècle* [*The Characters of Theophrastus Translated from the Greek, with the Characters or Manners of This Century*]. And only in the sixth edition (1691) was La Bruyère's text set in larger type than Theophrastus's.
18 It is true that the handwritten copy given to the Maréchal de Luxembourg had *La Nouvelle Héloïse* on its first page, then *Julie ou la Nouvelle Héloïse* on its second page – a sign of the author's own hesitation.

70

Time

appear on the Dumesnil edition of 1945, the Masson edition of 1964, or the Bardèche edition of 1971.[19]

More legitimate in principle, and clearly inevitable, are the abbreviations of the long synopsis-titles characteristic of the classical period and perhaps especially of the eighteenth century. It is hard to imagine these titles being quoted *in extenso* in a conversation or even in an order placed at the bookstore, and their reduction was definitely expected, if not planned, by the authors. Actually, some of these original titles are easily analyzable into elements varying in status and importance. For example, d'Urfé's *Astrée* bore on the title page of its first book [part], in 1607, *L'Astrée de Messire Honoré d'Urfé, Gentilhomme de la Chambre du Roy, Capitaine de cinquante hommes d'armes de ses Ordonnances, comte de Chasteauneuf et baron de Chasteaumorand ... où par plusieurs histoires et sous personnes de Bergers et d'autres, sont déduits les divers effets et l'honneste amitié* [The *Astrée* of Monsieur Honoré d'Urfé, Gentleman ..., Captain ..., Count ... and Baron ... *whereby with several stories and in the persons of shepherds and others, various effects and true friendship are inferred*] – in which we can easily distinguish a short title (but without being too sure whether the definite article at the beginning is or is not part of it), the author's name followed by his titles and functions, and something like a subtitle. But analysis is more difficult for the original title of what today we call *Robinson Crusoe*, which in 1719 was *The Life and Strange Surprizing Adventures of Robinson Crusoe, of York. Mariner: Who lived Eight and Twenty Years, all alone in an un-inhabited Island on the Coast of America, near the Mouth of the Great River of Oroonoque; Having been cast on Shore by Shipwreck, wherein all the Men perished but himself. With An Account how he was at last as strangely deliver'd by Pyrates.*

The fashion for these synopsis-titles seems to have died out early in the nineteenth century, as we see in the works of Walter Scott and Jane Austen, but during the rest of the nineteenth and even in the twentieth century such titles reemerged from time to time as pastiches, used either ironically or affectionately, at least in the works of authors imbued with a sense of tradition or inclined to wink – authors such as Balzac (*Histoire de la grandeur et de la décadence de César Birotteau, Marchand parfumeur, Adjoint au*

[19] The C. Gothot-Mersch edition for Garnier did not have the subtitle when it came out in 1971, but in 1980 it put the subtitle back on the title page.

71

maire du deuxième arrondissement de Paris, Chevalier de la Légion d'honneur, ...), Dickens (*The Personal History, Adventures, Experience & Observation of David Copperfield The Younger Of Blunderstone Rookery [Which He never meant to be Published on any Account]*), Thackeray (*The Memoirs of Barry Lyndon, Esq., of the Kingdom of Ireland. Containing an account of his extraordinary adventures; misfortunes; his sufferings in the service of his late Prussian majesty; his visits to many of the courts of Europe; his marriage and splendid establishments in England and Ireland; and the many cruel persecutions, conspiracies, and slanders of which he has been a victim*), or Erica Jong (*The True History of the Adventures of Fanny Hackabout-Jones In Three Books Comprising her Life at Lymeworth, her Initiation as a Witch, her Travels with the Merry Men, her Life in the Brothel, her London High Life, her Slaving Voyage, her Life as a Female Pyrate, her eventuel Unravelling of her Destiny, et cetera*). But in the last two cases, the titular pastiche is unavoidably called for by the textual pastiche.

On all of these and numerous other occasions, an irresistible tendency toward reduction is evident. If we exclude *La Nouvelle Héloïse*, which, as we have seen, follows a different route, the only contrary example – but what an example! – as far as I know is that of Dante's *Comedy*, which did not become the *Divine Comedy* until more than two centuries (1551) after the author's death (1321) and almost one century after its first printed edition (1472).

To finish up with the time of the title's appearance: a work can incorporate its date of publication into its title. The author must simply consider the date particularly relevant and must want to indicate as much by bringing it to the fore in this way. Hugo does so for *Les Châtiments*, or rather for *Châtiments*, the original collection published in 1853. The title of this collection, in large letters in the middle of the page, is *Châtiments / 1853*. In the Hetzel edition of 1870, which includes five new pieces, the definite article appears and, legitimately or not, the date disappears. The two elements come together in the first critical edition (Berret, for Hachette, 1932), which is perhaps inconsistent. In principle, editors have a choice of either the text and title (without date) of 1870 or the text and title (with date) of 1853. Jacques Seebacher, in his 1979 GF edition, chose the second alternative, although he included the date in parentheses.

The practice of incorporating the date of publication into the title is not to be confused with the much more common practice of including within a title (or even limiting a title to) the date of the work's action: Hugo's *Quatre-vingt-treize* [*Ninety-three*], Orwell's *1984*, Anthony Burgess's *1985*, Mérimée's *1572 / Chronique du règne de Charles IX*, Hugo's *Notre-Dame de Paris / 1482* (the date is not on the original edition of 1831 but is on the manuscript, and modern editors have acted properly in restoring it), *Les Chouans ou La Bretagne en 1799*, and so forth.[20] These dates are obviously thematic. The date of *Châtiments* is more complex: it is both thematic (the collection deals with the condition of France in 1853) and – the term escapes me at the moment; let us say, provisionally, "within the publisher's purview": the book is published in 1853.

Senders

The titular situation of communication, like any other, comprises at least a message (the title itself), a sender, and an addressee. Admittedly the situation here is simpler than in the case of other paratextual elements, but even so, a few words about sender and addressee are doubtless a good idea.

The title's (legal) sender, of course, is not necessarily its actual producer. We have already come across one or two cases in which the publisher supplied the title; and many other members of the author's circle may play this role, which, in principle, is of no interest to us here unless the author discloses the fact with a piece of information – itself necessarily paratextual – that no one, afterward, will be utterly able to disregard. But that is merely a lateral circumstance that can never exempt the author from the need to assume legal and practical responsibility for the title.

Let us not be too quick to infer from that that the sender of the title is always and necessarily the author and only the author. Dante, as I have said, never entitled his masterpiece *Divine Comedy*, and no retroactive judgment can hold him responsible

---

[20] Flaubert, following Michel Lévy's advice, gave up the idea of subtitling *Salammbô* "241–240 avant Jésus Christ" ("It was to accommodate the bourgeois reader, to tell him exactly when the story took place" – October 1862). His first idea, as a letter from October 1857 reveals, had been *Salammbô, Roman carthaginois*.

for conferring this title on his work. The title's actual creator is unknown (to me), and the person responsible for it is the first publisher – considerably posthumous – to have adopted it.

This holds for every entitling or posthumous re-entitling, but I would quickly add that responsibility for the title is always shared by the author and the publisher. It is shared in actual fact, of course, save when there has been a complete and forceful takeover; it is shared in the strict legal sense because nowadays at least the contract signed by both of these parties mentions the title (and not the text!); and it is shared in the broader legal sense, it seems to me, because the position and social function of the title give the publisher stronger rights and obligations to the title than to the "body" of the text. There must be particular laws, rules, customs, legal precedents pertaining to the title that I am unaware of but the existence of which I take for granted and the existence of which, above all (and this is what matters to us), everyone more or less takes for granted. Besides, this special relationship between the title and the publisher is expressed and symbolized by an object – a book: the *catalogue*. A catalogue is a collection of titles attributed, properly, not to an author but to a publisher. The publisher, not the author, can say, "This book is" or "is not" or (horrors!) "is *no longer* in my catalogue."

Addressees

The addressee of the title is obviously "the public," but this obviousness is a little oversimplified because, as I have said, the very notion of the public is oversimplified – which is perhaps not entirely a disadvantage. For the public is not the totality or the sum of readers. In the case of a dramatic performance, a concert, or a film showing, the public (or, to be more precise, the audience) is indeed the sum of the people present, and therefore, in theory, the sum of the viewers and/or listeners (in theory, because some of the people present may be present only physically and, for various reasons, may fail to see or hear – but let us skip over that, which is *de facto* and not *de jure*). For a book, however, it seems to me that the public is nominally an entity more far-flung than the sum of its readers because that entity includes, sometimes in a very active way, people who do not necessarily read the book (or at least not in its entirety) but who

participate in its dissemination and therefore in its "reception."
My list of such people is not exhaustive: it includes, for example,
the publisher, the publisher's press attachés, the publisher's
agents, booksellers, critics and gossip columnists, and even (and
perhaps especially) the unpaid or unwitting peddlers of reputation that we all are at one time or another. The text of the book is
not necessarily, not constitutively, meant for all those people;
rather, their role is, in a broad (but strong) sense, intermediary: to
get others to read what they themselves have not always read.
We have already met, or will soon meet, texts of accompaniment
(like the please-insert) whose function is almost officially to
relieve these same people of the need to read completely what
their very job responsibilities sometimes prevent them from
reading, without anyone feeling insulted or even really bothered
by such omission: nobody can reasonably require a publisher's
agent to read all the books he distributes. And the public for a
book includes yet another sometimes very broad category: people
who buy the book but do not read it (or at least not in its entirety).
The reader as conceived of by the author (and *this* reader, on the
other hand, has *not* always bought the book) is, to the contrary,
and constitutively by the deepest management of the text, a
person who reads the book *in toto* – unless certain introductory or
other provisions expressly give him permission, as we will see, to
exercise this or that type of selectivity. The public as defined here,
therefore, extends well and often actively beyond the sum total of
readers.[21]

It has long been clear where I wanted to end up: if the
addressee of the text is indeed the reader, the addressee of the
title is the public in the sense I have just specified, or rather
expanded. The title is directed at many more people than the
text, people who by one route or another receive it and transmit
it and thereby have a hand in circulating it. For if the text is an
object to be read, the title (like, moreover, the name of the
author) is an object to be circulated – or, if you prefer, a subject
of conversation.

[21] One can undoubtedly say as much about the public (in the broad sense) of a
play or movie; nonetheless, for the arts of visual performance, the term *public*
in the strict sense designates the set of actual receivers in a more active way
than for literature, where it is more relevant to distinguish between the public
and readers, and also (though this is not exactly the same distinction) between
purchasers and readers.

Functions

With regard to the function – or rather, functions – of the title, a sort of theoretical vulgate seems to have been established. Charles Grivel formulates it roughly like this: the functions of the title are (1) to identify the work, (2) to designate the work's subject matter, (3) to play up the work. And Leo Hoek incorporates Grivel's formulation into his definition of the title: "A set of linguistic signs ... that may appear at the head of a text to designate it, to indicate its subject matter as a whole, and to entice the targeted public."[22] This function-vulgate seems to me an acceptable starting point, but it calls for some comments, additions, and amendments.

In the first place, the three functions mentioned (to designate, to indicate subject matter, to tempt the public) are not necessarily all fulfilled at the same time: only the first is obligatory. The other two are optional and supplementary, for the first function can be fulfilled by a semantically empty title that does not at all "indicate its subject matter" (and serves even less to "entice the public"). In a pinch, the first function can be fulfilled by just a code number.

In the second place, these functions are surely not set forth here in any hierarchical order, for the first and third may manage very well without the second. For example, one might consider *L'Automne à Pékin* [Vian] to be tempting even though (or perhaps because) it has no connection with the subject matter ("as a whole" or not) of the novel to which it serves as the title.

In the third place: however undemanding the first function may seem, it is not always rigorously fulfilled, for many books share the same homonymous title, a title that is therefore no better at designating any one of them than are certain names of people or places which, without a distinguishing context, remain highly ambiguous. Ask a bookseller point-blank if he sells the *Satires* and, very logically, you will get from him in return only a question.

In the fourth place: if the function of designating is sometimes in default, the other two functions are always more or less open to debate, for the relation between a title and the "subject matter as a whole" is highly variable, ranging from the most straightfor-

---

[22] Grivel, *Production de l'intérêt romanesque*, 169–70; Hoek, *La Marque du titre*, 17.

ward factual designation (*Madame Bovary*) to the most doubtful symbolic relationship (*Le Rouge et le noir*); and that relation always depends on the receiver's hermeneutic obligingness. It may be argued that Goriot is not the main character in the novel bearing his name,[23] and conversely the case may be made that the text of *L'Automne à Pékin* is a subtly metaphorical evocation of that season in that place. As for tempting the public, or playing up a work, the subjectivity of such a function is already very obvious.

In the fifth and last place, our list of functions is no doubt incomplete in one way or another, for the title may "indicate" something else about its text besides the factual or symbolic "subject matter": it may equally well indicate the text's form, either in a traditional and generic way (*Odes, Elegies, Novellas, Sonnets*) or in an original way that is meant to be purely singular (*Mosaïque, Tel quel* [*As Is*], *Répertoire*) [Mérimée, Valéry, Butor]. So it would be advisable to make room – alongside of or perhaps in competition (alternation) with the indication of subject matter – for a more formal type of indication: a new function, then, to be slipped in between the former second and third ones, or at least a variant of the second, which accordingly would have to be redefined as an indication of either the subject matter or the form or sometimes (*Elegies*) of both at once.

Now, this variant – let us say, more ponderously, this particular type of semantic relation between title and text – was very clearly identified by Hoek in his 1973 article, but it is not included in his 1981 book; and I confess I don't perceive his reasons for silently abandoning it. Hoek, therefore, on the level he rightly calls *semantic*, at one time distinguished two classes of title: "subjectal" ones, which designate the "subject of the text," like *Madame Bovary*, and "objectal" ones, which "refer to the text itself" or "designate the text as object," like *Poèmes saturniens* [Verlaine].[24] These terms seem to me poorly chosen because,

---

[23] "The titles that show most respect for the reader are those that confine themselves to the name of the hero ...; but even this reference to the eponymous character can represent an undue interference of the author. *Père Goriot* focuses the reader's attention on the figure of the old father, though the novel is also the story of Rastignac; or of Vautrin" (Umberto Eco, *Postscript to "The Name of the Rose,"* trans. William Weaver [San Diego: Harcourt Brace Jovanovich, 1984], 2).

[24] John Barth, using other terms, proposes an equivalent distinction between ordinary titles, which he does not characterize (except as "straightforward," or

among other reasons, they are likely to create confusion: Emma
Bovary can just as well (or just as improperly) be called the
"object" as the "subject" of the novel to which she gives her
name. But the idea seems sound to me, so here I will propose
merely a (new) terminological reform: the titles that in any way at
all indicate the "subject matter" of the text will be called, as
simply as possible, *thematic* (as we will see, this simplicity is not
free of gradations); the others could, without much harm, be
termed *formal*, and quite often *generic*, which in effect most of
them are, especially during the classical period. But it seems to
me necessary to grant the justice of Hoek's observation that such
titles refer to *the work itself*, and mentioning its form or its genre
category is only a means of referring to the work – perhaps the
only means possible in literature, although music is familiar with
at least one other – the opus number; and there is no reason a
writer could not imitate this device or some analogous one. The
main point is for us to note in theory that the choice does not
exactly lie between a title that refers to subject matter (*Le Spleen de
Paris*) and a title that refers to form (*Petits Poèmes en prose*);[25] more
precisely, the choice lies between alluding to the thematic subject
and alluding to the text itself, considered as a work and as an
object. To designate this choice in its full scope, without limiting
its second term to a formal designation that could, if necessary,
be sidestepped, I will borrow from certain linguists the contrast
between *theme* (what one talks about) and *rheme* (what one says
about it). I know that this borrowing, like all others, entails some
amount of distortion, but I commit the offense in exchange for the
effectiveness (and economy) of this terminological pair.[26] If the
theme of *Le Spleen de Paris* is indeed what the title designates (and
for the sake of the hypothesis, let us grant that it is), the rheme is
... what Baudelaire says (writes) about it, and thus what he *makes*
of it, that is, a collection of short poems in prose. If Baudelaire,
instead of naming the work for its theme, had named it for its

literal), and titles that he calls, somewhat incorrectly, "self-referential ... which
refer not to the subject or to the contents of the work but to the work itself"
(*The Friday Book*, x).

[25] I substitute this double example for the ones Hoek used; his seem to me less
pure (*saturniens* is an obviously thematic indication).

[26] On the linguistic use of the term *theme* and its possibilities of extension, see
Shlomith Rimmon-Kenan, "Qu'est-ce qu'un thème?" *Poétique* 64 (November
1985); and for the relationship between theme and "subject matter" as a whole,
see that entire special issue of *Poétique* ("Du thème en littérature").

rheme, he would have called it, for example, *Petits Poèmes en prose*. That is what he did as well, thereby hesitating, for one and the same work (and for our greater satisfaction as theorists), between a *thematic* and a *rhematic* title.[27] So I propose to rename Hoek's former "subjectal" titles *thematic* and his "objectal" ones *rhematic*.[28] I do not yet know whether these two types of semantic relation (between title and text) must be considered two distinct functions or two species of the same function, but this question (which is secondary) will come up again in a little while. For the moment, let us return to – and finish our discussion of – Hoek's and Grivel's first function, the function of designating.

Designation

A title, as everyone knows, is the "name" of a book, and as such it serves to name the book, that is, to designate it as precisely as possible and without too much risk of confusion. But people are not sufficiently aware that *to name* a person (among other things) covers two very different acts, and here it is essential to differentiate the two acts more carefully than natural language does. One act consists of choosing a name for the person. Let us call this the act of *baptizing* – one of the rare occasions when we have the opportunity to affix a name (in this case, a first name) to something, for the age of the onomaturges is long past. And this act, of course, is almost always motivated by something – a preference, a compromise, a tradition: rarely is a child's first name left up to the luck of a dart thrown at a calendar (Purif, Epiph, Fêtnat).[29] But after the name is chosen, affixed, and duly

[27] This hesitation was brought to an end only in 1869, by Asselineau and Banville for the posthumous Michel Lévy edition, in favor of *Petits Poèmes en prose*; but other, later editions return to *Spleen de Paris* or refuse to choose: H. Lemaitre, in the Garnier edition, puts *Le Spleen de Paris* in parentheses, as J. Milly does with *Albertine disparue* for *La Fugitive* [see note 14].

[28] This distinction does not apply only to titles, and perhaps we will come upon it again. At this point, let us say, retroactively and to fill in a gap on page 73 above, that the date *1482* for *Notre-Dame de Paris* is thematic and that the date for *Châtiments* is at one and the same time thematic and rhematic. The publication dates normally printed on title pages are obviously rhematic, like everything that concerns the book as such and not its subject.

[29] [In France, every date from January 1 to December 31 is associated with a saint's name or the name of a major liturgical or secular holiday; these names, or their abbreviations, appear on the post office's calendar distributed every year to every household; and *only* these names or abbreviations may be entered on birth certificates. "Purif" is the calendar abbreviation for "Purifica-

registered, it will be used by all in a spirit and for purposes that will then bear no relation to the reasons for which it was chosen. The purposes for which it will be used are for sheer identification; and in relation to them, the motive behind the initial naming is wholly immaterial and generally unknown, with no great harm done: naming as *using* a name is wholly unrelated to naming as baptizing, or choosing a name; and the most motivated names are in no way the most effective ones, that is, the surest identifiers.

The same applies to the titles of books. When I ask a bookseller, "Do you have *Le Rouge et le noir?*" or when I ask a student, "Have you read *Le Rouge et le noir?*" the meaning attached to this title (the title's semantic relation to the book whose title it is) counts for nothing in my question, either in my mind or in my interlocutor's. That meaning is activated only if I explicitly summon it up, for example, in a question such as "Do you know why this book is entitled *Le Rouge et le noir?*" Now, it is clear that the first type of statement is infinitely more common than the second type. The relation – in this case, purely conventional – that governs the first type is one of sheer and strict designation, or identification. We have already noted that this function is not always fulfilled unambiguously by the title alone, for cases of homonymy do exist.[30] But suppose this function is in fact unambiguously fulfilled by the title alone: the title then does neither a better nor a worse job than any other identifying device, such as libraries' call numbers or the ISBN of modern publishing, both of which also have an initial motivation (classification) that, while quite useful in facilitating research, is immaterial to identification as such.

In actual practice, identification is the most important function of the title, which could if need be dispense with any other

tion" (January 2), "Epiph" the abbreviation for "Epiphanie" (January 6), and "Fêtnat" the abbreviation for "Fête nationale" (national holiday: July 14).]

[30] And also of synonymy, for certain books, as we have already seen, waver between two titles to such an extent that it would be quite arbitrary, considering common practice, to downgrade one to a "subtitle": *The Golden Ass* / *The Metamorphoses* [Apuleius]; *Ars poetica* / *Epistle to the Pisones* [Horace]; *Contr'un* / *Discours de la servitude volontaire* [La Boétie]; *Celestina* / *The Tragi-Comedy of Calisto and Melibea* [Rojas]; *Dorval et moi* / *Entretiens sur Le fils naturel* [Diderot]; *Julie* / *La Nouvelle Héloïse*; *Le Spleen de Paris* / *Petits Poèmes en Prose*; *Albertine disparue* / *La Fugitive*; *Aethiopica* / *The Loves of Theagenes and Chariclea* [Heliodorus].

function. Let us return to our act of baptizing, and let us suppose that my friend Théodore had been baptized at random, by the method of throwing a dart at the calendar. This initial *non-motivation* would make no difference in my use of his name, and in fact I am wholly unaware of the reasons for his having been named as he was. Likewise, if Stendhal had drawn lots to find a title for *Le Rouge et le noir*, that would make no difference in the title's function of identification and in the practical use to which I put the title. I suppose many surrealist titles have been chosen by lot, and they identify their texts just as well as the most carefully devised titles do – and the reader is then free, if the fancy takes him, to find a reason for them, that is, a meaning. Hans Arp, asked one day what title he planned to give a just-completed sculpture, replied sensibly, "*Fork* or *Asshole*, whichever you like." History doesn't reveal which of the two was chosen.

Thematic titles

Used to describe titles that bear on the "subject matter" of the text, the adjective *thematic* is not unimpeachable, for it assumes an extension of the notion of theme which might be thought excessive: if the Republic, the French Revolution, the cult of the self, or Time regained [Plato, Michelet (or Carlyle), Barrès, Proust] are indeed, in varying degrees, the main themes of the works that owe them their titles, the same thing cannot be said, or not in the same way, about the Charterhouse of Parma, the Place Royale [Corneille], the satin slipper, the Radetzky March [Joseph Roth], or even Madame Bovary: a place (backward or not), an object (symbolic or not), a leitmotif, a character (even a central one) are not themes strictly speaking but elements of the diegetic universe of the works for which they serve as the titles. Nevertheless, I will characterize all the titles thus evoked as *thematic*, by a generalizing synecdoche that, if you like, will be a tribute to the importance of theme in the "subject matter" of a work, whether the work be narrative, dramatic, or discursive. From this point of view, no doubt, everything in the "subject matter" that is not the theme, or one of the themes, is empirically or symbolically related to it or them.

There are many ways, therefore, for a title to be thematic, and each of them requires an individual semantic analysis in which interpretation of the text plays a major role. But it seems to me that good old tropology supplies us with an effective principle we can use to come up with a general set of distinctions. There are literal titles, which directly and nonfiguratively designate the theme or the central object of the work (*Phèdre* [Racine], *Paul et Virginie* [Bernardin de Saint-Pierre], *Les Liaisons dangereuses* [Laclos], *La Terre* [Zola], *War and Peace*), sometimes to the extent of revealing the denouement (*Jerusalem Delivered*, "The Death of Ivan Ilych" – proleptic titles). Other thematic titles are attached, by synecdoche or metonymy, to an object that is less unquestionably central (*Le Père Goriot*), or sometimes to an object that is resolutely marginal (*Le Chasseur vert* [*The Green Hunter*], *Le Rideau cramoisi* [*The Crimson Curtain*], *Le Soulier de satin*).[31] Lessing praised Plautus for often taking his titles from "circumstances of the least possible importance," and concluded, perhaps hastily, that "the title really is nothing." Hastily because the detail thus upgraded is *ipso facto* invested with a sort of symbolic value and therefore with thematic importance.[32] A third type of thematic title, constitutively symbolic in nature, is the metaphoric: *Sodome et Gomorrhe* for a narrative whose central theme is homosexuality (even if this symbolic evocation was originally – that is, well before Proust – a metonymy of place), *Le Rouge et le noir* undoubtedly, *Le Rouge et le blanc* definitely (Stendhal says so), *Le Lys dans la vallée* [*The Lily in the Valley*: Balzac],[33] *La Curée* [*The Booty*: Zola], *Germinal* [Zola],[34] *Sanctuary*. A fourth type functions

[31] [*Le Chasseur vert* is the title Stendhal used for *Lucien Leuwen* when the first chapters were published. *Le Rideau cramoisi* is one of the stories in Barbey d'Aurevilly's *Les Diaboliques*.]

[32] Another formation by synecdoche, but one whose function is instead rhematic, consists of giving a collection the title of one of its parts. This practice is common for collections of short stories, such as *La Chambre des enfants* [Des Forêts] or *Le Rire et la poussière* [M'uzan].

[33] Here the title is evoked in the text of the work so named, in disregard of the narrative convention that would require this text, an epistolary novel, to be unaware of its literary nature and, consequently, of the existence of its paratext: "She was, as you already know without knowing anything yet, THE LILY OF THIS VALLEY." In this contradictory or disavowing turn of phrase, we clearly perceive the author's discomfort at having his title (in capital letters!) cited by the letter-writer–hero. On this type of transgression, see Randa Sabry, "Quand le texte parle de son paratexte," *Poétique* 69 (February 1987).

[34] Zola clearly indicates, in a letter of October 6, 1889, to Van Santen Kolff, the semantic power of this delayed brainstorm: "As for this title of *Germinal*, I adopted it only after a lot of hesitating. I was looking for a title to express the emergence of new men, the effort the workers make, even unconsciously, to extricate themselves from the painful, toiling darkness where they are still

by antiphrasis, or irony, either because the title forms an antithesis to the work (*La Joie de vivre*, for the gloomiest of the novels
by Zola, who himself underscores its antiphrastic nature: "At first
I wanted a direct [literal] title like *Le Mal de vivre*, but the irony of
La Joie de vivre made it seem preferable"; and, creating the same
effect, *La Joie*, about which Bernanos himself said, "There is
everything in it except joy") or because the title displays a
provocative absence of thematic relevance. According to Boris
Vian himself, this is the case, already alluded to, of *L'Automne à
Pékin* and also of *J'irai cracher sur vos tombes* [*I Will Spit on Your
Graves*]; it is the case of most surrealist titles; of *La Cantatrice
chauve* [*The Bald Soprano*: Ionesco]; and of many others these days,
such as the *Histoire de la peinture en trois volumes* [*The History of
Painting in Three Volumes*] by Mathieu Bénézet, a slim little
volume that says nothing about painting. The antiphrasis may
take the form of an explicit disavowal, like the celebrated *Ceci
n'est pas une pipe* [*This Is Not a Pipe*: Magritte] – which, to tell the
truth, is not a title, either. The nonrelevance also may be only
apparent and may reveal a metaphorical intention. This is
obviously the role of *Ulysses*, which functions in accordance with
the figural mechanism Jean Cohen has correctly described:
because no one in this novel is called "Ulysses," the title, literally
not relevant, must certainly have a symbolic value – and, for
example, the hero, Leopold Bloom, must certainly be an Odyssean figure.[35] The nonrelevance may also, in a fairly twisted way,
plead literal truth: in a Truffaut film, a fellow asks a perplexed
author, "Does your book have a drum in it? A trumpet? No?
Okay, the title is obvious: *Without Drum or Trumpet*."[36] According

moving about. And one day, by chance, the word Germinal came to my lips.
At first I wanted none of it, thinking it too mystical, too symbolic; but it
represented what I was looking for, a revolutionary April, a flight of decaying
society into springtime. And little by little I got used to it, so much so that I
was never able to find another title. If it is still obscure for some readers, for me
it has become like a ray of sunlight illuminating the whole work" (quoted by
C. Becker, *La Fabrique de Germinal* [SEDES, 1986], 495). ["Germinal" is the name
of the seventh month (the first of the three spring months) in the French
Revolutionary calendar.]

[35] I strongly insist: Ulysses is a perfectly proper first name; therefore, a psychological novel of the *Adolphe* [Constant] type could very well, from the name of its
hero, be entitled *Ulysses* without alluding at all to Homer. In Joyce's novel,
what pulls one up short is certainly the fact that this title does not correspond
to the name of any character.

[36] [In French, "without drum or trumpet" is an idiom meaning "without fuss."]

to this irrefutable principle, one could rename some of the classics as follows: *Ulysses* itself as *Far from Auckland*, or *Le Roman de la rose* as *The Absence of d'Artagnan*.

Of course, the thematic relation may be ambiguous and open to interpretation: we have met two or three cases in which metaphor and metonymy overlap, and no one can prevent an ingenious critic (nowadays that means all of them) from giving a symbolic meaning to, for example, the erasers of *Les Gommes* [*The Erasers*: Robbe-Grillet] (it's already been done). Inversely, Proust thought that in reading Balzac's books one must reduce the apparently symbolic titles to a literal meaning: Lucien's illusions in (*Illusions perdues* [*Lost illusions*]) are thus "quite personal, quite arbitrary illusions ... the nature of them gives the book a powerful stamp of reality, but they slightly abate the transcendentalism of the title. So each title should be taken literally: *Un Grand Homme de province à Paris, Splendeurs et misères des courtisanes, A combien l'amour revient aux vieillards*, etc. In *La Recherche de l'absolu*, the absolute has more the nature of a formula, an alchemical rather than a philosophical affair."[37] Ambiguity may also be the aim of the titular phrase in and of itself, through the presence of one or several words with double meanings: *Fils, L'Iris de Suse, Passage de Milan*.[38] Less obvious, urged (and perhaps discovered) after the event, is the ambiguity of *Les Communistes*: Aragon announced one day that the gender of the noun was feminine – which would, instead, be literally a disambiguitizing because until then the noun had been considered bisexual. Another agent of ambiguity: the presence in the work of a second-degree work from which it takes its title, so that one cannot say whether the title refers thematically to the diegesis or, in a purely designative way, to the second-degree work: see, among others, *Le Roman de la momie* [Gautier], *Les Faux-Monnayeurs* [*The Counterfeiters*: Gide], *Doctor Faustus*,[39] *Les Fruits d'or* [Sarraute], or *Pale Fire*.

---

[37] *Contre Sainte-Beuve* (Pléiade), 269 [tr. *Marcel Proust on Art and Literature 1896–1919*, trans. Sylvia Townsend Warner (New York: Meridian Books, 1958), 169].

[38] The fact that the two meanings of "fils" are *pronounced* differently [see note 4] does not diminish this title's *written* ambiguity. [For *L'Iris du Suse* (Giono), "iris" designates a flower, the membrane of the eye, and a rainbow. For *Passage de Milan* (Butor), "Milan" is both the Italian city and the bird (English kite).]

[39] Here I am cheating a little in order to include an additional title on this list:

I have been considering only single titles, those without subtitles. But with double titles (doubly thematic), each element may play its own part. Classical titles generally organized this division of labor according to a clear principle: to the title went the name of the hero (or, in Plato, the name of Socrates' interlocutor),[40] and to the subtitle went the indication of theme (*Theaetetus or On Knowledge* [Plato], *Candide ou L'optimisme, Le Barbier de Séville ou La précaution inutile* [Beaumarchais]). We find the same thing in the twentieth century, as an archaizing allusion (*Geneviève ou La confidence inachevée* [Gide]). More broadly and flexibly, the subtitle nowadays often gives a more literal indication of the theme that the title evokes symbolically or cryptically. This is a very common practice and has become virtually routine for titles of scholarly works: *Les Sandales d'Empédocle, Essai sur les limites de la littérature* [*The Sandals of Empedocles: Essay on the Limits of Literature*: Magny]; *Miroirs d'encre, Rhétorique de l'autoportrait* [*Mirrors of Ink: Rhetoric of the Self-portrait*: Beaujour]; and so forth. American publishers have a name for this kind of first title: they call it *catchy*, indeed *sexy*, which says it all. They have felt no need to describe the subtitle, which is often a complete cure for love. But the relationship may also be reversed, depending on taste: if the title *Paludes* [*Marshlands*: Gide] is not bad, its subtitle, *Traité de la contingence* [*Treatise on Contingency*], is wonderful.

This division between title and subtitle is also not unheard of in works of fiction. Its most characteristic illustration is undoubtedly *Doctor Faustus*, a title that is obviously symbolic (the hero is no more Faust than Bloom is Ulysses, but only a sort of modern avatar of the Faust figure) and is immediately amended by a literal subtitle: *The Life of the German Composer, Adrian Leverkühn, as Told by a Friend*. The whole constitutes a genre contract (of hypertext by transposition)[41] with perfect exactness. A little as if *Ulysses* had this subtitle: *Twenty-four Hours in the Life of Leopold Bloom, Irish Sales Representative, Told using various more or less original Narrative Strategies*.

Leverkühn's work *en abyme* is actually called *The Lamentation of Dr. Faustus* (*Weheklag Dr. Fausti*).

[40] I do not know whether Plato's titles are "authentic," that is, chosen by the author. In my opinion it is more likely that they are delayed but, in any case, earlier than Diogenes Laertius, who cites them.

[41] [Hypertextuality is the subject of Genette's *Palimpsestes* (Seuil, 1982); see Richard Macksey's foreword above.]

4 *Titles*

Rhematic titles

Ambiguous or not, thematic titles easily dominate the field nowadays, but we must not forget that the classical custom was completely different, if not the reverse. Poetry (except epics and long didactic poems with thematic titles) was dominated by collections with formally generic titles: *Odes, Epigrams, Hymns, Elegies, Satires, Idylls, Epistles, Fables, Poems*, and so forth. The practice of using formally generic titles extends well beyond lyric poetry and classicism, with numerous collections of *Tales, Novellas, Essays, Thoughts, Maxims, Sermons, Funeral Orations, Dialogues, Conversations, Miscellanies*, and more unitary works called *Histories, Annals, Memoirs, Confessions, Recollections*, and so forth. The plural dominates, no doubt, but in this area we still find titles in the singular, such as *Journal, Autobiography, Dictionary*, and *Glossary*. In all these titles, rhematism takes the path of a genre designation – but other titles, inescapably less classical, require a less restrictive type of definition in that they display a sort of genre innovation, and for that reason they could be termed *parageneric: Méditations, Harmonies, Recueillements*,[42] *Unfashionable Observations, Divagations, Approximations, Variété, Tel quel [As Is], Pièces, Répertoire, Microlectures [Microreadings]*.[43] If our own period were not more enamored of originality than of tradition, each of these titles, like Montaigne's *Essais* (which broke new ground), could have given rise to a sort of genre formula and to a series of homonymic titles. This is perhaps the case with *Situations* (Péguy, Sartre): if it appeared a third time, people would begin to speak of "a collection of situations" as they speak of "a collection of essays" (an expression that no doubt would have greatly surprised Montaigne).

Other rhematic titles are still a bit more removed from any genre description, designating the work by a more purely formal

42 The exact titles of Lamartine's collections are, we should remember, *Méditations poétiques, Harmonies poétiques et religieuses*, and *Recueillements poétiques [Poetic Self-Communings]*. The rhematic nature of the second one is certified by this sentence in the foreword: "These Harmonies, taken separately, seem to have no connection with one another." I dare not add to this list *Les Contemplations* by Hugo, a title whose definite article (I will come back to this) draws it toward the thematic. As for *Recueillements poétiques*, I wonder whether it is not simply a stylish variation on the literal formula, which is *recueil de poèmes* [collection of poems].

43 [*Unfashionable Observations* is by Nietzsche; *Divagations*, by Mallarmé; *Approximations*, by Du Bos; *Variété* and *Tel quel*, by Valéry; *Pièces*, by Ponge; *Répertoire*, by Butor; *Microlectures*, by J.-P. Richard.]

– indeed, more fortuitous – feature: *Decameron, Heptaméron* [Margaret of Navarre], *Enneads* [Plotinus], *Attic Nights* [Aulus Gellius], *The Friday Book, En français dans le texte* [*In French in the Text*: Aragon], *Manuscrit trouvé à Saragosse* [*Manuscript Found in Saragossa*: Potocki]. Hence this still-open series: *Manuscript Found in a Bottle* (Poe), *in a Brain* (Valéry), *in a Hat* (Salmon). Or the title may be still more indefinite, but always patently directed at the text itself and not at its object: *Pages* [J.-P. Richard], *Ecrits* [*Writings*: Lacan], *Livre* [*Book*] (D. Barnes: *A Book*; Guyotat: *Le Livre*), or Raymond M. Smullyan's simultaneously interrogative and self-referential title, *What Is the Name of This Book?*

In addition, if imitation and recycling tend to turn thematic titles into rhematic ones as I have just shown for *Situations*, the use of sequels and continuations cannot avoid doing so. The title *Le Menteur* [*The Liar*: Corneille] was perfectly thematic; in *La Suite du Menteur* [*Sequel to the Liar*: Corneille], which is rhematic (this play is the sequel . . .), *Le Menteur* becomes itself rhematic (this play is the sequel to the play entitled . . .). The same effect is created by many of the synonymous formulae, such as *La Nouvelle Justine* or *Le Nouveau Crève-Cœur*,[44] and undoubtedly already by a simple volume-number, such as *Situations I.*

This is not the case with all titles that begin *Nouveau . . .*, for the adjective may have a wholly thematic value: see *La Nouvelle Héloïse* or *The New Robinson Crusoe*. But one can play on the uncertainty: which is it for *Nouvelles Nourritures* [*New Fruits*]? New fruits, or new *Fruits*? And for *Les Nouvelles Impressions d'Afrique*: new impressions, or new *Impressions* (to say nothing of the clever ambiguity of *impressions*)? And for *The New Sorrows of Young Werther*: new sorrows, or new *Sorrows*? And for *The New Adventures and Misadventures of Lazarillo de Tormes*? And for *Le Nouveau Contrat social*? And what would a *Nouvelle Vie de Marianne* be? Or a *Nouvel Amour de Swann*?

[44] [*Nouveau/nouvelle* means "new." *Justine* and *La Nouvelle Justine* are both by de Sade. *Crève-Cœur* and *Le Nouveau Crève-Cœur* are both by Aragon. In the next paragraph, *The New Robinson Crusoe* is by J. H. von Campe; both *Les Nourritures terrestres* [*Fruits of the Earth*] and *Les Nouvelles Nourritures* are by Gide; *Impressions d'Afrique* and *Les Nouvelles Impressions d'Afrique* are by Raymond Roussel; *The New Sorrows of Young Werther* is by Plenzdorff; *The New Adventures and Misadventures of Lazarillo de Tormes* by Camilo José Cela; and *Le Nouveau Contrat social* by Faure. *La Vie de Marianne* is by Marivaux. In the paragraph after that one, both of the *Chéri* books are by Colette, *Lamiel* is by Stendhal, and *La Fin de Lamiel* is by Jacques Laurent.]

Other ambiguities are possible with *Fin de* ... [*End of* ...].
How should we read *La Fin de Chéri*? Is it the end of Chéri, or
the end of *Chéri*? And *La Fin de Lamiel* – is it the end of Lamiel,
or the end of *Lamiel*? It is obvious that *end* can apply with equal
validity to a person or a book. That would not be the case with
sequel, which does not take an animate noun as its complement:
Sequel to Marianne can be only rhematic. But *Sequel to the Life of
Marianne* would, again, be ambiguous. Certain terms, in fact,
designate at one and the same time the object of a discourse and
the discourse itself. Hence the ambiguity of such titles as *History
of* ..., *Life of* .... Or again, under cover of polysemy: *Feuilles
d'automne* [*Leaves of Autumn*: Hugo]. But Hugo's title is actually
Les Feuilles d'automne, which reduces the ambiguity in favor of
the thematic: *Feuilles d'automne* could designate the pages of the
book, but *Les Feuilles d'automne* could hardly designate anything
but the dead leaves of autumn. The same effect is created, as I
have said, by *Les Contemplations* [Hugo], and in addition by *Les
Chants du crépuscule* [*Sunset Songs*: Hugo], *Les Chansons des rues
et des bois* [*Songs of Streets and Woods*: Hugo], and so on. I
remember serious editorial arguments when Wellek and Warren's book was being translated into French. *Théorie de la littérature* (the literal translation, but it had already been used) would
have been rhematic (this book *is* a theory of literature); *La Théorie
littéraire* is obviously thematic (this book *talks about* literary
theory). The same subtle difference between *La Logique du récit*,
which is thematic (narrative has its logic, which I am studying in
this book), and *Logique du récit* [Bremond], which is ambiguous.
The same choice for (*La*) *Grammaire de* ..., (*La*) *Rhétorique de* ...,
and so forth. English (or German) is more clear-cut and rhema-
tizes by means of an indefinite article, which is rarely used in
French: *The Rhetoric of Fiction* is the rhetoric peculiar to fiction,
whereas *A Rhetoric of Fiction* would be a rhetoric applied to
fiction. Furthermore, both English and German turn to the
indefinite article to introduce the genre indication proper, which
by definition is always rhematic from its application to the work
(if not from its content): *Ivanhoe, A Romance*, or *Lucinde, ein Roman*
[F. Schlegel].

This brings us to mixed titles, that is, titles containing two clearly
distinct elements, one rhematic (most often indicating genre) and

one thematic: *Treatise of Human Nature* [Hume], *Essay Concerning Human Understanding* [Locke], *Etude de femme* [Balzac], *Portrait of a Lady, Introduction à l'étude de la médecine experimentale* [Bernard], *Contribution to Political Economy* [Marx], *Regards sur le monde actuel [Reflections on the World Today:* Valéry], and so forth. All titles of this kind begin by designating the genre and there-fore the text, then go on to designate the theme. This formula – eminently classical and extremely clear-cut – was used especially for theoretical works. To tell the truth, over the years some of these titles have been truncated and have lost their rhematic element. For example, Copernicus's work *De revolutionibus orbium coelestium Libri sex* (1543) is reduced nowadays to its first four words and thus to its thematic aspect. Which gives me an opportunity to point out that Greek titles beginning *Péri ...,* Latin titles beginning *De ...,* French titles beginning *De . . .* or *Sur ...,* and so forth, are always mixed titles whose rhematic part is implied.

Connotations

In the final analysis, it seems to me that the contrast between the two *types* – thematic and rhematic – does not give rise to a parallel contrast between two *functions,* one of which would be thematic and the other rhematic. Rather, the two types fulfill the same function, but they do so differently and concurrently (except in cases of ambiguity and syncretism). That function is to describe the text by one of its characteristics, whether thematic (this book talks about ...) or rhematic (this book is ...). So I will call this shared function the *descriptive* function of the title. But thus far we have paid no attention to semantic effects of another type – secondary effects that may supplement equally well the thematic or the rhematic nature of the primary description. These effects can be called *connotative* because they stem from the *manner* in which the thematic or rhematic title does its deno-tating.

Let us take the title of an adventure novel: *Déroute à Beyrouth,* say, or *Banco à Bangkok* [both by Jean Bruce]. The title is obviously thematic, and as such it promises us an adventure set in one of those two capitals that are exotic and reputedly dangerous (in various ways). But the manner in which it makes the promise, a manner based on an obvious homophony, supplements the denotative value with another value, either (for a poorly informed reader) "This author is having fun with his title" or (for a more competent reader) "This author has to be Jean Bruce or someone imitating his titular manner."[45] Now let us take a rhematic title: *Spicilège*. If my *Littré* dictionary is to be trusted, this title denotes a collection of texts or unpublished fragments belatedly "gleaned" (that is the etymology) from the author's desk drawers by the author himself or by his heirs. But also, and perhaps especially, it connotes a style of title that is old (Montesquieu)[46] or, if used in our own time (Marcel Schwob), a studied archaism. For the modern public, this stylistic connotation is probably stronger than the original and entirely technical denotation, whose value has been almost entirely lost.

Now, the connotative capacities of titles are considerable and of all kinds. There are titular styles peculiar to certain authors: the case of Jean Bruce is exemplary because it is based on a simple and almost mechanical method, but there are many others. For example, a title like *La Double Méprise* irresistibly evokes Marivaux (it is Mérimée's); and the parageneric titles of Lamartine's collections all have a family resemblance, so that *Les Contemplations* [Hugo] must have struck Lamartine as a pastiche. There are connotations of a historical kind: the classical dignity of generic titles, the romanticism (and postromanticism) of parageneric titles, the eighteenth-century flavor of long narrative titles à la Defoe, the nineteenth-centuryish tradition of full names of heroes and heroines (*Eugénie Grandet* [Balzac], *Ursule Mirouët* [Balzac], *Jane Eyre*, *Thérèse Raquin* [Zola], *Thérèse Desqueyroux* [Mauriac], *Adrienne Mesurat* [Green]), the cliché-titles of surrealist collections (*Les Champs magnétiques* [*Magnetic Fields*: Breton and Soupault], *Le Mouvement perpétuel* [Aragon], *Corps et Biens* [*With All Hands on Board*: Desnos]). There are also genre connotations: the single name of the hero in tragedy (*Horace* [Corneille], *Phèdre* [Racine], *Hernani* [Hugo], *Caligula* [Albert Camus]); the name of the dramatized characteristic in comedy (*Le Menteur, L'Avare* [*The Miser*: Molière], *Le Misanthrope* [Molière]); the suffix *-ad(e)* or *-id(e)* in the titles of classical epics (*Iliad, Aeneid, Franciade* [Ronsard],

---

[45] On this manner, see J. Molino, "Sur les titres de Jean Bruce."

[46] Although Montesquieu's *Spicilège* was not published until 1944, Montesquieu had chosen its title.

Henriade [Voltaire], and so forth), which very economically link a thematic indication (the name) with a rhematic one (the suffix); the cocky violence of the titles in the *Série noire;* and so forth. But other connotative values require more subtlety to describe individually and are more difficult to classify by group: see the cultural effects of quotation-titles (*The Sound and the Fury, The Power and the Glory, Tender Is the Night, The Grapes of Wrath, For Whom the Bell Tolls, Bonjour tristesse* [Sagan]), of pastiche-titles (as we have already seen with Balzac, Dickens, Thackeray, and others), or of parodic titles (*La Comédie humaine, Le Génie du paganisme* [Augé], and so forth).[47] These are all echoes that provide the text with the indirect support of another text, plus the prestige of a cultural filiation, and do so as effectively as and more economically than an epigraph (which often, as a matter of fact, completes them, and I will come back to this).

These several insights into connotative value have been presented in no particular sequence, nor are they meant to be an exhaustive typology. The follow-up, it seems to me, would lie with historical and critical investigations, for the study of titular styles and their evolution no doubt basically proceeds by way of the study of connotative features – the features most laden with intentions but also most fraught with unintended effects, possible traces of an individual or collective unconscious.

Temptation?

The function of tempting, of inciting one to purchase and/or read, is both so obvious and so elusive that it hardly prompts me to comment. The canonical formula for this function was expressed three centuries ago by Furetière: "A lovely title is a book's real procurer."[48] I am not sure that a title's potential power to allure is always due to its "loveliness," if one really can objectively define such a value: Proust admired the title *L'Education sentimentale* for its compact and seamless "solidity," despite

---

[47] [*Le Génie du christianisme* is a work by Chateaubriand.] On the forms taken by parodic titles, see *Palimpsestes*, 46. A recent variant consists of modeling the title of a study on the title of the work studied: see Derrida, "Force et signification" (on [Rousset's] *Forme et signification*), Tzvetan Todorov, "La Quête du récit" (on *La Quête du Saint-Graal* [*The Quest for the Holy Grail*]), or Christine Brooke-Rose, "The Squirm of the True" (on *The Turn of the Screw*).

[48] Antoine Furetière, *Le Roman bourgeois* (Pléiade), 1084.

its grammatical "impropriety."[49] Another means of tempting has been conventional at least since Lessing: "A title must be no bill of fare [*Küchenzettel*]. The less it betrays of the contents, the better it is."[50] Taken literally, this advice would put the functions of tempting and of describing squarely at odds with each other. Here the vulgate intends, instead, to praise the mouth-watering powers of a certain amount of obscurity or ambiguity: a good title would say enough about the subject matter to stimulate curiosity and not enough to sate it. "A title," says Eco in a sentence that must sound even better in Italian, "must muddle the reader's ideas, not regiment them."[51] That muddling undoubtedly depends on a knack that is appropriate to each author and each object: no formula can spell it out in advance, and it cannot ensure the success of any formula after the fact. All publishers will tell you this: no one has ever been able either to predict a book's success or failure or, *a fortiori*, to assess the title's contribution to that success or failure. I would more readily believe in a more indirect efficacy, which we have already seen Giono evoke and which has been confirmed more recently by Tournier, apropos of his *Goutte d'or*: I find it to be a nice title (he said, approximately); it inspired me all during the book's gestation, and in general I can't be enthusiastic about my work unless I'm sustained by the thought of a title that pleases me.[52] In this particular circumstance people may have varying opinions about the result, but the motivating power of such a phantasm seems unquestionable. Anticipating "the finished product" is no doubt one of the (rare) ways to exorcise the nausea of writing, and the sense of gratification one gets from the title doubtless plays a role.

---

[49] *Contre Sainte-Beuve* (Pléiade), 588.
[50] Lessing, *Hamburg Dramaturgy*, Letter 21, trans. Helen Zimmern (New York: Dover, 1962).
[51] Eco, *Postscript*, 3.
[52] Tournier, comments made during an appearance on the television program *Apostrophes* on January 10, 1986. Let us note in passing that the ambiguity of this title, which is the essence of its "loveliness," is not proof against our mode of transcription. To safeguard the ambiguity, one would need to retain the original written form of the letters, all in capitals, which avoids imposing a choice between upper and lower case for the first letter of GOUTTE. An oral reference to the title does not pose this problem. [Rue de la Goutte d'or (capital "G") is a street in Paris, and *goutte d'or* (lower-case "g") means "golden droplet" – and both of these meanings of the titular phrase are significant to the novel.]

But this function, we realize, is not exactly a matter for the paratext.

Here it would undoubtedly be a good idea to bring a little order to our list (drawn up as we groped our way along) of the functions of the title. The first function, the only one that is obligatory in the practice and institution of literature, is the function of designating, or identifying. The only obligatory function, but one impossible to separate from the others because, under the ambient semantic pressure, even a simple opus number can be invested with meaning. Second is the descriptive function, which is thematic, rhematic, mixed, or ambiguous, depending on which feature or features the sender chooses as the bearer(s) of this description – inevitably always partial and therefore selective – and depending also on the addressee's interpretation, which appears most often as a hypothesis about the motives of the sender, who, for the addressee, is the author. This function of describing, in theory optional, in reality is unavoidable: "A title," Eco rightly says, "unfortunately, is in itself a key to interpretation. We cannot escape the notions prompted by *The Red and the Black* or *War and Peace*."[53] Third is the connotative function attached (whether or not by authorial intent) to the descriptive function. This connotative function, too, seems to me unavoidable, for every title, like every statement in general, has its own way of being or, if you prefer, its own style – and this is the case even with the most restrained title, which will at least connote restraint (at best; and at worst, the affectation of restraint). But perhaps we go too far in calling a sometimes unintended effect a function, and it would no doubt be better to speak here of connotative *value*. The fourth, of questionable efficacy, is the so-called temptation function. When present, it doubtless depends more on the third function (connotation) than on the second (description). When absent, too, I may add. Let us say, then, that the temptation function is always present but may prove to be positive, negative, or nil depending on the receiver, who does not always conform to the sender's own idea of his addressee.

But the main reason for skepticism about the temptation

---

[53] Eco, *Postscript*, 2.

function would perhaps be this: if the title is indeed the procurer for the book and not for itself, what one must necessarily fear and avoid is the possibility that its seductiveness will work too much in its own favor, at the expense of its text. John Barth, whose presentational affectations do a poor job of masking his healthy common sense, wisely claims that a book more tempting than its title is better than a title more tempting than its book; well, things (in general, and these things in particular) always become known. The procurer must not overshadow its protégé, and I know of two or three books (which will remain nameless) whose too-clever titles have always deterred me from reading them and possibly ending up disappointed. To Mme Verdurin, who asked him if he couldn't unearth some penniless baron as a doorman for her, Charlus answered, roughly speaking, that too distinguished a concierge might deter her guests from going farther than the porter's lodge,[54] and we know why he himself preferred to stop at Jupien's shop. With this "Jupien effect" of the too-tempting title we are surely verging on one of the ambiguities, paradoxes, or twisted effects of the paratext in general, an effect we will meet again, for example, in connection with the preface: procurer or not, the paratext is a relay and, like every relay, it may sometimes – if the author is too heavy-handed – impede and ultimately block the text's reception. Moral: let's not polish our titles too much – or, as Cocteau neatly put it, let's not spray too much perfume on our roses.

Genre indications

As we have already briefly noted, the genre indication is an appendage of the title, more or less optional and more or less autonomous, depending on the period or the genre; and it is rhematic by definition because its purpose is to announce the genre status decided on for the work that follows the title. This status is official in the sense that it is the one the author and publisher want to attribute to the text and in the sense that no reader can justifiably be unaware of or disregard this attribution, even if he does not feel bound to agree with it. From *Le Cid*,

---

[54] *Recherche* (Pléiade), 2:967 [tr. *Remembrance of Things Past*, trans. C. K. Scott Moncrieff and Terence Kilmartin (New York: Random House, 1981), 2:1000].

"Tragédie,"[55] to *Henri Matisse, Roman*, there is no lack of examples of official genre indications that the reader cannot accept without a mental reservation – in the case of *Le Cid* because the play ends too happily, in the case of *Henri Matisse* because the text is obviously a collection of essays whose flaunted novelistic intention or pretension is but one suggestion of meaning among others, to be set off against these others without being directly or indirectly privileged. But here we will disregard this feature of the official genre status (ultimately always questionable) to deal only with the indication itself, accepted at the very least by the most refractory public as information about an intention ("I look on this work as a novel") or about a decision ("I decide to assign the status of novel to this work").

The use of autonomous indications of genre seems to go back to the classical period, when it basically affected the "major genres," especially plays, which were always carefully labeled "tragedy" or "comedy" by a notation external to the title itself, in contrast to incorporated indications of the type *The Tragedy of King Richard the Second* or *The Comedy of Errors*. Long narrative poems likewise bore the indication "a poem" (the *Adone* of Marino, the *Adonis* of La Fontaine) or some variant that was either more specific (*Le Lutrin*, "Poème heroï-comique" [Boileau]) or more subtle (*Moyse sauvé*, "Idylle héroïque" [Saint-Amant]). Collections of short poems, as we have seen, incorporated the indication into titles that were wholly generic (*Satires, Epistles, Fables*) or parageneric (*Amours*). The other genres, particularly the novel, avoided flaunting a status Aristotle had never heard of, and contrived to suggest their genre status more indirectly by way of parageneric titles in which the words *history, life, memoirs, adventures, voyages*, and some others generally played a role; French subtitles of the type *Chronique du XIXe siècle* or *Mœurs de province* clearly derive from that model. *The Waverley Novels* is a delayed designation, and the indication "A Romance" that makes *Ivanhoe* conspicuous is no doubt meant to emphasize that work's historical, and more precisely medieval, flavor. Jane Austen – who, together with Scott, initiates the use of short titles – believes as he does that it is unnecessary to pair the title with an

---

[55] This indication was adopted in 1660 in obedience to the classical norm, which does not accept the hybrid "tragi-comédie," which was the original indication for *Le Cid* as well as for *Clitandre*, which underwent the same realignment.

autonomous indication of genre. No novel by Balzac,[56] Stendhal, or Flaubert contains such an indication: their titles are either unaccompanied (*La Chartreuse de Parme, Illusions perdues, Salammbô*) or supplied with a partly generic or parageneric subtitle. The use of such subtitles tends to disappear, except as an archaizing affectation, during the second half of the century. Thus, no novel by Dumas, the Goncourts, Zola, Huysmans, Gobineau, Barbey, Dickens, Dostoevsky, Tolstoy, James, Barrès, or Anatole France includes a genre indication. The exceptions to this norm of restraint appear, rather, in the late eighteenth and early nineteenth century in Germany: *Anton Reiser*, by Moritz (1785), "A Psychological Novel"; both F. Schlegel's *Lucinde* (1799) and Goethe's *Elective Affinities* (1809), "A Novel" (but no indication for Goethe's *Wilhelm Meister*). In England, *Jane Eyre* appears in 1847 (under the asexual pseudonym of Currer Bell) with this fanciful indication: "An Autobiography." The first indication "A Novel" put forward in France might have been this one, as reluctant as could be, by Nodier: *Moi-même, Roman qui n'en est pas un* [*Myself, A Novel That Isn't One*].[57] For more than another half century, in conformity with that exemplary formula, no novel will admit to being one. This durable semi-apologetic reluctance obviously does not mean that novelists of the eighteenth and nineteenth centuries (except perhaps Balzac) did not consider their works to be novels, and this status was, moreover, often acknowledged in other elements of the paratext: in the preface (Gautier, foreword of *Le Capitaine Fracasse*: "Here is a novel, the announcement of which ..."; the Goncourts, preface to *Germinie Lacerteux*: "This novel is a true novel"; Zola, preface to *Thérèse Raquin*: "I had naively thought this novel could do without a preface"), in the epigraph (the well-known epigraph of book 1, chapter 13, of the *Rouge*: "A novel is a looking-glass ..."), in the delayed overarching title (*Waverley Novels* or, on a 1910 edition of *Manette Salomon*: "Novels by E. and J. de Goncourt"), or even – and I will come back to this element – in the list of other works by

56 Who systematically shunned the term *roman*, even in his correspondence, using instead *œuvre, ouvrage*, or, more technically, *scène*. I will return to this in connection with his prefaces.
57 ... *pour servir de suite et de complément à toutes les platitudes littéraires du XVIIIe siècle* [*to serve as a sequel to and extension of all the literary platitudes of the eighteenth century*]. But this text remained unpublished until 1921, and its first accurate edition is the one provided by D. Sangsue (Corti, 1985).

the same author (in the 1869 original edition of the Goncourts' *Madame Gervaisais*, such list is entitled "Novels by the same authors"). But undoubtedly the truth is that the classical taboo still lay heavy on this genre and that authors and publishers did not consider the indication "a novel" sufficiently glittering to warrant their bringing it to the fore.

Its delayed promotion seems to date from the twentieth century, particularly the 1920s, even if Gide's *Immoraliste* (1902) and *Porte étroite* (1909) already bore the indication *roman*, which Gide subsequently withdrew for exclusive use with *Les Faux-Monnayeurs* (1925; but as early as 1910 he specified in a draft preface to *Isabelle* that the more modest, or purer, category of *récit* [story] applied to those two works that he had previously called "novels"). *A la recherche du Temps perdu*, as we know, includes no genre indication, and this restraint is perfectly consistent with the highly ambiguous status of a work that lies halfway between the autobiographical and the novelistic.[58]

We would need a long and painstaking survey of original editions to be able to specify the evolutionary stages (no doubt varying according to country) that have brought us to the present situation and to the triumph, as we know, of the autonomous indication of genre, especially for the genre "novel," which today is rid of all its complexes and is universally said to be more of a "seller" than any other genre. Collections of novellas, for example, are apt to conceal their nature with an absence of genre indication or with the putatively more appealing, or less repellent, indication "stories" – indeed, with the more or less misleading singular "a story." As for collections of poems, they sometimes seem to proclaim their nature only because in any case it jumps out at us the minute we glance at a page of text, and a fault quickly confessed is half redressed.

We could also note quite a few inconsistencies – calculated or not – in the publishers' recording of the genre indication: changes from one edition to another, of course (an example: the indication *récit* in the original [1957] edition of Blanchot's *Dernier Homme* was subsequently deleted), but also discrepancies between cover and title page or between dust jacket and cover. These days, the genre

[58] We will meet this question of the genre status of the *Recherche* again. It is a question Proust took great pains to keep open.

indication seems to fall more often on the cover than on the title page, particularly with Gallimard, Grasset, or Minuit, but Seuil is generally more thorough and, indeed, goes against the stream; for example, for Sollers's *H*, the indication *roman* is mentioned only on the title page. Here, no doubt, allowances have to be made for the Sollersian strategy: *Paradis* has *roman* only on its jacket, as if this alluring indication were supposed to disappear after fulfilling its function: "You said novel. – I? I said novel?" I am assured that when the author was asked about this fundamental point during a Friday evening televised literary program, he answered that this way of being a novel without being one was a powerful means of subverting the genre and thus, to say the least, of subverting society. I do not vouch for the literal accuracy of this reported remark, but the record will settle the question, and the exact content, whatever it is, appears henceforth in the paratext.

Another typical feature of our period is innovation, not so much as regards genre (for that, one must be named Dante, Cervantes, or perhaps Proust) but rather as regards genre designations. Some of these innovations are masked by those parageneric titles evoked above – *Méditations, Divagations, Moralités légendaires* [Lamartine, Mallarmé, Laforgue], and so forth. In a more self-contained form, we are familiar with Lamartine's *Jocelyn*, "épisode" (the foreword insists, without other justification, "This is not a poem, it is an episode," and then specifies, "a fragment of a private epic"), and with Gide's "récit" [story] or "sotie" [satirical farce]. Giono is anxious to distinguish his novels from his "chronicles." Perec calls *La Vie mode d'emploi* "romans," in the plural; Laporte calls the set *Fugue*, etc., "biographie"; Nancy Huston, *Les Variations Goldberg*, "romance"; Ricardou, *Le Théâtre des métamorphoses*, "mixte" [a mixture] (of fiction and theory, I suppose). An author such as Jean Roudaut is apparently committed to innovating with each title: "parenthèse," "paysage d'accompagnement" [companion landscape], "passage," "proposition," "relais critique" [critical relay] (but the text *Ce qui nous revient*, called "relais critique" on the cover, is called "autobiographie" on the title page). And so forth. It's been suggested that I go back as far as *Vanity Fair*, "A Novel Without a Hero," or *Rebecca and Rowena* (Thackeray's ironic sequel to *Ivanhoe*), legitimately called "A Romance upon a Romance." Perhaps in both cases Thackeray had in mind a real innovation in genre, such as (let us keep going back) romantic drama, bourgeois drama, the *genre sérieux*,[59] or tearful comedy. It is true that none of these designations is entirely official. But the one for Corneille's *Don Sanche d'Aragon*, *Pulchérie*, and *Tite et Bérénice* is: "comédie héroïque." Again (already) a "mixture," as is the "idylle héroïque" of Saint-Amant. To innovate is often to unite two old things. A recent movie, John Huston's *Prizzi's Honor*, is designated a "bloody comedy" – and it keeps that double promise.

The normal location for the genre indication, as we have seen, is the cover or title page, or both. But this indication can be repeated in other places, the most captivating of which (for those who are easily captivated) is the list of works "By the same author," generally placed at the beginning of the volume (facing the title page) or at the end, where the list takes the form of a classification by genre. By definition, this reminder (if there is one) should appear only in books other than the one(s) to which it refers, but occasionally from carelessness this logic is contravened: for example, the list in the Folio edition of Aragon's *Beaux Quartiers* mentions *Les Beaux Quartiers* itself.

The ancestor of this heading we can take to be the first four lines – according to Donat and Servius – of the manuscript of the *Aeneid*, lines that Varius allegedly suppressed when "editing" the poem:

> Ille ego qui quondam gracili modulatus avena
> Carmen et egressus silvis vicina coegi
> Ut quamvis avido parerent arva colono,
> Gratum opus agricolis, at nunc horrentia Martis
> Arma virumque cano ...

("I am he who once tuned my song on a slender reed [*Bucolics*], then, leaving the woodland, constrained the neighbouring fields to serve the husbandmen, however grasping – a work welcome to farmers [*Georgics*] – but now of Mars' bristling ...").[60]

59 [The *genre sérieux* "is situated midway between the traditional, amusing comedy, which takes the ridiculous and vice as its objects, and tragedy, which depicts public catastrophes and the misfortunes of the great" (Peter Szondi, *On Textual Understanding and Other Essays*, trans. Harvey Mendelsohn [University of Minnesota Press, 1986], 124).]

60 [Loeb Classical Library.] This incipit is generally looked on as apocryphal or as having been ultimately repudiated by Virgil, but not so the ending of the *Georgics*, where the author not only states his name, as I have said, but also recalls and cites his previous work, the *Bucolics*:

Perhaps Chrétien de Troyes was imitating that incipit, apocryphal or not, when he offered this list at the head of *Cligès* – a list that makes us feel especially wistful because most of the titles, or rather their texts, have disappeared: "He who wrote *Erec and Enide*, who translated Ovid's *Commandments* and the *Art of Love* into French, who wrote *The Shoulder Bite*, and about King Mark and Isolde the Blonde, and of the metamorphosis of the hoopoe, swallow, and nightingale, begins now a new tale."

Of course, classifying by genre is not the main function of "By the same author" lists, which classify that way only in exceptional cases. The list's main function is to announce to the reader the titles of the author's other books (possibly inciting him to read them) – or sometimes only the titles of the author's other books that are published by the same house. The list is therefore a sort of personal catalogue of the author's; it may include an announcement of books "to be published," "in press," or "in preparation" (subtle differences it is always better not to take literally); it may include the more melancholy reminder of books that are "out of print" (which sometimes means pulped); and it may omit works the author no longer wishes to mention, definitively or provisionally. For example, it is amusing to follow the comings and goings of *Une curieuse solitude* in the Sollers canon.[61]

Classification by genre is used by Gallimard for the major authors in its contemporary stable, such as Gide, Cocteau, Aragon, Drieu, Giono, Sartre, Camus, Leiris, and Queneau. I have no information about the role those authors themselves played in preparing the classifications, but no list for the authors I have just mentioned seems to me neutral enough to have been decided on without some authorial or para-authorial advice, at least mut-

Illo Vergilium me tempore dulcis alebat
Parthenope studiis florentem ignobilis oti,
Carmina qui lusi pastorum audaxque juventa,
Tityre, te patulae cecini sub tegmine fagi.

("In those days [when I was writing that poem] I, Virgil, was nursed of sweet Parthenope, and rejoiced in the arts of inglorious ease – I who dallied with shepherds' songs, and, in youth's boldness, sang, Tityrus, of thee under thy spreading beech's covert" [Loeb]).

61 In 1974 Sollers announced he was eliminating this little book from his bibliographies; in 1983 he reintroduced it in the "By the same author" list of *Femmes*. The term *canon* means, among other things, "official list of the works of an author or a group." A work disowned by its author, such as Borges's *Inquisiciones*, departs from the canon – without, it seems to me, thereby leaving its author's bibliography.

tered. For example, Gide's list, unveiled in 1914 for *Les Caves du Vatican*, includes a typically Gide-like distinction between "satirical farces," "stories," and "novel." Cocteau's list is governed almost entirely by the wish to assign his whole œuvre to a poetic universe: "poésie," "poésie de roman," "poésie critique," "poésie de théâtre," and so forth. Aragon's list, which fluctuates greatly, is generally classified under "poems" (from *Feu de joie* to *Les Chambres*), "novels" (the *Monde réel* set), and "prose" (all the rest) – a three-fold classification that, among other things, ends up excluding from the category "novels" such titles as *Anicet ou Le panorama, Roman*, and *Henri Matisse, Roman*, or such works as *La Semaine sainte* and *Blanche ou L'oubli*, although individually each of these is designated "a novel": is there a subtle distinction between the term used to describe a single work and the term used to describe the genre to which the single work belongs? But other versions of Aragon's list do record all these excluded works as novels, and the list printed in 1961 for *La Semaine sainte* includes even this text in the *Monde réel* set. Giono, as we know, distinguishes "novels," "stories," "novellas," and "chronicles," but the "By the same author" list in *L'Iris de Suse* combines these four genres in a single sublist, at whose head, however, are the names of all four – a sign, at least, of uncertainty and confusion; the other genres invoked in separate sublists under this "By the same author" are "essays," "history," "travel," "theatre," "translations." Sartre's works are classified under the headings "novels," "novellas," "theatre," "philosophy," "political essays," and "literature," this last very significantly grouping the critical essays with *Les Mots* [memoirs of Sartre's childhood]. Leiris's list puts *L'Age d'homme* and *La Règle du jeu* [books of self-ethnography] under "essays." For both Sartre and Leiris, we see that autobiography, when the author prefers not to identify it openly as such, creates some confusion about genre. And in Gide's case, *Si le grain ne meurt* [*If It Die*, Gide's first autobiography] appears, along with the *Journal*, in the category "miscellaneous." Queneau elegantly dodges that catchall by refraining from naming it, whence this tripartition: "poems," "novels," "*"*. Here the asterisk becomes a genre, and not the least important one.

The genre indication may also (finally?) be reinforced or replaced by a means available only to the publisher: publication of the work in a series dedicated to a specific genre, such as, for example, Gallimard's Série noire, Essais, and Bibliothèque des idées, or Seuil's Pierres vives, Poétique, Travaux linguistiques, and so forth (although in each series, generic categories generally coexist with disciplinary categories). Fiction & Cie [Fiction and Company] advertises its open-mindedness with a debonair elegance, as the exquisite series Métamorphoses (set up a while ago within Gallimard by Jean Paulhan) has done, with greater restraint. All these indications, then, are to be kept somewhat at arm's length, as are those of the specialized "pocket" series (Idées, Poésie, Points Roman) and the various sets of subclassifications used for almost half a century by the major pocket series in every country. This brings us back to the implicit and thus very unofficial genre indication that choice of format has provided since the classical period. The genre indications provided by delayed composites of the type "*Waverley Novels* by Walter Scott," "Novels and Tales of Henry James," and so forth, whether the author's doing or a posthumous editor's, are definitely more official – more official but, strictly speaking, sometimes very vague, as with the Pléiade designation "novelistic works," which inevitably ends up embracing every sort of prose that is more or less fictional. Malraux's volume *Romans* [*Novels*], a grouping that was no doubt authorial, or at least anthumous (1969), originally consisted of *Les Conquérants*, *La Condition humaine*, and *L'Espoir* (of those three, at least the second contained no genre indication in its first edition) but did not include either *Le Temps du mépris* or *Les Noyers de l'Altenburg*. Since that time, *La Voie royale* has joined the "Romans": thus, a text does not come into the world as a novel, it becomes one later.

Aragon and Elsa Triolet's *Œuvres romanesques croisées* [*Intersecting Novelistic Works*] no doubt establishes the most official (authorial) list of Aragon's novels and novellas. This list is broader than those usually found under the heading "novels" in "By the same author" lists, but for all that it is not wholly predictable, as it includes *Le Libertinage* but not *Les Aventures de Télémaque* or *Le Paysan de Paris*; *Théâtre/Roman* but not *Henri Matisse, Roman*. All these varying genre indications must definitely, as we say, be "taken into account" by the attentive reader, who no doubt can make neither head nor tail of them. And must also be taken into account by future editors of a possible *Œuvres complètes* – unless these editors prudently resign themselves to chronological order, without making genre distinctions. For I challenge the most determined genologist, if any still exists, to frequent for long this genre of the list, or these lists of genres, without finding that not only can he make neither head nor tail of them but that in fact he is utterly and completely in danger of being driven out of his mind.

Having thus touched on the genre indication, an appendage of the title, and on its own appendages or surrogates, we have not, even so, finished with titles: I have spoken here only of general titles, those at the head of a book or group of books. But titles also appear within books: titles of parts, chapters, sections, and so forth. These are internal titles, or, as we will call them (taking a short cut), *intertitles*. We will meet them again in their proper place – that is, in a later chapter.

5

❖❖❖

The please-insert

❖❖❖

The four stages

The please-insert [*le prière d'insérer*][1] is definitely, at least in France, one of the most typical elements of the modern paratext. It is also one of the most difficult to consider in historical detail, for in some stages of its evolution it takes a particularly fragile form; thus, to my knowledge, no public collection has been able to accumulate these PIs for purposes of research. The classic definition of the please-insert – the one given, for example, in the *Petit Robert* dictionary – is narrow and describes only one of its stages, the one that was typical in the first half of the twentieth century: "A printed insert that contains information about a work and is attached to the copies addressed to critics." Current usage extends the meaning of the word to cover forms that no longer fit that definition inasmuch as they no longer consist of an "insert" and are no longer addressed only to "critics." I will extend the meaning still further by applying the term to other forms, older ones, which perhaps did *not yet* consist of the insert. But what remains constant in all these various stages, it seems to me, is the definition's functional part (rather vague, to be sure): "printed ... contains information about a work." In other words (in my words), the please-insert is a short text (generally between a half page and a full page) describing, by means of a summary or in some other way, and most often in a value-enhancing manner,

---

[1] I will use this term in the masculine, which is suitable for an elliptical locution that has the value of a verb ("One is requested to insert"). As a publisher whose name I have forgotten once said, "This is not a request" (implying, no doubt, that it is, instead, an order). But the masculine is not certain, and many writers use the term in the feminine. Another uncertainty has to do with the meaning of the verb *insert*: it is sometimes – wrongly – related to the fact of inserting a loose sheet into a volume; actually, it has to do with inserting the text of the please-insert into the newspapers, and I will come back to this matter. I will sometimes shorten "please-insert" to PI.

the work to which it refers – and to which, for a good half-century, it has been joined in one way or another.

We may think it surprising that, according to the *Robert* definition, the copies of a work intended for the press should have to be accompanied by "information" that critics would certainly have no need of if they simply read the work, unless the information in question were supplementary, dealing (for example) with the circumstances of the work's composition; but we already know that that is generally not the case. The definition, therefore, seems to assume either that the please-insert could, on the contrary, spare critics the need to read the work before talking about it – an assumption unkind to critics – or that the work would be of such a nature that simply reading it would not suffice to disclose what it consists of – an assumption unkind to the work, save for a *fin-de-siècle* premium on obscurity. One will perhaps dodge this aporia by making another and more generous assumption: that the please-insert serves to "inform" critics, before they undertake a reading that may prove unprofitable, about the *sort* of work they are dealing with and therefore about the sort of critic toward whom it would be appropriate to direct the book for a reading – that the please-insert is, in short, for editors-in-chief.

In this case, what still needs explaining is the strange name: please-*insert*. "Please-review" would seem more appropriate, although it's a bit self-evident that the mere fact of addressing a work to critics is enough to constitute such a request. The explanation is undoubtedly that for the purpose described by the *Robert*, the name is already a little out-of-date and lagging behind its object, or, if you prefer, that the definition is a little anachronistic (in advance) in relation to the term it defines. *Please-insert* refers, it seems to me, to an earlier practice, one quite characteristic of the nineteenth century, when this type of text was addressed not exactly to "critics," and not in the form of an "insert," but to the press in general (newspaper editors), in the form of a press release meant to announce a work's publication. The forerunner of this please-insert, therefore, would be the *prospectus*, some traces of which remain in the history of publishing (for example, for Chateaubriand's *Essai sur les révolutions* and *Atala*, or for *La Comédie humaine*).[2] And at that time *please-*

---

[2] The *prospectus* was a note to the reader which was printed in newspapers before a work was published. The three prospectuses mentioned here are

insert was a completely clear and literal expression, indicating to newspaper editors that the book's publisher was asking them to insert this little text, in whole or in part, into their columns to inform the public of the work's appearance. I do not know whether at that time the practice was free of charge (probably not), but it certainly could have been because it amounted to the swapping of services: the newspaper received an already written piece of news, and the publisher received an "advertisement" that, by definition, met his wishes.

The Zola paratext gives us an invaluable illustration of this first stage of the PI. In Henri Mitterand's Pléiade edition of *Les Rougon-Macquart*, he cites, for example, a sentence that appeared in *Le Bien public* of October 11, 1877, announcing the serial publication of *Une Page d'amour* – "It is an intimate episode that will appeal especially to the sensibility of female readers, in a tone that contrasts with that of *L'Assommoir*. You won't have to be afraid to leave this novel on the family table" – and Zola's comment, to Flaubert, about that reassuring notice: "Don't those chaps have a style! But the ad seemed good, the minute they said my novel could be left on the family table." That ad, plus others in the same vein for Zola's *Pot-Bouille* (in *Le Gaulois* of January 5, 1882), *Au bonheur des dames* (in *Gil Blas*, November 23, 1882), and *L'Argent* (*Gil Blas*, November 16, 1890), all announce serialization in the newspaper itself, which somewhat reduces the circuit described above, but not the ultimate intended purpose of these texts. And though we see this author, perhaps as a function of the presumed view of his correspondent, wax ironic about the announcement of *Une Page d'amour*, the announcement of *L'Argent*, in Mitterand's view, is "without doubt by Zola" himself; if Mitterand is right, it would show that the PI written by the author is not a twentieth-century innovation. But note that I say *written by*, not *openly acknowledged by*, the author: the announcement of *L'Argent* is in the third person, and its putative sender is obviously the editorial staff of *Gil Blas*, conditions that no doubt explain why the historian can point to no material proof of a *de facto* authorship but (as a Zola specialist) can infer this authorship from his reading of the text – which is as follows:

generally published as appendixes in modern scholarly editions of their respective works.

Emile Zola's new novel, *L'Argent*, is a very dramatic and vivid study of the world of the Paris stock exchange, in which, exercising the historian's right, he has painted full-length portraits of several of the very odd personalities known all over Paris. The author has told the story of one of our major financial catastrophes, the story of one of those joint-stock companies that are started up, that conquer the kingdom of gold within a few years, thanks to a fit of madness on the part of the public, and that then collapse, crushing a whole crowd of shareholders in mud and blood.

For Emile Zola, money is a blind force capable of good and evil, the very force that contributes to civilization, in the midst of the ruins that humanity is always leaving behind itself. And he has conveyed his idea in a gripping way, with the help of a great central drama, accompanied and completed by a whole series of individual dramas. This is one of the author's major works.

But I am not forgetting that that is still an announcement of serial publication. In contrast, apropos of *L'Œuvre*, Mitterand draws attention to an announcement of book publication which appeared in several newspapers in April 1886 and which he likewise attributes to the author:

L'Œuvre, the novel by Emile Zola that is being published today by the Bibliothèque Charpentier, is a simple, poignant story, the drama of a bright mind battling against nature, the long struggle within an innovative painter (one who brings in a new style) between his passion for a woman and his passion for his art.

The author has set this drama in the milieu of his youth, he has presented us with his own story; he has told of fifteen years in his life and the lives of his contemporaries. These are the kinds of memoirs that go from the Salon des Refusés of 1863 to the exhibitions of these most recent years, a picture of modern art, drawn in the very midst of Paris, with all the episodes that that entails. The work of an artist, but the work of a novelist, and it will enthrall you.

As we can see, the characteristic features of these notices, whether they constitute a direct announcement of serialization by the newspaper or a press release inserted in the papers at the "request" of the publisher, are absolutely identical and, thanks to the professionalism with which Zola composed even the least of his pages, here these features jump right out at us. First comes a descriptive paragraph as factual as possible, then a paragraph of commentary on theme and technique, and in the closing words a laudatory assessment – a really good piece of work and, for "critics" (I would imagine), a challenge rather than an incentive. But those texts, as we are aware, were not (yet) addressed to the critics. They were addressed, via the papers, directly to the public, a little like today's "just published" notices that the literary journals do or do not publish and that are most often inspired by, and condensed from, our current PIs, that is, our jacket copy. But let's not skip the intermediary stage, the one that, in point of fact, the *Robert* definition describes.

To this second stage, I have – going by the look of things – assigned a historical spot: the first half of the twentieth century, especially the period between the two world wars. The state of my knowledge does not allow me to set a *terminus a quo*, which might be a little earlier; the *terminus ad quem* is in the hands of fate, and some publishers, like Minuit, still commonly use the inserted sheet, but this practice already deviates from the *Robert* definition, for these inserts are no longer reserved for the press's copies but are made available to all buyers. That, it seems to me, is a phenomenon of remanence, a lagging of form behind function,[3] for the characteristic function of this second stage of the PI, which justified its being printed as an insert, was indeed aimed at "critics." These inserts were therefore printed in limited numbers; they were no longer meant for publication (a fundamental difference); and their addressees, after using them however they saw fit, really had no reasons to hold on to them – hence our difficulty in finding them. Here, as in other areas, private collectors could help scholarship, for surely collections of these inserts exist.

Curiously enough, even though the change in intended purpose brought about a change in presentation (the insert), it does not seem to have brought about any noticeable change in the composition of the PI. I will not bore the reader with characteristic examples from the period before World War II, for

---

[3] But the precariousness of the insert, like the precariousness of the band, may have its function, even with respect to the reader: Robbe-Grillet emphasizes that the PI of *Projet pour une révolution* was printed "on a piece of paper to be thrown out," and gets half annoyed at the fact that some people thought they had to stick it into the book. That PI was the reprint of an article that had previously appeared in *Le Nouvel Observateur*, "apropos of something else, anyway," and the author believes "there is, perhaps, no reason to talk about it so much" (*Colloque Robbe-Grillet* 1:85).

it would take fifty to illustrate the point properly. I prefer to borrow from Raymond Queneau a version that is somewhat synthesized, albeit perhaps slightly exacerbated by the "parodic" purpose of his *Exercises de style*:

> In his new novel, handled with the brio that is all his own, the well-known novelist X, who has already given us so many masterpieces, has taken pains to set on stage only well-drawn characters living in a milieu easily understood by everyone, both adults and children. The plot turns on the encounter, in a bus, between the hero of this story and a fairly enigmatic person who quarrels with all and sundry. In the final episode, we see this mysterious person listening with the greatest attention to the advice of a friend of his, a consummate dandy. The whole creates a charming impression that novelist X has chiseled from his material with rare felicity.

In that intermediary period, the PI's function of providing inspiration was undoubtedly not very clear or (therefore) very easy to fulfill. The author would have done just as well to write the newspaper article himself, as Stendhal did in the case of the *Rouge* for the Italian journalist Salvagnoli, who as a result did not publish it. But writing the article oneself would also have been a little absurd, for an author would then risk having a number of strangely similar reviews appear under several signatures. So during this period the writers of PIs continued to write for "critics" in the same terms (except for stylistic evolution) they had used earlier for "the public." As a result (I continue to be free with my assumptions, where not much is known: a working hypothesis) the habit caught on, no doubt little by little, of going back to the initial addressee (the public) by this new route that only had to be broadened by the insertion of a PI in *all* copies: the third stage. This, it seems, was the common practice immediately after World War II and in the 1950s; and – as I have said – it is still continued today by some publishers. But economics inevitably brought this practice to an end: it is unnecessarily expensive to insert by hand texts that could, more cheaply and effectively, be imprinted someplace else, most often on the back cover. This is the current stage, the one most common in France and, it seems to me, throughout the world.

This displacement of one stage by another, which I have roughly described, was no doubt more complex or more chaotic than my summary suggests: today there are not only PIs that are still inserted, but there are also books without any PI, books in which an inserted PI echoes the PI on the back cover, and even books with two distinct PIs, one inserted and the other printed on the cover (this is often the case with books published by Minuit – for example, Jean-François Lyotard's *Différend*, 1983). But amidst all this diversity and flux, we have at least one firm date: Gallimard is said to have abolished the inserted PI in 1969.

This transfer from the extratextual epitext (a press release for the papers) to the precarious peritext (an insert for critics, then for anyone and everyone) and finally to the durable peritext (the cover) is definitely, in and of itself, a promotion that entails, or manifests, some other promotions. With respect to the addressee, we have passed from "the public," in the broadest and most commercial sense, to "critics," regarded as intermediaries between author and public, then to a more indistinct entity partaking of both the public and the reader. For the modern PI, placed closest to the text, on the cover or jacket of the book, is hardly accessible except to that already limited fringe of the public that frequents bookstores and consults covers: if the person who reads the PI makes do with that information, apparently deterred from going beyond it, the addressee remains "the public"; if reading the PI induces the person to buy the book or get hold of it in some other way, the addressee becomes a potential reader; and once he becomes an actual reader, he will perhaps finally put the PI to a more sustained use, one more relevant to his understanding of the text – a use the writer of the PI may anticipate and prepare for.

The sender, too, may well have changed. In Zola's time, as we have seen, the author could in actual fact write some of his own PIs, but it was not customary for him to assume that responsibility. During an initial period (when the target was "the papers"), the putative sender of the PI was the publisher; during a second period (target: the public), the putative sender was the paper itself. The PI's promotion to the peritext gradually modified these particulars, and some inserted PIs were already obviously taken on by the author and even signed with his initials. Thus we have signed PIs for Supervielle's *Gravitations* (1925), Michaux's *Ecuador* (1929) and *Un Barbare en Asie* (1933), and Drieu's *Gilles* (1939).[4] The practice expands when the PI moves to the cover, but here we have no statistics, and sometimes no certainty, for an anonymous PI-writer will naturally more or less imitate the author's manner. The authorial act of writing an unsigned PI is, moreover, a subtle and fairly oblique gesture, marked by stylistic features that are *sui generis*: a tone apt to be godlike, which is very prevalent in the 1960s (I will speak a little more about this below) and looks down on the text from on high, majestically yet with restraint, a tone the reader can logically, or very probably, attribute only to the author but which the author can always, if necessary, disavow. The signed PI, by the mere fact of the signature, is doubtless bound to take a more straightforward approach to the text: here the main formal distinction is use of the first person, but even so, there are mixed or intermediary states. These include signed PIs in the third person (*Gilles, Un barbare en Asie*) and nonsigned PIs in the first person (?).

Rarer, but likewise symptomatic of a literary promotion of this element of the paratext, is the case of the *allographic* PI, I mean a PI that is officially allographic and signed by its author.[5] For example, Mathieu Bénézet's *Dits et récits du mortel* (Flammarion, 1977) contains, on the one hand, a PI on the cover which is anonymous but has a distinctly authorial look and, on the other hand, an inserted PI four pages long, explicitly entitled "Please-Insert" and signed Jacques Derrida. This practice resembles that of the blurb, already mentioned. But in the United States the blurb is entirely ritualistic and, as it were, automatic, which deprives it of much of its power. The allographic PI is much rarer and therefore more meaningful. It is a gesture comparable to that of the allographic preface, which we will encounter again, and perhaps more persuasive as an endorsement because the preface, too, is fairly ritualistic. To write and sign the PI for someone else's book signifies, besides: "See, on his behalf I'm even doing a task

---

4   See P. Enckell, "Des textes inconnus d'auteurs célèbres," *Les Nouvelles littéraires* (April 14, 1983). The author of this valuable little collection cites other PIs, not signed but apparently authorial, by Cocteau, Bousquet, Paulhan, Jouhandeau, Queneau, Robin, Larbaud, and Nabokov. And we learn from Julien Green's journal (May 18, 1926) that he himself wrote (at least) the PI of *Mont-Cinère*: "If I don't do it, someone else will instead, and will do an even worse job of it."

5   I also mean: for an original edition. Allographic PIs for translations or reprintings, especially posthumous ones, are a different matter, and we will meet them again below.

that's usually menial, which tells you how highly I value his work."

The golden (or vermeil) age of the PI printed on the cover (or, as we sometimes say, on the flap) was doubtless, in the intellectual–avant-garde milieu (around the New Novel, *Tel quel, Change, Digraphe,* and other Parisian precincts), the 1960s and 1970s. Future historians will no doubt get much pleasure determining how much in all this precious hodgepodge had to do with profundity and how much with sham, megalomania, deliberate or unwitting caricature; but it's still too early to speculate on that. Some of the culprits are still making the rounds, and not far from here.

We even see PIs with their own titles. The title for the PI of Jean-Claude Hémery's *Anamorphoses* (Denoël, 1970) is, further-more, well chosen: "A foreword free of charge" – in contrast to the titles of prefaces, for which it is often too late: the book has already been bought. We also see PIs with their own epigraphs, like that for Derrida's *De la grammatologie* (Rousseau) or the one for Laporte's *Quinze variations sur un thème biographique* (a Chinese proverb). This says a lot about the importance acquired by this practice, once considered secondary, and about the investment that has suddenly been made in it. We see PIs made responsible for explaining and justifying the title (those of Robbe-Grillet's *Dans le labyrinthe*[6] and Pinget's *Passacaille,* for example) or, like the PI of Robbe-Grillet's *Jalousie,* for providing the author's thematic and narrative key to the text: "The teller of this tale – a husband who spies on his wife ... Jealousy is a passion for which nothing ever vanishes: everything jealousy sees, even the most innocent thing, remains imprinted on it once and for all." Or even, like the PI of Doubrovsky's *Fils,* for indicating the book's genre: "Autobiography? No, for that's a prerogative of the important people of this world, in the evening of their lives, and written with class. Fiction of events and of strictly real facts, or if you wish, autofiction ..." (Galilée, 1977). Possibly the most delectable PI, in its ironic treatment of the topos of amplification (see p. 199), is that of Claude Simon's *Leçon de choses* (1975): "Sensitive to the reproaches directed at

---

[6] This PI is signed "the editors," a rare form of signature that is both very conspicuous and very ambiguous; at Minuit, only if used facetiously could this plural include the author himself.

writers who disregard 'big problems,' the author has tried here to tackle some of them, such as housing, manual labor, food, time, space, nature, leisure, speech, education, news, adultery, and the destruction and reproduction of the human and animal species."

Perhaps I am wrong to use the past tense to designate procedures that could indeed, and very legitimately, outlive their flamboyant and high-voltage opening phase. On the whole, the back cover is a highly appropriate – and strategically highly effective – place for a sort of brief preface, one that, as Hémery suggests, can be read without much trouble by someone who hangs around bookstalls and finds such brevity quite sufficient. Some PIs themselves, moreover, insist on their status as quasi preface, as the PIs of Aymé or Drieu were doing even in the period of the inserts. "At this moment when I am writing my please-insert," said Aymé, "I now regret not having written a preface to *Le Bœuf clandestin*..." Then comes an abridgment of that missing preface, which will be missing no more. And the PI of *Gilles* is presented at one and the same time as a preterition of the PI and a preterition of the preface. I can but reproduce it here, adding only, for piquancy, that the book's second edition, in 1942, did contain a preface (in response to the critics):

A please-insert is hard for a novelist to write if he knows the critics will read it as a preface. Indeed, a novel does not allow a preface. It can only be sufficient unto itself.

What would the novelist talk about in his preface? About his intentions. But he had a hundred or he had none.

A novel is a story; and that's all. The very title must not mean anything. It must not point in one direction, when the work is written in all directions.

It's not the author's job to dismember his book; that's the critics' job.

For the critics, it's perhaps a duty, no doubt the highest duty, to reduce to ideas certain images, the arabesque of the narrative, the sudden stillness of a character, or the mood pervading the whole. But for the artist, painting passions and moods will never be the same thing as expressing an opinion or a judgment, will never be the same thing as forming a system.

That said, the simplest way of writing a please-insert would be to summarize that story which is all that matters.

But then, what false modesty on the author's part. Perhaps he fears no one will read him? Or what unkindness toward critics.

Tangents and appendages

Everything in this chapter so far bears on the *original* please-insert, which means, of course, the one appended to the work's original publication, not to mention, as in Zola's case, to the work's serialization before publication. But like many other elements of the paratext, the PI, even when printed on the cover, has a very transitory mission and can disappear when the book is reprinted, when the series changes, when a pocket book comes out. On each of these occasions, the PI may also be replaced by a new "flap"; or the PI may appear only on one of those occasions. The first edition of Des Forêts's *Bavard* (Gallimard, 1946) had no PI; the reprint in the 10/18 series (1963) has one, which is anonymous; and the reprint in the Imaginaire series (1983) has another, which is signed Pascal Quignard.

The reprinting of classical works in pocket series is similarly accompanied by much paratextual activity, including the production of PIs that are as diverse in their guiding principle as the series themselves – in their guiding principle and in their placement, for some series, like the Livre de poche, generally prefer not to touch the illustrations on the back cover and to transfer their PIs to the flyleaf, and other series use both of these locations for the paratext, each with a slightly different function. Sometimes, as is self-evident for these posthumous reprints, there is an allographic text, signed (Imaginaire, GF) or unsigned; sometimes (often, with Folio) there is a revealing excerpt – indeed, for *Moll Flanders* (a felicitous move), the original title in its entirety, a perfect PI before the term existed;[7] sometimes a laudatory quotation taken from a critic, a blurb after the event; and sometimes ... But it would not be very useful to draw up an inventory of practices that are highly changeable (for at any moment a series can revise its policy), an inventory that would be meaningless except on a worldwide scale.

The please-insert is not to be confused with the possible bio-

---

[7] Reciprocally, in 1936 Queneau wrote the PI for *Les Derniers Jours* in the form of a series of titles in the earlier style: "How two old Men met each other at the Corner of Dante Street and died two hundred fifty Pages later; How Vincent Tuquedenne went from being an atheistic Thomist to being a Hypochondriac and then a Billionnaire"; and so forth.

graphical and/or bibliographical summary (although the summary and PI may be placed side by side on an insert or a cover), for the summary, in contrast to the PI, does not bear specifically on the text it accompanies but aims, rather, to place that text in the larger context of a life and an œuvre. A study of the paratext is certainly not the most opportune place to address the biographical or bibliographical summary, but it should be addressed, by other hands than mine, without delay.

Also not to be confused with the please-insert of the work itself are some elements that must instead be considered the program or manifesto of the series in which the work appears and that are in fact found, at least during a certain period, on the covers of all the works published in that series. This is the practice today for, among others, the Ecriture series at the Presses universitaires de France and the Philosophie series at Galilée. The Métamorphoses series, established by Paulhan in 1936, had its PI but did not put it on the books in the series.[8] There are also manifestos of journals, carried for years on the journals' covers. It is only recently that *Communications* dropped its manifesto, which no longer corresponded much to its practice.

Lastly, one should not assume that the PI, or rather, any given PI, frequents only a single place, insert or cover. I have already mentioned the possibility that these two locations can double for each other. But in addition, the periodic catalogues of some major publishing houses are given to reproducing all or part of the PIs of the works published during the relevant interval. In that regard, therefore, a collection of these catalogues could be invaluable to paratextologists of all stripes and opinions. And the PIs of an author (whether or not he assumed official responsibility for them) can be collected, courtesy of the author, in a later work (see Char, *Recherche de la base et du sommet*, or Jabès, *Le Livre des ressemblances* – the latter contains the seven PIs of *Le Livre des questions*); or courtesy of a critic, in a work he devotes to the author (see the special issue of the journal *Exercises de la patience* devoted to Blanchot, or Pol Vandromme's study of Marcel Aymé [Gallimard, 1970]); or courtesy of those responsible for critical editions, such as the Pléiade editions of Zola, Giono, or Sartre. I have no need to say here how fortunate I think we are to have

---

[8] See P. Enckell, "Des textes inconnus d'auteurs célèbres."

these republications, when they are faithful.[9] The please-insert is a highly fragile and precarious paratextual element, an endangered masterpiece, a baby seal of publishing, for which no amount of solicitude will be superfluous. This is indeed an appeal to the public.

At the moment, as Marcel Aymé said,[10] I see nothing else to ask you to please insert.

[9] Unfortunately, Vandromme's is not. He admits to forging the PIs he could not locate and then mixing them indiscriminately with the genuine ones. In his collection, therefore, the only ones that can now be trusted are those Aymé officially signed.

[10] In the signed PI for *Les Contes du chat perché*.

6

Dedications and inscriptions

The French noun *dédicace* designates two practices that, while obviously related, have important differences. Both practices consist of offering the work as a token of esteem to a person, a real or ideal group, or some other type of entity. But one of these practices involves the material reality of a single copy and, in principle, ratifies the gift or consummated sale of that copy, whereas the other involves the ideal reality of the work itself, the possession of which (and therefore its transfer, gratis or not) can quite obviously be only symbolic. Some other features, which we will encounter below, also distinguish the two practices from each other. But although the French nouns, unfortunately, are identical, very happily the verbs distinguish these two actions: *dédier* [to dedicate] for the action that involves the work, *dédicacer* [to inscribe] for the action that involves the copy. I will begin with dedications, after excluding from the definition those works that are entirely *addressed* to a specific addressee – works such as epistles, certain odes, certain hymns, elegies, and other poems of amorous lyricism, as well as Wordsworth's *Prelude* (addressed to Coleridge), all of which are genres in which the text and its dedication are inescapably consubstantial. I know of no example of a work addressed to one person and dedicated to another, but perhaps I haven't searched patiently enough. In the realm of works of passion, in any case, that situation could prove quite interesting.

The dedication of the work

The origins of the dedication of the work go back at least to ancient Rome. We know, for example, that *De rerum natura* was dedicated to Memmius Gemellus, *Ars poetica* (which in fact is an epistle) to the Pisones, and the *Georgics* to Maecenas. Already in place was the classical regime of the dedication as tribute to a protector and/or benefactor (acquired or hoped for, whom one tries to acquire with the tribute itself) – and Maecenas's name, as it happens, came to be attached to this function.[1] In a more private way, Cicero dedicated the *Academica* to Varro, *De officiis* to his son, *De oratore* to his brother.

But I said we know: in that historical period, the recording of the dedication was not codified as it would be later. Thus, the existence of the dedication is more factual than textual, unless the name of the dedicatee is mentioned in the text itself and, more precisely, in its preambles – in many respects the forebears of our peritext. (That is where we have already encountered some names of authors and some titles [Chapters 3 and 4], and it is where we will encounter some kinds of prefaces [Chapter 8].) Gemellus's name appears in line 42 of *De rerum natura*, and many opening passages of medieval romances or chronicles (as we will see when considering the prehistory of the preface) testify to a princely commission, the mention of which is equivalent to a dedication of the work. In the sixteenth century as well, it is in the early stanzas (after the overview of the subject) that we find the dedication of *Orlando Furioso* to Ippolito d'Este (supposedly descended from the poem's hero, Ruggiero) and of *Jerusalem Delivered* to Alfonso d'Este, worthy "equal of Godfrey."

In the classical period, dedicating the work to a rich and powerful protector remains customary, from Ronsard's *Franciade* (1572), dedicated to Charles IX, to Austen's *Emma* (1816), dedicated to the prince regent. Compared with Roman and medieval practice, the classical innovation consists – once again – of officially and formally recording the dedication in the peritext, ratifying the modern (and current) sense of the term: the dedication becomes an autonomous statement, either in the short form of a simple mention of the dedicatee or in the more expanded form of a discourse addressed to him and generally called *dedicatory epistle* – or in both forms together, with the simple mention appearing on the title page. The dedicatory epistle is, as a matter of fact, *de rigueur* until the end of the eighteenth century, for reasons we will encounter below; and the proof of this is that

---

[1] [The French word for "patronage" is *mécénat*, and the word for "patron" is *mécène*.]

the two terms *dedication* and *dedicatory epistle* are at that time wholly synonymous.

In periods when literature was not really looked on as a profession and when the practice of giving the author rights to a percentage of the sales was almost entirely unknown[2] (those rights, we should remember, would be won at the end of the eighteenth century, thanks to the lawsuit brought by Beaumarchais),[3] the dedicatory epistle was regularly counted among a writer's sources of income. There were three other sources: the direct sale of several dozen author's copies (I will return to this apropos of the private inscription); the lump-sum sale of the work to the "bookseller," who at that time served as publisher (Scarron is said to have sold *Le Roman comique* for one thousand livres and *Virgile travesti* for ten thousand, and Corneille, Molière, and Racine regularly sold their works, but others, like Boileau, thought the practice beneath them); finally, payment by the piece for a defined project like the *Encyclopédie*, which yielded Diderot a life annuity. I mention only as a matter of interest an additional source, one not tied to the specific production of a work, which consisted of the writer's going into service with some high-ranking personage (or becoming one of his "dependents") for a semi-sinecure: Chapelain was tutor to the sons of the marquis de La Trousse, amd Racine and Boileau were the king's historiographers.

So the dedication was generally a tribute that was remunerated, either by protection of the feudal type or by the more bourgeois (or proletarian) coin of the realm. The classic example of a tribute receiving the second type of remuneration is the rather fawning epistle at the head of Corneille's *Cinna*, to M. de Montoron, financier. The theme of the flattery was simple and practical: a comparison between Augustus's generosity and ... the dedicatee's. To Corneille it was worth a bonus of two hundred pistoles or two thousand écus (I cannot vouch for the exchange rate) and the reputation of being an author who was

[2] However, A. Viala cites, among dramatists who obtained a percentage of the receipts, the example of Tristan L'Hermite in 1653 (*Naissance de l'écrivain* [Minuit, 1985], 111).

[3] [Beaumarchais "defended with success the financial rights of dramatic authors against the chicanery of the actors' companies" (*The Oxford Companion to French Literature*, comp. and ed. Sir Paul Harvey and J. E. Heseltine [New York: Oxford University Press, 1959]).]

more flexible in his behavior than in his work – or, as Voltaire would more or less say, more sublime in verse than in prose. The ironic expression "a dedication à la Montoron," needing no exegesis, long remained standard. But this type of comparison between the work's dedicatee and its hero was an almost inevitable topos of the dedication, an almost automatic effect of the pressure of the context: Saint-Amant, dedicating his *Moyse sauvé* to Queen Marie of Poland and playing on the metonymical relationship between the poem and its hero, asks her to "save him again from all the insults of Slander and Envy, Monsters no less formidable than the ones that attacked him in his Cradle."

Very significantly, Corneille abandons the practice after *Don Sanche d'Aragon* (1650), in other words, two-thirds of the way through his writing career, and the 1660 edition of his "complete" *Théâtre* suppresses almost all the dedicatory epistles in favor of more technical "examinations." Racine abstains after *Bérénice* (1670). If a curve can be plotted from two points, we can say that the dedicatory epistle seems at that time to be already considered a somewhat degrading expedient that an author hastens to forget about once he has attained the height of glory or is assured of other resources. Molière, for his part, dedicated only three of his plays: *L'Ecole des maris*, *L'Ecole des femmes*, and *Amphitryon*. La Fontaine, as everyone knows, dedicated the first collection of his *Fables* to Mgr. le Dauphin, the second to Mme de Montespan, and the twelfth book to the duke of Burgundy. I am not presenting that as a statistic.

At the end of Furetière's novel *Le Roman bourgeois* [*The Bourgeois Novel*] (1666) the titles of books by Mythophilacte are read out, and among them is a *Somme dédicatoire, ou Examen général de toutes les questions qui se peuvent faire touchant la dédicace des livres* [*General Survey of Dedications, or A General Examination of All the Questions That May be Asked about the Dedication of Books*]. For that imaginary work in four volumes and seventy-four chapters, Furetière gives (that is, invents) only the table of contents – a list of chapter titles that begin with *Si* [If] and *Quoi* [What], titles that are more like questions than answers but are clearly satirical in intent. Generous dedicatees are called *mécènes* (Maecenas), and the Montoron example is in good standing among them, but the author bitingly deplores their gradual disappearance. Volume 3 is supposed to be a study of remuneration for dedications according to the quality of the author, the work, and the work's material embodiment. Among other points of law, Furetière examines authors' recourse against forgetful or recalcitrant patrons. Volume 4 looks at the relation between the praises contained in the dedication (and possibly, more subtly, in the pages of the work) and the total amount of the remuneration. He maintains, not incorrectly, that undeserved praises must receive more remuneration than other praises, not so much for the imaginative effort required as to counterbalance the loss of credit the flatterer is exposing himself to. Finally, he asks a question that is very pertinent even today, dedication or not: can the patron pay for the praises in the same coin, or idle conceit – that is, with compliments in return? To the extent that these compliments are as public as the praises they reward, the answer seems obvious. But the thing we call author's ego is often satisfied by more private flattery, which nothing prevents the author from boasting of afterward.

Furetière included as an appendix a "parody," that is, a satiric pastiche of the genre (for genre it is): a dedicatory epistle to the executioner, punctuated with various mock-heroic praises of this notorious benefactor of humanity.

This *Somme dédicatoire* must certainly have contributed somewhat to the discrediting – which it already reflects – of the classical dedication and to its progressive disappearance. This progression (or here, rather, *regression*) is, as a matter of fact, quite elusive because, for one thing, the dedicatory epistle may fade by degrees into a modern-style simple mention without losing its function of hunting after kindness; in addition, some expanded dedications may fulfill another function; and finally, many payments, even strictly financial ones, have remained so discreet that an economic and social history of flattery is not within our reach. On this matter opinions are more discernible than facts – but they may also happen to be more significant. As a point of reference, here is Montesquieu's opinion, recorded in his *Pensées*: "I will not write a dedicatory epistle: those who profess to tell the truth must not be hoping for any protection on this Earth." In question, apparently, is a plan for a history of the Jesuits (whom to dedicate that to?), but in fact there is no dedication at the head of any work by Montesquieu (the introduction of the *Lettres persanes* begins like this: "I am not writing a dedicatory epistle here, and I am not requesting any protection for this book"), and to all appearances there are very few dedications in the entire production of Enlightenment writers, except in novels such as *Tom Jones* or *Tristram Shandy*. And in a reversal whose sociopolitical significance is very obvious, Rousseau dedicates the second *Discours* "à la République de Genève."

Although the dedication of Chateaubriand's *Génie du christianisme* – or more precisely, the dedication of its second edition, in March 1803 – is not positively the last dedication to a man in a high place (very high), I would be quite tempted to attribute that symbolic role to it. This distinctive feature of its publication was even then not very common, and we might as well come out with it at once: a dedication ordinarily appears in an original edition, at the risk of disappearing from later editions if the dedicatee, in the interval, has fallen from grace in one way or another. The original edition of *Le Génie* bore no dedication, but a copy inscribed to Louis XVIII is said to have brought the author a bonus of three hundred livres.[4] The second edition bears a dedicatory epistle to First Consul Bonaparte: "Citizen First Consul, you have graciously taken under your protection this edition of *Le Génie du christianisme*. It is a fresh token of the favour towards the august cause which is triumphing in the shelter of your power. None can fail to see in your destiny the hand of that Providence which marked you from the first for the accomplishment of its vast designs. The eyes of the nations are upon you.... I am, with deep respect, Citizen First Consul, your very humble and very obedient servant." Moreover, Chateaubriand had the grace to append this dedication to the definitive edition of 1826 – accompanied, to be sure, by this excuse: "No book could be published without the mark of praise for Bonaparte, like a stamp of slavery."[5] This might warrant a counter-investigation, but it is

[4] André Maurois, *René ou La vie de Chateaubriand* (Grasset, 1938), 160 et seq. [tr. *Chateaubriand: Poet, Statesman, Lover*, trans. Vera Fraser (New York: Harper and Bros., 1938), 114-15; in the next sentence, the quotation from the dedicatory epistle to Bonaparte is from the same source].

[5] In the foreword of *La Vie de Rancé*, Chateaubriand again brings up this dedication, but in more favorable terms: "I have written only two dedications in my whole life: one to Napoleon [no longer "Bonaparte"], the other to Abbé Séguin. I admire the obscure priest as much ... as the man who won victories."

also known that that second edition of the *Génie*, with its dedication, partook of an active campaign, orchestrated by Fontanes, to
obtain some official position for the author – who on May 4, 1803,
was appointed secretary of legation in Rome. This allowed Peltier
to note in his journal that, if the inscription to Louis XVIII had
been worth a bonus of three hundred livres to Chateaubriand, the
dedication to Bonaparte had yielded "a position paying fifteen
thousand francs." The conscientious reader will (again) make the
conversion.

Of the "death" of the classical dedication, there is posthumous
evidence: from Balzac, in an unpublished work that must date
from 1843 or 1844. The evidence is a dedication by preterition to
Mme Hanska, entitled "Envoi," and the work being dedicated is
Le Prêtre catholique, a novel that would remain unfinished. The
dedication begins in these terms: "Madame, the time of dedications is past." Such a claim by so great a writer of dedications
may be surprising, but the follow-up shows that here Balzac is
using the word in its classical sense. The modern writer, he says,
invested with immense power over public opinion, "is therefore
no longer answerable either to kings or to those in high places but
derives his authority from God....."[6] That is a very Balzacian
death certificate: the writer no longer addresses himself to kings
or to those in high places not because he despises greatness but
because he possesses it himself. Deriving his authority from God,
he can dedicate only to Him – or to Her, God's most worthy
emanation: "Thus I have not written you a dedication, but I have
obeyed you."

Tending to disappear at the beginning of the nineteenth
century, therefore, are two features, obviously connected: the
most direct (economic) social function of the dedication, and its
expanded form of laudatory epistle. Connected, but not wholly
inseparable: a simple, well-placed mention on the title page could
be sufficiently gratifying in itself, and inversely the classical
dedicatory epistle, by the very fact of its textual expansion, could
accommodate other messages besides praise for the dedicatee.
These might include information about the sources and creation
of the work, or comments on the work's form or meaning –
messages by which the function of the dedication clearly en-

[6] Pléiade 12:802.

croaches on that of the preface. This slide in function is even almost inevitable, to the extent that the author should want to justify the choice of dedicatee by a statement relevant to the work: we have seen that Corneille, to justify the dedication of *Cinna*, had at least to mention the theme of generosity. Likewise, to justify the dedication of *Pompée* to Mazarin, he must mention the excellence of the play's hero: "I present ... the greatest personage of ancient Rome to the most illustrious personage of the new Rome." Finally, the eighteenth century offers at least one case of a dedicatory epistle with a wholly private function: the respectful and affectionate tribute of a son to his father, at the head of the younger Crébillon's *Egarements du cœur et de l'esprit*. It is true that in this instance the father was an elder colleague and therefore to some extent a mentor.

In the case of *Tom Jones*, which is dedicated "To the Honorable George Lyttleton, *Esq.*; One of the Lords Commissioners of the Treasury," the prefacing function of the dedicatory epistle to a person in a high place is very noticeable and, moreover, avowed. For that matter, this epistle is dedicatory only by preterition, for Lyttleton had refused to accept the official dedication. Fielding gets around the refusal by mentioning it in the first line and then continuing as if nothing had happened, which he certainly could not have taken the liberty of doing if the objection had been very serious. As with Corneille's *Cinna* and *La Place Royale*, so too with *Tom Jones*: the theme of the dedication is resemblance, the role of model being attributed to the dedicatee, who is supposed to have inspired the character Allworthy, the perfect gentleman. Hence the slide toward defining the purpose of the work: "[I have endeavoured] to recommend Goodness and Innocence [and] to laugh Mankind out of their favourite Follies and Vices. How far I have succeeded in this good Attempt, I shall submit to the candid Reader...." We see that here the author forgets about the addressee-despite-himself to speak over that addressee's shoulder to the "candid reader" in general. This substitution of addressee marks the passage from one genre to another, which Fielding, always sensitive to these features of genre, immediately takes note of and accounts for: "Indeed I have run into a Preface, while I professed to write a Dedication. But how can it be otherwise? I dare not praise you; and the only Means I know of to avoid it, when you are in my Thoughts, are either to be entirely silent, or to turn my Thoughts to some other Subject."

From the nineteenth century on, the dedicatory epistle barely hangs on except by its prefacing function, and as a result the addressee is more apt to be a colleague or a mentor capable of appreciating its message. We see a felicitous transition with Balzac, who in 1846 dedicates *Les Parents pauvres* to the prince of Teano but specifies that "it is neither to the Roman prince nor to the heir of the illustrious house of Cajatani that has provided Christianity with popes, but to the learned connoisseur of Dante that I dedicate this little fragment of a long story." Then come an implied parallel between *La Comédie humaine* and the *Divine Comedy* (a parallel of which this is undoubtedly one of the first versions) and the statement of the link between the two novels *Cousine Bette* and *Cousin Pons*: "My two novellas are balancing each other, like twins of different sexes." In the same year, Michelet dedicates *Le Peuple* to Quinet [a historian]; in 1854, Nerval, *Les Filles du feu* to Dumas; in 1862, Baudelaire, the (future) *Petits Poèmes en prose* to Houssaye [a man of letters]. All of these are preface-epistles that we will perhaps encounter again in the chapter on prefaces. And even in 1889, Barrès offers *Un homme libre* "To some schoolboys of Paris and the provinces"; then come two pages of commentary on the difficulty of adolescence and the remedy proposed in this novel.[7]

But we should not draw too stark a contrast between the classical form of the dedicatory epistle and the modern form of a simple mention of the dedicatee. The nineteenth century (at least) was familiar with an intermediary form, an atrophied dedicatory epistle, if you will, but I would call it, rather, a motivated dedication, with the motivation generally taking the form of a brief characterization of the dedicatee and/or of the work being dedicated. An example is Balzac dedicating *Les Chouans* to

[7] One must undoubtedly distinguish between dedicatory epistles with a prefacing function and some letters of accompaniment that fulfill the same function without amounting to a dedication – for example, the "Letter to M. Léon Bruys d'Ouilly serving as a preface" to Lamartine's *Recueillements poétiques*. In that letter, the addressee is referred to as a mere messenger responsible for bringing the volume to the publisher. The volume he will convey "in his luggage" is obviously not dedicated to him. This practice is rather inelegant and (therefore?) rare, but Lamartine will use it again in 1849, with a letter to M. d'Esgrigny which serves as a delayed preface to *Les Harmonies poétiques et religieuses*.

Théodore Dablin with this very youthful phrase: "My first book to my earliest friend"; or Baudelaire dedicating *Les Fleurs du mal* to Théophile Gautier: "To the impeccable poet, to the perfect magician of French letters"; but we know that Gautier had refused a first, more elaborate version, objecting that "a dedication must not be a profession of faith" – a profession that would in fact risk pushing the dedicatee into the background or, worse, compromising him.

This intermediary form seems today to be gradually falling into disuse, but we still find a trace of it in Proust, who turns the in-memoriam dedication of *Les Plaisirs et les jours* to his friend Willie Heath into a veritable little preface, and who – not without some restrictive intention – dedicates *Swann* "To M. Gaston Calmette, as testimony of deep and affectionate gratitude" (for having played a role in the search for a publisher) and *Guermantes* "To Léon Daudet, the author of *Le Voyage de Shakespeare* ...., the incomparable friend" (implying, perhaps: "and not the politician"). We also find a trace of this intermediary form in Gide, who dedicates *Les Caves du Vatican*, among others, to Jacques Copeau, with an epistle that is something of a manifesto for the *sotie* [satirical farce] genre as a type of "ironic or critical book," and *Les Faux-Monnayeurs*, his "first [and last] novel," to Roger Martin du Gard, who, during that work's creation, had been both mentor and foil as Gide was learning to work in the *roman* genre. Also in Aragon: *Les Cloches de Bâle* is dedicated "To Elsa Triolet, without whom I would have been silent." And especially, this formula still dominates the practice of inscribing a copy of a book, where the minimal formula ("To X, Y") would smack a little too much of the "signing," the churning out of one inscription after another. We will come to this point again.

Place

Where does one dedicate? Since the end of the sixteenth century, the canonical site of the dedication has obviously been at the head of the book, and today, more precisely, on the first right-hand page after the title page. But as we have seen, during the classical period a first mention of the dedicatee was readily accommodated on the title page itself, to be deducted, as it were, from the epistle that generally followed. On the title page of *Don*

Quixote, the mention of "the Duke of Bejar, Marquis de Gibraleon, Count of Benalcazar and Bañares, Viscount of the Town of Alcocer, and Lord of the Towns of Capilla, Curiel and Burguillos" takes up much more space than the author's name.

A dedication at the end of the book is infinitely rarer, but it does have its letters patent of nobility: for example, at the end of *Waverley* is the dedication to "our Scottish Addison[,] Henry Mackenzie," and at the end of *Le Rouge et le noir, Promenades dans Rome*, and *La Chartreuse* this dedication, of a slightly different sort: "To the happy few"[8] – whence, by a parodic reversal, we find "To the unhappy many" at the head of Larbaud's *Poèmes de Barnabooth* (in 1908); and in larger numbers, for Aragon's *Blanche ou L'oubli*, "To the unhappy crowd." It was also Aragon who, back in 1936, had put the dedication of *Les Beaux Quartiers* (to Elsa, of course) as a postface. Yourcenar's dedication of *Mémoires d'Hadrien* to Hadrian himself (and I will come back to this) is likewise at the end of the volume.

Other sites? Within the book, and at the head of one of its parts (when one part or several bear a special dedication). For example, *Tristram Shandy* is dedicated to Pitt but volumes 5 and 6 to John, Lord Viscount Spencer, and volume 9 to "A Great Man" who remains unspecified. And we have stopped counting the collections of poems, novellas, or essays in which almost every component bears its own specific dedication – sometimes over and above a general dedication of the collection, which does not then seem to bear on much of anything.

Time

When does one dedicate? I touched on this apropos of the second edition of *Le Génie*, which is an exception to the rule, for the canonical time for the dedication to appear is obviously the original edition. Any other choice, except possibly an advance dedication for the work's publication in parts (I have not tried to

---

[8] The phrase comes from Shakespeare (*Henry V*, 4.3.60), but apparently Goldsmith's *Vicar of Wakefield* was where Stendhal found it applied to an elite group of readers: "The vicar, too, was writing with the thought that one day he would be read by the happy few" ["I published some tracts ... which ... I have the consolation of thinking are read only by the happy Few" (*Vicar*, ch. 2)]. What we are dealing with here is the choice of a public (we will find the same thing in certain prefaces) rather than a dedication in the strict sense.

discover any examples of this), unavoidably gives the impression of clumsily making amends, a delayed and therefore suspect nomination: for the convention of the dedication is that the work was written for its dedicatee, or at least that the tribute became imperative as soon as the writing was done. Even so, *Le Génie* is certainly not the only exception one can spot. We will make do with it, however, and not take the easy way out of looking for illustrations in collections where one or another element did not meet up with its dedicatee until the whole was being assembled.

The later deletion of the dedication is doubtless more common and easier to explain. Before *Le Génie*'s dedication to Bonaparte found a final place in the documentary appendixes of the Ladvocat edition, it disappeared from the intervening editions after the assassination of the duke of Enghien. So did the dedication of the *Eroica* Symphony, after the coronation. Most of Corneille's epistles, as I have said, were thrown out in 1660, and one could probably find many other, more private examples by taking a fine-tooth comb to successive editions of collections of poems, a *genus irritabile*. This practice is common enough for Aragon, in the delayed preface to *Le Libertinage*, to be able to comment *a contrario* on retaining the dedication to Drieu: "It may be thought strange that I have left at the head of this book a dedication to a man whose ultimate behavior could justify my tearing up that page of the book. I cannot bring myself to do it: he whose name I wrote at the head of *Libertinage* was my friend, and I will not let the Fascist he became wipe out today the lineaments of our youth."

Deletion + later addition: that is obviously the formula for substitution of the dedicatee, an operation that is no doubt rarer than deletion alone, because substitution intensifies the abandonment by reinforcing it with actual infidelity. To undertake the search for instances of that operation, one would have to be a little keener than we are on the minor footnotes of history, but my attention has been called to two cases in which treachery was wrapped in a veil of quasi anonymity: Louÿs's *Chansons de Bilitis*, at first dedicated to Gide, was subsequently (after a quarrel) dedicated "To the young ladies of the future," and a certain poem by Borges, which originally bore the initials I.J., substitutes for them an S.D. that is (to us) equally mysterious. Let's stop right there.

Dedicators

Who dedicates? This question may, as a matter of fact, be understood in at least two senses. The first, external to the work, is historical in kind and perhaps generic – let us say broadly typological and distributional: certain periods, certain genres, certain authors use the dedication more than others. The invention of the dedication, as I have said, seems Latin, which excludes earlier and perhaps parallel cultures. No distribution by genre seems to me relevant *a priori*, unless perhaps we note a marked holding back for drama (classical tragedy excepted), which could be due to the difficulty of indicating a dedication in performance. To this wholly hypothetical explanation could be linked an appreciable difference in attitude among France's great classical dramatists: the one who is most strictly a "man of the theatre" – Molière, of course – is the one who dedicates least.

Also detectable, it seems to me, is a certain restraint, here as elsewhere and for very obvious reasons, on the part of writers who represent what Auerbach called "a serious realism." Balzac stays closer to readily exhibitionist authorial postures, but Stendhal (more modest?) really does not dedicate at all, except to the anonymous "happy few" (if it is dedicating, and we have seen in how discreet a location). Flaubert dedicates only *Bovary* and the *Tentation*, the former to Bouilhet[9] and the latter, which lies outside the category of serious realism, to Le Poitevin in memoriam. Zola, unless I have overlooked something, dedicates only *Madeleine Férat* to Manet and, *in extremis* and as if from remorse, *Le Docteur Pascal*, the final volume of *Les Rougon-Macquart*, to his mother (in memoriam) and his wife. I think I detect in James a significant reserve, but to verify that, one would have to go to the original editions.

In its other sense, the question "who dedicates?" might seem pointless, but I will formulate it anyway: in a book, who assumes responsibility for the dedication? (To know, if need be, who *writes* the dedication would be another – and truly pointless – question.)

---

[9] And in addition – and for reasons of special gratitude – to his lawyer, Senard: "Allow me to inscribe your name at the head of this book, before the dedication: for it is to you, above all, that I owe its publication." [See Chapter 10, note 4.] The dedication proper, therefore, was still to Bouilhet.

The answer will no doubt seem obvious: the dedicator is always the author. False: some translations are dedicated by the translator. Confining myself to French translations of Conrad, I see that the translation of *Typhoon* [*Typhon*] is dedicated by Gide to A. Ruyters, and the translation of *Youth* [*Jeunesse*] by G. J. Aubry to Valéry. But the answer is false particularly because the notion of "author" is not always clear and univocal. For us, the author of *Gulliver's Travels* is obviously Swift, but we will see that in some paratextual elements this term designates the hero. Narrator-hero, of course, and this is where a healthy uncertainty may creep in. At the head of a first-person fictional narrative, what would prevent the narrator-hero from shouldering responsibility for a dedication? Or, to speak more precisely and realistically, what would stop the author (let's say Swift) from attributing to the narrator (Gulliver) the responsibility for a dedication? A dedication to some other character in the (same) fiction: for example, "To my friends from Lilliput" or, to change corpus, "To Monseigneur the Archbishop of Grenada" [Lesage's *Gil Blas*] or "To my teacher Bergotte" [the *Recherche*]. Or to a real person, who could even be the author – some novelists address themselves, in dedications, to their creations (I will come back to this), so why not the reverse: "To Daniel Defoe, signed Crusoe," "To Monsieur Proust, without whom, etc., signed Marcel." But let us not encroach on the discussion below about the dedicatee. The difficulty of such a practice (the reluctance to accept it) would obviously be due to its more or less metaleptic nature, with the narrator set up as an "imagined author" à la Mérimée's Clara Gazul or Queneau's Sally Mara, endowed with all the functions and prerogatives of the author (who mostly prefers to keep them in his own hands). For example, Walter Scott, here clearly determined to stay concealed behind the curtain, has *Ivanhoe*'s alleged author Laurence Templeton dedicate the book to Reverend Dryasdust.

In fact, it seems to me significant that, on the contrary, the dedications of homodiegetic narratives are very often signed with the name or initials of the (real) author, as if to avoid all equivocation: so it is with the dedications of *Le Lys dans la vallée* (signed De Balzac), *Henry Esmond* (signed W. M. Thackeray), *Swann* (Marcel Proust), and *Guermantes* (M.P.). The unsigned dedications of Gide's *Symphonie pastorale*, Gide's *Thésée*, and

Sartre's *Nausée* can be easily attributed on account of the identity of the dedicatee (Schlumberger, Heurgon and Amrouche, Castor), but still, these attributions are only likelihoods. A more neutral or more universal dedicatee, as in the "To music" of Lévi-Strauss's *Mythologiques*, would – if at the head of a first-person fiction – leave us in complete uncertainty.

I have drawn attention to the multiple dedications of *Tristram Shandy*, all of which Laurence Sterne lays claim to. But there is one other, in chapter 8 of volume 1, that is signed Tristram Shandy, who insists that it is indeed a dedication, "notwithstanding its singularity in the three great essentials of matter, form, and place." Singular also in its fictive sender, and in its addressee, whose name is ... left blank: this dedication is offered (in chapter 9) to whichever lord will offer for it the exact (and substantial) sum of fifty guineas.

Dedicatees

To whom does one dedicate? If we consider obsolete the early practice of the supplicant dedication, there remain two distinct types of dedicatees: private and public. By private dedicatee I mean a person, known to the public or not, to whom a work[10] is dedicated in the name of a personal relationship: friendship, kinship, or other. For example, Balzac offers (among others) *Le Médecin de campagne* to his mother, *Louis Lambert* to Mme de Berny, *Séraphîta* to Mme Hanska, *La Maison Nucingen* to Zulma Carraud. The public dedicatee is a person who is more or less well known but with whom the author, by his dedication, indicates a relationship that is public in nature – intellectual, artistic, political, or other. For example, Balzac also dedicates (again, among others) *Birotteau* to Lamartine, *Ferragus* to Berlioz, *La Duchesse de Langeais* to Liszt, *La Fille aux yeux d'or* to Delacroix, *Le Père Goriot* to Geoffroy Saint-Hilaire, *Le Curé de Tours* to David d'Angers, and *Illusions perdues* to Victor Hugo. The two types of relationship are obviously not mutually exclusive, for the author may have a private relationship with a public dedicatee: Crébillon *fils* with his father, Melville (for *Moby-Dick*) with

---

[10] Here I will systematically use the word *work* to avoid the ambiguity of *book*, which may designate either a work or a copy, and one can't always tell which of the two is meant.

Hawthorne, Aragon with Elsa Triolet, and so forth. And I will make no attempt to sort out, in the list of Balzac's public dedications, how much is professional and how much is a matter of friendship.

The dedication, in theory, is not put into print without prior agreement by the dedicatee, but there are undoubtedly many infringements on that rule of courtesy – a rule we have already seen Fielding get around under cover of preterition. Also an exception is the dedication in memoriam, like those we have already met by Flaubert to Le Poitevin or by Zola to his mother; or like the one by Hugo, in *Les Voix intérieures*, to his father. Those dedications are private, but the posthumous dedication also allows the author to produce an intellectual lineage without consulting the precursor whose patronage he is bestowing upon himself in this way. Dujardin, for example, dedicates *Les Lauriers sont coupés* to Racine, "In tribute to the supreme novelist of souls," and one may wonder what Racine would really have thought of such a definition – and of such a legacy. Borges, in 1960, dedicates *El hacedor* [published in English as *Dreamtigers*] to Lugones, who died in 1938, but takes the very subtle precaution of providing his dedication with a sort of dream narrative: in Lugones's office at the Library he visits the master who, for a change, shows him a few signs of begrudging approval. It is only a dream, of course, but "[when] I too will have died, and our times will intermingle and chronology will be lost in a sphere of symbols . . . , it will be right to claim that I have brought you this book, and that you have accepted it."

A fortiori going without authorization is the dedication to a group – the dedications in Stendhal, Barrès, Larbaud, or Aragon which we have already cited, and many others as well: Chateaubriand's *Essai sur les révolutions* (on the title page) "To all parties"; Vallès's *Bachelier* "To those who, nourished with Greek and Latin, died of hunger"; Péguy's *Jeanne d'Arc* to all those who struggle against universal evil and on behalf of the universal socialist republic;[11] Barthes's *S/Z* to the participants in a two-year seminar. Or the dedication to collective entities: *A Tale of a Tub*

---

[11] I have not put this formulation inside quotation marks because it is a concise abridgment; the actual dedication is more complex and a page long, and ends with a sentence very broad in its application: "Anyone who wants may now have his share of the dedication."

"To His Royal Highness Prince Posterity," Hugo's *Légende des siècles* "To France.*"* Or even the dedication to beings outside the human race: *Pierre* to Mount Greylock, [Aragon's] *Mouvement perpétuel* to poetry,[12] *Mythologiques* to music, [Ristat's] *Lord B* "To the nettle and music of Klaus Schultze." We no longer bother to count the dedications to God, to his saints, to the Virgin[13] – and I suppose, in a roundabout way, we should put into that class, if it is a class, the dedication by preterition of Barbey d'Aurevilly's *Diaboliques* [*The Diabolical Women*]: "Whom to dedicate this to?" One may also, very simply (too simply, perhaps), dedicate to the reader, and no doubt certain notes "to the reader" should be read as dedicatory epistles as much as prefaces: see those of Montaigne's *Essais*, of Quevedo's *Buscón*, or of Balzac's *Elixir de longue vie*. Some works of fiction are dedicated, by metalepsis, to one of their characters: the first part [1607] of d'Urfé's *Astrée* includes a dedicatory epistle to the heroine; the second part [1610], to the hero Céladon; and the third part [1619], to the little river Lignon, which both links and separates the lovers. Strictly speaking, those three are mostly prefaces in the form of epistles; the real dedicatees are, in 1607, Henry IV as restorer of the peace in Europe and, in 1619, Louis XIII as Henry's worthy successor. But the third edition of Sorel's *Francion* bears a real dedication to the hero: "To Francion. Dear Francion, whom could I dedicate your story to but you yourself?"[14] The terminal dedication of *Mémoires d'Hadrien*, as I said above, has this same type of addressee.

Dedication to the reader, that is, to the real addressee of the work, and dedication to the hero, that is, to the work's main subject – the only thing I see missing from this slightly deviant and no doubt playful set is self-dedication, or dedication to the

---

[12] To be exact: "I dedicate this poem to poetry, and to hell with whoever reads it." The second of these assertions is not precisely a dedication but perhaps a notice to the reader. In any case, it posed delicate problems for the relation between dedication and inscriptions. J. Ristat specifies (*Œuvre poétique*, vol. 2) that Aragon crossed the dedication out in copies for his friends, which does not evince much firmness of mind. He adds that the back cover of the copies meant for journalists bore handwritten erotic phrases. The current edition bears, printed, this retrospective note: "Here I had put some obscenities for the gentlemen of the press: they did not appear grateful."

[13] J. Delteil, *Sur le fleuve amour*: "To Mother, to the Virgin Mary, and to General Bonaparte"; Chateaubriand had not dared formulate such a parallel.

[14] 1633. The second edition (1626) bore a dedication that was equally whimsical, by preterition: "To men in high places: I write this epistle not to dedicate this book to you, but to let you know that I am not dedicating it to you."

author by the author himself. That would often be the most sincere formula, and it is more or less the one Joyce uses for his first work, a play entitled *A Brilliant Career* and dedicated like this: "To My own Soul I dedicate the first true work of my life."[15] That would also be the formula of *Mémoires d'Hadrien* if we took the work's autobiographical status literally – which, of course, the author does not at all wish us to do.

One can also dedicate the work to itself, if one believes it deserves the dedication, in other words, if one believes the work deserves *itself* – and how could it not? One always deserves oneself, alas! That is just about what Horace did: *Ad librum suum* [*To his book*]. But let's be honest: that is not a dedication, but the head of an epistle (the twentieth).

Some of Scott's novels have the distinctive feature of being dedicated to an imaginary character: Reverend Dryasdust, member of the Antiquarian Society, for *Ivanhoe* and *The Fortunes of Nigel*, and Captain Clutterbuck for *Peveril of the Peak*. But the point is that the dedication, or the dedicatory epistle fulfilling the function of a preface, or the prefatory letter, forms part of the pseudonymous game that, after 1816, Scott substituted for or superimposed on the anonymity of the early *Waverley Novels*. The main loaner name, Jedediah Cleishbotham, therefore shoulders responsibility for (for example) the introductory chapter of *Old Mortality* and the dedication to the reader of the introduction of *The Heart of Midlothian*. The dedications of *Ivanhoe* and *Nigel* to Dryasdust are signed Laurence Templeton and Cuthbert Clutterbuck, respectively, signatures that indirectly cause Templeton and Clutterbuck to be presumed the authors of these novels. Then the game gets complicated by inversions and other diversions that we will evoke more justifiably under the heading of the preface.

Whoever the official addressee, there is always an ambiguity in the destination of a dedication, which is always intended for at least two addressees: the dedicatee, of course, but also the reader, for dedicating a work is a public act that the reader is, as it were, called on to witness. A typically performative act, as I have said, for in itself it *constitutes* the act it is supposed to describe; the formula for it is therefore not only "I dedicate this

[15] R. Ellmann, *James Joyce*, new and rev. edn. (New York: Oxford University Press, 1982), 78.

book to So-and-So" (that is: "I am telling So-and-So that I am
dedicating this book to him") but also, and sometimes even
more, "I am telling the reader that I am dedicating this book to
So-and-So." But by that very fact, the formula is likewise "I am
telling So-and-So that I am telling the reader that I am dedicating this book to So-and-So" (to put it another way: "I am
telling So-and-So that I am publicly dedicating the work to
him"). But as a result, and not less so: "I say to the reader that I
say to So-and-So . . ." – ad infinitum, of course. The dedication
always is a matter of demonstration, ostentation, exhibition: it
proclaims a relationship, whether intellectual or personal, actual
or symbolic, and this proclamation is always at the service of the
work, as a reason for elevating the work's standing or as a
theme for commentary (in the latter respect, it is obviously not
immaterial that Balzac's *Duchesse de Langeais* is dedicated to
Liszt and his *Fille aux yeux d'or* to Delacroix, rather than the
reverse).[16] In all of that there is something basically oblique,
which Proust called the "insincere language of (prefaces and)
dedications" and which perhaps one cannot escape even by
avoiding a dedication – for the absence of a dedication, in a
system that includes the possibility of one, is significant as
degree zero. "This book is not dedicated to anyone" – isn't such
an implied message loaded with meaning? Take your choice:
either "I don't see anyone who deserves this book" or "I don't
see anyone whom this book deserves."

Functions

I was expecting to follow those few comments on the relationship between the dedication and its players with a section on
the semantic and pragmatic functions of the dedication itself. I
realize there is nothing left to say that I have not already said or
implied, and after all, this is not a coincidence: the dedication, I
said, is the proclamation (sincere or not) of a relationship (of one
kind or another) between the author and some person, group, or
entity. Except for additional encroachments on the functions of
the preface, the dedication's own function – which, for all that,

[16] [The heroine of *La Duchesse* demonstrates virtuosity at the keyboard; the events
of *La Fille* are intensely colored (i.e., they involve a scandalous affair between
two women).]

is not unimportant – is exhausted in that proclamation. This is so whether the proclamation is explicit or not – that is, whether it states precisely the nature of the relationship (as in classical dedicatory epistles or in particularizing, or indeed restrictive, formulae of the type "To So-and-So, for this reason [and not some other]") or whether it prefers to be elusive and indefinite about the relationship, depending on the reader (and perhaps the dedicatee himself) to try to pin it down. Certainly, if nowadays the dedication's directly economic function has disappeared, its patronage role or its role as moral, intellectual, or aesthetic backing has for the most part persisted: on the threshold or at the conclusion of a work, one cannot mention a person or a thing as a privileged addressee without invoking that person or thing in some way (as the bard of old invoked the muse – who couldn't do anything about it) and therefore implicating the person or thing as a kind of ideal inspirer. "For So-and-So" always involves some element of "By So-and-So." The dedicatee is always in some way responsible for the work that is dedicated to him and to which he brings, willy-nilly, a little of his support and therefore participation. This little is not nothing: is it necessary to bring to mind again that the Latin for "guarantor" is *auctor*?

The inscription of the copy

The distinction between dedication and inscription is obviously bound up with the possibility of distinguishing between these two realities, the work and the copy. This is not the place to take up the far-reaching questions raised by that second distinction; rather, more simply, I recall that the mode of existence of a unique work, such as Vermeer's *View of Delft*, is not the mode of existence of a work in multiple copies, such as the *Recherche*. In the case of a unique work, which pictorial works generally are, the possible dedication (I have little knowledge of what is actually done) can only be of the work and the copy simultaneously. A work in multiple copies – let us say, liberally, three thousand – can be dedicated as a work to one person, and each of its copies can be inscribed to three thousand others, or at least two thousand nine hundred ninety-nine. Strictly speaking, the number has nothing to do with the matter, and not even production by scribes, as practiced before Gutenberg, with its dozens or hundreds of not strictly identical copies, could invalidate the fundamental distinction: Virgil could dedicate the *Georgics*, as a work, to Maecenas, and could inscribe each of the handwritten copies to its individual purchaser. I have no further knowledge about this other practice; I imagine simply that the scribe's role – perhaps not more active than the modern printer's, but surely more individual – in making each copy might have given him some right to the inscription, I mean a right to inscribe the copy for which he was responsible, at least if each manuscript had been the work of a single copyist, which, as we know, quite early ceased to be the case. I also imagine (ignorance is a great stimulant of the imagination) that the birth of printing, by multiplying the number of (almost) identical copies, must at the same time, to offset that standardization of the product, have multiplied the demand for inscriptions. In short, the inscription, as we still know it today, constitutes the only part of a printed book that is handwritten and therefore, in a way, individual ("unique"). Hence its value. We also know, as I have already mentioned, that in the sixteenth century the sale of authors' copies, also called – and rightly so – "presentation copies," was among the resources to which authors were entitled. Erasmus, for example, had, we are told, "a network of agents across the length and breadth of Europe who were active in the distribution of his works and in the collecting of his rewards."[17] I imagine, too, that this trading on the inscription must also have gradually disappeared at the end of the classical period, when authors' royalties were instituted. On this point as on others, the lack of a history of the inscription is sorely felt. For an obvious reason (the difficulty of collecting the material), writing such a history would be no small matter, but it seems to me that the great benefit – better knowledge of the customs and institution of literature – would be well worth the trouble. It is clear, in any case, that two vestiges of this early trading remain: the signing of press copies (I will write you a nice inscription so that you will write me a nice review) and the signing sessions in bookstores, where the presence of an inscription is definitely a selling point.

[17] L. Febvre and H.-J. Martin, *The Coming of the Book*, 16.

Place, time

There is nothing but the obvious to say about the place of the inscription, put nowadays on the flyleaf or, better, on the half-title page, which gives the author the possibility of incorporating the half title, with or without embellishment, into the phrasing of the inscription. Nor is there anything more than the obvious to say about the time of the inscription, which is basically when the book is released, that is, first printed (press copies and author's copies), but may be later, on the occasion of a signing session or when an individual asks for an autograph. The duration of the inscription is, paradoxically, more certain than the duration of the dedication: it is indefinite, save for wear and tear or accident. An author can always, in fact – like Chateaubriand in 1804 – delete or modify a dedication when a new edition comes out. Deletion is certainly not retroactive, short of the author's being able to find and destroy all previous copies (and even then, indirect evidence may survive and be sufficient), but it at least reduces the application of the original dedication: for example, we say that Chateaubriand dedicated to Bonaparte only the second and third editions of the *Génie du christianisme*. But unless the inscribee consents, the author cannot touch an inscription: too late for any possible regrets or second thoughts, what is signed is signed. I know more than one author (and how many don't I know) who could kick himself for more than one inscription.

Gide's biography is rich in changeful inscription-related episodes, authentic or apocryphal, that may illustrate this type of embarrassment or conflict. An example: having had a falling out with André Ruyters, he inscribes a copy of his *Voyage au Congo* to Ruyters with this single word: "Nonobstant" [notwithstanding]. Another example: Claudel having inscribed a volume of his correspondence with Gide to his grandson with the words "My regrets at being in such bad company," and the inscribee having had the good taste to bring the volume to Gide for him, too, to sign, Gide is alleged to have simply added this pithy retort: "Idem." True, Claudel had already much annoyed him by sending him a copy of what was indeed their common work with this very insolent inscription: "With the author's compliments" – an occasion, if there ever was one, for Gide to feel (in his word) "suppressed." And we know that in 1922 Gide held a public sale of part of his library, particularly all the books inscribed by former friends with whom in the meantime he had had a falling out. One of them, Henri de Régnier, took his revenge by sending Gide *nonobstant* his next book, but with this biting inscription: "To André Gide, for his next sale."[18]

Inscriber, inscribee

In contrast to the dedication, the inscription (except for forgery) leaves no room for uncertainty about the identity of its inscriber, for it has the characteristic – one that is obvious and therefore misunderstood or disregarded – of being always signed or, more exactly, of including always and at least one signature. Always? One must never say never, but it seems to me that the only exceptions can be accounted for by forgetfulness or a spiteful simulation of it. At least one? Yes, for the autograph at its bare minimum is, precisely, not an unsigned phrase but rather simply a signature without a phrase. Immediately above it in the hierarchy is the signed formula without any mention of the inscribee: "With best wishes, So-and-So." Not very gratifying. The canonical phrase obviously includes the name of the inscribee (without which it would perhaps be better to speak of an autograph rather than a true inscription), with endless variations on the outline "To X, Y" – where X may be an individual or a collectivity (a couple, a group, a library) but is less likely than the dedicatee to be a nonhuman entity or even a dead person: no inscription to God, Mount Greylock, music, France, Jeanne d'Arc, my grandfather in memoriam, or even really my cat, although he would know what to do with it. All of which proves yet again that one may be able to do the greater (dedicate a work) without being able to do the lesser (inscribe a copy). In contrast to the dedicatee, the inscribee must be human and alive because, in contrast to dedicating a work, inscribing a copy is not only a symbolic act but also a real act, accompanied in principle by a

---

[18] I take these anecdotes from J. Lambert, *Gide familier* (Julliard, 1958). Naturally, other versions are in circulation: in R. Mallet, *Une Mort ambiguë* (Gallimard, 1955), Claudel's grandson is a girl, and Gide's rejoinder is, more gently, "With Gide's apology." In his conversations with Amrouche, Gide specifies that the special purpose of his sale of these copies was to make public (by putting them in the catalogue) these private inscriptions by former friends who had broken with him for reasons of morals and religion.

real gift, or at the very least by a past or present sale. Accompanied, that is, by an ownership that the inscription in fact stamps and ratifies. One does not (knowingly) inscribe to someone a book that does not belong to him; hence the frequent and very accurate phrase: "X's copy." In contrast, of course, the dedication is not at all accompanied by the gift or the sale of the whole set of printed copies: like the work itself, it is of another order, ideal and symbolic. Hence the strangeness of this phrase of dedication, for the *Duino Elegies*: "Property of Princess Marie von Thurn und Taxis-Hohenlohe." Strange by way of hyperbole, as in "I am all yours," or by way of litotes: to be the dedicatee of a literary work is not at all to be the owner of it – which one cannot be. The dedicatee of the work is both much more and much less than its owner. The dedicatee is of another order, and so forth.

Functions

For lack of the investigation mentioned above, which I continue to advocate, I will make no attempt here to propose a "theory" of the form or function of the inscription: the material available would be much too erratic and contingent. I will merely say a word about a statement I ventured to make above: nowadays, except in purely commercial or professional situations (review copies), it seems harder for the inscription than for the dedication to settle for the minimal formula "To X, Y,"[19] which, in this actual relationship, always appears *too* minimal. The friendly inscription, and *a fortiori* the tribute to a mentor, always calls, therefore, for more or less of a specification: a specification (even by a single adverb) either about the relationship between inscriber and inscribee or (better) about the relationship between the inscribee and the work itself or (better still) about both relationships at the same time. For example, from Zola to Flaubert for *L'Assommoir*: "To my great friend Gustave Flaubert, in hatred of good taste." Obviously and necessarily, these specifications by motivation ("To X, for such and such a reason") include an (authorial) comment on the work and thereby enter, by right and on an equal footing, the field of the paratext. It is unnecessary to add how valuable for each work an itemized account of all its

[19] As we know, a modern variant of this formula (no doubt more common for the inscription than for the dedication) is "*For* X, Y."

inscriptions would be. An account that – if we are talking about a complete one – would certainly be out of the question, but literary history does not seem to me to have made all the efforts in this direction that one might expect it to have made. To be continued, therefore.[20]

Modesty is undoubtedly one of the requisite attitudes, so the apology is one of the established topoi of the inscription. There are also authors who are sincerely modest or – more precisely, perhaps – particularly attentive to the interest one or another reader may bring, or not bring, to one or another work. The inscribee, after all, in contrast to the dedicatee, is always a potential reader at the same time that he is a real person, and one of the presuppositions of the inscription is that the author expects, in exchange for the gratification, a reading. Moreover, it would be unseemly, even from modesty, to give an inscribee the impression that nothing was expected of him: that would be to treat him as a philistine, or as a common autograph-chaser.

Roland Barthes was one of these attentive authors, always ready to apologize for offering a book that might not be of particular interest to his inscribee. One of his inscriptions in the form of an apology has been very subtly and (even better) very appropriately commented on by the inscribee, Eliseo Veron. I would be open to reproach if I commented, in turn, on that comment, but I invite the reader to look it up forthwith: Eliseo Veron, "Qui sait?" *Communications* 36 (1982).

As we now understand – as we already knew – the function of an inscription is markedly different from the function of a dedication. The main reason for this difference, or these differences, is the private nature not only of the relationship but also of the inscription's situation of communication, which, in principle, is confidential. Barring possible posthumous publication, there is nothing of the indirect movement I drew attention to above ("I inform the reader that I dedicate ..."). No one besides the

---

[20] On the particular case of the long inscription of *Swann* to Mme Scheikévitch, written in 1915 to give the inscribee a partial summary of the rest of the *Recherche*, see my *Palimpsestes*, 291 et seq. In status, that text (written two years after the book was published) falls midway between inscription and letter (it can be found, moreover, in the editions of Proust's correspondence). For more details on inscriptions and their fringes, see J.-B. Puech and J. Couratier, "Dédicaces exemplaires" (*Poétique* 69, February 1987).

inscribee is supposed to know that he is the inscribee, and in what terms; and in contrast, every inscribee knows very well that he is not the only one. Here, therefore, there is nothing of the public-backing effect that attaches to the dedication. Private backing? I doubt that that phrase has any meaning here. The request, as I have said – for here as elsewhere, there is a request – is more simply and more directly for a reading, and this relationship is altogether rather healthy. It remains to be seen whether finding a reader is not more difficult than finding a patron.

This point also involves a fairly comical paradox: the inscription accompanies the gift of a copy but accounts for this gift with a comment not, of course, about the copy but about the work itself. This paradox may even end up creating a somewhat awkward situation for the author (the hard-to-please inscribee: "Since this work suits me so well, why not dedicate it to me instead of simply inscribing this one copy to me?" or conversely, the disdainful dedicatee: "One copy would have sufficed!") – not to mention the embarrassment there always is in inscribing to Y a copy of a work already dedicated to X. The paradox has at least the merit of emphasizing the very special relation between copy and work: the copy derives its value from the work – not its entire value (after all, no two published copies of a single work are absolutely identical) but, literally, the essence of its value. Or rather, by the mere fact that the copy represents the work, the copy has value both *by means of* and *on behalf of* the work. The inscription, justifying itself by a reference to the work, insists simultaneously, therefore, on the work's two aspects, material ("Here is a book") and ideal. The inscription enhances the work's material value by making this book different (as we know, in this respect only the numbering of deluxe copies can compete – poorly – with the inscription), saying, in effect, "Here is the unique copy of Mr. So-and-So"; at the same time, the inscription designates the work's ideal aspect for whatever purpose that may serve, saying, in effect, "Here is a copy of such and such a work – a copy that is worth what it's worth above all because of what *the work* is worth." In other words: "Despite appearances and insofar as humanly possible, what I am offering you is not only a book, but indeed a work." In still other words: "Possession of this book is but a means, because this book is not only an object but is also a sign. The end is another possession, which is not at all a possession, and the only route to it is by reading." In other words, finally, in an attempt every now and then to exorcise the disdain for the text which is so common among bibliophiles: "Don't imagine for a moment that owning this book excuses you from reading it."

7

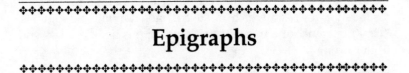

Epigraphs

I will define the epigraph roughly as a quotation placed *en exergue* [in the exergue], generally at the head of a work or a section of a work; literally, *en exergue* means *off* the work, which is going a little too far. Here the exergue is, rather, at the *edge* of the work, generally closest to the text – thus, following the dedication, if there is one. Hence the metonymy, so common nowadays, of *exergue* for "epigraph" – a metonymy that does not seem to me very felicitous, for it confuses the thing with the place. But I will come back to this matter of location after the requisite informal historical survey. I will also come back to the term *quotation*, which calls for some specifications, or rather some broadening.

Historical survey

At first glance, the epigraph seems more recent than the dedication. I find no trace of it, at least as defined above, before the seventeenth century. But perhaps something older still, the author's coat of arms, must be seen as its forerunner. The text of the coat of arms -- its motto – may indeed be a quotation, like the "Ab insidiis non est prudentia" from Pliny that Mateo Alemán incorporated into the title page of at least two of his works, *Guzman de Alfarache* and *Ortografía castellana*. What distinguishes the motto, therefore, is not necessarily its autographic characteristic but its independence in relation to the singular text – the fact that it can appear at the head of several works by the same author, who puts it, as it were, *en exergue* of his career, or of his entire life. This close link between motto and career or entire life is obviously the case for Rousseau's "Vitam impendere vero," which to my knowledge appears on none of his works and which, according to the second preface to *Julie*, he refused to allow his publisher to put at the head of that novel.

I know of no more recent example of the authorial motto, but some certainly exist; and everyone knows the mottoes of publishers or series which still adorn some covers today: "Rien de commun" ["Nothing ordinary"] (Corti), "Je sème à tous vents" ["I sow to the four winds"] (Larousse), "Je ne bastis que pierres vives, ce sont hommes" ["I build only with live stones; that is men"] (Seuil's Pierres vives series). This last motto, taken from Rabelais,[1] serves to comment on and justify the title of the series, a function we will later find at work with the epigraph. An intermediary state would be that of the epigraph that accompanied (on cover 2) the title of the literary journal *Tel quel*: a quotation, authentic or not, that changed with each issue but always included the expression "tel quel" [as is].

To my knowledge, then, the first epigraph of a work,[2] at least in France, was probably the one for La Rochefoucauld's *Maximes*, or rather *Réflexions, ou Sentences et maximes morales*, the 1678 edition (I do not think it appears in previous editions): "Nos vertus ne sont, le plus souvent, que des vices déguisés" ["Our virtues are usually only vices in disguise"]. But this first example is still, or already, deviant, for the sentence thus placed *en exergue* is not presented as a quotation (an allographic one, with its author named) and sounds rather like a maxim by La Rochefoucauld himself – it would constitute fairly well the typical La Rochefoucauld maxim, would be an emblem and condensation of his whole doctrine. An autographic epigraph, then, or an epigraph written by the author himself: this is a variant we will encounter again, along with the questions it raises. The first famous epigraph in the current sense of the term was probably, instead, the one for La Bruyère's *Caractères* (1688). It is a quotation from Erasmus, duly attributed to its author: "Admonere voluimus, non mordere; prodesse, non laedere; consulere moribus hominum, non officere" ["We have wished to warn and not to bite; to be useful and not to wound; to benefit the morals of men, and not to be detrimental to them"].

The custom of using epigraphs becomes more widespread during the eighteenth century, when we find them (generally in

---

[1] [*Tiers livre*, ch. 6.]

[2] At least, the first at the head of a famous work; but my attention has been called to one, taken from Horace, in Bardin's *Lycée du sieur Bardin* (1632). The investigation remains open.

Latin) at the head of some major works, such as Montesquieu's *Esprit des lois*: "Prolem sine matre creatam" ("A child created without a mother"), a quotation from Ovid but with no mention of the author;[3] Buffon's *Histoire naturelle*: "Naturam amplectimur omnem" ("We embrace all of nature"), with no mention of the author; *La Nouvelle Héloïse*: two lines in Italian from Petrarch, "Non la connobe il mondo, mentre l'ebbe: / Connobill'io ch'a pianger qui rimasi" (Rousseau's translation: "Le monde la posséda sans la connaître, / Et moi, je l'ai connue, je reste ici bas à la pleurer" ["The world possessed her without knowing her, / And I, I knew her, but am left here below to mourn her"]; Diderot's *Neveu de Rameau*: "Vertumnis, quotquot sunt, natus iniquis" ("Born when every single Vertumnus was out of sorts"), from Horace, *Satires* 2.7.14; and Rousseau's *Confessions*: "Intus et in cute" ("Inside out"), taken, with no mention of the author, from Persius, *Satires* 3.30. The use of Latin epigraphs continues in this postclassical phase at least up to Chateaubriand's *Mémoires d'outre-tombe*: "Sicut nubes ... quasi naves ... velut umbra," which is a potpourri from Job, 30.15, 9.26, 14.2: "[My welfare passeth away] as a cloud, [my days are passed away] as the swift ships, [man fleeth also] as a shadow."

A somewhat late-developing custom, then, which more or less replaces the classical custom of using dedicatory epistles and which, in its beginnings, seems a little more typical of works of ideas than of poetry or the novel. In the major novels of the eighteenth century other than *La Nouvelle Héloïse*, I find scarcely any epigraphs except the ones at the head of *Tom Jones* ("Mores hominum multorum vidit" [he "saw the customs of many men"], with no indication of the source [*Ars poetica* 141-42]) and *Tristram Shandy* ("It is not things themselves that disturb men, but their judgments about these things," from Epictetus's *Encheiridion*). Apparently the gothic novel, a genre simultaneously popular (in its themes) and erudite (in its settings), is the channel by which epigraphs in large number get into prose narrative: Radcliffe's

---

[3] The right meaning of this quotation is not obvious. "A work without a model" is sometimes how it is interpreted. But Montesquieu is also said to have glossed it like this: to write a great work, one needs a father, genius, and a mother, liberty; "my work was missing the latter" (Mme Necker, *Nouveaux Mélanges*). This paratext of a paratext casts a curious light (or shadow) on the text.

Mysteries of Udolpho (1794), Lewis's *Monk* (1795), and Maturin's *Melmoth the Wanderer* (1820) all contain an epigraph for every chapter.[4] Walter Scott follows suit, with the same frequency. His epigraphs are generally attributed to a real author, which does not automatically guarantee their accuracy or authenticity – even if we must no longer completely trust this "avowal" from the introduction to *Chronicles of the Canongate*:

The scraps of poetry which have been in most cases tacked to the beginnings of chapters in these novels are sometimes quoted either from reading or from memory, but, in the general case, are pure invention. I found it too troublesome to turn to the collection of the British poets to discover apposite mottoes, and, in the situation of the theatrical mechanist, who, when the white paper which represented his shower of snow was exhausted, continued the storm by snowing brown, I drew on my memory as long as I could, and, when that failed, eked it out with invention. I believe that, in some cases, where actual names are affixed to the supposed quotations, it would be to little purpose to seek them in the works of the authors referred to.

The English fashion of the novelistic epigraph passes into France at the beginning of the nineteenth century – via Nodier and other champions of the gothic, "frenetic," or fantastical genre – as is fairly well attested by Hugo's *Han d'Islande*. Each of that work's fifty-one chapters is duly armed with at least one epigraph (the record is four), and all these epigraphs are very characteristic in terms of authors chosen. In the lead is Maturin, quoted nine times unless I've miscounted, followed by Shakespeare and Lessing, seven times each. According to a principle we will encounter again, these choices of author are more significant than the texts of the epigraphs themselves, which are apparently distributed without much concern for their connection to the contents of their respective chapters. Hugo, moreover, does not fail to indicate as much in his preface, commending the "strange and mysterious motto [at the head of each chapter], which adds singularly to the interest and gives more expressiveness to each part of the composition."

Stendhal, too, takes from Scott the habit of using chapter epigraphs: he uses them in *Armance* for all but four chapters; in

---

[4] The earliest gothic novel, Walpole's *Castle of Otranto* (1764), did not include one.

the *Rouge* for all chapters except the final four, as well as for each of the two books ("Truth, bitter truth," Danton, and "She isn't pretty, she wears no rouge," an undoubtedly fanciful attribution to Sainte-Beuve); in the *Chartreuse* for the two books as well as for chapter 2 of the first book. And this doesn't count the epigraphs in his non-novelistic works and the epigraphs that the manuscripts of the two uncompleted novels, *Leuwen* and *Lamiel*, seem to anticipate. Balzac's position seems more restrained.[5] His youthful works (*Jean-Louis, L'Héritière de Birague,* and so forth) bear many epigraphs, sometimes several per chapter – often anonymous or of fanciful attribution. Of the works later brought together in *La Comédie humaine,* twenty-three – particularly historical narratives of the Scott type (*Les Chouans,*[6] *Le Martyr calviniste*) and fantastico-"philosophical" ones (*Sarrasine, L'Histoire des Treize, Louis Lambert, L'Envers de l'histoire contemporaine*) – bore an epigraph in their pre-original edition, according to Lucienne Frappier-Mazur. Of the big novels of manners, only *Le Père Goriot* observes the ritual, but with a phrase (in English) that emphasizes the realistic purpose of the narrative: "All is true" (Shakespeare – an epigraph Balzac first thought of using for *Birotteau*). But above all, these epigraphs are often deleted in the original edition, or at the latest in the Furne edition of *La Comédie humaine* (with only two exceptions: the epigraph of *La Peau de chagrin* is retained, and that of *Le Réquisitionnaire* is added in Furne). Balzac seems, therefore, to repudiate the epigraph as he abandons the historical, fantastic, or "philosophical" narrative in favor of the big novel – or rather (as he would put it), the big *study* of manners. As with the dedication and undoubtedly more so, this restraint vis-à-vis the epigraph will characterize the great modern realistic tradition: the epigraph is more or less absent from the works of Flaubert, Zola, and James, as it was already

---

[5]   See L. Frappier-Mazur, "Parodie, imitation et circularité: Les épigraphes dans les romans de Balzac," in *Le Roman de Balzac,* ed. R. Le Huenen and P. Perron (Montreal: Didier, 1980).

[6]   In the foreword of *Gars* – the first title, we should remember, of *Le Dernier Chouan,* which was the first version of *Les Chouans* – Balzac had the imagined author, Victor Morillon, say: "I abhor epigraphs. They interfere with my satisfaction, to use a Parisian expression, but I wanted to challenge imitation and, although careful not to let them give anything away to the reader, I pushed the indulgence to the point of ridicule. They are the first and the last ones I will encumber my narratives with."

from Fielding and Jane Austen, and the interlude opened by Ann Radcliffe and Walter Scott closes more or less in the middle of the nineteenth century.

Place, time

The usual place for the epigraph of a work is, as I have said, closest to the text, generally on the first right-hand page after the dedication but before the preface. In its early days, however, the epigraph was still allowed on the title page, as in the original editions of *La Nouvelle Héloïse* or *Oberman* ("Study mankind, not men," Pythagoras), and this practice has not been entirely abandoned in our time: see Aragon's *Fou d'Elsa* ("I play with her name the game of love," Djâmî). Another possible location, as for the dedication, is the end of the book: the last line of the text, set off by white space, as with the quotation from Marx that Perec put at the end of *Les Choses* (in addition to an introductory epigraph taken from Malcolm Lowry). Perec, moreover, named these terminal quotations (about ten of which he put at the end of *La Disparition*) "métagraphs" (*méta* for "after"). It goes without saying that this change in location may entail a change in role. For the reader, the relationship between introductory epigraph and text is still prospective, whereas in theory the significance of the terminal epigraph, after the text has been read, is obvious and more authoritatively conclusive: it is the last word, even if the author pretends to leave that word to someone else. The terminal epigraphs of *La Disparition* could hardly have appeared at the head of the work without running the risk of giving the game away too soon, but the terminal epigraph of *Les Choses* is indeed a conclusion or, as they say in fables, a moral. And the terminal epigraph of Giono's *Un roi sans divertissement* [*A King without Diversion*] is even more of a conclusion: presented, in fact, as belonging fully to the text, it is a quotation (from Pascal, of course, and a justification of the title) in the mouth of the narrator, who freely admits to not knowing its author: "Who said, 'A king without diversion is a man sunk into wretchedness'?"

Epigraphs of chapters, or of parts, or of individual works assembled in a collection, are placed even more regularly at the head of the section, and that is all there is to say about their location – or almost all: one could no doubt find two or three other more or less suitable locations for them. I have already mentioned the quotation from Sartre on the band of Hollier's *Politique de la prose*; this use of an epigraph on the band, a place that is very exposed (in all senses) and therefore very strategic, goes back at least to 1929, when Julien Green put on the band of *Leviathan* the famous sentence from act 4 of Maeterlinck's *Pelléas*: "If I were God, I would have pity on men's hearts." A distinguished colleague (Mauriac, if I am not mistaken) happened to denounce that sacrilegious epigraph.[7]

The epigraph is generally original in the sense agreed to here, that is, adopted (and definitively so) with the first edition. But Balzac has already provided us with an exception to each of these norms, and it would no doubt be easy to find other cases of epigraphs delayed or deleted by an author's decision or a publisher's oversight (not to mention changes from one edition to another). I have a pocket edition of *For Whom the Bell Tolls* in French translation (*Pour qui sonne le glas*), and the epigraph from Donne, despite its fundamental importance, is missing. We will encounter this epigraph below, for it is not really lost.

From the fact that the epigraph is a quotation, it almost necessarily follows that it consists of a text. But one may, after all, use as an epigraph a quotation – or reproduction – of a nonverbal work, such as a drawing or a musical score. An example is Corporal Trim's "flourish with his stick" in volume 9, chapter 4, of *Tristram Shandy*, which Balzac put more or less faithfully *en exergue* of *La Peau de chagrin*; or the three bars from *The Rite of Spring* reproduced at the head of the novel *La Consagración de la primavera* by Alejo Carpentier; or the words and music of the fishermen's hymn "Hear us, O Lord" that justifies the title of a collection of stories and novellas by Lowry.

The "epigraphed"

From that same fact (that the epigraph is a quotation), it follows that the attribution of the quotation raises two theoretically distinct questions, although neither is as simple as it appears to be: Who is the author, real or putative, of the text quoted? Who

[7] Julien Green, *Journal* (May 2, 1929), *Œuvres* (Pléiade), 4:46. [Green does not identify the colleague.]

chooses and proposes that quotation? I will call the author the *epigraphed*; and the person who chooses or proposes, I will call the *epigrapher*, or sender of the epigraph (its addressee – no doubt the reader of the text – being, if you insist, the *epigraphee*).

The epigraph is most often allographic, that is, according to our conventions, attributed to an author who is not the author of the work – let us say Erasmus for La Bruyère. That is what makes it a quotation and even, as Antoine Compagnon rightly says, "a quotation par excellence."[8] If this attribution is genuine, the epigraph is authentic; but the attribution may be false, and may be false in several ways. The epigrapher may quite simply, as we have seen Scott pride himself on doing, make up the quotation in order to attribute it, with or without plausibility, to a real or imaginary author. As I have said, the epigraph of the second part of the *Rouge* is suspected of being apocryphal – of being falsely attributed to Sainte-Beuve. It would be equally false, or fictive, if – still made up by Stendhal – it had been attributed to an imaginary or "imagined" author. It would still be false or fictive (but more subtly so) if it were attributed to Sainte-Beuve but had in fact been taken from another author, let us say Byron. Or the epigraph may be authentic but inaccurate (this often happens), if the epigrapher – either because he is quoting erroneously from memory or because he wishes to make the quotation fit its context better or for some other reason, such as an unfaithful intermediary – correctly attributes an epigraph that is inaccurate, in other words, an epigraph that is not a literal quotation: as if Sainte-Beuve had actually written "She is not pretty, she wears no black." Or the epigraph may be authentic and accurate but incorrectly referenced, when referenced at all.

For the customs of presentation of the epigraph are highly variable. It seems, however, that the most common custom is to name the author without giving a specific reference – unless the identity of the epigraphed goes without saying, as at the head of a critical or biographical study, when the anonymous epigraph can come only from the author being studied. In this case the elegant thing to do is omit the name and give the (more or less precise) reference. Jean-Pierre Richard does this at the head of

[8] Compagnon, *La Seconde Main*, 30.

151

Proust et le monde sensible, giving simply *La Prisonnière* as the source of this preparatory quotation: "A phrase ... so profound, so vague, so internal, almost so organic and visceral, that one could not tell at each of its re-entries whether it was a theme or an attack of neuralgia."[9]

Furthermore, the epigraph may be printed within quotation marks, in italics, or in roman type, and the name of the author being epigraphed may be within parentheses, in capital letters, and so forth, with all possible combinations of these variables. I do not think a norm has been established for these matters, at least in France.

The theoretical alternative to the allographic epigraph is obviously the autographic epigraph, one explicitly attributed to the epigrapher himself – that is, roughly speaking, to the author of the book. I know of no perfect illustration of this type of self-attribution, which would be grossly and totally lacking in modesty. The closest thing to it would perhaps be the page from *Fragments d'un "Déluge"* that Giono puts *en exergue* of *Noé*; or the inaccurate, or rough, quotation from chapter 23 of the *Chartreuse* that opens book 2 of this novel.[10] Most often the epigraph by oneself is more modestly disguised, either (as we have seen) as an apocryphal or fictive epigraph (like that of *The Great Gatsby*, attributed to Thomas Parke d'Invilliers, a character in Fitzgerald's earlier *Far Side of Paradise*) or as an anonymous epigraph. In actuality, therefore, the alternative to the allographic epigraph is the anonymous (that is, unattributed) epigraph, a miscellaneous category that lumps together empirical realities as different as the epigraph of the *Maximes* (which we attribute to La Rochefoucauld), the epigraph of *L'Esprit des lois* (which we know is taken from Ovid), the epigraph of a book that would bear *en exergue* a well-known proverb whose author would be unknown to everyone, and God knows what else.

Here, therefore, anonymity covers situations that are in actu-

---

[9] [Pléiade 3:260; tr. Scott Moncrieff and Kilmartin, 3:262.]

[10] I do not put into this category John Barth's two "epigraphs" for *The Friday Book*, which are in fact two statements by Barth on (against) the use of epigraphs, presented as excerpts from the epigraphs of *The Friday Book* itself, that is (we realize), as extracts from themselves; these, therefore, are not only epigraphs written by oneself but also epigraphs that are strictly self-referential and circular, clearly in this author's (very plain) style.

ality very diverse, and thanks to common knowledge or patient scholarship, the name of the epigraphed may be unearthed and assigned. The ordinary reader, when not helped by some editorial note, most often remains in a state of uncertainty as the epigrapher intended, and is left to his conjectures or his indifference. Here am I, for example, confronted with the epigraph of Sollers's *Drame* – "The blood that bathes the heart is thought" (an epigraph whose quotation marks, which are in the original, in all likelihood indicate that it is an allographic quotation) – and incapable on the spur of the moment of identifying its author. This epigraph, Sollers specifies in an interview published in *Le Monde* on August 12, 1984, "is a Heraclitean expression." To be doubly sure, one would need to verify this source, but in any case the attribution appears from then on in the paratext. We are awaiting, by the same or some other route, attributions of the epigraphs of Sollers's *Nombres* ("Seminaque innumero numero summaque profunda") and *Logiques* ("It is from all sides and in all ways that a world in motion wants to be changed").

A last word on the epigraph that is officially anonymous but clearly written by the epigrapher himself, of the type used by La Rochefoucauld – or by Ducasse, at the head of *Poésies*: "I replace melancholy with courage, doubt with certainty..." The fact that the autographic nature of these epigraphs is scarcely concealed (a whimsical signature would have already testified to an effort to simulate) confers on this type of epigraph, it seems to me, a level of personal commitment far beyond that of the ordinary epigraph, to which I will return. These epigraphs that are (almost) openly accepted by authors as their own belong, rather, to authorial discourse, and for this reason I would readily say that their function is that of a succinct preface.

Epigraphers

The second question of attribution is of a wholly different order, but we have already encountered it: it is the question of identifying not the epigraphed, but the epigrapher. Once again, we are dealing with legal responsibility, not actual fact. If an epigraph has been found or chosen for the author by a third party, no one necessarily has to attribute the responsibility for it to that third person. Here the epigrapher is indeed the author of the book, who accepted the suggestion and assumes full responsibility for it, unless he explicitly expresses a reservation of this type (I know of no examples): "My publisher, or my little cousin, proposes this epigraph and I don't dare reject it, but it seems to me to be quite unfitting." Even at that, such a clause would no doubt probably be thought a tolerably ambiguous joke.

Let us not necessarily conclude from this that it is always the author who claims to be the epigrapher, for here, as for the dedication, in the case of a homodiegetic narrative it is advisable to hold out at least the possibility of an epigraph put forward by the narrator-hero. But in contrast to the dedication, here the author does not have the option of ruling out all misunderstanding by signing his epigraph – I mean, by adding his name as epigrapher to the name of the epigraphed author. In the absence of the epigrapher's name, nothing prevents us, for example, from supposing that the epigrapher of the line from Vigny which opens *Sodome et Gomorrhe* ("Woman will have Gomorrah and man will have Sodom") is not Marcel Proust, but the narrator-hero of the *Recherche*.

All of this is, on my part, a hypothesis created purely for the sake of the theory. But depending on the reader, other situations may raise more relevant questions, and I admit that it seems to me more interesting, for example, to attribute the epigraph of *Doctor Faustus* (nine lines from Dante) to the narrator Serenus Zeitblom than to the author Thomas Mann. For Thomas Mann, the double merit of having "in reality" chosen the epigraph and, as it were, offered it to his witness-narrator seems to me quite sufficient. This is one application among others of a more general narratological principle: to attribute (in fiction, of course) to the author only what it is physically impossible to attribute to the narrator – granting that, in reality, everything comes down to the author, for he is also the *author of the narrator*.

I am not, moreover, the first person to ask such questions. Indeed, in the preface in dialogue to *Julie* (an epistolary novel, hence a polyhomodiegetic one), Rousseau himself wondered – or rather, invited the reader to wonder – who the epigrapher was: "Who can know," he asks, "whether I found this epigraph in the manuscript or whether I put it there?" Given the content of those lines of Petrarch I quoted above, the question suggests quite clearly the possibility of attributing the choice of the epigraph to

Saint-Preux [Julie's lover]. The same comment as for *Doctor Faustus*. ·

Epigraphees

Determining the epigrapher more or less determines the epigraphee – the addressee of the epigraph. More or less: when the epigrapher is the author of the book, it goes without saying that for him the epigraphee is the potential reader and, in practice, every real reader. One could, though, imagine cases in which the epigraph would, through some contrivance, be so closely tied to the dedication that it would be obviously, and exclusively, meant for the dedicatee, but I know of no actual case of this sort. If an epigraph were clearly attributed to the narrator, its addressee would equally clearly be the narratee, that is, again, the reader; for the typically literary act of assuming responsibility for choosing and offering an epigraph (as with a dedication, and more generally as with any element of the paratext) would automatically establish the narrator as the author (which does not mean identifying him with the real author but rather making him, like Mérimée's Clara Gazul, an imagined author) – an author inevitably seeking, and expecting, a reader. For example, attributing the epigraph of *Doctor Faustus* to Zeitblom would make him out to be the imagined author of a manuscript intended for publication, a manuscript of which Thomas Mann, like Sainte-Beuve with *Joseph Delorme*, would pretend to be only the editor. In this case of first-degree (extradiegetic) narration, the potential reader himself would be extradiegetic and therefore, once again, offered up for identification with the real reader.[11] Among cases of intradiegetic (second-degree) narration, for our present purpose we must definitely exclude oral narrations, which scarcely lend themselves to epigraphs – but let us suppose that Des Grieux [in Prévost's *Manon Lescaut*] began his narrative with a statement of this kind: *"En exergue* of my story, I propose this epigraph ..."* The addressee would very obviously be his narratee, M. de Renoncour. So that leaves us with written

[11] [The comments in this paragraph on extradiegetic and intradiegetic narratives build on the author's discussion of narrative level in *Narrative Discourse* (Ithaca: Cornell University Press, 1980), 227–31, and *Narrative Discourse Revisited* (Ithaca: Cornell University Press, 1988), 84–85.]

intradiegetic narrations, more specifically, those written in the form and under the name of literary works, such as the unforgettable *Tale of Foolish Curiosity* in *Don Quixote* or *L'Ambitieux par amour* in Balzac's *Albert Savarus*. An epigraph at the head of one of these works-within-a-work would be addressed, again, to a potential reader, but one who is intradiegetic just as the author of each of these second-degree works is, a Spaniard in the Golden Age or a resident of Besançon. The real reader of *Quixote* or *Savarus* could identify with that potential reader only by crossing through the relay screen of the primary narrative, in which a complete literary (fictive) situation is represented with its fictive author, text, and public. In other words, the real reader of *Don Quixote* or *Savarus* could identify with the intradiegetic potential reader only by reading the epigraph in question – as he reads the narrative it would head – *over the shoulder* of the intradiegetic reader. In short, the addressee of the epigraph is always the addressee of the work, who is not always its actual receiver.

Functions

No doubt because I didn't look for more, I see four functions of the epigraph, none of which is explicit; for the use of an epigraph is always a mute gesture whose interpretation is left up to the reader. The first two functions are fairly direct; the other two are more oblique.

The most direct function is certainly not the oldest; all the examples I have collected date from the twentieth century. This function is one of commenting – sometimes authoritatively – and thus of elucidating and thereby justifying not the text but the *title*. For example, the title *Sodome et Gomorrhe* is echoed and (for the most impoverished readers) clarified in the line from Vigny I have already quoted. Clarified not only by the prescribed separation of roles but also, and especially, by the preliminary indication that this volume will not be a historical novel or the tale of a trip along the Dead Sea but rather an evocation of contemporary homosexuality – in other words, by the indication that the title is meant figuratively. This function was much illustrated in the 1960s, when the entries in the *Littré* dictionary (in a pinch the *Robert*, rarely the *Larousse* – not stylish enough) were extensively canvassed for citations that could be used to reinforce certain titles with a meaning that was more precise, or more profound, or more ambiguous: see *Le Parc, Analogues, Fugue* [by Sollers, J.-P. Faye, Laporte], and many others that I forget.

A rarer effect is the reverse one, when the title modifies the meaning of the epigraph. We find a particularly juicy (if I may say so) illustration of this in Sollers's *Intermédiaire*, where a novella bears *en exergue* the celebrated precept of Saint Teresa of Avila, "Do what is within you": the novella is entitled *Introduction aux lieux d'aisance* [*Introduction to the Lavatory*]. Gide had envisaged an effect of this kind for a chapter from *Les Faux-Monnayeurs*, which was to have as its epigraph a phrase attributed to Paul Bourget: "La famille ... cette cellule sociale" ["The Family ... That Social Unit"], which would have been fairly brutally interpreted by the title of the chapter: "Le Régime cellulaire" ["Confinement"].

This use of the epigraph as a justificatory appendage of the title is almost a must when the title itself consists of a borrowing, an allusion, or a parodic distortion (as was obviously the case for *Sodome et Gomorrhe*). For example, *Le Voleur d'étincelles* of Brasillach bears *en exergue* the line from Tristan Corbière from which the book takes its title; *For Whom the Bell Tolls*, its quotation from Donne; Queneau's *Dimanche de la vie*, from Hegel; Sagan's *Merveilleux Nuages*, from Baudelaire; Sagan's *Bonjour tristesse*, from Eluard; and so forth. Some do without: *The Sound and the Fury*, *Tender Is the Night*, or *The Power and the Glory*; and these abstentions almost seem like elegant ellipses. The best example, perhaps, is O'Hara's *Appointment in Samarra*, which explains its title by quoting a page – a splendid page – from Somerset Maugham.

The second possible function of the epigraph is undoubtedly the most canonical: it consists of commenting on the *text*, whose meaning it indirectly specifies or emphasizes. This commentary may be very clear, as with the autographic epigraph of the *Maximes* or the quotation from Pindar's *Pythian Odes* that opens Valéry's *Cimitière marin* ("My soul, do not seek immortal life, but exhaust the realm of the possible"); as with the epigraph of Sartre's *Nausée*, taken from Céline ("This is a boy with no collective importance, he is simply an individual"); or the epigraph of Des Forêts's *Bavard* [*The Chatterbox*], attributed to

Rivarol ("He has a raging itch to talk, he suffocates, he croaks if he isn't talking"). More often the commentary is puzzling, has a significance that will not be clear or confirmed until the whole book is read. This is obviously the case of the two epigraphs of Claudel's *Soulier de satin*: "Deus escreve direito por linhas tortas" ["God writes straight, through twisted lines"] and "Etiam peccata" ["Even the sins"]. The attribution of relevance in such cases depends on the reader, whose hermeneutic capacity is often put to the test – as it has been from the very beginnings of the novelistic epigraph, with Scott, Nodier, Hugo, and Stendhal, who seem to have cultivated the appeal of epigraphs that are definitively puzzling or, as Hugo said, "strange and mysterious." "The function of the exergue," writes Michel Charles, "is easily to give food for thought, without one's knowing what the thought is."[12] Less bluntly, in a marginal note to *Armance* but with the *Rouge* in mind, Stendhal wrote, "The epigraph must heighten the reader's feeling, his emotion, if emotion there be, and not present a more or less philosophical opinion about the situation."[13] This evasive function, more affective than intellectual and sometimes more ornamental than affective, may indeed be assigned to most epigraphs of the type that, to save time, we will call romantic. This is also, to my mind, the function of the epigraph of *Drame*, quoted above on page 153. The semantic relevance of epigraphs is often, as it were, random; and without the least ill will, one can suspect some authors of positioning some epigraphs hit-and-miss, of believing – rightly – that every joining creates meaning and that even the absence of meaning is an impression of meaning, often the most stimulating or most rewarding: to think without knowing what you are thinking – is that not one of the purest pleasures of the mind?

The third function, I said, is more oblique. By that I mean, of course, that its basic message is not the message presented as basic. If I say to you, "Last night at dinner, So-and-So seemed to me in top form," and if So-and-So is someone famous whose company is considered flattering, it is certainly clear that here the

[12] Michel Charles, *L'Arbre et la source* (Seuil, 1985), 185.
[13] Stendhal, *Œuvres intimes* (Pléiade), 2:129. On Stendhal's use of the epigraph, cf. M. Abrioux, "Intertitres et épigraphes chez Stendhal" (*Poétique* 69 [February 1987]).

main information conveyed is not his apparent good health but indeed the fact that I dined with him. Likewise in an epigraph, very often the main thing is not what it says but who its author is, plus the sense of indirect backing that its presence at the edge of a text gives rise to – a backing that, in general, is less costly than the backing of a preface and even of a dedication, for one can obtain it without seeking permission.[14] Consequently, with a great many epigraphs the important thing is simply the name of the author quoted. When John Fowles puts *en exergue* of *The French Lieutenant's Woman* this sentence of exemplary insignificance, "Every emancipation is a restoration of the human world and of human relationships to man himself," let us understand that the value of such a quotation lies simply in the name of its author, Karl Marx, which functions here a little like a dedication in memoriam. Blanchot's book *L'Amitié* is not dedicated to Georges Bataille but opens with a sentence from Bataille, the function of which is analogous. So one could draw up some interesting statistics, individual or historical, this time not on the content of epigraphs but on the identity of their authors.[15] The romantic period took many epigraphs from Scott, Byron, and especially Shakespeare, and Nodier put a passage from Shakespeare (who probably holds the world's record for number of times quoted in epigraphs) at the head of each part of *Smarra*. Closer to our own time, Hemingway dips into the preface to *Joseph Andrews* for the epigraphs of all four parts of *The Torrents of Spring*. Such gestures are obviously deliberate, and I have recollections of a time when a young writer would have thought it beneath him not to take his epigraphs from Mallarmé (preferably *Crise de vers*), Lautréamont (preferably *Poésies*), Hölderlin, Joyce, Blanchot, Bataille, Artaud,

---

[14] However, there exists at least one well-known case of a protest that led to a deletion. Gide's *Caves du Vatican* had begun appearing in *La Nouvelle Revue française* with an epigraph taken – with Claudel's permission – from *L'Annonce faite à Marie*: "What King are you speaking of and what Pope? For there are two and we don't know which is the good one." As publication continued, Claudel showed growing embarrassment at seeing himself associated with such a work, and when one passage, confirmed by an epistolary confidence, revealed to him Gide's homosexuality, he insisted on deletion of the epigraph upon book publication.

[15] On a more technical ground, at the head of Robbe-Grillet's *Les Gommes* we note an epigraph whose content ("Time that sees all has found you out against your will") matters less than its author: Sophocles. [The novel *Les Gommes* has been called a modern retelling of the Oedipus story.] Thus the epigraph, just like a title, may bear the genre contract (here, the contract of hypertextuality).

Lacan (preferably anywhere), even piling up five or six (to be on the safe side) at the head of the same chapter. The fashion for that has now passed, what was very stylish yesterday is today very boorish, but the wheel turns, and what today is good-for-nothing will surely melt our hearts tomorrow or the day after. Don't throw out your old epigraphs: they could be useful to your grandchildren, if they still know how to read.

The most powerful oblique effect of the epigraph is perhaps due simply to its presence, whatever the epigraph itself may be: this is the epigraph-effect. The presence or absence of an epigraph in itself marks (with a very thin margin of error) the period, the genre, or the tenor of a piece of writing. I have already mentioned the relative restraint, in this regard, of the classical and realistic periods. In contrast, the romantic period, especially in prose fiction, is distinguished by a great consumption (I do not say "production") of epigraphs, undoubtedly equaled only by the short avant-garde phase with intellectual pretensions, and vice versa, from which we are only now emerging. People have rightly seen the epigraphic excess of the early nineteenth century as a desire to integrate the novel, particularly the historical or "philosophical" novel, into a cultural tradition. The young writers of the 1960s and 1970s used the same means to give themselves the consecration and unction of a(nother) prestigious filiation. The epigraph in itself is a signal (intended as a *sign*) of culture, a password of intellectuality. While the author awaits hypothetical newspaper reviews, literary prizes, and other official recognitions, the epigraph is already, a bit, his consecration. With it, he chooses his peers and thus his place in the pantheon.

8

❖❖❖❖❖❖❖❖❖❖❖❖❖❖❖❖❖❖❖❖❖❖❖❖❖❖❖❖❖❖❖❖❖❖❖❖❖❖

The prefatorial situation of communication

❖❖❖❖❖❖❖❖❖❖❖❖❖❖❖❖❖❖❖❖❖❖❖❖❖❖❖❖❖❖❖❖❖❖❖❖❖❖

Definition

Here, generalizing from the term most commonly employed in French, I will use the word *preface* to designate every type of introductory (preludial or postludial) text, authorial or allographic, consisting of a discourse produced on the subject of the text that follows or precedes it. The "postface" will therefore be considered a variety of preface; its specific features – which are indisputable – seem to me less important than the features it shares with the general type.

I said the term most commonly employed in French: the list of that term's French parasynonyms is very long, reflecting changing fashions and innovations, as this haphazard and not at all exhaustive sample may suggest: *introduction, avant-propos, prologue, note, notice, avis, présentation, examen, préambule, avertissement, prélude, discours préliminaire, exorde, avant-dire, proème* – and for the postface, *après-propos, après-dire, postscriptum,* and others. Naturally, many nuances distinguish one term from another, especially when two or more of these texts appear together, as in the didactic type of work, where the preface takes on a function simultaneously more formal and more circumstantial, preceding an introduction that is tied more closely to the subject of the text. This is a distinction Jacques Derrida makes very well apropos of the Hegelian paratext:

The *preface* must be distinguished from the *introduction.* They do not have the same function, nor even the same dignity, in Hegel's eyes, even though the problem they raise in their relation to the philosophical corpus of exposition is analogous. The Introduction (*Einleitung*) has a more systematic, less historical, less circumstantial link with the logic of the book. It is *unique*; it deals with general and essential architectonic problems; it presents the general concept in its division and in its self-

161

differentiation. The Prefaces, on the other hand, are multiplied from edition to edition and take into account a more empirical historicity; they obey an occasional necessity ...[1]

But didactic texts are not the only works that may contain several introductory discourses: a preface and a postface, or two prefaces that differ in their enunciating status – one allographic and the other authorial (as with Proust's *Les Plaisirs et les jours*) or one authorial and the other attributed to a narrator-character (as with Lesage's *Gil Blas*). I will, of course, come back to this.

Aside from such cases of co-presence, the nuances are for the most part connotative: *exorde, avant-dire,* and *proème* are more mannered, pedantic, or affected; *introduction, note,* and *notice* more modest – their modesty either sincere or feigned, depending on the case. But an introductory text does not even have to be labeled. What we refer to for the sake of convenience as the "preface" to La Bruyère's *Caractères* contains no mark other than a repetition of the title, and many a modern preface is distinguished as such only by the use of roman numerals for page numbers (a practice that first appeared in the mid-eighteenth century and that, in France, is still used with the critical paratext of some scholarly editions) and/or by recourse to italics (in France today, this is more common): see Blanchot's *Espace littéraire* or Barthes's *Degré zéro de l'écriture*.[2] One may also give a preface a title, not a generic one like all the designations I have mentioned so far, but a thematic one: the (preludial) introductory text of Blanchot's *Faux pas* is entitled "From Anguish to Language" and the (postludial) introductory text of his *Part du feu* is entitled "Literature and the Right to Die"; the paratextual function of these sections is indicated, or rather suggested, only by the italics, without which they would seem ordinary chapters. To finish up with these questions of definition and terminology, I call to mind that many extended dedications, like that of *Les Plaisirs et les jours* referred to just above, may play the role of a

---

[1] Jacques Derrida, *La Dissémination* (Seuil, 1972), 23 [tr. *Dissemination*, trans. Barbara Johnson (University of Chicago Press, 1981), 17]. Cf. J.-M. Schaeffer, "Note sur la préface philosophique," *Poétique* 69 (February 1987).

[2] This statement applies to *Le Degré zéro* in the original edition of 1953 and in the 1972 republication in the Points series, although there the running head is "Introduction." In the Médiations edition of 1965, this introductory text is in fact entitled "Introduction." Here as elsewhere, status may vary from one edition to another.

preface – later we will consider some of these dedications in this light – and that the recent promotion of the please-insert often allows it to serve as a preface.

Prehistory

In contrast to the title and the name of the author, both of which are virtually essential nowadays, a preface is obviously never obligatory, and the observations that follow are not meant to eclipse the countless cases in which a preface is absent – countless because we lack statistics that would, perhaps profitably, clarify for us the distribution of this custom according to period, genre, author, and national tradition. Thus I lack the means, as well as the desire, to sketch here a history of the preface. Besides, and not to make a virtue of necessity, my readings give me the impression that such a history would not be very meaningful: after a (very long) period of prehistory that I will speak of briefly, most of the themes and techniques of the preface are in place as of the mid-sixteenth century, and the subsequent variations do not reflect a true evolution but rather a set of varying choices within a repertory that is much more stable than one would believe *a priori*, and in particular much more stable than authors themselves believe – for often they resort, unwittingly, to well-tested formulae.

By "prehistory" I mean here the whole period that, for us, extends (let us say) from Homer to Rabelais, a period when for obvious material reasons the prefatorial function is taken on by the opening lines or pages of the text. What holds true for all the other paratextual elements holds true for the preface as well: its separation from the text by the presentational means familiar to us today (some of which I have already mentioned) is tied to the existence of the book, that is, the printed text. Here again the manuscript era is characterized by an easily comprehensible economy of means. But we cannot say of the preface, as we can of other elements such as the title or the name of the author, that this poverty of presentation (setting aside illustrations) entirely stifled its use; what we can say, and more accurately, is that the poverty of presentation concealed its use by depriving it of the means of drawing attention to itself with an appearance *en exergue*. Thus the beginnings (and possibly the endings) of texts are where one must seek these statements in which the author presents, and sometimes comments on, his work.

This use of the incorporated preface is illustrated by, for example, the opening lines of the *Iliad* and the *Odyssey*: the invocation of the muse, announcement of the subject (the wrath of Achilles; the wanderings of Odysseus), and establishment of the narrative starting point (for the *Iliad*, the quarrel between Achilles and Agamemnon; for the *Odyssey*, this phrase, perhaps indicative of a structure that, as we know, is more complex: "From some point [*amothèn*] here, goddess, daughter of Zeus, speak [of these adventures]"). This latter stance, of course, becomes the norm for the epic opening; and we know the first line of the *Aeneid*, monumental in its restraint: "Arma virumque cano, Trojae qui primus ab oris" ["I sing of warfare and a man at war / From the seacoast of Troy in early days"] – a line that, as I called to mind in an earlier chapter, had perhaps originally been preceded by a sort of list, also incorporated into the text, of other works "by the same author." Again in the sixteenth century, the opening stanzas of *Orlando Furioso* and *Jerusalem Delivered* contain such statements of the subject, paired (as we have seen) with justifications for the dedication.

Oral transmission by rhapsodists also certainly included these kinds of preambles and, perhaps, other presentational elements that have not come down to us. Classical Greek rhetoric had its own preamble, customarily called *exorde* [exordium], which included, among other commonplaces, some that were characteristically prefatorial: the difficulty of the subject, the statement of purpose, and the approach the speaker will take. In the *Antidosis* of Isocrates, a fictive speech for the defense, the exordium itself is preceded by a veritable foreword to the speaker-reader describing the nature of this text, a foreword the speaker undoubtedly was not meant to include in his public reading of the speech: here we see a difference in register that anticipates our thresholds of written presentation.

The opening pages of the *Histories* of Herodotus, traditionally called "proem," certainly constitute a preface, with a statement of purpose and method which begins, contrary to the custom for epics, with the name of the author and a sort of announcement of the title: "What Herodotus the Halicarnassian has learnt by inquiry is here set forth: in order that so the memory of the past may not be blotted out from among men by time, and that great and marvellous deeds done by Greeks and foreigners and especially the reason why they warred against each other may not lack renown." Thucydides provides the same kind of thing at the head of the celebrated "introduction" composed of the first twenty-two chapters of his *Peloponnesian War*: "I, Thucydides, an Athenian, wrote the history of the war waged by the Peloponnesians and the Athenians against one another...." Then comes a justification of the work based on the importance of its subject, and a statement of method. Livy will extend that custom – to which tradition gives the name *praefatio* (obviously the origin of our term) – to the openings of several of the books of his *Roman History*; in all these passages he comments on his work in the first person, already taking a stance that would become characteristic of the modern preface.

Perhaps it is to imitate these incipits of histories, even down to the statement of identity, that the first known romance-writer, Chariton, begins his *Chaereas and Callirhoe* like this: "My name is Chariton of Aphrodisias, secretary to Athenagoras the lawyer, and my story is all about a love affair that started in Syracuse." The other ancient romances seem in general more chary of preambles: the narratives of *The Aethiopica* by Heliodorus, *Leucippe and Cleitophon* by Achilles Tatius, and *The Life of Apollonius* by Philostratus begin *ex abrupto*. But the first paragraph of Lucian's *True History* constitutes a kind of polemical preface, accusing all previous travel narratives (beginning with Odysseus's tale to the Phaeacians) of lying, and taking ambiguous credit for being open about its own fabricating. The first paragraph of the *Golden Ass* of Apuleius contains a kind of genre identification (a "Milesian Tale") and ends with a very explicit – and rather good-natured – demarcation between the preface and the narrative: "We begin...." The opening passage of Longus's *Daphnis and Chloe* justifies what will follow by mentioning the author's desire to compete with a certain painting that depicts a love scene.

The status of the preface (if any) in dramatic works is constitutively very different, for nowadays what we consider a preface is a text that is not meant for performance and appears only at the head of a published edition, most often (at least in the classical period) after the work has already been staged in the theatre.[3] Ancient and medieval drama therefore are wholly unacquainted with anything like a preface. The term *prologue*, which in ancient drama designates everything that, in the play itself, precedes the entrance of the chorus, must not mislead us: its function is not to make a presentation, and still less to comment, but to provide an exposition in the dramatic sense of the word – most often (for example, in Aeschylus and Sophocles) in the form of a scene in dialogue, but sometimes (in Euripides) in the form of a character's monologue. Apparently only comedy can endow this monologue with the function of warning the public, in a slick and possibly polemical or satirical comment about fellow playwrights, so that here the monologue must be regarded as a true theatrical paratext, necessarily anticipating one of the most artful forms of the modern preface: the actor's preface, delivered by someone we assume is outside the action of the play but who then turns out to be one of the characters. Examples are the monologue of Xanthias at the head (or almost) of Aristophanes' *The Wasps*, and many of Plautus's and Terence's theoretical-polemical prologues. What has come down to us of the prologue of Plautus's *Pseudolus* gives the name of the author; the prologue of his *Asinaria* gives that play's title, sources, and genre status; the prologue of his *Amphitryon* is the best-known one because in it Mercury defines this play as – a major innovation – a "tragi-comedy"; the prologue of Terence's *Phormio* counters criticisms made by a rival; and the prologue of his *Heauton Timorumenos* reacts to the charge of "contamination" (mixing the plots of two earlier plays to produce a third and more complex one) by invoking the example of others. In the last two of these cases, the prologue ends with a plea for calm and for the public's attention, which certainly shows, if there was any need to, that the play itself begins here.

This partly paratextual function of the prologue scarcely survives classical antiquity except sporadically and often playfully. Shakespeare presents only traces of it in *Romeo and Juliet* and *2 Henry IV*; of the various types of prelude used in Spanish drama (the *entremes*, the *introito*, the *paso*, the *loa*), only the *paso* seems to

[3] As an exception and somewhat playfully, Francis Huster's production of *Le Cid* (November 1985) has a Corneille in modern dress take the stage to read his preface.

have fulfilled a function comparable to that of Plautus's prologues.[4] The practice of publishing plays will very quickly offer
authors an opportunity that is less ... dramatic, but perhaps more
effective, of settling scores with critics or members of a cabal, but
at that point we will already be in the thick of the modern phase
of the preface. To my (quite incomplete) knowledge, the two
most characteristic survivals from the early phase are the first
prologue of Goethe's *Faust*, "Prologue on the theatre," a wholly
businesslike discussion among the manager, the Poet-Playwright,
and the Player of Comic Roles about what can appropriately be
staged today (the second prologue, "Prologue in Heaven," with
the Lord and Mephistopheles laying bets on Faust's fate, already
belongs to the action), and the monologue of the Announcer of
Claudel's *Soulier de satin*, who, as we have seen, gives the
complete title of the play and ends with this delectable parody of
the ancients' appeals to the public: "Listen well, do not cough,
please, and try to understand a bit. It's what you won't understand that is the finest; it's what is longest that is the most
interesting, and it's what you won't find amusing that is fun-
niest." This, perhaps, is true not only in the theatre. But let us
return to our prehistory or, as Thucydides would say, our
archeology of the preface.

Medieval epic and romance seem to use indiscriminately the
incorporated prologue and the opening *ex abrupto* – more abrupt
than the opening of the ancient epic, which always included at
least an invocation of the muse and a statement of the subject. *La
Chanson de Roland* dives in headfirst: "Carlon the King, our
Emperor Charlemayn, / Full seven years long has been abroad in
Spain ...," but conversely *La Prise d'Orange* [a *chanson de geste* of
the cycle of William of Orange] opens with a prologue whose
regime is typical of oral texts:[5]

Listen, lords, so that God, the glorious one, son of the holy Mary, may

---

[4] On the Spanish prologues, see A. Porqueras Mayo, *El prólogo como género
   literario. Su estudio en el siglo de oro* (Madrid, 1957); see also the same author's
   later works: *El prólogo en el Renacimiento español* (Madrid, 1965), *El prólogo en el
   manierismo y el barroco españoles* (Madrid, 1968), and *Ensayo bibliográfico del
   prólogo en la literatura* (Madrid, 1971).
[5] The Régnier edition (Klincksieck, 1983), as a matter of fact, gives us a choice of
   two prologues, the second of which is more subdued but just as typical of oral
   texts: "Listen, my lords, noble honored knights!"

bless you, listen to the exemplary tale I will now tell you. It is not about a preposterous or senseless action, it is not based on sources that lie, nor is it undertaken from a taste for lying; but it treats of brave knights who conquered Spain ...

The second *laisse*[6] begins in a strongly contrasting narrative style: "It was in May, with the advent of fine weather ..." Chrétien de Troyes is equally eclectic: the narratives of *Erec et Enide* and *Yvain* are taken up *ex abrupto*, but *Cligès* opens with the prologue whose list of works by the same author I have already quoted – a prologue that also contains a reference to its source which is characteristic of the way medieval romance-writers vouched for the authority of their work: "This story that I wish to relate to you we find written down in one of the books in my lord St Peter's Library in Beauvais; the tale from which Chrétien fashions this romance was taken from there. The book containing the true story is very old, therefore it is all the more worthy of belief."[7] In *Lancelot* Chrétien begins by invoking a commission from "my lady of Champagne," an invocation that obviously is equivalent both to a dedication and to an acknowledgment of his debt regarding the subject: "Chrétien begins his book about the Knight of the Cart; the subject matter and meaning are furnished and given him by the countess." We find the same type of effect at the head of *Perceval*, commissioned by Philip of Flanders: "Therefore Chrétien ... aims and strives by command of the count to put into rhyme the greatest story that has ever been told in royal court: it is the Story of the Grail, the book of which was given to him by the count. Hear now how he acquits himself." We know how this choice between the two types of incipit is handled a

---

6 [The type of stanza used in *chansons de geste*.]
7 On these prologues of medieval romances, see P.-Y. Badel, "Rhétorique et polémique dans les romans du moyen âge," *Littérature* 20 (December 1975). The author addresses himself especially to "the modernists with whom one would like to resolve the question of whether [these prologues] resurfaced in the long term or whether, when, and in what conditions there has been, in this area, a rupture." If a mere generalist may offer a response, mine (which is already known – and the reason for it will gradually become more obvious) inclines toward the first hypothesis. The only ruptures, here, between the medieval (and ancient) archaeopreface and modern prefaces result from the change in regime (from the oral and the handcopied to the printed book) and from the change in the stance the poet adopts vis-à-vis his text: the modern novelist no longer takes cover, as did Chrétien and so many others (even Cervantes, perhaps in satirical imitation), behind a preexisting "tale" that he claims merely to have "put into verse." But the functions of the ancient and medieval prologue are, indeed, already typically prefatorial.

century and a half later, in the most illustrious narrative (I dare not say novel) of the Middle Ages: "Nel mezzo del camin ..." ["Midway upon the journey ..."]. I will not tug that *mezzo* toward the *in medias res* of the ancient epic, for it is truly the beginning of the story, but there we have at least a narrative without a prologue, even if the absence of a prologue may be due to the fact that the work was not entirely finished. As for the *Decameron*, it contains a kind of general preface in which the author lays out the personal motives for his undertaking (his memory of an amorous adventure) and for his choice of a female reading public – two themes destined to have an enormous number of descendants. The introduction to the first day confirms the orientation toward "the charming ladies" in accordance with an age-old apportionment: to men goes the heroic, to women the romantic.

Medieval historians, too, seem to waver between the incorporated prologue and the abrupt beginning, unless we ought to find a significant evolution here: Villehardouin abstains, Robert de Clari says a word about his subject, Joinville begins with a dedication to Louis X and an announcement of his plan, Froissart gives his name and justifies his undertaking the way Herodotus did ("In order that the honourable enterprises, noble adventures and deeds of arms which took place during the wars waged by France and England ..."), and Commynes dedicates his memoirs of Louis XI to the archbishop of Vienna, who had commissioned them from him.

It seems to me appropriate to conclude this survey with the texts that – already squarely in the age of the printed book – proclaim in the most striking and representative manner the advent of the modern preface: Rabelais's prologues.[8] The one to *Pantagruel* is hardly more than a kind of pledge to renew the *Grandes Chroniques*, offering us "another book of the same caliber, were it not that it is a little more objective and trustworthy." *Gargantua*'s prologue is much more ambitious, albeit ambiguous (and I will come back to this): as everyone knows, it is the

---

[8] Here I am not claiming that these "prologues" are chronologically the first separate prefaces in the history of the book, for I do not know exactly when a separate preface first appeared. The inaugural value of Rabelais's prologues is obviously symbolic.

semifarcical invitation to an interpretive reading "in a higher sense." After this dazzling move, the next one will be harder to pull off, for that invitation would have to be indefinitely renewed. Rabelais manages it with a brilliance that in the future will likewise be much imitated, if not equaled: at the head of the *Tiers livre* there is a kind of yarn that is somewhat evasive about the work's theme. The yarn: at the siege of Corinth, where everyone was thrashing about, Diogenes, so as not to be outdone, rolled his earthenware barrel in all directions; and that is what I am doing here, during the present war, instead of fighting (this is already the argument of the paradoxical usefulness of the useless work). For the *Quart livre*, a prologue "To Readers of Good Will" pushes the impertinence much further. A long amplification of the old fable of the woodsman's three hatchets is followed by this *simplissime* transition: and now, "cough one good cough, drink three drinks, give your ears a cheery shake, and you shall hear wonders ..." In other words: a preface is necessary, but I no longer have any prefatory message to give you, so here is a story without any connection to what will follow. Without any connection? I imagine that innumerable exegetes who are more ingenious than I (this is no longer Rabelais speaking) have found connections equally innumerable and ingenious, but I much prefer to read this as the first example of a functional type we will encounter again: the elusive preface.

Form

Incorporated prefaces of the pre-Gutenberg era, which are in fact sections of text with a prefatorial function, precisely because they are incorporated raise no problem with respect to location (necessarily, the opening – or sometimes the closing[9] – lines of the text), or date of appearance (date of the text's first "publication"), or formal status (the text's own), or establishment of the sender (the author – real or imagined – of the text) and the addressee (again, obviously, the addressee of the text, except for sections used as invocations or dedications, where a relay-addressee – the muse, the dedicatee – may momentarily come

---

[9] Like the famous *explicit* of *Roland*: "Ci falt la geste que Turoldus declinet" ["Here ends the geste Turoldus would recite"], a paratext as typical as it is puzzling.

between author and reader). But as soon as the preface becomes free to attain a relatively autonomous textual status, these questions begin to arise, and we must consider them more or less briefly before addressing the main issue, which, here as elsewhere, is that of function.

The most common formal (and modal) status of the preface is, clearly, that of a discourse in prose, which in its discursive features may contrast with the narrative or dramatic mode of the text (examples are the prologue of *Gargantua* and the preface to Racine's *Britannicus*),[10] and in its prose form may contrast with the poetic form of the text (the preface to Hugo's *Feuilles d'automne*). But there are exceptions. Some prefaces take the dramatic form of a dialogue (Diderot's *Entretiens sur le fils naturel*, Rousseau's second preface to *La Nouvelle Héloïse*) or, indeed, of a short play (see the "Comedy about a Tragedy" at the head of the second edition of Hugo's *Dernier Jour d'un condamné*). Others may, in whole or in part, adopt the narrative mode – for example in order to account, truthfully or not, for the circumstances in which the work was written (prefaces by Scott, Chateaubriand, James, Aragon) or the circumstances in which the text was discovered, when it is attributed to a fictive author (*Gulliver's Travels*, Constant's *Adolphe*, Eco's *Name of the Rose*); indeed, it is rare for a preface not to contain such narrative germs here and there. If the text itself is discursive in type, the preface may even contain the only narrative elements of the book: see Chateaubriand's prefaces to his *Essai sur les révolutions* and *Génie du christianisme*. Finally, nothing prevents an author from endowing the introductory poem of a collection with a prefatorial function, as Hugo often does: "Prélude" (following the preface in prose) of *Les Chants du crépuscule*, "Fonction du poète" at the head of *Les Rayons et les ombres*, "Nox" and "Lux" at the beginning and end of *Les Châtiments*, "Vision d'où est sorti ce livre" ["The Vision That Led to This Book"] at the head of *La Légende des siècles*, and others. This is also the status of the "Au lecteur" ["To the Reader"] of *Les Fleurs du mal*. Huysmans's

---

[10] On the strictly linguistic aspects of this discursivity, see H. Mitterand, "La Préface et ses lois: Avant-propos romantiques" (1975), in *Le Discours du roman* (PUF, 1980). This study, based on Benveniste's categories, examines three nineteenth-century prefaces: Bignan's for *L'Echafaud*, Balzac's for *La Comédie humaine*, and Zola's for *Thérèse Raquin*.

Drageoir aux épices, a collection of prose pieces, is even provided with an "introductory sonnet" that has a typically prefatorial function,[11] which reverses the customary contrast – and this case is not unique: we find a sort of preface in verse at the head of *Treasure Island*.

Place

The choice between the two locations, preludial or postludial, is obviously not neutral, but we will take up the significance of this choice under the heading of functions. At the moment, let us note only that many an author considers the terminal location more tactful and modest. Balzac describes the final note of the 1830 edition of *Scènes de la vie privée* as an "immodest note but in a humble place." Walter Scott, entitling the last chapter of *Waverley* "A Postscript, Which Should Have Been a Preface," plays on this effect of place a little more ambiguously: like a driver who asks for a tip (he says, roughly speaking), I ask here for one last minute of attention; but (he adds) people rarely read prefaces and often begin a book at the end; as a result, for those readers this postscript will serve as a preface. Besides, many works (an example is Klossowski's *Lois de l'hospitalité*) include both a preface and a postscript. And huge works of a didactic kind, like *Le Génie du christianisme* or Montesquieu's *Esprit des lois*, frequently contain a preface at the head of each major section ("The Idea of This Book," "The Subject of This Book"). But so, too, does a work of fiction like *Tom Jones*, each "book" of which opens with an essay-chapter whose function is, in one way or another, prefatorial. These are all, so to speak, internal prefaces, warranted by the magnitude and subdivisions of the text. More gratuitously and playfully, Sterne inserts a preface between chapters 20 and 21 of volume 3 of *Tristram Shandy*; and early in *A Sentimental Journey* there appears a "Preface [Written] in the Desobligeant" (a chaise that holds only one person). More indirectly, one may also give a metatextual status to any section of the text, as Blanchot does when, in an introductory note to *L'Espace littéraire*, he designates the chapter

[11] This was only rarely the case with the introductory poems for novels in the classical period; those poems were on the whole dedicatory, formal, or ornamental.

"Le Regard d'Orphée" as the "center" of that work. Another way an author can give a metatextual status to a section of text is by using the title of one of the parts (whether the initial part or not) for the title of the whole – thus indirectly putting the particular part *en exergue* (see, also by Blanchot, *Le Livre à venir*).

"Location" means the possibility, over time and particularly from one edition to another, of a change in location, which sometimes involves a change in status. A preface, authorial or allographic, may become after the event a chapter in a collection of essays: see Valéry's prefaces in *Variété*, Gide's in *Incidences*, Sartre's in *Situations*, and Barthes's in *Essais critiques*; indeed, after the event a preface may become a chapter in a collection of prefaces, either all autographic, such as James's in *The Art of the Novel* (posthumous collection of 1934), or all allographic, such as Borges's in his *Prólogos* of 1975. In all these cases, the preface comes to have two sites, the original and the one in the collection; the original site, however, may be abandoned in a later edition. For example, the 1968 reprinting of Frantz Fanon's *Damnés de la terre* deletes Sartre's 1961 preface because a disagreement had arisen between the preface-writer and the author's widow – but in the meantime, the ex-preface had found an early place of refuge in *Situations V*. Conversely, an originally autonomous essay may subsequently be adopted as a preface: an article by Gilles Deleuze on Michel Tournier's novel *Vendredi* was first published in a magazine (1967) and then reprinted in Deleuze's *Logique du sens* (1969) before becoming in 1972 the postface to the pocket edition of the novel. Montesquieu's *Défense de "L'Esprit des lois"* and Chateaubriand's defense of *Le Génie du christianisme*, both published separately, become kinds of later postfaces at the earliest opportunity. The same thing for Rousseau and Tolstoy, both of whom were prevented, for various reasons, from publishing at the head of the first editions of *Julie* and *War and Peace*, respectively, the "Préface de *Julie* ou Entretien sur les romans" and "Some Words about *War and Peace*";[12] each has since caught up with the official peritext of its work. Finally, some prefaces are copious enough to constitute an autonomous volume, either right from the beginning (Sartre's *Saint Genet*, 1952, presented as the first volume of the complete works of Genet) or at a later time

[12] The "Préface de *Julie*" was published separately in 1761 by Rey; "Some Words ..." was published in 1868 in the journal *Russian Archive*.

(Sartre again, whose "Introduction" to the *Ecrits intimes* of Baudelaire became, a year afterward, a book that was itself provided with a preface, by Leiris).[13] Other types of transformations have probably escaped my notice.

Time

It is a commonplace to note that prefaces, as well as postfaces, are generally written after the texts they deal with (perhaps exceptions to this sensible norm exist, but I know of none that has been formally attested to); that's not what we're talking about, however, for the prefatorial function is directed at the reader, and accordingly the relevant time is the time of publication. After the date of the first edition and throughout the indeterminate length of the ensuing eternity, the time of a preface's appearance may occupy any of an infinity of moments, but this indefiniteness seems to me, in effect (as I indicated in Chapter 1), to focus on certain typical and functionally significant temporal positions. The most common case, no doubt, is that of the *original* preface – for example, the authorial preface of Balzac's *Peau de chagrin*, August 1831. The second typical time is that of what I will call, for lack of a better term, the *later* preface. Its canonical occasion is the second edition, which may come on the heels of the original edition but which often presents a very specific pragmatic opportunity (I will return to this): examples are the preface to the second edition (April 1868) of Zola's *Thérèse Raquin* (original edition: December 1867) and the preface to the regular first edition (November 1902) of Gide's *Immoraliste* (limited edition: May 1902). Or the occasion may be a translation – for example, the preface to the French edition (1948) of *Under the Volcano* [*Au-dessous du volcan*] (1947), or the preface to the 1982 American edition of Kundera's *The Joke* (1967). But some original editions may be published later than the first public appearance of a text: this is the case with plays performed before they are printed; with novels published first in serial form (in a newspaper or magazine); with collections of essays, poems, or stories, whose components first appeared in periodicals. In all these cases the original

---

[13] The Baudelaire volume with Sartre's preface appeared in the Incidences series, Point du jour edition, 1946. Sartre's preface was published separately as a book by Gallimard in 1947.

edition may, paradoxically, be the occasion for a typically later preface.

The third relevant moment is that of the *delayed* preface, which may be for the delayed republication of a single work (Montesquieu's *Lettres persanes* in 1754, Gide's *Nourritures terrestres* in 1927, Green's *Adrienne Mesurat* in 1973) or for the delayed original edition of a work that long remained unpublished (Chateaubriand's *Natchez* in 1826) or for the delayed completion of a work written over a long period and published at intervals (Michelet's *Histoire de France* in 1869) or finally – this is perhaps the most common situation, and undoubtedly the most typical – for a delayed collection of complete or selected works: see the "examinations" in the 1660 edition of Corneille's plays, Chateaubriand's prefaces for the Ladvocat edition (from 1826 to 1832) of his "complete" works, Scott's prefaces (from 1829 to 1832) for his novels, Nodier's prefaces for the Renduel edition (1832–37), Balzac's for *La Comédie humaine* in 1842, James's for the New York Edition (1907–9), and Aragon's for his novelistic works (1964–74) and for the beginning of his poetic œuvre (1974–81).

In contrast to later prefaces, which belong to a period as soon after the original edition as possible, delayed prefaces are generally the place for a more "mellow" consideration, which often has some testamentary or, as Musil said, *pre-posthumous* accent: one last "examination" of his own work by an author who will perhaps have no further chance to return to it. The pre-posthumous is obviously an anticipation of the posthumous, a way to confront posterity. Scott says, rather amusingly, that his collected novelistic works should have been posthumous but that circumstances (legal and financial) did not allow them to be. We know, too, that Chateaubriand wanted the *Mémoires d'outre-tombe* [*Memoirs from beyond the Grave*] to be posthumous, and one version of the preface to that work is rightly called "testamentary." Thus some delayed prefaces illustrate a variety we call the *posthumous* preface – posthumous as to its publication, needless to say: for the paratext as for the text itself, this is the standard meaning of that adjective, short of a resort to séances. But in contrast to the text, a preface – if it is allographic – may be a posthumous *production*, a case we will meet again. At the moment, let us bear in mind only this: the allographic preface, too, may be original (Anatole France for Proust's *Les Plaisirs et les jours*), later (Malraux for *Sanctuary*), or delayed anthumous (Larbaud for Dujardin's *Lauriers sont coupés*); in addition it is unique in that it can be produced posthumously, whether near in time (Flaubert for the *Dernières Chansons* of Louis Bouilhet) or remote (Valéry for the *Lettres persanes*) or better – I mean more remote (Pierre Vidal-Naquet for the *Iliad*).

This distribution of the times when the preface appears may entail matters of duration, for a preface produced for some particular edition may disappear, definitively or not, in some later edition if the author decides it has done its job: either a disappearance plain and simple or a substitution. The record for brevity is held, as I have said, by the preface to *La Peau de chagrin*,[14] published at the head of the original edition in August 1831 and deleted one month later when the work was reprinted in the collected *Romans et contes philosophiques*. All of Balzac's original prefaces were, moreover (for a reason we will come across below), meant to disappear, and they really did disappear in the edition of *La Comédie humaine*, in favor of the famous foreword of 1842. That is a typical case of substitution, but by no means an unprecedented one: Corneille's original forewords gave way in 1660 to a series of delayed "examinations"; and in 1676, for the first collected edition of his works, Racine carried out an analogous substitution for *Alexandre, Andromaque, Britannicus*, and *Bajazet*. In all these cases one can entertain oneself, on a day when there's a storm or a general strike, by calculating how long each preface lasted. But some authors prefer to add a new preface without deleting the old one: for various reasons, that is what Scott, Chateaubriand, Nodier, Hugo (for the *Odes et ballades*), and Sand (for *Indiana*) did. These cases of coexistence entail, in turn, choices as to relative location and, therefore, arrangement. From one edition to another, Hugo arranges his prefaces sequentially in chronological order (1822, 1823, 1824, 1826, 1828, 1853) to allow the reader, he says in 1828, to "observe, in the ideas put forward, an advancement of liberty that is neither insignificant nor uninstructive"; the significance, which at that time was for the most part aesthetic in nature (the transition from classicism to romanti-

[14] On this subject, see N. Mozet, "La Préface de l'édition originale [de *La Peau de chagrin*]. Une poétique de la transgression," in C. Duchet, ed., *Balzac et "La Peau de chagrin"* (CDU-SEDES, 1979).

cism), was itself revised in 1853 in a political direction (the movement from monarchism to democracy). Other authors, such as Scott or Nodier, put the latest preface first to express the present state of their thinking about the work, and the preceding ones after it, thus pushing these earlier prefaces back into the past and at the same time drawing them closer to the text to the point of almost absorbing them into it, illustrating this general principle: in the course of time and by losing its initial pragmatic function, the paratext, unless it disappears, is "textualized" and incorporated into the work. Still other authors, such as Chateaubriand, prefer to shift the earlier paratext back into an appendix, thereby conferring on it more of a documentary value. But in both these cases (Scott/Nodier and Chateaubriand), the concern is (also) not to lose anything.

Whether the author retains or deletes the various prefaces, it is customary (and properly so) for posthumous scholarly editions to keep or restore them (at least the ones written by the author himself). Here again, the editor is compelled to choose an arrangement, which will vary with the situation and will generally be determined by the choice of text. When one adopts the text of the last edition revised by the author, it more or less goes without saying that one adopts his arrangement – indeed, that one respects his final wish for deletion. Maurice Regard's editions of Chateaubriand for Pléiade respect the sequence of 1826; Marcel Bouteron's edition of Balzac (the first Pléiade edition, 1935–37) very logically, if not very happily, deleted all the original prefaces – which had to be restored (an act of repentance dictated by the demand for completeness) in 1959 in a complementary volume put together by Roger Pierrot. As a result, the new Pléiade edition supervised by Pierre-Georges Castex, although likewise based on the Furne text, restored the original preface at the head of each work, transferring to the appendix only the prefaces (authorial or allographic) of the intermediary collections – *Scènes de la vie privée, Romans et contes philosophiques, Etudes philosophiques*, and *Etudes de mœurs au 19e siècle* – that had been superseded by the final structure of *La Comédie humaine*; those were prefaces for which a relevant location somewhere else could no longer be found.

To insist here on these philological details may seem fussy, but the increasing success of scholarly editions and complete sets justifies one's concern with their effects on the act of reading; and experience shows that these effects are greatly influenced by choices of location. Besides, I am only skimming over questions of much greater complexity which are the daily torment of editors. The preface to La Bruyère's *Caractères*, a preface present in the original edition of 1688, sustained (almost as frequently as the text itself) diverse successive additions (without prejudice to the variants) in 1689, 1690, 1691, and 1694 – in other words, in the fourth, fifth, sixth, and eighth editions of the work. This situation is probably not entirely unique, but in any case it is enough to disrupt our classification: here is a preface that, in the form in which people have been reading it since 1694, is at one and the same time (or rather, according to segment) original, later, and delayed. All of that, it is true, over a span of six years, but it is equally true that four times in those six years La Bruyère felt the need to enrich, or at the very least expand, his prefatorial discourse. The name for that is professional conscientiousness, and it ought to induce us to act with equal conscientiousness.

Senders

Determining the sender of a preface is a tricky matter, first, because there are numerous types of preface-writers (real or otherwise), and second, because some of the situations thus created are complex – indeed, ambiguous or indeterminate. Hence the need, here, for a cumbersome typology, which we can make clearer with a tabular presentation. But in considering the examples I put forward, one has to bear in mind that the prefatorial apparatus of a work may vary from one edition to another; in addition, that the same text may include in the same edition two or more prefaces due or attributed to different senders; and finally, that here (as elsewhere) the sender we are interested in is not, save for exceptions to be mentioned below, the actual writer of the preface, whose identity is sometimes less well known to us than we suppose, but indeed its alleged author, identified by an explicit reference (a full name or initials, the phrase "author's preface," etc.) or by various indirect signs.

The alleged author of a preface may be the author (real or alleged, hence some twists and turns in perspective) of the text: this very common situation we will call the *authorial*, or *auto-*

graphic, preface. Or the alleged author of a preface may be one of the characters in the action, when there are characters and action: this is the *actorial* preface. Or the alleged author of a preface may be a wholly different (third) person:[15] the *allographic* preface.

But I spoke above of preface-writers real or otherwise, and I must now explain that stipulation. A preface may be attributed to a real person or to a fictive person. If the attribution to a real person is confirmed by some other (if possible, by *every* other) paratextual sign, we will call the preface *authentic*. If the attribution to a real person is invalidated by some paratextual sign, we will call the preface *apocryphal*. And if the person to whom the preface is attributed is fictive, we will call the attribution, and therefore the preface, *fictive*. I am not sure that the distinction between fictive and apocryphal has universal relevance, but it seems to me useful in the area we are dealing with now, and we will use it henceforth in this sense: *fictive* applies to a preface attributed to an imaginary person, and *apocryphal* to a preface attributed falsely to a real person.

The intersecting of these two categories – the preface-writer's role in relation to the text (author, actor, or third party) and his regime with respect to, shall we say ingenuously, "truth" – gives rise to a double-entry table containing three possibilities under each category, hence (for the moment) nine types of preface according to the status of the sender. I set them out in the chart below in order of canonicity or, more simply, of decreasing ordinariness, supplying each type with an illustrative example that, in certain cases, will quickly prove unsatisfactory. For the authentic authorial preface, let's be simple: Hugo's preface to *Cromwell*; for the authentic allographic, Sartre's preface to Nathalie Sarraute's *Portrait d'un inconnu*; for the authentic actorial, lacking an example of a real person writing the preface to his own (hetero)biography,[16] let us invoke Valéry's preface to a

---

[15] In fact, I am not altogether sure that only a "person" – that is, no doubt, a human being – can be the alleged source of a preface. In principle, nothing would prevent an author from attributing a preface to an animal, for example, Moby-Dick (but that would be a variety of the fictive actorial preface) or to an "inanimate" object, for example, the ship *Pequod* (the same comment applies) or, to stick with the same author, Mount Greylock (that would be a fairly apocryphal allographic preface). But as yet I know of no examples of any of this, and I have no wish to complicate unduly an already tricky situation.

[16] No doubt there exist some fine examples of this situation that I am not yet

work in which he is, in a way, the hero: the *Commentaire de Charmes* [*Commentary on (Valéry's) "Charmes"*] by Alain. For the fictive authorial preface, the one by "Laurence Templeton" (here quotation marks of disbelief become necessary) to *Ivanhoe*,[17] a novel of which Templeton claims, by means of this very preface, to be the author; for the fictive allographic, "Richard Sympson," alleged cousin of the hero, writing the preface to the narrative of *Gulliver's Travels*; for the fictive actorial, let us cite the second preface of *Gil Blas*, known as "Gil Blas to the Reader." For the apocryphal authorial, let us imagine a preface wrongly attributed to Rimbaud at the head of the apocryphal *Chasse spirituelle*[18] or, more simply, let us imagine that some author – any author – one day "signed" a preface actually written by one of his friends or ghostwriters; I know of no real example, but some such must certainly exist, under seal of professional secrecy. In any case, this is what Balzac imagines in *Illusions perdues*, where d'Arthez writes for Lucien, at the head of *L'Archer de Charles IX*, "the splendid preface which perhaps overshadows the work but which brought so much illumination to writers of the new school."[19] For the apocryphal allographic, let us imagine that that same *Chasse spirituelle* had had a preface attributed – still wrongly – to Verlaine; or more simply, that the preface to *Portrait d'un inconnu*, signed Sartre, had in fact been written by Nathalie Sarraute or by some other person of goodwill, as Mme de Caillavet is sometimes alleged to have written the preface to Proust's *Les Plaisirs et les jours* for Anatole France. But here we

aware of. A partial biography is sufficient – that is, one published before the death of its hero – and that subgenre is more and more in evidence; that situation (a real person writing the preface to his own heterobiography) also presumes good relations between the biographee and his biographer. When discussing functions, I will cite two or three not particularly striking cases.

17 A preface, we should remember, in the form of a "dedicatory epistle" to the equally fictive Dr. Dryasdust.

18 [See Chapter 3, under "Pseudonymity."]

19 Pléiade 5:335 [tr. *Lost Illusions*, trans. Herbert J. Hunt (Penguin, 1971), 238]. This sentence of Petit-Claud's (Pléiade 661 [Penguin 603]) proves that we are not dealing with an allographic preface signed d'Arthez: "The preface could only have been written by one of two men: Chateaubriand or yourself! – Lucien accepted this eulogy without revealing that the preface was by d'Arthez. Ninety-nine out of a hundred authors would have done the same."

Another instance of the apocryphal authorial, this one real, is the preface to the third edition of Sorel's *Francion* (1633): both text and preface (in the form of a dedicatory epistle to Francion, which I have already mentioned) are attributed to the obscure and deceased Moulinet du Parc.

have available a real, or almost real, example: the prefaces for
two collections of Balzac's works, *Etudes philosophiques* and *Etudes
de mœurs*, both signed by Félix Davin, who – as we know today
from a more or less reliable source and by paratextual means –
was hardly more than a loaner name for Balzac himself:[20] a
pseudo-allographic and crypto-authorial situation, the reverse of
that of *L'Archer de Charles IX*, which was pseudo-authorial and
crypto-allographic. For the apocryphal-actorial, I must again
imagine a situation for which there is no example but that is very
conceivable: the situation that would exist if Valéry's preface to
the *Commentaire de Charmes* were shown to have been concocted
either by Alain or by someone else and to have been accepted by
the author of *Charmes* out of either laziness or indifference. Here,
then, is the promised chart, in which I mark each cell with a letter
that will represent it in the pages to follow, each fictive or
apocryphal preface-writer's name with quotation marks of disbelief, and each example of my own devising with a monitory
asterisk.

Regime \ Role	Authorial	Allographic	Actorial
Authentic	A Hugo for *Cromwell*	B Sartre for *Portrait d'un inconnu*	C Valéry for *Commentaire de Charmes*
Fictive	D "Laurence Templeton" for *Ivanhoe*	E "Richard Sympson" for *Gulliver*	F "Gil Blas" for *Gil Blas*
Apocryphal	G *"Rimbaud" for *La Chasse spirituelle*	H *"Verlaine" for *La Chasse spirituelle*	I *"Valéry" for *Commentaire de Charmes*

---

[20] Thus this letter of January 4, 1835, from Balzac to Mme Hanska: "You will
easily guess that the Introduction [to the *Etudes philosophiques*] cost me as much
as it cost M. Davin, for I had to teach him his notes and correct him over and
over until he had properly expressed my thoughts" (R. Pierrot, ed. [Delta,
1967], 1:293); the editor specifies that the Davin manuscript of this introduction
is lost but that the Davin manuscript of the introduction to the *Etudes de mœurs*
is much shorter than the final text, which indicates that, in the proofs, Balzac
expanded the loaner name's text.

But this chart calls for some observations, additions, and perhaps corrections. To begin with, the presence of senders described as "fictive" or "apocryphal" may seem to run counter to the general principle that requires us to take the paratext at its word and to the letter, suspending all disbelief – indeed, all hermeneutic capacity – and accepting it as given. According to this rule, "Laurence Templeton," given as the preface-writer–dedicator–author of *Ivanhoe*, ought to be accepted as such, without reservation or quotation marks, and any question on this point would be as misplaced as an inquiry into the true identity of, say, the writer of the preface to *Cromwell*. In reality, these two questions are not of the same order: responsibility for the preface to *Cromwell* is, in one way or another, claimed by Hugo without any public objection, and that must suffice for us; in contrast, "Templeton's" authorship is explicitly refuted by Scott's claims – I should say, by his delayed admissions – and after 1820 few readers took "Templeton's" authorship seriously. As for "Gil Blas's" authorship, from the very first it is contradicted by the presence, preceding "Blas's" notice to the reader, of a "Declaration by the Author," an author identified as Lesage as early as the original edition, on the title page – but in this situation anonymity would in no way diminish the force of the "declaration." In all these cases, then, and in all other similar cases, the paratext – and therefore the status of the preface – is self-contradictory: diachronically (by developments over time) in the case of "Templeton," synchronically in the case of "Gil Blas." In other words, the official version of the status of the paratext is in some cases an official *fiction* that the reader is invited to take no more (and undoubtedly even less) seriously than we take, for example, some "diplomatic" pretext that is meant by general agreement to conceal a truth that everyone perceives or guesses but whose disclosure would benefit no one. The status of apocrypha is by definition bound to the discovery or later admission of forgery. The status of fiction, which obviously governs novelistic *texts* (no one is seriously asked to believe in the historical existence of Tom Jones or Emma Bovary, and the reader who would take it into his head to do so would most certainly be a "bad" reader, one who does not conform to the author's expectation or abide by what must indeed be called the contract – the bilateral contract – of fiction), likewise governs certain elements of the paratext, often implicitly and with dependence on the shrewdness of the reader, who, for example, will find in the actual text of the prefatory epistle by "Templeton" indications of its fictitiousness, but just as often explicitly, by the mere fact of the obvious contradiction between, for instance, one preface (like that by "Gil Blas") and another (like that by Lesage) or between a preface (shall we say the original one to *Lolita*, signed "John Ray" and attributing authorship of the text to Humbert Humbert) and some other element of the paratext (in this case, the presence of the name of the author, Vladimir Nabokov, on the cover and title page). What one paratextual element gives, another paratextual element, later or simultaneous, may always take away; and here as elsewhere, the reader must put it all together and try (it's not always so simple) to figure out what the whole adds up to. And the very way in which a paratextual element gives what it gives may always imply that none of it is to be believed.

To illustrate this feature, I will present some other examples of fictive attributions in various contexts, but first, a more urgent matter, I should introduce a fundamental distinction within the very category of the authentic authorial preface – that is, the preface that the real author of the text claims responsibility for, in one way or another: our cell A. The case of *Cromwell* (and of thousands of others: this is far and away the most common situation – so common that I will not needlessly weary my readers by mentioning other examples here) is unequivocal and cut-and-dried: the anonymous author of this preface, a preface it would be pointless and therefore foolish to sign, presents himself implicitly but obviously as the author of the play, whom we know in another connection to be Victor Hugo. Here and now I will point out some variants of this situation, ones that do not basically modify its status.

The text and preface may both be anonymous but clearly by the same author: as we know, this is the case for the early editions of *Les Caractères* or, for example, of *Waverley* and all the anonymous novels by Walter Scott.[21] The text may be pseudonymous

---

[21] The original edition of *Lyrical Ballads* (1798) by Wordsworth and Coleridge offers a curious, but perfectly logical, variant of this species: the preface-writer presents himself as the (sole) author of the poems that follow – a prefatorial fiction obviously brought about by the textual fiction of anonymity.

and the preface anonymous but implicitly authorial: see *La Chartreuse de Parme*.[22] The text may be onymous, like that of *Cromwell*, but constituted by a homodiegetic narrative with a hero- or witness-narrator. This is the typical case in which, to avoid all confusion – that is, any attribution of the preface to the narrator – the author signs his preface (a bit the way Proust signs the dedications of the *Recherche*) with his name or initials: see the postface to the second edition of *Lolita* (the verb *sign* is much more appropriate here than in connection with the name of the author on the title page). Finally (unless I have omitted something), responsibility for the text may be claimed by two or more people and responsibility for the preface by only one of them: this is the case of the 1800 edition of *Lyrical Ballads*, whose preface (which we will come upon again) was signed only by Wordsworth and was thus, if you wish, semi-authorial. This is also the case of the 1875 preface for *Renée Mauperin* (1864), a preface signed only by Edmond de Goncourt; the novel was written by both brothers, and this preface is semi-authorial because it is later and semiposthumous, Jules having died in the meantime, whereas Coleridge, although strenuously shoved aside by his distinguished colleague, was still very much alive in 1800. In all these situations and perhaps in one or two others that have escaped me, the real author, in his preface, claims (or more simply, assumes) responsibility for the text, and this, of course, constitutes one of the functions of this type of preface – so obvious a function that we will not mention it again, except incidentally. Besides, the term *function* is perhaps too strong to designate what is here only an *effect*: the author feels no need at all to state positively what goes without saying; for him to speak implicitly of the text as his own is enough.[23] I will call this type of authentic authorial preface *assumptive* and will give the label A^1

---

22 Another logical variant: George Sand, signing with a man's name, always writes her prefaces using masculine forms.

23 I know of only one case of an *explicitly* assumptive preface, that is, one in which the author feels the need to *assert* in a preface that he is the author of the text, but this case is obviously playful. It is the preface to *Jean Sbogar* by Nodier: "The chief result of all these long and boring lucubrations [on these instances of plagiarism] is that *Jean Sbogar* is not by Zchoke, or by Byron, or by Benjamin Constant, or by Mme de Krudener; it is by me. And it was very essential to say that, for the honor of Mme de Krudener, of Benjamin Constant, of Byron, and of Zchoke."

to the half of cell A that this type will henceforth have to make do with. ·

For there exists another kind of authorial preface, just as authentic in its status of attribution in that its declared author is indeed the real author of the text, but much more fictional in its discourse because in this preface the real author claims – here again without really inviting us to believe him – not to be the author *of the text*. He denies his authorship not, of course, of the preface itself, which would be logically absurd ("I am not uttering this very sentence"), but of the text it introduces. This is the case, for example, with the original preface to Montesquieu's *Lettres persanes*, in which the author (in those days, anonymous) of the preface claims not to be the author of the text, which the preface-writer attributes to its several epistolary enunciators. Or, if one prefers a less murky situation, the case of *La Vie de Marianne*, where Marivaux, "signatory" of the text inasmuch as his name is present on the title page, claims in the introductory "foreword" to have received that text just as it is from a friend who allegedly found it. This second type of authentic authorial preface we will call the *disavowing* preface (implied: disavowing the text), and we will award it the half-cell A^2, as indicated by this enlargement of our cell A:

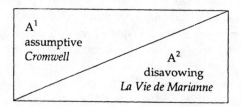

A^1
assumptive
Cromwell

A^2
disavowing
La Vie de Marianne

This type of preface could no doubt equally well be called *crypto-authorial*, for the author uses it to conceal (or deny) his authorship; it could also be called *pseudo-allographic*, for the author uses it to present himself as an allographic preface-writer, claiming responsibility only for the preface, not for any other part of the work. It goes without saying that this disavowing operation is the first, the main, and sometimes the only function (this time in the strong sense of the word) of this type of preface, but we will return to the matter. In this kind of preface the author, as I say, claims to be an allographic preface-writer, but this alleged role is generally supposed to follow from another one, whose possible diversity determines some further variants. The author (onymous, anonymous, or pseudonymous) may present himself as just the "editor" of a homodiegetic narrative (autobiography or journal) whose authorship he naturally attributes to its narrator: see *Robinson Crusoe, Moll Flanders, Adolphe,* Sainte-Beuve's *Volupté,* Lamartine's *Jocelyn,*[24] Taine's *Thomas Graindorge* (preface signed H. Taine), *Treasure Island* (by way of a disavowing dedication signed "the author"), Mirbeau's *Journal d'une femme de chambre* (preface signed O.M.), Larbaud's *Barnabooth* in its 1913 version ("foreword" signed V.L.), Gide's *Geneviève,* Sartre's *Nausée* (but here the disavowing foreword is signed "the editors" and is thus apocryphal allographic instead), or Eco's *Name of the Rose.* The author may likewise take on the role of editor with regard to an epistolary novel, claiming to have discovered and tidied up a real correspondence: see the *Lettres persanes* already mentioned, *Pamela, La Nouvelle Héloïse* (whose contract is, to tell the truth, ambiguous, for the titular note "Letters ... collected and published by Jean-Jacques Rousseau" is deliberately blurred by the preface: "Although my title here is only that of editor, I myself worked on this book, and I make no secret of the fact. Did I write the whole, and is the entire correspondence a fiction? People in society, what does it matter to you? For you it is surely a fiction"), Laclos's *Liaisons dangereuses* (where there is a striking contradiction between the "Editor's Preface," in which the editor claims only to have pruned and arranged this correspondence, and the "Publisher's Note," in which the publisher asserts he doesn't believe anything in the correspondence and sees it only as pure fiction), *Werther, Oberman,* and certainly many others, some of which we will encounter below. The author may, as well, but more rarely, attribute the text to an anonymous writer, more or less an amateur, who supposedly asked him for help and advice. This is the case with *Armance* (as of the original edition of 1827): an anonymous text with a "foreword" [avant-propos] signed

---

[24] With *Jocelyn,* authorial disavowal takes a rather devious route, for the work's paratext is complex: the subtitle (*Journal found at the home of a village priest*) is disavowing, and so is the verse prologue, which develops the subtitle by recounting the circumstances of the discovery; but slipped in between the two is a more or less clearly assumptive prose foreword. On the specific case of the journal-novel, see Yasusuke Oura, "Roman journal et mise en scène éditoriale," *Poétique* 69 (February 1987).

Stendhal ("A woman of intelligence ... has begged me ... to edit the style of this novel"); or again, with Balzac's *Gars* (the first version [1828] of *Les Chouans*), which its (unpublished) "foreword" [avertissement] attributed with a fair number of details to the man named Victor Morillon. Finally, the author may attribute the work to a foreigner whose translator he claims to be: see Macpherson for *Ossian*, Nodier for *Smarra*, Pierre Louÿs for *Bilitis*. The case of *Madame Edwarda* is doubly exceptional here because the disavowing preface by George Bataille is later (1956, for a text published in 1941) and because the supposed author, "Pierre Angélique," is not presented as a foreigner. Bataille, that is, presents himself as neither translator nor editor but as an ordinary allographic preface-writer.

Now it is no doubt easier to see why I divided cell A diagonally: this layout is meant to express how much the disavowing preface, albeit authentic, inclines toward fiction (with its fictional disavowal of the text) and also toward the allographic, which it simulates by its (just as fictional) claim not to have been written by the author of the text. But this fictionality has degrees of intensity: in cases of initial anonymity (as for the *Lettres persanes*) the fictionality is weaker and is not fully revealed until the moment when the text and its preface are, finally, officially (although often posthumously) attributed to their real author; the fictionality is stronger, and even entirely blatant, when the name of the author on the title page (as for *Marianne*, *Volupté*, *La Nausée*) quietly contradicts the fictive attribution of the text to its narrator.[25] Consequently, when I take up disavowing prefaces from the point of view of function, I will group them with fictive and apocryphal prefaces. But let's not get ahead of ourselves.

To conclude this discussion of the sender of the preface, I will say a word about the other types. The *authentic allographic* (cell B), whereby one writer presents to the public the work of another

---

[25] The case of *La Nouvelle Héloïse* is obviously different, for the title includes "Letters collected by Jean-Jacques Rousseau," which, in contrast, is meant to confirm in advance the (partial) disavowals in the preface. The same effect for *Oberman*, "Letters published by M. de Senancour," and for *Adolphe*, "An anecdote found among the papers of an unknown person, and published by M. Benjamin de Constant." More (but not very) cryptic is the title of *Les Liaisons dangereuses*, which includes "Letters collected in one section of society and published for the edification of others by Monsieur C— de L—."

writer, here offers no mystery, for its official attribution is always explicit, whether its occasion be original, later, or delayed – indeed, posthumous. A special case is that of the "editor's [or publisher's] note"[26] – often of dubious authenticity – such as the "Publisher's Note to the Reader" at the head of La Fayette's *Princesse de Clèves* justifying the anonymity of the work, or the "Editor's Note" at the head of *Le Rouge et le noir*, falsely attesting that this novel, published in 1830, was written in 1827. In this latter case at least, a transfer to cell H (apocryphal allographic) would not be at all inappropriate if we hadn't on principle forbidden ourselves to intervene on the basis of a mere suspicion. About the *authentic actorial* preface (cell C) as well, I have little to add here, except to deplore the lack or poverty of examples of biographees who supply prefaces for their heterobiographies. The case of autobiography is obviously different, for there – even though by definition the biographer and biographee are one and the same person filling two roles – it is in reality always the former who lays claim to the discourse and therefore to the preface as well as the narrative: see the introductory notice of Rousseau's *Confessions* and the preface to Chateaubriand's *Mémoires d'outre-tombe*. That is indeed a pity, for one would sometimes like to know the young hero's opinion of how he is being treated by the mature man – indeed, the old man – who writes about him unfairly; a scrupulous or exceptionally cunning autobiographer could indeed contrive such a paratext, but that would put us, inescapably, in the realm of fiction, or rather of apocrypha, as in "The Other" in *The Book of Sand*, where the old Borges holds a dialogue with the young Borges on the banks of the Rhône, or the Charles. As the first of these self-devouring scribes, Saint Augustine, said, more or less, "The child I was is dead, and I – I exist." One cannot be more cruel, or more truthful.

In the *fictive authorial* preface, the alleged author and his preface-writer are the same fictive character. This cell D is preeminently illustrated by the works of Walter Scott, starting with the *Tales of My Landlord* (first series, from 1816, including *The Bride of Lammermoor*, 1819), attributed to "Jedediah Cleishbotham," who will pass his pen on to the "Templeton" of *Ivanhoe*, the "Clutterbuck" of *The Fortunes of Nigel*, and the "Dryasdust" of *Peveril of the Peak*. In the

---

[26] [On the ambiguity of the French word *éditeur*, see Chapter 12, note 24.]

fictive allographic preface (cell E), the preface-writer is fictive, as is the alleged author of the text, but these are two distinct persons. This fictive preface-writer may be anonymous (but provided with distinct biographical features), such as the French officer presented as the author of the "foreword" of Potocki's *Manuscrit trouvé à Saragosse*, the Dalmation presenter of Mérimée's *Guzla*, or the male translator of Sallenave's *Portes de Gubbio*. But these cases are rather rare. If an author is going to take the trouble to make up an allographic preface-writer, he generally prefers to grant him the solid identity that a name confers: "Richard Sympson" for *Gulliver*, "Joseph l'Estrange" for Mérimée's *Théâtre de Clara Gazul*, "Marius Tapora" for Beauclair and Vicaire's *Déliquescences d'Adoré Floupette*, "Tournier de Zemble" for Larbaud's *Barnabooth* in 1908, "Gervasio Montenegro" for Borges and Bioy Casares's *Chronicles of Bustos Domecq*, "Michel Presle" for Queneau's *On est toujours trop bon avec les femmes*, and so forth. A possible variant of this type would give a fictive preface-writer to a real author, as if *Le Père Goriot*, for which Balzac rightly took responsibility, were nevertheless prefaced by "Victor Morillon." This is somewhat the case for *Lolita*: the original edition indeed bore the name of the real author but included a preface by "John Ray." Ray, however, is very careful not to attribute the work to Nabokov: he attributes it to its narrator-hero Humbert Humbert, just as "Richard Sympson" attributes *Gulliver* to Gulliver. For the moment, then, my variant remains without an illustration, and for an obvious reason: the fictive attribution of a preface is a maneuver derived, as by the infectiousness of play, from the fictive attribution of the text. In the serious situation in which an author takes total responsibility for his text, it hardly occurs to him to contrive a fictive preface-writer: he writes and signs his preface himself, or he asks some authentic allographic preface-writer to provide one, or he does without.

Cell F is that of the *fictive actorial* preface, a relatively classic species. In principle nothing would prevent a heterodiegetic narrative – indeed, a stage play – from being prefaced by one of its characters: *Don Quixote* by Don Quixote (or Sancho Panza), *Le Misanthrope* by Alceste (or Philinte) – wonderful vacation assignments for Gisèle and Albertine.[27] A less striking example,

---

[27] [Characters in the *Recherche*.]

certainly, but one better equipped with the famous "merit of existing," is Svevo's *Confessions of Zeno*, prefaced by "the doctor who is sometimes spoken of in rather unflattering terms in this novel," a first-person narrative in which he is neither the hero nor the narrator;[28] and Borges's *Six Problems for Don Isidro Parodi* is prefaced by the "Gervasio Montenegro" I have already mentioned, who is one of the least striking characters in the narrative. But these cases are still exceptions: most often the character promoted to the role of preface-writer is the narrator-hero of a first-person narrative, which – via the preface itself – he claims to have written. That is the case for *Lazarillo*, the fictive nature of which, after all, in the absence of a solid attribution, is not absolutely proven by anything, and it is the case for Vicente Espinel's *Marcos de Obregon*. It is obviously the case for *Gil Blas*, the eponym of this cell, on account of its second preface; for *Gulliver*, on account of the preface of 1735, attributed to the narrator-hero in the form of a letter "To his cousin Sympson"; for *Tristram Shandy*, on account of its internal preface; for Poe's *Gordon Pym*; for the *Braz Cubas* of Machado de Assis; for Queneau's *Œuvres complètes de Sally Mara*.

Lacking real examples properly attested to, I will give no further consideration to the row of *apocryphal* prefaces (cells G, H, I), which I have included here mainly on theoretical grounds (to provide a sound distinction between the fictive and the apocryphal) and as a provisional step (while we await discoveries to come, or achievements not yet published). I say lacking real examples properly attested to because the Davin case is established as an apocryphal situation only by private and no doubt incomplete communications. In the same department as the suspect allographic prefaces we will naturally put many a "Notice from the Publisher [or Editor]," such as those already mentioned for *La Princesse de Clèves* and *Le Rouge et le noir* or the one for Balzac's *Provincial à Paris*, which we will meet again and which we have every reason to attribute *in petto* (but only *in petto*) to the author – all of which are in effect please-inserts, theoretically from the publishers. Henri Mondor has found

---

[28] The preface of *Henry Esmond* (1842), signed by the hero's daughter, Rachel Esmond Warrington, has a comparable status: she is mentioned, barely, on the last page of the novel. Were it not for this delayed and modest mention of her, the preface-writer, having no role in the diegesis, would be simply allographic.

among Mallarmé's papers the proof sheet of a preface (ultimately not published) to *Les Mots anglais* signed "The publishers," but its style leaves the critic in no doubt as to its real provenance. The presence of this page in the current Mallarmé peritext (Pléiade, p. 1329), accompanied by this kind of editorial certification of Mallarmé's authorship, is, for today's reader, no doubt the equivalent of a guarantee that the signature is apocryphal. But here we tread on the slippery ground of research into (real) authorship, which is neither within our province nor to our taste. More legitimate, in contrast, is consideration of the openly ambiguous or undecidable cases, to which I would be tempted to assign, off the table, a sort of supplementary cell (J).

I have already referred to the prefaces to autobiographies, prefaces that, in terms of the identity of person if not of role, are simultaneously authorial and actorial (A + C). Prefaces in dialogue, such as the one to *La Nouvelle Héloïse*, are always simultaneously authorial and allographic, for the author is pretending to share the discourse with an imaginary interlocutor (A + E) – indeed, with a real one (A + H), as Nodier does at the head of the *Dernier Chapitre de mon roman*, conducting a dialogue with his "bookseller." Diderot's *Entretiens sur le fils naturel* (or *Dorval et moi*) has a still more complex status, for the real disavowing author ("Moi") is carrying on a discussion with the imagined author, who is, moreover, one of the characters ("Dorval"); the formula for that would be $A^2 + D/F$.

Those are cases of prefaces with multiple attributions, prefaces made ambiguous by the very fact of this multiplicity. Other (authentic authorial) prefaces are ambiguous because the author, intentionally or not, seems to fluctuate between assumption and disavowal. That is the case of *La Nouvelle Héloïse* and *Les Liaisons dangereuses*, both of whose prefaces I have already mentioned. It is the case of the prologue to *Don Quixote*, in which Cervantes, apparently thinking of his alleged source, Cid Hamet, asserts he is only the "step-father" of his hero and therefore of his work; in other sentences, however, he clearly assumes responsibility for this work, as we will see below. It is the case of *Guzman de Alfarache*, whose multiple paratext is cleverly ambiguous: a dedication signed Mateo Alemán implicitly assumes responsibility for the text; two forewords, "To the vulgar" and "To the discreet reader," remain vague enough so that the reader – vulgar or discreet – is unable to settle the matter; and finally "A declaration for the better understanding of this book," presented by the author, speaks of the hero in the third person (the hero is thus not the author) but at the same time attributes authorship of the text to him. It is also the case of Hugo's *Dernier Jour d'un condamné*, the original preface of which consisted only and entirely of this contract, as resolutely alternating as the original preface to *La Nouvelle Héloïse*:

There are two ways to account for the existence of this book. Either there was indeed a bundle of yellowing papers of various sizes on which were found, recorded one by one, a poor devil's last thoughts; or there was a man, a dreamer who acquainted himself with nature for the benefit of his art, a philosopher, perhaps even a poet, whose imagination gave birth to this idea, and who took it, or more likely was possessed by it, until he could only wrestle free of it by flinging it into a book.

Of these two possibilities, the reader may choose the one that he prefers.

It is the case of *La Chartreuse de Parme*, in whose foreword Stendhal, claiming to be the author, maintains (like the officer at Saragossa) that he is transcribing a narrative, this one told by a nephew of the canon of Padua. It is also, but not finally, the case with the *Storia e cronistoria del Canzoniere* by Umberto Saba, an essay by the poet about his œuvre, an essay attributed to an anonymous critic and supplied with a preface that is in theory allographic, thus attributed to a third party, who little by little comes to be identified with the author of the essay. I am not sure whether, for the reader, the conviction that the preface is in reality written by Saba himself simplifies or confuses everything.

Uncertainty may also derive from the anonymity of the disavowing preface-writer when he is provided with no biographical feature – not even nationality (the French nationality of the preface-writer of *Saragossa*) or sex (the male sex of the preface-writer of *Gubbio*) – that would allow him to be definitely distinguished from the (real) author of the text and therefore to be definitely considered fictive allographic. The preface-writer of Sainte-Beuve's *Joseph Delorme*, for example, or of Proust's *Jean Santeuil* seems to waver between the fictive allographic and the disavowing authorial – or rather, seems to stop short of the very idea of such a choice, for nothing identifies him with Sainte-

Beuve or Proust, or with anyone else either. So it is only the
methodological principle of economy that will lead us to resolve
this question in favor of the disavowing authorial, that is, in favor
of the least costly hypothesis – the one that spares us an
unnecessary agent. The situation of *La Bibliothèque d'un amateur*
by Jean-Benoît Puech is certainly more subtle, or more complex.
An anonymous preface at its head states roughly this: the text
that follows is the work of one of my friends, whose name I won't
reveal. Is that Puech disavowing authorship of his text (A^2), or is
that a fictive (indeed, authentic) allographic preface-writer (E or
B) simply forgetting to sign his name and identify the preface's
real author? A later text by the same author removes this doubt
by stating after the fact that the preface-writer was Puech and
that the author of the text was his friend Benjamin Jordane[29] –
another case in which one paratext corrects another, leaving the
reader to decide how much credit it deserves.

   The next-to-last puzzler for diehard classifiers, of which I am
certainly not one: *Clotilde Jolivet*, the novel by Cecil Saint-Laurent,
is prefaced by (this was bound to happen) ... Jacques Laurent.[30]
Is this preface – which, for all that, is very sensible, and defends
the genre of the historical novel – allographic or authorial? I hear
whispers telling me that this uncertainty already hung heavy
over the preface of Bataille's *Madame Edwarda*, but I am not so
sure, for the status of imagined author is not exactly the same for
"Pierre Angélique" as it is for "Cecil Saint-Laurent."[31] It is true
that the latter, in the course of time, tends to fill out: it is no
longer a matter just of a pseudonym, and Jacques Laurent sometimes asks his interviewers, "Which of us two do you want to
speak with?" When all is said and done, it seems to me sound
poetics to put into the same bag two authors – or if you prefer,
four authors – whose critical stature is so different.

   I am still not too sure how to designate the preface Prévost
wrote to his *Cleveland* (1735): it is presented as disavowing

[29] Puech, "Du même auteur," *La Nouvelle Revue française* (November 1979):
151–64.
[30] [As explained in Chapter 3, Jacques Laurent is the legal name, Cecil Saint-
Laurent the pseudonym.]
[31] Pierre Angélique is the pseudonym Georges Bataille took for *Madame Edwarda*,
and Bataille himself signed the preface. But "Pierre Angélique" is a fiction who
tends to disappear for the benefit of the real author, Bataille, whereas in the
eyes of the public "Cecil Saint-Laurent" often passes for a real author – and
Jacques Laurent plays on this so-called double identity.

authorial, for the author claims to be only the editor-translator of Cleveland's memoirs. But Prévost does not claim responsibility for this preface; rather, it is implicitly attributed to M. de Renoncour, the (imagined) author of the *Mémoires d'un homme de qualité* (1728). Fictive allographic, then, as for *Clara Gazul*; but because Renoncour was, by definition, the narrator-hero of those pseudo-memoirs and therefore a fictive character in that work, there is something obliquely *actorial* about his preface to *Cleveland*: a fictive character of one work becomes the fictive preface-writer of another work by the same author, somewhat as if Robinson Crusoe supplied the preface to *Moll Flanders*, or Felix Krull to *Doctor Faustus*. Somewhat? Completely.

Addressees

Determining the addressee of a preface is, fortunately, much simpler than determining the sender. It all boils down almost to this truism: the addressee of the preface is the reader of the text – the reader, and not simply a member of the public, as is the case (with some slight differences I have already pointed out) for the addressee of the title or of the please-insert. And this is so not only *de facto* – because the reader of the preface already necessarily has the book (it is harder to read a preface than a please-insert while one is standing in the aisle of a bookstore), even if Stevenson did entitle the verse preface of *Treasure Island* "To the hesitating purchaser" – but also and especially *de jure*, because the preface, in its very message, postulates that its reader is poised for an imminent reading of the text (or, in the case of a postface, has just concluded a reading), without which its preparatory or retrospective comments would be largely meaningless and, naturally, useless. We will meet this feature again on every page, so to speak, of our study of the preface's functions.

But this ultimate addressee is sometimes spelled by a relay-addressee who is, as it were, his representative. This is obviously the case for the dedicatory epistles (authentic or fictive) with a prefatorial function, epistles mentioned above, such as those of Corneille, *Tom Jones*, Walter Scott, Nerval's *Filles du feu*, or Baudelaire's *Petits Poèmes en prose*; and we know that the set of prefaces Aragon wrote for his share of the *Œuvres romanesques croisées*[32] is addressed to a privileged reader – a reader who is female as well as his inspiration and something of a confessor. To those dedicatees who are identified or (as with Corneille's *La Suivante, La Place Royale,* and *Le Menteur*) anonymous, we can add collective or symbolic addressees, such as the addressee of Barrès's *Un homme libre,* the preface of which is entitled "To some schoolboys of Paris and the provinces I offer this book," or the addressee of Bourget's *Disciple:* "To a young man." But even the imaginary dedicatees of Scott, of d'Urfé, and of many others – when the text of the dedication broadens to the dimensions and functions of a preface – easily play this role of mediator: coexisting in the same text are messages meant for them alone (as when d'Urfé, in the preface to the second part of *Astrée,* reproaches Céladon for his paradoxical behavior – a reproach that is, even so, an indirect way of apologizing for him to the reader) and messages meant, by way of the intermediary, for the reader alone (as when d'Urfé, in that same preface, dissuades the reader/addressee from seeking keys in his novel or explains why his shepherds speak the civilized language of gentlemen). In all these cases, the reader, the main addressee of the preface, has no difficulty sorting things out and receiving what – through the third party or over the third party's shoulder – is quite obviously meant exclusively for him.

[32] [*Intersecting Novelistic Works* of Aragon and his companion, Elsa Triolet.]

The functions of the original preface

"But what do prefaces actually do?"[1] This diabolically simple question is what we will now try to answer. A preliminary inquiry, whose meanderings and hesitations I will spare the reader, has convinced me of this (highly foreseeable) point, that not all prefaces "do" the same thing – in other words, the functions of prefaces differ depending on the type of preface. These functional types seem to me for the most part determined jointly by considerations of place, time, and the nature of the sender. If we take as our base the chart of types of senders (type of sender remains the fundamental distinction) and make adjustments according to the parameters of place and time, we get a new and strictly functional typology divided into six fundamental types. Our cell A^1, which I have already said is the most heavily populated, will all by itself give us the first four functional types: (1) the *original authorial preface* (*authorial* is to be understood, henceforth, as meaning authentic and assumptive); (2) the *original authorial postface*; (3) the *later authorial preface* (or postface: at this stage, the distinction between preface and postface is hardly relevant); (4) the *delayed authorial preface or postface*. Cell B and, very secondarily, cell C give us functional type five: the *authentic allographic (and actorial) preface* (the preface-writer–character is little more than a variant of the allographic preface-writer). All the other cells (A^2, D, E, F, and, for the principle of the thing, G, H, and I) merge, except for some slight differences, to constitute the sixth and last functional type: *fictional prefaces*.

I will not attempt right now to state the grounds for this division; its rationale will, I hope, become apparent when it is put to use. Here I must simply specify three things. First, this wholly operational typology will sometimes be contravened, for func-

[1] Jacques Derrida, *La Dissémination* (Seuil, 1972), 14 [tr. *Dissemination*, trans. Barbara Johnson (University of Chicago Press, 1981), 8].

tional distinctions by their nature are less rigorous and watertight than the others: the date, the location, and the sender of a preface generally lend themselves to a simple and sure determination, whereas the functioning of a preface is often a matter of interpretation, and many functions may now and then slide from one type to another. For example, simply from the need to compensate, a later preface may take on a function that had been ignored by the original preface or, *a fortiori*, by the absence of an original preface. Second, the inventory of functions that appears below should not be taken as an inventory of prefaces that have only one function: most often, each preface fulfills several functions successively or simultaneously, and not surprisingly some prefaces will be referred to several times on several grounds. Finally, I should add that of our six functional types, some are more important than others because of the more fundamental nature of their functions. This is true particularly of the first type, which we may look on as *the* basic type, the preface par excellence. The others, like so many varieties, I will define – more expeditiously – in terms of their difference from the first.

The original assumptive authorial preface, which we will thus shorten to *original preface*, has as its chief function *to ensure that the text is read properly*. This simplistic phrase is more complex than it may seem, for it can be analyzed into two actions, the first of which enables – but does not in any way guarantee – the second (in other words, the first action is a necessary but not sufficient condition of the second). These two actions are *to get the book read* and *to get the book read properly*. These two objectives, which may be described, respectively, as minimal (to get it read) and maximal (... and, if possible, read properly), are obviously tied to three aspects of this type of preface: the fact that it is authorial (the author being the main and, strictly speaking, the only person interested in having the book read properly), the fact that it is original (a later preface runs the risk of being too late: a book that in its first edition is read improperly, and *a fortiori* not read at all, risks having no other editions), and the fact that its location is introductory and therefore monitory (this is *why* and this is *how* you should read this book). The two objectives imply, therefore, despite all the customary disavowals, that the reader begins by reading the preface. These objectives determine two groups of functions, one tied to the why and the other to the how, which I will examine in succession, although in the actual text of individual prefaces it is often hard to disentangle one from the other.

The themes of the why

Here it is no longer precisely a matter of attracting the reader – who has already made the considerable effort to procure a copy of the book by buying, borrowing, or stealing it – but of hanging onto him with a typically rhetorical apparatus of persuasion. This apparatus comes under what Latin rhetoric called *captatio benevolentiae* [a currying of favor], the difficulty of which was fully recognized: for the point is more or less (as we would say today) to *put a high value on* the text without antagonizing the reader by too immodestly, or simply too obviously, putting a high value on the text's author. To put a high value on the text without (seemingly) doing the same for its author implies making some sacrifices that, though painful to one's amour propre, generally pay off. For example, one refrains from dwelling on what could pass for a display of the author's *talent*. Among the numerous prefaces I had occasion to read when preparing for this study, none of them elaborated on either of these two themes: "Admire my style" or "Admire my craftsmanship." More generally, the word *talent* is taboo. The word *genius* also, of course. Montesquieu uses it once, as we will see shortly, but with a disarming simplicity that wholly redeems it.

How then can one place a high value on the work without seeming to implicate the work's author? The answer is obvious, even if it somewhat inverts our modern critical credo that everything is in everything and that form is content. One must place a high value on the *subject*, even if that means alleging, more or less sincerely, the inadequacy of its *treatment*: if I am not (and who would be?) equal to my subject, you must nevertheless read my book for its "matter." La Fontaine, in the preface to the *Fables*: "It's not so much by the form that I've given this work that its value can be measured as by its usefulness and its subject matter." Such a dichotomy is obviously more appropriate to works that are not in the category of fiction, so we encounter this rhetoric more often in prefaces to historical or theoretical works.

Importance

One can attribute high value to a subject by demonstrating its importance and – inseparable from that – the usefulness of examining it. This is the standard practice – well known to ancient orators – of *auxèsis*, or *amplificatio* [magnification or overstatement]: "This matter is more serious than it seems, it is exemplary, it calls into question lofty principles, fairness is at stake," and so forth. See Thucydides showing that the Peloponnesian War (or Livy, the Punic Wars) is the greatest conflict in human history; see Montesquieu asserting at the head of *L'Esprit des lois*, "If my work meets with success, I shall owe much of it to the majesty of my subject."[2] *Documentary usefulness:* to preserve the memory of past achievements (Herodotus, Thucydides, Livy, Froissart). *Intellectual usefulness:* Thucydides, "Whoever shall wish to have a clear view both of the events which have happened and of those which will some day, in all human probability, happen again in the same or a similar way"; Montesquieu, ". . . that men were able to cure themselves of their prejudices. Here I call prejudices not what makes one unaware of certain things but what makes one unaware of oneself"; Rousseau (the preamble of the Neuchâtel manuscript of the *Confessions*), "[I portray myself so that] people can have at least one thing to compare themselves with; so that everyone may know himself and one other, and I will be this other." *Moral usefulness*, the whole immense topos of the edifying role of dramatic fiction: see the preface to Racine's *Phèdre*, "I have composed [no tragedy] where virtue has been more emphasised than in this play. The least faults are severely punished in it. . . . Such is the proper aim that any man who works for the public should cherish"; the preface to Molière's *Tartuffe*, "If the function of comedy is to cure men's vices"; the preface to La Bruyère's *Caractères*, "We should neither write nor speak but to instruct"; or even, paradoxically or not, the preface to the younger Crébillon's *Egarements du cœur et de l'esprit*, "[The novel must become] a picture of human life, in which we censured vice and folly." We will meet this theme of moral usefulness again in connection with later prefaces, in which it is deployed even more – right on

2 This is where, humbly transgressing the rule of modesty, he continues, ". . . still, I do not believe that I have totally lacked genius."

up to the middle of the nineteenth century. *Religious usefulness:* see, inevitably, the introduction to Chateaubriand's *Génie du christianisme. Social and political usefulness:* again, *L'Esprit des lois*, "If I could make it so that everyone had new reasons for loving his duties, his prince, his homeland and his laws ..., that those who command increased their knowledge of what they should prescribe and that those who obey found a new pleasure in obeying"; Tocqueville, the advance of democracy being irresistible, the American example will help us plan for it and weather it; and so forth.

This argument of usefulness is so powerful that we see it used *a contrario*: Hugo, in the preface to *Les Feuilles d'automne*, paradoxically defends "the appropriateness of a volume of true poetry at a time [1831] when there is so much prose in people's minds"; and Montaigne, in a bold attempt at provocation, "I have set myself no goal but a domestic and private one. ... Thus, ... you would be unreasonable to spend your leisure on so frivolous and vain a subject" (we know how he will later contradict himself by arguing that "each man bears the entire form of man's estate").

Novelty, tradition

A preface's statement about the importance of the subject no doubt constitutes the main case for valuing the text highly. Ever since Rousseau, this statement has tended to be accompanied by an insistence on the originality, or at least the novelty, of the subject: "Here is the only portrait of man, painted justly according to nature and with complete truth, which is in existence, or, probably, ever will be. ... I am undertaking a work which has no example, and whose execution will have no imitator." But this motif is new, for as we know the classical age preferred to insist on the traditional nature of its subjects (an obvious guarantee of quality), going so far as to require, for tragedy, themes that are manifestly or demonstrably ancient; and because in the theatre people did not especially care to stage yet one more performance of the old works, each generation, each author, was set on offering its new version of a well-tried subject. In classical prefaces, as we will see, this argument from ancientness is handled indirectly, in the form of an indication of sources exhibited as precedents.

Unity

One theme of value-enhancement which, for an obvious reason, is characteristic of prefaces to collections (of poems, novellas, essays) consists of showing the unity – formal or, more often, thematic – of what is likely to seem *a priori* a factitious and contingent jumble of things that end up together primarily as a result of the very natural need and very legitimate desire to clean out a drawer. Hugo is a master of this technique, at least from the time of the original preface to *Les Orientales* (January 1829). In that preface he compares literature to an old Spanish city, with neighborhoods and monuments in all styles and from all periods, and evokes "on the other side of town, hidden amidst the sycamores and the palms, the oriental mosque, with copper and tin domes, painted doors, enameled inner walls, with its light from above, its delicate arches, its incense burners that smoke day and night, its verses from the Koran on each door, its dazzling sanctuaries, and the mosaic of its pavement and the mosaic of its outer walls; blooming in the sun like a large flower full of fragrances"; after offering some disavowals in the name of modesty, Hugo clearly leads us to understand that *Les Orientales* was, or was meant to be, that mosque. In this case the cause was not very hard to defend, for this collection's unity of tone is obvious. The four major collections of lyrics Hugo published before going into exile [late 1851] are less homogeneous, but nevertheless each strikes its basic note, provided by the title and confirmed by the preface. I have already mentioned the preface to *Les Feuilles d'automne* [*Autumn Leaves*, 1831]; for *Les Chants du crépuscule* [*Sunset Songs*, 1835], the theme is "the twilight state of the soul and of society in the century in which we live"; for *Les Voix intérieures* [*Inner Voices*, 1837], this triple aspect of life: the hearth (the heart), the field (nature), the street (society) – a well-organized trinity standing, as we know, for a (mysterious) unity; and for *Les Rayons et les ombres* [*Lights and Shadows*; 1840], the composite picture of an equally mysterious "complete poet ... compendium of the ideas of his time" – or unity by totality. *Les Contemplations* [1856], "memories of a soul," is organized, as we know, into a past and a present, separated and therefore linked by the abyss of a grave. The historical and polemical unity of *Les Châtiments* [*The Chastisements*, 1853] goes without saying, but *Les*

9 The functions of the original preface

Chansons des rues et des bois [*Songs of Streets and Woods*, 1865] is, again, organized as a diptych: on the right is youth, on the left, wisdom – here, too, united by the symmetrical double flying-buttress of the two introductory poems: "Le Cheval" / "Au cheval" ["The Horse" / "To the Horse"].

The dedicatory epistle of Baudelaire's *Petits poèmes en prose* displays a unifying rhetoric both more complex and more tortuous. The author first presents this collection as a work that "has neither head nor tail," in which everything is head and tail, and which "we can cut wherever we want": this is the very definition of the inorganic aggregate. But after this disavowal comes the claim to a double unity, formal ("a poetic prose, musical without rhythm and without rhyme, supple enough … to fit the soul's lyrical movements") and thematic (a collection born "in frequenting enormous cities") – so in this preface we find again the double motif of the double title.

Balzac, who was very anxious to unify (after the event, said Proust, only half unfairly) his multiform production as a writer of novels and novellas, entrusts his spokesmen with the responsibility for indicating the tone of his early collections. The introduction to the *Romans et contes philosophiques* of 1831, signed Philarète Chasles, insists that the intent of the collection is to portray "the disorganization produced by thought." Davin, in the preface to the *Etudes philosophiques* of 1835, an expansion of the 1831 volume just mentioned, adds that the author aspires to be the Walter Scott of the modern period. For *Etudes de mœurs* (also 1835), he justifies the work's internal arrangement as a closely interconnected and overdetermined thematic series – scenes of private life: the freshness of youth; provincial life: maturity; Parisian life: corruption and decay; country life: calmness and serenity. (The scenes of political life did not have a symbolic function in the unfortunately limited sequence of the stages of life.) Balzac will finally endorse this organizing theme in his preface to *Scènes de la vie de province* (also 1835) and in the foreword of 1842, which we will encounter again.

The genre that most insistently calls for a unifying preface is no doubt the collection of essays or studies, because this kind of collection is often most conspicuous for the diversity of its components and at the same time most anxious (as a sort of theoretical point of honor) to deny or compensate for that diversity. We know how Montaigne, right at the beginning, relates the dispersion of his interests to the (elusive) unity of his person. I have already mentioned the very indirect way in which Blanchot places each of his collections under the invocation – introductory or central – of an essay whose mission is to point out the collection's strongest or most serious note. One would need a whole chapter to study the functioning of this technique in, say, contemporary criticism. The version that, in its classicism, is most typical seems to me to be provided by the early collections of Jean-Pierre Richard: *Littérature et sensation*, a set of four studies that the author relates to the unity of their critical (thematic and existential) purpose; and *Poésie et profondeur*, again four studies, whose common methodological feature is both specified (the theme of depth) and diversified (each of the four authors studied illustrates a typical stance toward this theme). At the other extreme would be Roland Barthes, who was obsessed by his awareness – at first troubling, then accepted – of the patchwork character (*poïkilos*, motley, he said in Greek) of his work and whose attempts to "recuperate" the self were marked by a more restless attitude and a more circuitous approach. His preface to *Sade Fourier Loyola* emphasizes indirectly ("Here they are all three brought together") the incongruous – indeed, provocative – appearance of such a grouping, before highlighting some common features that are more formal than thematic: three logothetes, but not of the same language; three fetichists, but not for the same object. But his preface to *Essais critiques* – a text that, though it dates from the middle of his "semiological" period, in many respects foreshadows the final period – had already very subtly sidestepped the duty (the chore?) of justification. The author, he said, "would gladly elaborate ... but cannot," sensing some bad faith in any retrospective stance; he finds, on rereading himself, only "the meaning of an infidelity"; and, as a "writer postponed," prefers to lay claim to the inability (characteristic of every writer) to have "the last word." Moreover, in an interview on April 1, 1964, Barthes returns to this point (which obviously makes him uneasy), but he does so in a somewhat contradictory way: "I explained in my preface why I didn't want to give these texts, written at different times, a retrospective unity: I don't feel the need to *tidy up* the gropings or the contradictions of the past. The unity of this collection can only be a question: What is writing? How to write? On this one question I have essayed various responses, languages that may have varied over a ten-year period; my book is, literally, a collection of *essays*, of different experiments all of which, however, deal with the same question."[3] Here the retrospective unity that is virtuously shoved out the door sneaks back in through the window in the form of a "question."

Obvious discomfort, here, with the ideological cliché that *a priori* makes unity (of subject, method, or form) into a sort of dominant value, a value as imperious as it is unconsidered, almost never subjected to scrutiny, accepted from the beginning of time as a matter of course. Why would unity be superior in principle to multiplicity? I think in this unconsidered monism I glimpse – beyond the rather superficial rhetorical automatisms – some metaphysical (indeed, religious) motives. But perhaps I am wrong to draw a contrast between motives and automatisms: nothing is more revealing than cultural stereotypes.

Nonetheless, it would be nice to be able to draw a contrast between this nearly universal prizing of unity and an opposite theme of prizing diversity. What most resembles this contrasting theme seems to me to be found, but unobtrusively, in the prefaces by Borges – all of whose works, as we know, are collections. In the "prologues" or "epilogues" – original or more or less delayed – that accompany his collections, his most common stance consists of commenting quite specifically on one or another of the essays or stories making up the collection (in his view, poems call for lighter glossing). Some of his commentaries are very restricting – and I will come back to this – but Borges almost always refrains from singling out a general characteristic. Sometimes he singles out a partial grouping that, by contrast, accentuates the heterogeneity of the rest (*Discussion, The Garden of Forking Paths, The Aleph*). Or he emphasizes *two* features (*Other Inquisitions*: "As I corrected the proofs of this volume, I discovered two tendencies in these miscellaneous essays [*miscelaneos trabajos*] ...")*. More often he stresses the diversity, either to apologize for it (*El otro, el mismo*: "This book is nothing more than a compilation. Its pieces were written in accordance with various moods and moments, not to justify a volume") or to claim

---

[3] Barthes, *Le Grain de la voix*, 31.

responsibility for it (*El Hacedor* [published in English as *Dreamti-gers*]): "God grant that the essential monotony of this miscellany (which time has compiled – not I – and which admits past pieces ...) be less evident than the geographical and historical diversity of its themes." Monotony is the term (which Borges, in contrast to Proust, considers pejorative) that he most readily applies to a possible unity, which would be weakness (*Doctor Brodie's Report*: "The same few plots, I am sorry to say, have pursued me down through the years; I am decidedly monotonous"; *The Gold of the Tigers*: "To escape, or possibly to extenuate, that monotony, I chose to admit, perhaps with rash hospitality, the miscellaneous [*miscelaneos* once again] interests that crossed my everyday writer's attention"; *Prólogos*: Larbaud praised my first collection of essays for the variety of its themes; this one will be "as eclectic"; *Los conjurados*: "I profess no aesthetics. Each work imposes on its author the form it requires: verse, prose, a style baroque or plain"). This stance serves as an exemplary contrast with the way in which an allographic preface-writer, Roger Caillois, thought it necessary to describe *L'Auteur* [*El Hacedor*] as a "whole in which the concern for structure is not lacking." In discussing Borges's prefaces, one must of course make allowances for the sometimes fairly coquettish rhetoric of modesty (the person concerned, too modest or too coquettish to use that term, said "timidity") which constantly leads Borges to disparage his œuvre and, further, to systematically deny it the status of an œuvre. For œuvre means unity and completion. "You who are readers," Borges never stops saying, "you see unity and completion because you are unaware of the innumerable variants and hesitations concealed behind a version that one day, when I was tired or distracted, I affirmed was final; but I – I know all about that." To stress diversity is thus in certain respects to reject the reader's (banal and distressing) compliment, to regard it as a "generous error." But we have just seen the ambiguity that lies in this retreat, and the (timid) pride that lies in this spectacular humility.

The trap, or the ruse, of asserting the claim of diversity could, moreover, fall short of, or go beyond, any consideration involving psychology. The trap or the ruse could be that the very word *diversity* would become – from the inescapably unifying effect of discourse and language – a unifying theme. That is what Lamartine indicates, very simply and very firmly, in the foreword of *Les Harmonies poétiques et religieuses*: "Here are four books of poems written down as they were felt, without links, without follow-up, without apparent transition ... These Harmonies, taken separately, have no connection with one another; considered as a whole, one could find a principle of unity *in their very diversity...*"[4]

Truthfulness

Faced with these high valuations of subject, high valuations of treatment are rare or restrained for the reasons mentioned above. The only aspect of treatment an author can give himself credit for in the preface, undoubtedly because conscience rather than talent is involved, is truthfulness or, at the very least, sincerity – that is, the effort to achieve truthfulness. Taking credit for truthfulness or sincerity has been a commonplace of prefaces to historical works since Herodotus and Thucydides, and of prefaces to autobiographical works, or self-portraits, since Montaigne: "This book was written in good faith, reader." We have already glimpsed the form Rousseau gave to what may be considered a genuine pledge. Historians reinforce this pledge with a statement about method that serves as a guarantee (based on the particular means they used). Thucydides, for example, maintains that he relies only on direct observation or duly corroborated testimony; and for speeches, the literal text of which he is unable to quote, he makes sure to commit himself only on their overall content and plausibility.

Fiction itself is not wholly unfamiliar with this contract of truthfulness. The first Greek romance, as we remember, opens with the assertion – perhaps accurate – that this love story really did take place in Syracuse. In a "note" published as an appendix to *La Fille aux yeux d'or*, Balzac guarantees that this episode "is

---

[4]   In italicizing this phrase and cutting the quotation off here, I am perhaps stretching Lamartine's text toward my meaning. Here is the rest of it: "For in the author's mind, they were intended to reproduce a great many of the impressions that nature and life make on the human soul; impressions varied in their essence, uniform in their object, because all of them would have been absorbed and would have come to rest in the contemplation of God." Here, therefore, we find again the usual ground of all monistic valuing: the soul, God.

true in most of its details," and he adds, more generally: "Writers never make up anything, an admission the great Walter Scott humbly made in the preface where he tore off the veil in which he had long wrapped himself. Even the details rarely belong to the writer, for he is only a more or less successful transcriber [Proust will say "translator"]. The only thing that comes from him is the combination of events, their literary arrangement ..." And we know the formula the Goncourts placed at the head of *Germinie Lacerteux*: "This novel is a true novel." But even so, in claiming credit for realism they use the disavowing form of a so-called apology: "We must ask the public to pardon us for presenting it with this book, and must warn the public about what it will find herein. The public likes false novels: this novel is a true one." The novelist Edouard in Gide's *Faux-Monnayeurs* confesses, or rather declares, "I have never been able to make anything up," and even if Gide subsequently complained that that sentence was used against him, there is no doubt that it expressed his condition as a writer, a condition Julien Green accepted, more proudly or more cleverly, in declaring, "The novelist invents nothing; he guesses."[5]

Despite the Goncourts' claim, it is not so easy to know what kind of novel the public prefers; and the contract of truth is offset, or countered, by a reverse contract, of fiction, which we will encounter below along with some more or less canonical variations on the inevitable blending of the two. But at that point, theoretically we will no longer be in the realm of merit.

Lightning rods

The authorial discourse of valuation thus stops here, or almost. When an author is anxious to highlight his merit, talent, or genius, he generally prefers – not unreasonably – to entrust this task to someone else by way of an allographic preface, sometimes a highly suspect one, as we will see below. More in keeping with the topos of modesty, and more effective in many respects, is the stance that, in classical oratory, was the inevitable counterpart of the *amplificatio* of the subject [see p. 199]: rhetoric codified this reverse stance under the term *excusatio propter infirmitatem*

---

[5] Julien Green, *Journal*, February 5, 1933.

[excuse because of mental weakness]. Offsetting the importance of his theme, which he sometimes inordinately exaggerated, the orator pleaded his incapacity to handle it with all the necessary talent, apparently counting on the public to average everything out fairly. But the plea of incapacity was above all the surest way for an author to ward off critics, that is, to neutralize them – and indeed, to forestall criticism by taking the initiative. That paradoxically value-enhancing function is expressed by Lichtenberg in his own way, with a single term: "The preface could be entitled 'Lightning Rod.'"[6] Cervantes, in the prologue of *Don Quixote*, apologizes in no uncertain terms for not having produced the masterpiece he would have wished to produce: "But," he argues, "I could not counteract Nature's law that everything shall beget its like; [my] sterile, uncultivated wit [could beget nothing but] a dry, shriveled, eccentric offspring." Rousseau, presenting *Emile*, announces that the subject of the education of children, which "after Locke's book ... was still entirely fresh," will continue to be so after him, and he himself denounces his work as being "too big, doubtless, for what it contains, but too small for the matter it treats." In the preface to *Julie* he had already had recourse to what was undoubtedly the most effective form of this type of preventive autocriticism: the imaginary dialogue, which allows an author to answer objections he himself has chosen to raise. For the preface to *Proscrits*, Nodier produces a more flippant dialogue, in which he mixes the clever defense with the even more clever refusal to defend himself: "'Your work won't be approved by people of taste.' 'I'm afraid not.' 'You tried to be new.' 'That's true.' 'And you managed only to be odd.' 'That's possible.' 'People found your style uneven.' 'Passions are, too.' 'And strewn with repetitions.' 'The language of the heart is not rich. ...' 'Finally, your characters are poorly chosen.' 'I didn't choose.' 'Your episodes poorly invented.' 'I invented nothing.' 'And you wrote a bad novel.' 'It's not a novel.'"

The most accurate and effective remark, perhaps, is Balzac's, in the preface to *Le Cabinet des antiques*. Like Cervantes, he had dreamed of another book and then the subject drifted away, and this book, like all books, turned out to be what it turned out to be.

[6] G. C. Lichtenberg, *Aphorismen* [tr. *Aphorisms*, in *The Lichtenberg Reader: Selected Writings of Georg Christoph Lichtenberg*, trans. Franz H. Mautner and Henry Hatfield (Boston: Beacon Press, 1959)].

"It is as easy to dream a book as it is hard to write one." What answer can one give except, perhaps, that no one is required to write books? We already know Balzac's reply: "I am." But that, I'm afraid, is not an argument fit for a preface.

The themes of the how

However devious and paradoxical this rhetoric of value-enhancement may sometimes become, the dissociation it assumes between subject (always praiseworthy) and treatment (always unworthy) means that this rhetoric is hardly in fashion nowadays, for the reason indicated earlier in the chapter. Thus, since the nineteenth century the functions of enhancing the work's value have been relatively eclipsed by the functions of providing information and guidance for reading. In other words, arguments of the why have been eclipsed (but in the meantime, have found other vehicles than the preface) by themes of the how, which have the advantage of *presupposing* the why and therefore (by the well-known force of presupposition) of imperceptibly imposing it. When an author is so kind as to explain to you *how* you must read his book, you are already in a poor position to reply, even *in petto*, that you will *not* read it. The how is therefore in certain respects an indirect form of the why and may be substituted, without loss, for the direct forms – with which it initially coexisted.

"The preface," said Novalis, "provides directions for using the book."[7] The phrase is accurate but stark. The way to guide the reading, to try to get a proper reading, is not only to issue direct orders. The way to get a proper reading is also – and perhaps initially – to put the (definitely assumed) reader in possession of information the author considers necessary for this proper reading. And advice itself benefits from being presented in the light of information: information, for example (in a case in which this might interest you), about the way the author wishes to be read. Thus in the preface to *Les Contemplations*, Hugo approached the matter with all the necessary precautions but also with all possible clarity: "If an author could have some right to influence the frame of mind of the readers who open his book, the author

---

[7] Novalis, *Die Enzyklopädie*, vol. 1 of *Fragmente*, ed. E. Wasmuth (Heidelberg: Schnieder Verlag, 1957) (French tr. *Encyclopédie* [Minuit, 1966], 40).

of *Les Contemplations* would say merely this: this book must be read the way one would read the book of a dead man." That, no doubt, is the supreme piece of information, but there are others, more humble, that may in this way help guide a docile reader. *Roland Barthes par Roland Barthes*, not exactly in the preface but, as we have seen, in a snapshot of handwriting on the inside front cover: "It must all be considered as if spoken by a character in a novel." Coming from someone who, along with many others, had announced the "death of the author," that is a very authorial – not to say very authoritarian – order to give. True, no one took it literally.

Genesis

The original preface may inform the reader about the origin of the work, the circumstances in which it was written, the stages of its creation. "This collection of reflections and observations," Rousseau tells us in the preface to *Emile*, "was begun to gratify a good mother who knows how to think." Here we recall those medieval romances and chronicles that mentioned the commission right at the beginning and (in contrast to Rousseau) identified the person who issued it. The original foreword to Chateaubriand's *Vie de Rancé* informs us that the author had been ordered to write this final masterpiece by his director of conscience, the abbé Séguin – to whose memory it is of course dedicated. The original preface to *Le Génie du christianisme* contains what is undoubtedly the most famous and most dramatic (but also most disputed) information of this kind: it was the death of his mother, reinforced by the death of his sister ("which Providence made use of to recall me to my duties"), that brought Chateaubriand back to the way of faith. "I was not governed, I confess, by any mighty supernatural insight; my conversion came from the heart: I wept and I believed." The plan for the *Génie* came from this conversion of the heart, which obviously enlightened the mind. In the 1846 foreword to *Les Mémoires d'outre-tombe*, Chateaubriand mentions the more secular circumstances of this long-term work that he wrote in various places and at various times, and in which he constantly intermingled (as he himself informs us) the periods he was writing about and the periods during which he was writing, the narrated I and the

narrating I. The prefaces to his *Œuvres complètes* already emphasized this biographical context of the works, but those prefaces
were delayed, not original. Autobiographical information is in
fact always more typical of the retrospective paratext, and we
will find it there again when we discuss delayed prefaces, in
Chateaubriand always, and in some other authors.

A special aspect of this genetic information (an aspect that no
longer involves biography in such a direct way) is the indication
of sources. This is typical of works of fiction that draw their
subjects from history or legend, for "pure" fiction in theory lacks
sources, and strictly historical works indicate their sources,
instead, in the detail of the text or in the notes. The indication of
sources thus appears especially in the prefaces to classical tragedies and historical novels. Corneille and Racine never fail to cite
their sources, and Corneille's *Tite et Bérénice*, for example, has no
paratext other than the excerpts from Dio Cassius on which this
play is based. When, as an exception, the author has had to
supply a character who was foreign to the original action, he
either apologizes for doing so (Corneille for *Sertorius*: "To bring
in two [women], I had to resort to invention") or quotes a lateral
source (Racine says he found Aricie, a character in his *Phèdre*, in
Virgil, and Eriphile, a character in his *Iphigénie*, in Pausanias).
What perhaps prevents Walter Scott from indicating his sources
in his original prefaces is, initially, his anonymity, and later the
imagined authors, but in 1828 he makes good that deficiency – a
typical example of compensation. The original preface of Hugo's
Bug-Jargal mentions the witnesses and documents on which this
story of the revolution in San Domingo is based. For *War and
Peace*, Tolstoy neither cites nor precisely mentions his sources, but
he evokes them in a way meant to be intimidating and states he is
ready to produce them if anyone challenges him: "Wherever in
my novel historical persons speak or act, I have invented nothing,
but have used historical material of which I have accumulated a
whole library during my work. I do not think it necessary to cite
the titles of those books here, but could cite them at any time in
proof of what I say."

What we might want to look on as a special case of the
indication of sources is the thanks expressed to the people and
institutions that, in various ways, helped the author prepare,
write, or produce his book. Very various ways: with information,

advice, criticism; with typing or typographical assistance; with moral, emotional, or financial support; with patience or impatience, lucidity or blindness, tactful presence or substantial absence. Undoubtedly I am overlooking some forms of help, and I would reproach myself for riding roughshod over so delicate a matter were it not, it seems to me, undeniable that the public expression of these thanks, like the dedication of the work, certainly comes under the heading of information for the reader, and perhaps also, obliquely, of value-enhancement: an author who has so many friends of both sexes cannot be completely bad. But to be honest, I should add that this touching and (God knows why) typically academic item is occasionally – especially in English, under the heading *acknowledgments* – made the subject of a separate paratextual element, which I am somewhat cavalierly annexing to the preface.

Choice of a public

Guiding the reader also, and first of all, means situating him, and thus determining who he is. It is not always wise to cast one's net too wide, and authors often have a fairly specific idea of the kind of reader they want, or the kind they know they can reach; but also the kind they want to avoid (for Spinoza, for example, it was nonphilosophers).[8] Balzac, as we know (and as was better known in his own day), specially targeted the female public, whose most competent analyst he claimed to be, even if he does not make this claim in his prefaces. Targeting a female public is in many respects a practice as old as the novel itself (to men goes the epical, to women the novelistic). We have already seen Boccaccio illustrate this practice, addressing himself to "the charming ladies"; and we can see it in a parodic form in Rabelais's prologue to *Gargantua*, addressed to drunkards and syphilitics – symbol and not inconsiderable portion of the male sex. I have already mentioned (in Chapter 8 in the section on addressees) Barrès's and Bourget's choice of the adolescent public, a choice made explicit, for example, in the preface to Barrès's *Homme libre*: "I write for children and the very young. If I pleased grown-ups I would feel proud, but there is not much point in their reading

[8] Spinoza, preface to *Theological-Political Treatise*, cited by J.-M. Schaeffer, "Note sur la préface philosophique."

me. They have already had the experiences I am going to write about." Such determinations of a public, or more exactly of readers, are not necessarily always to be taken literally. Sometimes, by means of the publicity band [see Chapter 1, note 11], an author targets other readers whom he hopes in this way to cut to the quick ("Why not me?"), as with some snobbish advertisements or, no doubt, the classical shibboleth of writing for the ideal, or symbolic, public composed of departed masters: " 'What would Homer and Virgil say if they were to read these lines? What would Sophocles say, if he saw this scene enacted?' ... For, to quote an Ancient's thoughts, those are the true audiences whom we should bear in mind."[9] The shibboleth was reversed by Stendhal when he claimed (passim but, to tell the truth, not in a preface) that he was aiming at the public of 1880, or of 1950. And was splendidly renewed, via Stendhal, by Pascal Quignard: "I hope to be read in 1640."[10]

Commentary on the title

"A preface," said Jean Paul in, precisely, the preface to his *Jubelsenior: Ein Appendix*, "should be nothing more than a longer title page [but we know that title pages in the eighteenth century were themselves sometimes very long]. The present preface has one task only: to explain the word *appendix* that appears in my title." In its own way, that statement suggested a new function for the preface – if possible, the original preface: to account for the title, something that is all the more necessary when the title, long or short, is allusive, indeed, enigmatic. Aulus Gellius, in the preamble of *Attic Nights*, was already explaining his title in terms of the circumstances in which he had "amuse[d] [him]self by assembling these notes." I read somewhere that a novel by Paul de Kock entitled *Le Cocu* [*The Cuckold*] contained a "preface to explain the title"; not having checked it out myself (for the Bibliothèque Nationale is closed Sundays), I do not know what there is about this apparently lucid title that called for an explanation, which was perhaps an excuse. Cervantes, too, underestimated the hermeneutic capability of his readers when he specified, for his *Exemplary Stories*, "I have given these stories

---

[9] Racine, preface to *Britannicus*.   [10] Quignard, "Noèsis," *Furor* 1 (1980).

the title of *Exemplary*; and if you look closely there is not one of them that does not afford a useful example." More necessary, no doubt, is this gloss by Swift on his *Tale of a Tub*: sailors, to prevent whales from attacking their ship, have the habit of throwing an empty tub overboard to amuse and divert the whales; in the same way, this book was sent forth to trick Hobbes's *Leviathan*. In the introduction (first chapter) of *Waverley*, Scott gives a long explanation of his subtitle *'Tis Sixty Years Since*, an explanation that attests to his keen awareness of the genre connotations of his age: if I had chosen *A Tale of Other Days*, readers would have expected a gothic novel in the style of Mrs. Radcliffe; *A Romance from the German*, a story of the Illuminati; *Sentimental Tale*, a young heroine with an abundance of hair; *A Tale of the Times*, a person from the fashionable world; I prefer *Sixty Years Since* to announce a subject that is neither ancient nor contemporary, for "the object of my tale is more a description of men than manners."

Commentary on the title may be a defense against criticism undergone or anticipated. Corneille, for example, apologizes for having given the title *Rodogune* to a play whose heroine is named Cleopatra (people might have confused her with the queen of Egypt); and Racine apologizes for having given the title *Alexandre* to a play whose real hero, critics claim (the author disagrees), is Porus. Commentary on the title may also serve to explain why a title was changed from what was advertised or from what it had been in serial publication: in the "Quasi-Literary Foreword" (followed by an "Eminently Commercial Note") of *Le Cousin Pons*, Balzac accounts for this new title (the ad had said: *Les Deux Musiciens*) in terms of his desire to emphasize the work's symmetrical relationship to *La Cousine Bette* and thus to make "very visible the antagonism of the two parts of *L'Histoire des parents pauvres*." Commentary on the title may also serve as a kind of delayed repentance: in the preface to *Volupté*, Sainte-Beuve apologizes for a title that is a bit too enticing but could not be corrected in time; and Edmond de Goncourt, in his (later) preface to *Renée Mauperin*, wonders: "Is *Renée Mauperin* the right title, the proper title, for this book? Wasn't *La Jeune Bourgeoise*, the title under which my brother and I announced the book before it was finished, a better way to define the psychological analysis of contemporary youth which we were attempting in 1864? But by this time, it is really quite late to rename this volume." And Hugo, for *L'Homme qui rit*: "The right title for this book would be *L'Aristocratie*"; and Bourget, for *La Terre promise*: "If such a title would not have seemed too ambitious, this book would have been called *Le Droit de l'enfant*." Such admissions of hesitation obviously have the effect, and no doubt the purpose, of suggesting a kind of semiofficial subtitle. Or more subtly, of indicating a nuance that the pedestrian title originally envisaged did not convey: "In speaking of a *Poetics of Reverie*," writes Bachelard, "when the simple '*Poetic Reverie*' had been tempting me for a long time, I wanted to indicate the force of coherence which a dreamer feels when he is really faithful to his dreams, and that his dreams take on coherence precisely because of their poetic qualities." And Northrop Frye, at the head of *The Great Code*: " '*The Bible as Literature*' ... is not quite the subtitle of this book."[11] Finally, commentary on the title may be a warning against – and therefore a sort of partial correction to – the misleading suggestions of the title: everyone knows how Rabelais, at the head of *Gargantua*, diverts suspicion from the "mockeries, tomfooleries, and merry falsehoods" that the "outward sign (that is the title)" of his book may engender.

Nowadays (as we have seen) this function of commenting on the title has for the most part devolved to the please-insert – whose influence is obviously nearer to hand and more immediate – or, more obliquely (as we have also seen), to the epigraph.

Contracts of fiction

A function that is more or less inevitably reserved for works of fiction, particularly novelistic fiction, consists of what I will call (with the touch of suspicion that adheres to the term) professing the work's fictiveness. Innumerable classical works have prefaces warning the reader to resist any temptation to seek keys (or as it was more commonly put in those days, "applications") to the characters or situations. I have mentioned the preface to the first part of d'Urfé's *Astrée*. The publisher's note to La Fayette's

---

[11] It is in fact *The Bible and Literature*. As for the title, Frye explains it in his introduction, with a kind of incorporated epigraph that gives its source: "Blake ... said 'The Old and New Testaments are the Great Code of Art,' a phrase I have used for my title after pondering its implications for many years."

Princesse de Montpensier emphasizes the "entirely imaginary" nature of this narrative. La Bruyère (outside the fiction?) believes himself "able to protest against ... all false application" of his portraits. Lesage's *Gil Blas* ("The Author's Declaration"): "As there are some people who cannot read, without making applications of the vicious and ludicrous characters they meet with in works of this kind; I declare to these mischievous readers, that they will be to blame, if they apply any of the pictures drawn in this book. I publicly own that my purpose is to represent life as we find it: but God forbid that I should undertake to delineate any man in particular!" *Les Egarements du cœur et de l'esprit*: "There are subtle readers who never read except to apply what they see. ... Personal interpretations do not last long: either people get tired of making them, or they are so futile that they die of their own accord." Constant's *Adolphe*, preface to the second edition: "I have already protested against the allusions which malignity, aspiring to the merit of penetration, has, by absurd conjectures, believed it might discover in it. If I had really given occasion for such interpretations ... I should consider myself as deserving severe reproach ... To seek for allusions in a romance, is to prefer slander to nature, and to substitute mere gossip for observation of the human heart." The most unsophisticated form of "application" consists of attributing to the author the opinions or feelings of his characters: there are "subtle readers" too subtle to read the quotation marks, and I am not talking about the fine distinctions of free indirect style, to which, it is sometimes said, and with some truth, *Madame Bovary* owed its lawsuit;[12] nor am I talking about the amalgams of the author's way of thinking and the opinions ascribed to the narrator: "Even though the case for separation between an author and his characters was settled long ago, many people incur ridicule by making the writer a party to the feelings he attributes to his characters; and if he uses the *I* form, most of them are tempted to confuse him with the narrator" (Balzac's preface to *Le Lys dans la vallée*).

We still find professions of fictiveness in modern prefaces, such as the one to *Gilles*, where Drieu explains that there is no key in this novel and, at the same time, that "all novels have keys,"[13]

---

[12] [See Chapter 10, note 4.]
[13] Drieu, *Gilles*, preface to the new and unabridged edition of 1942 (original edition: 1939).

and the prefaces by Aragon, who exploits this facile paradox in a manner we will encounter again below. But the form used most frequently nowadays, perhaps borrowed from a practice customary in film, is that of a separate notice of this type: "The characters and situations in this narrative are wholly fictitious and any resemblance to real persons and situations is purely coincidental." Such a formula, as we know, has a legal function, for it aims – sometimes unsuccessfully – to avoid libel suits. In this case we are dealing with a real contract of fiction. By the luck of the stepladder I have found different variants of it at the head of, for example, Aragon's *Aurélien, Voyageurs de l'impériale*, and *Semaine sainte*, Céline's *Féerie pour une autre fois*, Henri Bosco's *Antiquaire*, Barth's *Sot-Weed Factor*, Modiano's *Boulevards de ceinture*, and Catherine Rihoit's *Bal des débutantes*. The formula may also be humorously reversed (*Green Hills of Africa*: "Unlike many novels, none of the characters or incidents in this book is imaginary"; Queneau's *Dimanche de la vie*: "The characters in this novel are real, and any resemblance to imaginary people would be coincidental"), or it may be subverted in various ways (Perec's *Vie mode d'emploi*: "Friendship, history, and literature have supplied me with some of the characters of this book. All other resemblances to living persons or to people having lived in reality or fiction can only be coincidental"; Alain Jouffroy's *Roman vécu*: "All the facts, all the feelings, all the characters, all the documents used in this novel that I have dedicated to all the women and men who have made my life possible have the strict accuracy of my imagination. I beg pardon of reality"). Robbe-Grillet's *Maison de rendez-vous* contains two notices that quite decidedly contradict each other. Francis Jeanson puts a deliberately inappropriate note at the head of his *Sartre dans sa vie* [*Sartre in His Life*]: "The main character in this story is wholly imaginary. One should not, however, underestimate the possibility that some correlations will emerge between the behavior of a person named *Jean-Paul Sartre* and the pure fiction contained herein: the author, in any case, is anxious to indicate that he would not easily agree to be held responsible for mishaps of that kind." And I have already quoted twice the disavowing phrase that opens *Roland Barthes par Roland Barthes*.

One can undoubtedly see why I have appended these autonomous formulations of the contract of fiction to the preface, for they seem only recently to have become detached from it. But certainly they could just as well be considered appendages of the genre indication, which they very often duplicate when they do not deliberately contradict it. We would, of course, do well to handle such confirmations and refutations gingerly or take them *cum grano salis,* for the denial of "any resemblance" has always had the double function of protecting the author from the potential consequences of the "applications" and, inevitably, of setting readers in search of them.

The order in which to read

It is sometimes useful to inform the reader, in the preface and as if to clarify the table of contents, about the order of the material in the book. Bachelard, for example, did this almost systematically. This didactic – indeed, pedagogic – stance is one we can hardly expect to find in a preface to a work of fiction or poetry. One may also indicate to the hurried reader which chapters he may, if necessary, pass up; indeed, one may suggest different paths through the book, as Aragon does for *Henri Matisse, Roman,* or Cortazar for *Hopscotch.* Or on the contrary, one may require a reading that is complete and in sequence, as Max Frisch does in his notice "To the Reader" of the *Sketchbook 1946–1949.* That notice is the most unvarnished form of the rhetoric of the how: "Follow the order as presented."

Contextual information

Sometimes, for one reason or another, an author may publish a work that in his mind constitutes part of a whole still in progress and that will acquire its full – indeed, its real – significance only in this context-to-come, of which the public still has no suspicion. This is a typically Balzacian situation,[14] and it calls for that equally Balzacian production, the provisional original preface, whose sole task is to alert the reader to the temporary situation

---

[14] The way around it, which I will call "Flaubertian" on the basis of a dream the young Gustave had, would be "that of the fellow who had published nothing until he was fifty years old and suddenly one day published his complete works, then left it at that" (letter to Du Camp, May 1846 [Pléiade 1:265]). This suggestion fascinated Gide (*Journal*, July 12, 1914), but I do not know if anyone has ever acted on it.

and to give him some idea of what lies ahead. "These forewords and prefaces are to disappear entirely when the work is finished and appears in its real and complete form," we read at the head of *Le Cabinet des antiques* (1839). But as early as 1833, Balzac provided *Ferragus* with a preface, despite his "aversion" to the genre, because this narrative was only a fragment separated from the episodes to follow. Every stage of the publication of *Illusions perdues* is punctuated with similar forewords:[15] for *Les Deux Poètes* (1837), wait for the second section; for *Un Grand Homme de province à Paris* (1839), wait for the third section; and *Les Souffrances de l'inventeur* (1843, under the title *David Séchard*) is accompanied, as well, by the announcement of other "scenes" that will shed light on this one. At the head of *César Birotteau*, the reader is asked to link this work with *La Maison Nucingen*, as he is asked to link *Le Curé de village* with *Le Médecin de campagne*, and *Le Cousin Pons* with *La Cousine Bette*. At the head of *Pierrette*, the author still complains about the separated publication that obscures the relation between part and whole. But it is doubtless the preface to *Une Fille d'Eve* (1838–39), the most important of Balzac's prefaces before the foreword of 1842 (which it anticipates in many respects), that best illustrates the use of "explanatory prefaces" to compensate for staggered publication. In these prefaces, Balzac says, the author must make himself the "cicerone to his œuvre" (a fine metaphor for the function of guiding), an œuvre where everything holds together, where everything (as in life) is "mosaic." Hence a reminder of the overall structure, which had already been announced in the prefaces of the early collections; hence the idea (which Balzac attributes to his publisher and which critics yet unborn would undertake to implement) that a biographical dictionary of the *Etudes de mœurs* would be useful: "RASTIGNAC (Eugène-Louis), elder son of the baron and baroness de Rastignac," and so forth.

But we know that Balzac did not rely solely on the monitory force of prefaces and that within the text itself he increased the number of asides (incorporated paratexts) referring from one novel to another. Proust, who pokes fun at this practice in his pastiche [in *Pastiches et mélanges*], perhaps mocks it so well only

---

[15] [*Illusions perdues* is a novel in three parts: *Les Deux Poètes, Un grand homme de province à Paris,* and *Les Souffrances de l'inventeur.* It belongs to the grouping *Scènes de la vie de province.*]

because he, too, was going to suffer from deferred publication. And if, in 1913, he forgoes a monitory preface, he does so in favor of taking another route, less official but perhaps more effective: an interview published on the very eve of *Swann*'s appearance, with exactly that kind of advisory message. We will meet this interview again in its proper place.

These directives urging the reader to wait for the whole before judging the fragment entail an obvious risk: that of deterring the public from reading the book immediately and inducing it to wait until the complete work appears and then make a bulk purchase, so to speak. Consequently, some authors accompany these directives with a very well balanced rhetoric, as Hugo does at the head of the first series (1859) of *La Légende des siècles*. This volume, he says, is only a beginning, but it is sufficient unto itself, just as a peristyle is already a monument: "It exists on its own and forms a whole; it exists with others and is part of a group." An invitation, in advance, to read it twice: the first time, right now, as "a whole," and the second time, later, as "part of a group." For *Les Rougon-Macquart*, Zola avails himself of another strategy, placing at the head of *La Fortune des Rougon* a preface that pertains in advance to the group. In this way the reader, beyond this first episode, feels himself already involved in a more comprehensive reading. This is also more or less Frye's stance in the introduction to *The Great Code*: "After considerable thought, I have decided to remove the ominous heading 'Volume One' from the title page, because I should want any book I publish to be a complete unit in itself. But a second volume is in active preparation nonetheless, and this introduction is partly to it as well."

Finally, other authors merely take advantage of the preface of one book to announce their next book. In the prologue of *Exemplary Stories*, for example, Cervantes promises the publication of *Persiles* and the second *Quixote*. Then in the prologue of the second *Quixote* he announces *Persiles* once again, plus the second part of *Galatea*. And in 1897 Gide's *Paludes* had an ephemeral later postface whose title was "Postface for the second edition of *Paludes* and for the announcement of *Les Nourritures terrestres*." Promises kept, mission accomplished. Such is not always the case, and that is the major danger of these "announcement effects." One should not be superstitious.

Statements of intent

The most important function of the original preface, perhaps, is to provide the author's interpretation of the text or, if you prefer, his statement of intent. Such an approach is apparently contrary to a certain modern vulgate, formulated in particular by Valéry, which refuses to grant the author any control over the "real meaning" – indeed, which absolutely denies the existence of such a meaning. I say a *certain* vulgate, for plainly it is not shared by everyone – and we won't even count those who profess it only grudgingly, from a modernist point of honor, but believe none of it in their heart of hearts and do not hesitate to hold it up to ridicule, if not from preface to preface then at least in interviews and conversations and at dinner parties. In any case, try to imagine how Proust – although strongly opposed to any bio-graphical criticism – would react to an interpretation of the *Recherche* that did not accord with the indigenous theory devel-oped in *Le Temps retrouvé* and carefully prepared for as early as 1913 in the interview mentioned above. What he reproached Sainte-Beuve for, as we know, was not that Sainte-Beuve resorted to an author's underlying intention but, indeed, that he forgot about, or failed to understand, that intention, favoring instead superficial chitchat about the external circumstances of a work's creation. I say, too, *apparently* contrary, for even Valéry did not claim to have no personal interpretation of his work; he refrained only from imposing his interpretation on his readers because he did not believe it had been shown to be the most accurate one. But we will encounter this point again.

Curiously, the first modern preface in the broad sense of modern (or, at least, the preface we have symbolically ordained as the first modern one – the prologue to *Gargantua*) was already taking the same kind of position, which it made into its main argument. I will not retrace here the very long and very involved controversy generated by this deliberately ambiguous text, a controversy that one of its most recent participants has rightly called a "critical hullabaloo."[16] We should remember only that Rabelais, after inviting his reader to go beyond the playful

---

[16] G. Defaux, "D'un problème l'autre: Herméneutique de l'altior sensus' et 'captatio lectoris' dans le Prologue de 'Gargantua,'" *Revue d'histoire littéraire de la France* (March–April 1985): 195–216.

promises of the title in favor of an interpretation "in a higher sense" and of a "more abstruse doctrine," immediately adds that these hermeneutic depths, like the ones people insist on finding in Homer or Ovid, are very likely to have escaped their author's notice. In these passages the author may be satirizing the interpretive excesses of scholasticism and may also be maneuvering to attract a new public more demanding than the public of *Pantagruel* by promising it hidden treasures that he himself, like La Fontaine's plowman, cared little about[17] – but that makes no difference to Rabelais's overall strategy, which consists of suggesting to the reader an interpretive approach by inviting him, even on the off chance, to "break the bone and suck out the substantific marrow."

Between Rabelais and Valéry (and beyond, of course), authorial practice is generally less subtle or less equivocal: it definitely consists of forcing on the reader an indigenous theory defined by the author's *intention*, which is presented as the most reliable interpretive key; and in this respect the preface clearly constitutes one of the instruments of authorial control. That this indigenous theory is not always sincere emerges quite plainly from the innumerable edifying professions in which the most licentious novels and most subversive essays of the eighteenth century envelop themselves – professions whose inescapable hypocrisy has left many a trace in nineteenth-century, and indeed twentieth-century, prefaces. Paul Morand complained about this not so very long ago in his own preface to *Nouvelles des yeux*: "A recent collection of the best-known prefaces of the nineteenth century has just shown how blatant their inanity is.[18] Their sole raison d'être, common to them all, is to prove that the work being offered is not immoral and that the author does not deserve to go to jail. In our day this is no longer a problem" (a statement that perhaps makes short work of some real dangers). That this indigenous theory is, as well, not always very lucid has been

---

[17] [In La Fontaine's *Plowman and His Sons* (book 5, no. 9), a plowman on his deathbed tells his sons that there is buried treasure somewhere on the land he is bequeathing them; he doesn't know where it is, and to find it, they will have to work the land over and over. They do – and reap not buried treasure (there is none) but a rich harvest.]

[18] This must be a reference to the *Anthologie des préfaces de romans français du XIXe siècle*, compiled in 1962 by H. S. Gershman and K. B. Whitworth, Jr. (Columbia: University of Missouri Press); French edition published by Julliard, 1964.

shown by Balzacian criticism since Zola, apropos of the well-known gulf between the ideological assertions of Balzac's 1842 foreword and the historical lessons of *La Comédie humaine*. Nonetheless, and just as obviously, these paratextual statements of intent are present, and no one – whether he denies it or not – can fail to take them into account.

Their common theme is thus, roughly, "Here is what I meant to do," and the short preface to *The Magic Mountain* is even entitled, as all of them could be, "Dessein" ["Purpose"].[19] Cervantes, as we know, defines his intention in *Quixote* as that of making "an attack upon the books of chivalry," however many doubts may have been cast on this aim by a long tradition of Cervantean exegesis. In the dedication of *Tom Jones* the author "declare[s], that to recommend Goodness and Innocence hath been my sincere Endeavour in this History; ... to inculcate, that Virtue and Innocence can scarce ever be injured but by Indiscretion; and ... to laugh Mankind out of their favourite Follies and Vices." *Le Génie du christianisme* is meant to prove "that Christianity is the most poetic religion, the most humane one, the one most favorable to liberty, and to arts and letters," and in its episode *René*[20] is meant "to denounce this sort of new vice [the vagueness of the passions] and to portray the fatal consequences of excessive love of solitude." Benjamin Constant, in the 1824 preface to *Adolphe*, declares: "What I wanted to describe was the pain inflicted upon even the hardest hearted by the suffering they cause to others, and the illusion which makes them think they are more fickle and corrupt than they really are." In 1842 Balzac invokes the political philosophy of Bossuet and Bonald as his inspiration for a work written "by the light of two eternal truths: Religion and Monarchy." Zola picks up the volitional formula again at the head of *Thérèse Raquin*: "I *tried* to study temperaments not characters." And again at the head of *Les Rougon-Macquart*: "I *wish* to explain how a family ... conducts itself in a given social system ... I *shall endeavour* to discover and follow the thread of connection which leads mathematically from one man to another." And everyone

---

[19] To tell the truth, the German term is a bit more ambiguous: *Vorsatz* is also used to designate a flyleaf. [In the two English translations of *The Magic Mountain* (the older one by H. T. Lowe-Porter and the newer one by John E. Woods), the preface has been entitled "Foreword."]

[20] [Originally part of *Le Génie*, *René* was later published separately.]

knows what Proust *meant* to show in the *Recherche*; but everyone also knows that he did not deign to entrust his profession of faith to a mere preface.

From two contemporary authors I will take two formulae of authorial interpretation that seem to me the most categorical, the least inhibited by the Valéryan scruple. The first appears, it is true, in a delayed preface, Aragon's preface to *Aurélien* in 1966: "The impossibility of being a couple is the very subject of *Aurélien*." Too bad for the people who thought they perceived two or three other subjects as well: henceforth they will have to make an effort to circumvent this inhibiting signpost, which won't be that easy to do.[21] The second is doubtless still more intimidating because it is offered somewhat as the key to a riddle, or at least as the translation of a figure: it is Borges revealing, in the prologue of *Artifices*, that " 'Funes, the Memorious' ... is a long metaphor of insomnia." Impossible after that to read the story without having the authorial interpretation hang over your reading, compelling you to take a position, positive or negative, in relation to it.

Genre definitions

Our final function could just as well pass for a variant of the preceding one, which it extends toward a more institutional characterization, or one more concerned with the field (thematic or formal) into which the single work fits. This concern with genre definition does not show up much in areas that are well marked out and codified, like the classical theatre, where a simple paratitular indication (*tragedy, comedy*) is thought sufficient; rather, it appears in the undefined fringes where some degree of innovation is practiced, and particularly during "transitional" periods such as the baroque or early romantic, when writers seek to define such deviations in relation to an earlier norm whose authority still carries weight. For example, we see Ronsard, reviving the ancient epic, say a little awkwardly in the

[21] *Entretiens avec F. Crémieux*, recorded from October 1963 to January 1964 (and published by Gallimard, 1964) was a little less intimidating, for it applied the same formula to *Voyageurs de l'impériale* as well (pp. 95–96). In the interval, Aragon must have thought it advisable to find a better "target" for his formula.

preface to *La Franciade* [an unfinished epic], "This book is a novel like the *Iliad* and the *Aeneid.*"[22] We see Saint-Amant justify the paradoxical genre indication of *Moyse sauvé* ("heroic idyll") by pointing both to the absence of an "active hero" and battles or a siege and to the predominance of the "lute" over the "trumpet," in other words, the lyrical over the epical. Or La Fontaine, justifying the genre indication of *Adonis* ("poem") on the basis of that play's adherence to the heroic genre, although its subject and dimensions would, instead, tip it toward the idyll;[23] or Corneille, justifying the genre indication of *Don Sanche d'Aragon* ("heroic comedy") with the fact that it has a comic plot involving people in high places – in other words, it manifests the intersecting of the two Aristotelian criteria of the level of dignity of the action and the level of dignity of the characters.

Bernardin de Saint-Pierre laconically calls *Paul et Virginie* a "sort of pastoral"; Chateaubriand calls *Atala* a "kind of poem, half descriptive, half dramatic," *Les Martyrs* an "epic in prose," and *Les Natchez* epical in its first part, novelistic in its second. But the sense of genre innovation may be stronger than it is in any of these examples, thus giving the preface the tone of a real manifesto. These founding texts are well known, and here I will merely mention them. There is the preface to *Joseph Andrews*, in which Fielding defines the new novel as a "comic epic poem in prose" (comic à la Hogarth, not burlesque like his French predecessors: a critique of affectation and hypocrisy). There is Diderot's *Entretiens sur le fils naturel*, in which the author, in a dialogue with the play's protagonist, Dorval, outlines a "poetics of the *genre sérieux*," a category of drama midway between the comic and the tragic[24] but one that he regards as wholly different from the tragicomedy of Corneille, which "blends two genres, remote from each other and separated by an impassable barrier";

---

[22] Original preface of 1572. But the delayed preface, published posthumously in 1587 (and perhaps completed by Claude Binet), will be a real *ars poetica* of the "heroic poem," very Aristotelian in spirit: respect the unity of time of one year, seek not historical truth but what is possible and credible, coin new words, and prefer the decasyllabic line to the alexandrine, which "smacks too much of prose." On this set of prefaces to *La Franciade*, see F. Rigolot, "L'Imaginaire du discours préfaciel," *Studi di letteratura francese* (Florence, 1986).

[23] Chapelain had already justified such a genre indication in his preface to Marino's *Adone* (which we will come upon again), but La Fontaine seems to have forgotten that.

[24] [See Chapter 4, note 59.]

then Diderot's *Discours sur la poésie dramatique*, the postface to his play *Père de famille*, a new variety of bourgeois drama, which is situated between the *genre sérieux* and comedy; and also Beaumarchais's *Essai sur le genre dramatique sérieux*, the preface to *Eugénie*, in which – following in Diderot's footsteps – the author insists on the *genre sérieux*'s difference from classical tragedy (let us abandon the fear and keep only the pity) and on the necessity of writing in prose. There is Wordsworth's preface to the second edition of *Lyrical Ballads*, a real manifesto of romantic lyricism, poetry defined as "the spontaneous overflow of powerful feelings," the rejection of neoclassical "poetic diction" in favor of a language as straightforward as that of prose and distinguishable from it only by the pleasure of meter, an inexhaustible play of similitude and difference. There is also (undoubtedly the most famous one of all) Hugo's preface to *Cromwell*, a manifesto of romantic drama defined, as we know, in terms of the Christian sense of the conflict between body and soul, the blending of the sublime and the ridiculous (the same blending that Diderot condemned), and the rejection of the unities of time and place; primitive times were characterized by lyric utterance, ancient times by epical, and modern times by dramatic: a whole philosophy of History at the service of the invention, or rather the resurrection (Shakespeare), of a genre.[25]

Walter Scott, for the reasons mentioned earlier, did not draw attention to his (relative) invention of the historical novel with any manifesto in the form of an original preface, except for some modulations in the dedication of *Ivanhoe*, which we will encounter again; and even his delayed prefaces are still very modest about the full significance of an innovation that had such a powerful effect all across Europe.[26] What we might consider as just such a manifesto would perhaps be Vigny's later preface (1827) to *Cinq-Mars* (1826), even if there he seems especially anxious to emphasize his originality vis-à-vis the Scottish model by insisting on the presence of real historical people in the fore-

---

[25] "Prefaces, like manifestos, never stop writing the history of literature – along the lines of mythic narrative" (J. M. Gleizes, "Manifestes, préfaces," *Littérature* 39 [October 1980]).

[26] See the special issue of *Revue d'histoire littéraire de la France* entitled "Le Roman historique" (March 1975); and particularly, on the prefatorial accompaniments of a genre that was especially lavish with them, C. Duchet's "L'Illusion historique: L'enseignement des préfaces (1815–1832)."

ground of his novel (Scott had in fact led the way in *Quentin Durward*). But the important things here are the distinction Vigny proposes between "the True in fact" and "Truth in art" (in art men are "stronger and greater, ... more determined for good or for evil," "raised to a higher and ideal power, which concentrates all their forces") and the famous (and often misunderstood) expression "History is a romance of which the people are the authors" – an intermediary degree between factual accuracy and the artistic truth of fiction, with posterity attributing to the heroes of History words and actions that, for the most part, are imaginary but that neither the participants nor historians after them have any power to eradicate from popular belief. Tolstoy, equally anxious to differentiate his work from a generic type as inhibiting as it is illusive, refuses to define *War and Peace* positively as a historical novel. Nonetheless, perhaps he writes the (delayed) charter for the genre by defining the necessary conflict between the novelist and the historian: the novelist must remain faithful to the disorder of the facts as the participants actually experienced them (the implicit model, of course, is the Waterloo of the *Chartreuse*), independent of the artificial constructions developed after the event by general staffs and ingenuously endorsed by the historian. In short, it could well be that the historical novel was more apt to give rise to disavowing stances, beginning with Scott's incognitos. The characteristic expression of these stances is formulated by Aragon apropos of *La Semaine sainte*: "[This] is not a historical novel, it is simply a novel"[27] – a statement that, to tell the truth, is qualified by what follows: "All my novels are *historical*, although they are not *in period dress*. La Semaine sainte, appearances to the contrary, is *less* of a historical novel."

If this is so, of course no novel is historical, for every novel is historical. Balzac doubtless saw it this way, regarding himself as the Walter Scott of contemporary reality – as secretary to the historian whose name was "French society," determined to "write the history forgotten by so many historians: the history of manners." But as we know, he did not much like to define his works as novels.[28] Consequently he does not characterize his

---

[27] Interview in the periodical *Two Cities* (1959), reprinted as a preface for the ORC [*Œuvres romanesques croisées*, the novelistic works of Aragon and Elsa Triolet] and for later editions.

[28] He almost never uses this term, except to designate just that historical subgenre

undertaking in explicitly generic terms (but rather in epistemological and ideological terms). The manifesto of the "realistic" novel, if there is one after the preface to *Joseph Andrews*, could be considered instead, though it is very laconic, the preface to the Goncourts' *Germinie Lacerteux*, this "true novel": "The Novel [note the capital letter] is beginning to be the major serious form ["serious" had already been Diderot's word], passionate, full of life ..., contemporary moral History" (that last phrase is entirely Balzacian). Or, more loquacious, Maupassant's preface to *Pierre et Jean*, the preface most faithful to the spirit of a manifesto because its purpose is not to "make any plea here for the little novel which follows" but "to deal with the Novel in general" – this preface is, moreover, entitled "A Study of the Novel." It praises realism, which it contrasts with the novel of adventure and defines in terms of the substitution of a thousand "fine, hidden and almost invisible threads ... for the single piece of string that used to be called 'the plot.' " But this realistic technique that aims to give "a total illusion of truth" must choose between two paths: that of psychological analysis and that of "objectivity"; the latter eschews all "dissertation upon motives" and limits itself as a matter of methodology "to showing us people and the things that happen," leaving psychology "concealed in the book as it is in reality behind the events of life." We see that this delayed manifesto of the realistic or naturalistic novel is also a very premature manifesto of the so-called behaviorist novel.[29]

Finally, the preface-manifesto may argue for a cause broader than that of a literary genre. Gautier's preface to *Mademoiselle de Maupin* is an attack on moral hypocrisy, progressive utilitarianism, and the press, and a profession of faith in "art for art's sake": "There is nothing truly beautiful but that which can never be of any use whatsoever; everything useful is ugly." The preface-manifesto of *The Picture of Dorian Gray* sings exactly the same tune: "There is no such thing as a moral or an immoral

à la Scott ("When *Les Vendéens* will have grabbed the prize for the novel from W.S.," to Mme Hanska, January 26, 1835) or to describe a philosophical-fantastic work like *La Peau de chagrin*, incorporated in 1831 into the collection entitled *Romans et contes philosophiques*.

29 The naturalistic manifestos of Zola, as we know, did not take the form of prefaces. They can be found mainly in the articles collected in 1880 under the title *Le Roman naturaliste*.

book. Books are well written, or badly written. That is all. ...
All art is quite useless." More engagé is the preface to *The
Nigger of the "Narcissus*,"[30] a passionate and somewhat grandilo-
quent charter of the mission of the writer and of the artist in
general ("The artist, then, like the thinker or the scientist, seeks
the truth and makes his appeal"), which never once mentions
the text it is attached to and could pertain equally well to
Conrad's whole œuvre: a kind of Nobel acceptance speech
minus the occasion. As for Hugo's 1832 preface to *Le Dernier
Jour d'un condamné* [*The Last Day of a Condemned Man*], it is as
we know a manifesto against the death penalty and thus is
certainly not unrelated to the subject of the novel, but it goes
well beyond any literary consideration. And in 1860 Hugo
planned for *Les Misérables* a "philosophical preface," never
completed, that was intended as a defense of religion and more
precisely, no doubt, as a development of what could be called
the "democratic argument": "Man is bound up with the planet,
the planet is bound up with the sun, the sun with the star, the
star with the nebula, and the nebula – a stellar group – with
infinity. Remove one term from that chain and the polynomial
goes to pieces, the equation totters, creation no longer means
anything in the cosmos, and democracy no longer means anything on earth."[31] Nothing less.

Dodges

This overlong (albeit incomplete, and somewhat randomly illustrated) review of the functions of the original preface could lead
one to think that all authors feel equally compelled to provide
such a preface. Fortunately that is by no means the case, and here
we should remember the great abundance of works without
prefaces – and the smaller but significant number of authors who
refuse as much as possible to get involved with this paratextual
form: a Michaux, a Beckett, and already a Flaubert, who very

[30] This preface, under the title "Author's Note" and intended as an afterword,
was published with the last section of the novel in the *New Review* of December
1897 but was not reprinted in the early editions of the novel in book form; it
was published separately in 1902, and in 1921 it served as preface to the third
volume of the *Works of Joseph Conrad*.

[31] Cf. P. Albouy, "La 'Préface philosophique' des *Misérables*" (1962), in *Mythogra-
phies* (Corti, 1976).

clearly explains his refusal in a letter to Zola, on December 1, 1871, apropos of *La Fortune des Rougon*: "I find fault only with the preface. In my opinion, it spoils your book, which is so impartial and so lofty. You give away your secret: that is carrying candor too far; and you express your opinion, something which in my poetics a novelist hasn't the right to do."

We must also note – and I will conclude the chapter by calling attention to this paradoxical function – the revealing frequency with which many preface-writers express a kind of reservation, sincere or pretended, about the obligation to provide a preface, an obligation they are reminded of by the publisher and often feel is either a duty that is onerous to perform[32] or an exercise that yields a text too tiresome to read even when the author (as is doubtless the case for a Fielding, a Scott, or a Nodier) has, nevertheless, devoted himself to it with obvious pleasure, though a pleasure he deems perverse. In all these (and perhaps some other) cases of bad conscience, the most appropriate and most productive compromise consists of expressing the sense of unease in the preface itself, in the form of apologies or protests.

Apologies about length: "God spare thee, reader, long prefaces" (a remark attributed to Quevedo by Borges in the preface to *Doctor Brodie's Report*); "too long a preface" (Chateaubriand, *Essai sur les révolutions*). About dullness: in the introduction to *Lettres persanes*, Montesquieu says he is not bothering to praise the text ("It would simply be adding tediousness to what is in itself necessarily tedious, namely, a preface"); at the head of book 5 of *Tom Jones*, Fielding explains the presence of these eighteen prefaces, or preparatory chapters, or "digressive Essays," which he deliberately made "laboriously dull" (they are there to make what follows them seem more entertaining by contrast, like the stylish women of Bath, who "endeavour to appear as ugly as possible in the Morning, in order to set off that Beauty which they intend to shew you in the Evening"). About irrelevance: my prefaces, says Fielding again (bk. 16, ch. 1), are interchangeable, like prologues in the theatre, but that does not entirely lack advantages: the public gains a quarter of an hour at the dinner table, the critics do their hissing, and the reader may, without regret, skip several pages, "a Matter by no means of trivial

---

[32] "Those twenty-six pages," said Balzac apropos of the 1842 foreword, "gave me more trouble than a whole work" (to Mme Hanska, July.13, 1842).

Consequence to Persons who read books with no other View than to say they have read them." About uselessness: "For a long time now people have been inveighing against the uselessness of prefaces – yet they keep on writing them," says Théophile Gautier.[33] Nodier preemptively entitles the preface to *Quatre talismans* "A Useless Preface" and entitles the one to *La Fée aux miettes* "To the Reader Who Reads Prefaces"; but with Nodier the theme of uselessness extends to the text itself and beyond, an extension that paradoxically – and ironically – reinforces the value of the preface: "I can hardly justify having written so many useless novels except by repeating often that they are like my prefaces, a kind of novel of my life which, too, is only a useless preface. ..."[34] About presumptuousness (again, Nodier): "I think I said somewhere that a preface was a monument to pride: I willingly repeat it."[35] About hypocrisy: this is the place to recall Proust's famous line about "the insincere language of prefaces and dedications" – but this line does not appear in a preface.[36]

Protests of various kinds: Cervantes would have liked to deliver his *Quixote* bare, "without the embellishment of a prologue"; Marivaux devotes almost the whole preface of *La Voiture embourbée* to a quite lively and quite ambiguous diatribe against the obligation to write a preface and against the commonplaces of the genre. This is a preface that deserves to be quoted at length:

The first lines I address to my friend at the beginning of this story ought to spare me the burden of writing a preface, but a preface is necessary: a book printed and bound without a preface – is it a book? No, without doubt, it does not yet deserve that name; it is a sort of book, a book without proper authorization, a work of the same species as those that are books, an applicant, aspiring to become a book, and only when vested with this last formality is it worthy to truly bear that name. Only then is it complete: whether it be dull, mediocre, good or bad, with its

[33] Quoted by Derrida, *La Dissémination*, 33 [*Dissemination*, 27]; having been unable to find the source of the quotation, I don't know whether it appears in a preface.

[34] Nodier, the (delayed) "New Preface" to *Thérèse Aubert*. At the head of the *Vicaire des Ardennes* (1822), Balzac places a "Preface That One Will Read If One Can."

[35] Nodier, "Preliminaries" to *Jean Sbogar*; here again a self-mocking modalization: "Harmless pride, besides, and almost worthy of tender compassion – pride that's based on the fuss about a little book and that lasts just long enough to escort that little book from the store to the pulping machine."

[36] *Le Temps retrouvé*, Pléiade, 3:911; trans. Andreas Mayor (New York: Random House, 1981), 3:949.

preface it bears the name of book wherever it goes. ... And so, Reader, since a preface is necessary, here is one.

I don't know if people will like this novel, the turn it took seems to me rather pleasing, its comedy seems entertaining, its fantastic element fairly original, its transitions fairly natural, and the odd mixture of all these different styles gives it an utterly exceptional air, which leads me to hope that it will entertain more than bore, and ... But it seems to me that this is a really bad beginning for my preface: there is nothing to do except stick to my conclusions; it is a book in which the comedy is pleasing, the transitions natural, the fantastic element original; if that is so, the work is beautiful: but who says so? I, the author, say so. Ah, you will say, how funny these authors are with their prefaces that they fill with praise for their own books! But you yourself, Reader, how bizarre you are! You insist on a preface and you are indignant because the author says what he thinks of his book; you must understand that if he did not think this book *good*, he would not produce it. ... But stop, a peevish misanthropist will perhaps exclaim: if you know that in offering your book you are not offering anything beautiful, why produce it? Flattering friends made you do it, you say; well, you should have broken with them, they are your enemies; or else, since they were putting so much pressure on you, why didn't you resort to the fire that could do away with the wretched object of their insistent demands? These pleas are some excuse! I can't abide this varnish of humility, this ridiculous mixture of hypocrisy and arrogance that we see in almost every Mr. Author. I would prefer an avowed feeling of conceit to the circumlocutions of bad faith.

And I, Mr. Misanthropist, I prefer making a prefaceless book to sweating over something that satisfies nobody. If I hadn't been hampered by my plan to write this preface, I would have spoken of my book in more natural, more accurate terms, neither humble nor vain; I would have said that it had imagination, that I didn't presume to decide if that imagination was good; that, furthermore, I had truly been entertained while writing it, and that I wished it would be entertaining to others; but this hindrance of a plan made my mind rigid, so that I ran aground on insignificant reefs.

Thank God, now I am released from a great burden, and I am still laughing at the part I would have played had I been obliged to go through with my preface. Farewell. I infinitely prefer stopping short to boring you by going on at too great length. Let's move on to the work.

And another protest, Stendhal's draft preface to *Lucien Leuwen*: "What a dismal age it is when the publisher of a light novel has to urge on the author a preface of this sort" (since *Leuwen* was published posthumously, we see that Stendhal anticipates the publisher's request and screams even before he's hurt). The later preface to Zola's *Thérèse Raquin*: "It takes all the deliberate blindness of a certain kind of criticism to force a novelist to write a preface. Since I have committed the sin of writing one because I am a lover of light, I crave the forgiveness of men of intelligence who do not need me to light a lamp for them in broad daylight to help them see clearly." The delayed preface to *The Portrait of a Lady*: "It is dreadful to have too much, for any artistic demonstration, to dot one's i's and insist on one's intentions, and I am not eager to do it now." Another delayed preface (called "After the Event"), this one to Blanchot's *Ressassement éternel* [published in English as *Vicious Circles*] (dating from 1951, for two texts from 1935 and 1936): after citing Mallarmé ("'I abhor prefaces that come from the author himself, but those that come from someone else I find even more distasteful. My friend, a real book needs no introduction ...'"), Blanchot argues that a writer, who does not exist before his book, no longer exists after it: "Then how can he turn back (ah, the guilty Orpheus) to what he believes he is leading into the light – to judge it, to consider it, to recognize himself in it and, in the end, to make himself the privileged reader of it, the principle [*sic*] commentator or simply the zealous helper who gives or imposes his version, resolves the enigma, reveals the secret and authoritatively interrupts (we are, after all, talking about the author) the hermeneutic chain, since he claims to be the adequate interpreter, the first or the last? *Noli me legere.* ..." However, continues Blanchot, even Mallarmé, and Kafka, and Bataille, taking various routes, have commented on their own works. And then, in keeping with these examples chosen to prop up the inconsistency ("Yes, I know, but even so"), there follows an authorial commentary on the text thus prefaced.

These forms of protest, in which oratorical wariness and literary coyness are no doubt exposed a little more than the authors intended, will not unreasonably be thought slightly indiscreet and somewhat suspect.[37] Undoubtedly Malcolm Lowry's more affable manner at the head of the French transla-

---

[37] In his preface to *Cleveland*, Prévost had already denounced this wariness and coyness: "I will not imitate the affectation of numerous modern authors who seem to fear offending or at least disturbing the public with a preface, and who reveal as much repugnance and embarrassment when they have one to write as if they really had to fear their readers' distress and disgust. I have trouble imagining what their fears and difficulties may be due to. For if their works don't require the preliminary clarifications of a preface, who is forcing them to go to the useless trouble of composing one? And if, on the contrary, they think their readers need some explanation in order to understand what is being

tion of *Under the Volcano* [*Au-dessous du volcan*] will seem preferable, even though basically it is equally (or more) negative: "I like
Prefaces. I read them. Sometimes I do not read farther, and it is
possible that you may do the same. In that case, this preface will
have failed in its purpose, which is to make your access to my
book a little more easy."[38] Here the topos "I hate prefaces and so
do you" is inverted, but the presumed effect is worse, for the lure
of the preface may deter one from reading the text that follows it.
So again we find the Jupien effect. The simplest approach
ultimately is the one Dickens takes in the original preface to
David Copperfield, stating quite frankly that in his book he said
everything he had to say, and he has nothing to add except his
regret at parting from such dear companions and so engrossing
an "imaginative task." The simplest, and perhaps the sincerest.

Another sophisticated evasion: preterition. This is the art of
writing a preface by explaining that one is not going to write it, or
by conjuring up all the prefaces one could have written. There
was a little of that in Marivaux. Cervantes opens his heart to a
friend about his aversion to prefaces, the friend makes an
eloquent response, and Cervantes finds the friend's discourse so
apt that he turns it into ... the preface to *Quixote*. The same tactic
for *La Nouvelle Héloïse*: "Write down this conversation for your
whole preface," suggests Rousseau's interlocutor at the end of
their conversation; or for Jules Janin's *Ane mort et la femme
guillotinée*, whose preface sums up a conversation between the
author and "The Critics" ("They listened to me as well as can be
expected and, when I had said everything, they added that I was
awfully obscure. 'That is the beauty of a preface,' I answered
brazenly"). For the preface to the second edition of *Han d'Islande*
[April 1823; first edition, January 1823] Hugo lists various drafts
that came to nothing: a discourse on the novel in general (preface-
manifesto), a laudatory note signed by the publisher (apocryphal
allographic), and others. Finally, he merely points out some
corrections and closes by mentioning some capers that, a decade

presented to them, why be afraid of displeasing them by offering assistance
that they cannot fail to welcome as soon as they recognize the need for it?"
[38] [*Malcolm Lowry: "Under the Volcano," A Casebook*, ed. Gordon Bowker (London:
Macmillan Education, 1987), 29. This preface is translated by George Wood-
cock from the French version of Lowry's English notes.]

later, would justify the delayed judgment (preface of 1833) that
"'Han d'Islande' is the work of a young man – a very young
man."[39]
The last evasion is truly a way out: it consists of speaking
squarely of something else. An elusive preface, we may remember, was already what Rabelais put at the head of *Quart
Livre*. So too, in a sense, was Nerval's dedication (to Dumas) of
the *Filles du feu*, a dedicatory preface containing a fragment of an
abandoned novel (but also a comment, or a refusal to comment,
on the sonnets *Les Chimères*, which were appended to the volume:
the sonnets "would lose their charm if they were explicated").
Completely elusive was the text Aragon placed at the head of *Le
Libertinage*, a long manifesto entitled "Scandal for Scandal's
Sake," thundering and disjointed, which ends with this innocuous challenge: "It will certainly be said that there is some
disproportion between this preface and the book that follows it. I
couldn't care less." Again a book by a young man, a very young
man.
Another way to speak of something else is to speak of the
preface as a genre, and here we pass from the elusive preface to
the self-referential preface: a preface about prefaces. See the
"Hors-livre" ["Outwork"] of Derrida's *Dissemination*, already
mentioned, or the three prefaces of Barth's *Friday Book*, perfect
illustrations of paratextual coyness, on the obviously compulsory
theme of criticism of all paratextual coyness. See also – or rather,
even earlier – the "Preface to the Reader" by Pierre Leroux for *La
Grève de Samarez* (1863): that preface is intended as a history of
the preface. A history that to my mind is inaccurate, for in it we
read that the ancients did not write prefaces because they were
not thinking about posterity! But I do find in it a nice piece of
advice, although hard to apply: "A good preface must be like the
overture to an opera."As a matter of fact, Leroux's long preface is
itself preceded by a "prologue," in which I find nothing to quote
except this sensible remark: "Voltaire did not want people to use

[39] The original preface, which is shorter, already used preterition in a humorous
way: rereading his novel, the author suddenly became aware of its "insignificance" and its "frivolity"; he therefore abandoned the idea of "elaborat[ing] a
long preface, which should be the shield of his work" and resigned himself,
"after making a proper apology, to say[ing] nothing at all in this so-called
preface, which the publisher will consequently be careful to print in large
letters."

the expression 'Grab your pen.' He thought that phrase barbaric. However, if one is going to write, one must certainly grab something."

Still, make sure you don't (as some people do) grab in the wrong place.[40]

[40] Having once or twice paid tribute to works without prefaces, I should perhaps mention the opposite and naturally paradoxical case of prefaces without works. We know that Ducasse's *Poésies* has sometimes, rather apocryphally, been presented as a "preface to a future book"; and that Nietzsche, for Christmas 1872, dedicated to Cosima Wagner *Five Prefaces to Five Books That Have Not Been Written*. It is said that in the accompanying letter Nietzsche added, "and are not to be written," which casts doubt on the prefatorial character of these "prefaces." Total emancipation of the preface has no doubt yet to be illustrated and, in any case, can only be the product of playfulness or defiance.

10

Other prefaces, other functions

✦✦✦

Postfaces

The main disadvantage of a preface is that it constitutes an unbalanced and even shaky situation of communication: its author is offering the reader an advance commentary on a text the reader has not yet become familiar with. Consequently many readers apparently prefer to read the preface after the text, when they will know "what it's all about." The logic of this situation should then lead the author to acknowledge such an impulse and offer a postface instead; here he could expatiate on his subject knowing that both sides were fully informed: "Now you know as much about it as I, so let's have a chat." Further, I admit that at the start of this investigation I was expecting to encounter a corpus of original postfaces almost as abundant as the corpus of prefaces. But I found nothing of the kind: even given the very amateurish nature of my investigation, the meagerness of the corpus of original postfaces is conspicuous enough to be significant. I have already mentioned the "postscript" to *Waverley* and some "epilogues" by Borges – including that of *The Book of Sand*, which, moreover, invokes a supplementary motive peculiar to this genre: "Prefacing stories a reader has not yet read, since it demands the analysis of plots that it may be inconvenient to deal with in advance, is a somewhat impossible task. I therefore prefer an afterword." Let us add the postface to *Lolita*, a postface that first appeared in 1956 as an article and was united with its text only in the first American edition of 1958 (original edition: Paris, 1955); so here we have, typically, a later postface, and we will consider it below under that heading. Pretty much the same is true of two paratexts we have already mentioned, often printed nowadays as postfaces: "Entretien sur les romans ou Préface de *Julie*," which, because of technical difficulties, Rousseau had been unable to place at the head of the original edition, and "Some Words about *War and Peace*," first published in a journal while the novel was appearing in serial form and later reprocessed into an "appendix." These last three cases are, therefore, examples of false original postfaces: prefaces manqué, or later postfaces. The celebrated "Postface to the Second Edition" of *Capital*, too, is later, as its title indicates; similarly, the final text of Klossowski's *Lois de l'hospitalité* (1965) is, like the initial "foreword," a paratext later than the three narratives brought together under this title (1953–60),[1] and its discourse is characteristically retrospective. I can also mention, alongside Borges, Severo Sarduy, for the final "note" of *De donde son los cantantes* [published in French as *Ecrit en dansant*]: Sarduy justified this note's placement at the end the same way Borges justified the postface to *The Book of Sand*. Still considering Borges, we can point to the "epilogue" of his *Obras completas* (1974), a rare example of an apocryphal paratext (apocryphal inasmuch as it is pseudo-allographic posthumous): this epilogue is a bogus article "Borges" in an encyclopedia of the twenty-first century, with its inevitable share of errors both factual and judgmental.

Undoubtedly I should doggedly pursue the two or three outstanding specimens of original postface that have so far escaped my notice. But doing so would mean succumbing to a collector's compulsion that lacks theoretical significance, for on this level there seems to be nothing more to add: the original postface is a rarity, and rather than try to reduce the shortage artificially, we would do better to explain it.

Ultimately, the basic reason for the shortage seems to me very clear: placed at the end of a book and addressed to a reader who is no longer potential but actual, the postface certainly makes more logical and more relevant reading for that reader. But for the author, and from a pragmatic point of view, the postface is much less effective, for it can no longer perform the two main types of function we have found the preface to have: holding the reader's interest and guiding him by explaining why and how he should read the text. If the first function is not fulfilled, the reader will perhaps never have an opportunity to reach a possible postface; if the second function is not fulfilled, it will perhaps be

---

[1] [The three are *Roberte ce soir* (1953), *La Révocation de l'edict de Nantes* (1959), and *Le Souffleur ou Le théâtre de la société* (1960).]

too late for the author to rectify *in extremis* a bad reading that has already been completed. Given the postface's location and type of discourse, it can hope to fulfill only a curative, or corrective, function; understandably, most authors think the difficulties and awkwardnesses of the preface are preferable to this final corrective. At the cost of these flaws, the preface has the virtue of at least being monitory and preventive. Here as elsewhere, an ounce of prevention is worth a pound of cure, or of rectification. Or indeed, if one is going to wait in any case, it's better to wait a little longer and be able to remedy the damage duly noted by the reactions of the public and critics. This will be the typical function of the later preface. But for the postface, it is always both too early and too late.

Later prefaces

Logically, because a work's second edition (and, for that matter, each of its subsequent editions) addresses new readers, nothing prevents the author from adding to that second or subsequent edition a preface that is "later" in date but "original" for these new readers, to whom the author would tell the tale that, for one reason or another, he had originally thought could be dispensed with. That is roughly what Nodier points out, with his customary irony, in his preface to the second edition of *Adèle*: "This reprinting is a new appeal to goodwill. ... It is entirely up to you to take this edition as the first one, the other *first* never having stirred from the bookseller's stockrooms, except for about fifty copies that my friends did me the favor of accepting." In this precise sense, it is never too late to inform a new public, and the later preface can be the place in which to express one's afterthoughts. That is a little how Wordsworth uses his 1800 preface to *Lyrical Ballads*, where – after the event – he puts the manifesto he had apparently not thought of in 1798 (the earlier edition contained a much more modest anonymous advertisement; but it is true that the second edition is appreciably enlarged, which justifies a more ambitious paratext). That is, as well, how Tolstoy proceeds in his 1890 preface to *The Kreutzer Sonata* (1889), a typical example of making up for a missing statement of intent: As I have been asked to do, he said, I propose "to explain in clear, simple terms what I think of the story I wrote entitled *The*

Kreutzer Sonata. This I shall endeavor to do; that is, I shall attempt briefly to express, within the limits of the possible, the substance of what I was trying to say in that story, and the conclusions which in my view may be drawn from it" (one cannot get more didactic than that). This basic message, as we know, is a manifesto in favor of continence, outside marriage and within marriage. "This is the substance of what I was trying to say, and of what I thought I had indeed said, in my story."

But this compensatory attitude is apparently quite rare, and for a simple reason already intimated in that last sentence. The author never approaches a new public without having more or less strongly felt the reaction of the first one – in particular the reaction of the kind of reader who is hardly likely to take another look and correct himself on the occasion of a new edition: the critic. Most often, therefore, later compensation for the absence or shortcomings of an original preface inevitably takes the form of a response to the first reactions of the first public and the critics. Without any doubt that is the main function of the later preface or postface (as I have already said, at this stage the distinction between preface and postface is hardly relevant), and I will come to it in a minute – as soon as I have mentioned two other functions, no less typical but relatively minor.

The first minor function consists of calling attention to the corrections, material or other, made in this new edition. We know that in the classical period, when it was hardly common to correct proofs, original editions were usually very inaccurate. The second edition (or sometimes an even later one) was therefore the opportunity for a typographical cleanup that it was entirely to the author's benefit to point out. In his preface to the fifth edition (1765) of the *Dictionnaire philosophique* (1764), Voltaire affirms that this edition is the first correct one. In the foreword to the second edition (1803) of the *Génie* (1802), Chateaubriand gives an account of various corrections and apologizes for not having been able to remove two basic errors (they will be removed in the next edition); he takes the same approach in his "examination" (1810) of *Les Martyrs* (1809). I have already mentioned in another connection the April 1823 preface to Hugo's *Han d'Islande*, in which the anonymous author states that "the term 'first edition' should really be applied to this reprint, inasmuch as the four variously sized bundles of grayish paper blotted with black and white, which the indulgent public has hitherto kindly consented to consider as the four volumes of 'Hans of Iceland,' were so disfigured with typographic errors by a barbarous printer that the wretched author, on looking over his own production, altered as it was beyond all recognition, was perpetually subjected to the torments of a father whose child returns to him mutilated and tattooed by the hand of an Iroquois from Lake Ontario." Hugo again, in the "note" of the Renduel edition (1832) of *Notre-Dame de Paris*, draws attention to the addition of three chapters "lost" in 1831 and "found" since then – including the famous "This Will Kill That." In a later preface authors may also openly declare their refusal to make corrections other than typographical ones. This is the theme, still common today (for the use of proofs has made the preceding theme obsolete – not that original editions have become flawless, but now authors have no one to blame but themselves): "I am republishing this (more or less) old text without changing anything in it." Chateaubriand takes that position for the *Essai*, and George Sand for *Lélia* (the preface of 1841) and *Indiana* (the preface of 1842); allowing themselves only corrections of style, both authors decline to reconsider the substance of opinions they have outgrown.

A second minor function, which is, rather, a secondary effect: in a later (or delayed) preface, the author implicitly assumes responsibility for a text he had originally disavowed: see, for example, Montesquieu in 1754 for *Lettres persanes*, Constant in 1816 for *Adolphe*,[2] Nabokov in 1956 for *Lolita*, Eco in 1983 for *The Name of the Rose*. In general this change is simply a regularization – usually readers hadn't been taken in by what was only a transparent convention – but a regularization that nonetheless modifies the official status of the text.

Thus the most important thing here, it seems to me, is the response to critics. That was the main business of prefaces to plays in the classical period, and those prefaces are, we should remember, both original in the published edition and subsequent to production on the stage. The response to critics is in fact a delicate business, for one risks seeming either thin-skinned or

---

[2] Fictive second edition (London), in which a new preface, implicitly assumptive, replaces the original note by the editor.

immodest. Hence the resort to various counterattacks, or covers. For example: I am not defending myself against critics, who are free to say what they want, but I am anxious to correct some errors (Corneille, the foreword to *Le Cid*: it is false that I accepted the arbitration of the Academy, and false that I violated Aristotle's rules). Or this: I accept criticism, but I observe that those who find fault with me contradict one another (that is Racine's specialty: for *Alexandre*, "I refer my enemies to my enemies"; for *Britannicus*, I have been reproached sometimes for making Nero too cruel, sometimes for making him too mild). Or this: what I am reproached for is what the best of the ancients have already done (implying: to attack me is to attack them). Or finally, and especially: the critics are overwhelmingly against me, but the public is on my side.

This appeal from the critics' judgment to the public's is characteristic of classical doctrine, which holds that the "learned" can never prevail against "plain folks," nor dusty pedants against King, Court, and Town; but in all periods it has a formidable effect, for it puts critics in a difficult position – making them look ridiculous – and, in particular, suggests they are acting from pettiness and jealousy. In the delayed examination of *Le Cid*, Corneille argues that Rodrigue's two visits to Chimène, which critics deemed shocking, were received by the public with "a certain quivering that betokened a wonderful curiosity, and a redoubling of attention to what they had to say to each other in so pathetic a state." In contrast, the patent failure of *Pertharite* leaves him with nothing to say: "It is not my custom to resist the public's judgment." For *Alexandre*, Racine notes that "one does not make so much commotion over a work of which one has no opinion" and that some fault-finders came to see it six times. For *Andromaque*: they have reproached me for a Pyrrhus who is too little like Céladon [a character in d'Urfé's *Astrée*], but "what could I do? Pyrrhus had not read our novels." For *Britannicus*, they claimed that the play was over when the hero died and that "one should not listen to the rest. None the less one does listen to it and even with as much attention as the end of any tragedy." For *Bérénice*: "I ... cannot imagine that the public will bear me a grudge for having given it a tragedy honoured by so many tears and the thirtieth performance of which has been followed with as much attention as the first." Molière, the preface to *L'Ecole des femmes*: "Many people at first jeered at this comedy; but those who laughed were on its side, and all the bad things one could say about it couldn't keep it from being a success with which I'm satisfied." Beaumarchais, "A Reasonable Letter on the Fall and Criticism of the *Barbier de Séville*" (preface to the original edition of 1775): the critics complain, but the public laughed. Preface to *Le Mariage de Figaro*: "An author who is distressed by the cabal and the squawkers but sees his play do well regains courage, and that's what I've done," for nothing is more pleasing than to note the vexation of one of those cabalists shouting from his box, exactly as in Molière's *Critique de l'Ecole des femmes*: "Go ahead and laugh, public,[3] go ahead and laugh!"

Moreover, an appeal to the judgment of the public – or of some unassailable protector – allows the author to conceal his own defense behind his defense of others whom it would be cowardly to abandon to the critics. On my side, said Racine, are "the Alexanders of our age": could I betray them by accepting criticisms that they apparently do not endorse? "No doubt," said Molière, "I am enough indebted to all those people who gave [*L'Ecole des femmes*] their approval, to think myself obliged to defend their judgment against that of others."

The criticisms to which classical playwrights responded by taking shelter beneath the umbrella of success were generally aesthetic and even technical ("This play is badly made"), and it is for that very reason that the argument of success was so valuable to them: "It is not so badly made after all, for it works." On this ground, recourse to the public was unanswerable. But refuting ideological (moral, religious, or political) criticism is an entirely different matter. An author attacked on this ground can hardly defend himself by invoking success. That would, in fact, be an argument against him, as proof of his dreadful influence. An author of tragedies is a public poisoner, they were saying at Port-Royal in Racine's time. Consequently, in the preface to *Phèdre*, Racine must enter the plea not that this play is "the best of my tragedies" – that is, the most successful and most warmly received – but indeed that it is the one in which "virtue" is most "emphasised," where "the least faults are severely punished," where "the mere

---

[3] Molière actually said "pit"; but in the classical period, the public in the pit is the public par excellence.

thought of crime is here regarded with as much horror as crime itself. ...." Molière encountered critics of this kind with *Tartuffe*, but those critics were much more fearsome, and we can see in the preface of 1669 how close a game it was. Here the protection of the king, or of prince ***, is more effective than the approbation of the public. But what Molière must do above all is demonstrate the purity of his intentions and show, if possible, that his accusers are in the wrong with regard to their own principles, or rather, with regard to principles that no one can publicly challenge. Hence Molière's insistence on the theme of "faux dévots" ["religious hypocrites"]: those are the people I mock in my play, and whoever attacks it thereby puts himself in their company. Beaumarchais deploys an analogous casuistry in support of *Figaro*: accused of having attacked the court in that play, he responds by distinguishing among "the man of the court," "the courtier," and "the professional sycophant." I attacked, he said, only the last; "not the states themselves, but the excesses of each state." He was accused of having held morality up to ridicule; but nothing of the sort: the Count is not held up to ridicule, he is punished and pardoned; the Countess remains faithful despite the excuses she could invoke for not being so; Figaro is honorable, Suzanne virtuous, and Chérubino still only a boy ... where is the evil, if not in the hearts of those who see evil where it does not exist?

It is this moral, religious, or political defense that we find in most later prefaces of the eighteenth and nineteenth centuries, a defense that partly justified the harsh words of Paul Morand I quoted in the preceding chapter. Montesquieu's *Défense de "L'Esprit des lois,"* first published separately in 1750 and then appended to the text, responds to the charge of Spinozaism and ungodliness. The defense of the *Génie du christianisme* (1803) opens with a very characteristic disavowal: I had decided, says Chateaubriand, not to respond to critics, but the criticisms are such that I must defend not myself but my book, not on the literary level but on the religious level. There follows a defense in proper form – backed up by the precedents of Origen, Francis of Sales, Pascal, Fénelon, Montesquieu – against the criticism that Chateaubriand placed the merits of Christianity on too aesthetic and too human a level. The same tactic in his "examination" (1810) of *Les Martyrs*, which had been faulted for its syncretism (I did not blend Christianity and paganism: I showed them in

juxtaposition, as they really were during the early Christian
period) and for its recourse to the Christian supernatural (I am
not the first – see *Jerusalem Delivered, Paradise Lost,* [Voltaire's]
Henriade; and if I myself had not drawn attention to that aspect,
in my original preface and with my ill-considered title of *Les
Martyrs, ou Le triomphe de la religion chrétienne,* no one would have
noticed it; "If I had entitled my book *Les Aventures d'Euloge,*
people would have sought in it only what is actually there") –
here, then, the author defends the text by giving an autocritique
of the title.

We find the same note of a speech for the defense in the later
prefaces of novels, whose general tone is fairly well represented
by Senard's real defense in the trial of *Madame Bovary.*[4] Balzac, in
the preface to *Le Père Goriot* (after the work's serial publication),
denies having favorably depicted "women of too-little virtue"
and provides an early statistic on the female complement of *La
Comédie humaine.* Dickens, for *Oliver Twist* (1837), asserts in 1841
he had a moral purpose, like the purpose Cervantes had, or
Fielding; he returns to this matter in 1867 to contend that he
depicted debased and criminal milieux in the repellent light that
is the best deterrent. Zola begins his preface to the second edition
of *Thérèse Raquin* with a protest that could serve as the emblem of
every later preface: "I was simple enough to suppose that this
novel could do without a preface," for I found its lesson clear
enough. I was no doubt mistaken, for the critics have accused me
of immorality. So here, for the use of imbeciles, I must "light a
lamp in broad daylight" and set forth my intentions: my purpose
is purely scientific, and so forth. And he imagines, in a very
revealing way, the literary tribunal by which he would like to be
judged "for what I have tried to do, and not for what I have not
done." At the head of *L'Assommoir,* as well, he responds to his
critics by invoking his "aims as the author. I wanted to depict the
inevitable downfall of a working-class family. ... But I am not
defending myself. My work will do that for me. It is a work of
truth, the first novel about the common people which does not

---

[4] [The charge against Flaubert was "offense to public and religious morality and
to good morals." The same charge was brought seven months later against
Baudelaire for *Les Fleurs du mal.* Flaubert was acquitted; Baudelaire was not –
and six of the poems in his volume remained unpublishable in France until
1949. For a brief account of the two cases, see *A New History of French Literature,*
ed. Denis Hollier (Cambridge, MA: Harvard University Press, 1989), 726–31.]

tell lies but has the authentic smell of the people" (that is not very kind to the Goncourts' *Germinie Lacerteux*).

The atmosphere of a trial is still noticeable in the later postface of *Lolita*. Here we must remember that this novel, rejected by American publishers on grounds of immorality, at first could be published only in France. Nabokov responds to the charges of pornography and anti-Americanism by asserting that he does not share his hero's taste for nymphets and that in this narrative, the fruit of his love affair simply with the English language, his purpose was purely aesthetic.

Another celebrated defendant, one duly convicted in a real trial, was Baudelaire, who long contemplated writing a later preface to *Les Fleurs du mal*, several sketches of which exist. In these we see him hesitate between various defensive strategies: pleading not guilty by invoking the argument of the simple formal exercise ("Certain illustrious poets have long since divided among themselves the more flowery provinces of the realm of poetry. I have found it amusing, and the more pleasant because the task was more difficult, to extract *beauty* from *Evil*"); displaying the *delectatio morosa* of failure ("If there is any glory in not being understood, or in being only very slightly so, I may without boasting say that with this little book I have at a single stroke both won and deserved that glory"); the purely aesthetic intention ("How poetry is related to music through prosody, whose roots go deeper into the human soul"); the immoralist provocation ("It is not for my wives, my daughters, or my sisters that this book has been written"); the abandonment of any response ("Suddenly an indolence of the weight of twenty atmospheres fell upon me, and I was stopped, faced by the appalling uselessness of explaining anything whatever to anyone whatever"); the rejection of a suggestion he undoubtedly made up himself ("My publisher insists that it might be of some use, to me and to him, to explain why and how I have written this book. . . . But, on second thought, doesn't it seem obvious that this would be a quite superfluous undertaking for everyone concerned since those are the minds that already know or guess and the rest will never understand?"); and so forth. We can see these hesitations as the sign of a vacillator ready to procrastinate about everything, indeed, to deny everything, and as the obvious announcement of his final renunciation. But above all this text seems to me characteristic of the discomfort and distress felt by several generations of writers who, faced with criticism that is inquisitorial and persecutorial, are constrained to base their pleas more often on what is likely to gain them acquittal than on what they really think. Therefore, reading the repertory of the later preface is generally something of an ordeal, and it is quite comforting to note that the later preface seems to be dying out. It is disappearing in large measure for lack of functions: material corrections are now made on proofs, or silently from one edition to another; moralizing criticism is no longer the fashion (Nabokov will have been one of its last victims), or its last adherents no longer deserve an answer; as for strictly literary or aesthetic criticism, today authors can hardly reply by invoking, as Molière and Racine did, the argument of success, which in high literary circles would be taken as frankly demagogic. Can we imagine Maurice Blanchot responding, "The critics have pulled me to pieces, but what counts is that my concierge really liked it"? We leave those arguments to the adherents of a so-called popular literature, who have scarcely any need to appeal to them because critics pay little attention to such works. But from another point of view, modern authors' indifference to the content of the criticism they receive is not a very good omen. At least in France, this indifference marks the advent of a purely media-oriented and PR state of mind in which criticism is held to be nothing but a mere promotional article: reviews are valued according to the number of pages, lines, or characters and the placement of a photograph. As a result the "debate" languishes, or in any case flows through channels other than the decidedly obsolete one of the later preface.

Delayed prefaces

The delayed – or preposthumous, or testamentary – preface, like the later preface, may fulfill the function of compensating for omissions from an earlier preface or for the omission of the earlier preface itself; but here I will consider only the delayed preface's own particular functions, those warranted by the long temporal interval and the approach of death, which makes the delayed preface generally, and in the strict sense, a final preface.[5]

[5] "What I am writing now are my posthumous works," said Aragon in the 1965

247

The first of these functions is autobiographical: "The prefaces in this edition," says Chateaubriand in 1826, "are in the nature of memoirs." Actually, that is the most striking aspect of the series of prefaces Chateaubriand wrote to accompany the publication of his *Œuvres complètes*, and of the wonderful "general preface" that opens them and, in a few pages, presents a kind of advance synthesis of the *Mémoires d'outre-tombe*.[6] The same autobiographical purpose informs each preface in the series, particularly the one to the *Essai sur les révolutions*, a youthful work (1797) whose very immaturity and strongly pronounced ideological character justify a careful positioning of it. I will examine the preface to the *Essai* again, from another angle, but now I wish to emphasize the obvious fact that in a set such as Chateaubriand's, and all the sets I will mention in this chapter, the prefaces are *unequally* delayed; more precisely, because the works collected are generally arranged in chronological order, their prefaces are less and less delayed as the interval between the date of the work and the date of its preface diminishes. The 1831 preface to the *Etudes historiques*, a work that was itself completed in 1831, is no longer delayed at all in our sense of the word. And in terms of our concern here, the prefaces that are most delayed – that is, most distant – are almost always the most interesting ones, and not only in Chateaubriand. Chateaubriand himself, moreover, seems sensitive to this dwindling of the distance; and we will see Aragon, at least, twice give up the job, no doubt for this reason among others.

At the head of a similar undertaking and at more or less the same time (1829), Walter Scott, in the general preface to his complete novelistic works, sets about retracing the origin and vicissitudes of his literary vocation, which goes back to his sickly adolescence. Just as Chateaubriand had long ago lost, then found, his "terrible" manuscript of *Les Natchez*, so Scott in 1805 had written, then left in a desk that was moved to a garret, a first

preface to *Les Beaux Quartiers* – and we cannot quite tell whether the comment applies to the works contemporaneous with this preface (*La Mise à mort*, to be precise) or to this preface itself.
6 The general preface was published, along with a "foreword by the author" that has a more technical function, in June 1826 at the head of the first volume to appear (volume 16). This preface is one of Chateaubriand's most beautiful pieces of writing, and it is unfortunate that, because of its circumstantial status, it has been excluded from the most accessible modern editions.

version of *Waverley*, which he finds some years later when looking for – a very "Abercrombian" touch – some fishing-tackle; he then decides to complete the manuscript, eager to do for Scotland (as a footnote to his poetic œuvre) something equivalent to what Maria Edgeworth had done for Ireland. The rest of the general preface is therefore the history of the *Waverley Novels*, of the author's persistence in retaining anonymity or pseudonymity, and of his inevitable unmasking, which we looked at in Chapter 3. Here Walter Scott (or at least the master of Abbotsford) apologizes for having to speak of himself in the first person; coming from this author who is fanatical about incognitos, the regret is doubtless sincere and will be confirmed by the succession of individual prefaces: they are devoted almost exclusively to a very technical account of the sources and documentation of his narratives.

The *grande mortalis aevi spatium*[7] may also attend the creation of a single work when that work is huge, like Michelet's *Histoire de France*, begun in "the blitzkrieg of July" 1830 and completed in 1869 with the celebrated preface that Proust, normally harsher toward this type of performance, rated much more highly than he rated the work itself. This preface, simultaneously original and delayed, is actually not only a statement of purpose and method (History as "integral resurrection," bound up less with political events than with imperceptible economic and social developments) but also an evocation of the circumstances in which the whole work was written (the years Michelet spent "buried in the National Archives" in the company of the dead) and of the development of an idea thanks to "useful tasks" that, by holding up his work, made it more mature.

To date, the most recent example of this autobiographical function is surely provided by the set of delayed prefaces Aragon produced first for the collected *Œuvres romanesques croisées* and then for his *Œuvre poétique*.[8] Then and especially, for the prefaces in the first set are more technical and more literary, focused more

---

7   [Tacitus, *Life of Agricola*, ch. 3: "For the term of fifteen years, *a large space in human life*, chance and change have been cutting off many among us" (Loeb Classical Library).]

8   The ORC [*Intersecting Novelistic Works*] of Aragon and Elsa Triolet [Aragon's companion from 1928 until her death in 1970] (Laffont, 1964–74); the *Œuvre poétique* of Aragon (Livre Club Diderot, 1974–81). On the paratext of the ORC, see M. Hilsum, "Les Préfaces tardives d'Aragon," *Poétique* 69 (February 1987).

on the works than on their circumstances – just as the author, in the foreword to *Libertinage*, in fact says they will be: "I will not tell the story of my life. My subject here is my books, and writing"; and at the head of *Les Cloches de Bâle* he justifies this restraint simply with the fact that his novels are themselves less autobiographical than his poems. The retrospective discourse is, in any case, broken off with *La Semaine sainte* (1958), for which Aragon merely reuses the paratext of 1959, typically later in that it responds to the critics and corrects misunderstandings; for *La Mise à mort* (1965), in 1970 he shies away from any preface ("As a routine matter, I had agreed to write a preface to *La Mise à mort* ... an absurd thing to do. That novel is its own preface, I mean perpetually, one page prefacing another" – a classic motivation for refusing to write a preface) and substitutes for it some excerpts from *Les Incipit*, published in 1969. For *Blanche ou L'oubli* (1967), the "afterword" is more of a threnody to Elsa, a song of despair by Orpheus the survivor, and here again, the same theme: "There can't possibly be a preface to *Blanche ou L'oubli*, as there can't possibly be a preface to life. A preface to *Blanche* would have to be the book repeated all over again." Finally, for *Théâtre/Roman*, which he returns to in the very year of its original publication (1974), he reprints all of *Les Incipit* as a postface – an epitext is thus rapidly incorporated into the peritext.

In contrast, the prefatorial apparatus of his *Œuvre poétique* is almost entirely autobiographical, and the very presentation accentuates this feature, for here the texts, whether poetic or not, are wrapped in and sometimes smothered by the discourse that serves more to present than to comment on them, as they are swept along in the torrent of a tormented existence. These texts cover the stormy years when he was a leading surrealist, then his support for Communism, the trips to the Soviet Union, the conferences, the dubious missions, the questioning, the frustrations, the suppressed bitterness, and the occasional poems (*Front rouge, Hourra l'Oural*) that in no way brighten the picture, for to Aragon they constitute (in their excessive verbal violence and political irresponsibility) the most reprehensible part of his entire œuvre. Moreover, the last two volumes for which he wrote prefaces (7:1936–37, 8:1938) contain virtually no poems, for during those three years the texts of articles, pamphlets, proposals, and political speeches replaced poetry. Saddest of all is that at that point in his retrospective project (May 1979), and for reasons that are obviously a state secret, Aragon lays down the preface-writer's pen just when the œuvre would have begun to be worth the trouble. Let us not expatiate upon this waste.

The *Œuvres romanesques croisées*, more refreshing in every respect, illustrates yet a second typical function of the delayed preface, even if we have already glimpsed this function at work in some original prefaces: describing the genesis of the text and indicating its sources. Accurate or not, the delayed preface to the ORC provides invaluable evidence about Aragon's methods of working and their evolution toward "realism"; about the fate of rough drafts now missing (the famous *Défense de l'infini*, a "gigantic serial" burned, totally or not, in Madrid in 1928, a matrix-work comparable to the manuscript of Chateaubriand's *Natchez*); about the models (which, of course, "are not keys") for characters such as Aurélien (a little Aragon, a little Drieu, but a Drieu who would not have gone all the way)[9] and the hero of *Les Voyageurs de l'impériale* ("It is the imaginary story of my maternal grandfather") and the Géricault of *La Semaine sainte* (James Dean!) – or about the absence of models: Blanche is not Elsa, I am not Gaiffier, and so forth. In all these revelations and disavowals there is a curious mixture of the author's pursuit and denial of control over his past work, with the denial (especially apropos of the most recent works) perhaps a final detour – both pathetic and histrionic – by the will to control.

More tranquil, apparently, was the project undertaken by Henry James, who in the last decade of his life wrote a set of eighteen prefaces for the monument of his selected works.[10] Here we have, typically, a set with decreasing "delayedness," for the works being prefaced were published, if I am not mistaken, between 1874 (*Roderick Hudson*) and 1904 (*The Golden Bowl*); but in this case the author's stance scarcely shows the effects of the decreasing interval. James's steady purpose, remote from any extraliterary autobiographical confidence, is to retrace the stages

---

[9] [Pierre Eugène Drieu la Rochelle collaborated with the Nazis and committed suicide in 1945.]

[10] *The Novels and Tales of Henry James* (New York: Scribner, 1907–9). The collected prefaces were published by R. P. Blackmur under the title *The Art of the Novel* (New York: Scribner, 1934) and were translated into French by F. Cachin, *La Création littéraire* (Denoël, 1980).

of creation starting with what he always designates "the germ of my idea": the main character for *The Portrait of a Lady* ("This single small corner-stone, the conception of a certain young woman affronting her destiny, had begun with being all my outfit for the large building of 'The Portrait of a Lady' ") and for *The Wings of the Dove* ("The idea, reduced to its essence, is that of a young person conscious of a great capacity for life, but early stricken and doomed"); a simple anecdote for "The Pupil," *Maisie, The Awkward Age, The Ambassadors*. Then the development, making one's way through difficulties; the complementary characters needed for the sake of symmetry (*Maisie*); the "ficelle" characters, confidants who are always available, like Maria Gostrey of *The Ambassadors*; the selection of point of view (Maisie, Strether) and of narrative method (the temptation – resisted – to entrust the narrative to these two "reflectors") ... Rarely has a set of prefaces so much resembled a poetics, and it is not without reason that the posthumous book in which these prefaces are collected could be entitled *The Art of the Novel* (in French, *La Création littéraire*).

Reconstituting the genesis of a work becomes even more theoretical in *Postscript to "The Name of the Rose,"* a postface that in its date is later[11] but in its function is typically delayed – which, from a mind as fast-moving as Umberto Eco's, will not be a surprise. This postface is in effect an ideal account, in the manner of Edgar Allan Poe or Raymond Roussel, of the creative "process" of *The Name of the Rose*; for if Eco, in keeping with current doctrine, refrains from interfering in any way with the "path of the text," he does not forgo illuminating this path with a very well thought out account of its creation. "The author must not interpret. But he may tell why and how he wrote his book" (we have already encountered these precautions of the day). Here the seminal idea was the very praiseworthy one of "poisoning a monk." Hence the choice first of the historical framework ("I know the present only through the television screen, whereas I have a direct knowledge of the Middle Ages"), then of the

---

[11] It was published first in a journal – "Postille al *Nome della rosa*," *Alfabeta* 49 (June 1983) – and was then appended to the later editions as a postface. [Its English translation was published as a separate volume: *Postscript to "The Name of the Rose,"* trans. William Weaver (San Diego: Harcourt Brace Jovanovich, 1984).]

narrative system (a first-person narrative told by a witness-narrator à la Watson, and for good reason), the authorial fiction in several layers ("I am saying what Vallet said that Mabillon said that Adso said ..."), the genre (the most philosophical one possible: the detective story), the hero (a cross between Occam and Sherlock Holmes), and so forth. All this as if the book had been mapped out from first line to last. The only thing the author does not claim to have calculated is the culmination (albeit unavoidable) in that magisterial postscript, the obvious goal and supreme achievement of the entire undertaking.

It sometimes happens that after a work, particularly an early one, is published, an author's tastes or ideas evolve – indeed, undergo a sudden conversion. More generally, a middle-aged or elderly writer, when the time has come to compile his Complete Works, sees a delayed preface as an opportunity to express his thoughts, at a safe distance, about some past work. Now is the moment not for the afterthought written when one is rushed and busy but for the fair and dispassionate second thought, the effect of a re-reading *after forgetfulness*[12] – that is, after an interval of detachment and separation that transforms the author into an (almost) ordinary and (almost) impartial reader: "For as one grows older, one acquires the impartiality of that future to which one is drawing closer."[13] The author no longer dwells on rejoinders but on the portals of death, no longer dreams of responding with fury to critics but of assessing his own works, without heat or passion, in the serenity of what Satie rightly calls "next-to-last thoughts."

To gauge the difference in tone between vigorous polemic and Olympian appraisal, one need only compare, in Corneille and Racine, the set of original or later prefaces with the set of

[12] "To reread, therefore; to reread after having forgotten – to reread *oneself*, without a shadow of tenderness, without paternity; coldly and with critical acumen, and in a mood terribly conducive to ridicule and contempt; one's air hostile, one's eye destructive – is to recast one's work, or feel that it should be recast, into a very different mould." Thus Valéry describes his state of mind in the "Note and Digression" that serves as a delayed preface (1919) to his *Léonard* of 1895 – and that in fact outlines a sort of rewriting of that work. But Chateaubriand had already noted in his *Mémoires d'outre-tombe*, apropos of the delayed edition of *Les Natchez*: "What has happened to me has perhaps never happened before to an author: to reread thirty years later a manuscript I had totally forgotten."
[13] *Mémoires d'outre-tombe* 18:9.

"examinations" of 1660 [Corneille] and the set of prefaces of 1676 [Racine]. For Corneille, the edition of 1660 is the opportunity – with regard to his first twenty-three plays (up to *Œdipe*, 1659) – for some professional soul-searching of sorts that is serious, technical, almost objective in its balance of severity and, sometimes, amused indulgence; and the examinations, together with the three accompanying general discourses, constitute a kind of dramaturgical last will and testament. Corneille reflects on the ups and downs of the composition and style of his plays, which sometimes run counter to and sometimes complement each other: the style of *La Galerie du palais* is plainer than that of *La Veuve*, and the style of *La Suivante* is weaker but the play is more consistent. *L'Illusion* is extravagant, "caprices of that nature can be risked only once." *Horace* would perhaps be the best, if the closing acts were as good as the opening ones. *Cinna* is so unanimously considered my best play that I would be reluctant to criticize it: it is truly the one that most perfectly conforms to probability, and its lines are "more direct and less affected" than those of *Le Cid*. The style of *Polyeucte* is less strong, but more moving. *Héraclius* is "so cluttered that it requires prodigious concentration," and so forth. Racine, less the technician or more sure of himself, for *Alexandre*, *Andromaque*, and *Britannicus* merely replaces the polemical preface with one that is more neutral and more reserved, noting only that the last of the three did indeed outlive its critics.

These delayed and comparative examinations are sometimes the occasion for a kind of personal list of prizewinners, or more simply for a statement of preference: Corneille admits to a special "fondness" for *Rodogune*, and *Nicomède* is "one of the [plays] for which I have most affection." Chateaubriand admits his partiality for the early chapters of *Les Mémoires*. Dickens, with his customary directness, says of *Copperfield*: "Of all my books, I like this the best. ... Like many fond parents, I have in my heart of hearts a favorite child. And his name is David Copperfield." James decides in favor of *The Portrait of a Lady* and, especially, *The Ambassadors*. Conrad, more ambiguous, is unwilling to say whether *Lord Jim* is the work he likes best, but he adds, "I don't feel grieved and annoyed by the preference some people give to my *Lord Jim*." For Aragon, "Among my writings, *Aurélien* has always been a favorite." I would be quite happy to extend this

Delayed prefaces

touching series, but for the time being my collection (as drawn from prefaces) stops there.

Authorial preference (for that is what we must call it), from a conscious or subconscious concern to compensate, easily inclines toward the works less valued by everyone else. Despite the classical doctrine of the public's infallibility, such is somewhat the case with Corneille's *Rodogune* and *Nicomède*, and with many other preferences not expressed in delayed prefaces (nowadays authorial preference is a cliché of interviews, and we will doubt-less come upon it again). But often authorial preference also inclines toward the oldest works, which an aging author quite naturally tends to prefer to the works that followed because in those early books he finds the charm of youth and of an innocence or freedom that in later books he somewhat relin-quished. We find a bit of that indulgence even (already) in Corneille, in his forbearance toward his early comedies; and Renan's fondness for his "old Purana" of *L'Avenir de la science* is quite well known. Aragon shows more interest in *Le Mouvement perpétuel* [poetry published in 1926] or *Le Paysan de Paris* [a novel published in 1926] than in the works he wrote from a sense of duty in the 1930s. But the most typical case is perhaps that of Borges: he removed some of his collections of the 1920s from his list of works (to the point of making their exclusion the chief raison d'être for his *Obras completas* and of buying up at any price the copies still in circulation), but he never disavowed his very first published work, *Fervor de Buenos Aires* (1923), about which he would say, in the delayed preface of 1969, that the *muchacho* [kid] who wrote it was already "essentially – what does *essentially* mean? – the man who today puts up with or corrects: I have stayed the same"; and in his "Autobiographical Essay" [in *The Aleph*] of 1970: "I seem never to have gone beyond that book. I feel that everything I have written since has been nothing more than a development of the themes I took up then for the first time; I feel that for my whole life I have been rewriting that book." More sarcastically, Thomas Pynchon, rereading the short stories in *Slow Learner: Early Stories*,[14] begins by exclaiming, "Oh my God" – before saving them as a catalogue of errors for beginners to avoid, and observing (in a semi-ironic reversal of the

14 Delayed original preface (1984) to a collection of old stories (1958–64) [*Slow Learner: Early Stories* (Boston: Little Brown, 1984)].

255

Borgesian topos), "Most of what I dislike about my writing is present here in embryo." The thing is that he, too, experiences "one of those episodes of middle-aged tranquility, in which I now pretend to have reached a level of clarity about the young writer I was back then. I mean I can't very well just 86 this guy from my life. On the other hand, if through some as yet undeveloped technology I were to run into him today, how comfortable would I feel about lending him money, or for that matter even stepping down the street to have a beer and talk over old times?" Again a Borgesian theme.

Precocious in everything, Hugo in 1833 writes a (third) preface to *Han d'Islande* (1823), one that, in its calm forbearance, has the ring of a delayed preface, despite the author's still-tender years [he was 30] and the short interval. For him this "work of a young man – a very young man" testifies more to inventiveness than to experience, "for youth, having neither facts nor experience nor models behind it, can only divine by means of its imagination." For Hugo, the golden age of the creator is, rather, the "second period of life. ... Still young, and yet mature – this is the precious phase, the intermediate and culminating point, the warm and radiant hour of noon, the moment when there is the least possible shade, and the most light" – definitely the phase in which he finds himself now – this summit where "supreme artists" remain for their whole life. *Han d'Islande* has, for him, all the features of adolescence, when a youth is "in love for the first time, when the commonplace and ordinary obstacles of life are converted into imposing and poetic impediments, when his head is full of heroic fancies which glorify him in his own estimation, when he is already a man in two or three directions, and still a child in a score of others." In short, a work that is "naive first and foremost" – this flaw that no skill can ever replace.

The theme most strongly distinguishing the retrospective (in some cases, one could say retroactive) discourse of the delayed preface is doubtless the theme of "I have not changed," of emotional permanence and intellectual continuity – and this theme appears particularly, of course, when an author most strongly feels the need for it, that is, when he has in fact quite obviously changed. In this post-conversion discourse an author does not, of course, aim to erase the conversion but to temper its abruptness by discovering in his past the foreshadowings and premonitions of his present. When Chateaubriand can finally, in 1826, republish his tempestuous *Essai sur les révolutions* (1797), he refrains from making the slightest correction in it but provides it with an ample paratext designed to reclaim it, a paratext in the form of notes (to which I will return) but also a preface meant, first, to place the work in its historical context and, second and especially, to defend it against the major charge of atheism. "Besides, this work is a veritable chaos; every word contradicts the word that follows it"; and the job of the notes will be to sift out, in all the details, the errors of youth from the early intuitions of truth. But nothing shows it to be the work of an atheist or an opponent of Christianity. In that book I was already what I still am – a supporter of liberty whose only failing was that I had not yet discovered the cornerstone of my convictions: that Christianity is, precisely, a religion of liberty, and that representative monarchy is the only bulwark against all types of despotism. "There is no true religion without liberty, and no true liberty without religion."

The conversion effected by George Sand between the original (1832) edition of *Indiana* and the new edition in 1842 is of the opposite type, let's say a rarer type, although it is illustrated as well by Hugo for the *Odes et ballades*. To put it in heavy-handed political terms, we can call it a passage from right to left. The original preface to this novel about the condition of women was Sand's attempt to forestall all criticism by pleading harmlessness and by denying all subversive – indeed, all reforming – intent. In 1842 we find a change in outlook: the earlier preface, the author now states, had been written "under the influence of a remnant of respect for society as it was constituted." But "my present duty is to congratulate myself for having been as daring as I was, then and later."[15] Today, rereading myself with severity, "I found instead that the feelings which dictated *Indiana* then are so completely in accord with my present feelings that ... I would do it the same way." The fact is that *Indiana* was indeed written "out of deep and genuine feelings – not very carefully reasoned, it is true – about the barbaric injustice of the laws that still control a

---

[15] [The French reads, in part, "... hardiesses auxquelles je me suis cependant *laissé* emporter" (emphasis added), and Genette inserts the comment, "Note the masculine pseudonymic" – i.e., the masculine ending of the past participle.]

woman's existence within marriage, family, and society." But we must add that a third preface, the "notice" of 1852, will again attempt to adjust the line of fire, this time in a direction more "respectful of society as it was constituted," by attacking critics, who are "much too subtle [and] are never content to judge what is directly in front of their eyes but go out of their way to look for what is not there. ... Some people chose to see the book as a carefully reasoned argument against marriage." A second palinode, which brings us back to the starting point.

In 1890, Renan finally makes up his mind to publish *L'Avenir de la science* as is; this was a work he had finished in 1849 and had left in his drawer because it was unpolished and huge. He provides a preface that, like the preface of Chateaubriand's *Natchez* (another old Purana), will therefore be simultaneously original and delayed. On rereading himself after so many years, he finds the text has a thousand defects of youth, including an excess of optimism. "But when I try to draw up the balance sheet of what, in those dreams of half a century ago, has remained a fantasy and what has come true, I experience, I confess, a feeling of quite appreciable mental joy. In short, I was right all along. ... At the beginning of my intellectual career I was then right to believe firmly in science and to take it as the object of my life. If I were to start all over, I would do what I have done all over again, and during the few years left for me to live, I will continue. Immortality is to work at an eternal undertaking."

In 1865, Barbey d'Aurevilly writes a preface for a new edition of *Une vieille maîtresse* (1851), a work composed before his conversion to Catholicism, so here again we have an example with a more classic look. The "Free Thinkers" claim this work is in conflict with Barbey's present convictions. Sheer calumny: his aim was "to show not only the madness of passion, but its enslavement ..., in depicting it, on every page he condemns it," and this work is accordingly a work of morality. In 1903, Huysmans, likewise a convert to Catholicism, republishes *A rebours* [*Against the Grain*] (1884) with a "Preface Written Twenty Years after the Novel" (that is its title: the time period is canonical). I believed at the time, he explains, that I was indeed a long way from religion, but I was mistaken: "I might quite well sign my name at the present moment to the pages of 'Against the Grain' relating to the Church, for they appear in very deed to have been written by a Catholic. ... [A]ll the romances I have written since 'Against the Grain' are contained in embryo in that book." The action of grace was ripening unbeknown to me, and unbeknown to all critics save one – Barbey – who wrote: "After such a book it only remains for the author to choose between the muzzle of a pistol [suicide] or the foot of the cross." And Huysmans concludes: "The choice has been made." Let us do him the justice of saying that here he does not try to reclaim all of his previous work, for everything before *A rebours* he leaves in the naturalist "blind alley."

The conversion of Barrès, unlike the conversions of Chateaubriand, Barbey, and Huysmans, is not exactly religious but ideological and political. Publishing the "definitive" edition of *Sous l'oeil des barbares* in 1892, he adds an "Examination of the Three Ideological Novels" known as *Le Culte du Moi*, dedicated, not without reason, to Paul Bourget.[16] This preface is not so very delayed, but Barrès, too, was an express, not a local. These three volumes, received as a breviary of skepticism, "were not able to say all they meant." Their alleged egotistical nihilism was in reality a first stage, like Descartes's doubt (or *cogito*?). One must start from the only sure reality, which is the self. "I mean that people are going to speak to me of interdependence. The first point was to exist. ... Furthermore, consider the Self a temporary ground on which you have to stand until someone energetic has reconstructed a religion for you." Apparently, as Huysmans would say, "The choice has been made." Barrès extends the maneuver in his preface to the 1904 edition of *Un homme libre* by aligning *Le Culte du Moi* with the nationalist positions he took in *Les Déracinés* (1897). Bourget, who definitely is to Barrès what Barbey was to Huysmans (what a chain!), had appraised *Un homme libre* as "a masterpiece of irony that lacks only a conclusion." We know what the alternatives are [suicide or Christianity], but for Barrès the choice will be, instead, the mouth of the cannon [militarism]. In the meantime, "This deferred conclusion is furnished by *Les Déracinés*: in *Les Déracinés*, the free man recognizes and accepts his determinism. A candidate for nihilism pursues his apprenticeship, and from analysis to analysis he experiences the nothingness of the self, until acquiring a social

---

[16] The three are *Sous l'oeil des barbares* (1888), *Un homme libre* (1889), and *Le Jardin de Bérénice* (1891).

consciousness." And in an appendix to this edition, "A Reply to M. René Doumic" can conclude like this: "No fatted calf!" For the prodigal son had never left; he was only flexing the muscles of his mind. Hence the phrase that sums everything up, with a play on words that has already been useful and will continue to be so for a long time to come: "Penser solitairement, c'est s'acheminer à penser solidairement" ["To think in solitude is to move toward thinking in solidarity"].

From Barrès to Aragon the chain continues, and the filiation is, as we know, insisted on – by the latter, of course. But Aragon's discourse of reclamation is more complex and – as we have already glimpsed – more anguished. The truth is that the author of *Les Incipit* has *several* pasts to reclaim, and the hardest is not the oldest: from surrealist anarchism to Communist solidarity, the formula of transition is indeed that of Barrès; and on the literary level, the passage from automatic writing to socialist realism is still of the same order, reinforced by a vigorous dialectic of "lying true" [*mentir vrai*] and by a clever evasion "in the style of Hugo: that in surrealism there is realism." Accordingly there is no repudiation here, only straightforward progress and development: "To those who would conclude that I repudiate my early writings, I will say that the man is not the negation of the child, but his development." More difficult to redeem is the "leftist" *Front rouge* phase, which Aragon quite plainly prefers to condemn, although autocriticism is an "acrobatic exercise that, as a matter of fact, I have never been in the habit of or had respect for." Finally, more difficult to condemn – for whatever one may say, it goes to the heart of the commitment to Communism – is the Stalinist "deviation" and the multiple dishonest compromises with their most ignoble consequences. Here the discourse becomes Dostoevskyan, mingling the retrospective inclination for revolt with the voluptuously masochistic submission to "that voluntary hell that is mine." But this, perhaps, no longer directly concerns the œuvre. The life, too, has its paratext, and posterity is a very long postface, which one cannot write oneself.

The delayed preface to one work may also be the last preface to the entire œuvre, and (with a little luck) the last word. That is more or less the case with Ronsard, who died upon writing the delayed preface to *La Franciade*; and we have seen (p. 175) that that was ideally the aim of Chateaubriand and Walter Scott. Aragon breaks off, abruptly and definitively, at volume 8 of his *Œuvre poétique*, some three years before his physical death. Leaving the stage is an art "entirely of execution."[17]

The "last preface," or the one presumed to be last, is thus frequently felt by the author to be his last "address" to the reader – his final opportunity to communicate with his public. In what was, on the contrary, his first authorial preface (unless I am mistaken) – the one to *Inquisiciones* (1925) – Borges wrote that the preface is the place in his work where the author is "least the author." That must be understood, perhaps, as least the *creator* but, conversely, most the *communicator*. Even so convivial a novelist as Fielding seems to experience the sense of a breaking off of contact, a suspension of the "discourse," during the strictly narrative, and fictional, chapters of his work. Consequently he presents the last "preface" of *Tom Jones* (the introductory chapter of the eighteenth and last book) as his final situation of communication. The end of this novel, under pressure of the "Variety of Matter," will contain no more pleasantries or "ludicrous Observations": "All will be plain Narrative only." So it is here that we part from each other, if possible as good friends, "like Fellow-Travellers in a Stage Coach, who have passed several Days in the Company of Each other; and who, notwithstanding any Bickerings or little Animosities which may have occurred on the Road, generally make up all at last, and mount, for the last Time, into their Vehicle with Chearfulness and Good-Humour; since after this one Stage, it may possibly happen to us, as it commonly happens to them, never to meet more." Accordingly, this last preface – the last stop before the last trip – is entitled, logically, "A Farewel to the Reader."

For an author who knows how to live, and how to die in time, the last preface is therefore the moment for the ceremony of leave-taking. No one, to my knowledge, has carried it off better than Boileau in the preface to the 1701 collection of his *Œuvres*. He would in fact live for another twelve years, but to a sixty-three-year-old poet in the eighteenth century, it seemed urgent to go into retirement. "As this is probably the last edition of my

---

[17] [As Napoleon said of politics or war.]

works that I shall prepare for publication,[18] and as it is not likely that at my age of more than sixty-three years, and bowed under many infirmities, I can have very far to go, the public will approve of my taking leave of it in the customary way and thanking it for its kindness in so often purchasing[19] works that are so little worthy of its admiration." Then follows a serious inquiry into the reasons his works found such favor. There is only one: "the care I have taken always to comply with [the public's] feelings and, so far as I could, to acquire its taste in all things." For it is not a matter of "being approved by a small number of connoisseurs"; one must stimulate "the general palate of mankind." And the best way of doing that is "in never presenting the reader with any but true thoughts and accurate phrasing." Everything else (and here Boileau attacks lines by Théophile and Benserade which, as a result, have remained famous) is frozen like "all the icebergs of the North put together" and can please only momentarily. Works based on truth and justice are, on the contrary, immortal, and they weather all cabals, "as with a piece of wood that one forces under water with one's hand: it stays down as long as one holds it down; but soon, when the hand grows tired, the wood rises and comes to the top." Accordingly Boileau confidently awaits the judgment of posterity. Yes, the judgment: "What does it really mean to publish a work? Isn't it, in some sort, to say to the public, 'Judge me'? Why then take offense at being judged?"

Contrary to the hope expressed by the author of the *Satires*,[20] nowadays such a remark may well appear quite old-fashioned. But how will it be tomorrow, and especially the day after, with whatever "comes to the top"? In any case, it seems to me appropriate to end this too-long journey through authorial prefaces with such an engaging demonstration of the art of taking leave.

---

[18] In 1710 he began to prepare another (the posthumous edition of 1713), but it is thought that he did not get past the fifth sheet before he died, in March 1711.

[19] The word is indeed *acheter* [to purchase], not *achever* [to complete]. Such frankness would undoubtedly be shocking today, when we like to engarland the business of literature with hypocritical wreaths; but we know that Boileau was someone who liked to call a purchase a purchase.

[20] [The preface to the 1701 collection of Boileau's works includes this sentence: "But I have put this whole argument into rime in my ninth Satire, and all I need do is send my censurers there."]

Allographic prefaces

The authorial preface had a prehistory: centuries of "hidden life," buried in the first or last pages of text. Nothing comparable seems to exist in the history of the allographic preface, the first examples of which, at least in France, appear to go back only to the sixteenth century – that is, to the period when the authorial preface itself becomes detached from the body of the text. If an investigation with more information at its disposal were to confirm this impression, the explanation for it would be contained, so to speak, in the fact, for allography is in its own way a separation: a separation between the sender of the text (the author) and the sender of the preface (the preface-writer). It is even possible that the first physically separate prefaces were allographic – for example, the preface (anonymous, but doubtless by Marot) accompanying the translation (printed in 1526) of the *Roman de la Rose* and suggesting a set of symbolic interpretations of that work. Let us also mention, still in France, the (purely philological) preface, again by Marot, to his edition of Villon's works (1533); and then, also by Marot, a preface to his translation of Ovid (1534); and from pens other than his, prefaces to various translations of Homer, Sophocles, Euripides, Horace, and Terence. In 1547, Amyot heads his translation of *Théagène et Chariclée* with a kind of manifesto in support of the Greek romance, regarded as a salutary moral and aesthetic antithesis to the shapeless nonsense of chivalric romances. Amyot's prefaces to his translations of Diodorus (1554) and Plutarch (1559) also become manifestos, in support of History.[21] Thus the production of prefaces seems to have been closely tied to the humanist practice of publishing and translating the classic texts of the Middle Ages and classical antiquity. If this hypothesis were verified, the Italian Renaissance would doubtless allow us to push back the date of the first allographic prefaces by several decades.

All those prefaces are obviously produced posthumously, that

[21] Most of the prefaces mentioned here are conveniently brought together in B. Weinberg's collection, *Critical Prefaces of the French Renaissance* (Evanston, IL: Northwestern University Press, 1950). On the preface to [the French translation of Heliodorus's] *Théagène et Chariclée*, see M. Fumaroli, "Jacques Amyot and the Clerical Polemic against the Chivalric Novel," *Renaissance Quarterly* (spring 1985).

is, after the death of the author of the text. That possibility, from which the authorial preface is, of course, excluded, is the one thing that distinguishes the temporal occasions of the allographic preface; thus an allographic preface may be original (for a first edition), later (for an anthumous republication or for a translation),[22] or delayed (these are generally posthumous). As I have said, to my knowledge the first original allographic preface could have been the one that Chapelain wrote for the *Adone* of Marino,[23] but here again it must be possible to go back further than that. Let us likewise note (and I will not mention it again) that an original allographic preface may coexist with an authorial preface. This phenomenon is undoubtedly rare in fiction, where one introduction is rightly thought sufficient, but it is not rare in theoretical or critical works, which allow (and I will come back to this) a significant apportioning of prefatorial discourses. We find something of that division of labor even in Proust's *Les Plaisirs et les jours*, where a preface by Anatole France precedes a kind of dedicatory epistle from Proust to Willie Heath. In all these instances, for obvious reasons, the allographic preface takes precedence over the authorial preface.

Despite the case of *Adone*, the allographic preface does not seem to have been very common in the classical period. Its age of abundance begins in the nineteenth century, but this abundance is quite relative: making an equal effort on behalf of both authorial and allographic prefaces, I came across many more of the former than of the latter, and on this point I calmly await the statistics to come. At the moment, the hypothetical explanation for this disproportion is a matter for "common sense," that is, for such commonplaces as "It is harder to bother two people than one," "We are never so well served as by ourselves," or (more debatably) "To do a preface for a book, you need to have read a few pages of it." Our study of functions will perhaps help us refine these truisms.

Basically, the functions of the allographic preface overlap with, but at the same time add some specificity to, the functions of the

---

[22] In the case of a translation, the preface may be signed by the translator, as we have just seen. The translator–preface-writer may possibly comment on, among other things, his own translation; on this point and in this sense, his preface then ceases to be allographic.

[23] Published in Italian in Paris in 1623.

original authorial preface (to promote and guide a reading of the work), for the functions characteristic of the later and delayed authorial prefaces hardly fall within the province of an allographic preface-writer (henceforth referred to simply as *preface-writer*). The added specifications are obviously attributable to the change in sender, for two types of people cannot carry out exactly the same function. Here, therefore, high praise of the text becomes a recommendation, and information about the text becomes a presentation. For a reason that escapes me, I will begin with the second.

The informational functions connected with the role of presenter are multiple and perhaps heterogeneous. Providing information about the creation of the work is for the most part characteristic of posthumous prefaces, for while the author is alive it would seem unsuitable for a third party to perform that task for him. This, however, is what Grimm does in 1770 apropos of the work that, ten years later, would become Diderot's *Religieuse* [*The Nun*], but we know how distinctive the creation of that work was; and besides, only at that later date will Grimm's disclosures, duly corrected by Diderot, become the "Preface to the Preceding Work."[24] Nowadays, providing this type of information is the basic role of the prefaces (more modestly called "notices" or "introductions") supplied by editors of scholarly editions, who retrace the stages of the work's conception, writing, and publication and move on logically to a "history of the text" and an account of their own editorial decisions (establishment of the text, choice of pre-texts and variants, documentary and critical notes, and so forth). In series that aim at both philological rigor and (relatively) wide circulation, the functions of emphasizing the value of the text were until recently entrusted to another presenter who, in an actual "preface," took on the task of providing a discourse that was more general and, as a rule, more enticing: for example, André Maurois for Proust, Armand Lanoux for Zola. This division of duties is now tending to disappear – an

---

[24] [Friedrich Melchior Grimm's newsletter (circulated in manuscript), *La Correspondance littéraire*, contained in 1770 an early version of *La Religieuse* and an (untruthful) account of the work's origin. A revised text of *La Religieuse* appeared in Grimm's newsletter in 1780–82, along with Diderot's revised account of its origin. *La Religieuse* was published as a book in 1796.]

obvious sign of the promotion of philological labor which we noted earlier apropos of pocket series.

A second type of information, similarly characteristic of posthumous prefaces, is strictly biographical. Publication of a work, and *a fortiori* of the complete works, of an author has for a long time – at least since the troubadors' *vidas* [biographies] were inserted into thirteenth-century collections – been the almost obligatory occasion for informing readers about the circumstances of that author's life. In the classical period all the major editions opened with a ritual "Life of the Author," which served as a critical study. At the head of the first collection of his *Fables*, La Fontaine places a "Life of Aesop the Phrygian"; La Bruyère opens his *Caractères* with a "Discourse on Theophrastus"; in 1684 a "Life of Blaise Pascal" by his sister Gilberte appears at the head of the *Pensées*; in 1722 an edition of Racine is embellished with a biography that the family immediately denounces as insufficiently edifying; in 1783 the Kehl edition of the works of Voltaire opens with a "Life of Voltaire" by Condorcet; and we know that in 1825 Balzac, for editions of Molière and La Fontaine in which he was a financial partner, writes a biographical notice several pages long about each of them, adding little to either their glory or his own. Flaubert, in his preface for the simultaneously original and posthumous edition of the *Dernières Chansons* by his friend Louis Bouilhet (1872), starts out by exorcising the prefatorial practice, which he finds detestable and of whose antiquity he seems to have no inkling: "Hasn't 'information' been overworked? History will soon absorb all of literature. The excessive study of what made up a writer's ambiance prevents us from considering the very originality of his genius. In La Harpe's time, people were persuaded that, thanks to certain rules, a masterpiece comes into the world without owing anything to anything, whereas now people believe they are discovering its raison d'être when they have spelled out in detail all the circumstances surrounding it" (this sort of protest will later be called a *Contre Sainte-Beuve*, and we may also enjoy seeing La Harpe [1739–1803] credited with an idea that would nowadays be called "Valéryan"). Then Flaubert himself hastens to make his sacrifice on the altar of the contemptible rite, telling us about his friend's life and opinions: his demanding nature, his scruples, his disgust with a "mediocratic" century, his hatred of proclamations that never go beyond words ("He would hang himself rather than write a preface"). But Flaubert, hardly more drawn to this genre than Bouilhet was, has given many signs of resistance (we will look at them again below), and in fact this preface – the only one he ever wrote – exudes piety more than enthusiasm. Mallarmé's preface for *Vathek*[25] is almost exclusively biographical (and bibliographical), and Sartre's preface for *Aden Arabie* is essentially a biographical statement about Nizan as Sartre knew him. Most of Borges's posthumous allographic prefaces that make up the collection *Prólogos* contain biographical notices; the most interesting is the one devoted to Macedonio Fernandez, which is explicitly presented as a biographical notice: "No one has yet written the biography of Macedonio Fernandez. ... I want nothing that touches Macedonio to be lost. I who stay up late recording these absurd details continue to believe that their protagonist was the most extraordinary man I have ever met. No doubt Boswell thought the same about Samuel Johnson."

A final type of information, already closer to critical interpretation, consists of situating the presented text either within the context of the author's entire œuvre – as Larbaud does in 1926 for the French translation of *Dubliners* [*Gens de Dublin*] and as Todorov does in 1984 for the French translation of *The Great Code* [*Le Grand Code*] – or within the broader context of a genre or the literature of a period: a typical example is Georges Poulet's preface for Jean-Pierre Richard's *Littérature et sensation*, where Poulet defines Richard's criticism in relation to other currents (Blanchot, Béguin, Bachelard) in contemporary criticism.

The other function of the allographic preface is without doubt far more important, especially for original allographic prefaces; above all it is more specific, and accounts for the resort to a preface-writer. This is the function of recommending: "I, X, tell you that Y has genius and that you must read his book." In this explicit form – which, strictly speaking, is quite rare and characteristic of the most unsophisticated sectors of the institution of literature – the prefatorial discourse may well elicit a double expression of ridicule, provoking the "save me from my friends" effect associated with immoderate praise and the backlash effect

[25] [Beckford's oriental tale was written in French, although the English translation was published first.]

that strikes the preface-writer presumptuous enough to pro-
nounce on some other writer's genius. The 1847 edition of
Provincial à Paris, a minor work by Balzac,[26] opened with an
"avant-propos by the publisher" in which the latter (?) swung the
incense-burner with a delicacy wholly ... Balzacian: "There is one
who, perhaps more than the others, deserves the colossal reputation he enjoys. This writer is M. de Balzac. ... No other has
sounded more deeply than M. de Balzac the thousand recesses of
the human heart. ... Now that the edifice is just about finished,
everyone may admire its elegance, power, and solidity. ... M. de
Balzac is a writer who can be compared to no one else living
today. We see only one name we would readily match with M. de
Balzac. And this name is Molière. ... If Molière were alive in this
day and age, he would write *La Comédie humaine*. Of what other
contemporary writer could one say as much?" The probable
apocryphalness of this pseudo-publisher's allography does not
help matters: in the eyes of posterity, Balzac alone shoulders the
burden of a ridicule ordinarily heaped on two people.

Fortunately, the function of recommending usually remains
implicit because the mere presence of this type of preface is in
itself a recommendation. For an original preface, this support is
generally provided by a writer whose reputation is more firmly
established than the author's: Flaubert for Bouilhet, Anatole
France for Proust, Borges for Bioy Casares, Sartre for Sarraute.
For a translation, it is generally provided by a writer who is
better known in the importing country: Baudelaire for Poe,
Malraux or Larbaud for Faulkner, Larbaud again for Joyce,
Aragon for Kundera. For a considerably posthumous republication of a classic text that the publisher has a contemporary author
"revisit," the role of advocate falls to this (by definition) more
current writer: Valéry for Montesquieu's *Lettres persanes*, Stendhal's *Lucien Leuwen*, and Flaubert's *La Tentation de Saint Antoine*;
Sartre for Baudelaire's *Journaux intimes*; Queneau for Flaubert's
Bouvard et Pécuchet. Or also (all question of relative fame set
aside) by a writer who is capable of adding value to a work – of
adding an interpretation, and therefore an exemplary theoretical
status. This is apparently the significance we must give to the
preface Chapelain wrote for Marino's *Adone*.[27] At the time,

---

[26] It later became *Les Comédiens sans le savoir*; see Pléiade 8:1709.
[27] "Lettre ou discours de M. Chapelain à M. Favereau ... portant son opinion sur

Allographic prefaces

Chapelain was only a young disciple of Malherbe, who had been approached about the preface but preferred to pass on to his disciple a task he himself doubtless found rather uninspiring. The deal proved successful: Chapelain produced a long text that, although fairly ponderous, demonstrated with full Aristotelian orthodoxy that Marino's poem was "animated and fabricated in its innovativeness according to the general rules for epics" – was in fact a new kind of epic inasmuch as its action was not heroic but was sufficiently "illustrious" (the life and death of Adonis) to furnish the subject of a long narrative poem, just as the nonmartial action of *Oedipus* could furnish a subject for tragedy (here we note once again the generative capacity of the Aristotelian combinatorial framework).[28] Having completed his demonstration, Chapelain, who at the very beginning had apologized for his lack of authority, concluded by protesting with fairly haughty modesty that he had not undertaken to "praise" the knight Marino but only to say wherein he was worthy of praise: "My intention has not been to crown him but to show you succinctly that I knew why he deserved the crown." *Mutatis mutandis*, adding value is also the function of Larbaud's preface for the 1925 republication of Dujardin's *Lauriers sont coupés* (1887), a preface that focuses on the history of the interior monologue; and of Deleuze's preface for Tournier's *Vendredi*, which promotes Tournier's book to the status of an illustration of "a certain theory of the Other" – and of perversion as absence of the Other. And some may recall that in the 1960s the 10/18 pocket series specialized in this kind of introduction with a high intellectual coefficient: Blanchot providing commentary for Des Forêts's *Bavard*, Barthes for Cayrol's *Corps étrangers*, Ricardou for Simon's *Route des Flandres*, and so forth. But Sartre's monumental "preface" for the *Œuvres complètes* of Genet [625 pages in its English translation, entitled *Saint Genet*] remains forevermore the most imposing, or most inhibiting, example of philosophical support for a literary work. Forevermore? Unless someday someone takes it into his head to print *L'Idiot de la famille* [Sartre's

le poème d'*Adonis* du chevalier Marino," reprinted in *Opuscules critiques*, ed. Hunter (Droz, 1936).
28 [Genette's *The Architext: An Introduction* (Berkeley and Los Angeles: University of California Press, 1992) is, among other things, an extended analysis of the workings of the Aristotelian combinatorial framework.]

269

study of Flaubert, consisting of five volumes in its English translation] as a preface to *Madame Bovary* ...

In his *Prólogo de prólogos*, Borges notes in passing that "no one, as far as I know, has yet formulated a technique of the preface," and he sensibly adds, "This lacuna is not serious, given that we all know what we are dealing with." That remark, which ought to discourage anyone from expressing himself on so trivial a subject, does not discourage Borges himself from continuing: "Most of the time, alas! the preface resembles an after-dinner speech or a funeral oration, and it abounds in gratuitous hyperbole that the reader, who is no fool, takes as only a manner of speaking. But there are cases in which the preface ... sets out and comments on an aesthetic." And he mentions Wordsworth and Montaigne, examples that indicate he is not thinking only of allographic prefaces, which the phrase "funeral oration" obviously alludes to. "When a preface is successful," he concludes, "it is not a type of toast; it is a lateral form of criticism." Various examples that we have already mentioned, among which we could include Borges's own allographic prefaces in *Prólogos*, show well enough that the two functions of attributing high value and supplying critical commentary are by no means incompatible and even that the second may be the most effective form of the first – most effective because indirect, the commentary bringing to light "deep" meanings that are for that very reason rewarding. We know, for example, how much Faulkner's intellectual "price" in the French literary stock market owed for a time to Malraux's well-known phrase about "the intrusion of Greek tragedy into the detective story."

Nevertheless, the critical and theoretical dimension of the allographic preface clearly draws it toward the border that separates (or rather, toward the absence of a border that does not sharply separate) paratext from metatext and, more concretely, preface from critical essay. This proximity to the critical essay is particularly noticeable in posthumous prefaces written for the republication of ancient works:[29] the fact that the author has long been dead frees the preface from any sort of semiofficial status and (almost) from any obligation to attribute high value to

---

[29] I am not speaking of posthumous prefaces in the form of homage (after a short interval) to a deceased friend, such as the one Flaubert wrote for Bouilhet, which Borges would rightly assign to the "funeral oration" model.

the work. It is well known, for example, that the presence of a preface, even possibly a harsh one, signed by Valéry was always more of an incentive than a deterrent. It is not by chance that I mention Valéry. His long prefaces, for Montesquieu, Stendhal, and Flaubert, are all in the nature of critical essays – and are nowadays very legitimately and indistinguishably combined with his autonomous essays, such as those on La Fontaine or Voltaire. Moreover, in these prefaces his approach is very high and mighty and sometimes even very remote, particularly with respect to the *Lettres persanes* – or rather with respect to the mind in general, then the mind of the eighteenth century, before he arrives at Montesquieu and then Montesquieu's book. The "Stendhal" preface has an equally broad range and presents the author of *Leuwen* more as a type of mind than as a writer. "The Temptation of (St.) Flaubert" is even quite openly disparaging: it is an indictment of realism, *Salammbô*, and *Bovary*, and even of *Saint Antoine*, a work in which Flaubert, "carried away by the accessories at the expense of the main point," quite simply "lost the soul of his subject." It is characteristic that Valéry's "Stendhal," for example, was first published in a journal and was subsequently reprinted in a separate booklet before finding a place in *Variété* [a five-volume collection of Valéry's miscellaneous critical writings]. One sees the same sort of publishing trajectory with Sartre's prefaces reprinted, along with old articles, in *Situations*, and with Barthes's, reprinted in *Essais critiques*, and so forth. And once again, there are those two masterpieces of criticism by Sartre, formerly prefaces, the *Baudelaire* and the *Saint Genet* – but I will not risk discussing those two at greater length under the rubric of the allographic preface, for examining them here would inflate this section to such an extent that it would burst like a balloon.

But sometimes it also happens that the preface-writer – emboldened by the commanding position his fame generally confers on him and by the fact that he is always responding to a request and is therefore sure of being more or less able to "do as he pleases" – takes advantage of the circumstances to go somewhat beyond the supposed subject of his discourse and argue in support of a cause that is broader or possibly wholly different. The prefaced work then becomes simply the pretext for a manifesto, a confidence, a settling of accounts, a digression. This is Mallarmé exactly, forgetting about René Ghil's (slight) *Traité du verbe* (1886) to advance, in an *avant-dire*, his own theory of language and verse. It is also Proust favoring *Tendres Stocks* with a discourse on his doctrine of style, which deals a bit less with Morand than with Stendhal, Baudelaire, and Flaubert. It is Valéry transcending Leo Ferrero's *Léonard de Vinci ou L'œuvre d'art*[30] in a perfectly autonomous essay on "Léonard et les Philosophes." And Borges exploiting the opportunity provided by Bioy Casares's *Invention of Morel* to assail the arbitrariness of the psychological novel ("The Russians and their disciples have demonstrated tediously that no one is impossible. A person may kill himself because he is so happy, for example, or commit murder as an act of benevolence. Lovers may separate forever as a consequence of their love. And one man can inform on another out of fervor or humility ...") and to glorify the novel of adventure. It is Sartre enrolling Sarraute's *Portrait d'un inconnu*, which can't answer back, under the banner of the anti-novel.[31] And Sartre again, crushing Fanon's *Damnés de la terre* under the weight of his own extreme anticolonialist rage in a discourse that has not unreasonably been called "a verbal highjacking."[32] And it is Aragon taking advantage of the opportunity provided by the French translation of Kundera's *The Joke* [*La Plaisanterie*] to express his anguish over the imminent danger of a certain "Biafra of the mind."[33]

Even so, one should not think that, when it comes to the question

---

[30] Published by Kra in 1929. Valéry's preface was subsequently incorporated into the collection of his studies on Leonardo; see Pléiade 1:1234 et seq.

[31] Nathalie Sarraute's reservations, which one can easily guess, were finally expressed with the greatest clarity in an interview conducted by J. L. Ezine, *Les Ecrivains sur la sellette* (Seuil, 1981), 37: "I already disagreed with that when he wrote it, in the preface to *Portrait d'un inconnu*; that novel is not an 'anti-novel,' and neither are the others. ..."

[32] G. Idt, "Fonction rituelle du métalangage dans les préfaces 'hétérographes,'" *Littérature* 27 (October 1977); in this study of the preface to Fanon's *Damnés de la terre*, the author very correctly describes Sartre's function as "master prefacewriter": "Author of about fifty prefaces, from one to five hundred pages in length, written or spoken, extolling classics, promoting unknowns, or introducing foreign authors, in the institution of literature Sartre stands in first place and not on the sidelines." In the gallery of master preface-writers of this century, in quantity Sartre probably surpasses all his predecessors, including Anatole France and Valéry.

[33] For Aragon, this phrase designated the annihilation, by the Stalinist or post-Stalinist dictatorship, of all thought. [Biafra was the name of a region of Nigeria whose attempted secession led to a bloody civil war fought between 1967 and 1970.]

of a clear conscience, the allographic preface-writer has the advantage over the authorial preface-writer, or that all writers, famous or not, consent to this role of literary or ideological "godfather" without any discomfort or qualms. Some writers evade the role without much ado, and their restraint naturally excludes them from our survey.[34] Others evade it more explicitly, for example, Flaubert, whom we see flatly refusing the intrusive request of a Mme Régnier: I have already refused to do it for others, he explains, and "this 'great-man' behavior, this manner of recommending a book to the public, this Dumas style of doing things, in a word exasperates me, disgusts me"; besides, "the thing is perfectly useless and doesn't help sell even one additional copy, the savvy reader knowing perfectly well what to make of these acts of obliging compliance which disparage a book right away; for the publisher gives the impression of having doubts about the book since he resorts to an outsider to sing its praises."[35] This last argument does carry weight, even if we have no way of evaluating the benefits and drawbacks of using an allographic preface. Other authors, less categorical or more perverse than Flaubert, express their qualms or reservations (as we have seen so many writers of authorial prefaces do) in the actual text of the preface, which will at least have the merit of lucidity. Borges, in a 1927 preface to an anthology of Uruguayan poetry, wondered publicly what he was doing "in this *zaguán* [vestibule]"; and T. S. Eliot, in his introduction to Djuna Barnes's *Nightwood* (1937), puts the question in the form – for me, definitive – of an aporia: "The few books worth introducing are exactly those which it is an impertinence to introduce."

The reverse corollary is self-evident, and it unambiguously points to the other source of discomfort: not the preface-writer's

---

[34] We know that Balzac, for *La Comédie humaine*, asked Nodier for a preface and then, after he refused, asked Sand, who accepted but then backed out. As a result of this double withdrawal we gained the foreword of 1842 but lost what would perhaps have been the most dazzling example of an allographic preface.

[35] September 7, 1877. We must note, however, that in 1853 Flaubert had toyed with three projects for prefaces: one was allographic, a preface on Ronsard, which would have been a sort of "essay on French poetic genius," or a "history of poetic feeling in France"; another was for Bouilhet's *Melaenis*; and a third was an authorial preface for his own *Dictionnaire des idées reçues*, perhaps a remote ancestor of *Bouvard et Pécuchet*: in this preface he envisaged "spouting the critical ideas that are on my mind." The idea of absolutely refusing to express any theory in a preface thus came to him later.

embarrassment at playing a role that is basically immodest and superfluous, but his reluctance to perform a task from which he was unable to excuse himself. That, at least, is how I interpret the clause, at best condescending and at worst unkind to the author, with which so many preface-writers seem to clear their names by carefully indicating that, in writing the preface, they are granting a pressing request. "Why did he ask me to present his book to curious minds?" asks Anatole France at the head of Proust's *Les Plaisirs et les jours*. "Why should he ask me to introduce his book to discriminating minds? And why have I promised to undertake this most agreeable but perfectly useless task? His book ... is its own recommendation." For Dujardin's *Lauriers sont coupés*, Larbaud writes, "It is the author himself ... who did his young colleague the honor of requesting this preface." Valéry, at the beginning of the "Lettre à Leo Ferrero" that serves as a preface to *Léonard de Vinci ou L'œuvre d'art*, says, "You are venturing into still more dangerous territory when you ask me to introduce your work to the public." Sartre: "I agree with pleasure to add some words to Stéphane's remarkable essay on the Adventurer. Not to praise or recommend it: it recommends itself. ..." And Sartre again, at the head of *L'Artiste et sa conscience*: "My dear Leibowitz, you have asked me to add a few words to your book. ... [I agreed from friendship and] solidarity. ... But now that I must write, I admit to feeling very uneasy." Sartre's tact was, as we know, boundless; the source of his uneasiness here is, in theory, his musical incompetence, but another source is quickly revealed: an obscure disagreement about the modalities (indeed contributing to uneasiness) of the musician's political commitment.[36] Again and still Sartre, for *Le Traître* by André Gorz: "The book appealed to me and I said yes, that I would preface it, because we must always pay [the word is gracious] for the right to love the things we love. But as soon as I seized the pen, an invisible carousel began turning just above the paper. It was *the Foreward* [*sic*] *as a literary genre*, which was seeking its specialist, a serene and handsome old man, an Academician. ..."

Sometimes one is more the Academician than one imagines and, as Satie (I think it was) or Jules Renard said, it is not enough

[36] "It is certainly not one of my better essays" ("Autoportrait à soixante-dix ans," *Situations X*, 171 [tr. *Life/Situations: Essays Written and Spoken*, trans. Paul Auster and Lydia Davis (New York: Pantheon Books, 1977), 40]).

to refuse honors, you must not deserve them. But for us the interesting thing is to see here, once again, how the prefatorial malaise, whether it proceeds from sincere modesty or from unavowed disdain, turns into a kind of generic hyperconsciousness. No one writes a preface without experiencing the more or less inhibiting feeling that what's most obvious about the whole business is that he is engaged in writing a preface. Roland Barthes, who wrote nothing that was at all ritual and "coded" (be it preface, journal page, autobiography, letter of condolence or of congratulations) without immediately feeling the weight and force – at once paralyzing and inspiring – of the code, reveals it in his own way, a way as precise as it is evasive, in the first paragraph of his preface to *La Parole intermédiaire* by François Flahault. This paragraph, to which I will very carefully avoid adding a single word, is a veritable little organon of the allographic preface:

I tend to believe that the preface-writer's role consists of expressing what the author, from a sense of propriety, modesty, discretion, etc., cannot say. Now, despite the words, I am not referring to psychological scruples. An author can certainly say "I," but it is hard – without causing some vertigo – for him to comment on this *I* with a second "I," necessarily different from the first. An author can speak of the knowledge of his time, can indeed adduce his own relations to it, but he does not have the power to situate himself there declaratively, historically, he cannot *assess himself*. An author can produce an ethical vision of the world, but he cannot make a display of it, first, because in the current state of our prejudices that would appear to diminish his scientific objectivity, and then, because a "vision" is never anything but a synthesis, a secondary state of discourse, which can be attributed to the other person but not to oneself. That is why the preface-writer, acting as a second voice, maintains with the author and the public a very special particular speech-relation, inasmuch as he is ternary: as preface-writer, I designate one of the places where I would very much like François Flahault to be recognized by a third party, who is his reader. I thus illustrate in an apposite way the theory defended in this book. The preface is in fact one of those "illocutionary" acts that our author analyzes here.[37]

---

[37] A nice performance by Barthes the preface-writer appears at the head of Bruce Morrissette's *Romans de Robbe-Grillet* (Minuit, 1963 [tr. *The Novels of Robbe-Grillet*, trans. Bruce Morrissette (Ithaca: Cornell University Press, 1975)]). The preface was clearly solicited, for once not by the author but by the "hero," to dispel any idea that the interpretation presented in the book is semiofficial. Barthes distinguishes two interpretations of Robbe-Grillet: the "thingist" one

Actorial prefaces

I said above (p. 196) that the authentic actorial preface could be considered a special case of the allographic preface: a case in which the "third" party, between author and reader, happens to be one of the real persons discussed in a referential text. I also said that, for lack of striking examples of a "biographee" supplying a preface for his biography,[38] Valéry offered us the neighboring, or cousinly, example, of a "commentee" providing the preface for a commentary. As a matter of fact, he offers two such examples: the preface to Alain's commentary on *Charmes* (1928) and the *avant-propos* to Gustave Cohen's commentary on *Le Cimitière marin* (1933). I will not claim that these two performances can illustrate the full scope of the actorial preface's functions. One could imagine that the chief function of an actorial preface to a heterobiography – in addition to making the requisite polite remarks and protestations of modesty – would be to correct, in a straightforward way, a few errors of fact or interpretation and to fill in a few gaps. Such an approach presupposes some understanding between the biographer and his model, without which there would in any case be no such preface. Shifting to the sphere of commentary, one could then imagine that a Valéry-type preface would be a kind of second-degree commentary in which the author would say whether he agrees with his critic on the meaning the latter finds in his text, and would in this way either authorize it as official commentary or challenge and correct it. As we already know, serving as this sort of arbiter is exactly the role Valéry twice turned down, professing (and perhaps improvising for the occasion) the extremely famous doctrine – which subsequently became one of the most firmly

(obviously his own, but he does not say so) and the humanist one (Morrissette's). Is it necessary to choose between them? No, he asserts, for the literary work rejects all response – a rejection of response that obviously dismisses the humanist's claim and therefore responds in effect with the greatest clarity.

38 Let us note, however, a preface by Claudel (two fairly superficial pages) to J. Madaule's *Drame de Paul Claudel* (Desclée de Brouwer, 1936); a letter by Gide at the head of P. Iseler's *Débuts d'André Gide vus par Pierre Louÿs* (Le Sagittaire, 1931); and a letter by Malraux at the head of S. Chantal's *Coeur battant: Josette Clotis–André Malraux* (Grasset, 1976). A letter is obviously a convenient way to handle a prefatorial obligation, but some letters almost give the impression of being negative responses surreptitiously turned into letter-prefaces. Mme Régnier indeed should have put Flaubert's refusal at the head of her book.

entrenched principles in our critical vulgate – according to which the author has no right to comment on his work and therefore can only listen in amazement to the comments inflicted on it: "My verses have the meaning attributed to them. The one I give them suits only myself and does not contradict anyone else" (*Charmes*); "There is no true meaning to a text – no author's authority. Whatever he may have wanted to say, he has written what he has written" (*Cimitière marin*); and so on. I will not be so bold as to claim here that this nice theory is purely an *ad hoc* subterfuge Valéry devised to avoid taking a position on the soundness of a commentary, but I can't help thinking that a bit of that is involved, and we know that Valéry was somewhat disposed toward this kind of improvisation. On the other hand, it has not been sufficiently noted that, in the preface for Alain, this theory was closely linked to the equally famous definition of poetry as an intransitive and noncommunicational state of language – in other words, that this dismissal of the author as critic was, at least originally, theoretically reserved for the domain of poetry and that its extension since then, valid or not, to every kind of text slightly subverts its Valéryan endorsement.

There is another difference between Valéry's use of his theory and ours. When Valéry decreed the author's lack of authority, he carried abstention to the limit (the details he gives about *Le Cimetière marin* involve genesis, not meaning: how the poem came to him in a decasyllabic rhythm). Current use of the theory, almost anywhere in prefaces, interviews, and lectures, is of a less rigorous type that often has something in common with a kind of exorcising preterition: at first, of course, I have no authority to comment on my work; subsequently, this is how it is, and whoever thinks otherwise is a priggish pedant, a retarded Stalinist, a gas-station philosopher, and other terms of abuse. This composite discourse is (almost) a complete fabrication, and any resemblance to the discourse of a real author is the result of coincidence, objective or not. But experience shows that it is not so easy or so gratifying for an author to *truly* lay aside his authority.

Fictional prefaces

Our last functional type encompasses (from the chart of types of senders) cells A^2, D, E, F, and, for the time being, G, H, and I –

that is, the disavowing authorial prefaces and all the fictive and apocryphal prefaces. With this type we thus return to the category of authorial prefaces, or, more precisely, prefaces that we are authorized (or rather required) – by data external and/or subsequent to the official original status of the preface – to regard as authorial. The quality that assumptive authorial prefaces and allographic prefaces had in common, despite their difference in sender, is what I will call (once again, for lack of a better term) the *serious* nature of their transmitting regime; the prefaces we are now going to look at for their functions are distinguished by their *fictional* or, if you prefer, playful regime (here the notions of fictional and playful seem to me more or less equivalent) – fictional in the sense that the reader is not really, or at least not permanently, expected to take the alleged status of their sender seriously.

I seem to be substituting the contrast between serious and fictional for the contrast between authentic and fictive (or apocryphal), but what we are dealing with is not exactly a substitution, for the category of the serious does not encompass all types of authenticity: the disavowing authorial preface is authentic in the sense previously defined (its author, even if anonymous or pseudonymous, is indeed who he claims to be), but it is not serious in its discourse, for its author claims not to be the author of the text – although he will later admit he is, and it is almost always obvious that he is. Assumptive authorial prefaces and authentic allographic and actorial prefaces are serious in the sense that they say (or imply) the truth about the relation between their author and the text that comes after. The other prefaces – all the others – are either authentic, fictive, or apocryphal, but they are all fictional (a category that thus extends beyond that of the fictive) in the sense that they all – each in its own way – offer a manifestly false attribution of the text.

Their fictionality thus concerns essentially questions of attribution: of the text alone, in the disavowing authorial preface; of the text and of the preface itself, in the preface with a fictive sender; and when all is said and done, of the preface alone, in the possible apocryphal preface of the Davin type.[39] But then again, their functionality consists essentially of their fictionality, in the sense

[39] [Davin was a loaner name Balzac used in signing some of his prefaces: see Chapter 8 under "Senders."]

that they exist essentially *to effect a fictional attribution*. In other words: the preface to Marivaux's *Vie de Marianne* essentially serves to claim fictionally that these memoirs were not written by Marivaux, who signs them, but by Marianne herself; the preface to *Ivanhoe* essentially serves to claim fictionally that this novel is not by Walter Scott but by "Laurence Templeton"; and so forth. Now, we have already considered these fictions of attribution thoroughly enough (in Chapter 8 under the heading "Senders"), where they had a legitimate place, and so the inevitable conclusion would seem to be that we have already, ahead of time, treated the functions of the fictional preface and that all we have left to do now is move on to the next topic.

If that is not entirely the case, the reason is, first, that here as elsewhere, *effecting* a fiction is not just a matter of *stating* it in a sentence of the type "I, Marivaux, am not the author of the memoirs that follow" or "I, Templeton, am the author of the novel that follows." To effect a fiction, one must (as all novelists know) do a bit more than make a performative statement: one must *constitute* this fiction by dint of fictionally convincing details; one must, therefore, *flesh it out* – and the most effective way of doing so seems to be to *simulate a serious preface*, with all the paraphernalia of discourses and messages (that is, functions) which such a simulation entails. Thus the primary function of the fictional preface, which is to effect a fictional attribution, is supplemented with and reinforced by secondary functions arising from simulation of the serious preface – or more precisely, as we will see, from simulation of one or another type of serious preface. For example: "I, Marivaux, will tell you what I think of the memoirs of Marianne" (simulation of an allographic preface); or "I, Templeton, dedicate this narrative to Mr. Dryasdust, antiquarian, and I justify to him my new subject matter of a novel set in medieval England" (simulation of an authorial preface); or "I, Gil Blas, will tell you how you should read the story, which follows, of my life" (simulation of a preface to an autobiography); and so on.[40] And at the same time, and under cover of this fictional simulation, nothing prevents the (real) author of the preface from saying in it, or from having it say, apropos of the text of which he is likewise the real author, various things he

[40] [*Gil Blas* is by Lesage; below, *Adolphe* is by Constant, and *Les Liaisons dangereuses* by Laclos.]

seriously believes – for example, that "the great question in life is the sorrow we cause" (*Adolphe*) – or even (better yet) various things he does not believe but wishes, this time seriously, to have the reader believe (for a lie is as serious as the truth, or as an honest error) – for example, that the aim of the letters published under the title *Les Liaisons dangereuses* is to warn young maidens against corrupt men. Thus here we again encounter, though under cover of simulation, the functions (already identified) of the serious preface, and obviously I will not repeat my earlier discussion of them here. Instead, let us simply pay our respects to some of their reincarnations in the simulated forms, reincarnations that may be sincere or deceitful – in other words, serious.

Disavowing authorial prefaces

The fictions of attribution and the supplementing and reinforcing activities of simulation vary by type of sender. The disavowing authorial preface, which bears a fictive attribution *of the text* only, by the same token presents itself as an allographic preface and in most cases as, more precisely, a simple editorial note. A pseudo-editorial preface, then, for a text presented most often as a simple document (an autobiographical narrative, a diary, a correspondence) without any literary aim, a document attributed to its narrating character(s), diarist(s), or letter-writer(s). Its first function, then, consists of explaining – that is, recounting – the circumstances in which the pseudo-editor acquired possession of this text. Prévost asserts that the *Mémoires d'un homme de qualité* fell into his hands during a trip he took to the abbey of ***, where the author (Renoncour, of course) had gone to withdraw from the world. Marivaux obtains the story of Marianne from a friend, who quite simply found it. For *Adolphe*, Constant gives the details of a stay in Calabria. Scott received the manuscript of *Rob Roy* in the mail (to my knowledge, this is his only disavowing preface). For *Le Vicaire des Ardennes*, Balzac – or rather, "Horace de Saint-Aubin" – took possession of the manuscript of a young man who had just died. Georges Darien stole (what else?) from a hotel room the manuscript of Georges Randal (*Le Voleur* [*The Thief*]), who had, besides, foreseen if not wished for the theft. The rough copy of *Armance* was entrusted to Stendhal for correction by "a woman of intelligence." The manuscript of *Gaspard de la nuit*

[*Gaspard of the Night*] was handed over to Louis Bertrand (that is how he signs his preface)[41] in a public garden in Dijon by a poor devil who disappears in the night and must ever after roast in Hell.[42] It was, apparently, the *Mémoires de M. d'Artagnan* (in reality, as we know, pseudo-memoirs fabricated by Courtilz de Sandras) that put Dumas *père* on the track of the memoirs of the Count de La Fère, "a folio manuscript with the reference number of 4772 or 4773, I have forgotten which," the alleged source of *Les Trois Mousquetaires*. It is during a stay at Kerengrimen (or at Beg-Meil) that Proust becomes acquainted with the writer C. (or B.), who passes on to him the manuscript of *Jean Santeuil*.[43] It is the heroine's daughter who sends Gide the journal of *L'Ecole des femmes*. The original text of "The Immortal" [in *Labyrinths*] "is written in English and abounds in Latinisms," and was transmitted to Borges by the antiquarian Joseph Cartaphilus, whom a note, toward the end of the text, will identify as the narrator-hero. It is on August 16, 1968, that an anonymous go-between puts into the hands of Umberto Eco "a book written by a certain Abbé Vallet, *Le Manuscrit de Dom Adson de Melk, traduit en français d'après l'édition de Dom J. Mabillon* (Aux Presses de l'Abbaye de la Source, Paris, 1842)," a manuscript that the author of *The Name of the Rose* translated into Italian while sailing up the Danube from Vienna to Melk with a woman he cared for, who finally carried off the original when she walked out of his life in, as he says, an "abrupt and untidy way. ... And so," he continues, "I was left with a number of manuscript notebooks in my hand, and a great emptiness in my heart." I refrain from summarizing a follow-up that can be found in any good library under the inevitable title "Naturally, a manuscript" and that is the last word in the whole history of the genre, as Strauss's *Four Last Songs* are in the history

41 [Louis Bertrand was known as Aloysius Bertrand.]
42 Published in 1842 (some months after the author's death) thanks to Victor Pavie, *Gaspard de la nuit* presents a fairly complex paratext: after the disavowing authorial preface there is a second preface – fictive authorial – signed Gaspard de la nuit, then a short dedicatory epistle to Victor Hugo, unsigned and provided with two epigraphs. All of that is preceded by an authentic allographic preface by Sainte-Beuve. But we know from Bertrand's correspondence that he wished to make major revisions in this work and, in particular, to delete the disavowing preface. Cf. Richard Sieburth, "Gaspard de la nuit: Prefacing Genre," *Studies in Romanticism* 24 (summer 1985): 249.
43 *Jean Santeuil* contains two different drafts of a disavowing preface, hence these alternatives. Of course, the posthumous nature of this publication gives its paratext a wholly hypothetical status.

of the romantic lied; but I fear that this swan song in no way discourages imitations.

The details – more or less picturesque – of these circumstances of acquisition obviously give the preface-writer an opportunity to provide the more or less expanded narrative through which this type of preface already participates in the novelistic fiction, furnishing the textual fiction with a kind of frame narrative, generally at only one end. But we know that the "editors" of *Werther* and of Bataille's *Abbé C.* eventually reappear to assume responsibility themselves for the denouement; and that the editor of Flaubert's *Novembre*, who had provided no preface, comes on stage *in fine* ("The manuscript stops here, but I knew the author …") to take the narrative all the way to the hero's death; and some prefaces, like those of *Moll Flanders* or Sainte-Beuve's *Volupté*, serve in advance as epilogues, which by definition are precluded from appearing in autobiographical narratives, whether real or fictive.

The second function of the disavowing authorial preface, a function whose fictionality is less novelistic and strictly editorial in type, consists of indicating the corrections made, or not made, in the text: translation and stylistic simplification for *Lettres persanes*; excision of indecent details for *Les Liaisons dangereuses* – but no correction that would have risked homogenizing the styles of the diverse letter-writers (the author can thus stress the excellence, which obviously is all his doing, of the letters' stylistic diversity); entire rewriting of the work for *Rob Roy*; no corrections at all for *Adolphe*.

The third function of the disavowing authorial preface is rarer than the other two, undoubtedly because the text itself generally takes care of it. This function is to provide a brief biography of the alleged author, which I find only at the head of nonautobiographical works. Nodier attributes *Smarra* to "a Ragusan nobleman who has hidden his name under that of Count Maxime Odin," and Balzac, in the foreword to *Gars*,[44] invents a very detailed biography (and a very autobiographical one, foreshadowing *Louis Lambert* in many respects) of the imagined author "Victor Morillon." I cannot refrain from quoting here one page of that foreword, in a context that makes it particularly delectable:

---

[44] The discarded title of the first version of *Les Chouans* (1828). See Pléiade 8:1667.

The public has been caught so many times in the traps set for its good faith by authors whose self-esteem and vanity increase, hard as that is to imagine, as soon as they have to hand over a name to the public's curiosity, that we think we are serving the public well by taking an opposite tack.

We are happy to be able to own that our feeling was shared by the author of this work – he always expressed deep aversion to those prefaces that are like pageants, where their authors try to make readers believe in the existence of abbots, soldiers, sextons, people who died in dungeons, and discoveries of manuscripts, and that elicit a wealth of fellow-feeling that is showered upon the sham creatures. Sir Walter Scott had this obsession, but he himself had the sense to make fun of these excesses that deprive a book of truth. If one is impelled to become an actor, one must, it is true, resolve to play the charlatan, but without using a puppet. We greet with more seriousness and respect a man who introduces himself modestly by saying his name, and today there is modesty in giving one's name, there is a certain amount of nobility in offering Critics and one's fellow citizens a genuine life, a pledge, a man and not a shadow, and in this respect no more submissive a victim has ever been brought before the Critics' hatchets. Even if there was once some charm in the mystery a writer wraps himself in, even if the public once respected his veil as if it were a dead man's shroud, so many scribblers have made use of the curtain that right now it is soiled, crumpled, and all that's left for a man of intelligence to do is find a new tactic against this prostitution of thought called *publication*.

We also receive the impression of a disguised autobiography from the portrait Sainte-Beuve sketches at the head of *Joseph Delorme*; but not, I suppose, from the biography of the Greek poetess which Pierre Louÿs dreams up for *Chansons de Bilitis*.

The last function, in which the simulation of an allographic preface is strongest, is that of providing a more or less value-enhancing commentary on the text. Defoe stresses the moral value of *Moll Flanders*, in which every fault is severely punished; and I have already mentioned the analogous commentaries for *Les Liaisons* and *Adolphe*. Sainte-Beuve follows suit for *Volupté*, a salutary analysis "of a propensity, of a passion, of a vice itself ..." (I have not fully grasped which ones). In his "observations" on *Oberman*, Senancour is careful not to express a moral judgment, but he lays his literary cards on the table and warns critics: in this set of letters you will find no action, but descriptions, feelings, passions, and also ... tedious passages and contradictions. But the disavowing preface that most rigorously imitates a classic allographic preface is without doubt the preface to *Madame Edwarda*. In Chapter 8 under "Senders," I drew attention to the temporal distinctiveness of this preface: in a genre (that is, the genre of fictional prefaces in general) that is ordinarily inseparable from a temporary attributive fiction, this is to my knowledge the only later preface devoted after an interval to an explicit or implicit denial. Georges Bataille does not intervene as preface-writer for "Pierre Angélique" until fifteen years after the novel was first published, and this fact alone excludes the "editorial" fiction. He cannot present himself as publishing the manuscript of some unknown person; rather, he must appear as the author of a later allographic preface on the occasion of a republication, like Larbaud for Dujardin or, even better, Deleuze for Tournier – even better because Bataille's preface, like Deleuze's, is highly "theoretical," a preface-manifesto that could almost be called (as some of Sartre's prefaces have been called) a preface-highjacking, except that this is a self-highjacking, for the sake, as we know, of an exposition (as serious as they come, and even solemn in its naïveté) of the Bataillean philosophy of "eroticism contemplated gravely, tragically," of ecstasy achieved through horror, and of that great discovery – who would have thought it? – that "horror reinforces attraction!" (the exclamation mark is in the text).

Fictive authorial prefaces

The fictive authorial preface (cell D) is, as I have already said, eminently – and even, to my knowledge, exclusively – represented by Walter Scott in a great many of his novels, from 1816 on. The most important examples – all by virtue simply of dedications or dedicatory epistles with a prefatorial function – are *Tales of My Landlord*, *Ivanhoe*, *The Fortunes of Nigel*, and *Peveril of the Peak*. It is here, with these prefaces, that the paratextual game of imagining the author gets complicated in a way that makes them, for us, the most novelistic and fascinating part of an œuvre that has otherwise been somewhat affected by the age limit. In the dedicatory epistle of *Ivanhoe*, already mentioned above, what is most vivid is undoubtedly the person of the dedicatee, "the Rev. Dr Dryasdust, F.A.S. residing in the Castle-Gate, York," carefully selected by the fictive author Templeton for his archeological competence, which establishes him as a truly experienced judge of what was, we should remember, our author's first strictly historical novel. *The Fortunes of Nigel* opens with an "Introductory Epistle" addressed to that same Dryasdust by Captain Cuthbert Clutterbuck, who takes pride in the fact that they are "all one man's bairns" – we see whose. The mention of kinship is not misplaced at the head of this voluminous epistle wholly devoted, first, to describing the meeting, on the premises of some bookseller (whom all the details point to as Constable, Scott's publisher), between the aforementioned captain and ... the illustrious but anonymous "author of *Waverley*" (who will never be designated otherwise than by that famous "precise description") and, second, to recapitulating the long conversation that ensues:

I at length reached a vaulted room, dedicated to secrecy and silence, and beheld, seated by a lamp, and employed in reading a blotted *revise*, the person, or perhaps I should rather say the eidolon, or representative vision, of the *AUTHOR OF WAVERLEY!* You will not be surprised at the filial instinct which enabled me at once to acknowledge the features borne by this venerable apparition, and that I at once bended the knee, with the classical salutation of, *Salve, magne parens!* The vision, however, cut me short by pointing to a seat, intimating at the same time that my presence was not unexpected, and that he had something to say to me.

What follows is, as one might guess, nothing other than the imagined author's imaginary interview with the real author, who welcomes him as "the person of my family whom I have most regard for, since the death of Jedediah Cleishbotham" (the imagined author of the *Tales of My Landlord*) and declares his intention of naming him "godfather to this yet unborn babe – (he indicated the proof-sheet with his finger)" – this is, as it were, the contract of supposition, and the anointing of the preface-writer. The conversation will touch on every topic of Scottian concern: the reception of *The Monastery*; the art of the novel since its founding by Fielding ("He [Fielding] challenges a comparison between the Novel and the Epic"); the strengths and weaknesses of the work to which this epistle serves as preface; the speculations that are circulating about the identity of the author of *Waverley*, and his determination "to be silent on a subject which, in my opinion, is very undeserving the noise that has been made about it"; his opinions of critics; the public's loyalty and how to retain it; his reasons for not writing for the theatre; the rightful income he draws from his work:

> *Captain.* ... Are you aware that an unworthy motive may be assigned for this rapid succession of publication? You will be supposed to work merely for the lucre of gain.
>
> *Author.* Supposing that I did permit the great advantages which must be derived from success in literature to join with other motives in inducing me to come more frequently before the public, that emolument is the voluntary tax which the public pays for a certain species of literary amusement; it is extorted from no one, and paid, I presume, by those only who can afford it, and who receive gratification in proportion to the expense. If the capital sum which these volumes have put into circulation be a very large one, has it contributed to my indulgences only? or can I not say to hundreds, from honest Duncan the paper-manufacturer to the most snivelling of the printer's devils, "Didst thou not share? Hadst thou not fifteen pence?" I profess I think our Modern Athens much obliged to me for having established such an extensive manufacture; and when universal suffrage comes in fashion, I intend to stand for a seat in the House on the interest of all the unwashed artificers connected with literature.

Finally, about the prospects for his inspiration in the future: "The world say you will run yourself out. *Author.* The world say true; and what then? When they dance no longer, I will no longer pipe; and I shall not want flappers enough to remind me of the apoplexy."

The delayed "introduction" of 1831 will apologize for the somewhat overly whimsical and self-satisfied nature of that conversation, but the same device governs the "Prefatory Letter" of *Peveril of the Peak*, a preface this time addressed by Dryasdust – definitely our most faithful "hero of a preface"[45] – to Clutterbuck and recounting a visit from the author of *Waverley*, "our common parent," to the person he calls "the creature of my will." This time the letter contains a portrait of the aforementioned author, but it is as unlike Scott as possible. Here the conversation is shorter, and perhaps it suffers from being a rehash of an earlier one. But the antiquarian, to whom the author of *Waverley* had previously submitted his manuscript, shows himself to be more exacting than Clutterbuck about the historical truth, and his

---

[45] "Not being a valetudinarian, the author would make a poor hero of a preface" (Balzac, preface to *La Peau de chagrin*).

interlocutor, the author, has to defend the usefulness of the genre in which he writes, invoking the example of Shakespeare's history plays, which the Duke of Marlborough claimed were "the only English history I ever read in my life," and maintaining that "by introducing the busy and the youthful to 'truths severe in fairy fiction dressed,' I am doing a real service to the more ingenious and the more apt among them; for the love of knowledge wants but a beginning – the least spark will give fire when the train is properly prepared; and having been interested in fictitious adventures, ascribed to an historical period and characters, the reader begins next to be anxious to learn what the facts really were, and how far the novelist has justly represented them."

We have seen that Scott's game of imagining the author gradually dissolved, from *Ivanhoe*, of which Templeton explicitly claims to be the author (or from *The Bride of Lammermoor*, one of whose notes is signed Jedediah Cleishbotham), to *Nigel*, where Clutterbuck is only a transparent "godfather," and then to *Peveril*, where Dryasdust becomes almost an allographic preface-writer. And in all these cases, in one way or another, Scott uses the prefatorial fiction to deliver his own message, from the pen of Templeton or from the mouth of the author of *Waverley*. The situation of *Quentin Durward* is even more ambiguous. The author – this time anonymous, as in the days of *Waverley* – reports in a long narrative preface how, during a trip to France, he paid a visit to an old gentleman in the latter's château on the bank of the Loire and how this gentleman, in his library, showed the visitor certain documents about his distant Scottish connections – the alleged source for the novel. During this conversation, the old gentleman alludes several times to Sir Walter, to whom he attributes *The Bride of Lammermoor*. The anonymous preface-writer protests that his host's assertion is totally erroneous:

I had next the common candour to inform my friend, upon grounds which no one could know so well as myself, that my distinguished literary countryman, of whom I shall always speak with the respect his talents deserve, was not responsible for the slight works which the humour of the public had too generously, as well as too rashly, ascribed to him. Surprised by the impulse of the moment, I might even have gone farther, and clenched the negative by positive evidence, owning to my entertainer that no one else could possibly have written these works, since I myself was the author, when I was saved from so rash a commitment of myself by the calm reply of the marquis, that he was glad to hear these sort of trifles were not written by a person of condition.

Quentin Durward, as I have said, appeared in English under the (already quite perforated) cloak of anonymity. But in the same year, French readers received its French translation (by Defauconpret) with a cover that was duly (or rather, unduly, but very visibly – and very truthfully) adorned with the name of Walter Scott. I imagine that a French reader had to make two tries before understanding that sentence – or rather, before not understanding it in the least. We see, perhaps, why I said that these prefaces are the most fascinating part of Scott's œuvre. This intoxication with incognito, this proof of otherness by identity ("It cannot be I, for it is I"), is a form of extravagant humor that prefigures the most unsettling masquerades of a Pessoa, a Nabokov, a Borges, a Camus (Renaud, of course).[46]

Fictive allographic prefaces

Despite the isolated example of Walter Scott, it seems that when one has made the effort to imagine a fictive author and wishes to add a fictive preface to his text, the most common (I don't dare say the most natural) impulse is to imagine, in addition, a separate allographic preface-writer. Like the disavowing authorial preface, the fictive allographic simulates the authentic allographic, except that it is attributed to an imaginary third party; and this imaginary third party, whether given a name (such as "Richard Sympson" or "Joseph L'Estrange") or not (for example, the officer of the *Manuscript Found in Saragossa* or the translator of *Portes de Gubbio*), is always supplied with a separate biographical identity (the officer of *Saragossa* is French, the presenter of *La Guzla* is Dalmatian, the translator of *Gubbio* is a man, and so forth).[47] And, as I have said, if we did not have that separate biographical identity to take into account, the principle of economy would induce us to group this kind of preface with

---

46 Let us add that the preface to the first of the *Tales of the Crusaders* (1825) will contain a kind of report on a meeting of all the imagined authors of Scott's novels.

47 [All titles and characters mentioned but not identified in this section are identified on pp. 189–90].

the disavowing authorial prefaces (as we did for *Delorme* or *Santeuil*). Further, if the fictive allographic preface, like the disavowing authorial and the authentic allographic, can present a text that is supposed to be a simple document without any literary aim (*Gulliver, Saragossa, André Walter* [*Les Cahiers d'André Walter*, Gide's first work],[48] *Lolita, Gubbio*), and if it can therefore (like them) simulate a simple editorial note, it can also, and more easily, apply to a text offered as a literary work, whether in translation (*Clara Gazul, La Guzla, On est toujours trop bon avec les femmes*) or not (*Déliquescences d'Adoré Floupette, Œuvres françaises de M. Barnabooth, Pale Fire, Chronicles of Bustos Domecq*), and can accordingly assume the look of a classic allographic preface.

Except for the fictive identity of the sender, the first case (simulation of a simple editorial note) offers us nothing especially new in comparison with the functions of the disavowing preface: it gives details about the discovery or transmission of the manuscript (entrusted to his cousin by Gulliver himself, found at Saragossa during the war and conveyed to the presenter by a descendant of the narrator, transmitted to "John Ray" by Humbert Humbert's attorney after Humbert's death, handed over to the translator of *Gubbio* by an anonymous intermediary in a public garden); it mentions the corrections made, if any ("I ... made bold to strike out innumerable Passages relating to the Winds and Tides, ..." says "Sympson"; "Save for the correction of obvious solecisms and a careful suppression of a few tenacious details, ... this remarkable memoir is presented intact," asserts "John Ray"); it makes moral comments comparable to those that Rousseau, Laclos, and Constant include with the "documents" they present to us (thus, according to "John Ray," Humbert Humbert's "memoir" – a term that indicates a convention of nonliterariness[49] – "should make all of us – parents, social workers, educators – apply ourselves with still greater vigilance

---

[48] At least, if we decide to consider the preface to *André Walter* as fictive allographic: it is signed P.C., and we know that those are the initials of Pierre Chrysis, pseudonym of Pierre Louÿs, who must have actually written a preface that, in its discourse and its function, enters into the game of the fiction.

[49] The indication of nonliterariness is, to tell the truth, only one aspect of this preface, in which "John Ray" also happens to call this "memoir" *Lolita* and to "view ... it simply as a novel" and "as a work of art" – which Marivaux would certainly not have done for *Marianne*, or Constant for *Adolphe*.

and vision to the task of bringing up a better generation in a safer world").

The second case (the look of a classic allographic preface) appears in its most clear-cut form when the text is presented as a work that has already been published in its original language, as in Merimée's *Théâtre de Clara Gazul* (the "extremely rare" original edition, "Joseph L'Estrange" tells us, appeared in Cadiz "in two small quarto volumes") or his "Illyrian poems" that make up *La Guzla*. But the literary status of works that have been "unpublished" up to that point, such as *Déliquescences, Barnabooth, Pale Fire*, or *Bustos Domecq*, is a little more uncertain; the only thing that attests to it and distinguishes these works from simple documentary "memoirs" is their form: it is resolutely novelistic (a third-person narrative) or poetic. Following the lead of *Barnabooth's* subtitle [*Ses œuvres complètes: Poèmes par un riche amateur*...], we could define this intermediary status as that of a "work by an amateur," rich or poor, if in literature the notion of amateur meant anything very relevant, which seems to me highly unlikely. In any event, these texts are indeed presented, in general, more as literary works than as documents, which should open the door to strictly critical evaluations or commentaries. But whether from modesty or inability, the "Joseph L'Estrange," "Tournier de Zemble," and other "Gervasio Montenegro" types of preface-writers rarely take that route. Rather, their contribution (in keeping with the classical custom) is testimonial-biographical in nature: "L'Estrange" evokes Clara Gazul as he used to know her, "Marius Tapora" recounts the life of Adoré Floupette, and "Tournier de Zemble" composes a long and minutely detailed hagiography of Barnabooth. To my knowledge, only "Charles Kinbote" produces a real commentary (on the poem by John Shade), but this commentary is basically conveyed by his notes at the end of the volume, and we will come to them later, in our chapter on notes. Kinbote's preface is instead modestly editorial and strictly academic (technical description of the manuscript, chronology of composition, controversy about its degree of completion, note about variants) – up to the point where he evokes his personal relations with the deceased author and asserts the importance of his own commentary for an understanding of the poem ("a reality that only my notes can provide"), a shift that announces and initiates the paranoid tailspin that will follow, when the pseudo-allographic preface will prove little by little – but on another level – to be pseudo-actorial.

Fictive actorial prefaces

Logic, or symmetry, would require that the fictive actorial preface be a simulation of the authentic actorial preface – that is, of the preface to a heterobiography provided by the work's "hero." This symmetry would not take us very far, however, for the model itself is missing. Save in exceptional cases, the fictive actorial preface is in reality reserved for narrator-heroes; in other words, it simulates a more complex but more natural situation, in which the hero is at the same time his own narrator and his own author. In short, the fictive actorial preface simulates the preface to an autobiography, in which the preface-writer, as I have already had occasion to complain, expresses himself more as the author ("here is what I wrote") than as the hero ("here is what I lived through"). It is as the author that Lazarillo presents – as an innovation contrary to the epic custom of beginning *in medias res* – his decision "not to begin in the middle but at the beginning, so as to present a complete narrative of myself"; it is as the author that Gil Blas exhorts the reader, in keeping with the fable of the two schoolboys of Salamanca, to make an interpretive reading of what follows and to "perceiv[e] the moral instructions [my adventures] contain"; as the author that Gulliver protests the cuts and additions made by his cousin and in the end regrets publishing a work that failed to produce any improvement in the behavior of the Yahoos; it is as the hero, without doubt, that Gordon Pym vouches for the veracity of the pieces written and already published as fictional by Mr. Poe but, indeed, as the author that he claims to have written all the rest; again, it is as the author that Braz Cubas announces a "diffuse work in which I, Braz Cubas, having adopted the free style of a Sterne or Xavier de Maistre, am not sure that an underlying vein of pessimism does not come to the surface here and there. It is possible. The work of a deceased being. Written with the pen of cheerfulness, dipped in the ink of melancholy, it should not be difficult to predict the result of such a conjugal union. Add to this, that serious-minded people will write it off as pure romance whilst the frivolous will miss their favourite romantic strain." It is certainly as the heroine that Sally Mara refutes some assertions made about her and shifts the responsibility for *Sally plus intime* to Raymond Queneau but very much as the author that she assumes responsibility for the rest of the collection, making her position clear in these words: "It is not often that an author alleged to be imaginary is allowed to preface his or her complete works, especially when they appear under the name of a supposedly real author. Thus I must thank Gallimard for offering me the opportunity."[50] In short, there is nothing about the fictive actorial preface that we would not also find in the usual authorship of prefaces to autobiographies, in which, as we clearly perceive, writing one's life consists less of putting the writing at the service of the life than vice versa. Narcissus, after all, is not in love with his visage, but, in fact, with his image – which means, here, with his œuvre.

Mirrors

I would definitely say the same for the fictional preface in general, where we have continually seen the prefatorial act mirroring and mimicking itself, in a sympathetic reenactment of its own operations. In this sense, the fictional preface – a fiction of a preface – does nothing but aggravate, by exploiting, the preface's underlying bent toward a self-consciousness both uncomfortable and playful: playing on its discomfort. I am writing a preface – I see myself writing a preface – I describe myself seeing myself writing a preface – I see myself describing myself ... This endless reflecting, this self-describing in a mirror, this staging, this playacting of the prefatorial activity, which is one of the truths of the preface – all these the fictional preface brings to their ultimate fulfillment by passing, in its own way, over to the other side of the mirror.

But this self-depiction is also, and to a very high degree, that of the activity of literature in general. For if (as has surely been apparent ever since the beginning of this chapter) in the preface the author (or his "godfather") is, in the words we have put into Borges's mouth, "least the creator," it is perhaps there that,

---

[50] We should remember that when this work came out in 1963 it had the following on the cover: Raymond Queneau / de l'Académie Goncourt / *Les Œuvres / complètes / de Sally Mara.*

paradoxically or not, he is and shows himself to be most the literary man. Consequently we see the preface, like all other overly obvious paratextual elements, carefully avoided as much as possible by those authors who are most closely associated with classical dignity and/or realistic transparency: an Austen, a Flaubert, a Zola, a Proust, the Balzac of 1842, James up to the New York Edition. This is just about the only distributional feature we have been able to discover, but this feature seems to me very revealing inasmuch as it conveys a concern to avoid as much as possible that perverse effect of the paratext – its "impediment" effect – which we have dubbed, in reference to the porter's lodge that Charlus speaks of, the Jupien effect.[51]

In varying degrees and with various inflections depending on type, the preface is perhaps, of all literary practices, the one that is most typically literary, sometimes in the best sense, sometimes in the worst, and usually in both senses at once. (Degrees and inflections depending on type: the assumptive authorial preface is basically inseparable from the author's concern to force his intention on the reader; the allographic preface, inseparable from the routines of protection and patronage as well as – sometimes – from those of highjacking and interception; the fictional preface, inseparable from the staging of the fictional exercise itself.) I see only one other literary practice that has the capacity to outdo the preface in those various extremes of literariness. That one is, obviously, the practice of writing *about* the preface. Accordingly, I have carefully avoided doing so here and have merely listened to the preface do what it does so well: speak of itself.

[51] [For an explanation of Charlus's porter's lodge, see Chapter 4 under "Temptation?"] One could equally well call it the George Moore effect, in honor of the author who once said, "Don't put a preface at the head of your work, or the critics won't talk about anything else." This advice is quoted as the epigraph of the preface to *Sandales d'Empédocle* by C. E. Magny, who claims, somewhat excessively, that "since naturalism, authors no longer dare write prefaces – except to other people's books."

11

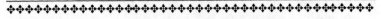

Intertitles

Intertitles, or internal titles, are titles, and as such they invite the same kinds of remarks I made earlier, which I will avoid systematically repeating but will allude to now and then. And inasmuch as they are internal to the text or at least to the book, they invite other kinds of remarks, to which I will devote more attention.

First and most obviously: in contrast to general titles, which are addressed to the public as a whole and may have currency well beyond the circle of readers, internal titles are accessible to hardly anyone except readers, or at least the already limited public of browsers and readers of tables of contents; and a good many internal titles make sense only to an addressee who is already involved in reading the text, for these internal titles presume familiarity with everything that has preceded. For example, the title of the thirty-seventh chapter of *Les Trois Mousquetaires* is "Milady's Secret," and this name, or nickname, obviously sends the reader back to a previous encounter with the character who bears it.[1]

The second and more important remark stems from the fact that, in contrast to the general title (which is a paratextual element that has become indispensable, if not to the material existence of the text then at least to the social existence of the book), intertitles are by no means absolutely required. Their potential presence extends from impossible to indispensable, and here we should quickly run through these different degrees.

---

[1] That is, it has an anaphoric, or reminding, value: this woman who is already familiar to you. A novel could certainly be entitled *Milady's Secret*, in which case this name would take on a cataphoric value, that is, the name would serve as an advance notice. The reader would receive it entirely differently, as a slight puzzle. The same regime can also apply to an intertitle, as we see with the first chapter of the *Mousquetaires*, "The Three Gifts of Monsieur d'Artagnan the Elder," which introduces a name as yet unfamiliar.

Cases of absence

The intertitle is the title of a section of a book: in unitary texts, these sections may be parts, chapters, or paragraphs; in collections, they may be constituent poems, novellas, or essays. It follows, therefore, that a completely unitary text – that is, an undivided one – can contain no intertitle. To the best of my knowledge this is the case, for example, of most medieval epics, at least in the state in which they have come down to us, but it is also the case of some modern novels, such as Sollers's *H* and *Paradis*. It would be tempting to say the same of *Ulysses*, but as we know, its situation is a bit more subtle. Conversely, some texts are apparently *too* highly segmented – I mean chopped too fine – for each section to bear its own intertitle. This is the case for collections of fragments, aphorisms, thoughts, and other maxims when the author, like La Rochefoucauld, did not deem it necessary to group them – as La Bruyère would for his *Caractères* – into thematic subgroups forming chapters and warranting the assignment of an intertitle to each.

Next there are types of texts that are inseparable from their basic orality, texts intended for or derived from an oral delivery, and for them – speeches, dialogues, plays – the very fact of oral performance would make it hard to indicate the presence of intertitles. The case of drama is the most nuanced, for the traditional divisions, mute in performance, in published form have a sort of minimal, or purely rhematic, titling that consists of the number assigned to an act, a scene, and/or a tableau. And some playwrights, such as Hugo or Brecht, are given to providing titles for their acts. In Hugo's *Hernani*: Act 1 – "The King," Act 2 – "The Bandit," Act 3 – "The Old Man," Act 4 – "The Tomb," Act 5 – "The Wedding"; in his *Ruy Blas*: 1 – "Don Salluste," 2 – "The Queen of Spain," and so forth. Brecht gives titles,[2] for example, to the parts of *Caucasian Chalk Circle*, *Puntila*, and *The Mother*; and in *Mother Courage*, *Threepenny Opera*, *Mahagonny*, and *Galileo* he provides kinds of summaries that are generally meant to be posted during the performance for the benefit of the audience. This presence could be connected to the well-known narrative ("epical") stamp with which Brecht wanted to mark his plays. In

---

[2] In this chapter I often shorten *intertitle* to *title* when the context prevents any misunderstanding.

Hugo's case, I would be more apt to attribute the presence to a passion for titles in all genres – a passion we will encounter again in other manifestations. But there are certainly other instances of this practice, one that Diderot did not illustrate in his own plays but was very well able to justify: "If a poet has thought well about his subject and divided his action up well, to none of the acts in his play will he be unable to give a title; and just as with respect to the epic poem people speak of the descent to the underworld, the funeral games, the enumeration of the army, the apparition of the departed soul, so with drama people would speak of the suspicions act, the rages act, the act of the recognition or the sacrifice. I am surprised that the ancients did not decide to give titles to their acts: doing so would have been consistent with their style. If they had, they would have rendered a service to the moderns, who would not have failed to imitate them, and once the nature of the act was settled, the poet would have been forced to compose accordingly."[3] I add that indications of place or time, completely standard at the head of an act or scene, may sometimes enter tradition as kinds of intertitles. This is clearly what happened with regard to Goethe's *Faust*: "Night," "Outside the City Gate," "Faust's Study," and so forth. But these few cases of titling remain exceptions.

Next there are genres in which textual division is, as it were, mechanical and accompanied by indications that cannot be considered titles – indeed, that preclude the presence of titles: the epistolary novel, in which each letter bears the mention of its writer, its addressee, and possibly the date and place of writing; the journal, authentic or fictive, whose rhythm is marked, theoretically, only by dates; the travel narrative, punctuated by dates and names of places. But here, too, various fancies may be indulged: Hugo's *Rhin* is presented as a travel narrative in letters, with numbers and titles that play various roles. *Par les champs et par les grèves* [the account of a walking tour its two authors took in Brittany], an amoeboid work, is divided into numbered chapters, the odds by Flaubert and the evens by Maxime Du Camp.

---

[3] Diderot, *De la poésie dramatique*, ch. 15, "Des entr'actes."

Degrees of presence

The presence of intertitles is possible, but not obligatory, in unitary works divided into parts, chapters, and so forth, and in most types of collections. In collections of novellas, however, intertitles may be obligatory, for in these works their absence could easily cause the text to be mistaken at first for one continuous narrative. We shall now make a quick survey of these cases of the possible or necessary presence of intertitles; and generic categories – here obviously the most determining ones – will serve as our controlling framework.

But first, an essential precaution. The distinction between (general) titles and (partial) intertitles is itself less absolute than I have implied, unless one is willing to be blindly guided by the bibliological criterion alone: the title is for the book, the intertitles are for the sections of the book. I say blindly because this criterion varies considerably according to edition, so much so that a "book" like the 1913 *Du côté de chez Swann* became a "section of a book" in the 1954 Pléiade edition of the *Recherche*, and conversely a "section" like "Un amour de Swann" quickly enough became, in some presentations, a self-contained book. So the material criterion is fragile, or unstable; but the undoubtedly more sophisticated criterion of the unity of the work is likewise quite slippery: is Zola's *Germinal* a work or a part of a work? And as a result, is "Germinal" a title or an intertitle? And Flaubert's "Un coeur simple"? And Hugo's "Tristesse d'Olympio"? And so forth. We all know where custom comes down, more heavily than legitimately, and we will abide by custom willy-nilly, but it is appropriate at least to harbor some suspicion, a feeling of guilt, or a mental reservation.

There are, then, works without intertitles, and by definition we will no longer be concerned with these, once we recall the obvious fact that absence, here as elsewhere, may be as meaningful as presence. But there are still degrees – or at least modalities – of intertitular presence, illustrated here, as with general titles, by the contrast among the thematic regime (example: the chapter title "A Small Town"), the rhematic ("Chapter 1"), and the mixed (the actual title of the first chapter of the *Rouge*: "Chapter 1 / A Small Town").[4] These two or three regimes may also coexist in the same work: this is very often what we find in collections such as Hugo's *Contemplations* or Baudelaire's *Fleurs du mal* in which poems with titles and poems without titles (that is, in this case, poems designated numerically) alternate apparently without discomfort. We are going to track some avatars of the distribution of different kinds of intertitular presence across four major generic types, which upon investigation reveal a certain homogeneity of regime: fictional narratives, referential (historical) narratives, collections of poems, and theoretical texts. This order is more or less arbitrary.

Narrative fiction

Not very much is known about the presentation of the first written (transcribed?) versions (in the time of Peisistratus) of the first long continuous narrative texts, the Homeric poems; and modern editors are hardly lavish with details on this point. But tradition, transmitted by the Alexandrian scholiasts or by Eustathius in the twelfth century, has handed down thematic titles of episodes, some of which undoubtedly go back to the origins of the poems, that is, to the period of bardic recitations, when the thematic titles may have served as titles of performances. The episodes so entitled may consist of large narrative masses, such as the "Telemachy" (nearly three books) or the "Recitals at the Palace of Alkinoos" (four books), or shorter segments; these may be the length of a single book (such as the "Meeting of Hector and Andromache," book 6 of the *Iliad*), or they may be even shorter still ("Duel between Paris and Menelaus," end of book 3). No doubt it was the Alexandrian period that measured out this narrative continuity or discontinuity and produced a fairly mechanical division into twenty-four books, each marked simply by a letter of the Greek alphabet, equivalent to the numerals we now

[4] Thematic intertitles not preceded by rhematic indications of the "Chapter Number Thus-and-Such" type are in reality very rare in any period, perhaps because without such indications the narrative text could easily be taken for a collection of separate novellas. The original titles of Balzac's *Eugénie Grandet*, however, were thematic without an accompanying rhematic indication (and no explanation has been given, as far as I know). Closer to our own time, the same situation exists with two of Yourcenar's books, *Mémoires d'Hadrian* and *L'Œuvre au noir*; and outside of fiction (?), with Leiris's *Biffures*.

use. A second, or third, tradition then tried to salvage the original thematic titles by attributing to each book, after a fashion, one or several titles corresponding to the essence of its action. Accordingly lists circulate, more or less official ones, saying, for example, for the *Iliad*: Book 1 – "Plague and Anger," Book 2 – "Dream and Catalogue of the Ships," and so forth. Some of these unofficial intertitles are venerable because they designate the actions by irreplaceable technical terms – "Aristéia" (heroic feats), "Hoplopoiia" (fabrication of arms), or "Nekuya" (descent into Hades) – which connoisseurs prefer to any translation. What's more, the general titles – *Iliad* and *Odyssey* – are of the same type, transliterated rather than translated.

I do not know how this matter was handled in the post-Homeric epics whose texts have not come down to us, but the titles that modern editions give to the books of Virgil or Quintus seem to have no foundation in the ancient written tradition, even if here the official division into books is more closely aligned with the thematic sequence of episodes (*Aeneid*: Book 1 – "The Tempest," Book 2 – "The Capture of Troy," and so forth). Little by little, it seems to me, numbered mechanical division submerged thematic titling and served as a model, for centuries, for the whole classical epic tradition and – well beyond that – for the whole serious novelistic tradition. We find numbered mechanical division in Latin epics, Dante, Ronsard [*La Franciade*], Ariosto, Tasso, Spenser, Milton, Voltaire [*La Henriade*], and on up to Chateaubriand's prose epic, *Les Natchez*. Greek and Latin romances conform to the great ancient model established by the Alexandrians, as do baroque and classical novels (d'Urfé's *Astrée* has five parts that group the numbered books), including La Fayette's *Princesse de Clèves*, Sorel's *Francion* and Furetière's *Le Roman bourgeois*, *Robinson Crusoe* and *Moll Flanders* (which have hardly any divisions), and also *Tristram Shandy* – to say nothing of the long medieval verse narratives: the *chansons de geste*, as I have said, but also the romances, which seem most often to dispense with any division.

A special case is that of the great composite narrative works like the *Decameron* or the *Canterbury Tales*, which are actually collections of novellas. The *Decameron*, as its title indicates, is divided into ten days, each of which bears as its title the name of its narrator; in modern editions, the ten novellas that constitute each of these days bear titles whose authenticity seems questionable, and are accompanied by summaries a few lines long which are perhaps equally delayed and which, although they indeed belong to the current paratext, obviously no longer have the status of intertitles. The *Canterbury Tales* is divided into tales, each of which has a title that simply identifies the occupation of its narrator: the "Knight's Tale," the "Miller's Tale," and so forth. Margaret of Navarre's *Heptaméron*, divided into seven days, seems to have had no original titles. The anonymous *Cent Nouvelles Nouvelles* [*One Hundred New Novellas*], whose titles are perhaps original, is an artificial collection. The investigation remains open.

In contrast to the main classical tradition of numbered divisions – which are basically rhematic inasmuch as they indicate (by way of a numeral) only a relative place and a type of textual section (book, part, chapter, and so forth) – there is another, more recent and more popular tradition, apparently originating in the Middle Ages, that resorts to a thematic titling (or a mixed one, with the rhematic element elided), perhaps parodying serious texts by historians and by philosophers or theologians. I am referring to descriptive intertitles in the form of noun clauses: "How ...," "Wherein Is Seen ...," "Which Tells ...," "About ..." (implying: "Chapter ..."). For example, the anonymous *Roman de Renart*, which first appeared in collections during the thirteenth century, is divided into mute (untitled) books that are themselves divided into "adventures" with descriptive (narrative) titles: "First Adventure: How Renart Carried Off in the Night Ysengrin's Bacons," and so forth.[5]

Ahead of this type of intertitle lay a destiny almost as rich as that of the classical type, but almost always in the ironic register

[5] It is hard to say how early in the Middle Ages this type of title emerged, for we do not begin to find it until it appears in delayed manuscripts or in the first printed versions of prose romances or historical texts. It would be tempting, Bernard Cerquiglini tells me, to imagine that titles beginning "How ..." are derived from captions to text illustrations: for example, figure 182 in Jacques Le Goff's *Civilisation de l'Occident médiéval* is a picture of an open medieval book (the book's title is *Histoire en prose des quatre fils Aymon* [*Prose History of the Four Aymon Sons*], incunabulum of 1480), and on the photographed book's left-hand page is an illustration above which, faithfully describing it, is this caption: "How the Four Aymon Sons Were Chased out of Paris by Charlemagne, King of France." But this hypothesis cannot account for all noun-clause titles.

of popular and "comic" narratives: we see it in Rabelais, whose titles, which almost systematically begin "How ...," come straight from the *Grandes Chroniques*, a burlesque that his own early work was a continuation of; we see it in the Spanish picaresque writers, imitated in this respect by Lesage; in Cervantes,[6] who, in *Quixote*, introduces a highly playful or humorous model ("A chapter in which is related what will be found set forth in it," "Which treats of many and great things," "Which treats of matters having to do with this history and none other"), one that will flourish in Scarron's works and, most spectacularly, in Fielding's, particularly *Tom Jones* ("Containing five Pages of Paper," "Being the shortest Chapter in this Book," "In which the Reader will be surprized," "Containing various Matters," and so forth – all the titles in this novel are quoteworthy). Here, however, we must note a kind of homage to the serious tradition in the fact that the eighteen books of *Tom Jones* have no titles: the ironic and loquacious titling is authorized only at the level of chapters.

Cervantes's model, after becoming the norm (the antinorm) of comic narrative, lived on well into the nineteenth and twentieth centuries, with variously sustained teasing effects: we find examples in Dickens (*Oliver Twist, Pickwick, David Copperfield*), Melville (*Mardi, Pierre, The Confidence-Man*), Thackeray (*Henry Esmond, Vanity Fair*), Anatole France (*La Révolte des anges*), Musil (in direct style), Pynchon (*V.*), Barth (*The Sot-Weed Factor*), Jong (*Fanny Jones*) – and in Eco (*The Name of the Rose*), the last one, as of now.

In first-person (homodiegetic) narratives, these clausal intertitles may raise the question (much more often than general titles do) of the identity of their enunciators. When these intertitles are written in the third person ("Of the birth and education of Gil Blas"), this choice – which contrasts with that of the narrative text itself – obviously makes the author the enunciator of the intertitles. This is the case with most picaresque novels, with Tristan L'Hermite's *Page disgracié* (in which the hero is systematically designated in intertitles by the phrase "the disgraced page"), and in our own time with *The Name of the Rose*. The wording adopted in *Gulliver's Travels* is more complex and paradoxical, for it designates the narrator-hero as "the author" [e.g., "The Author

---

[6] Or his editor, for the authenticity of his intertitles is sometimes questioned.

shews his Skill in Navigation"]; Swift therefore assigns this function of enunciating the intertitles to his character, but he does not go so far as to grant the character the right to use intertitles in the first person.

In contrast, the character does fully receive this right in Quevedo's *Buscón* (a noteworthy infringement of the picaresque norm), in *Mardi*, in the pastiche-novels of Thackeray, in *Treasure Island*, in *David Copperfield* (the first intertitle of *Copperfield* is "I Am Born"). As we have already seen in connection with other elements of the paratext, the inevitable effect of this concession is to establish the narrator-hero as someone with not only narrative authority but also literary authority, as an author responsible for putting together, managing, and presenting the text and aware of his relation to the public. He is no longer, as Lazarillo is, only a character who recounts his life in writing; he is a character who makes himself a writer by establishing his narrative as a literary text that, thanks to him, is already provided with one part of its paratext. At one and the same time the real author is relegated to the fictively modest role of simple "editor," or presenter – at least when his name, different from the hero's, continues likewise to appear in the paratext, the presence of the two names together setting up a fictive division of responsibilities even if the reader, experienced in literary conventions, knows no one really expects him to be fooled by it.

This situation, all in all a classical one, is not exactly the situation established by the intertitles of the *Recherche*, either those we find in 1913 as synopsis-advertisements of the volumes to come or those appearing at the head of the published volumes of *Les Jeunes Filles*, *Guermantes*, and *Sodome*.[7] Here, as with *Copperfield* or *Treasure Island*, the intertitles are all in the first

---

[7] [The titles and dates of publication of the works making up the *Recherche* are as follows: published anthumously were *Du côté de chez Swann* (1913), *A l'ombre des jeunes filles en fleurs* (1918), *Le Côté de Guermantes I* (1920), *Le Côté de Guermantes II* (1921), *Sodome et Gomorrhe I* (1921), and *Sodome et Gomorrhe II* (1922); published posthumously were *La Prisonnière* (1923), *Albertine disparue*, later changed to *La Fugitive*, the title Proust had originally wanted (1925), and *Le Temps retrouvé* (1927).] The announcement of 1913 (opposite the title in the Grasset *Swann*) appears in Pléiade 1:xxiii; the list of the actual contents of *Les Jeunes Filles* (1918) appears at the head of each "part" (Pléiade 1:431 and 642); the list of prospective contents carried at the head of *Les Jeunes Filles* for the volumes to come is in Pléiade 3:1059; the list of actual contents of *Guermantes* and *Sodome* is where it should be, 2:1221–22. A comparative table of these different content listings is given by J.-Y. Tadié, *Proust* (Belfond, 1983), 23–26.

302

person ("Decline and Death of My Grandmother," "How I Cease for the Time Being to See Gilberte," and so forth), but because of the relative anonymity of the hero, no clear demarcation is effected between him and the author.[8] Such a mode of enunciation – confirmed by that of Proust's correspondence, of some of his inscriptions, and of some articles, and not contradicted by a conflicting genre indication (as we have already mentioned, there is no genre indication) – obviously draws the regime of this narrative closer to that of autobiography pure and simple. Here it is entirely as if Proust had passed imperceptibly from the officially autobiographical (although undoubtedly already fictive) situation of *Contre Sainte-Beuve* ("I have a conversation with Mama about Sainte-Beuve") to that of the *Recherche* ("I finally realize I've lost my grandmother"), in which the former undergoes a transfusion but not a transformation. In the face of that, Proust's official professions of heterobiography carry little weight, for sometimes they themselves are ambiguous; for example, to René Blum: "There is a gentleman who recounts and who says *I*"; to Elie-Joseph Bois: "... the character who recounts, who says *I* (and who is not me)"; but in the 1921 article on Flaubert: "... passages in which a few crumbs of 'madeleine,' dipped in an infusion, recall to me (or at least recall to the narrator who says 'I' but who is not always myself) a whole period of my life...."[9] I have proposed elsewhere to call this typically ambiguous status *autofiction*,[10] borrowing the term from Serge Doubrovsky. Here I don't want to go back over my reasoning, but the very possibility of autofiction indicates, it seems to me, the importance of (among other things) these features of the (inter)titular enunciation: in some states of relation between text and paratext, the selection of a grammatical regime for the wording of the intertitles may help settle (or unsettle) the genre status of a work.

[8] We should remember that twice in the *Recherche* the hero is called *Marcel*, with some disavowing contortions; moreover, this ambiguous first name is used at least one other time – an occasion that has received less attention although it is much more revealing – in a sketch that Bardèche cites (*Proust romancier* [Les Sept Couleurs, 1971], 1:172) and dates from 1909: "Man of letters near Cabourg ... Marcel will see him without having read anything by him." So to my knowledge, the only times Proust does not call his hero *I*, he calls him *Marcel*.

[9] *Contre Sainte-Beuve* (Pléiade), 599.

[10] *Palimpsestes* (Seuil, 1982), 291 et seq.

11 Intertitles

The intertitular apparatus of the *Recherche* provides another lesson, which concerns the structure of the work and its evolution. In Chapter 4, I mentioned the initially unitary structure Proust wanted and its gradual drift toward a more segmented division into three, then five, then seven "volumes." This movement is evident also at the level of chapters, for only the first volume, *Du côté de chez Swann*, is simply divided into three parts supplied with subtitles: "Combray" (I and II), "Un amour de Swann," and "Noms de pays: Le nom." The remaining volumes, starting with *Les Jeunes Filles en fleurs*, will be much more distinctly segmented, with a hierarchical division into parts, chapters, and sections as evidenced by the synopses, prospective or actual, mentioned above. Starting with *Guermantes*, the parts and chapters no longer bear subtitles, and the last three volumes, by the mere fact of their posthumous publication, present neither parts nor chapters. However, for everything that follows *Du côté de chez Swann* we have available a very voluminous set of intertitles: for *Les Jeunes Filles*, these intertitles are furnished by the content summaries of the 1918 edition; for all the rest, by the advertisement-synopses appended to that 1918 edition; for *Guermantes II* and *Sodome*, both by these advertisements and by the tables of contents in the editions of 1921 and 1922, notwithstanding some discrepancies of detail that attest to final adjustments made after the war. However undependable these intertitles may be on account of the genetic drift, the publisher's negligence, and the posthumous publication, we know that from 1918 on, Proust indeed considered them intertitles and would have wanted to put them at the heads of the sections to which they pertain – or at least, in a concession to the publisher, into summary tables of contents with page references. Attesting to that is this letter to a typist apropos of the proofs of *Les Jeunes Filles*: "Almost a month ago I asked Gaston Gallimard whether he agreed that I should intersperse the text with chapter headings giving the same information as that in the printed summary. He replied that he didn't much like the idea, and, after thinking the matter over, I am inclined to agree with him. We are of the opinion that the **** which I have introduced throughout wherever a fresh piece of narrative begins, will be enough, and that the reader, thanks to the summary and to the page numbers to be inserted in it ... will be in a position to affix to each section of the whole the appropriate title."[11]

Even this very concessive request was not met when the book was in press, and it must be admitted that in the text's present state, the correct positioning of some of the intertitles is not entirely obvious. Nevertheless, in theory Proust envisaged – well after the war, and in contrast to his first intentions – a work much more distinctly segmented, and supplied with an abundant titular apparatus. It is as if, gradually or belatedly, he had gotten caught up in the game of division and paratextual proliferation, a game he had first joined reluctantly and under pressure of necessity.

This fact seems to me interesting in itself. In attempting to explain it, we may speculate that Proust found with experience that the architectural unity of his work – which we know he valued so highly (and in fact more and more highly as it was breaking up under the influence of his own additions) – would be better demonstrated and emphasized by the titular presentation of its underlying structure than by the initial plan of a long textual flow without breaks or markers. Hence his swing to the opposite choice, one that some people may see as going too far in the other direction. In any case, it is clear (and significant) that, each time, his publishers brought him back, willy-nilly, to the middle ground. But as we know, the publication history of the *Recherche* is only beginning ...

We have seen that the classical norm for intertitles in narrative fiction was divided into two strongly contrasting positions with very pronounced generic connotations: in serious fiction, parts and chapters received only numbers; in comic or popular fiction, expanded intertitles were used. This classical contrast was replaced by a new one at the beginning of the nineteenth century: narrative intertitles (and titles) in the form of summaries or outlines almost entirely died out (the more recent examples I have mentioned clearly give the impression of being archaizing exceptions) in favor of a type of intertitle that is more restrained,

[11] Quoted by Maurois, *A la recherche de Marcel Proust* (Hachette, 1949), 290–91 [tr. *Proust: Portrait of a Genius*, trans. Gerard Hopkins (New York: Harper, 1950; reprint, Carroll and Graf, 1984), 277–78].

or at least shorter, purely nominal, and reduced in most instances to two or three words, or even only one.

The architect of this intertitular shrinkage seems, here again, to have been Walter Scott,[12] whose *Waverley Novels* are divided between novels with mute chapters (by that I will mean, henceforth, chapters headed only by numerals), such as *Ivanhoe, Rob Roy, The Bride of Lammermoor,* and novels with short intertitles, such as *Waverley* or *Quentin Durward.* By way of example, here are the first three intertitles of *Quentin Durward*: 1 – "The Contrast," 2 – "The Wanderer," 3 – "The Castle." The contrast between this table of contents and the one for *Tom Jones* is striking.

In the nineteenth and twentieth centuries, divisions with short intertitles will become the novelistic norm, always in competition with mute divisions. This new contrast therefore replaces the old one but has a decidedly weaker genre connotation, reflecting not only the relative weakness of the new formal contrast but also the relative disappearance of the (sub)genre of the comic or picaresque novel. Henceforth "serious realism" reigns almost unchallenged, and this new novelistic mode does just about as well with short intertitles as with none, except for certain slight differences that we should undoubtedly not bother with. Among Stendhal's novels, for example, the chapters of the *Rouge* bear titles whereas the chapters of *Armance* and the *Chartreuse* are mute, but it would be truly rash to draw any conclusion whatsoever from this difference. The contrast is perhaps more significant in Flaubert, between the mute chapters of *Bovary* and *L'Education,* which are novels of contemporary manners, and the thematic intertitles of *Salammbô,* a novel more "historical" in type although not very Scottian in its ways. The same contrast, perhaps, with Aragon, between the intertitles of *La Semaine sainte* and *Blanche* and the mute chapters of the *Monde réel* set. We note, also, the systematic restraint shown by the Goncourts, Zola, Huysmans, Tolstoy, by Jane Austen, by James, by Conrad.

More difficult in itself is the case of Balzac. The pre-original serial editions and a good many of the original editions (for example, *Grandet, Goriot, La Vieille Fille, Birotteau, Illusions perdues,*

[12] But we already find a model for it in Voltaire's *Zadig*: "The One-Eyed Man," "The Nose," "The Dog and the Horse." The intertitles of *Candide,* on the contrary, are in the old style.

Cousine Bette, Cousin Pons) have chapters, generally numerous and, it seems, from one book to another becoming even more numerous and shorter, with intertitles that are often loquacious in the old "comic" manner. The collected edition of *La Comédie humaine*, which Furne began publishing in 1842, systematically deletes the chapter divisions and at the same time, of course, the original intertitles.[13] This gesture could be read as Balzac's renouncing the affectations of the old sort of title and adopting a more restrained regime that conformed more closely with the "serious" intention of the whole. But Lovenjoul, in his *Histoire des œuvres de Balzac* (1879), writes that "the chapter divisions were eliminated, to the author's great regret, on the ground that they took up too much space.... He always regretted it." According to this somewhat indirect testimony, the deletion of chapters and titles must therefore have been purely circumstantial and economic, with no deep significance. And it is true that once or twice (for *Savarus* in 1843, for *Les Souffrances de l'inventeur* in 1844), separate editions subsequent to the corresponding volume of *La Comédie humaine* reinstate the chapters, with their titles. But conversely, the Charpentier edition of *Grandet*, in 1839, which is the first separate edition (the original was in volume 5 of *Etudes de mœurs* in 1834), deletes the intertitles for no obvious economic reason. So here we are spinning our wheels, getting nowhere on the question of Balzacian intertitles.[14]

The largest investment in the titular apparatus is certainly Hugo's. His early novels – *Han d'Islande, Bug-Jargal,* and *Le Dernier Jour d'un condamné* – had only mute chapters. But in *Notre-Dame de Paris* he inaugurates a more complex mode of titling, calling on all the forms handed down by tradition – short titles à la Scott, narrative titles in the old style – plus a few innovations more or less of his own devising, such as titles in Latin, pseudo-proverbial formulae, and so forth. This more complex mode will come into its own in his post-exile novels,

---

[13] The Pléiade edition, which bases its text on that of the Furne copy that Balzac corrected after the event, quite naturally maintains the deletion and gives the intertitles only as variants; the Garnier editions, in contrast, restore the intertitles, an approach that is not very logical but is invaluable to fanciers of the paratext, even an apparently outdated one.

[14] We should not, in any case, imagine that chapter divisions were forced on Balzac by serial publication: *La Cousine Bette,* which appeared in 41 parts in *Le Constitutionnel,* contained in that form 38 chapters; the original edition would contain 132; likewise, *Le Cousin Pons* went from 31 chapters to 78.

thanks to structures organized into hierarchies of parts, books, and chapters, and in *La Légende des siècles* [three series of epic poems]. The table of contents of *Les Misérables* is exemplary in its intertitular complexity, and of unsurpassed diversity in its lack of restraint; no sample could evoke its flamboyant proliferation. All I can do, therefore, is refer the reader to this paratextual monument itself, which has no fewer than five parts divided into 48 books divided into 365 chapters, but because the books and the parts also have their own titles (no opportunity should be missed), we end up, unless I've miscounted, with 418 titles in all, propelled by an obvious frenzy of playfulness. This is poles apart from the titular restraint characteristic of classicism and serious realism: this is the return to a Cervantean sense of humor, but reinforced by all the resources (I mean: by a minuscule part of the resources) of Hugo's rhetoric and imagination. The text itself, after that, may well seem a little colorless – indeed, a little shallow.

The contemporary period has not much disturbed the use of divisions and the contrast between thematic intertitles[15] and numbered chapters. The main innovation is doubtless the introduction of totally mute divisions, lacking both intertitles and numerals. The author indicates these divisions either by simply starting a new page – as in Céline's *Voyage au bout de la nuit* or Joyce's *Finnegans Wake* (though in the latter, the "chapters" thus established are grouped into three numbered "parts"), as in Claude Simon's *Histoire*, as in Robbe-Grillet's *Jalousie* (of which the table of contents consists of a list of chapter incipits) – or by simply inserting asterisks or extra white space between sections of text. This is what Proust does, for lack of a better alternative, in *Les Jeunes Filles*, and what Joyce does in the definitive presentation of *Ulysses* – but unofficial tradition has preserved the memory of the pre-original intertitles ("Telemachus," "Nestor," "Proteus," and so forth), which each reader is always free to enter by hand in the proper place. The use of totally mute divisions is also and especially the most common and most

---

[15] A variant of thematic intertitles which we find in narratives consisting of interior monologues, like *As I Lay Dying* or *The Sound and the Fury*, is the use of intertitles that indicate the identity of the "speaker" – an approach inspired, very logically, by the norm for drama.

characteristic practice of the French "New Novel." Perhaps strictly speaking such a presentation deprives us of the right to speak of "chapters":[16] what we are dealing with here is a type of division that is appreciably fainter and subtler, no longer intended to mark the narrative except with a kind of respiratory scansion. One more step (but this step matters) and we reach the continuous text of *H*; another step, and we reach the unpunctuated text of *Paradis* (yet another, and we would be back at the texts of antiquity, when written words were not separated from each other); obviously, as I have already said, at that point there is no longer any room for any kind of intertitle.

History

Throughout classical antiquity, the practice of historians seems to have been as restrained as that of the epic poets, or rather of their delayed "editors." The nine books of Herodotus, a division that dates likewise from the Alexandrian period, were marked by the names of the nine muses, obviously without any thematic relationship. The eight books of Thucydides were marked by letters and divided into short numbered chapters, an approach Latin historians imitated. Apparently the use of descriptive titles was initiated in the delayed editions (late fifteenth century, and sixteenth) of the medieval chroniclers: the titles in these editions are synopses in indirect style, noun clauses introduced with "How ..." or complements introduced with "About ... ." For example, Commynes, I.1 – "About the occasion for the wars between Louis XI and the Count of Charolais"; I.2 – "How the Count of Charolais, with several powerful barons of France, raised an army against King Louis XI, under pretence of the common good." The next change is in the direction of briefer and more direct titles, apparently initiated by Machiavelli in his *History of Florence* and displayed by (for example) Voltaire and Gibbon. In Voltaire's *Précis du siècle de Louis XIV*, we find 1 – "Introduction," 2 – "About the states of Europe vis-à-vis Louis

---

[16] As a matter of fact, absolute rigor would forbid us to speak of "chapters" when, as with Zola's *Rougon-Macquart*, we are faced with sections that have only a numeral, without the indication *Chapter Number Thus-and-Such*. But custom takes no notice, and custom is quite right: those are chapters that do not declare themselves such.

XIV," 3 – "Minority of Louis XIV. Victory of the French under the great Condé, at that time the duke of Enghien," and so on. This style of direct (nominal or propositional) titles – but apt to be divided into several juxtaposed elements, each announcing a particular section of the chapter – is likewise the style used by memorialists, as we see in Saint-Simon, in Casanova (whose intertitles were supplied in 1826 by his editor, Laforgue), and even in Chateaubriand and Dumas, whereas personal autobiography is more apt to adopt a numbered division, perhaps inherited from Saint Augustine: Rousseau, Musset, Gide, and Nabokov take this course. Intertitular style is undoubtedly a piece of evidence one can use in making the often fine distinction between memoir and autobiography. But one must be careful: Giono's *Jean le Bleu*, for example, a work whose status is ambiguous (the content is generally known to be autobiographical, but the genre indication is "a novel"), features memoir-style intertitles; thus, chapter 6: "The ring that was a little lettuce leaf – The heralds – The girl who smelled of musk – The animal fair," and so forth.

Among historians, Michelet is conspicuous for titles that are more concise, more terse (many nouns without articles), and also more diversified. Here as an example are the first few titles from the first chapter of *L'Histoire de France*: "Celts and Iberians – Gallic or Celtic Race; likeable genius; tendency to action; ostentation and rhetoric – Iberian Race; less sociable genius; spirit of resistance – The Gauls push back the Iberians and follow them beyond the Pyrenees and the Alps." This freedom will become much more pronounced in Michelet's delayed works, such as *La Sorcière*, *La Montagne*, or *La Mer*: "Circle of Waters, Circles of Fire," "Rivers of the Sea," "Pulse of the Sea," "Fecundity," "The Milky Sea," "The Bloody Flower"... These titles are as idiosyncratic as Hugo's but in a wholly different manner: Michelet's are less rhetorical, more abrupt, as if issuing directly from a high-strung sensibility. Via the book *Michelet* by Barthes, who borrows from his subject as if by osmosis, the Michelet model holds sway today over the titling and the very conceptual apparatus of French thematic criticism.

I said a word in passing about autobiography. Biography – released, after a still greater delay, from the constraints of the historical model – deserves particular mention. Classical biographies display restraint: we find a division into years with Boswell, numbered chapters in Chateaubriand's *Vie de Rancé*, very factual titles in Renan's *Vie de Jésus* (1 – "Place of Jesus in the History of the World," 2 – "Infancy and Youth of Jesus. His First Impressions," 3 – "Education of Jesus"). But modern biographers often yield to the temptation to use highly symbolic titles. See Maurois's *Balzac* (in other respects very restrained), in four parts: "The Upward Climb," "Fame," "The Human Comedy," "Swan-Song"; the chapters in the fourth part: "The Torment of Tantalus," "Reunion in St Petersburg," "Chorus of Wolves," "Perrette and the Milk-Pail," and so forth.[17] We find the same effects in Painter's *Chateaubriand* (first volume, *The Longed-for Tempests*: "The Flowers of Brittany," "The Judgement of Paris," "The Noble Savage," "The Wilderness of Exile"...). As for Painter's *Marcel Proust*, here the biographer systematically takes his titles (among other things) from the world of the *Recherche*, thus unrestrainedly transferring episodes from "Marcel's" story into Proust's life: "Balbec and Condorcet," "Bergotte and Doncières," "Visits from Albertine," "The Death of Saint-Loup," and so forth.

Didactic texts

The major didactic prose works of classical antiquity, works of philosophy or rhetoric (Platonic dialogues, treatises by Aristotle, Cicero, Quintilian), likewise respect the rule of restraint. Here too, it is the Middle Ages that inaugurate the use of thematic titles, a good example of which is provided by Saint Thomas's *Summa Theologica*, with its chapters beginning "De ..." and its paragraphs beginning "Utrum ... ." The same type of title appears in Machiavelli, Descartes, Montesquieu (whose *Esprit des lois* presents a heavy titular apparatus segmented into six parts, thirty-one books, and roughly five hundred chapters), Rousseau, Kant, and even (barely lightened) in Chateaubriand and Mme de Staël, and (once again very heavy) in Toqueville and Gobineau. The modern regime, characterized by brevity together with a predominance of nouns, appears perhaps in Taine, whose *La Fontaine*

---

[17] [André Maurois, *Prométhée, ou La vie de Balzac* (Hachette, 1965); tr. *Prometheus: The Life of Balzac*, trans. Norman Denny (New York: Harper and Row, 1965).]

et ses Fables has 1 – "The Gallic Spirit," 2 – "The Man," 3 – "The Writer," and so forth. With these titles we are on familiar ground.

The exceptions are rare. Among them are Paulhan's archaizing titles (a playful return to the classical regime) and, in Barthes's *Michelet* (a book I have already drawn attention to), the short sections with "rubrics" (which is what Barthes called his brief titles at the heads of paragraphs: "Migraines," "Work," "Michelet a History Freak," "I'm in a Hurry"...). These rubrics started the fashion with which we are familiar in thematic criticism as well as in Blanchot's *Livre à venir* or *Espace littéraire*. We have also witnessed a brief vogue – inspired by the mode of presentation used in scientific articles – of chapters with subdivided, analytical numbering: 1.1.1, 1.1.2, and so on. That system, it must certainly be said, was a formidable deterrent to reading in a genre that surely didn't need one; the emblematic masterpiece of this style of titling remains Barthes's *Système de la mode*. But an entire generation thus gave itself the thrill of ostentatious rigor and illusory scientificity.

Collections

In a collection of short poems, the autonomy of each piece is generally much greater than the autonomy of the constituent parts of an epic, a novel, or a historical or philosophical work. And even though the thematic unity of the collection may be more or less strong, the effect of sequence or progression is usually very weak,[18] and the order of the constituent parts is most often arbitrary. Each poem is in itself a closed work that may legitimately claim its own title.

Apart from some individual or generic exceptions, however, putting titles on short poems is a phenomenon quite a bit more recent than putting titles on chapters. Here too, classical antiquity is conspicuous in its restraint in almost all genres: odes (even the Pindaric epinicia, albeit devoted individually to clearly identified victors, are classified only by the set of games in which their subjects competed: *Olympic, Pythian, Nemean*), satires, elegies, iambics, epigrams, and on up to Horace's epistles, have reached

---

[18] Among the rare exceptions, let us mention La Ceppède's collection of *Théorèmes* (1613–22), a narrative sequence of 315 sonnets on the Passion and Resurrection of Christ – a collection we will meet again for its notes.

us in collections whose parts are merely numbered. The major didactic poems, *De rerum natura* and the *Georgics*, number their books as epics do. The only exceptions seem to involve hymns (Callimachus), which are brief epics; Theocritus's *Idylls*, a delayed collection (second century A.D.) whose components circulated for a long time individually (thematic titles, of course: "Thyrsis," "The Spellbinders," "The Goatherd's Serenade"...) – but not Virgil's *Bucolics*; and of course fables, an eminently popular genre and likewise one involving long periods of erratic circulation.

The Middle Ages seem to have innovated less in this type of work than in the others: most collections, from those of the troubadours and *trouvères* of the twelfth century to those of Villon and Charles d'Orléans in the fifteenth century (with the exception, it seems, of Rutebeuf), come down to us with no intertitles other than genre indications: *canso, aube, sirventes, ballade, rondeau,* and so forth. The Renaissance and classicism will therefore not have to try very hard to revive the practice of the ancients: the *canzonieri,* from Petrarch to the Pléiade poets, number their pieces, even if (as in some editions of Petrarch) that means supplementing the numerals with synopses a few lines long, synopses that are reminiscent of those of Boccaccio and that cannot be regarded as titles. Titles appear only (in Ronsard) at the head of odes, hymns, and discourses. Boileau innovates with respect to Horace by indicating at the head of each epistle the name of the addressee. All in all, not much. At the end of the eighteenth century André Chénier's work provides a good inventory of the classical norm, for Chénier used almost the whole palette of canonical intertitular genres: numbers for elegies, epigrams, iambics; names of addressees for epistles and hymns; thematic titles for love poems, pastoral poems, and odes.

In the meantime, however, the baroque interlude had distinguished itself by a fairly heavy investment in titles. We see this in Marino and his followers, in the English Metaphysicals (but Donne gives titles only to his secular pieces: elegies, songs, and sonnets; he gives numbers without titles to his *Holy Sonnets* – undoubtedly a significant differentiation), in Quevedo (but his titles, often very detailed, might well, as in Petrarch, be synopses or editorial glosses; and Góngora remains very restrained). In France the master titler is the Marinist Tristan L'Hermite: the table of contents of his *Amours* is a fireworks display of baroque titling, all quips and oxymorons ("Pleasant Torments," "The Beautiful Sick Woman," "Useless Remedies," "Hollow Pleasures," etc.), with a grace or charming elegance that foreshadows Couperin. But as we have seen, the norm quickly regains the upper hand.

The great rupture, here, is romanticism's doing, starting with the youthful poems of Hölderlin ("The Laurel," "Hymn to Liberty," "Greece") and Wordsworth and Coleridge's *Lyrical Ballads* ("Lines Written a Few Miles above Tintern Abbey," "The Rime of the Ancient Mariner"). In France, it was apparently Lamartine's *Méditations* that for more than a century provided a model (short, restrained, and solemn) for lyric titling: "Isolation," "Man," "Evening," "Immortality," "Memory," "The Lake," "Autumn"... This model held sway over the work of all the romantics and postromantics, from Baudelaire (some of whose inflections are personal and provocative: "Une Charogne," "Le Guignon" ["A Carrion," "Ill Luck"]; others are neo-baroque – "La Muse vénale," "La Lune offensée," and "Remords posthume" ["The Venal Muse," "The Moon Offended," "The Remorse of the Dead"] – and Tristan could have written them) to Verlaine and Mallarmé and on up to the young Rimbaud. Hugo, here as elsewhere, is distinguished by the structural complexity of his major collections: *Les Contemplations* is divided into two parts of six books each, *Les Châtiments* into seven parts with titles ironically taken from imperial propaganda ("Society Is Saved," "Order Is Reestablished," "The Family Is Restored"...), and *La Légende des siècles* into sixty-one parts in which some of the poems, like "The Romances of El Cid," "The Little King of Galicia," "The Satyr," are themselves subdivided into sections with intertitles – an inflation that is very far removed from Lamartinian restraint.

But Hugo is also distinguished by a reticence that is itself dramatic: some of his poems have no titles, particularly in the second part of *Les Contemplations*, as if the solemnity of the subject (one thinks of Donne's *Holy Sonnets*) required this reserve. An analogous approach is evidently taken by Verlaine, two of whose collections are entirely without intertitles, and these two happen to be *La Bonne Chanson* [lyrics written for his wife before their marriage] and *Sagesse* [poems marking his recommitment to Catholicism]. The contrast – and often the alternation within a single collection – between poems with titles and poems without has persisted up to our own time. Whitman rarely uses titles, but – rather redundantly – places his incipits as titles. Frost and Stevens most often give their poems titles, as do the surrealists and Lorca and Ungaretti. In some collections the absence of intertitles signals an intention to maintain classical dignity: Rilke's *Duino Elegies* and *Sonnets to Orpheus*, Bonnefoy's *Douve*, almost everything by Emily Dickinson and Saint-John Perse. But we must not overemphasize the significance of these choices.

Along with Tristan and Hugo, the great expert in these matters could be Jules Laforgue. His register, as we know, is comical and woebegone humor. His best poem (and this is saying a lot) could be the table of contents of *Les Complaintes*: "Autobiographical Preludes" (homage to Wordsworth?), "Propitiatory Complaint to the Unconscious," "Complaint-Petition of Faust the Younger," "Complaint to Our Lady of the Evenings," "Complaint of the Voices under the Buddhistic Fig Tree," "Complaint of That Lovely Moon," "Complaint of Pianos Heard in the Suburbs"... Someone has to stop me. Tristan evoked Couperin, and Laforgue, of course, foreshadows Satie and his entourage.

I will not further try the patience of my unlikely reader by proposing a new ramble through the intertitles of other "genres," such as collections of novellas or essays. Besides, these types of collections are too recent to introduce any very significant diversity into a survey whose main lesson seems to me by now fairly clear.

It all boils down more or less to the antithesis we have continually encountered between rhematic, or purely designative, titling (which consists simply of numbering the divisions or, indeed, leaving them altogether mute) and thematic titling – wordy or restrained – which, since the beginning of the nineteenth century, has moved roughly from the wordy to the restrained. With a thousand slight differences and various exceptions, this formal antithesis corresponds to a contrast in authorial positioning: with thematic titling goes a demonstrative – indeed, insistent – stance on the part of the author toward his work, whether or not a screen of humor muffles this insistence; on the other side is a more restrained stance that initially betokened classical dignity, then realistic seriousness.

315

Here as elsewhere, the "impediment" aspect of the paratext could easily cause it to direct a little too much attention not to the text but to the fact of the *book* as such: "This is a novel by Victor Hugo," proclaims the table of contents of *Les Misérables*. "This," says the paratext more generally, "is a book." Such a statement is not, of course, false, and no truth is better left unsaid. But an author may also wish his reader to forget about this particular truth, and one sign of a paratext's effectiveness is no doubt its transparency: its transitivity. The best intertitle, the best title in general, is perhaps the one that goes unnoticed.

Tables of contents, running heads

I have just said "the table of contents of *Les Misérables*," and earlier I spoke of "the table of contents of *Les Complaintes*," etc. This provides me with an opportunity to end where I ought to have begun: with the location of intertitles. Potentially, there are at least three: at the head of a section, of course – and I will not dwell on this, although it has endless formal and graphic variations – but also, serving as announcements or reminders, in the *running heads* or in the *table of contents* [which appears at the back in contemporary French books]. A few words on these two types of element will spare us the need for a separate study of them.

Running heads may serve as reminders, at the top of the page and sometimes necessarily in abbreviated form, of the general title of the work (if they are on the left) and (if on the right) of the title of the section, generally the chapter. In theory they are only reminders, handy when one is reading and consulting the text, but sometimes running heads transcend this role and play their own part, by surreptitiously giving a title to a chapter that is in theory untitled, or by highlighting details that change from page by page (variable running heads), or by playing a tune that differs from that of the chapter's official intertitle. In the original edition of the *Chartreuse* (a novel without intertitles) the running heads are distributed more or less capriciously; in the original edition of the *Rouge*, the running heads are unfaithful, or fairly liberated. Of course, every new edition for which the type has been reset entails a deletion or reshuffling of variable running heads.[19] The most sensible solution would doubtless be, in scholarly editions, deletion plus a reminder in the notes, a little as the Pléiade edition of Balzac lists among the variants the intertitles that were deleted in 1842.

The table of contents, too, is in theory no more than a device for reminding us of the titular apparatus – or for announcing it, when the contents page appears at the front of the book, as it once did in France[20] and as it still does in German and Anglo-American books. These two types of reduplication (back and front) are certainly not equivalent, and the second unquestionably seems more logical, even if it goes against the grain with French readers, for whom, aesthetically, it feels vaguely inelegant. But let us not overestimate these effects of positioning: nothing is easier or more common, at least for readers who take an intellectual type of approach, than to cast a preliminary glance at a table of contents placed at the back of the volume.

But the table of contents is not always a faithful listing of the intertitular apparatus. It may misrepresent this apparatus by making cuts, as in some inexpensive or careless editions in which the numbered chapters without titles are quite simply not in a table of contents; or by making additions, attributing titles to chapters that *in situ* do not contain any: this, we should remember, is the approach Proust took for *Les Jeunes Filles*; or by cavalierly making changes, as sometimes happens with Stendhal; or again, and especially, by creating – with a list of incipits – the illusion of a set of titles. Actually, the incipit as ersatz title, in collections of poems or in a novel like Robbe-Grillet's *Jalousie*, is typically an effect created by the table of contents. At the spot itself (except with Whitman, as already mentioned) there is only a text without a title, for at that place nothing must privilege the first line or the first phrase. In the table of contents and then in the designative use that derives from it, this first line, as incipit, breaks away and takes on an

---

[19] On running heads in Stendhal, see M. Abrioux, "Intertitres et épigraphes chez Stendhal," *Poétique* 69 (February 1987).

[20] As a matter of fact, the classical custom was, instead, to put a table of chapters at the beginning of a work and, at the end, an actual table of contents, a sort of detailed index. Our modern table of contents is in reality a table of chapters, and its name is a little misappropriated.

unduly emblematic value, as if it were always, according to Valéry's statement, god-given.[21] Hence the large number of poems of which we know only the first lines, and sometimes less: "Demain, dès l'aube, à l'heure où blanchit la campagne," "J'ai cueilli cette fleur pour toi sur la colline," "Je n'ai pas oublié, voisine de la ville," "La servante au grand cœur dont vous étiez jalouse"...[22]

[21] [See Chapter 4, note 12.]
[22] [The first and second are from Hugo's *Contemplations*, the third and fourth from Baudelaire's *Fleurs du mal*.]

12

Notes

> Too many notes!
> Joseph II

With notes we doubtless reach one – indeed, several – of the borders, or absences of borders, that surround the eminently transitional field of the paratext. Their strategic importance will perhaps offset the inevitably disappointing nature of a "genre" whose occurrences are by definition irregular, divided up, crumbly, not to say dustlike, and often so closely connected to a given detail of a given text that they have, as it were, no autonomous significance: hence our uneasiness in taking hold of them.[1]

Definition, place, time

For the moment, I will give the note as formal a definition as possible, without broaching the subject of function. A note is a statement of variable length (one word is enough) connected to a more or less definite segment of text and either placed opposite or keyed to this segment. The always partial character of the text being referred to, and therefore the always local character of the statement conveyed in a note, seems to me the most distinctive formal feature of this paratextual element, a feature that contrasts the note with, among other paratexts, the preface – including

[1] A cliché we will not mention again: "A note is the mediocre attached to the beautiful" (Alain, quoted in the *Robert* dictionary). Hatred of notes is one of the most unchanging stereotypes of a certain anti-intellectual Poujadism (or sometimes dandyism). That had to be said in a note. ["Poujadism" – after Pierre Poujade, who led a 1950s political movement supported mainly by small shopkeepers – is now a pejorative term connoting narrow-mindedness and negativism (*Petit Robert* dictionary).]

those prefaces or postfaces that are modestly entitled "Note," as Conrad's very often are. But the formal distinction between note and preface obviously reveals an affinity of function: in many cases, the discourse of the preface and that of the apparatus of notes are in a very close relation of continuity and homogeneity. This relation is particularly evident in later editions, such as that of Chateaubriand's *Martyrs*, or in delayed editions, such as that of the same author's *Essai sur les révolutions*. In both of these examples, a single discourse – a defensive one for *Les Martyrs*, an autocritical and reclaiming one for the *Essai* – is divided between the preface and the notes, the preface dealing with general considerations and the notes taking responsibility for points of detail.

Under the older name of *glose* [gloss] (the *Robert* dictionary dates the word *note* from 1636), the use of notes goes back to the Middle Ages, when the text – placed in the middle of the page – was apt to be surrounded, or sometimes larded in various ways, with explanations written in smaller letters; and this layout is still common in the incunabula of the fifteenth century, where the gloss can be distinguished only by its smaller type size. In the sixteenth century "side notes," or marginal notes, appear; they are shorter and appended to more definite segments of text. In the eighteenth century it became customary to put the notes at the bottom of the page. But our present-day practice remains highly varied: notes are still placed in the margins (see Barthes's *Fragments d'un discours amoureux* or *Chambre claire*, magazines like *Degrés* or *Le Débat*), between the lines (in many a didactic work or textbook), at the end of a chapter or book, or in a special volume.[2] Francis Ponge mentions a Bible in which the notes occupied a middle column between two columns of text.[3] "Scientific" practice often involves a two-tiered reference apparatus in which the notes at the bottom of the page refer concisely, by name and date, to a bibliography at the end of the volume. It is also possible to keep the right-hand page for the text and put the notes on the facing left-hand page: that is the layout adopted for Gaétan Picon's *Malraux par lui-même*, which we will come upon again; and Monique Wittig's *Guerrillères* reverses this arrangement. Nothing, moreover, prohibits long infrapaginal

[2] See P. Hazard, *La Pensée européenne au XVIIIe siècle* (Boivin, 1946).
[3] *Entretiens avec Philippe Sollers* (Gallimard-Seuil, 1970), 105.

notes from spilling over onto several pages: on page 173 of *Echanges* by Renaud Camus a note begins that will occupy precisely the lower half of all the book's subsequent pages, or roughly a sixth of the volume. Nor does anything preclude annotations in several degrees, that is, notes on notes: Renaud Camus again, in *Travers*, carries the game to the sixteenth degree. Finally, nothing precludes the coexistence of several systems in a single book: short notes at the bottom of the page, more detailed ones at the end of the chapter or volume,[4] and very often, in scholarly editions, author's notes at the bottom of the page and editor's notes at the end of the volume. Chapter 10 of *Finnegans Wake* has some notes in the two margins and others at the bottom of the page, with each of these three locations reserved for a separate enunciator.[5]

Our most common practice consists of putting "callouts" in the text,[6] using one or another system (numbers, letters, or symbols) and pegging each note to the text by repeating the identifying marker or mentioning one of the text's words or lines. But marginal notes, placed opposite the textual segment in question, easily dispense with such pegging, and even notes with callouts may in their relevance extend beyond the word or phrase to which the callout is attached: references at the end of a paragraph may bear on the entire paragraph, or a note bearing on an entire chapter or article may be pegged to the first sentence or to the title. The last note of Rousseau's *Nouvelle Héloïse* actually bears on the whole work: it is a brief postface disguised as a note. Finally, notes at the end of a chapter, without callouts in the text and supplied with headings that pick up successive key phrases from the text, may bear more or less freely on one detail or another or on the chapter as a whole: see Michel Charles's *L'Arbre et la*

---

[4] This is the approach taken, for example, by J.-P. Richard in his *Univers imaginaire de Mallarmé* (Seuil, 1961), an approach he explains very precisely (p. 28, n. 25).

[5] See S. Benstock, "At the Margin of Discourse: Footnotes in the Fictional Text," *PMLA* 98 (1983): 204–25.

[6] ["Callout" is the term U.S. publishing professionals use (the British equivalent is "indicator") to designate the specific reference in the text to information that is presented extratextually (information such as notes, figures, tables, sidebars). The callout for notes generally consists of a superscript number or other symbol; for the other kinds of extratextual information, the callout generally consists of a phrase along the lines of "See table 1."]

source. In these last two cases, we are clearly on one of the borders of the note.[7]

Like prefaces, notes can appear at any time during the life of the text, if a new edition should offer an occasion for them. Again, therefore, we have a temporal distribution that accords with the three relevant occasions: original notes, or those in the first edition – this is the most common situation and requires no example; later notes, or notes for the second edition, such as those in *Les Martyrs* (1810 [original edition: 1809]) or in Rousseau's *Emile* (1765 [original edition: 1762]); delayed notes, such as those in the Cadell edition of the *Waverley Novels* (1829–33), in the Ladvocat edition of the *Essai sur les révolutions*, or in Valéry's *Léonard*. Sometimes, too, notes disappear from one edition to another: in 1763, for *La Nouvelle Héloïse*, Rousseau leaves out a great many of the original notes, which had displeased readers (but he reinstates them by hand in his personal copy, and modern editions follow suit). And I am not considering posthumous deletions, unfortunate initiatives undertaken by hasty "editors" such as Michelet's editor for the Bouquins series. But sometimes – indeed, more often – notes from various periods coexist, with or without an indication of date: for example, in Scott, in Chateaubriand, in Senancour.

Senders, addressees

The chart of possible senders of notes is the same as the chart of senders of prefaces (see page 181 above). There are assumptive authorial notes, very certainly the most common ones, such as the notes to *Tom Jones*; and there are disavowing authorial notes, such as those to *La Nouvelle Héloïse* or to Senancour's *Oberman*, and these obviously extend the disavowing fiction of the preface. There are authentic allographic notes: all the notes by editors in more or less critical editions, or the notes by translators. Authentic actorial notes: the notes contributed to a biography or critical study by the person who is its subject – Malraux's notes

---

[7] An article by J.-M. Gleizes, "Il n'y a pas un instant à perdre," *TXT* 17 (1984), contains terminal notes that are numbered but not called out in the text, and the first one specifies (if we can put it this way): "The notes refer to any place in the text. And just as easily to any of the text's white spaces." Gérard Wajeman's novel *L'Interdit* (1986) consists solely of an apparatus of notes for an absent text – that was bound to happen someday.

for *Malraux par lui-même*, for example, a work I have already mentioned. Fictive authorial notes: in Scott, certain notes signed "Laurence Templeton" for *Ivanhoe* or "Jedediah Cleishbotham" for *Lammermoor*. Fictive allographic: those by "Charles Kinbote" to the poem by "John Shade" in *Pale Fire*. Fictive actorial: the notes of narrator-characters such as Tristram Shandy or those in chapter 10 of *Finnegans Wake* (Dolph in the left margin, Kev in the right margin, Issy at the bottom of the page). I am not really aware of any apocryphal notes, but (to go back to our prefatorial hypotheses) notes attributed to Rimbaud (apocryphal authorial) or to Verlaine (apocryphal allographic) for *La Chasse spirituelle* would suffice, as would notes attributed to Valéry for *Commentaire de Charmes*. And sometimes for fun an author attributes to his publisher an assessment expressed in a note: see Aragon in *Anicet* (Gallimard, 1920, p. 53) or Sarduy in *Colibri* (French translation, Seuil, 1986, p. 68).

Inasmuch as the annotated segments of text may themselves have one or another enunciative status, the combinatorial set of possible relations is obviously very rich. One possibility is an authorial note to an authorial text (this is the most common case in discursive works); another is an authorial note to a narratorial text (*Tom Jones*); or an authorial note to an actorial text or to a speech by a character (Stendhal); a pseudo-editorial note to an actorial text (*La Nouvelle Héloïse*); an editorial note to an authorial, narratorial, or actorial text (critical editions); or an actorial note to a narratorial text (*Finnegans Wake*). And this list does not preclude other, rarer situations or the coexistence (very common and already considered) of notes attributed to several senders: author + editor (critical editions), fictive author + real author (Scott), author + actor (*Tristram Shandy*), multiple actors (*Finnegans Wake*), and others. Finally, there are cases of notes with embedded enunciating: this is the situation for all notes that include quotations (third party cited by author) or for critical notes mentioning, for example, an epitextual authorial commentary (author cited by third party).

The addressee of the note is undoubtedly, in theory, the reader of the text, to the exclusion of any other person (to whom – and this is even more obvious than for the preface – the note might well, most often, make no sense). We must, however, consider the case of second-degree texts, those quoted with their notes in the primary text: the notes of these second-degree texts are addressed in the first place to the reader of the quoted text and reach the reader of the quoting text only by proxy or rebound. This could be the status of actorial notes in an epistolary novel, if custom did not rule out, in theory, placing notes at the bottom of a letter. And there is nothing to prevent a written metadiegetic narrative, such as *L'Ambitieux par amour* in Balzac's *Albert Savarus*, from containing such quoted notes.

Above all, we must observe that notes, even more than prefaces, may be statutorily optional for the reader and may consequently be addressed only to certain readers: to those who will be interested in one or another supplementary or digressive consideration, the incidental nature of which justifies its being bumped, precisely, into a note. Moreover, sometimes the author – Rousseau, for example, in the foreword to the *Second Discours* – gives his reader permission in advance to disregard such excursuses.[8] But ordinarily the reader himself initiates and is responsible for his choices, making guesses and taking each as it comes. And conversely, and with no regard for the obviousness of what I've just mentioned, some readers read only the notes – when an index is lacking, for example, to see whether they themselves are cited. But these considerations are already encroaching on the study of functions.

Functions

With the note as with the preface, our study of functions can avoid mix-ups and various irrelevancies only by distinguishing a certain number of functional types, whose main criteria are provided, here again, by the status of the sender and by temporal characteristics. Accordingly, I will consider, in succession, assumptive authorial notes, subdivided into original, later, and

---

[8]   Which for this reason are printed at the end of the volume. "Those who have the courage to begin again will be able to amuse themselves the second time in beating the bushes, and try to go through the notes. There will be little harm if others do not read them at all." It is true that these notes are often long digressions occupying several pages, for example on humanity's biped condition (note 3), on humanity's natural goodness (note 7), or on racial diversity (note 8) [note numbers given here are those in vol. 3 of *The Collected Writings of Rousseau*, ed. Masters and Kelly (Hanover, NH: University Press of New England, 1992)].

delayed; then allographic (and secondarily, actorial) notes; and finally the various kinds of fictional notes. But given the almost always discursive nature of the note and its very intimate relation to the text, it seems to me necessary to introduce here a new distinction, one not required in the study of the preface, between notes connected with texts that are themselves discursive (history, essays, and so forth) and notes – as a matter of fact, far less common – that adorn or mar, as you like, works of narrative or dramatic fiction or lyric poetry.

Discursive texts: original notes

The original note to a discursive text is the note par excellence, the basic type from which all the others derive to a greater or lesser degree;[9] this is also the type with which we all are most familiar, as consumers or producers of notes, and I do not expect to bring any staggering revelations to the subject. I have studied this type of note over a small, arbitrary corpus, fairly classic and basically French, extending from La Bruyère to Roland Barthes. I believe this corpus to be more or less representative and significant in its consistencies and rare deviations, and I herewith present as synthetic an account of my findings as possible.

What we find in notes, then, are definitions or explanations of terms used in the text, and sometimes the mention of a specific or figurative meaning; in a note to the sentence "Not all countryside is rustic," for example, La Bruyère specifies: "Here this term is meant metaphorically" (for in the literal sense, all countryside is necessarily rustic). In their display of caution, such restrictions of meaning may take on a polemical nuance; in another example from La Bruyère, on each occurrence of the word *dévot* [a pious person] or *dévotion* [piety], the author stubbornly specifies: "faux dévot" [religious hypocrite], "fausse dévotion" [religious hypocrisy]. We also find translations of quotations that appear in the text in their original language, and vice versa. And references for quotations; indications of sources; and presentation of supporting authorities, corroborating or supplementary information, and documents. Most of the notes by Montesquieu, Buffon, Michelet, or Tocqueville fulfill this documentary function, sometimes at

---

[9] This should be understood in a structural and not historical sense: the earliest notes may very well have been allographic.

great length; see the note at the end of Tocqueville's *Ancien Régime et la Révolution*: several pages on the *cahiers de doléances* [registers of grievances].[10] And we find details about an event that in the text is evoked more vaguely or cavalierly – details that sometimes go as far as the restrictive nuance: for example, Chateaubriand (*Essai sur les révolutions*, Pléiade 326), having spoken of the "innocence" of Charles I, specifies in a note that this king was innocent at least of what he was accused of. The discursive text's note may also mention uncertainties or complexities that the author ignored in the text, considering them misgivings not likely to interest the ordinary reader, but that he is anxious to bring up in a note aimed at more exacting scholars. We find examples again in the *Essai*, regarding various points of chronology (57, 180), Pythagoras (177), or Hanno's expedition (156; this note ends with a very significant mention of the addressee: "This does not matter much to the reader"). Discursive texts' notes may also provide additional arguments or attempts to forestall objections (54, on the Flood). They may contain digressions on the subject, or sometimes off it: still in the *Essai*, Chateaubriand slips in, years before his *Mémoires d'outre-tombe*, portraits of Chamfort (122), of Malesherbes (329), of Louis XVI (337), reflections on the origins of the American people (147), speculations on Sanskrit (208), and memories of his trip to America. This last is apropos of Abélard (351–55), and "since the fault [of digression] is already committed, an additional half-page will expose me no further to criticism" – then comes the well-known description of Niagara Falls; a delayed note of 1826 contains this comment: "It must be acknowledged that that is subtly hooking a note to a word" (the same autocriticism could be applied to the strange note in his *Génie* on the vowel A). Michelet, too, sometimes grants himself autobiographical asides that, in his notes as in his prefaces, contribute so much to the vividness of his work. In a note in *La Sorcière* [published in English as *Satanism and Witchcraft: A Study in Medieval Superstition*], for example, Michelet lingers over his evocation of Toulon, where he lived while writing that book: "I have twice spoken of Toulon; but I can never speak enough of a place which

---

[10] ["Every electoral assembly ... was entitled to draw up an address to the crown (*cahiers de doléances*) embodying its complaints and demands" (J. M. Thompson, *The French Revolution* [Oxford: Basil Blackwell, 1943]).]

has brought me such happiness. It meant much for me to finish this gloomy history in the land of light. Our works feel the influence of the country where they were wrought. Nature labours with us; and it is a duty to render gratitude to this mysterious comrade, to thank the *Genius loci.*" One would wish to happen upon this kind of genetic counterpoint more often. Stendhal's *De l'amour* offers us another type of it: remarks by real or imagined reader-friends (" 'Cut out this bit,' they tell me," or "Cut out this word [*crystallization*]"), fictive attributions to "Léonore" and "Lisio Visconti," and other confidences imparted out of the blue, which as a matter of fact appear just as frequently in the text, for in this book the division of the discourse between text and notes seems quite random, or capricious. In our whole corpus, Stendhal is undoubtedly the author whose use of the note is most idiosyncratic; he carries to its ironic extreme the eighteenth-century tradition of reserving the most polemical or sarcastic barbs of the discourse for the notes (see Bayle, Voltaire, Gibbon),[11] making equivocal use of "prudent" notes aimed at censors or the police[12] – notes sometimes attributed to a fictive or apocryphal third party. The ostentatious and somewhat hyperbolic prudence of those notes could certainly have produced perverse effects, attracting what Claudel (I think) later called "the thoughtful eye of the constabulary" to an often innocuous text. Stendhal's twisted and frequently bizarre use of the note in his novels is obviously much akin to the almost fanatic delight this author takes in pseudonymity and cryptography.

What can we conclude from all of this? Undoubtedly that the basic function of the original authorial note is to serve as a supplement, sometimes a digression, very rarely a commentary: as has often been observed, there would be nothing absurd about incorporating this kind of note into the actual text – and besides, we know that many authors, rather than appear pedantic, prefer either to abstain from using notes or to limit them to a minimal apparatus of references. Nothing absurd, to be sure, but I will nonetheless add (if this is the place for a brief defense of the object

[11] On Gibbon's practice, see G. W. Bowersock, "The Art of the Footnote," *The American Scholar* (winter 1983–84).

[12] "Gentlemen of the police, there is nothing political here. I study: wines, cuckoldry, and Gothic and Romanesque churches. The author is thirty-five years old and is traveling on business; he is an ironmonger" (the first note in *Le Voyage dans le Midi de la France*).

we are discussing): incorporation into the text would entail some loss or impairment. The obvious impairment, at least from the point of view of a classicizing aesthetic of discourse, is that incorporating a digression into the text might well mean creating a lumpish or confusion-generating hernia. The loss might consist of the elimination pure and simple of particular digressions, even though these could be valuable in themselves. But above all, the main loss seems to me that in denying himself the note, the author thereby denies himself the possibility of a second level of discourse, one that sometimes contributes to textual depth. The chief advantage of the note is actually that it brings about local effects of nuance, or sourdine, or as they also say in music, of *register*, effects that help reduce the famous and sometimes regrettable linearity of discourse. Given all that notes have to offer – registers of intensity, degrees in the obligation to read, potential for reversibility and for paradoxical turns (the main points getting put into a note) – we can certainly see why so many writers, including some of the greatest, have been unwilling to deprive themselves of these possibilities. If the note is a disorder of the text, it is a disorder that, like some others, may have its proper use.

But as is no doubt clear, this justification of the (original) authorial note at the same time, to some extent, calls into question its paratextual character. The original note is a local detour or a momentary fork in the text, and as such it belongs to the text almost as much as a simple parenthesis does. With this kind of note we are in a very undefined fringe between text and paratext. Our guiding principle, one of economy and relevance – to allocate to a new category (the paratext) only what cannot, without a loss, be assigned to an existing category (here, the text) – must lead us in this case to a negative decision: other types of notes, as we will see, belong more appropriately to the paratext, but the original authorial note, at least when connected to a text that is itself discursive and with which it has a relation of continuity and formal homogeneity, belongs more to the text, which the note extends, ramifies, and modulates rather than comments on.

Discursive texts: later notes

It is quite another matter with (the much rarer) later and delayed notes: their relations of continuity with the accompanying preface (of the same date) are generally very pronounced. We could define the difference between the two systems like this: the original preface presents and comments on the text, which the notes extend and modulate; the later or delayed preface comments on the text taken as a whole, and the notes of the same date extend and explain this preface in detail by commenting on the particulars of the text; and on the strength of this function of commenting, such notes clearly belong to the paratext. The function of this localized commentary is generally identical (except for its point of application) to that of prefaces of the same occasion: the later notes and preface perform the function of responding to critics and possibly of making corrections; the delayed notes and preface, the function of providing long-range autocriticism and putting the author's own achievement into perspective.

Responding to critics: this function is exemplified by some notes Rousseau added to a copy of the first edition of *Emile*, with an eye to a new edition and as a response, sometimes a very vigorous one, to Formey's attacks in the latter's *Anti-Emile* of 1763. This category also includes the far more numerous "remarks" Chateaubriand made on matters of detail throughout his examination of *Les Martyrs* for the third edition of 1810.[13] The critics had focused mainly on points of history (and geography) and secondarily on questions of form. Chateaubriand defends himself against the criticisms based on form by invoking illustrious precedents (Homer, Tasso, Milton) and sometimes takes note of the critics' points by calling attention to corrections made in the text of this new edition, stressing his modesty in the face of justified remarks; to the criticisms on points of history or geography, he generally makes point-by-point replies, producing his sources or adducing his own knowledge of the places depicted in his book – replies that, after the event, give this highly academic text a sort of autobiographical and "things seen" counterpoint that is bound to enliven it. The later notes on the "confidential copy" of his *Essai historique*, jotted down immediately after publication in 1797, do not fulfill the same function: written before any critical response, they involve, instead, spontaneous

---

[13] [*Les Martyrs* is a prose epic.] I mention this work here in violation of the distinction between discursive texts and fictional texts – a violation justified by the fact that the feature of being later often makes this distinction irrelevant, and retaining it would involve us with uselessly cumbersome subdivisions.

modifications and various additions. In short, they are not so much later notes as corrections made with an eye to a new edition (we will encounter this sort of thing again). For various reasons – including, no doubt, Chateaubriand's desire to disguise the loyalty he continued to feel for at least a year or two toward this compromising text – they were not incorporated into the republication of 1826.[14] De Staël's *De l'Allemagne* presents another interesting variation: the original edition of 1810 had been quite heavily blue-penciled by the imperial censors before being simply banned and destroyed. One set of proofs was saved, which allowed a new edition to be printed in London in 1813. In this edition, which restored the censored pages, the notes serve basically to specify what had been suppressed and to spell out the passages that an impulse of preemptive self-censorship had made too allusive. This response to censorship may indeed, I think, count as one way of responding to criticism.

Discursive texts: delayed notes

The delayed note, it seems, is a slightly more canonical and more fertile genre. It may be restricted to biographical and genetic information, which we should not necessarily always take for gospel truth: such is more or less the case of the notes known by the initials I.F. which Wordsworth dictated to Isabella Fenwick in 1843 apropos of *Lyrical Ballads*. But as with the delayed preface, the most obvious function of delayed notes is to review one's past, half-critically and half-compassionately. Here again we come across the *Essai sur les révolutions*, whose 1826 apparatus is probably the model of the genre. Chateaubriand is severe toward formal errors (inaccuracies, anglicisms, obscurities, digressions), toward defects in attitude (excesses of every kind, arrogance and self-importance, unwarranted liberties, "a young man's presumptuousness," an unhappy adolescent's misanthropy, the youthful flaunting of various abilities), and especially, of course, toward fundamental mistakes: the work's absurd system of comparison between antiquity and modern France, its shallow irreligiousness in the tradition of Rousseau and the *philosophes*, its excessive

---

[14] Conversely, it is to bring this loyalty to the surface that Sainte-Beuve publishes the bulk of them in 1861 in his edition (Garnier) of Chateaubriand's *Œuvres complètes*.

indulgence toward the Jacobins, its confusion between liberty and democracy, its failure to grasp the political superiority of constitutional monarchy. But he is also happy to recognize in certain textual details the basic continuity of thought he has already mentioned in his preface: the substratum of attraction to Christianity and of political liberalism ("a permanent feature of my opinions"); and to note here and there signs, or promises, of intellectual and literary excellence ("I would write this still"; "Good: away from my system, I am rational again") and of precocious proficiencies (in law, in economics) that he will rejoice in throughout his life. In essence, the *Essai*'s "mass of contra-dictions" does not put him too much to shame, and this slightly muddleheaded text – like, on another level, the famous manu-script of *Les Natchez* – is seen as providing the "raw material from which I drew a part of the ideas I have spread among my other writings" (Pléiade 257). In short, if the child, as we know, is father to the man, reciprocally it is as a father that the adult judges the child he was: "From a wholly paternal weakness, I was ready to pardon myself for these remarks" (259).

Renowned in their own way, Lanson's delayed notes (1909 and 1912) to the *Histoire de la littérature française* (1894) display a less complex retrospection: they are essentially, as described in their foreword, "notes of repentance or conversion," bearing on the assessment of one or another work. Accordingly, Lanson con-siders himself – after the event – too harsh on the art of the *trouvères*, or the *chansons de geste*; "Today I would no longer dare say" that Rabelais is not profound; "the more I read Montaigne," the more I do him justice; the same for Montesquieu, for Voltaire (having no head for metaphysics has become a kind of virtue), for Hugo, for Zola: these are all reevaluations that illustrate fairly well the leftward ideological shift with which we are familiar, a shift solemnized by the way Voltaire and Rousseau are reconciled in the republican pantheon. "There is no need for us to keep fighting their war in our minds": as was said in Lanson's day when the Republic had triumphed, the time had come to take the eighteenth century as a unit.

Nor would we expect to find Valéry displaying toward his youthful essays the same kind of dramatic contrast in attitude that Chateaubriand had displayed toward his. The 1931 notes to Valéry's *Introduction à la méthode de Léonard de Vinci* show above all a maturation and a concern with clarifying his thought.[15] He repudiates just about none of his youthful intuitions and is anxious even to confirm the most provocative ones, which in their day were thought scandalous (that "enthusiasm is not a state of mind for a writer," that Pascal "wasted hours sewing papers into his pockets, at a time when he might have honored France by discovering the infinitesimal calculus" – "where would mankind be if all the others of equal talent had followed his example?"). But he generally finds their expression regrettably obscure and very *fin de siècle*. He therefore tries to gloss certain passages in simpler and more transparent terms: "I didn't find the right word, I meant ...," "In reality, ..." "That is, ..." "Today I should write ...," "What I wished to designate ..." The exercise is exemplary and, all in all, fairly typical of a common evolution, which takes the writer (see Borges) from recondite and flamboyant beginnings to a maturity that is more classical and endeavors to be limpid.

Texts of fiction

Whether original, later, or delayed, the authorial annotation of a text of fiction or poetry, by dint of its discursive nature, unavoidably marks a break in the enunciative regime – a break that justifies our assigning it to the paratext.[16] Even so, we must specify that this type of note, quite obviously rarer than the preceding type, is still used most often with texts whose fictionality is very "impure," very conspicuous for its historical references or sometimes for its philosophical reflections: novels or poems whose notes for the most part bear precisely on the nonfictional aspect of the narrative. A typical case is the *Waverley Novels*: here the notes, whether original or added in the Cadell edition, always play a corroborative role, adducing both testi-

---

[15] These are marginal notes in an autograph facsimile for Sagittaire's reissue of the entire group of Valéry's texts on Leonardo, which date from 1895, 1919, and, for the letter-preface to Ferrero, 1929. The layout in the Pléiade edition, incidentally, is a good example of marginal notes without a system of callouts [these notes are set in the outside column of each page, in italics, alongside the passages on which they comment].

[16] I will not consider here the case – which we often have in Borges (*Tlon, Menard, Babel*) – of notes that are assigned to fictional texts presented in the form of essays or critical reviews: except for their fictionality, these notes have the same regime as "ordinary" notes.

mony and supporting documents. The same role is played by the
notes in Hugo's *Han d'Islande*, *Bug-Jargal*, and *Notre-Dame de Paris*
and by those in other historical novels of the nineteenth century
(historical novels in our century more often forgo notes – but see,
however, the notes in Tournier's *Roi des aulnes*). And we find
notes playing this role even as far back as the eighteenth century,
with the very numerous and sometimes very copious notes in La
Ceppède's *Théorèmes* (a recounting in 315 sonnets of the Passion
and Resurrection of Christ, obviously based on the Gospel); here
the system of "historical" references is supplemented with a
scrupulous apparatus of theological commentaries, which are
comparable to the doctrinal paraphrases of the mystical poems of
Saint John of the Cross. For example, for sonnet 37 there is a
twenty-five-page explanation of the word *agonie* [death throes].
Less obtrusive is Eliot's annotation of *The Waste Land*, which also,
for the most part, bears on the bookish sources – from the Bible to
Wagner by way of *The Golden Bough* and Jessie Weston's *From
Ritual to Romance* – of this poem, which is "historical" in its own
way (history of the Fisher King) and stuffed with various
allusions and borrowings. Eliot no doubt preferred to produce
these himself, rather than face critical reproach. Authorial notes
are harder to find in texts of "pure" poetry, poetry without a
historical foundation or background. Coleridge's notes to the
Ancient Mariner, relatively delayed (1817) and apparently introduced to clarify a narrative intention that Wordsworth had
deemed confused, are not really notes but rather kinds of
marginal intertitles announcing the successive episodes of the
narrative. Saint-John Perse's notes for the Pléiade edition of his
works are obviously delayed and (a bit like Wordsworth's I. F.
notes) more documentary than interpretive: they include information about the circumstances of the writing, references, quoted
allographic commentaries, excerpts from letters.[17]

I am not really aware of any examples of authorial notes in plays.
The well-known "It is a scoundrel who says this" in *Tartuffe*
[4.5.1487] is presented in every respect as a stage direction, and I

---

[17] In this example, which is unique so far (and I hope it will not set a fashion, for
in its arbitrary censorings and choices it may very well prevent a true critical
edition for a long time to come), the notes are at one and the same time written
in the third person (pseudo-allographic) and attributed (p. xliii) to the author.

see no reason to credit that category in general to the account of
the paratext. Dramatic texts are normally made up of two
registers: "dialogue," which is spoken on the stage by the actors,
and stage directions, or *didascalies*, which are carried out (more or
less faithfully) by the actors and director, and the text of which
appears literally only when the play is read. The "note" in
Tartuffe, which evidently serves as commentary, is nonetheless
provided – in parentheses between two lines of verse – as a
direction for the actor: please deliver this monologue in such a
way that the public clearly perceives the speaker to be a scoundrel and not the gentleman and truly pious person he claims to
be.[18]

This note, then, is not one, but I evoke it because Stendhal often
used it as a formal model for the notes in his novels, notes whose
basic aim was to clear the author, ironically or not, of responsibility for the behavior and opinions of his characters: "It is a
malcontent who says this," "It is a Jacobin speaking" (Julien, in
the *Rouge*), "a passionate individual" (Fabrice, in the *Chartreuse*),
"a republican," "a Jacobin," "a conceited person" (in the margins
of *Leuwen*), "He will mend his ways" (Octave, in *Armance*). Other
notes are more historical in type, for no novel by Stendhal is
"pure fiction" – and one note in the *Rouge* apropos of something
M. de Rênal says even specifies eloquently: "Historical." Finally,
others, which are very personal and generally cryptic, strike one
as having been printed inadvertently – I am not claiming that
they were, but at least they are formulated as if they were.[19]

The notion of "pure fiction," a term I use loosely in quotation
marks, undoubtedly does not mean much until we clarify it
somewhat, but this is not the place. Let us say more simply that
historical and geographical references[20] are more or less present

[18] On the question – too rarely taken up – of stage directions, see M. Issacharoff,
"Texte théâtral et didascalecture," in *Le Spectacle du discours* (Corti, 1985). But
we lack a study of the oral stage directions authors give actors during
rehearsals – directions that must surely be recorded here and there. We know,
for example, that Beckett never gives his characters psychological motivations
and that once he got upset with an actor who gestured toward the sky while
uttering the name of Godot.
[19] See my "Stendhal," *Figures II* (Seuil, 1969), 170 [tr. "Stendhal," in *Figures of
Literary Discourse*, trans. Alan Sheridan (New York: Columbia University Press,
1982), 160]; cf. C. W. Thompson, "Expression et conventions typographiques:
Les notes en bas de page chez Stendhal," in *La Création romanesque chez Stendhal*
(Droz, 1985).
[20] Or technical ones: see the thirty-four notes, almost all of them medical, by John

depending on the novel in question, and that, between *Ivanhoe* at one extreme and, say, Gide's *Porte étroite* or Beckett's *Molloy* at the other, *Le Rouge et le noir*, *Le Père Goriot*, and *Madame Bovary* obviously belong in an intermediary zone. The more a novel gets clear of its historical background, the more the authorial note may seem peculiar or transgressive, a referential pistol-shot during the fictional concert. Thus, Fielding's notes in *Tom Jones* seem justified when they provide historical or philological explanations, references, or translations of quotations in the text. They are more surprising when – in digressions comparable to those in the introductory chapters of all the books – they introduce an opinion the author holds about some particular point of manners. And they are more surprising still when they admit to some uncertainty about what is in a character's mind ("[Sophia] mean[t], perhaps, ..." [bk. 6, ch. 5]), contrary to the commitment to omniscience displayed in the narrative – or perhaps contrary to the identity, in theory, between author and narrator, inasmuch as such a note suggests that the former, who is responsible for the note, knows less than the latter, who is responsible for the narrative. A reverse dissociation is introduced by a note in Beckett's *Watt* where the author seems to correct a narrator from whom, until then, he had not been differentiated in any way: "The figures given here are incorrect. The consequent calculations are therefore doubly erroneous." In Gide's *Isabelle*, a similar clarification ("Gérard is mistaken; the beak of the *Phoenicopterus antiquorum* is not spatula-shaped") does not in the least produce this effect of metalepsis, for "Gérard" is an intradiegetic narrator, from the very beginning distinct from the extradiegetic author-narrator who is responsible for the note, as when Sterne contradicts or corrects Tristram Shandy.

To sum up: in all of these authorial notes in fiction we find a great many documentary supplements and very few authorial comments. One could imagine a more emancipated regime in which the note would no longer come under the heading of this documentary type of discourse but would be narrative in type and would – in itself and for its own account – pursue some

Irving for *The Cider House Rules*; or theoretical ones: in *The Kiss of the Spider Woman*, Manuel Puig inserts a half-dozen notes on the various explanations for homosexuality.

momentary fork in the narrative. Valéry, complaining about the overly servile linearity of fictional narratives, may have unwittingly given us the possible formula for this other type of note: "Perhaps it would be interesting, *just once*, to write a work which at each juncture would show the diversity of solutions that can present themselves to the mind and from which *it chooses* the unique sequel to be found in the text. To do this would be to substitute for the illusion of a unique scheme which imitates reality that of the *possible-at-each-moment*, which I think more truthful."[21] I am not aware of any actual notes illustrating this possibility.[22] The long note in *Echange* mentioned early in this chapter – and many other of Renaud Camus's notes – might seem to come close, but what we have here is instead a definitive fork (a text that is evenly and symmetrically bifid from page 173 on) and it somewhat exceeds the localized status a note ordinarily has (in the same way, the "log" that runs at the bottom of the pages of Derrida's *Parages* is not, despite its position, a local note but is clearly an appendage to the text as a whole). And above all, Camus's text is itself not purely narrative enough -- rather, it mixes narrative and essay – to satisfy our hypothesis. What would satisfy it best would still be the pretexts of a Flaubert or a Proust, where here and there we see the narrative setting out along a path, then abandoning it and returning to the point of bifurcation. Such effects, of course, are artifacts of genetic excavation, but nothing prohibits us from expecting them to reverberate, in one way or another, on practices to come. In any case, the fact remains that this way of using notes has more to do with managing the text than with laying down a paratext.[23]

21 *Œuvres*, Pléiade 1:1467 [tr. "Memoirs of a Poem," in *The Art of Poetry*, trans. Denise Folliot, vol. 7 of *The Collected Works of Paul Valéry*, Bollingen series (New York: Pantheon, 1958), 104].

22 On various deviant or playful aspects of notes in Perec, see V. Colonna, "Fausses notes," *Cahiers Georges Perec* 1 (POL, 1985).

23 We learn from a letter to L. de Robert in July 1913 that Proust had fleetingly contemplated relegating to the notes what he looked on as "tedious passages" in his text: "Send me a line and let me know if the idea of putting some tedious passages into notes (which would make the volume shorter) is a bad one (I think it is)." Such a course would undoubtedly have produced a text in two narrative registers, unless the "tedious passages" in question were generally discursive kinds of passages.

Allographic notes

The allographic note is almost inevitably an editorial note, for the addition of notes far exceeds what an author may expect (or wish) from the kindness of an ordinary third party – which hardly goes beyond a preface. The production of an apparatus of allographic notes is, as a matter of fact, along with establishment of the text, what defines the editorial function.[24]

Solely because it is allographic, the editorial note draws us toward another fringe of the paratext, for it consists of an external commentary (most often posthumous) that in no way involves the responsibility of the author. Still, this picture has to be qualified, for the vogue of scholarly editions has recently produced, for example, anthumous Pléiades that, as such, are established with the help (and are therefore to some degree under the control) of the author being pléiadized. For example, Julien Green participated in Jacques Petit's editorial work "with constant and congenial attentiveness. [Green] allowed me to consult his manuscripts and gave me a great many details and clarifications, which have enriched this work" (note to the introduction). We find a similar degree of cooperation in at least the early Giono volumes, in the preparation for the Sartre, and perhaps even more in the Char – every possible degree, therefore, between the strictly allographic posthumous edition and self-pléiadization à la Saint-John Perse, and therefore between an apparatus of notes consisting simply of critical and historical commentary entered into the peritext and a purely authorial paratext.

I shall not inflate this chapter unduly with a "theory" of the editorial note after having stated as a principle that this note falls outside the definition of the paratext. I wish simply to repeat that this practice goes back to the Middle Ages and that posterity has remembered at least one more-than-respectable monument to the genre: the *Commentaire de Corneille* by Voltaire, who in 1764 appointed himself editor of Corneille's œuvre to

[24] [The French word *éditeur* means both "editor" and "publisher," and in the text at this point, after specifying that here *éditoriale* is to be taken in the first sense of the term, the author continues: "There can never be enough complaints about the confusion the French language maintains between the two meanings (*editor/publisher*) of the word *éditeur*, but there will always be illiterate Academicians to uphold the position that French is a perfect language and should not be messed with."]

help "satisfactorily establish the descendant of that great man."[25] What we find here, typically, are notes of evaluative commentary: Voltaire emphasizes achievements, indicates obsolete turns of phrase, and criticizes improprieties, implausibilities, inconsistencies, defective transitions between scenes, scenes without action, multiplicity of actions (as in *Horace*), errors of language and style. Voltaire's is a very representative expression of the taste and dramaturgical doctrine of classicism; his main grievance – here stripped of d'Aubignac's pettiness – is the "coldness" of some baroque contrivances. Voltaire speaks here like Boileau finding fault with Saint-Amant: "In the examinations of his plays, after *Théodore* and *Pertharite* [both failures], Corneille always assumes some small defect that damaged his works; and he always forgets that what kills them is lifelessness, which is the greatest defect" (this is apropos of *Don Sanche d'Aragon*); and again, apropos of *Nicomède*, this, which is a perfect match for the Corneillean aesthetic: "Admiration barely moves the soul, does not arouse it. Of all the feelings, admiration is the one that cools off most quickly."

I have emphasized this commentary because it also represents a type of annotation that latter-day critical editions have more or less abandoned in favor of a much more objective type, ideally rid of evaluation and limited to the function of providing clarification (encyclopedic and linguistic) and information – information about the history and establishment of the text, with presentation of pre-texts and variants; about sources; and (by way of quotations from the private epitext) about the author's own assessments or interpretations. The relative proportions of these several functions naturally vary, depending not only on the period during which the edition is published (in the early twentieth century, some Classiques Garnier editions still gave stylistic, psychological, or moralizing assessment more than its due) but also on the intended public and therefore the type of series (clarification and information are more emphatic in textbook editions, more restrained in scholarly ones), the type of text (Balzac lends himself more to historical commentary, Proust to

---

[25] Voltaire's commentary was expanded in 1774. It bears on all of Corneille's plays starting with *Médée*, on the three *Discours*, and sometimes on the examinations and dedications. The "descendant" of Corneille whom Voltaire took up was in reality a more distant relative.

genetic information), and the editor's inclination (some recent Pléiade editions still – or again – devote much space to interpretation, whether psychoanalytic or other). But the most pronounced trend leads to a spectacular enrichment of the genetic aspect: as many pre-texts as possible are included, in response to the educated public's growing curiosity about the "making" of the text and about the unearthing of versions the author had abandoned. In this way, critical editions paradoxically (and I will come back to this) help blur the notion of text.

Actorial notes

The (authentic) actorial note is obviously a variety of the allographic note, but a very distinctive variety: even if it does not, strictly speaking, bear any stamp of the authorial (except perhaps the indirect sanction bestowed by the author's having generally solicited it in principle and accepted it in detail), it takes on a highly unsettling type of authority – the authority not of the author but of his subject, who is himself often an author. Examples of this kind of situation are not very numerous,[26] but the forty-five notes Malraux added to Gaétan Picon's study *Malraux par lui-même* are a striking illustration of the genre, although Malraux's remarks most often are not very closely connected to Picon's text. When he happens to indicate agreement or disagreement, or more generally – apropos of Balzac, Dickens, or Dostoevsky – when he expresses himself about his aesthetics of the novel, he provides Picon's study with a second-degree commentary that, if you like, falls within the province of ordinary metatext (an allographic one, for Malraux is not Picon), but a metatext that is indeed intimidating, for what it deals with is Malraux: a point of view whose authority is certainly easy to challenge (we remember that Valéry, on a like occasion, took care not to exercise such authority) but hard to disregard. We have there, from within and as if *en abyme*, a kind of "unbypassable" paratextual agent. Furthermore, of course, the remarks in question belong fully to the paratext, and now we're talking not about Picon's, but Malraux's. The Picon study that concerns him and

[26] We call attention to Matisse's notes for Aragon's *Henri Matisse, Roman*, and to Aragon's own notes for D. Bougnoux's study *"Blanche ou L'oubli" d'Aragon* (Hachette, 1973).

interrogates him, not without getting a response, thus ends up functioning as a "conversation" between Malraux and Picon.

Fictional notes

By *fictional*, we should remember, I mean not the serious authentic notes that may accompany a work of fiction but, for a text that may or may not be fictional, notes whose sender himself is, on some ground, fictional: disavowing, fictive, or apocryphal.

The disavowing, or pseudo-editorial, authorial note is a fully classic genre and, from Rousseau's *Nouvelle Héloïse* to Sartre's *Nausée*, is particularly well illustrated in epistolary novels or novels in the form of journals. As in fictional prefaces, in fictional notes the author presents himself as an editor, responsible in detail for establishing and managing the text he claims to have taken or been given custody of. Rousseau, Laclos, Senancour, Bernanos, Sartre, and others thus mention supposed gaps in the text[27] and the deletions or restorations for which they accept responsibility, explain allusions, supply references for quotations, and ensure – by the use of recalls and announcements – the reader's perception of the text's coherence, behaving in a way that obviously simulates allographic commentary. Rousseau definitely carries this commenting function further than anyone else – further in quantity (more than 150 notes) and in density, unrestrainedly interpreting and appraising the conduct, feelings, opinions, and style of his characters, having his say on their native country, their language, their customs, their religion, and so forth. Here the note becomes the place and medium for what elsewhere would be the narratorial-authorial discourse, a discourse that the epistolary form shuts Rousseau off from – unless he were to make one of his heroes his spokesman, which he abstains from doing much more than people generally assume. It is a place and a medium, then, for "author's intrusions." Stendhal will remember it, but without giving himself the editorial pretext.

The fictive authorial note, as Walter Scott uses it under cover of

---

[27] Sometimes Rousseau, fortified by the overtly fictional nature of his role as editor, plays shamelessly with this type of function: "One sees that several intervening letters are missing here as well as in many other places. The reader will say that a writer gets out of difficulty quite easily with such omissions, and I am completely of his opinion" (letter v-6).

his imagined authors, presents no distinctive functional characteristic, for the disguised author merely attributes to his loaner
name, Cleishbotham and other Templetons, a documentary apparatus exactly like the one he takes responsibility for elsewhere as
"the author of *Waverley*." The fictive allographic note is more
interesting but, strictly speaking, except for the identity of the
enunciator, it takes us back to the disavowing pseudo-editorial
function. For example, in *Les Bêtises*,[28] the apparatus of notes (like
the set of prefaces and postfaces) that accompanies the texts of
the anonymous fictive author is attributed to a certain A.B., who
in this way is distinguished from [the real author] Jacques
Laurent but takes on the same functions that Rousseau does in
Héloïse, or Senancour in *Oberman* – functions that Laurent
himself, therefore, could just as easily take on in this book. The
investment in the fiction of the allographic note-writer would, in
one sense, be stronger in an openly satirical simulation such as
the one Reboux and Muller produced in their pastiche of Racine
(*Cléopastre*),[29] an apocryphal text accompanied by fictive allographic notes attributed to the pen of "Mr. Dragonfly, a third-rate
teacher at the high school in provincial Romorantin." This is a
juicy caricature of textbook annotation as it still (or already) was
being practiced in that *fin de siècle*. Dwelling on it here would be
unwise, for one is always oneself a little more Dragonfly than one
might wish, so instead I briefly call to mind the presence amid
the throng of another caricature, one no less sarcastic but
certainly considerably more accomplished as a literary achievement: the commentary in notes to John Shade's poem provided
by Shade's nuisance of a colleague and neighbor, Charles
Kinbote, in *Pale Fire*. This commentary, as we know, furnishes the
essence of what indeed ends up constituting a kind of novel,
despite Kinbote's disavowals. "I have no desire," he says, "to
twist and batter an unambiguous *apparatus criticus* into the
monstrous semblance of a novel." In reality, of course, what we
have is a novel in the form of a monstrous semblance, or cruel
caricature, of an *apparatus criticus*. Having failed to get John
Shade to use his (Kinbote's) history, real or mythical, as the

[28] [*Les Bêtises* has four parts, or texts, some of which have prefaces and some of
which have postfaces.]
[29] [The authors' three volumes of pastiches, called *A la manière de* ..., appeared
between 1908 and 1913.]

subject of Shade's poem and having acquired the manuscript after Shade's death, Kinbote tries, half-veraciously and half-mendaciously, to force upon the poem a commentary that relates as many details as possible to himself, his native land, his fate – so much so as to ultimately make *Pale Fire* a kind of indirect, allusive, or cryptic narrative of his experiences. A perfect example of textual appropriation, this *apparatus* is also an exemplary staging of the abusiveness and paranoia always found in any interpretive commentary, supported by the unlimited submissiveness of any text to any hermeneutic, however unscrupulous the latter may be. I am not sure but what some truths, since then, may have been stranger than that fiction.

I have little to say about fictive actorial notes, generally attributed to a narrator-character, as are two or three in *Tristram Shandy* (apropos of Tristram's father); they simply give this narrator a wholly plausible authorial function – were it not that in this novel they interfere with the notes that Laurence Sterne, for his part, assumes responsibility for. Still to be written are more heavily fictional notes, those attributed to a non-narrating character, such as the ones that a Julien Sorel or an Emma Bovary might sign with their initials saying what they think of the text by Stendhal or Flaubert. The notes in chapter 10 of *Finnegans Wake* are apparently of this type, but that text is too impenetrable for me to get involved in commenting on its paratext. Besides, are we really dealing there with a paratext? Here again, the semblance of notes obviously is part of the fiction – and therefore, indirectly, of the text.[30]

As we see, therefore, the note is a fairly elusive and receding element of the paratext. Some types, such as later or delayed authorial notes, do indeed fulfill a paratextual function, that of providing defensive commentary or autocriticism. Other types, such as original notes to discursive texts, instead constitute modulations of the text and are scarcely more distinct from it than a phrase within parentheses or between dashes would be.

---

[30] Among the *curiosa* offered by a certain pathology – deliberate or not – of the note, my attention is drawn to *Mulligan Stew* by Gilbert Sorrentino, one chapter of which displays a conspicuous lack of connection between text and notes. Sometimes, too, a typesetter's or proofreader's goof systematically shifts an entire apparatus of notes off kilter. In all these cases, the burden of making sense of the happenstance falls on the reader.

Fictional notes, under cover of a more or less satirical simulation of a paratext, contribute to the fiction of the text except when they constitute that fiction through and through, such as those of *Pale Fire*. As for allographic notes, they slip out the other side of the paratext: this time not the side turned toward the text, but the side turned toward the critical metatext, of which they are, as I have said, only a kind of peritextual appendage, always potentially reconvertible into autonomous commentary. This is the case with Voltaire's notes on Corneille, which are nowadays separated from their booster text and have a status hardly distinct from that of Voltaire's remarks on Pascal in the twenty-fifth philosophical letter [in *Lettres philosophiques*] – remarks that have obviously never been notes for an edition of the *Pensées*.

This situation, I must make clear, is not at all paradoxical, and still less is it perplexing: if the paratext is an often indefinite fringe between text and off-text, the note – which, depending on type, belongs to one or the other or lies between the two – perfectly illustrates this indefiniteness and this slipperiness. But above all, we must not forget that the very notion of paratext, like many other notions, has more to do with a decision about method than with a truly established fact. "The paratext," properly speaking, does not *exist*; rather, one chooses to *account in these terms* for a certain number of practices or effects, for reasons of method and effectiveness or, if you will, of profitability. The question is therefore not whether the note does or does not "belong" to the paratext but really whether considering it in such a light is or is not useful and relevant. The answer very clearly is, as it often is, that that depends on the case – or rather (and this constitutes a great step forward in the rational description of facts) that that depends on the *type* of note. This conclusion, at least, will perhaps justify in the long run (with regular use) a typology that at first glance is cumbersome.

13

❖❖❖

The public epitext

❖❖❖

Definitions

The criterion distinguishing the epitext from the peritext – that is (according to our conventions), distinguishing the epitext from all the rest of the paratext – is in theory purely spatial. The epitext is any paratextual element not materially appended to the text within the same volume but circulating, as it were, freely, in a virtually limitless physical and social space. The location of the epitext is therefore anywhere outside the book – but of course nothing precludes its later admission to the peritext. Such admission is always possible, and we will encounter many examples of it: see the original interviews appended to posthumous scholarly editions, or the innumerable excerpts from correspondence or diaries quoted in the critical notes of such scholarly editions. This purely spatial definition, however, has some pragmatic and functional repercussions. When an author, such as Proust for *Du côté de chez Swann*, chooses to present his work (here, the beginning of his work) by way of an interview rather than a preface, he no doubt has a reason for making such a choice, and in any case his choice leads to these kinds of effects: reaching a broader public than the public of first readers, but also sending this public a message that is constitutively more ephemeral, destined to disappear when its monitory function is fulfilled, whereas a preface would stay attached to the text at least until deleted upon publication of a second edition, if any. Proust thus utilizes the medium of the newspaper for an interim advertising effect comparable to that of Balzac's provisional prefaces – comparable, but not identical: one could weigh all the ins and outs of the functional advantages and disadvantages of such a choice, as Proust conceivably (but not demonstrably) did.

Anywhere outside the book may be, for example, newspapers

344

and magazines, radio or television programs, lectures and colloquia, all public performances perhaps preserved on recordings or
in printed collections: interviews and conversations assembled by
the author (Barthes: *Le Grain de la voix*) or by the intermediary
(Raymond Bellour: *Le Livre des autres*), proceedings of colloquia,
collections of autocommentary (Tournier: *Le Vent Paraclet*). Anywhere outside the book may also be the statements contained in
an author's correspondence or journal, perhaps intended for later
publication, either anthumous or posthumous.

The temporal occasions of the epitext are as varied as those of
the peritext: they may be preceding (private or public statements
about an author's plans and the genesis of his work), original
(interviews granted when a book comes out, lectures, inscriptions),[1] or later or delayed (conversations, colloquia, spontaneous
and autonomous autocommentaries of every kind). The sender is
most often the author, aided or not by one or several interlocutors, relayed or not by a an intermediary, professional or not. But
the sender may equally well be the publisher (I will come to this)
or some *authorized* third party, as in the case of more or less
"inspired" reviews – those in the "more" category possibly even
being pseudo-allographic apocrypha. In all these instances the
addressee is never only the reader (of the text) but is some form
of the public, including perhaps nonreaders of the text: the public
for a newspaper or for one of the other media, the audience at a
lecture, the participants in a colloquium, the addressee(s) of a
letter or of a spoken confidence – indeed, in the case of the
journal, the author himself.

As we saw for the peritext, these various temporal and
pragmatic characteristics offer us a principle of functional typology. I will distinguish essentially the following categories of
epitext: *publisher's, semiofficial allographic, public authorial,* and
private authorial, without prejudicing some finer gradations that
we will come to in due course. But before discussing the several
categories, I have three preliminary observations to make. The
first is that the epitext – in contrast to the peritext – consists of a
group of discourses whose function is not always basically
paratextual (that is, to present and comment on the text), whereas
the more or less unchanging regime of the peritext is constitu-

---

[1] [Inscriptions, of course, have been discussed as part of the peritext (Chapter 6).
Their assignment to the epitext is explained on page 380.]

tively and exclusively inseparable from its paratextual function. Many a conversation bears less on the author's work than on his life, his origins, his habits, the people he encounters and frequents (for example, *other* authors) – indeed, bears on any other external subject explicitly put forth as a topic of conversation: the political situation, music, money, sports, women, cats, or dogs; and a writer's correspondence or journal is sometimes very sparing of comments on his work. Instead, therefore, we must look on these various exercises as occasions capable of furnishing us with paratextual scraps (sometimes of prime interest), though they must often be sought with a magnifying glass or caught with rod and line: here once again, we are dealing with a paratextual *effect* (rather than function).

The second remark, with an opposite emphasis, is that the epitext is a whole whose paratextual function has no precise limits and in which comment on the work is endlessly diffused in a biographical, critical, or other discourse whose relation to the work may be at best indirect and at worst indiscernible. Everything a writer says or writes about his life, about the world around him, about the works of others, may have paratextual relevance – including, therefore, both his critical œuvre (that of a Baudelaire, a James, a Proust, for example) and his allographic paratext (Mallarmé's preface to Ghil's *Traité du verbe* or Proust's preface to Morand's *Tendres Stocks*, as we have already seen). If our study of the note made us aware of the paratext's lack of internal borders, our study of the epitext confronts us with its lack of external limits: the epitext, a fringe of the fringe, gradually disappears into, among other things, the totality of the authorial discourse. Our use of the word and concept will unavoidably be more restrictive, and in a way more timid, but we would do well to bear in mind this potential for indefinite diffusion.

A last precaution: whereas on many occasions we have noted the relative neglect accorded the peritext by the literary world (including specialists), the situation of the epitext is obviously very different. Critics and literary historians have long made extensive use of the epitext in commenting on works – as evidenced, for example, by the systematic recourse to correspondence in the genetic notes of scholarly editions. In this sense, the study I now present will be less off the beaten track than those presented in previous chapters. A good reason, perhaps, to dispatch this one more quickly.

The publisher's epitext

I will not dwell on the publisher's epitext: its basically marketing and "promotional" function does not always involve the responsibility of the author in a very meaningful way; most often he is satisfied just to close his eyes officially to the value-inflating hyperbole inseparable from the needs of trade. What we are talking about here are posters, advertisements, press releases and other prospectuses (such as the one in 1842 for *La Comédie humaine*[2] – an ancestor of our please-insert), periodical bulletins addressed to booksellers, and "promotional dossiers" for the use of sales reps. Our media-oriented era will no doubt see other props exploited, and publishers' commercials have already been heard and seen on radio and television. Sometimes an author may participate in this type of production, undoubtedly in proportion to his professionalism and savoir faire – a Balzac, a Hugo, a Zola, to stay with past examples. But he does so anonymously and in the capacity (a paradoxical one, if you like) of assistant to the publisher, in such a circumstance writing texts for which he would no doubt refuse to accept responsibility and which express less his own mind than what he thinks the publisher's discourse ought to be. Here, therefore, consensus between author and publisher is still the rule, but history has left us some exceptional traces of disagreement. For example, after the Belgian publisher Lacroix deemed it necessary, in a press release put into *Le Temps*, to describe *Les Travailleurs de la mer* as "the most undisputed work by Victor Hugo," the latter, whose relations with his publishers were always marked by the most punctilious exactness, deemed it necessary to protest a superlative he judged inopportune. Writing on January 27, 1869, to Verboekhoven, Lacroix's associate, Hugo said: "Be good enough on my behalf to tell M. Lacroix, who evidently issued this clever advertisement, that in France it is not customary for a publisher himself to state that the author he publishes is more or less disputed. Tell him that paying to make such a statement is more than naive."

[2] See Pléiade 1:1109.

347

The semiofficial allographic epitext

The category of semiofficial allographic (that is, allography more or less "authorized" by some authorial assent or even inspiration) is much less clear-cut and indisputable in the epitext than in the peritext: in the epitext, there is nothing as open as the author's acceptance of an allographic preface, even though this acceptance is not always the sign of a complete identity of views. What would most resemble this acceptance would perhaps, sometimes, be the publication of a critical study under the logo of the author's usual publisher: Siegfried Unseld wrote somewhere that Hermann Hesse had once told him that he preferred to have critical studies of his works published by Suhrkamp [Hesse's own publisher] to ensure a certain standard and to make them seem from an outsider's perspective to be placed under the aegis of the works' publisher. Here the publisher's aegis is certainly an indirect form of authorial backing. We know that this would have been the effect created for Bruce Morrissette's study of Robbe-Grillet [the study was published by Robbe-Grillet's own publisher] – that is, Morrissette's study would have seemed to have Robbe-Grillet's backing – if Robbe-Grillet had not taken care to undercut the effect by asking Roland Barthes for the preface I have already mentioned [Chapter 10, note 37]; although very courteous, the preface clearly contradicted Morrissette's thesis.

Most often, the semiofficial epitext takes the form of a critical article that is somewhat "remote-controlled" by authorial instructions that the public is not in a position to know about, except from some posthumous disclosure. It is sometimes said that Mme de La Fayette had a lot to do with the anonymous study (attributed subsequently to the abbé de Charnes) *Conversation sur la critique de la Princesse de Clèves*, a book responding to Valincour's criticisms; but her involvement has not been confirmed. At the other extreme, it is known that Stendhal himself wrote and published (in *Débats* under cover of anonymity) a laudatory article on his *Histoire de la peinture en Italie* and another one (in the *Paris Monthly Review* and elliptically signed S.) on his *De l'amour*. The second piece stands out as a skillful balance of praise (for the book's profundity, innovation, accuracy, liveliness) and undoubtedly sincere criticism (there are too many ellipses, obscurity from the omission of "intermediary ideas"). Drafts of two other unpublished Stendhal puff pieces in the same spirit have also been found: "Never dull except when he is obscure. Bold ellipses often cause his style to lapse into this defect." We are especially familiar with the famous "Letter to Salvagnoli" of October or November 1832, a letter sent to this Italian journalist to (abundantly) jog his memory for an article on *Le Rouge et le noir* to appear in the review *Antologia* – an article that never did appear, perhaps because Salvagnoli did not deign to go along with the scheme. This "letter" is therefore a kind of aborted (pseudo-allographic) apocrypha, but in the state in which the text has come down to us it is above all a wonderful example of autocommentary for the specific use of a certain public, in this case the Italian public: the *Rouge* is presented as a picture of French manners since the Restoration in which provincial moralism favorable to "love from the heart" (Mme de Rênal) is contrasted with Parisian shallowness begetting "love from the head" (Mathilde de la Môle).

The publication of *Du côté de chez Swann* was greeted by a series of articles that were very ... friendly, signed Maurice Rostand, Jean de Pierrefeu, Lucien Daudet, or Jacques-Emile Blanche. Nothing in these articles lets us gauge the extent to which they reflect the author's suggestions, but we know that Blanche's article pleased Proust so much that he himself wrote several promotional items to draw attention to it and that he pressured Jacques Rivière at length (and in vain) to have the *Nouvelle Revue française* (NRF) remind readers of the article's existence. A letter to Calmette dated November 12, 1913, provides a good example of a Proustian attempt to inspire: "If you were to do an item on [*Swann*], I would like the epithets *refined* and *delicate* not to be included, nor the reminder of *Les Plaisirs et les jours*. [*Swann*] is a work of power, at least that's its ambition." Proust provides the same guidance in a letter to Robert de Flers at about the same time with an eye to a notice (the same one?) that was to appear in *Le Figaro* of November 16: "The thing to say is that it's ... a novel full of passion and meditation and landscapes all at the same time. And especially that it's very different from *Les Plaisirs et les jours* and is neither *delicate* nor *refined*."[3] As early

---

[3] This letter seems to be contradicted by another one, written on December 18 to André Beaunier, in which Proust, complaining about criticism that does not show much understanding, adds: "That's why articles give so little pleasure. I

as September, offering to place a possible article by Lucien Daudet in the papers, Proust specified very revealingly: "No one is more authorized than you."

Gide's journal for July 12, 1914, contains a curious entry, consisting of the copy of a letter to André Beaunier, who was supposed to write a review of *Les Caves du Vatican* for the *Revue des deux mondes*. In this letter, Gide gives his correspondent and future critic the gist of an abandoned preface, stressing the simultaneity of conception and the thematic complementarity of *Caves*, *L'Immoraliste*, and *La Porte étroite*, "soties" [satirical farces] and "récits" [stories] marked by their "ironic" or "critical" intent. "Then I suppressed this preface," adds the author, "thinking that the reader had no concern with such confidences. But perhaps the critic ... and that is why I am rewriting all this for you. But after all you are quite free not to pay any attention to it and you can go on as if you didn't know it if this upsets your article." This is a strange case of the migration of a paratextual message – an absolutely fundamental one – from preface to letter and from letter to journal, displaying an author's extreme awareness of the significance of the pragmatic choices available to him: confidences useless to the reader but perhaps useful to the critic, who could take them into account and in that way make them known indirectly, unless he would prefer – for his own convenience and so long as such mental suppression really is possible – to forget them and remain "as if [he] didn't know it." The balancing act is very delicate, and very precise. I admit that I, in turn, don't know what the critic did with it, but in this circumstance what matters to us is the authorial intent, and in Gide as in Proust or Stendhal the intent is very obvious: to clarify, and thereby to guide interpretation.

Likewise we know today, thanks to Richard Ellmann, that the parallels between Joyce's *Ulysses* and Homer's *Odyssey* (parallels that were put forward by Larbaud in a 1921 lecture, were later spelled out by Stuart Gilbert, and – along with the title and intertitles given in the serial publication and then deleted in the book publication – have continued ever since to govern our reading of the novel) were prompted by Joyce himself, clearly

have expressly asked several of my friends who wanted to write them, and Robert de Flers, and many others, to refrain." But even such a negative request would itself come under the heading of authorial intervention.

anxious both to circulate them and to evade any direct responsibility for making them public.[4] Here we find ourselves in the
presence of what in politics is typically called a system of "leaks"
organized at the source and maintained through unofficial channels. In theory the author has said nothing: it would be unworthy
of him to emphasize strenuously and in detail the hypertextual
nature of a work whose title (here the only officially paratextual
element) must suffice to enlighten readers worthy of being called
intelligenti pauca [those who understand, for whom few words
suffice]. But if the job does not end up getting done, it is better to
take charge – not to dot the *i*'s oneself, certainly, but to have
others dot them, duly *chaptered*: I don't want to say anything, but
nonetheless it is necessary that "that be known." What are
friends for?

The public authorial epitext

In theory, as we have seen, the publisher's epitext and the
semiofficial allographic epitext lie outside the declared responsibility of the author, even if he has participated more or less
actively in their production – unless, as in the case of Stendhal's
letter to Salvagnoli, undeniable traces of this participation have
come down to us. Even so, this particular situation remains
defective, for Salvagnoli made no use of the Stendhalian draft:
this deficiency is the reverse of the usual one, for in most cases we
know what came out (the "inspired" article) but not what went
in (the authorial recommendations). I know of no case in which
posterity has inherited a complete dossier, a lack easily explained.
But these two forms of epitext are obviously marginal and somewhat deviant. Basically the epitext is overwhelmingly authorial,
even if some of its forms involve the participation of one or
several third parties. I have already announced a division (using
a pragmatic criterion) into *public* and *private* authorial epitext, but
each of these species presents some varieties according to new
criteria, themselves pragmatic or temporal in kind.

[4] Ellmann, *Ulysses on the Liffey* (London: Faber, 1972), xvi–xvii and 187 et seq.;
the Larbaud lecture was reprinted first in the *NRF* in 1922 and then as the
preface to the 1926 French translation of *Dubliners* [*Gens de Dublin*], where it
may still be found; Gilbert, *James Joyce's "Ulysses": A Study* (New York: Knopf,
1930).

The public epitext is always, by definition, directed at the public in general, even if it never actually reaches more than a limited portion of that public; but this directing may be autonomous and, as it were, spontaneous, as when an author publishes (in the form of an article or volume) a commentary on his work, or it may be mediated by the initiative and intervention of a questioner or interlocutor, as is the case in interviews and conversations, not to mention some intermediate regimes. Moreover, these public epitextual messages, whether autonomous or mediated, may take different forms and fulfill different functions depending on the time of their production: original, later, or delayed. The intersecting of these two criteria could give rise to a chart like this one:

Time Regime	Original	Later	Delayed
Autonomous	1 Auto-review	2 Public Response	5 Autocommentary
Mediated	3 Interview	Conversations	4 Colloquia

I have filled in this chart without wanting to overly systematize an exceedingly fluid and often more intricate reality, and without claiming to include all the forms of public epitext: we will undoubtedly come upon one or two other forms whose assignment to a cell would prove problematic. But the most canonical forms, at least in our time, are indeed present. I will discuss them now in a wholly empirical sequence, as indicated by the numbers on the chart.

Auto-reviews

The original and autonomous public epitext is a rather rare species, at least in an open form: we are speaking here of a review, in a newspaper or magazine, produced by the author himself. We have seen how Stendhal carried it off in the more or less veiled form of an article signed S. but written in the third person, as if this S. were not Stendhal.[5] Much more openly

---

[5] We should remember that the original edition of *De l'amour* is signed by "The author of *Histoire de la peinture en Italie* and of *Vies de Haydn* ...."

authorial, although likewise written in the third person, is the review of *Roland Barthes par Roland Barthes*, signed Roland Barthes, which *La Quinzaine littéraire* of March 1, 1975, published under the appropriate title "Barthes to the Third Power."[6] Although this review was written in response to a request from the periodical, I call it autonomous in keeping with the pragmatic criterion: this is a text fully acknowledged by the author, without the participation of an intermediary. This curious performance was obviously justified, on a somewhat playful level, by the already autocommenting nature of the book, which the article was therefore an extension of as much as a commentary on (Maurice Nadeau said correctly, in an introductory paragraph, that the article "would show to advantage in the new edition, no doubt imminent, of the book"). In passing, we come across (in the article) a new illustration of the always artful way in which Barthes eluded the taboo – based on the presumption of non-competence – against auto-interpretation: "Since criticism, traditionally, is never anything other than a hermeneutic, how could he [R.B.] agree to give a meaning to a book that is entirely a refusal of meaning, a book that seems to have been written for no other purpose than to refuse meaning? Let us try to do it in his stead, since he throws in the towel...." Then he lays down a meaning (a "hermeneutic") as ambiguous as was fitting at such a time and in such a context. Humor (a fairly rare regime in Barthes) also sometimes helps one elegantly crush one's own principles.

---

[6] The combined use of the signature and the third person is obviously a transparent convention, but on occasion it seemingly suffices as an alibi. For example, the (anonymous) please-insert of Jean-François Lyotard's *Le Différend* begins with this sentence, whose form is particularly tricky but nevertheless leaves no room for doubt: "'My book of philosophy,' he says." After the book's publication, in a conversation with Jacques Derrida (*Le Monde*, October 28, 1984), Lyotard made this comment on his oratorical, or grammatical, cautiousness: "Since I couldn't put forth as my own the pretentious statement 'My book of philosophy,' I ascribe it to someone else for purposes of distancing." But in a please-insert, the third person could hardly designate anyone but the author; so we must await the epitext to learn that the person supposed to be Lyotard is the writer of the please-insert and not "he." This is all very confusing, but no matter: suffice it to say that we have here both a strong affirmation and, for form's sake, a weak disavowal.

Public responses

The public response to critics is just as delicate an exercise and is in theory prohibited. The grounds for the prohibition are well known: critics are free to say what they want, and an author who is treated badly (or well) by critics would be showing bad (or overly good) form in defending himself against reprimands (or uttering thanks for praises) that arise only from the free expression of opinion. Besides, most responses (for despite the theory, authors do very often respond) take the path (already a familiar one) of the later preface, or the path (which I am saving for the next chapter) of the private letter. The public response, either in the same organ (by virtue, precisely, of the well-known "right of response") or in another one, is considered legitimate only with regard to criticisms deemed defamatory or based on an inaccurate reading.

Flaubert's behavior in the face of criticisms of *Salammbô* certainly illustrates this range of reactions. To a review by Alcide Dusolier published in *La Revue française* of December 31, 1862 – a harsh but strictly literary criticism (Dusolier deems this novel labored, monotonous, a "triumph of immobilism") – Flaubert makes no response: one does not dispute a verdict based on taste. The long article by Sainte-Beuve, published in December 1862 in three issues of the *Constitutionnel* – equally harsh but raising various questions of fact – he answers in a private letter, which we will come upon again under that heading. To the article by the archeologist Froehner (*Revue contemporaine* of December 31, 1862), which attacked him basically with regard to historical accuracy, he responds publicly (in *L'Opinion nationale* of January 24, 1863) to affirm the reliability of his documentation and to denounce Froehner's errors of reading. "Despite my practice of never replying to reviews [a classic introductory remark], I find yours unacceptable": for the reason, obviously, that the issue here is one not of value judgments but of matters of fact on which he thinks his professional conscientiousness is being impugned, and he is entitled to defend himself.[7]

It is again on grounds of historical and sociological truth that Zola, throughout his career, produces a great number of public

---

[7] The controversy persists into February 1863, still in *L'Opinion nationale*, with the publication of Froehner's reply and a last counterattack by Flaubert.

responses (without prejudicing the private ones): for *L'Assommoir*, for *Nana*, for *Germinal*, for *La Débâcle*, among others. The criticism of *Nana*, in particular, had put him in a fairly delicate position, given the period and the subject matter [prostitution]: if he did not know what he was talking about, he was laying false claim to realism; if he did know what he was talking about, he was disclosing reprehensible associations; hence this apotropaic protest: "This is the first time a writer has been put on the hot seat and cross-examined about where he has gone and where he has not gone, what he has done and what he has not done. I do not owe the public my life, I owe it only my books."[8] A distinction, as a matter of fact, less solid than he claims in a type of literature whose champions base the value of books on their fidelity (even indirect) to life. As it happens, moreover, Zola frequently goes beyond the limits of self-defense in favor of a wholly literary justification, scoffing at those who, apropos of *L'Assommoir*, claim they miss the "small works of art" like his *Contes à Ninon* [an early collection of tales] ("I still have at home some works that are much more remarkable than the *Contes à Ninon*: my old school writings, stored at the bottom of a drawer. I even have my first penmanship notebook, in which the vertical lines already had a literary merit quite superior to that of my latest novels"), and protesting when one of his novels is judged on its serial publication, or independently of its context: "Perhaps the huge group of novels to which I have devoted myself has to be completely finished to be understood and to be judged."[9] There is always some bad faith in this Balzacian (and soon to be Proustian) argument, which, on each partial publication, would require critics to suspend all (unfavorable) judgment while awaiting the ultimate completion. Bad faith and also imprudence, for "critics" could respond by postponing every kind of review. After all, if one wishes to be judged neither by the serial text nor by the individual volume, the solution (called "Flaubertian," above [Chapter 9, note 14]) is self-evident.

These sometimes oblique uses of the right of response as a means of literary defense are obviously based on the fragility of the distinction between criticism and defamation, and some authors are not very scrupulous in the way they exploit this

[8] *Le Voltaire*, October 28, 1879.
[9] Letter to Fourcaud, September 23, 1876; see Pléiade 2:1559.

confusion, especially nowadays when the media temptation is so strong. To avoid supplying them with fresh opportunities, I will mention here only one name, that of the imaginary Passavant in Gide's *Faux-Monnayeurs*, a figure emblematic, or prophetic, of our *littérature à l'estomac*.[10] Here is how Edouard, in free indirect style and not, perhaps, without some touch of jealousy, describes Passavant's maneuvers: "In the fourth [newspaper] there is a letter from Passavant, complaining of an article which had recently appeared in the same paper and which had been a trifle less flattering than the others. Passavant writes defending and explaining his book. This letter irritates Edouard even more than the articles. Passavant pretends to enlighten public opinion – in reality he cleverly directs it" [pt. 1, ch. 8].[11]

Mediations

The critical appraisal of one's own text and the use – indeed, abuse – of the right of response constitute an autonomous recourse to the media, a recourse that on the whole is exceptional. For with respect to the media, the canonical situation consists of a dialogue between the writer and some intermediary whose job it is to ask him questions and record and transmit his answers.[12] The media epitext is therefore most often an epitext that is mediated, and doubly mediated: by the situation of interlocution, in which to a certain extent the questions determine the responses, and by the process of transmission, which gives the intermediary and the media apparatus on which he depends a sometimes very important role in the ultimate formulation of the "recorded remarks," depriving the author proportionally of control over his discourse – but not absolving him completely of responsibility, for if interviews are often a "trap," he who lets himself get caught in one cannot evade the onus. The form this

[10] Literary practices that aim at, and if possible manipulate, media coverage. [The phrase – literally, "literature that hoodwinks, bluffs, pulls a fast one" – is Julien Gracq's; his essay by that title was first published in 1950.]

[11] Pléiade 983.

[12] Here I use *media* in the broadest sense, with print journalism included. On the genres of the interview and the conversation, see Philippe Lejeune, "La Voix de son maître" and "Sartre et l'autobiographie parlée," in *Je est un autre* (Seuil, 1980); and J.-B. Puech, "Du vivant de l'auteur," *Poétique* 63 (September 1985). My perspective is naturally different from theirs, for they are basically looking at the autobiographical aspect of the epitext.

deprivation takes depends, moreover, less on the good or ill will of the intermediary than on the technique of transmission: to the author, the transcribed oral conversation is the most dubious form unless he personally looks to the faithfulness of the transcription, which gives him the possibility of correcting himself and thereby saying to the public not what he really said to the intermediary but what he decides after the fact he ought to have said; the oral conversation prerecorded for delayed distribution cannot be distorted except by cutting; the oral conversation transmitted live is by definition unfalsifiable, even by the author: what is said is said, what is not said cannot be belatedly set right. Still, in audiovisual forms we must not overlook the part played by "silent," that is, nonverbal, utterance: a facial expression may serve as a positive or negative response. Use of the mediated paratext – a use inevitably destined to spread – will have to take into account these particulars and undoubtedly some others.

A final characteristic of the media epitext, a characteristic whose effects on the message are hard to measure, lies in its very distinctive pragmatic situation as a "false dialogue" (or at least, a dialogue with an external addressee), which Philippe Lejeune describes like this: "The dialogue between subject and interviewer is not a true dialogue in the first degree but is the construction of a message meant by both jointly for a potential addressee," who is obviously the public. More bluntly, the editors of Thomas Mann's *Frage und Antwort* [*Questions and Answers*] speak of a "balance of power between ... the nonperson who takes the initiative and the VIP who reacts."[13] To call the interviewer a "nonperson" may seem ungracious, but this expression conveys the peculiarity of the interview situation: the journalist is truly questioning the writer, but the writer is not truly responding to the journalist, for the response is addressed in effect not to the journalist but, through him, to the public. Perhaps I ought not even say, moreover, that the journalist is truly questioning the writer; rather, the journalist is transmitting to the writer a question from the public, for that is indeed the journalist's automatic role. He is therefore not an autonomous "person" either going or coming, but instead simply a messenger.

[13] French tr. *Questions et réponses* (Belfond, 1986), 14.

This description, of course, applies only to the "ideal" situation of an interview or conversation, in which the journalist fairly rigorously effaces his "person" in order to (confine himself to) play(ing) his role and in which the writer disregards his interlocutor enough to aim, through him, only at the potential addressee. For obvious reasons, this ideal is never completely realized: no one can entirely efface himself as a person, and no one can entirely disregard the person of his interlocutor – *a fortiori*, I would say in an intentionally "sexist" way to introduce a factor perceptible to everyone, of his interlocutress. Consequently, it might be quite amusing to search a corpus of interviews and conversations for traces of those moments when some thickening of the real interlocution clouds the perfect transparency of the mediation. We clearly find such a thickening, for example, in the conversations between Paul Léautaud and Robert Mallet, when the two partners get so caught up in the game that the media dialogue sometimes becomes almost a rhubarb. The public does not necessarily lose in these instances of turbulence, which bring to a genre that is constitutively bland (from transitivity) a bit of the piquancy associated with any impurity.

Up to this point I have made no effort to distinguish between the terms *interview* and *conversation*, which are very often treated as synonyms. We should now acknowledge a distinction whose main ground, as our chart indicates, is temporal.[14] I will use *interview* to designate a dialogue, generally short and conducted by a professional journalist, entered upon in the line of duty on the specific occasion of a book's publication and, in theory, bearing exclusively on that book. *Conversation* will designate a dialogue that is generally more wide-ranging, taking place after a longer period of time, without any particular occasion (or going well beyond the limits of this occasion, if the publication of a book or the receipt of a prize or some other such event gives the pretext for a more far-reaching retrospection), and often conducted by an intermediary who is less interchangeable, more "personalized," more specifically interested in the œuvre in question, even possibly a friend of the author's, as Francis Crémieux more or less was for Aragon, Sollers for Francis Ponge,

---

[14] In other terms and with other emphases, this distinction is present in J.-B. Puech's "Du vivant de l'auteur."

Maria Esther Vasquez for Borges, and most of Sartre's delayed interlocutors for him. This distinction, naturally, often unravels in practice, so that many an interview is almost a conversation (but not vice versa). This distinction is also, most often, disregarded in the composition of the later collections that furnish me with the bulk of my corpus. As much as possible, however, I will hold to it: the "mixing of genres" is a proof of their existence.

Interviews

The interview (like the conversation, moreover) is a recent practice: it is said to have been introduced into France, on the basis of an American model, in 1884 by *Le Petit Journal*. At the turn of the century the genre spread rapidly in transcribed form, and during the twentieth century in the radio and then the audiovisual formats. An in-depth study of the subject would require copious archival digging, but such a study is not my present purpose; so I shall make do with a chance corpus and some later collections.[15]

When a writer takes the initiative for an interview – or vigorously seizes the opportunity provided by one – to send the public a message truly close to his heart, the genre may function (as I have said) as an advantageous substitute for a preface. This fairly rare use is perfectly illustrated by the interview Proust granted Elie-Joseph Bois, published by *Le Temps* of November 13, 1913.[16] Its main themes are well known: *Du côté de chez Swann* is

---

[15] Including M. Chapsal, *Les Ecrivains en personne* (Julliard, 1960) and *Quinze Ecrivains* (Julliard, 1963); J.-L. Ezine, *Les Ecrivains sur la sellette* (Seuil, 1981); R. Barthes, *Le Grain de la voix* (Seuil, 1981); P. Boncenne, *Ecrire, lire et en parler* (Laffont, 1985). These collections, as I have said, often contain more conversations than interviews. The reason is obvious: interviews are more dependent on specific circumstances and therefore lend themselves less readily to later collection. The celebrated television program *Apostrophes* [see below], because of its relation to the topical, comes under the heading of interview but is partly differentiated from this genre by the fact that the authors appear on the program in groups, so the set of interviews may become more like a discussion of sorts. That has been their strength and undoubtedly the reason for their success ever since the famous set-tos of 1977 on the "new philosophy": a small intellectual cause, a large media effect. [From 1975 to 1990, *Apostrophes* was an extremely popular Friday-night television program on which the moderator, Bernard Pivot, discussed with groups of authors their current books; authors who appeared on *Apostrophes* saw the sales of their works skyrocket.]

[16] See *Choix de lettres*, ed. Philip Kolb (Plon, 1965), 283 et seq.

only the beginning of a vast and unitary work, one that needs length to express the passage of time and one that we could call a "novel of the unconscious" because of the role involuntary memory plays in it; its narrator-character is not the author; its style is dictated by the originality of its vision; and so forth.

Most often, however, the initiative for an interview comes from the newspaper, and the author – who does not expect much more from it than some free publicity – goes along rather passively, and apparently without the underpinning of a strong intellectual motivation. In the late 1970s, one of the stars (on the "questions" side) of the genre complained of an inflation, for which he seemed to hold authors responsible: "Nowadays, we read and listen to long interviews with Michel Foucault. As recently as thirty years ago, we would have read only reviews of his books. In short, literary critics nowadays are circumvented by the creators themselves, who express their thoughts to the public directly in the form of interviews, *portraits*, discussions, and so forth."[17] I am not so sure that things really happen that way. Not only are authors hardly in a position to force their alleged desire for interviews on the media (writers not invited to appear on *Apostrophes* know something about that), but in addition, after we set aside the wholly exceptional appeal of that particular program, it seems to me that only the lack of something better leads most authors to endure what must indeed be called the drudgery of interviews. This "something better" that has failed to turn up is obviously the allographic review, which writers – if my private sources are to be believed – care more about than anything else (below we will find a signal example of this in Virginia Woolf) and for which, given a certain inadequacy on the part of professional criticism, especially nowadays in France, the interview tends to be substituted as an easy way out. Before accusing authors of moving diligently to "sell" their books themselves, we must wonder about the vacuum that such diligence fills somehow or other, without reversing the relation of cause and effect. During the heyday of French intellectual output, the

[17] Bernard Pivot, *Nouvelles littéraires*, April 21, 1977. [*Portraits*: French radio and television stations run programs on which an interviewer exhaustively questions someone prominent in one of the arts, seeking to build up a portrait of the subject's life and work. The most famous of these programs is the now-discontinued *Radioscopies* (*X Rays*), referred to in note 20. That two-hour-long program was broadcast five days a week to a large audience.]

perennial refrain of newspaper offices went roughly like this:
"No one understands anything about it, no one can talk about it
but the author: let's send him a tape recorder." But I am not
forgetting, either, that the "decline of criticism" is a commonplace
as old as criticism itself and is one of the perennial excuses of the
paratext. Writing a preface for the first edition of *Béatrix*, Balzac
was saying even then: "It is not always pointless to explain the
personal meaning of a literary composition, in a time when
criticism no longer exists."

In short, all these things are part of a close-knit system called
the Republic of Letters, of which Roland Barthes, in April 1979,
gave a description that is a trifle peevish but quite fairly balanced.
To the question "For you, what is an interview?" he answered:
"The interview is a practice that is fairly complex if not to
analyze, then at the very least to judge. Generally speaking, I find
interviews fairly trying and at one time I wanted to give them
up.... And then I realized that my attitude was excessive: the
interview is – to put it lightly – part of a social game that no one
can evade, or, to put it more seriously, part of a collaborative
intellectual venture between writers on the one hand and the
media on the other hand. There are meshing gears that have to be
accepted: from the moment one writes, one expects eventual
publication, and from the moment one is published, one must
accept what society asks of books and what it turns them into....
Your question comes under the heading of a general study that is
lacking of a subject I have always wanted to teach a course on: a
vast panorama, long reflected on, of the practices of intellectual
life in our day."[18]

Barthes, as we know, along with writers such as Sartre, Borges,
Tournier, and some others, belonged to that category of "great
communicators" – great dispensers of interviews and conversations of all kinds – in whom obligingness toward the media
proceeds not always, moreover, from a pursuit of publicity but
sometimes from a certain inability to refuse, or else from a sense
of militant urgency. My reader will work out the proportions for
himself, and as he sees fit, not without a respectful nod to those –
a Michaux, a Blanchot, a Beckett, for example – who have always,
or almost always, refused to get caught up in the "meshing

[18] *Le Grain de la voix*, 300; or Boncenne, *Ecrire, lire et en parler*, 366.

gears" and whom, by definition, we will not have occasion to meet in this piece of machinery.

The "social game" of the interview undoubtedly proceeds more from a need for information than from a need for true commentary: a book has come out, one must make it known and make known what it consists of – for example, by "talking about it" with its author. Hence the considerable role played by description (summarizing the plot of a novel or the thesis of a work of ideas and quoting some phrases to "give an idea of the style"), which has scarcely any function in other paratextual forms except the prospectus or the please-insert. And as the interviewer in any given case generally know more about interviews than about the author, the machinery is apt to run on reflexes – that is, on interchangeable clichés, an inventory of standard questions plus a symmetrical inventory of standard answers that emerged fairly quickly, the whole drastically reducing the part played by the unexpected. As regards fiction, the number one question is definitely "Is this book autobiographical?" – and the number one answer, "Yes and no" (Barthes for *Fragments d'un discours amoureux*: "It is I and it is not I"; Mauriac for Yves Frontenac [the hero of *Le Mystère Frontenac*]: "Both I and not I"; Sollers for *Portrait d'un joueur*: "Yes and no: it's Philippe Sollers if he were a character in a novel"; Truman Capote is more sly – I condense: My most autobiographical books are not the ones people think they are; and so forth). Another standard question: "Are the characters based on real people?" Standard answer: "No: there are certainly models, but I have blurred them." "Have you been influenced by X? – Not at all, I have never read him"; or more perversely, according to the technique of the backfire: "No, not by X, but by Y, whom no one has thought of."[19] "Does your book bring about, or illustrate, a return to ... (to Balzac, to narrative, to psychology, to the French classical tradition, to Kant, to Descartes, to Plotinus ...)? – Yes and no, History moves forward in spirals." "Did writing this book change you? – Yes and no, does one ever really change?" (Simone de Beauvoir, for *Le Deuxième Sexe*, answers quite simply *no*, which is bound to disappoint.) "Did you spend a long time writing it?" Here, two good answers: "Yes, I do an awful lot of crossing out," and "I wrote it very quickly after

[19] Gracq, for *Le Rivage des Syrtes*: Buzzati? No, Pushkin.

carrying it around in my head for a long time." "Which character
do you like best? – So-and-So, because he's least like me." But in
interviews with novelists, the question that is most productive –
because it does not lend itself to a *yes, no,* or *yes and no* answer –
consists of requiring the author to *explain* (as if he had not, most
often, already done altogether too much of that) the behavior of
his characters. Very rare are those who, like Faulkner, have the
firmness to evade that question. Most, transformed by urgency,
launch into motivational analyses in which the most commonplace psychology hobnobs with the boldest cock-and-bull stories,
to the great delight of an audience convinced it is at that very
instant penetrating the arcana of creation. That is the big
moment, the highlight of the evening; the characters – for
characters are always the issue – take on amazing substance for
those few moments, these "empty bodies" arrive on stage,
everyone auscultates them and palpates them, takes them apart,
puts them back together, loves them, hates them, rewrites the
story, walks in their shoes, and finally, as usual, recounts his life.
This is all very pleasant when it is happening but does not stand
the test of rereading – such is not its purpose, however. Here I
interrupt this synthetic evocation for fear of verging on satire.

Conversations

The conversation – as a rule more delayed, more thorough,
conducted by an intermediary whose motivation is more personal, fulfilling a less popularizing and less sales-oriented function – has a more prestigious pedigree than the interview.[20] This
is not to say that it is entirely devoid of more or less simplistic
commonplaces: "Which book is your favorite?" The usual response: "The last one" or "The next one" (but we also learn,
more specifically, that Claudel's favorites are *Tête d'or, Partage de*

---

[20] For the history of the genre, I again refer the reader to Philippe Lejeune, whose
list of radio conversations (*Je est un autre,* 122) is invaluable. I will add, among
others, the Thomas Mann collection, already cited, and Aragon–Crémieux,
Queneau–Charbonnier, Borges–Charbonnier and Borges–others, Ponge–
Sollers, the collections of interviews already mentioned, and two collections
that center for the most part on habits and methods of working: *Writers at
Work: The "Paris Review" Interviews* (French tr. *Romanciers au travail* [Gallimard,
1967]) and J.-L. de Rambures, *Comment travaillent les écrivains* (Flammarion,
1978). Although *Apostrophes* generally comes under the heading of the interview, some of its special programs (Nabokov, Cohen, Duras, Dumézil) belong
under the conversation, as does Jacques Chancel's *Radioscopies.*

13 The public epitext

midi, Le Soulier de satin, and *L'Art poétique* because it was not well received by the public; Henry Miller, *The Colossus of Maroussi*; or Barthes, among his early works, *Michelet* rather than the "abstruse" *Degré zéro*). "Don't your characters eventually get away from you and live an autonomous existence?" Jacques Laurent's answer: "Yes, a third of the way through." Faulkner's: "Yes, generally on page 275." And especially – because of the conversation's delayed temporal position and sometimes the interlocutor's own curiosity, or even the author's bad memory or reluctance to comment on himself – the conversation very often abandons the subject of the œuvre (unless an interlocutor like Jean Amrouche shows commendable insistence) in favor of a fairly autobiographical retrospection with a more indirect paratextual relevance: see Léautaud–Mallet or Breton–Parinaud. Nonetheless the (nowadays considerable) mass of collected conversations constitutes a mine of paratextual evidence, particularly on work habits (places, times, positions, surroundings, tools, rituals, rapidity or slowness of writing, and so forth) and on the interpretation or delayed or comprehensive assessment of the œuvre, often supplementing (Claudel, Faulkner, Sarraute) or confirming and nuancing (Barrès, Borges, Tournier) the interpretations or assessments given in a delayed preface. Undoubtedly the best authorial commentary on Barrès's *Culte du moi* appears in Jules Huret's inaugural survey of "literary evolution";[21] on Claudel's *Soulier de satin*, in Frédéric Lefevre's *Une heure avec Claudel* or in *Mémoires improvisés* (conversations with Amrouche); on Gide's *Cahiers d'André Walter* (very guarded), *Immoraliste, Caves,* or *Robert*, in the Gide–Amrouche conversations; on Aragon's *Fou d'Elsa*, in Aragon–Crémieux. And no critic – indeed, no careful reader – can be unaware of Nathalie Sarraute's clarification to Sartre's preface for her *Portrait d'un inconnu* (I mentioned this in Chapter 10), a clarification she made in conversation with Jean-Louis Ezine; or of the fantasy sketched by Faulkner, in conversation with J. Stein vanden Heuvel, of the ideal life a writer would lead if he were the manager of a brothel[22] – or more seriously, of his evocation of the

---

[21] *L'Evolution littéraire: Enquête sur le déclin du naturalisme et l'avenir du symbolisme naissant*, published in *L'Echo de Paris* in 1891; republished by Thot, 1982. This was the first notable example (at least in France) of a set of interviews.

[22] ["The best job that was ever offered to me was to become a landlord in a brothel. In my opinion it's the perfect milieu for an artist to work in ..." (*Lion*

seminal image of *The Sound and the Fury*, "the picture ... of the muddy seat of a little girl's drawers in a pear tree, where she could see through a window where her grandmother's funeral was taking place...." Philippe Lejeune rightly says that thanks to Amrouche, *Mémoires improvisés* is "a remarkable general overview of literary history and a codicil to Claudel's œuvre itself." The special relation between the author and his interlocutor (who then stops being a pure "nonperson" and becomes an accomplice or an inquisitor) sometimes contributes powerfully to the conversation's usefulness as a source of paratextual evidence, whether through the intermediary's insistence, or the excellent rapport between the two men, or – even better, perhaps – their disagreement. See Mallet getting Léautaud (who no doubt had a short fuse) to fly off the handle, or Amrouche, with his stubborn defense of Robert, forcing Gide to take a strong stand against his character: "That is one of his worst character traits: the need to dominate the situation, and to save the last word for himself, and to have things easy ..., a false nobility, a nobility without generosity, he *claims credit*...." In all these cases and in many others, the drawback of the genre (its situation of dialogue) turns into an advantage, so that a well-managed conversation (which sometimes means: one that appears to be badly managed) becomes an irreplaceable form of the paratext.

Colloquia, discussions

Here I use the terms *colloquium* or *discussion* to designate any situation in which an author is induced to "dialogue" not with one interlocutor[23] but with an audience of several dozen people, with or without taping and planned publication. Such a situation is most likely to arise following a lecture, or when a writer is invited to discuss his work before a group of students and professors, or at a colloquium expressly organized around and concerning an author. The first kind of situation (the discussion that follows a lecture) is often superficial and hurried and leaves hardly any traces; but the second kind leaves more of a mark and is surely best illustrated by the three volumes devoted to

in the Garden: Interviews with William Faulkner 1926–1962, ed. James B. Meriwether and Michael Millgate [New York: Random House, 1968], 239).]
[23] Or possibly two or three, as in the column "L'Express va plus loin ...."

Faulkner.[24] And the third kind has left quite a trace in the set of volumes based on the ten-day-long colloquia held at Cerisy and centered on the heroes of the New Novel (1971), on Michel Butor (1973), Claude Simon (1974), Alain Robbe-Grillet (1975), Francis Ponge (1975), Roland Barthes (1977), and Yves Bonnefoy (1983).[25]

The paratextual function of these colloquium-type situations is fairly similar to the paratextual function of conversations, and is in fact no more than a variant of it: like the conversation, the colloquium happens only to an author who is already famous enough to be clutched at by the public in its curiosity and fervor. The particular features of this variant obviously derive from the multiplicity of interlocutors, which entails three very marked effects. The first is the absence of "sustained dialogue": exchanges follow one after another, generally with no possibility that a topic can be explored in depth, for speakers jump disconnectedly from one subject to another (this is very noticeable around Faulkner). The second is the lack of intimacy, or at least of proximity, a lack that rules out too-personal questions and biographical tangents and keeps the discussion on the terrain of the œuvre (in Faulkner's case, with a very striking emphasis on *The Sound and the Fury*). The third, well known to regulars at Cerisy, is what can be called the *colloquium-effect* that is, the tendency in an audience that is academic and very Parisian, although cosmopolitan, to ask questions that do more to make the questioner look good than to stimulate the person being questioned. At Cerisy, this exhibition-effect is sometimes worsened by a touch of theory-based intimi-dation that some authors react to better than others: with humor and self-assurance, with one-upmanship, with disarming sin-cerity. Authors least equipped to deal with such a situation give the impression of being really outshone by their dazzling ex-egetes and seem to get winded in thinking beyond their capa-cities. More clever or more blasé, Gide sometimes blurted out, in front of Amrouche, an ironically admiring exclamation, which in no way disconcerted the hermeneut but sufficed to put the latter's

---

[24] *Faulkner at Nagano*, ed. Robert A. Jelliffe (Tokyo: Kenkyusha, 1956); *Faulkner in the University: Class Conferences at the University of Virginia 1957–1958*, ed. Frederick L. Gwynn and Joseph L. Blotner (Charlottesville: University of Virginia Press, 1959); and *Faulkner at West Point*, ed. Joseph L. Fant and Robert Ashley (New York: Random House, 1964). I have been able to consult only the second, which is regarded – credibly – as the most interesting.

[25] All published in the 10/18 series, except Bonnefoy, which was published by Sud.

victim in the clear. There are times when it is better not to pretend to understand.

Delayed autocommentaries

Ten-day colloquia centered on an author generally involve a statement by the "interested party" which, despite the aforementioned constraints, belongs more to what I call the delayed autonomous epitext, or autocommentary. This practice is relatively modern because the classical period, little given to critical commentary in general, had even less tolerance for commentaries that an author himself was so indiscreet as to take responsibility for: a taboo based on the presumption of impropriety. Even in the eighteenth and early nineteenth centuries, although we do indeed see Rousseau or Chateaubriand include in their memoirs information about the circumstances in which they wrote one or another book and the ups and downs of its reception (that is part of the events of their lives, which they have undertaken to recount), still, we do not see them embarking on a commentary that would smack too much of the studio from which the book came. The romantic period seems scarcely more favorable to autocommentary, for writers at that time were anxious (and Poe reproached them for this) to give the impression that their inspiration had been of quasi-miraculous spontaneity; they were therefore not especially eager to exhibit inspiration's workshop – a taboo based on the presumption of nonrelevance. The modern period is unquestionably more open to such confidences, subject in actual fact to a third taboo that we have already encountered, which is the taboo based on the presumption of noncompetence, prohibiting authorial interpretation. Consequently autocommentary most often takes another route, which is that of genetic commentary: I am not better (and am perhaps worse) qualified than someone else to say what my work means and why I wrote it; however, I am better equipped than anyone else to say *how* I wrote it, in what conditions, using what sort of process, indeed, employing what methods.[26]

---

[26] Robbe-Grillet expresses this defensive retreat very well: "Contrary to what has often been said here, I consider that a lucid and methodical author knows his work fairly well: he was the one who got it going. I don't mean that he will always know it better than everyone else on every point, but he has a

The initiator of this approach was obviously Edgar Allan Poe, who, in his essay "The Philosophy of Composition,"[27] appears very conscious of the revolutionary nature of his initiative:

I have often thought how interesting a magazine paper might be written by any author who would – that is to say who could – detail, step by step, the processes by which any one of his compositions attained its ultimate point of completion. Why such a paper has never been given to the world, I am much at a loss to say – but, perhaps, the autorial vanity has had more to do with the omission than any one other cause. Most writers – poets in especial – prefer having it understood that they compose by a species of fine frenzy – an ecstatic intuition – and would positively shudder at letting the public take a peep behind the scenes....

We know how the rest of the essay illustrates (truthfully or not – that is another matter) this purpose of unveiling – indeed, of demystifying – the secrets of the literary workshop: the wish to produce a poem acceptable to both the public and the critics; the advantages of a short poem, which can be read in a single sitting; the choice of an effective subject (the death of a young woman); the adoption of a refrain that can be inflected differently at each stanza (*Nevermore*); the movement toward a climax; and so forth. As a matter of fact, Poe's example was slow to set a fashion, and not until the middle third of the twentieth century do we see it resurface in particularly meaningful form: Raymond Roussel's book *Comment j'ai écrit certains de mes livres* [*How I Wrote Certain of My Books*], published posthumously in 1935, bears an emblematic title that will be echoed in our own time (Butor at Cerisy: "How Some of My Books Wrote Themselves," and Renaud Camus announcing in 1978 a "How Some of My Books Wrote Me" – variations characteristic of an affectation of the period). Roussel's book discloses the famous "method" that consists of producing two homophonous sentences and then imagining a narrative that arranges the transition from one to the other. Aragon, in *Je n'ai jamais appris à écrire ou Les incipit* [*I Never Learned to Write, or Incipits*] (1969), refers again to the Rousselian model to establish the generative power, for his works from *Télémaque* to *La Mise à mort*, of a first sentence bestowed by fate. In a more classical or

---

considerable amount of information about the work as a whole, especially if he writes slowly, which is the case for me" (Cerisy 2:412).

[27] Published in 1845 after the success of "The Raven." The title given it in Baudelaire's French translation ["Genèse d'un poème"] is more meaningful than the original, "The Philosophy of Composition."

less aggressively formalist manner, Thomas Mann had written in 1949 a *Genesis of "Doctor Faustus"* that meticulously laid out this novel's sources and principle of composition, the vicissitudes of a production extending from 1901 to 1947, and discussed its genre status and symbolic purposes.[28] To the same genre belong some talks given at Cerisy in 1971 by Nathalie Sarraute ("What I Am Trying to Do"), Claude Simon ("Fiction Word by Word"), Alain Robbe-Grillet ("On the Choice of Begetters"), Claude Ollier ("Twenty Years After"), Michel Butor (already mentioned), Robert Pinget ("Pseudo-principles of Aesthetics"), and Jean Ricardou ("Birth of a Fiction"), talks whose titles alone indicate fairly well both their inclusion within the tradition launched by Poe and the individual nuances of this filiation: the emphasis is placed sometimes on thematic intentions, sometimes on formal approaches. Michel Tournier's stance in *Le Vent Paraclet* is slightly deviant in that he supplements the genetic aspect (construction of the theme of the *phorie* for *Le Roi des aulnes*, of the three stages for *Vendredi*, the relation between *Météores* and Verne's *Autour du monde en 80 jours*) with a degree of symbolic interpretation that blithely disregards the doubts then in fashion about the legitimacy of authorial hermeneutics. But Tournier, as we know, likes to position himself counter to the avant-garde.

In comparison with the mediated epitext, these autonomous epitexts (and I am certainly leaving out dozens of them) have the obvious advantage of autonomy, which shields them from the constraints and hazards of dialogue: here the author firmly takes the initiative and retains control of his commentary. The disadvantage, conversely, is the absence of the dialogic excuse, but the public request (an invitation to deliver a lecture, a commission from a publisher)[29] often stands in for it to exempt the author from the reproach of indiscretion. Except for these nuances, the

---

[28] *Die Entstehung des Doktor Faustus* (Frankfurt: Fischer Verlag, 1949) [tr. *The Story of a Novel: The Genesis of "Doctor Faustus,"* trans. Richard and Clara Winston (New York: Knopf, 1961)]; the title of the French translation, *Le Journal du Docteur Faustus* (Plon, 1962), is a little misleading, for what we are dealing with is not a contemporaneous log but clearly a retrospective account. Also from Mann there exists a lecture, "The Making of *The Magic Mountain*," delivered at least at Princeton in 1939, the text of which I don't have.

[29] Commission from a publisher is especially the case with a series like Ecrivains de toujours, for Barthes (but *Roland Barthes par Roland Barthes* is not exactly a commentary on his work); or with a series like Les Sentiers de la création, for Aragon.

autonomous epitext shares with the mediated epitext the fundamental characteristic of place (outside the peritext), which gives
the author a chance to deliver a dissociated commentary, one
materially independent of the text. The paratextual pressure thus
becomes less heavy-handed, is offered but not imposed: the text
and its paratext go their separate ways, and the reader of the
former is not under any obligation to deal with the latter – at least
for a while. We know that *Les Incipit*, for example, was appended
to the collected *Œuvres romanesques croisées*. There the epitext
joins up with the peritext, and this is only a beginning, a first
installment against the epitext's inevitable arrival in the peritext
of scholarly editions, generally posthumous. I will return to this
irresistible evolution.

A whole separate study, for which, fortunately, I lack the means,
would perhaps be necessary to deal with another form – at least,
an indirect one – of the public epitext: that consisting, in all
periods, of authors' public readings of their works. I am not
referring here to the authorial commentaries that may accompany
public readings – these commentaries belong to categories I have
already mentioned. Rather, I am referring to the reading (or
recitation from memory) itself, which in its delivery, its stresses,
its intonations, in the gestures and facial expressions used for
emphasis, is already quite obviously an "interpretation." We
necessarily lack all traces of such performances earlier than the
late nineteenth century, but we do have some indirect pieces of
evidence that it would perhaps be useful to collect and compare;
and for the celebrated tours by Dickens (who was remembered as
a phenomenal actor), we also have at least some specially
abridged – indeed, modified – versions of the texts the author
used in his readings, which indirectly convey commentary.[30]
Throughout the twentieth century readings have been widely
recorded, live or in a studio. These recordings, like the notes that
accompany musical recordings or even simply the information
provided on record jackets or CD cases, are a mine of paratextual
information. Other researchers, I hope, will work that vein. It is
said – but here, as far as I know, no authenticating recording
exists – that Kafka *would laugh* while reading his works in public.

[30] See P. Collins, ed., *Charles Dickens: The Public Readings* (Oxford University
Press, 1975).

14

The private epitext

❖❖

What distinguishes the private epitext from the public epitext is not exactly that in the former the author is not aiming at the public and therefore does not have publication in view: many letters and many journal pages are written with clear foreknowledge of their publication to come, and undoubtedly this prescience does not affect the writing of these letters and journals in a way that undermines their private – indeed, intimate – character. For us, what will define this character is the presence of a first addressee interposed between the author and the possible public, an addressee (a correspondent, a confidant, the author himself) who is perceived not as just an intermediary or functionally transparent relay, a media "nonperson," but indeed as a full-fledged addressee, one whom the author addresses for that person's own sake even if the author's ulterior motive is to let the public subsequently stand witness to this interlocution. In the public epitext, the author addresses the public, possibly through an intermediary; in the private epitext, the author first addresses a confidant who is real, who is perceived as such, and whose personality is important to the communication at hand, even influencing its form and content. So much so that at the other end of the chain, when the public – eventually admitted to this confidential or intimate exchange – learns, always after the fact,[1] about a message that is not addressed essentially to it, it does so "over the shoulder" of a third party who is genuinely treated as an individual person. Flaubert does not address Louis Bouilhet as he does Louise Colet, Gide does not write for Valéry as he does for Claudel or for himself, and the reader of these letters or these

---

[1] Except in the form known as the "open letter," when publication accompanies – unless it takes the place of – the private mailing. Some public responses take this form, which by no means does away with the convention of the real addressee.

diaries cannot receive them correctly without taking these various persons into consideration. Of course, this distinction is by nature entirely relative: we have already evoked cases that slide in one direction (Léautaud facing Mallet), and we will encounter other, perhaps symmetrical, cases. We are not too sure, for example, whether Goethe considered Eckermann a confidant or an intermediary. But these in-between situations do not basically compromise the validity of our distinction and therefore the validity of the category of the private epitext, whose existence is sufficiently evident not to be refuted by its margins.

I will subdivide this vast corpus into two large clumps: the *confidential* epitext, in which the author addresses one (or more rarely, several) confidant(s), either in writing (correspondence) or orally (confidences, in the usual sense of the term), and the *intimate* epitext, in which the author addresses himself. This autodestination may, in turn, take two relatively distinct forms (but they too include many intermediary cases): the *journal* and what for some years has been very aptly called the *pre-text*.

Correspondence

The correspondence of writers is more or less as old a reality as literature itself (or at least written literature), but clearly – with some exceptions, and for reasons of propriety which we have already encountered – letters written before the nineteenth century contain hardly any confidences about the literary activity of their authors. Chateaubriand's correspondence, very *"ancien régime"* in this respect, remains remarkably discreet. In the romantic period we see a very notable change in attitude, perhaps intensified by circumstantial separations that favor the output of such confidences: Mme Hanska is off on her distant estate, Hugo is in exile, and Flaubert and Louise Colet are separated by his notorious discipline. We lack an in-depth study of the history of these sets of letters and the conditions in which they were published, but here again one date seems to me highly significant (that is, I make the decision to consider it such): 1876, the publication (obviously posthumous) of Balzac's correspondence, an event greeted by two commentaries whose diametrical contrast illustrates quite well its importance. The first is Zola's, in an article later reprinted in *Les Romanciers naturalistes*:

Ordinarily, one does not do illustrious men a favor by publishing their correspondence. In letters they almost always appear egotistic and cold, calculating and vain. In letters one sees the great man in his bathrobe minus his crown of laurel, no longer striking the official pose; and often this man is petty – nasty, even. No such thing has just happened for Balzac. On the contrary, his correspondence has heightened his stature. They rummaged around in every drawer and published all of it, yet they didn't diminish him by one jot. He comes out of this terrible test truly more likeable and even grander.

The second commentary is Flaubert's, in a letter to his niece, Caroline:

I have just read Balzac's *Correspondance*. Well! For me, what an *edifying* read. The poor man! What a life! How he suffered and toiled! What an example! ... But what a concern for money, and so little love of Art! Have you noticed that he doesn't speak of it a single time? What he sought was Fame, not Beauty. And he was Catholic, legitimist, a land-owner, dreaming of the Chamber of Deputies and the Academy; above all, an ignoramus, and provincial to the marrow of his bones: luxury dazzled him. His greatest literary admiration was for Walter Scott.[2]

To the extent that a letter from a writer bears on his work (this extent is eminently variable, and often fairly slight, even in the modern period), we may say that it exerts on its first addressee a paratextual *function* and, more remotely, on the ultimate public simply a paratextual *effect*. The author has an exact (particular) idea of what he wants to say about his work to a definite individual correspondent, a message that may even have no value or meaning except to that correspondent; he has a much more diffuse, and sometimes more casual, idea about the relevance of this message for the public to come. And reciprocally, the reader of an author's correspondence is very naturally led to make "allowances": for example, in a cover letter to a publisher, allowances for a high attribution of value, caution, or false modesty; in Balzac's letters to Mme Hanska, for boastfulness and self-glorification; in Flaubert's letters to Louise Colet, perhaps for expansive exaggeration of the difficulty of writing – Flaubert's message *ad usum delphinae*[3] is always to some extent this: "See the

---

2   December 31, 1876; the same criticism, the same day, in a letter to Edmond de Goncourt.

3   [Literally, "for the use of the dauphin" (son of Louis XIV). The phrase is used to refer ironically to publications that have been expurgated or arranged for the good of the cause and for pedagogical purposes.]

effort and suffering that are implicit in true literature, and take a page from this book." For us, in other words, the paratextual effect arises from an awareness – "adjusted for individual variations" – of the initial paratextual function.

Given this reservation, we can use the correspondence of an author (any author) – and this is indeed what specialists do – as a certain kind of statement about the history of each of his works: about its creation, publication, and reception by the public and critics, and about his view of the work at all stages of this history. I shall examine these topics in succession in the pages to come, first noting that the relative amount of epistolary space devoted to each of these types of information may vary greatly by author (or, for any given author, by work). For example, Flaubert's correspondence is very loquacious about the gestation of his works (and especially, thanks to Louise Colet, about the gestation of *Madame Bovary*) and more reserved about his dealings with publishers and about the public's reception; conversely, Proust's correspondence holds nothing back regarding the trials and tribulations of getting *Swann* published [in 1913] but after 1909 says almost nothing about the trials and tribulations of its creation. In Proust's case, however, I may be wrong to speak as if we are dealing here with indirect evidence. His letters to Calmette, René Blum, and Louis de Robert do not *testify* to a hunt for a publisher: they *constitute* it. If they testify to it, they do so only for us – another effect of the very particular pragmatic situation of the private epitext: what in its own day was action becomes for us simply information.

In the case of a work that never gets born, correspondence may testify also to a nonbirth: aborted works of which sometimes only these indirect traces, along with some rough drafts, survive. For Balzac, see *La Bataille*, premonitorily called (in a letter to Mme Hanska, January 1833) an "impossible work"; or for Flaubert, the sea monster known as the *Essai sur le sentiment poétique français* and the envisioned novels *Monsieur le Préfet* and *La Bataille des Thermopyles*. But the bulk of a writer's correspondence concerns the creation of works that do materialize; for some of these works, letters constitute (often better than most diaries do) a true log. Balzac's letters to Mme Hanska, from *Grandet* (1833) to volume 7 of *La Comédie humaine* (1844), contain confidences shared with the far-off beloved which, as I have said, are strongly characterized by a concern to attribute high value to whatever work he is writing about. Sometimes the basis for the valuation is literary ("*Eugénie Grandet* is a wonderful work," *Le Médecin de campagne* is "a great tableau," *La Recherche de l'absolu* "a wonderful piece of work," *Le Père Goriot* "a wonderful work," "In *Albert Savarus* I think I've got a masterpiece"), sometimes moral and religious ("Everything is pure" in *La Recherche de l'absolu*, "When you read [the foreword of 1842], you won't wonder any longer if I'm Catholic"), and sometimes social ("*Le Père Goriot* is a stunning success; my most determined enemies have knelt to me," and so forth). From Stendhal, who is generally not very talkative about his work, there are at least two letters of fundamental importance, one to Mérimée (December 23, 1826), which gives the key to *Armance*, the other to Mme Gaulthier (May 4, 1834), which tells us everything we know about the origin of *Leuwen* (his rewriting of a manuscript – now lost – by the aforementioned Mme Gaulthier). The letters from Flaubert to Louise Colet about the early stages of the creation of *Madame Bovary*, from January 1852 to April 1854, are too well known for me to dwell on them; what came after (the completion of *Bovary*, the elaboration of *Salammbô*, *L'Education*, and the *Trois Contes*) is less well known in detail because the confidences imparted to Mme Roger des Genettes or to Mlle Leroyer de Chantepie are more sparse – hence the erroneous impression that the creation of those works was less laborious.[4] Zola's correspondence is likewise rich in information about his work, particularly his letters to disciples like Paul Alexis or Henri Céard or to journalists like Van Santen Kolff, who from *Germinal* on would be a kind of professional confidant, half good friend and half intermediary, to whom Zola clearly entrusted the task of making known to the public his methods and work habits or, more precisely, the image of them he wanted to convey: again, a situation lying between the public and private epitexts.[5]

---

[4] In reality, Flaubert devoted four-and-a-half years to *Bovary*, five to *Salammbô*, six to the *Education*, the longest gestation but the one prompting the fewest moans and groans.

[5] The confidences shared with Alexis and with Edmondo de Amicis, an Italian, can be found in Paul Alexis, *Emile Zola, Notes d'un ami* (Charpentier, 1882); those shared with Van Santen Kolff ended up in various German publications that have not been translated. See the editions of the correspondence and R. J.

14 *The private epitext*

The happiest moment in the creation of a work is undoubtedly the moment of writing the final period – although this period is not always completely final, particularly with authors who make thoroughgoing corrections on transcripts or proofs; but to have "covered the canvas" is in a way a guarantee of imminent completion. It is the legitimate occasion for a sort of victory shout, the medium for which is often a letter. It would be entertaining to put together a set of these letters and to think about the addressees selected for the honor. Here are a few, noted in the course of my readings: Mme Hanska for *La Recherche de l'absolu*, Mlle Leroyer de Chantepie for *Salammbô* (Louise Colet, having shown herself unworthy, was not entitled to the cock-a-doodle-do for *Bovary* and therefore, unless I am mistaken, no one received it in writing), Jules Duplan for *L'Education sentimentale*, Henri Céard for *Nana* and *L'Œuvre*, Van Santen Kolff for *La Débâcle*. We will not take literally this line Proust sent to Mme Straus in 1909: "I've just started – and finished – a whole long book." If Céleste Albaret's recollections are to be believed, it was to her that he announced in person, in the spring of 1922: "Last night, I wrote the word *end*. Now I can die." This premonitory sentence [Proust died in November of that year] must perhaps temper our enthusiasm about the joy of finishing.

The "completed," or at least the presentable, manuscript is often submitted to the judgment of one's intimates. In the past undoubtedly more often than today, this test took the form of a reading aloud: we know about Flaubert reading the *Tentation* to Louis Bouilhet and Maxime Du Camp, and the negative outcome. This practice, of which the particulars (no doubt rich in private paratextual information) are unfortunately beyond our reach, was still very much in force among, for example, the Bloomsbury group or the *Nouvelle Revue française* (*NRF*) group. Gide did not shrink from traveling in order to read a manuscript to Martin du Gard, who might have been in le Perche [a region halfway between Paris and the Normandy coast] or on the Côte d'Azur; at other times, a guest's visit to Cuverville [Gide's family estate in Normandy] was graced by the same privilege: "Jacques Rivière

Niess, "The Letters of Emile Zola to Van Santen Kolff," *The Romanic Review* (February 1940). [Van Santen Kolff was a Dutchman living in Germany; Zola was "his literary idol," and he was "one of [naturalism's] chief propagators in the Netherlands and Germany" (Niess, "Letters").]

has just left me. He has been staying here for three days. I read him the first seventeen chapters of *Les Faux-Monnayeurs*" (*Journal des F.-M.*, December 27, 1923). But sometimes, too, the manuscript, or some copy of it, makes the journey alone – hence an epistolary exchange. On May 29, 1837, for *La Vieille Fille*, Balzac recommends to Mme Hanska that she imitate the laconic sternness of Mme de Berny [his first literary counselor]: "[She] did not argue, she wrote: *bad*, or *sentence to be rewritten*." At the beginning of September 1913, Proust responds to Lucien Daudet's comments on the proofs of *Swann* by insisting on the overall structure of the *Recherche* and on the effects created by very long-range recalls.

But to speak of proofs means that an author's approaches to publishers have had a happy, positive outcome. Hugo's correspondence during his exile, particularly the letters exchanged with Hetzel or Lacroix,[6] reveals among other things details of the prepublication phase, when as a matter of fact Hugo was more exacting than anguished. On November 18, 1852, he announces to Hetzel the beginning of what will become *Les Châtiments*: "It's a new caustic that I think must be applied to Louis Bonaparte. He is cooked on one side, and now it seems to me time for turning the emperor over on the grill."[7] On December 21: "I had told you 1,600 lines, but there will be nearly 3,000. The vein spurted – there's nothing wrong with that." On January 23, 1853, he supplies the final title, adding: "This title is threatening and simple, that is, beautiful." On February 6, because Hetzel, a little frightened, had suggested to him that "what is strong has no need to be violent," Hugo mounts his high horse: I will be violent, like Jeremiah, Dante, Tacitus, Juvenal; "like Jesus, I smite with all my strength, *Napoléon le Petit* is violent. This book will be violent. My prose is honest but not moderate. . . . I say to you that I am violent." In May 1855, apropos of *Les Contemplations*, he

6   See Victor Hugo–P.-J. Hetzel, *Correspondance* 1 (1852–53), ed. S. Gaudon (Klincksieck, 1979); and B. Leuilliot, *Victor Hugo publie "Les Misérables"* (August 1861–July 1862) (Klincksieck, 1970).
7   [*Les Châtiments* (*The Chastisements*) is a volume of satirical poems denouncing Napoleon III. Of the other works by Hugo referred to in this paragraph, *Napoléon le Petit* is a prose work lampooning Napoleon III and was published the year before *Les Châtiments*; *Les Contemplations* is a volume of lyric poems; *La Légende des siècles* is three series of epic poems; and *Petites Epopées* means "little epics."]

writes: "One must strike a great blow, and I take my stand. Like Napoleon (the first), I give it all I've got. I empty my legions onto the battlefield. What I had kept for myself I am now giving, so that *Les Contemplations* will be my most comprehensive work of poetry. ... I have not yet built on my sand anything besides Giseh. It is time to construct Cheops; *Les Contemplations* will be my great pyramid." In April 1859, apropos of the future *Légende des siècles*: "I have gone beyond the *Petites Epopées*. That was the germ. The thing is now bigger than that. I am writing quite simply Humanity, fresco by fresco, fragment by fragment, epoch by epoch. So I am changing the title of the book, and here it is: *La Légende des siècles, par Victor Hugo.* This is beautiful and will amaze you, I think. ...."

Prepublication exchanges between author and publisher may bear on projects that are less far along. For example, we see Zola, in 1869, send Lacroix a detailed summary of *La Fortune des Rougon* twelve pages long, accompanied by four pages on the general idea of the *Rougon-Macquart* and by the announcement of the nine volumes to come, which will end up being nineteen:[8] valuable evidence on the evolution of that multivolume work – an evolution by expansion, except that one of the anticipated volumes (about "an episode of the Italian war" [Napoleon III's Italian campaign of 1859]) was replaced by *La Débâcle* (about another and certainly more distressing war [the Franco-Prussian]). We are also familiar with the copious (more than 20,000 words) summary of *The Ambassadors* that James sent to Harper in 1900, a summary that in itself constitutes a kind of first version of the novel.[9]

The *Recherche* was undoubtedly further along (although by no means as near completion as he claimed) when Proust undertook his search for a publisher. This long quest is the most intensely paratextual period of his correspondence, which becomes quite discreet in 1909, that is, when the draft essay on Sainte-Beuve is turning into a semi-novelistic narrative. The silence is broken on October 25, 1912, by a letter to Antoine Bibesco in which we learn that Proust wants to submit to the *NRF* a work that is "a novel; if its freedom of tone seems to ally it with memoirs, in reality a very

[8] See Pléiade 5:1755 et seq.
[9] "Project of Novel," *The Complete Notebooks of Henry James*, ed. Leon Edel and Lyall H. Powers (Oxford University Press, 1987), 541–76.

378

meticulous (but too complex to be perceptible at first) structure distinguishes it, to the contrary, from memoirs: contingency is included only as necessary to express the role contingency plays in life." Three days later, a roughly identical letter to Louis de Robert, still with an eye to the *NRF*, presses the matter in these terms: "... a long work that I call a novel because it doesn't have the contingency of memoirs (it includes only the contingency necessary to represent the role played by contingency in life) and because it is very meticulously structured, although this structure, being complex, is not very perceptible; I really couldn't tell you its genre." On the same day, a letter to Fasquelle (as if Proust were knocking on several doors at once) stresses the "indecent" nature of the volumes to follow: the publisher must commit himself with full knowledge of the facts, so that later on he will not be able to plead surprise. On February 20, 1913, and then on the 23d and 24th, he finally targets the publisher Grasset, at first via René Blum and then directly, about publishing "an important work (let us say a novel, for it is a sort of novel).... I don't know if I told you that this book is a novel. At least, the novel is the genre from which it actually departs the least. There is a gentleman who narrates and says 'I'; there are a lot of characters; they are 'prepared for' in this first volume, that is, in the second volume they will do exactly the opposite of what, on the basis of the first, they were expected to do." For more than a year letters pile up in this way, to potential publishers and then to the real one (the agreement with Grasset is dated March 11) and to various benevolent intermediaries, insisting on the structural effects, on the choice of titles,[10] and especially, as we have seen, on the genre status (or rather the absence of genre status) of a "sort of novel" that "departs the least" (therefore does depart a little) from this genre – and that also, in a pinch, for lack of a more exact term, would deserve the label "novel" not because its content is fictive but because its narrative is more constructed than the narrative of a mere autobiography is. The same reserva-

---

[10] To L. de Robert, during the summer of 1913, Proust justifies the choice of *Du côté de chez Swann* in terms of the "down-to-earth poetry" of a title he calls "modest, real, gray, drab, like a tillage from which poetry could be launched." Quite obviously he has in mind only the Combrayian aspect of this title, an aspect that today is almost entirely overshadowed by the subsequent development of a character who is basically "Parisian," right up to the cosmopolitan sound of his name.

tion will be expressed in a more delayed confidence to Paul
Morand, who reported Proust's comment and his own observation: "This novel is not quite a novel (Proust was uncomfortable
when people spoke to him of his 'novel'; he was equally uncomfortable when they used the word Memoirs or Recollections of
childhood). ... It is a sort of novel."[11] There we find the same
ambiguity we encountered earlier in connection with the absence
of genre indication, the grammatical regime of the intertitles, and
all the descriptions Proust gave of his work – which goes to show
that he spared nothing to suggest in his own way its status as
very *sui generis*.

The actual time of publication is not very favorable to epistolary confidences, for the author is then busy tending to his review
copies – that is, writing his inscriptions. But strictly speaking,
these very inscriptions, which are sometimes copious (and are
also, and rightly so, called "envois"), are indeed a form of
missive, and the little I said about them in Chapter 6 could just as
well have been placed here; for the inscription, despite its
location, belongs less to the original peritext than to the group of
epitextual practices that accompany and orchestrate the book's
publication. Inscriptions directed at critics likewise partake of the
quest for reviews and possibly the attempt to inspire them, a
subject I have already discussed apropos of the semiofficial
epitext. This quest sometimes uses letters as its channel, as we
have seen, but if one were to consult review copies, one would no
doubt turn up numerous cases of inscriptions meant to guide
critics.[12]

Later correspondence, naturally more copious and often richer,
may in particular instances contain information (true or false) on
how the public and critics reacted to the book. I say in particular
instances because the presence of such information presupposes a
correspondent who is distant not only from the author but also
from the theatre of operations. The case of Hugo in exile is
obviously inverse (he is the one given information), but here
Balzac comes to mind, for example, announcing to Mme Hanska

---

[11] Paul Morand, "Le Visiteur du soir, Marcel Proust" (the account of a visit paid
in late 1915 or early 1916), in *Mon plaisir en littérature* (Gallimard, 1967), 137.
[12] For obvious reasons, it is undoubtedly even harder to consult review copies
than to consult copies with inscriptions to friends.

the triumph of *Le Père Goriot* the very day after it goes on sale. More commonly, later correspondence contains responses to individually expressed reactions – responses, that is, to private letters (most often, letters thanking the author for complimentary copies) and to public reviews.

Responses to private letters: we are familiar with the fundamentally important exchange of May–June 1909 between Claudel and Gide on the subject of the latter's *Porte étroite*.[13] Alongside literary compliments that were perhaps conventional, Claudel had forcefully noted what he saw as the absurd and blameworthy nature of the search for moral and religious perfection on its own account, with no hope of reward – a typically Protestant search (obviously illustrated by the behavior of Alissa). Gide is delighted by this reaction, which shows that his picture was accurate, and asserts that only Protestantism can generate such an internal drama. Much later he tells Amrouche that Claudel's letter had been a revelation to him on that point and therefore on the meaning of his work. Another well-known illustration of this type of letter is Proust's answer to Jacques Rivière (February 7, 1914): "At last I find a reader who *guesses* that my book is a dogmatic work and a structure. ... It is only at the end of the book, and when the lessons of life have been learned, that my thinking will be unveiled. The thought I express at the end of the first volume is the *opposite* of my conclusion. It is a stage, apparently subjective and casual, en route to the most objective and committed of conclusions. ..." Jacques Rivière (whose letter is lost) was not, perhaps, as deserving of praise as Proust says, for we know how the latter had multiplied his warnings *urbi et orbi*; but hyperbolic congratulations to good students have always been excellent pedagogy.

Responses to public reviews: the correspondence of Hugo or Zola overflows with them. For Hugo, I will mention only the superbly ambiguous response he gave to Lamartine's harsh criticism of *Les Misérables* in the latter's *Cours familier de littérature*: "There is much I could say to you in response. But to respond to Raphael, one has to be Michelangelo. I will limit myself to this, which has always summed up and concluded everything

13 *Correspondance Gide–Claudel* (Gallimard, 1949), 101–4 [tr. *The Correspondence 1899–1926 between Paul Claudel and André Gide*, trans. John Russell (New York: Pantheon, 1952), 89–93].

between you and me: a handshake" (April 19, 1863). And for Zola, I will mention a point-by-point refutation (April 26, 1892) of ... thirty-one criticisms directed at *Pot-Bouille* in a review printed in the daily *Gil Blas*. To each his own.

Proust, at least for *Swann*, will be almost as combative and fussy as Zola, insisting several times on the fact that he voluntarily forgoes using the right of public response. Writing to Paul Souday (December 11, 1913), he reproaches the latter for treating obvious typos as errors for which he is to blame; to Henri Ghéon (January 2, 1914) he protests against the mention of his "leisure activities," against the accusation of "subjectivity," against an error regarding Charlus's morals, and (to Ghéon) he tactlessly objects (and will apologize a few days later) to some compliments Francis Jammes had paid him; to Gaston de Pawlowski (January 11): I do not do "photography," and I am nothing less than "Bergsonian" (a pity: we will never know what a Bergsonian photographer might be like); to André Chaumeix (January 24), who chided him for his book's lack of structure: can you find one in *L'Education sentimentale*? And so forth.

But the most (justly) famous private responses are perhaps Flaubert's to Sainte-Beuve for *Salammbô* and Stendhal's to Balzac for the *Chartreuse*. Sainte-Beuve had devoted a fairly harsh three-part article to *Salammbô*. From a critic of his importance, such attention deserved a respectful and therefore private response. Flaubert is nonetheless very firm, justifying the historical coloring of his narrative, the psychology of his heroine, his descriptions, and his lexicon, drawing attention himself (a classic ploy) to errors Sainte-Beuve had not picked up (a lack of transitions; "the pedestal too big for the statue" – that is, his inadequate treatment of Salammbô; and other, more minor slips), and in fact defining the aesthetic aim of this work: "I, by applying to antiquity the technique of the modern novel, wanted to capture a mirage." Half-admiring, half-glib, the critic approves in these terms: "I no longer regret having written those articles, since by doing so I induced you to bring out all your reasons" – from our point of view, a fine tribute to the paratextual importance of Flaubert's response. Stendhal's private response thanks Balzac for a no less monumental review published September 25, 1840, in the *Revue parisienne*. We have three partly overlapping versions of the Stendhal letter and do not know which one Balzac received; he apparently did not keep it. Amidst the warmest praises, Balzac had criticized the style of the *Chartreuse* and its too-linear construction, advising the author to eliminate everything that comes before Waterloo and sum it up in an analepsis, and to do a better job at the outset of foreshadowing the characters who are introduced later on. Stendhal's reaction is apparently very spontaneous (despite the three drafts): "Your amazing article, such as no writer has ever received from another, caused me – I now dare to confess it – to burst into laughter as I read it, whenever I came upon a somewhat excessive piece of praise, which I did at every step. I could imagine the faces my friends would pull as they read it." He thanks his illustrious colleague "for your advice more than for your praise" and affirms his intention of turning it to advantage (we will see below that he actually undertook, right away, to make the recommended revision). But for all that, Stendhal does not fail to stand up for himself even on points on which he accepts Balzac's advice: my style aims at clarity and truth, "I shall correct [it], since it offends you, but I shall have great difficulty. I do not admire the style now in fashion, I am out of patience with it." Hence some jabs at Chateaubriand ("'the indeterminate crest of the forests'"), at George Sand ("If the *Chartreuse* had been translated into French by Mme Sand, she would have had some success, but to express what is told in the two present volumes she would have needed three or four. Carefully weigh this excuse"), and indeed, no doubt, at Balzac himself: "I have been told for the past year that I must sometimes give the reader a rest by describing landscape, clothes, etc. Such descriptions have bored me so much when written by others! But I shall try." Even the first fifty pages, which he obediently readies himself to condense, seemed to him "a graceful introduction" and no more encumbering than the celebrated exordia of Mme de La Fayette or Walter Scott. It's true that "the *Chartreuse* resembles a volume of memoirs: the characters appear as they are required. The fault into which I have fallen seems to me very excusable: is not this an account of Fabrice's life?" And as a bonus, Stendhal's letter contains, first, these few points of genetic information: the Sanseverina "is copied from Correggio," I "dictated [the book] in from sixty to seventy days," the epilogue was rushed because of the publisher's deadlines; and then this fundamentally important insight into the Stendhalian thematic, an insight that is equally valid for the *Rouge* or for *Leuwen*: "I had said to myself: to be at all original in 1880, after thousands of novels, my hero must not fall in love in the first volume, and there must be two heroines."[14] Clearly Stendhal's response to Balzac is as important for authorial commentary on the *Chartreuse* as his letter to Salvagnoli is for authorial commentary on the *Rouge*. Balzac could justifiably have prided himself, like Sainte-Beuve for *Salammbô*, on having induced the author to "bring out all [his] reasons." However the reader may want to use it, that is perhaps the best definition of the paratext.

In a more ironic register, I conclude by noting the response Gide made in January 1951 to Gabriel Marcel's review of the play based on *Les Caves du Vatican*: "You have made an effort to be obtuse which I confess I had hoped you were incapable of. Very cordially all the same."

For obvious reasons, writers' letters are less rich in delayed commentaries. But Flaubert (to Charpentier, February 16, 1879) does complain after twenty-two years of being always coupled with *Madame Bovary*: "I'm fed up with *Bovary*. The constant mention of that book gets on my nerves. Everything I wrote after it doesn't exist. I assure you that if I weren't in need of money I'd take steps to see that it was never reprinted." And we know of Baudelaire's fundamentally important reflection on *Les Fleurs du mal* [1857], made to his legal financial guardian, the lawyer Ancelle, on February 18, 1866: "In this *atrocious* book, I put all my *heart*, all my *love*, all my *religion* (travestied), all my *hate*. It is true that I will write the contrary, that I shall swear by all the gods that it is a book of *pure art*, of *mimicry*, of *virtuosity*, and I shall be a shameless liar."

Oral confidences

Compared with the corpus of authors' letters, the corpus of oral confidences is apparently less copious and, above all, more dispersed, for such remarks may be reported in all sorts of texts, of which only a relatively limited number (of the "Recollections of So-and-So" type) are specifically devoted to the source of these

14 [About the date 1880, see Chapter 9 under "Choice of a Public."]

confidences. This "Recollections" genre includes, partly, Boswell's *Life of Johnson* (1791) and, more massively, the *Gespräche mit Goethe in den letzten Jahren seines Lebens* [published in English as *Conversations with Eckermann*] (1836), *Monsieur Proust* by Céleste Albaret (1973), *Cahiers de la Petite Dame* [subtitled *Notes pour l'histoire authentique d'André Gide*] by Maria Van Rysselberghe (Gallimard, 1973–77), and, also concerning Gide, *Notes sur André Gide* by Roger Martin du Gard (1951), *Conversations avec André Gide* by Claude Mauriac (1951), *Gide familier* by Jean Lambert (1958), and *Une mort ambiguë* by Robert Mallet (1955) (the Mallet book concerns Claudel and Léautaud as well as Gide). Most often, remarks attributed to authors are scattered about in the correspondence or journals of the confidants: for example, the Goncourts' journal reports some conversations with Flaubert, Julien Green's journal reports numerous exchanges with Gide, and Simone de Beauvoir's memoirs report innumerable remarks made by Sartre. It is obviously the job of biographers to assemble these scattered pieces of evidence, and that is what they are doing.

The role played here by memory, by the possible predispositions and sometimes the embellishing imagination of those doing the reporting, suggests that we be prudent in utilizing these remarks, which almost never reach us exactly as spoken unless a hidden tape recorder was present. Conversely, we may suppose that the author keeps less watch over himself in oral confidences than in his correspondence, unburdens himself with more spontaneity, indeed, more sincerity – especially when he thinks, as Gide apparently did, that his remarks will never be reported.[15] But in reported remarks, the role played by commentary on the work is generally fairly slight. In his old age, Goethe comes out with some harsh words about *Werther* ("I have ... taken good care not to [read the book] again. ... [I] dread ... being involved once again in the pathological state of mind by which the novel was inspired") and about *Faust* ("Faust is crazy stuff") and finds scarcely anything to save except *Hermann and Dorothea*: "almost

---

[15] "At bottom, I have no luck ... all of those close to me: the Petite Dame, Martin, Elisabeth, you yourself [Pierre Herbart], all of them monuments of discretion, nothing that I may have said or done will ever be reported" (December 1948, *Cahiers de la Petite Dame* 4:116). Here we must naturally make allowances for coyness and the indirect request.

the only one of my longer poems that I still enjoy." As for Gide, the Petite Dame's recollections of him cover only his last thirty-three years [1918–51], and in 1918 the bulk of his work was already behind him; and among his intimates Gide hardly speaks about his works in progress except to mention the difficulties he is experiencing with *Geneviève*, the failure of which will, moreover, be glaringly apparent at a private reading.[16] Those close to him had to push him a little to extract delayed evaluations of his youthful works, or a kind of personal list of prizewinners: *Les Nourritures terrestres*, *Paludes*, and *Les Caves du Vatican* (as of July 15, 1922; but in 1928 he adds the *Journal*). These bits of information are naturally not always to be taken as gospel truth. For example, Gide asserts (April 1949) that, aside from the notes on Madeleine, he had "never eliminated anything from [his] journal," but a note by the editor Claude Martin indicates that a study of the manuscripts will prove the opposite. This author, who never stopped saying that he "did not believe in the posthumous" because he suspected friends and family of always finding "excellent reasons for doctoring, camouflaging, and whitewashing the dead person" and who, in turn, has long been suspected of having doctored and camouflaged his own life, not to whitewash himself but rather to blacken himself to advantage, might be surprised, if he were to return a century later, at how the work of the "posthumous" is righting, little by little, the image of him. As Martin du Gard once rather bluntly put it: attempting to fashion one's own image often turns out, in the end, to have been a waste of time, for "we shall none of us see our own death mask."[17] But these comments bring us to the very necessary distinction between statements and documents, a distinction that will now govern our entire study of the intimate paratext.

[16] We know that this work, which in 1930 Gide envisaged as a "novel of the *Nouvelle Héloïse* genre with long discourses," a broad ideological tableau of young intellectuals of the period, was to a great extent destroyed and ended up as the short narrative published in 1936. The confidences imparted to Claude Mauriac and Jean Lambert are very clear about this failure, which was undoubtedly the major literary disappointment of Gide's life, after Madeleine's destruction of his letters to her.

[17] Roger Martin du Gard, *Notes sur André Gide* (Gallimard, 1951), 94 [tr. *Notes on André Gide*, trans. John Russell (New York: Viking, 1953), 80–81].

Diaries

I use the term *intimate epitext* to designate any message bearing
directly or indirectly on an author's own past, present, or future
work which the author addresses to himself, with or without
the intention of publishing it later – for the intention does not
always ensure the result. A manuscript meant for publication
may disappear accidentally – or even because the author
changed his mind (as Thomas Mann apparently did with
respect to a large part of his journal); and conversely, a manuscript not meant for publication may accidentally escape destruction, such as the manuscripts of *The Trial* and *The Castle*.
This type of message is found basically in two types of
documents: diaries and dossiers of pre-texts. The distinction
between these two types is much less clear-cut in practice than
in theory, for many diaries, such as Kafka's, contain rough
drafts; and conversely, many dossiers of pre-texts, such as
Stendhal's, contain diary-type notes, information or commentary
on the work in progress. We will encounter these difficulties of
categorization when we focus on the intimate epitext that
precedes publication. But first, to start with what is easiest, I
will say a word about the later and delayed epitext, which – in
the author's journal – basically reveals his reactions to the
reception accorded his work as well as his own assessment of
his work after the event.

On a book's publication, the anguish an author feels while
waiting for critics and the public to express their judgment, and
the effect this judgment has on the author, are probably evidenced nowhere more intensely than in Virginia Woolf's diary.[18]
For Woolf, from *Night and Day* (1919) to *Between the Acts* (1941),
each publication is an occasion of real agony, apparently aggravated by the great closeness among members of the Bloomsbury
group. Anxious about the judgment – which, however, was
unfailingly favorable – of her husband (and publisher) Leonard
and of her friends E. M. Forster, Lytton Strachey, Roger Fry, and
Harold Nicolson, and in very keen competition with Katherine
Mansfield (who had once, rather cruelly, called her "Miss Austen
up-to-date" and whose death, in January 1923, she greets with

[18] [The source for these quotations is the five-volume *Diary of Virginia Woolf*, ed.
Anne Olivier Bell (New York: Harcourt Brace Jovanovich, 1977–84).]

very mixed feelings),[19] Virginia Woolf displays in her diaries a
paradoxical sensitivity: she is not much reassured by praise
("Lytton praises me too highly for it to give me exquisite
pleasure; or perhaps that nerve grows dulled," October 14, 1922),
is often more stimulated by criticism ("But I value blame. It spurs
one," April 15, 1920; "Already I am feeling the calm that always
comes to me with abuse: my back is against the wall: I am writing
for the sake of writing: &c. & then there is the queer disreputable
pleasure in being abused – in being a figure, in being a martyr. &
so on," October 11, 1934; "And there is the odd pleasure too of
being abused: & the feeling of being dismissed into obscurity is
also pleasant & salutary," October 14, 1934; "But the delight of
being exploded is quite real. One feels braced for some reason;
amused; roused; combative; more than by praise," April 2, 1937),
but above all is terrified by the waiting and is always set to
believe that no one will mention her book and that every silence
conceals a negative judgment (April 27, 1925, for *The Common
Reader*: "It is as if one tossed a stone into a pond, and the waters
closed without a ripple"; October 23, 1929, she is afraid that
Forster will refuse to review *A Room of One's Own*; November 16,
1931: "To be noted, as curiosities of my literary history: I
sedulously avoid meeting Roger & Lytton whom [sic] I suspect
do not like The Waves"; August 2, 1940: "Complete silence
surrounds that book [her biography of Fry]. It might have sailed
into the blue & been lost. 'One of our books did not return' as the
BBC puts it. No review by Morgan, no review at all. No letter.
And tho' I suspect Morgan has refused, finding it unpalatable,
still I remain – yes honestly, quiet minded, & prepared to face a
complete, a lasting silence"). Virginia Woolf's psychic vulner-
ability is expressed more on this level than on the subject of the
vicissitudes of her writing itself,[20] and undoubtedly it is not

---

[19] "At that one feels – what? A shock of relief? – a rival the less? Then confusion
at feeling so little – then, gradually, blankness & disappointment; then a
depression which I could not rouse myself from all that day. When I began to
write, it seemed to me there was no point in writing. Katherine wont read it.
Katherine's my rival no longer. More generously I felt, But though I can do this
better than she could, where is she, who could do what I can't!" (January 16,
1923).

[20] Not that she, too, was unfamiliar with the "torments of writing": "A good day
– a bad day – so it goes on. Few people can be so tortured by writing as I am.
Only Flaubert I think" (June 23, 1936). One of the most gratifying aspects of the
"job" was perhaps, for her, the steady increase in the amount of money her

pushing things too far to recall that she ended her life after putting the completed manuscript of *Between the Acts* in the mail, as if she found it finally unbearable to face the anguish of publication one more time.

After such heated passages, the statements in other diaries may seem more temperate, if not placid. In them we especially find judgments after the event, often going against the grain of popular and critical opinion. We see Jules Renard, for example, unhappy with *Poil de carotte* ("A bad book, incomplete, badly constructed," September 21, 1894) and displaying in comparison a preference for *Histoires naturelles* (October 14, 1907); or Gide complaining about having known only flops, "the flatness of the flop ... in direct ratio to the importance and originality of the work, so that it was to *Paludes*, *Les Nourritures*, and *Les Caves du Vatican* that I owed the worst ones. Of all my books the one that on the contrary brought me the warmest, most substantial, and promptest praises is the one that (not the least well turned out perhaps) remains the most outside my work, that *interests* me the least (I am using the word in its most subtle sense), and that, all things considered, I would be most willing to see disappear" (July 15, 1922; I admit I cannot definitely identify this undeserved success). His judgment of his early works, *André Walter* or the *Nourritures*, is, moreover, often harsh, at least on the level of style, which he deems intolerably bombastic;[21] *La Porte étroite* strikes him as uneven, like "a nougat in which the almonds are good (i.e., the letters and journal of Alissa), but in which the filling is pasty, nondescript writing" (November 7, 1909, an opinion confirmed in March 1913). *Corydon* is of prime importance but still too timid (August 1922, November 1927, October 1942). *Caves* was not understood by critics, perhaps for lack of a preface that would have spelled out its purpose (as we know, one had been planned and abandoned, then unearthed), but "there is a certain amusement and even some advantage in letting the critics make a mistake at first" (June 30, 1914). *Si le grain ne meurt* is full "of grammatical errors, ambiguities, bloomers. If it were not already

books brought in, money that – as co-director, with her husband, of Hogarth Press – she carefully keeps track of in the account books, figuring up sometimes the cost of buying a car, sometimes the cost of installing a bathroom ...
[21] The same judgment in *Si le grain ne meurt* ("inspired tone") and in the conversations with Amrouche.

printed, I should cut out three quarters of it" (June 23, 1924). As
for the relative failure of *Les Faux-Monnayeurs*, he thinks it short-
lived (March 5, 1927) and attributes it to his "too constant anxiety
for art, ... I had 'stretched my nets too high,' as Stendhal said"
(June 23, 1930). "What is easier than to write a novel like others! I
am loath to do so, that's all, and no more than Valéry can I resign
myself to writing: 'The Marquise went out at five o'clock,' or, and
this is of a quite different nature, but strikes me as even more
compromising: 'X. wondered at length whether ...'" (August 1,
1931). We have already encountered this tendency, so common
among modern authors, to offset other people's judgment with a
contrary one, disparaging the best-received works and putting a
high value on the others. This gesture is quite fair in public
controversy; it is also, apparently, good personal strategy, for it
establishes a "globally positive" balance sheet: some of my books
have been successful, which is gratifying, and the others are
good, which is even more gratifying. Classical writers, as we
know, as a rule rejected this type of consolation, at least in public
and with regard to the public and its long-term judgments. But
we know, too, that classical writers were not in the habit of
keeping diaries.

Anyone who searches in writers' journals for precise and detailed
information about the creation of their works is likely to be
disappointed, for at least two reasons. First, many a writer looks
on his journal rather as a complement to – indeed, as relief from –
the work, and uses it preferably to keep track of events ("intimate" or not) external to his work: see the journals of the
Goncourt brothers or of Jules Renard, which are useful especially
as pictures of contemporary literary life. Second, as a specialist in
the genre has observed, "It is very rare that a writer will be
occupied simultaneously in creating a book and in keeping a
journal."[22] Alternation between the two may involve a massive
interruption, such as that of Stendhal's journal from 1819
onward[23] or of Tolstoy's between 1865 and 1878, to say nothing
of an intentional destruction of material after the fact, as in the

[22] Alain Girard, *Le Journal intime* (Presses universitaires de France, 1963), 168.
[23] Unless one "reconstitutes" it, as V. del Litto does, that is, *puts together* as a
journal the notes and marginalia scattered after that date throughout Stendhal's whole library.

case of Thomas Mann between 1896 and 1917 and between 1922 and 1932. Usually, however, the exchange fits a looser pattern; the writer at work continues to keep his journal but largely refrains from mentioning his work in progress. This pattern is particularly obvious with Claudel, who mentions only his long-term projects in his journal, clearing them out of it as soon as the active phase of writing begins. As Jacques Petit has observed, "Once a work is under way it no longer has a place in [Claudel's] journal, which remains the province of everyday chance events, a collection of isolated impressions, of notes without a precise point, but a sort of 'reservoir' he will later draw from. And so we discover in the journal the preparations for a work, the traces of its maturation, more often than allusions or comments exactly contemporaneous with its writing."[24] The reason for this kind of incompatibility is fairly obvious, and almost physical. The actual labor of writing, or even of actively preparing to write, gets done by means of other vehicles, in places other than the journal: in drafts and sketches constituting the pre-text. Jacques Petit notes this again, apropos of [Claudel's play] *Le Père humilié*: the author jots down in his journal on May 17, 1915, "The shape of my drama is becoming clear," while on that same day he sketches the plot of his play on a separate piece of paper that today is kept with the manuscript. The only authors who do not apportion things in this way are those, such as Kafka, who use the same vehicle alternately as a journal of their life and as a notebook of sketches. But even so, in Kafka we clearly see that this juxtaposition involves hardly any comments in the journal about the sketches: the latter – sometimes very elaborate – are interspersed among the daily notes without warning in a kind of reciprocal ignorance; this has allowed some editors to publish post-humously the sketches alone or the daily notes alone. As for James's notebooks or Musil's journals, there is hardly anything diary-like about them except that dates are assigned to what is basically a notebook of sketches. Another factor, too, sometimes helps distort the evidence provided in journals – the factor that Gide mentions, in a conversation with Green: "[My diary] gives a completely false idea of me, for I hardly ever keep it except in moments of discouragement."[25] In this respect, the diary is a little

---

[24] Jacques Petit, "note" to the Pléiade edition of the *Journal*, lxiv.
[25] Julien Green, *Journal* (Pléiade), 4:474.

14 The private epitext

like the daily newspaper: it reports bad news more often than good, it discusses the train only when there is a derailment. Work that is going well does not really call for any comment, except a short note of the "worked well this morning" variety; it entirely absorbs the writer's time and energy and bears its own witness, as it were, in its effects. The times when the writer is "stuck," in contrast, are more conducive to a switching of desks, with the groans of Gide's journal or Kafka's (like those of Flaubert's correspondence) perhaps playing here a cathartic role.

For these and some other reasons, the "logbook" aspect of writers' journals is often fairly limited. The portion of Gide's journal or Woolf's or Mann's or Green's which is devoted to the author's labors is therefore discontinuous (in Green, on the order – a highly approximate statistic – of about ten lines every ten pages, or one-fortieth of the present version)[26] and fairly elliptical: that portion mentions, from time to time, how well or badly the work is going rather than describing it in detail or commenting on its subject. So from reading the pages of Virginia Woolf's diary that refer to *Flush* we are completely unable to guess that book's subject, which nevertheless is very distinctive; and this case is not at all exceptional.

Let us not conclude, however, that the journal in general is paratextually destitute. Woolf's, for example, contains valuable information about her methods of working, particularly her technique of doing the final revision by retyping the whole as quickly as possible ("a good method, I believe, as thus one works with a wet brush over the whole, & joins parts separately composed & gone dry" – December 13, 1924), and about her authorial judgments ("I daresay its true, however, that I haven't that 'reality' gift" – June 19, 1923, on *The Hours*; "I have written this book [*Orlando*] quicker than any: & it is all a joke; & yet gay & quick reading I think; a writers holiday"; "I began it as a joke, & went on with it seriously. Hence it lacks some unity"; "this

---

26 P. de Mendelssohn's edition of Mann's *Diaries* for the years 1918–21 and 1933–39 (Fischer, 1977–79; English translation published by Abrams, 1982) is only a selection, but the editor says he kept the same proportion of subjects as in the original. In the case of Green's *Journal*, one part of which – the most "personal," in the ordinary sense of the word – is held back for posthumous publication, the definitive version will no doubt reduce the proportion devoted to literary evidence. As for Woolf, the difference in bulk between the complete *Diary* (5 volumes) and the *Diary of a Writer* (1 volume) – even though the latter is not limited to her logbook – is eloquent in itself.

Orlando is of course a very quick brilliant book. Yes, but I did not try to explore" – March to November 1928). Judgments, more-over, that fluctuate, such as these – apropos of *The Years* – written only several weeks apart: "Never did I enjoy writing a book more, I think" (December 29, 1935), but on rereading it, "Such feeble twaddle – such twilight gossip it seemed; such a show up of my own decrepitude, & at such huge length" (January 16, 1936), and three months later, "It now seems to me so good ... that I cant go on correcting" (March 18, 1936).

To my knowledge and despite his restraint, Green's journal constitutes the most coherent, or the best organized, evidence about a labor of literature whose permanent features he clearly singles out: a slowness to which he is resigned (one day he worries about a "suspect fluency"); tireless rewriting ("I have indeed redone the beginning of *Moïra* eight or nine times," February 25, 1957); a Stendhalian refusal to write outlines, which "kill the imagination"; the need to have, for each novel, a generating image to refer to (for *Mont-Cinère*, the photograph of a house in Savannah; for *Adrienne Mesurat*, a canvas by Utrillo); the independence of the characters, whom their creator *observes* rather than directs (the author is "a little like someone who would listen behind doors and peek through a keyhole, but he never tries to intervene. To intervene, to change the course of an action determined by the characters, is to invent a novel. Everyone can do that. To me, that would be of no interest whatsoever" – April 8, 1955; for the true novelist "invents nothing, he guesses" – February 5, 1933); the autobiographical truth of fiction ("My real journal is in my novels," October 15, 1948)[27] – fiction takes as its material exactly what the journal passes over in silence ("A novel is made of sin as a table is made of wood," October 27, 1955).

The only "logbook" that is entirely and exclusively devoted to the creation of a work is, to my knowledge, Gide's *Journal des Faux-Monnayeurs*, a logbook kept from June 1919 to May 1925

[27] This commonplace in the form of a paradox – from which Philippe Lejeune derived the notion of *autobiographical space* – already appears in Gide (if not earlier). See, for example, the last note to the first part of *Si le grain ne meurt*: "Memoirs are never more than half sincere, however great one's desire for truth; everything is always more complicated than one makes out. Possibly even one gets nearer to truth in the novel."

and published in 1927. Whether taken from Gide's journal or not, these brief pages – which, as we know, are justified in the actual novel, thanks to the novelist Edouard[28] – slightly give the impression of being an *ad hoc* undertaking aimed more at demonstrating than at documenting. What's more, statements about the real labor take up less space than either the author's declaration of intention in the form of self-exhortation (somewhat as in Zola's sketches) or his profession of aesthetic faith.[29] Sustained by a kind of private controversy with Martin du Gard, Gide makes the decision that in this work, which he considers his "first novel," he will reject the panoramic technique of a Tolstoy in favor of a more focalized narrative, a picture in chiaroscuro governed by the point of view of certain characters. For models of this relativist technique Gide invokes Dickens and especially Dostoevsky, but today we would also think of James's precepts, codified during the same period by his disciples Percy Lubbock and Joseph Warren Beach. They are therefore precepts of their time (the autonomy of the characters, "Take constant care that a character speaks only for the benefit of the one to whom he is addressing himself" [*J. des F.-M.* January 13, 1921], "Never present *ideas* except in terms of temperaments and characters" [June 17, 1919], "Admit that a character who is exiting can be only seen from the rear" [January 2, 1921], and so forth) – precepts that, up to Sartre and doubtless beyond, will remain the aesthetic vulgate of one type of "modern" novel, a type inaugurated actually by *Madame Bovary* and characterized by the rejection of classical "omniscience" (although for the sake of contrast that omniscience is somewhat exaggerated, even with respect to Balzac's or Tolstoy's fiction). In short, Gide's *J. des F.-M.* is a "journal" very deliberately addressed (and dedicated) "to those who find questions of craft interesting" – a journal that, like certain prefaces, has much the quality of a manifesto.

[28] "Just think how interesting such a note-book kept by Dickens or Balzac would be; if we had the diary of the *Education Sentimentale* or of *The Brothers Karamazof*! – the story of the work – of its gestation! How thrilling it would be … more interesting than the work itself. …"

[29] The author specifies, moreover, that these pages contain only general remarks "on the planning, composition, and guiding motive of the novel," leaving the role played by detail to slips of paper that go straight into the category of the pre-text.

Pre-texts

The paratextual message of writers' journals, whether its subject be technical or (more rarely) thematic, has more to do with testimony than with documentation. And this testimony is always questionable, not only insofar as it is intended for publication (anthumous or posthumous) and is therefore directed in the final analysis at a public to which the author reveals only what he wants to reveal, but also more generally and more radically because, like any journal – indeed, like any interior monologue – it consists of telling oneself what one wants to tell oneself and wants to hear oneself telling oneself: it is a discourse whose pragmatics is no more shorn of strategic intentions than any other, is less dedicated to setting forth the truth than to producing an effect on its author. Even without being directed at the public, the intimate message of the journal, like all paratextual messages I have evoked so far, is therefore an intentional and persuasive message. Its typical content is something like "Here is what *I tell myself* about how I am writing this book, here is what *I tell myself* I think about both the book and what others have said of it" – in short, "Here are the feelings about this book which I exhibit to myself." One would have to be very naive about the inner life to assume that this exhibition is always in good faith and uncontaminated by any playacting. Besides, there are abundant signs to the contrary, as when Virginia Woolf declares so insistently that criticisms delight her or leave her calm and collected.

When we come to the dossier of pre-texts, we apparently abandon the always subjective and suspect terrain of testimony for the theoretically more objective terrain of the *document*; and at the same time – a new border – we apparently abandon the terrain of the conscious and organized paratext, or the paratext *de jure,* for that of an involuntary and *de facto* paratext. A manuscript page supposedly says to us, this time in the third person, "Here is how the author wrote this book." The irrefragable givens of archeology, shards and carved stones, supposedly take over now from historiographical chitchat: finally something solid.

Unfortunately or not, we must temper this optimism. Not only because some anthumous publications of pre-texts arouse a suspicion or two among the mischievous or because some official donations, from Hugo to Aragon, are a little too structured for us

to rule out all thought of authorial staging, but also because –
more simply and, here again, more radically – the pre-texts
available to us (except in very particular circumstances of which I
know no example) are by definition manuscripts that their
authors indeed wished to leave behind; and the variously
worded stipulation "To be burned after my death" carries only
relative weight and stands little likelihood of being fulfilled.
When an author – let us say Chateaubriand – wants one of his
manuscripts to disappear, he knows enough to attend to it in
person. The pre-texts retained by posterity are all, therefore, pre-
texts *passed on* by their authors, along with the degree of intention
that attaches to such a gesture and with no guarantee of compre-
hensiveness: nothing withstands the techniques of codicologists
and other experts ... except a missing page. In short, the objective
and real message of the pre-text has to be rewritten instead in this
form: "Here is what the author was willing to let us know about
the way he wrote his book." From "let us know" to *have us know*
is only a very small step, and as a result the *"de jure"* again fully
envelops the *"de facto"*: for one to visit a "workshop," the workshop must indeed exist, and someone must have opened it up.

Given these reservations (about the absolute veracity of the
pre-text but not – indeed, to the contrary – about its paratextual
value) and taking into account both the still-tender age of the
discipline known as "genetic criticism"[30] and my very poor
competence in a highly technical area where improvisation is not
acceptable, I think we can nonetheless rough out a kind of
inventory of the types of documents likely to go into a dossier of
pre-texts. They include hypotextual sources such as the Berthot
trial for the *Rouge* or the Farnese chronicle for the *Chartreuse*;
seminal anecdotes – sorts of oral hypotexts – such as those often
set down in James's notebooks; preparatory documents, such as
Flaubert's copious reading notes for *La Tentation*, for *Salammbô*, or
for *Hérodias* or Zola's sociological investigations ("My notes on
Anzin" for *Germinal*, and others); programmatic outlines, again

[30] For general methodological principles, see, among others, Jean Bellemin-Noël,
Le Texte et l'avant-texte (Larousse, 1972); "Genèse du texte" [the title of the
whole issue], *Littérature*, no. 28 (December 1977); the anthology *Essais de critique
génétique* (Flammarion, 1979); Louis Hay, "Le Texte n'existe pas," *Poétique*
(April 1985); and A. Grésillon and M. Werner, eds., *Leçons d'écriture: Ce que
disent les manuscrits* (Minard, 1985) – without prejudicing the (much more
numerous) individual studies.

such as Zola's – their status lies midway between pre-text and journal, for they fall within the domain of directives to oneself ("Proceed this way or that way") at least as much as, and often more than, within the domain of real outlines; plans and scenarios, sometimes preparatory, sometimes recapitulatory during the writing; "fictional documents" (I will come back to this in connection with Zola); "drafts" proper – that is, rewritten versions, often very numerous for the same final version, as we see in Flaubert or Proust, including numerous pages later discarded (see the "new version" of *Madame Bovary* that Pommier and Leleu put together on the basis of these discards); "clean" manuscripts, autograph or transcribed, and nowadays typescripts or computer printouts; page proofs that are more or less corrected; and in addition the special category of pre-texts that I propose to call *after-texts* and that we will encounter again below. This very empirical list is probably not exhaustive, and I imagine that modern word-processing techniques have begun producing some supplementary items that are still mysteries to me.

Were this list exhaustive, it would undoubtedly allow us to envisage a typology of pre-textual practices in which we would see each author (and sometimes each work) characterized by his choices, deliberate or instinctive. To illustrate with some well-known examples, let us say that Balzac is characterized by, among other things, his inordinate use of corrections on proofs; Stendhal, by the presence in the margins of explanatory comments called "scaffolds" or "construction piles" and carefully labeled with the English phrase *for me*, the most famous of which is, alas! this authorial response to the character Mme de Chasteller, who wondered where the horrible thought of raising Lucien's hand to her lips came from: "From the womb, my dear!" Zola, by what Henri Mitterand describes as a "nearly unalterable plan of action":[31] programmatic sketch, documentary notes, "fictional documents" (lists of possible titles or of names of places and characters), a brief plan of the whole, and detailed chapter-by-chapter plans (what seems to be missing here is any role for multiple rewrites, as if Zola, after the ground had been duly prepared, wrote as the ink flows, crossing nothing out); James – judging from his notebooks alone – by the slow work of amplifi-

---

[31] "Programme et préconstruit génétique: Le dossier de *L'Assommoir*," in *Essais de critique génétique.*

cation set in motion by the initial anecdote, of psychological motivation, of much pondered technical choices ("point of view," person, distribution of dramatic scenes and narrative summaries), and finally, of writing that is often so subtle and "indirect" that it ends up blurring a large part of the intermediary psychological construction into allusiveness and evanescence; Proust – to conclude – by an indefinite process of inflation and "supernourishment" (with the help of a great many paste-ons and "paperoles"),[32] a process involving a narrative framework whose broad outlines are imagined from the very beginning, and by a neverending play of displacements and transfers, erratic all-purpose pages that are the despair of geneticians and editors. For a shorter text, Ponge's *La Fabrique du Pré* [*The Making of "The Meadow"*] shows an evolution that is undoubtedly more specific and perhaps typical of the "creative method" of this particular author:[33] from August to October 1960, Ponge composes a set of sketches according to nature; in October, he has recourse to the *Littré* dictionary, searching for etymologies and homophones; on October 12, a remark by Philippe Sollers introduces the phrase taken from Rimbaud, "le clavecin des prés" ["the harpsichord of the meadows"], variously incorporated into the versions of November–December; then a two-year interruption until a new set of sketches is made during the winter of 1962–63; again an interruption, until the following winter; and then in May–June 1964, Ponge launches one last campaign (the final version will be published in 1967 in *Le Nouveau Recueil*).

These genetic dossiers (the study of which is no doubt destined to expand) must be supplemented by the dossiers of unfinished works,[34] works for which we have nothing else besides pre-texts (without any certain, final outcome), such as Stendhal's *Lucien*

---

[32] Very often introduced by a formula of deployment that becomes a kind of tic: "Capital, when I say ..." (or "When I do ... ," for here, too, the *I* designates the hero as well as the author: "To be put in when I meet Bloch ..."); Proust's systematic use of the formula involves a superlativization (*capitalissime, capitalissime, issime, issime*) that dissuades us from seeing it as an always meaningful assessment. ["Paperoles" are defined in Chapter 2, note 21.]

[33] Another dossier of the Pongean pre-text, *Comment une figue de paroles et pourquoi* (Flammarion, 1977), is much less usable at the present time, for most of its versions are undated. [*La Fabrique du Pré* has appeared in English as *The Making of the Pré*, trans. Lee Fahnestock (Columbia: University of Missouri Press, 1979). "Pré" means meadow, and the work with that title is a poem.]

[34] See *Le Manuscrit inachevé*, ed. L. Hay (Paris: CNRS, 1986).

Leuwen and *Lamiel*, Flaubert's *Bouvard et Pécuchet*, Kafka's *Amerika*, Musil's *The Man Without Qualities* – and strictly speaking, all of the *Recherche* starting with *La Prisonnière* – for which the task of establishing the "text" is largely conjectural, with editors' practices moving gradually toward greater fidelity to the unpolished version of the manuscript. The most recent (and most deviant) episode in this evolution is the publication, in the spring of 1986, of an "edition" of *The Garden of Eden*[35] consisting of 247 pages drawn by Tom Jenks from a typescript of 1,500 pages found in 1961 among Hemingway's papers. But as this pre-text is certainly preserved, for geneticians there remains a long row to hoe, and for us, the prospect of an edition undoubtedly less readable than Jenks's but more instructive about the paths – and impasses – of literary creation.

A last type of pre-text, as I have already indicated, consists of revisions and corrections made to an already published text. That is why I speak here of "after-texts," but it goes without saying that the *after* of one edition is (or is intended to be) the *before* of a later edition. When these corrections are used for a new anthumous edition, the last authenticated text generally becomes "the" official text of the work, with the earlier versions preserved only as variants, unless there are serious (aesthetic or other) reasons for occasionally republishing the original version, as has been done for Corneille's *Cid*, Senancour's *Oberman*, and Chateaubriand's *Vie de Rancé*.[36] When the author dies before having been able to prepare a new edition but has written down his corrections with enough care and certainty, posthumous editors take them into account, which brings us back to the preceding situation: see Montaigne's additions, made between 1588 and 1592, on the so-called Bordeaux copy, and Balzac's modifications, made after 1842, on his copy of the Furne edition (today this "corrected Furne" is the basis of all reliable editions of *La Comédie humaine*). But other corrections made after publication are more confused, less firmly decided on, and nothing indicates that the author would have stayed with them. In this situation, posthumous editors preserve the text of the original edition and relegate

[35] New York: Scribner's Sons.
[36] *Le Cid*, ed. Cauchie (Textes français modernes, 1946); *Oberman*, ed. Monglond (Arthaud, 1947); *Rancé*, ed. M.-F. Guyard (GF, 1969).

399

the author's stray corrective impulses to notes of variants. This is typically the case for Stendhal's three completed novels[37] – *Armance*, the *Rouge*, and the *Chartreuse* – for which we have marginal or interleaved notes on copies called, after their collectors, "Bucci" for the first two and "Chaper" for the third.[38] The *Armance* notes contain, among other things, various indications about the creation of the novel and especially a very clear outline that specifies in black and white (once again) the hero's impotence. The *Rouge* notes envisage corrections of detail, sometimes backed up by an assessment ("tone too offhand"), but they also contain marks of approval (the English phrase "very well") – both the former and the latter serving clearly as authorial comments. The *Chartreuse* notes have a more important purpose, for they try, among other things, to apply Balzac's advice, but they won't lead to anything: Stendhal proves to be very hesitant on the question of this novel's style, which seems to him "tedious like a translation of Tacitus" but, even so, preferable to the style of the novels then in fashion; and hesitant also on the distressing excision of an opening chapter that reminds him really too much of a time he is "passionately fond of." A fundamentally important note confirms, without spelling things out, what otherwise would be only a reading hypothesis: that Fabrice "was regarded as" the son of Lieutenant Robert. On this point as on Octave's impotence, the interpretive relevance of the pre-text – and more generally of the paratext – is decisive, whatever the critics' denials. One may even deem its relevance overpowering and excessive: "*Armance*. Obviously, when one has the key to the mystery (it is in everyone's hands), to a certain extent one has the impression of cheating. I don't think I would have guessed. ..."[39] This kind of scruple, or regret, is certainly shared by a good many readers, but (let us note) it is based solely on the paratextual nature of this "key." If Stendhal had introduced as clear a sentence into the actual text, the authorial interpretive nudge would have been just as indiscreet; and conversely, if he had kept his key in his own hands and made sure it stayed there, readers

[37] As a matter of fact, the first posthumous editions, courtesy of Romain Colomb for Lévy, more or less incorporated these corrections; but modern editions have not followed suit.
[38] For the *Chartreuse*, other, later corrections and additions exist, which editors put into appendixes.
[39] Julien Green, *Journal* (Pléiade), 4:1186.

would quite frankly have nothing to "guess," for "Octave's impotence," which everyone nowadays naively takes for a "fact," would have no more existence than the number of Lady Macbeth's children or the names of Hamlet's professors at Wittenberg. In any case, and once again, this kind of effect serves as a measure of how fragile the distinction between text and paratext is.

But the paratextual function of the pre-text does not boil down to these relatively exceptional effects of explanatory or evaluative comments. More fundamentally, the paratextual function of the pre-text consists of offering a more or less organized tour of the "workshop," uncovering the ways and means by which the text has become what it is – distinguishing, for instance, between what was there at the beginning and what turned up only along the way. For example, examination of the manuscripts and proofs of Balzac's *Béatrix* allows Maurice Regard to make the case that that novel's cultural references and "intellectual reflections" did not appear until fairly late, generally on proofs, and that "the first draft – what Jean Pommier calls *spontaneous writing* – is essentially physiological."[40] Another example is one we have already glimpsed: the chronology of the versions of *Pré* (assuming the chronology given in *La Fabrique du Pré* to be accurate) shows that in this case neither Ponge's recourse to suggestions from the lexicon (pré < *paratus* ["*paratus*: ... prepared"; the prefix "pré-" = "the syllable of pre-paration"]) nor his recourse to suggestions from the intertext (the "clavecin des prés") dates from the very beginning; rather, both of them come about only after a fairly long phase of "realistic" observation – the author "taking words into account" *after* "taking the side of things" [*Taking the Side of Things – Le Parti pris des choses* – is the title of an earlier book by Ponge]. Still another example: examination of Proust's manuscripts shows that the definitive names of the characters in the *Recherche* are most often not adopted until the last stage and therefore cannot play the triggering role sometimes attributed to them.[41] I find it hard to see how anyone could defend the

---

[40] Garnier edition, 463–64.
[41] See Roland Barthes, "Proust et les noms" (1967), in *Nouveaux Essais critiques*, published with *Le Degré zéro de l'écriture* (Seuil, 1972) [tr. "Proust and Names," in *New Critical Essays*, trans. Richard Howard (New York: Hill and Wang, 1980)].

legitimacy of a critical interpretation that, unaware of such particulars, would surmise a reverse order of creation in any of these cases. Of course, interpretation must be no less careful about using old versions of the text or early comments that may testify to intentions subsequently abandoned: if a scenario of January 1895 for *The Turn of the Screw* (published three years later) seems to decide the question that the final text carefully leaves open (the question of whether the ghosts really did appear), nothing proves that James did not change his mind in the interval.[42] What is oldest does not necessarily tell the truth about what is most recent, and the recovery of origins must not end up assigning any kind of hermeneutic privilege to what is earliest. Were that to happen, obviously we would be replacing the old finalist fetishism of the "last version," looked on as the inevitable culmination and as superior by definition, with a new and even less well founded fetishism, a kind of archaizing cult of the literary *Ur-Suppe* [primal soup].

For the most important but also most ambiguous effect of the pre-text is perhaps the way in which genetic study, surrounding the "final" text with the entire, sometimes enormous mass of its past versions, confronts what the text is with what it was, with what it could have been, with what it almost became, thus (in keeping with Valéry's wish) helping to relativize the notion of completion, to blur the "closure" that has been made too much of, and to remove the aura of sacredness from the very notion of Text. If Jacques Petit's formula "The Text does not exist" (a formula that, in turn, has perhaps been made too much of) is no doubt merely a provocation, it serves the altogether salutary purpose of warning us that the work and the œuvre are always to a greater or lesser extent in progress and that the cessation of this labor, like death itself, is always to some degree accidental.

One last word on the specificity of the epitext in general, whether public or private: this specificity itself is wholly relative, for the epitextual message often has the same content as the peritextual message, sometimes taking its place (an interview substituting for a preface) and sometimes intensifying it in a considerably repetitive authorial commentary (see Borges). In reality the main

---

[42] This reservation does not apply in the case of *Armance*, where the private "revelations" about Octave's condition are subsequent to publication.

difference between epitextual and peritextual messages lies in the choice of channel, and therefore (to water down McLuhan's old formula, likewise a provocative one), a large part of the message lies in the nature of the medium. The specificity of the epitext is relative as well in that recourse to the epitextual path (or voice) is very often only provisional: in the case of major works that find favor with posterity, posthumous editions tend more and more, as we have already noted, to incorporate into the critical peritext the most significant part – even the totality – of what was originally the public and private epitext. As a result, the post-humous peritext is gradually becoming the receptacle, and as it were the museum, of the totality of the paratext, whatever place may have been chosen for it first. Long ago Valéry used to say, "Everything ends up at the Sorbonne" – which (and let us add this to the unassuming glory of the old lady and her young sisters) is not exactly an end but an everlasting renewal: every-thing survives, or is revived, "in the curriculum." Today we would readily add, with the same degree of antonomasia and exaggeration, "Everything ends up in the Pléiade" (which is often the same thing): text, pre-text, and paratexts of all kinds. So we have come full circle: having started out with publishing, our investigation returns to publishing. The ultimate destiny of the paratext is sooner or later to catch up with its text in order to *make a book*.

15

❖❖❖

Conclusion

❖❖❖

However long – and, I fear, however fatiguing – this journey may
have been, I must not conceal the fact that it is by no means
exhaustive, nor was it meant to be. For one thing, each of these
chapters merely skims over its subject at the very general level of
a typology (this is really and truly only an introduction, and
exhortation, to the study of the paratext); for another thing, this
inventory of paratextual elements remains incomplete. Some
elements (for example, the practices of non-European cultures)
simply eluded me because I didn't pay much attention to them or
have enough information about them. Other elements are not
commonly used nowadays and my knowledge of them is too
erratic for me to be able to study them in any meaningful way.
For instance, certain elements of the documentary paratext that
are characteristic of didactic works are sometimes appended,
with or without playful intent, to works of fiction: Senancour's
Oberman includes a sort of thematic index called "Indications,"
arranged in alphabetical order (Adversité, Aisance, Amitié [Ad-
versity, Ease, Friendship] ...); *Moby-Dick* opens with a comprehensive documentary dossier about whales; Updike's *Bech: A
Book* ends with an imaginary bibliography of works by and
studies about the hero (the studies are attributed apocryphally to
real critics); the "appendix" of Perec's *Vie mode d'emploi* [*Life: A
User's Manual*] contains a floor plan of the building, an index of
persons and places, a chronology, a list of authors quoted, and an
"Alphabetical Checklist of Some of the Stories Narrated in this
Manual." Novelistic works like Zola's *Rougon-Macquart*, Thackeray's *Henry Esmond*, Nabokov's *Ada*, or Renaud Camus's *Roman
roi* contain family trees constructed by the authors themselves.[1]

---

[1] Actually, *Les Rougon-Macquart* contains two family trees, one published in 1878
with *Une Page d'amour*, the other in 1893 with *Le Docteur Pascal*, which shows
the development of the system. See Pléiade 5:1777 et seq.

For the *Portable Faulkner* of 1946, Faulkner drew a map of Yoknapatawpha County; and Umberto Eco drew a plan of the abbey in *The Name of the Rose*. Still other elements, used more regularly, figure as little more than announcements – such as the dramatis personae for plays (but some novels, such as *Green Hills of Africa*, imitate this practice), which from the classical period onward includes a useful direction about place and, in our own time, often an equally valuable mention of the first cast. Beaumarchais adds various directions about dress and, most important of all, about the characters; everyone knows at least the directions ["Notes on the Characters and Their Costumes"] for *Le Mariage de Figaro*.

I have likewise left out three practices whose paratextual relevance seems to me undeniable, but investigating each one individually might demand as much work as was required here in treating this subject as a whole. The first of the three practices is *translation*, particularly when it is more or less revised or checked by the author, as Groethuysen's German version of *Les Nourritures terrestres* was by Gide; and all the more so when the entire task is undertaken by the author alone, in keeping with the established practice of a bilingual writer such as Beckett, each of whose translations must, in one way or another, serve as commentary on the original text.[2] The second practice, wholly different in kind, is *serial publication*,[3] which is generally held to go back to *Robinson Crusoe* but which became widespread after 1836 and has continued right on up to our own day, with some vicissitudes.[4] The operations – cuts and deletions – performed on texts at these times certainly do not always have the blessings of the author, who sometimes complains about them, but the particulars of the negotiations deserve close examination. Specialists (for France, notably specialists in Balzac[5] and Zola) have already provided such examinations, but to my knowledge we

---

[2] But a commentary to be used with care, for the right to be unfaithful is an authorial privilege.

[3] The norm is prepublication, but a book may be just as likely to go into serial publication *after* appearing in bookshops. This was exactly the case with *Robinson Crusoe* in 1719, and we know that Gide's *Caves du Vatican*, published in 1914, was reprinted in 1933 in *L'Humanité* after Vaillant-Couturier had somewhat forced the author's hand.

[4] The first French novel published in serial form seems to have been Balzac's *Vieille Fille* in *La Presse*.

[5] See R. Guise, *Balzac et le roman-feuilleton* (Plon, 1964).

lack a comprehensive historical study of the phenomenon – one that is of the utmost importance, for the massive fact is that, for a century and a half, hundreds of writers, including some of the greatest, accepted the disadvantages of such a system, which often ended up presenting the public first with a disfigured text pending publication in book form.[6]

The third of the three practices in itself constitutes an immense continent: that of *illustration*. This practice goes back at least to the ornamental capitals and illuminations of the Middle Ages, and its value as commentary, which sometimes has great force,[7] involves the author's responsibility, not only when he provides the illustrations himself (Blake, Hugo, Thackeray, Cocteau, and many others) or commissions them in precise detail (see Rousseau's "subjects for engravings" for *La Nouvelle Héloïse*, a collection of instructions whose evocative liveliness is not always equaled by the engraver's performance) but also, and more indirectly, each time he accepts their presence. We know that such authors as Flaubert or James rejected illustrations on principle, either because they feared an unfaithful visualization or, more radically, because they objected to any kind of visualization whatsoever.[8] All these positions indicate the authors' very keen sense of the paratextual capacity – whether apposite or ill advised – of illustrations. To examine this subject in its full scope, one would need not only the historical information I don't have but also a technical and iconological skill (think of the illustrations and frontispieces of the classical period) I will never have. Clearly, that study exceeds the means of a plain "literary person."

[6] But we know that pirated editions, generally made in Belgium and called "préfaçons" [unauthorized preprints], often put into circulation volumes that had been typeset from the text of the serial. See P. Van der Perre, *Les Préfaçons belges* (Gallimard, 1941).

[7] To measure the degrees of this force, we need only compare, for example, two cover illustrations: one (drawn by the author himself) is for *The Flounder* by Günther Grass, and the other is for *La Pensée sauvage* [*The Savage Mind*] by Lévi-Strauss. The illustration for *The Flounder* represents a flounder and therefore has only a corroborating, or redundant, value; the illustration for *La Pensée sauvage* represents a flower, and this immediately introduces an ambiguity that otherwise would probably have escaped some readers until they reached the pages where the author explains.

[8] The second position is that of Flaubert, who expressed it several times and with the greatest energy. In one letter, for example, he describes himself as "fundamentally a born enemy of texts that explain drawings and drawings that explain texts." He continues, "My conviction about this is radical, and forms part of my aesthetic" (to A. Baudry, 1867 or 1868).

This is all the more true, undoubtedly, for the paratext outside of literature. For if we are willing to extend the term to areas where the work does not consist of a text, it is obvious that some, if not all, of the other arts have an equivalent of our paratext: examples are the title in music and in the plastic arts, the signature in painting, the credits or the trailer in film, and all the opportunities for authorial commentary presented by catalogues of exhibitions, prefaces of musical scores (see the 1841 foreword for Liszt's *Years of Pilgrimage*), record jackets, and other peritextual or epitextual supports. All of them could be subjects for investigations paralleling this one.[9]

What makes me all the less inclined to regret these provisional lacunae is that one of the methodological hazards attendant on a subject as multiform and tentacular as the paratext, it seems to me, is the imperialist temptation to annex to this subject everything that comes within its reach or seems possibly to pertain to it. Whatever the desire – inherent in any study (in any discourse) – to justify one's subject by magnifying it, to me the sounder and methodologically better course seems to be to react in the reverse way and, as I said apropos of notes, to apply the Occamian principle of economy, which deters us from multiplying "theoretical objects" unless the reason for doing so is of the utmost importance. Inasmuch as the paratext is a transitional zone between text and beyond-text, one must resist the temptation to enlarge this zone by whittling away in both directions. However indeterminable its boundaries, the paratext retains at its center a distinctive and undisputed territory where its "properties" are clearly manifest and which is constituted jointly by the types of elements I have explored in this book, plus some others. Outside of that, we will be wary of rashly proclaiming that "all is paratext."

The most essential of the paratext's properties, as we have observed many times (but, in concluding, I still want to insist on it), is functionality. Whatever aesthetic intention may come into play as well, the main issue for the paratext is not to "look nice" around the text but rather to ensure for the text a destiny consistent with the author's purpose. To this end, the paratext

[9] See Françoise Escal, "Le Titre de l'œuvre musicale," and Charles Sala, "La Signature à la lettre et au figuré," both in *Poétique* 69 (February 1987).

provides a kind of canal lock between the ideal and relatively immutable[10] identity of the text and the empirical (sociohistorical) reality of the text's public (if I may be forgiven these rough images), the lock permitting the two to remain "level." Or, if you prefer, the paratext provides an airlock that helps the reader pass without too much respiratory difficulty from one world to the other, a sometimes delicate operation, especially when the second world is a fictional one. Being immutable, the text in itself is incapable of adapting to changes in its public in space and over time. The paratext – more flexible, more versatile, always transitory because transitive – is, as it were, an instrument of adaptation. Hence the continual modifications in the "presentation" of the text (that is, in the text's mode of being present in the world), modifications that the author himself attends to during his lifetime and that after his death become the responsibility (discharged well or poorly) of his posthumous editors.

The relevance I accord to the author's purpose, and therefore to his "point of view," may seem excessive and methodologically very naive. That relevance is, strictly speaking, imposed by my subject, whose entire functioning is based – even if this is sometimes denied – on the simple postulate that the author "knows best" what we should think about his work. One cannot travel within the paratext without encountering this belief or, in a way, without assuming it as one of the elements of the situation, as an ethnologist does with an indigenous theory: the correctness of the authorial (and secondarily, of the publisher's) point of view is the implicit creed and spontaneous ideology of the paratext. This view, held almost unconditionally for centuries, is today, as we know, assailed for fairly diverse reasons, wherein a certain formalist approach ("There is no true meaning to a text") and a certain psychoanalytic approach ("There is a true meaning, but the author cannot know it") paradoxically hit it off well. This debate leaves me personally fairly perplexed, if not indifferent, but I don't think it has to be pursued here: valid or not, the author's viewpoint is part of the paratextual performance, sustains it, inspires it, anchors it. Once again, the critic is by no

---

[10] Very relatively, of course, and very diversely: one has only to think of those medieval works of which no two texts are absolutely alike. But this "*mouvance* of the text" (Zumthor) has no connection to the *mouvance* of the public, which justifies the *mouvance* of the paratext.

means bound to subscribe to that viewpoint. I maintain only that, knowing it, he cannot completely disregard it, and if he wants to contradict it he must first assimilate it. Several times I have evoked the hermeneutic power of intimidation contained in just the title of *Ulysses*; and in Chapter 1, I suggested that a reader who was unaware of this title would perhaps no more "guess" the novel's Homeric reference than Julien Green would have guessed the "real" theme of Stendhal's *Armance* without the presence of some key. This unaware reader would read the novel differently, and to me this adverb involves no value judgment (Borges, if I am not mistaken, regarded the Homeric reference as factitious and useless). But that's how it is, this reader does not exist, and save for an experiment – itself factitious – à la Condillac,[11] he cannot exist. In a way, our study's whole thesis (if it is one) can be summed up in this obvious fact; and its whole lesson (if it is one) in this advice à la Wittgenstein, which follows from it: what one cannot ignore, one is better off knowing – that is, of course, acknowledging, and knowing that one knows it. The effect of the paratext lies very often in the realm of influence – indeed, manipulation – experienced subconsciously. This mode of operation is doubtless in the author's interest, though not always in the reader's. To accept it – or, for that matter, to reject it – one is better off perceiving it fully and clearly. Such a consideration suffices, I hope, to justify if not this study of the paratext then at least another, or others, for which the deficiencies or defects of this one could provide the impetus.

From the fact that the paratext always fulfills a function, it does not necessarily follow that the paratext always fulfills its function well. Several years of frequenting the paratext have at least convinced me of one thing that was not at all obvious to me *a priori*, and that is the great conscientiousness with which writers perform their paratextual duty (some would call it their paratextual drudgery). Contrary to the impression that could be created here and there by some behavior that is far too accommodating, most writers set their sights not on an immediate or facile success but indeed on a more fundamental and more "noble" success: having their work be interpreted correctly (according to their lights). The main impediment to the effective-

---

[11] [A (fictive) experiment that presumes a subject who is reared under a special artificial set of conditions.]

ness of the paratext generally does not arise from a poor understanding of its objectives but rather from the perverse effect (hard to avoid or control) that we have met several times under the whimsical name of the *Jupien effect*: like all relays, the paratext sometimes tends to go beyond its function and to turn itself into an impediment, from then on playing its own game to the detriment of its text's game. The way to neutralize this danger is obvious, and most authors manage to do it: use a light touch. Actually, the same principle holds (or should hold) for the author as for the reader and is summed up by this simple slogan: *watch out for the paratext!*

Nothing, in fact, would be more unfortunate, in my opinion, than to replace some idol of the closed Text – which held sway over our literary consciousness for one or two decades and which has now been destabilized, thanks in large part (as we have seen) to scrutiny of the paratext – with a new and even more hollow fetish: the paratext. The paratext is only an assistant, only an accessory of the text. And if the text without its paratext is sometimes like an elephant without a mahout, a power disabled, the paratext without its text is a mahout without an elephant, a silly show. Consequently the discourse on the paratext must never forget that it bears on a discourse that bears on a discourse, and that the meaning of its object depends on the object of this meaning, which is yet another meaning. A threshold exists to be crossed.[12]

---

[12] [On *threshold*, see Chapter 1, note 3.] *Postscript of December 16, 1986.* Like Walter Scott's postillion who asks for a tip, I take advantage of this last bit of space available for communication to draw attention to two undoubtedly important volumes that I have become aware of only now, when returning the proofs of this book: Margherita Di Fazio Alberti, *Il titolo e la funzione paraletteraria* (Turin: ERI, 1984), and Arnold Rothe, *Der Literarische Titel: Funktionen, Formen, Geschichte* (Frankfurt: Klostermann, 1986). I also draw attention to two articles: Laurent Mailhot, "Le Métatexte camusien: Titres, dédicaces, épigraphes, préfaces," *Cahiers Albert Camus* 5 (Gallimard, 1985), and Jean-Louis Chevalier, "La Citation en épigraphe dans *Tristram Shandy*," in *L'Ente et la chimère* (Université de Caen, 1986). Finally, I add this to the list of titles inspired by Raymond Roussel's title (on page 368): the wonderful *Pourquoi je n'ai écrit aucun de mes livres* [*Why I Have Not Written Any of My Books*] by Marcel Bénabou (Hachette, 1986).

Additional references

[This list contains works published in English originally or in English translation which are cited in the text but not referenced in the notes.]

Alemán, Matheo. *The Rogue, or The Life of Guzman de Alfarache*. Translated by James Mabbe. New York: AMS Press, 1967.

Apuleius. *Golden Ass*. Translated by Jack Lindsay. Bloomington: Indiana University Press, Midland Book, 1962.

Auerbach, Erich. *Mimesis: The Representation of Reality in Western Literature*. Translated by Willard Trask. 1946. Reprint. Garden City, NY: Doubleday Anchor, 1957.

Aulus Gellius. *Attic Nights*. Loeb Classical Library.

Bachelard, Gaston. *The Poetics of Reverie*. Translated by Daniel Russell. New York: Orion Press, 1969.

Balzac, Honoré de. *Albert Savarus*. Vol. 3, *The Works of Honoré de Balzac*. New York: McKinlay, Stone, and MacKenzie, 1915.

Les Chouans. *La Comédie humaine of Honoré de Balzac*. New York: Century Company, 1906.

Barthes, Roland. *Roland Barthes by Roland Barthes*. Translated by Richard Howard. New York: Hill and Wang, 1977.

Sade / Fourier / Loyola. Translated by Richard Miller. New York: Hill and Wang, 1976.

Foreword to *The Novels of Robbe-Grillet*, by Bruce Morrissette. Translated by Bruce Morrissette. Ithaca: Cornell University Press, 1975.

Baudelaire, Charles. *The Flowers of Evil*. Edited by Marthiel Mathews and Jackson Mathews. New York: New Directions, 1955.

Baudelaire's Prose Poems: The Esthetic, the Ethical, and the Religious in the Parisian Prowler, by Edward K. Kaplan. Athens: University of Georgia Press, 1990.

Beaumarchais, Pierre-Augustin Caron de. *The Barber of Seville and The Marriage of Figaro*. Translated by John Wood. Harmondsworth: Penguin, 1964.

Beckett, Samuel. *Watt*. New York: Grove Press, 1959.

Blanchot, Maurice. *Vicious Circles: Two Fictions and "After the Fact."* Translated by Paul Auster. Barrytown, NY: Station Hill Press, 1985.

Boccaccio, Giovanni. *Decameron*. Translated by G. H. McWilliam. Harmondsworth: Penguin, 1972.

Boileau: Selected Criticism. Translated by Ernest Dilworth. Indianapolis: Bobbs-Merrill, 1965.

Borges, Jorge Luis. *The Book of Sand*. [Contains *The Book of Sand* and *The Gold of the Tigers*.] Translated by Norman Thomas di Giovanni [*The Book of Sand*] and Alastair Reid [*The Gold of the Tigers*]. Harmondsworth: Penguin, 1979.

   Doctor Brodie's Report. Translated by Norman Thomas di Giovanni. New York: E. P. Dutton, 1972.

   Dreamtigers. Translated by Mildred Boyer and Harold Morland. Austin: University of Texas Press, 1964.

   Ficciones. Edited by Anthony Kerrigan. New York: Grove Press, 1962.

   Labyrinths. Edited by Donald A. Yates and James E. Irby. New York: New Directions, 1962.

   Other Inquisitions 1937–1952. Translated by Ruth L. C. Simms. Austin: University of Texas Press, 1964.

   Foreword to *The Invention of Morel and Other Stories*, by Adolfo Bioy Casares. Translated by Ruth L. C. Simms. Austin: University of Texas Press, 1964.

Cervantes, Miguel de. *The Adventures of Don Quixote*. Translated by J. M. Cohen. Harmondsworth: Penguin, 1950. Also translated by Samuel Putnam. New York: Viking, 1949. Also Norton Critical Edition.

   Three Exemplary Novels. Translated by Samuel Putnam. New York: Viking, 1950.

Chariton. By Gareth L. Schmelling. New York: Twayne Publishers, 1974.

Chateaubriand. *The Genius of Christianity: Poetic and Moral Beauties of the Christian Religion*. Translated by Irving Putter. Berkeley and Los Angeles: University of California Press, 1952.

Chrétien de Troyes. *Arthurian Romances*. Translated by William W. Kibler, except *Erec and Enide* translated by Carleton W. Carroll. Harmondsworth: Penguin, 1991.

Claudel, Paul. *The Satin Slipper, or The Worst Is Not the Surest*. Translated by Fr. John O'Connor. New Haven: Yale University Press, 1931.

   The Tidings Brought to Mary, in *Two Dramas*. Translated by Wallace Fowlie. Chicago: Henry Regnery, 1960.

Conrad, Joseph. *Lord Jim*. Edited by Thomas C. Moser. Norton Critical Edition, 1968.

   The Nigger of the "Narcissus." Edited by Robert Kimbrough. Norton Critical Edition, 1979.

Constant, Benjamin. *Adolphe*. Translated by Leonard Tancock, except the preface of 1816 translated by Alexander Walker. Harmondsworth: Penguin, 1964.

Crébillon, Claude-Prosper Jolyot de. *The Wayward Head and Heart*. Translated by Barbara Bray. Westport, CT: Greenwood Press, 1978.

Additional references

Dante. *The Divine Comedy*. Translated by Charles Eliot Norton. Chicago: Henry Regnery, 1951.

Deleuze, Gilles. *The Logic of Sense*. Translated by Mark Lester with Charles Stivale. New York: Columbia University Press, 1990.

Derrida, Jacques. *Dissemination*. Translated by Barbara Johnson. University of Chicago Press, 1981.

Dickens, Charles. *David Copperfield*. New York: New American Library, Signet Classics, 1962.

Dumas, Alexandre (*père*). *The Three Musketeers*. Translated by Lowell Bair. Bantam Books, 1984.

Eco, Umberto. *The Name of the Rose*. Translated by William Weaver. San Diego: Harcourt Brace Jovanovich, 1983.

Eliot, T. S. Introduction to *Nightwood*, by Djuna Barnes. 1937. Reprint. New York: New Directions, 1961.

Epictetus. *Encheiridion*. Translated by Ian Watt. Epigraph to *Tristram Shandy*, by Laurence Sterne. Boston: Houghton Mifflin, 1965.

Faulkner, William. In *Twentieth Century Interpretations of "The Sound and the Fury."* Edited by Michael H. Cowan. Englewood Cliffs, NJ: Prentice-Hall, 1968.

Fielding, Henry. *Joseph Andrews*. New York: Random House, Modern Library, 1950.

Tom Jones. Edited by Sheridan Baker. Norton Critical Edition, 1973.

Flaubert, Gustave. *The Letters of Gustave Flaubert, 1857–1880*. Translated by Francis Steegmuller. Cambridge, MA: Harvard University Press, Belknap Press, 1982.

November. Translated by Frank Jellinek. New York: Carroll and Graf, 1987.

France, Anatole. Preface to *Pleasures and Regrets*, by Marcel Proust. Translated by Louise Varese. New York: Crown (Lear), 1948.

Frisch, Max. *Sketchbook 1946–1949*. Translated by Geoffrey Skelton. New York: Harcourt Brace Jovanovich, 1977.

Froissart, Jean. *Chronicles*. Translated by Geoffrey Brereton. Harmondsworth: Penguin, 1968.

Frye, Northrop. *The Great Code: The Bible and Literature*. New York: Harcourt Brace Jovanovich, 1982.

Gautier, Théophile. *Mademoiselle de Maupin and One of Cleopatra's Nights*. New York: Random House, Modern Library, n.d.

Gide, André. *The Counterfeiters with Journal of "The Counterfeiters."* Translated by Dorothy Bussy [the novel] and Justin O'Brien [the journal]. New York: Knopf, 1951.

If It Die ... . Translated by Dorothy Bussy. London: Secker and Warburg, 1950.

The Journals of André Gide, 1888–1949. Translated by Justin O'Brien. 4 vols. New York: Knopf, 1949–1951.

Isabelle, in *Two Symphonies* [*Isabelle* and *La Symphonie Pastorale*]. Translated by Dorothy Bussy. New York: Random House, Vintage Books, 1977.

Giono, Jean. *Blue Boy*. Translated by Katherine A. Clarke. 1946. Reprint. San Francisco: North Point Press, 1981.

Giono: Master of Fictional Modes. By Norma Goodrich. Princeton University Press, 1973.

Goethe, J. W. von. *Faust*. Translated by Stuart Atkins. Boston: Suhrkamp/Insel, 1984.

Goethe: Conversations and Encounters. By J. P. Eckermann. Translated by David Luke and Robert Pick. Chicago: Henry Regnery, 1966.

Goldsmith, Oliver. *The Vicar of Wakefield*. Harmondsworth: Penguin, 1982.

Hemingway, Ernest. *Green Hills of Africa*. New York: Charles Scribner's Sons, 1935.

Herodotus. Loeb Classical Library.

Homer. *The Odyssey*. Translated by Richmond Lattimore. New York: Harper and Row, 1965. Reprint. Harper Colophon Book, 1975.

Horace. *Ars Poetica*. Translated by Sheridan Baker. Epigraph to *Tom Jones*, by Henry Fielding. Norton Critical Edition, 1973.

Satires. Loeb Classical Library.

Hugo, Victor. *Hans of Iceland*. Volume 9, the Valjean Edition of the Novels of Victor Hugo. New York: Collier and Son, n.d.

"The Last Day of a Condemned Man" and Other Prison Writings. Translated by Geoff Woollen. Oxford University Press, World's Classics, 1992.

Huysmans, Joris-Karl. *Against the Grain*. New York: Three Sirens Press, 1931. Reprint. Dover, 1969.

James, Henry. *The Art of the Novel: Critical Prefaces*. Introduced by Richard P. Blackmur. New York: Charles Scribner's Sons, 1934.

Job. King James Version.

La Bruyère, Jean de. *The Characters of Jean de la Bruyère*. Translated by Henri van Laun. New York: Brentano's, 1929.

Laclos, Choderlos de. *Les Liaisons Dangereuses*. Translated by P. W. K. Stone. Harmondsworth: Penguin, 1961.

La Fayette, Madame de. *The Princesse de Clèves*, "Publisher's Note to the Reader." Translated by Terence Cave. Oxford University Press, World's Classics, 1992.

La Fontaine, Jean de. *The Complete Fables of Jean de la Fontaine*. Translated by Norman B. Spector. Evanston, IL: Northwestern University Press, 1988.

Laforgue, Jules. *Selected Writings of Jules Laforgue*. Translated by William Jay Smith. Westport, CT: Greenwich Press, 1972.

La Rochefoucauld, François, duc de. *Maxims*. Translated by Leonard Tancock. Harmondsworth: Penguin, 1959.

[*Lazarillo*.] *The Life of Lazarillo de Tormes: His Fortunes and Adversities*. Translated by W. S. Merwin. Gloucester, MA: Peter Smith, 1970.

Additional references

Lesage, Alain-René. *The Adventures of Gil Blas de Santillana*. Translated by Tobias Smollett. London: Oxford University Press, World's Classics, 1907.

Machado de Assis, Joaquim Maria. *Posthumous Reminiscences of Braz Cubas*. Translated by E. Percy Ellis. Rio de Janeiro: Instituto Nacional do Livro, 1955.

Malraux, André. "A Preface for Faulkner's *Sanctuary*." Reprinted in *Faulkner: A Collection of Critical Essays*, edited by Robert Penn Warren. Englewood Cliffs, NJ: Prentice-Hall, 1966.

Mann, Thomas. *Doctor Faustus: The Life of the German Composer, Adrian Leverkühn, as Told by a Friend*. Translated by H. T. Lowe-Porter. New York: Alfred A. Knopf, 1948.

Mansfield, Katherine. *Novels and Novelists*. Edited by John Middleton Murry. London: Constable, 1930.

Maupassant, Guy de. *Pierre and Jean*. Translated by Leonard Tancock. Harmondsworth: Penguin, 1979.

Maurois, André. *Prometheus: The Life of Balzac*. Translated by Norman Denny. New York: Harper and Row, 1965.

Michelet, Jules. *Satanism and Witchcraft: A Study in Medieval Superstition*. Translated by A. R. Allinson. New York: Walden Publications, 1939.

Montaigne, Michel Eyquem de. *The Complete Works of Montaigne*. Translated by Donald M. Frame. Stanford University Press, 1948.

Montesquieu, Charles-Louis de Secondat, baron de. *Persian Letters*. Translated by John Davidson. London: Routledge, n.d.

The Spirit of the Laws. Translated by Anne M. Cohler, Basia Carolyn Miller, and Harold Samuel Stone. Cambridge University Press, 1989.

Nabokov, Vladimir. *Lolita*. New York: Berkley Publishing Corporation, 1966.

Pale Fire. New York: G. P. Putnam's Sons, 1962.

Painter, George D. *Chateaubriand: A Biography*. Vol. 1, *The Longed-for Tempests (1768–1793)*. New York: Knopf, 1978.

Marcel Proust: A Biography. 2 vols. New York: Random House, 1959.

Perec, Georges. *Life: A User's Manual*. Translated by David Bellos. Boston: David R. Godine, 1987.

Persius. *The Satires of Persius*. Translated by Gus Lee. Liverpool: Francis Cairns, 1987.

Poe, Edgar Allan. "The Philosophy of Composition." In *The American Tradition in Literature*, revised, vol. 1, edited by Sculley Bradley, Richmond Croom Beatty, and E. Hudson Long. New York: W. W. Norton, 1956.

Proust, Marcel. *Against Sainte-Beuve and Other Essays*. Translated by John Sturrock. Harmondsworth: Penguin, 1988.

Marcel Proust: Selected Letters. Vol. 2, 1904–1909. Edited by Philip Kolb and translated by Terence Kilmartin. Oxford University Press, 1989.

Rabelais, François. *The Complete Works of François Rabelais*. Translated by Donald M. Frame. Berkeley and Los Angeles: University of California Press, 1991.

Racine, Jean. *The Complete Plays of Jean Racine*. 2 vols. Translated by Samuel Solomon. New York: Random House, 1967.

Robert de Clari. *The Conquest of Constantinople*. Translated by Edgar Holmes McNeal. New York: Columbia University Press, 1936.

Rousseau, Jean-Jacques. *The Confessions of Jean-Jacques Rousseau*. Revised by A. S. B. Glover. New York: Heritage, 1955.

Discourse on the Origins of Inequality. Translated by Judith R. Bush, Roger D. Masters, Christopher Kelly, and Terence Marshal. Vol. 3 of *The Collected Writings of Rousseau*, edited by Roger D. Masters and Christopher Kelly. Hanover, NH: University Press of New England, 1992.

Emile or On Education. Translated by Allan Bloom. New York: Basic Books, 1979.

La Nouvelle Héloïse: Julie, or the New Eloise. Abridged and translated by Judith H. McDowell. University Park: Pennsylvania State University Press, 1968.

Sand, George. *Indiana*. Translated by Eleanor Hochman. Signet Classics, 1993.

Sartre, Jean-Paul. *Life/Situations: Essays Written and Spoken*. Translated by Paul Auster and Lydia Davis. New York: Pantheon Books, 1977.

Situations. Translated by Benita Eisler. Greenwich, CT: Fawcett World Library, 1966.

Scott, Walter. "Introduction to *Chronicles of the Canongate*." In *The Prefaces to the Waverley Novels*, edited by Mark Weinstein. University of Nebraska Press, 1978.

The Fortunes of Nigel. London: Macmillan, 1930.

Ivanhoe. Harmondsworth: Penguin, 1986.

Quentin Durward. Chicago: Rand, McNally, n.d. Also Oxford University Press, World's Classics, 1992.

Peveril of the Peak. Chicago: Rand, McNally, n.d.

Rob Roy. Everyman's Library, 1991.

Waverley. New York: New American Library, Signet Classics, 1964.

The Song of Roland. Translated by Dorothy L. Sayers. Harmondsworth: Penguin, 1957.

Sophocles. Epigraph to *The Erasers*, by Alain Robbe-Grillet. Translated by Richard Howard. New York: Grove Press, 1964.

Stendhal. *Armance*. Translated by Gilbert Sale and Suzanne Sale. Chester Springs, England: Merlin Press, Dufour Editions, 1961.

The Charterhouse of Parma. Translated by Margaret R. B. Shaw. Harmondsworth: Penguin, 1958.

Love. Translated by Gilbert Sale and Suzanne Sale. Harmondsworth: Penguin, 1975.

Lucien Leuwen. Translated by H. L. R. Edwards. Harmondsworth: Penguin, 1991.

Red and Black. Translated by Robert M. Adams. Norton Critical Edition, 1969.

To the Happy Few: Selected Letters of Stendhal. Translated by Norman Cameron. Westport, CT: Hyperion, 1979.

Svevo, Italo. *Confessions of Zeno*. Translated by Beryl de Zoete. London: Secker and Warburg, 1962.

Swift, Jonathan. *Gulliver's Travels and Other Writings*. Edited by Ricardo Quintana. New York: Random House, Modern Library, 1958.

Theocritus. *The Poems of Theocritus*. Translated by Anna Rist. Chapel Hill: University of North Carolina Press, 1978.

Thucydides. Loeb Classical Library.

Tolstoy, Leo. *The Kreutzer Sonata*. Translated by David McDuff. Harmondsworth: Penguin, 1983.

"Some Words about *War and Peace*," in *War and Peace*. Translated by Louise Maude and Aylmer Maude. New York: Simon and Schuster, 1954.

Valéry, Paul. *The Collected Works of Paul Valéry*. Bollingen series. 15 vols. Volume 1: *Poems*. Translated by David Paul. Princeton University Press, 1971. Volume 8: *Leonardo Poe Mallarmé*. Translated by Malcolm Cowley and James R. Lawler. Princeton University Press, 1972. Volume 9: *Masters and Friends*. Translated by Martin Turnell. Princeton University Press, 1968.

Vigny, Alfred de. *Cinq Mars*. New York: Current Literature Publishing Company, 1910.

Virgil. *The Aeneid*. Translated by Robert Fitzgerald. New York: Random House, 1981. Reprint. Vintage Books, 1984.

Wilde, Oscar. *The Picture of Dorian Gray*. New York: Airmont Publishing Company, 1964.

Zola, Emile. *L'Assommoir*. Translated by Leonard Tancock. Harmondsworth: Penguin, 1970.

The Fortune of the Rougons. Edited by Ernest A. Vizetelly. New York: Albert and Charles Boni, 1925.

Thérèse Raquin. Translated by Leonard Tancock. Harmondsworth: Penguin.

Emile Zola. By Elliott M. Grant. New York: Twayne, 1966.

Zumthor, Paul. *Oral Poetry: An Introduction*. Translated by Kathryn Murphy-Judy. University of Minnesota Press, 1990.

Index

With the usual portion of errors and omissions, this index lists the instances when authors' names actually appear and the instances when – through the mention of a title – they implicitly appear. It would have been more useful to have an index of titles (sometimes several per work), along with an indication of names (likewise) and dates (ditto), but I'm told that such an index would have been longer than the book. In any case, the real function of this index, as of most, is to save the author from the taunt: "No index."

Index

Bayle, P., 327
Beach, J. W., 394
Beardsley, A., 25
Beauclair, H., and Vicaire, G., 189, 289–90
Beaujour, M., 85
Beaumarchais, P., 85, 119, 226, 243–44, 405
Beaunier, A., 349, 350
Beauvoir, S. de, 362, 385
Becker, C., 66, 83
Beckett, S., 229, 334, 335, 361, 405
Beckford, W., 267
Béguin, A., 61, 267
Bellemin-Noël, J., 396
Bellour, R., 345
Bénézet, M., 83, 111
Benstock, S., 321
Benveniste, E., 171
Bergson, H., 382
Bernanos, G., 83, 340
Bernard, C., 89
Bernardin de Saint-Pierre, J.-H., 18, 82, 225
Bertrand, A., 281
Bibesco, A., 378
Bignan, A., 171
Binet, C., 225
Bioy Casares, A., 189, 268, 272, 289, 290
Blackmur, R. P., 251
Blake, W., 215, 406
Blanche, J.-E., 349
Blanchot, M., 97, 115, 159, 162, 172–73, 203, 233, 247, 267, 269, 312, 361
Blum, R., 62, 303, 374, 379
Boccaccio, G., 87, 169, 212, 299, 313
Boileau, N., 42, 95, 119, 261, 313, 338
Bois, E.-J., 303, 359
Bonald, L. de, 223
Boncenne, P., 359, 361
Bonnefoy, Y., 60, 315, 366
Booth, W., 88
Borges, J. L., 2, 100, 128, 132, 173, 188, 189–90, 204–5, 224, 230, 237–38, 255, 261–62, 267, 268, 270, 272, 273, 288, 289–90, 292, 332, 359, 361, 363, 364, 402, 409
Bosco, H., 217
Bossuet, J. B., 223
Bost, P., 69
Boswell, J., 57, 267, 311, 385
Bougnoux, D., 339
Bouilhet, L., 129, 176, 266, 268, 270, 273, 371, 376
Bourget, P., 157, 195, 212, 215, 259

Bousquet, J., 111
Bouteron, M., 177
Bowersock, G. W., 327
Brasillach, R., 157
Brecht, B., 295
Bremond, C., 88
Breton, A., 90, 364
Brod, M., 66
Brontë, C., 90, 96
Brooke-Rose, C., 91
Bruce, J., 89–90
Buffon, G., 146, 325
Burch, N., 28
Burgess, A., 73
Butor, M., 19, 25, 34, 77, 84, 86, 366, 368–69
Byron, G. G., 151, 159

Caillois, R., 205
Callimachus, 313
Calmette, G., 126, 349, 374
Campe, J. H. von, 87
Camus, A., 90, 100
Camus, R., 53, 288, 321, 336, 368, 404
Capote, T., 362
Carpentier, A., 150
Casanova, J., 310
Castex, P.-G., 177
Cayrol, J., 269
Céard, H., 375–76
Cela, C. J., 87
Céline, L.-F., 157, 217, 308
Cendrars, B., 38
Cent Nouvelles Nouvelles, 300
Cerquiglini, B., 300
Cervantes, M. de, 98, 127, 156, 168, 189, 191, 208, 213, 220, 223, 231, 234, 245, 301
Chancel, J., 363
Chanson de Roland, La, 167, 170
Chantal, S., 276
Chapelain, J., 47, 119, 225, 264, 268–69
Chapsal, M., 359
Char, R., 60, 115, 337
Charbonnier, G., 363
Chariton of Aphrodisias, 37, 165, 206
Charles, M., 158, 381
Charles d'Orléans, 313
Charnes, abbé de, 348
Chasles, P., 202
Chateaubriand, F.-R., 6, 18, 67, 105, 122–23, 127–28, 132, 133, 138, 146, 171, 172, 173, 175, 176–77, 188, 200, 210–11, 223, 225, 230, 240, 241, 244–45, 248, 251, 253, 254, 257, 258,

420

Index

259, 261, 299, 310, 311, 320, 322, 326,
  329, 330–31, 367, 372, 383, 396, 399
Chaucer, G., 299–300
Chaumeix, A., 382
Chénier, A., 313
Chollet, R., 61
Chrétien de Troyes, 4, 37, 100, 168
Cicero, 118, 311
Claudel, P., 58, 81, 82, 138–39, 158, 159,
  167, 276, 327, 363–64, 365, 371, 381,
  385, 391
Cocteau, J., 94, 100–1, 111, 406
Cohen, A., 363
Cohen, G., 276–77
Cohen, J., 83
Coleridge, S. T., 183, 184, 314, 333
Colet, L., 371–76
Colette, S.-G., 41, 88
Collins, P., 370
Colomb, R., 400
Colonna, V., 336
Commynes, P. de, 169, 309
Compagnon, A., 2, 5, 151
Condillac, E. de, 409
Condorcet, A. de, 266
Conrad, J., 130, 229, 254, 306, 320
Constant, B., 83, 171, 186–87, 216, 223,
  241, 280, 282–83, 289
Copernicus, 89
Corbière, T., 157
Corneille, P., 81, 87, 90, 94–95, 99, 119–20,
  124, 128, 166, 175–76, 194–95, 211, 214,
  225, 242, 253–55, 337–38, 343, 399
Cortazar, J., 218
Couratier, J., 141
Courier, P. L., 54
Courtilz de Sandras, 281
Crébillon (fils), 124, 131, 199, 216
Crémieux, F., 224, 358, 363–64
Curtius, E. R., 38

Damisch, H., 20
Dante, 37, 72–73, 98, 125, 154, 169, 299
Danton, G., 148
Darien, G., 280
Daudet, Léon, 126
Daudet, Lucien, 349–50, 377
Davin, F., 181, 190, 202, 278
Debussy, C., 65
Defaux, G., 221
Defoe, D., 43, 55, 71, 90, 114, 186, 194,
  282, 283, 299, 405
Deguy, M., 59
Deleuze, G., 173, 269, 284
Delteil, J., 133

Derrida, J., 91, 111–12, 161–62, 196, 231,
  235, 336, 353
Descartes, R., 311, 362
Des Forêts, L. R., 82, 114, 157, 269
Desnos, R., 90
Dickens, C., 72, 91, 96, 234, 245, 254,
  301–2, 339, 370, 394
Dickinson, E., 315
Diderot, D., 43, 80, 119, 146, 171, 191,
  225–26, 228, 265, 296
Dio Cassius, 211
Diodorus of Sicily, 263
Diogenes Laertius, 85
Djâmî, 149
Donat and Servius, 99
Donne, J., 150, 157, 313–14
Dorgelès, R., 28
Dostoevsky, F., 96, 339, 394
Doubrovsky, S., 59, 84, 112, 303
Doyle, A. C., 253
Drieu La Rochelle, P., 100, 111, 113,
  128, 216, 251
Du Bos, C., 86
Du Camp, M., 218, 296, 376
Duchet, C., 2, 55, 56, 66, 176, 226
Ducourneau, J. A., 61
Dujardin, E., 132, 176, 269, 274, 284
Dumas, A. (père), 47, 96, 125, 235, 273,
  281, 294, 310
Dumesnil, R., 71
Dumézil, G., 363
Duras, M., 50, 363
Dusolier, A., 354

Eckermann, J. P., 372, 385
Eco, U., 77, 92–93, 171, 186, 241, 252,
  281, 301, 405
Edgeworth, M., 249
Eliot, G., 50
Eliot, T. S., 273, 333
Ellmann, R., 134, 350–51
Eluard, P., 34, 157
Enckell, P., 111, 115
Epictetus, 146
Erasmus, 137, 145, 151
Escal, F., 407
Espinel, V., 190
Euripides, 166, 263
Ezine, J.-L., 272, 359, 364

Fanon, F., 173, 272
Faulkner, W., 82, 91, 157, 176, 268, 270,
  308, 363–66, 405
Faure, E., 51, 87
Faye, J. P., 157

421

Index

Hume, D., 89
Huret, J., 364
Huster, F., 166
Huston, J., 99
Huston, N., 98
Huysmans, K. J., 96, 171, 258–59, 306

Idt, G., 272
Ionesco, E., 83
Irving, J., 335
Iseler, P., 276
Isocrates, 164
Issacharoff, M., 334

Jabès, E., 59, 115
Jaffray, P., 24
James, H., 89, 91, 96, 102, 129, 148, 171, 173, 175, 233, 251–52, 254, 293, 306, 346, 378, 391, 394, 396, 397, 402, 406
Jammes, F., 382
Janin, J., 234
Jeanson, F., 217
Jenks, T., 399
Job, 146
Johannot, Y., 20
John of the Cross, Saint, 333
Johnson, S., 267, 385
Joinville, J. de, 169
Jong, E., 72, 301
Jordane, B., 193
Jouffroy, A., 217
Jouhandeau, M., 111
Joyce, J., 2, 5, 10, 20–21, 66, 83–84, 85, 134, 159, 267, 268, 295, 308, 321, 323, 342, 350–51, 409

Kafka, F., 66, 233, 370, 387, 391–92, 399
Kant, I., 311, 362
Kantorowicz, C., 55
Kierkegaard, S., 52
Klingsor, T., 48–49
Klossowski, P., 60, 172, 238
Kock, P. de, 213
Kolb, P., 62, 359
Kundera, M., 174, 268, 272

Labarre, A., 17
Labé, L., 50
La Boétie, E. de, 80
La Bruyère, J. de, 42, 70, 145, 151, 162, 178, 183, 199, 216, 266, 295, 325
Lacan, J., 87, 160
La Ceppède, J. de, 312, 333
Laclos, C. de, 43, 82, 186, 187, 191, 280, 282, 283, 289, 340

La Fayette, Mme de, 42, 188, 190, 215–16, 299, 348, 383
La Fontaine, J. de, 18, 95, 120, 198, 222, 225, 266, 271
Laforgue, J., 98, 315, 316
Lagny, G. de, 37
La Harpe, J.-F. de, 266
Lamartine, A. de, 44, 49, 57, 86, 90, 98, 125, 131, 186, 205–6, 314, 381
Lambert, J., 139, 385–86
Lanoux, A., 265
Lanson, G., 331
Laporte, R., 98, 112, 157
Larbaud, V., 10, 48, 111, 127, 132, 176, 186, 189, 205, 267, 268, 269, 274, 284, 289–90, 350–51
La Rochefoucauld, F. de, 42, 46, 145, 152–53, 157, 295
Laufer, R., 35
Laugaa, M., 48
Laurent, J., 51, 88, 193, 341, 364
Lautréamont, 51, 153, 159, 236
Lawrence, T. E., 53
Lazarillo de Tormes, 42, 47, 87, 190, 291, 302
Léautaud, P., 358, 364–65, 372, 385
Lefèvre, F., 364
Le Goff, J., 300
Leibowitz, R., 274
Leiris, M., 100–1, 174, 298
Lejeune, P., 2, 13, 41, 45, 356, 357, 363, 365, 393
Lemaitre, H., 79
Leroux, P., 235
Lesage, A. R., 43, 48, 162, 180–83, 190, 216, 279, 291, 301
Lessing, G. E., 82, 92, 147
Leuilliot, B., 377
Levenston, E. A., 55
Levin, H., 55
Lévi-Strauss, C., 131, 133, 406
Lévy, M., 73
Lewis, M. G., 147
Lichtenberg, G. C., 208
Liszt, F., 407
Litto, V. del, 390
Livy, 165, 199
Locke, J., 89, 208
Longus, 54, 165
Lorca, F., 49, 315
Lorris, G. de, 37, 57, 84, 263
Louÿs, P., 128, 187, 283, 289
Lovenjoul, C. de, 307
Lowry, M., 149, 150, 174, 233–34
Lubbock, P., 394

Index

426

Index

Urfé, H. d', 71, 133, 195, 215, 299

Valéry, P., 67, 77, 86, 87, 89, 130, 157, 173, 176, 179–81, 221–22, 253, 266, 268, 271, 272, 274, 276–77, 318, 322, 323, 331–32, 336, 339, 371, 390, 402, 403
Valincour, J.-B. de, 348
Vallès, J., 132
vanden Heuvel, J. S., 364
Vandromme, P., 115–16
Van Santen Kolff, J., 66, 82, 375–76
Varius, 99
Vasquez, M. E., 359
Verlaine, P., 77, 180, 181, 314, 323
Verne, J., 369
Veron, E., 141
Viala, A., 119
Vian, B., 76–77, 83
Vidal-Naquet, P., 176
Vigny, A. de, 154, 156, 226–27
Villehardouin, G. de, 169
Villon, F., 263, 313
Virgil, 37, 90, 99, 117, 137, 164, 211, 213, 299, 313
Voltaire, 23, 43, 50, 52, 55–56, 57, 70, 85, 91, 120, 235, 240, 245, 266, 271, 299, 306, 309, 327, 331, 337–38, 343

Wajeman, G., 322
Walpole, H., 147
Weinberg, B., 263
Wellek, R., and Warren, A., 88
Weston, J., 333
Whitman, W., 315, 317
Wilde, O., 228
Wittgenstein, L., 409
Wittig, M., 320
Woolf, V., 50, 360, 387–89, 392–93, 395
Wordsworth, W., 117, 183, 184, 226, 239, 270, 314, 315, 330, 333

Yourcenar, M., 49, 127, 133–34, 298

Zola, E., 5–6, 8, 30, 60–61, 63, 66, 82–83, 90, 96, 106–7, 110, 114, 115, 129, 132, 140, 148, 171, 174, 220, 223, 228, 230, 232–33, 245, 265, 293, 297, 306, 309, 331, 347, 354–55, 372–73, 375–76, 378, 381–82, 394, 396–97, 404, 405
Zumthor, P., 408

CPSIA information can be obtained at www.ICGtesting.com
Printed in the USA
238132LV00001B/23/A

9 780521 424066